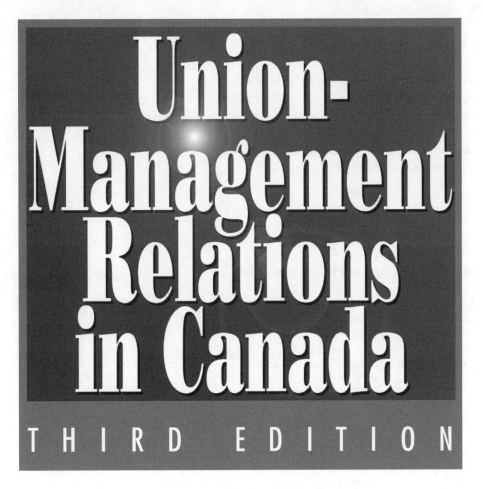

Union-Management Relations in Canada

THIRD EDITION

Morley Gunderson
University of Toronto

Allen Ponak
University of Calgary

Addison-Wesley Publishers Limited

Don Mills, Ontario • Reading, Massachusetts
Menlo Park, California • New York • Wokingham, England
Amsterdam • Bonn • Sydney • Singapore • Tokyo
Madrid • San Juan • Milan • Paris

Executive Editor: Joseph Gladstone
Managing Editor: Linda Scott
Acquisitions Editors: Shirley Tessier, John Clelland
Editors: Ed O'Connor, Michael Cuddy, Suzanne Schaan
Design: Anthony Leung
Production Coordinator: Melanie van Rensburg
Manufacturing Coordinator: Angela Booth Malleau
Printing and Binding: Friesen Printers

Canadian Cataloguing in Publication Data

Gunderson, Morley, 1945–
    Union–management relations in Canada

3rd ed.
Includes bibliographical references and index.
ISBN 0-201-76607-8

1. Industrial relations — Canada.   I. Ponak, Allen M., 1949–.
II. Title.

HD8106.5.G85 1995   331'.0971   C95-930944-6

ISBN 0-201-76607-8

Printed and bound in Canada.

  B C D E -FP- 99   98   97   96

———

To our families:

Melanie Brady and Brendan, Rory, Jesse, and Brady Gunderson

and

Margaret, David, and Matthew Ponak

And to the memory of our parents:

Ann and Magnus Gunderson

and

Sarah and Sam Ponak

———

CONTENTS

GENERAL EDITORS

MORLEY GUNDERSON (*B.A.*, *QUEEN'S UNIVERSITY*; *M.A.*, *PH.D.*, *UNIVERSITY OF WISCONSIN–MADISON*) is the director of the Centre for Industrial Relations and a professor in the Department of Economics at the University of Toronto. During 1977–78, he was a visiting scholar at the International Institute for Labour Research in Geneva, Switzerland, and during 1984–85 and 1991–93, he was a visiting scholar at Stanford University.

His publications include the books *Comparable Worth and Gender Discrimination: An International Perspective* (1995), *Labour Market Economics: Theory, Evidence and Policy in Canada* (3rd ed., 1993), *Pay Equity* (1990), *Women and Labour Market Poverty* (1990), and *Economics of Poverty and Income Distribution* (1983). He has published numerous journal articles on various topics: gender discrimination and comparable worth; the aging workforce, pensions and mandatory retirement; public sector wage determination; the determinants and impact of immigration; the causes and consequences of strikes; child-care arrangements and labour market behaviour; workers' compensation and reasonable accommodation; labour market adjustment and training; and the impact of free trade on labour markets, industrial relations, and workplace practices.

Currently Professor Gunderson is on the editorial advisory board of the *Journal of Labor Research* and the *International Journal of Manpower*, and he is co-editor of the *Labour Arbitration Yearbook*. He is a member of the executive board of the Industrial Relations Research Association, and has been an advisor/consultant to various organizations: Labour Canada; the Ontario Ministry of Labour; the Canadian Human Rights Commission; the Macdonald Commission on the Canadian Economy; the Abella Commission on Employment Equity; the Ontario Pay Equity Commission; the Canadian Labour Market and Productivity Centre; the Ontario Task Force on Hours of Work and Overtime; the Ontario Task Force on Mandatory Retirement; the British Columbia Task Force on Employment and Training; the British Columbia Task Force on Health Care and Costs; the Centre for Policy Studies on Youth and Family; the Prime Minister's Roundtable on Governments and Competitiveness; the Advisory Group on Working Time and the Distribution of Work; the North America Forum at Stanford; and the International Labour Organization.

ALLEN PONAK *(B.A., MCGILL UNIVERSITY; M.L.I.R., MICHIGAN STATE UNIVERSITY; PH.D., UNIVERSITY OF WISCONSIN–MADISON)* is professor of industrial relations in the Faculty of Management, University of Calgary, and director of the university's Industrial Relations Research Group. Previously, he held faculty positions at the University of British Columbia and McGill. In 1978–88, he was a visiting scholar at the National Institute of Labour Studies at Flinders University in Adelaide, Australia, and in 1994 he was a visiting scientist at the Technion in Haifa, Israel.

Professor Ponak's research has been widely published in scholarly journals and industrial relations volumes, and he has made numerous presentations of his research at both academic and professional conferences. His work has covered a number of topics including collective bargaining goals of unionized professionals; employee attitudes to collective bargaining; impact of interest arbitration on settlement propensities; discharge and reinstatement in grievance arbitration; delay in grievance arbitration; essential service dispute strikes and dispute procedures; and public sector industrial relations. Professor Ponak is a member of the editorial boards of *Relations industrielles/Industrial Relations* and the *Employee Responsibilities and Rights Journal.* In 1991–92 he was the national president of the Canadian Industrial Relations Association.

In addition to his academic duties, Professor Ponak is experienced in labour dispute resolution, serving as an arbitrator and mediator. Many of his decisions have been reported in *Labour Arbitration Cases* and, in 1992, he was admitted to the National Academy of Arbitrators. Professor Ponak co-chairs an annual labour arbitration conference in Calgary that has become one of the largest in Canada. He also is chair of the editorial board of *Worksight,* an Alberta quarterly publication devoted to workplace issues.

CONTRIBUTORS

ROY J. ADAMS (*PH.D., UNIVERSITY OF WISCONSIN*) IS PROFESSOR OF INDUSTRIAL RELATIONS at McMaster University. A "serious comparativist," he has carried out research and published articles on various aspects of industrial relations and labour policy in several countries including Canada, the United States, the United Kingdom, Sweden, Germany, France, New Zealand, Japan, and China. He is the editor of two books, *Comparative Industrial Relations: Contemporary Research and Theory* and (with Noah Meltz) *Industrial Relations Theory: Its Nature, Scope and Pedagogy*, and author of the recently published *Industrial Relations under Liberal Democracy*. A member of the editorial board of several journals including *Employee Responsibilities and Rights Journal, Employee Relations, International Journal of Human Resource Management, Journal of Individual Employment Rights*, and the *International Journal of Comparative Labour Law and Industrial Relations*, he is a past president of the Canadian Industrial Relations Association, consultant to various trade unions, governments, and quasi-governmental agencies, and currently editor of *Comparative Industrial Relations Newsletter*.

JEAN BOIVIN (*PH.D., CORNELL UNIVERSITY*) IS CO-AUTHOR, WITH JACQUES GUILBAULT, OF *Les relations patronales-syndicales au Québec* (1989). He is professor of industrial relations at the Département des relations industrielles, Université Laval, Quebec. He has published articles and contributed chapters to several books on industrial relations in both French and English. He is a former president of the Canadian Industrial Relations Association and a former member of the Industrial Relations Research Association's executive board. He was visiting scholar at the University of Toronto's Centre for Industrial Relations in 1987–88 and is presently chairman of the editorial board and book review editor of *Relations industrielles/Industrial Relations*.

DONALD D. CARTER (*B.A., LL.B., QUEEN'S UNIVERSITY; B.C.L., OXFORD UNIVERSITY*) is now dean of the Faculty of Law, Queen's University. From 1985 to 1990 he was director of the Industrial Relations Centre/School of Industrial Relations at Queen's University. He has also served as president of the Canadian Industrial Relations Association (1991–92) and as chair of the Ontario Labour Relations Board (1976–79). He is the author of numerous articles and monographs relating to labour law and industrial relations in Canada and has contributed to the *International Encyclopaedia for Labour Law and Industrial Relations* and to the casebook *Labour Law: Cases, Materials and Commentary*, now in its fifth edition. He has also served as a labour arbitrator on numerous occasions.

RICHARD P. CHAYKOWSKI (*PH.D., CORNELL UNIVERSITY*) IS ASSOCIATE PROFESSOR IN the School of Industrial Relations at Queen's University. He has also been a Queen's National Scholar at Queen's University and a visiting scholar at the University of Toronto, McGill University, and the Massachusetts Institute of Technology. He has been invited to speak about his research in a wide range of public forums, including student organizations, executive groups of major corporations, the Conference Board of Canada, Queen's University Industrial Relations Centre continuing education, and the Government of Canada.

His general teaching and research interests include public policy in labour markets, and theoretical and empirical analyses of issues in industrial relations and human resources, labour economics, and comparative economic systems. His published work has appeared widely in such journals as the *Industrial and Labour Relations Review*, *Industrial Relations*, the *Journal of Labour Research*, *Relations industrielles/Industrial Relations*, and *Advances in Industrial and Labor Relations*. His book *Industrial Relations in Canadian Industry* (co-edited with Anil Verma) was published in 1992, and his volume *Research in Canadian Workers' Compensation* (co-edited with T. Thomason) is scheduled for publication in 1995.

ESTHER DÉOM (*PH.D., UNIVERSITÉ DE MONTRÉAL*) IS A PROFESSOR OF INDUSTRIAL RELA-tions and director of the Département des relations industrielles at Université Laval. She was secretary-treasurer of the Canadian Industrial Relations Association for many years and was president of CIRA in 1993. She is a member of the editorial board of *Relations industrielles/Industrial Relations*. Her current research is in the area of pay equity and job evaluation, employment equity, and work organization and women. She also acts as a neutral third party in many employment equity committees and is the spokesperson for the Quebec Coalition for Pay Equity.

GENEVIEVE EDEN (*PH.D., UNIVERSITY OF TORONTO*) IS AN ASSOCIATE PROFESSOR IN THE School of Public Administration at the University of Victoria. She has published in various academic journals in the areas of employment law, human rights in the workplace, and dispute resolution. Current research interests also include gender issues in the workplace. She has had several years of experience in both the private and public sectors holding senior positions in human resource management and labour relations and has acted as a third-party neutral. She has been a member of the executive of the Canadian Industrial Relations Association.

GEOFFREY ENGLAND (*LL.B., LL.M., M.A.*) IS PROFESSOR OF LABOUR RELATIONS AT THE School of Management, University of Lethbridge. His chief research interests are in labour law and industrial relations, with most of his writings appearing in law journals. Professor England has also edited *Essays in Labour Relations Law* and *Essays in Collective Bargaining and Industrial Democracy*, and he is an experienced arbitrator.

ANTHONY GILES (*PH.D., UNIVERSITY OF WARWICK*) IS AN ASSISTANT PROFESSOR AT Université Laval in Quebec City. He teaches undergraduate and graduate courses on industrial relations, industrial society, labour markets, and comparative labour market policy. Professor Giles has published articles on a variety of topics and is presently engaged in research on workplace innovations in multinational corporations and the impact of globalization on industrial relations.

DOUG HYATT (*PH.D., UNIVERSITY OF TORONTO*) IS ASSISTANT PROFESSOR OF ECONOMICS AND industrial relations at the University of Wisconsin–Milwaukee and a research associate of the Institute of Policy Analysis at the University of Toronto. His articles have appeared in a number of scholarly journals including *Industrial and Labor Relations Review, Industrial Relations*, and *Relations industrielles/Industrial Relations*. His current areas of research include public sector collective bargaining, labour supply and the impact of child-care costs, public and private pension plans, occupational health and safety, and workers' compensation.

CARLA LIPSIG-MUMMÉ (*B.A., BRANDEIS UNIVERSITY; M.A., BOSTON UNIVERSITY; PH.D., UNIVERSITÉ DE MONTRÉAL*) is professor of labour studies and director of the Centre for Research on Work and Society, York University, a research centre working in partnership with the labour movement. Her areas of research and publication have been labour and politics in Quebec, Australia, English Canada, and the United States; trade union strategic repositioning; women, work, and unions; new organizing strategies for labour; the problem of labour internationalism, cultures of militancy, and precarious employment. She has published in *Studies in Political Economy* (Canada), *Journal of Industrial Relations* (Australia), *Relations industrielles/Industrial Relations* (Quebec), *Labour/Le travail* (Canada), *Monthly Review* (United States), *Sociologie du travail* (France), *Sociologie et société* (Quebec), and *Possibles* (Quebec). Formerly a union organizer with the United Farmworkers and International Ladies' Garment Workers Union, she has more recently been a consultant to the executive of the Centrale de l'enseignement du Québec and the Confédération des sydicats nationaux (Québec), as well as a research supervisor of the Technology Adjustment Research Project of the Ontario Federation of Labour. As well as co-editing *Acquisition ou fusion de l'entreprise et emploi*, she is currently at work on a textbook, *The Political Economy of Labour: An Introduction to Labour Studies in the New Social Order*.

DAVID C. MCPHILLIPS (*B.A., M.B.A., LL.B., LL.M.*) IS AN ASSOCIATE PROFESSOR IN the Faculty of Commerce and Business Administration, University of British Columbia. He is also a barrister and solicitor and is an active labour arbitrator and mediator in British Columbia. His teaching and seminar interests include labour law, employment law, industrial relations, and human rights. His articles have appeared in the *Industrial and Labour Relations Review, Relations industrielles/Industrial Relations*, the *Canadian Bar Review, McGill Law Journal*, and *Osgoode Hall Law Journal*.

NOAH M. MELTZ *(B.COMM., UNIVERSITY OF TORONTO; PH.D., PRINCETON UNIVERSITY)* is professor of economics and industrial relations in the Department of Economics and the Centre for Industrial Relations, University of Toronto, and principal of Woodsworth College, University of Toronto. He was director of the Centre from 1975 to 1985. His recent books include *The State of the Art in Industrial Relations* (co-editor), *Human Resource Management in Canada* (3rd ed., co-author), *Unemployment: International Perspectives* (co-editor), and *Economic Analysis of Labour Shortages: The Case of Tool and Die Makers in Ontario*. Recent articles include "Inter-State vs. Inter-Provincial Differences in Union Density" and "Labour Movements in Canada and the United States." He is a past president of the Canadian Industrial Relations Association and is the chair of the Advisory Committee on Labour Statistics of Statistics Canada.

DESMOND MORTON *(PH.D., UNIVERSITY OF LONDON)* IS PROFESSOR OF HISTORY AT THE University of Toronto, specializing in political, military, and industrial relations history. He is the author or co-author of 29 books including *Working People: An Illustrated History of the Canadian Labour Movement* (3rd ed.). He is former principal of the University of Toronto's Erindale Campus and is currently director of the McGill Institute for the Study of Canada in Montreal. His most recent books are *A Short History of Canada* (3rd ed.) and *When Your Number's Up: The Canadian Soldier in the First World War*.

GREGOR MURRAY *(PH.D., UNIVERSITY OF WARWICK)* IS ASSOCIATE PROFESSOR IN THE Département des relations industrielles, Université Laval, in Quebec City. He conducts research on trade unionism, comparative industrial relations, and industrial relations theory. He has also worked closely with a number of trade unions on problems of internal structure and strategic adjustment. His recent publications include articles and co-edited volumes on these themes as well as on the legal framework for union representation and transformations in collective bargaining and trade unionism. Forthcoming publications include volumes with A. Giles on the critical political economy approach to industrial relations and with M.-L. Moris et al. on industrial relations research traditions in France and Canada.

FRANK REID *(M.SC., LONDON SCHOOL OF ECONOMICS; PH.D., QUEEN'S UNIVERSITY)* IS A professor in the Centre for Industrial Relations and the Department of Economics at the University of Toronto. His publications have appeared in industrial relations journals, such as *Relations industrielles/Industrial Relations*, *Industrial and Labour Relations Review*, and *Journal of Industrial Relations*, as well as economic journals, such as *Canadian Journal of Economics*, *Journal of Labor Economics*, and *American Economic Review*. He is also the author of books and chapters of books in the industrial relations area and has served as a consultant to numerous federal and provincial government agencies on labour-related topics.

AKIVAH L. STARKMAN *(PH.D., UNIVERSITY OF KENT AT CANTERBURY)* IS THE EXECU-
tive director of the Bureau of Labour Information, Human Resources Development
Canada. He was also the executive coordinator of the federal Advisory Group on Working
Time and the Distribution of Work. His principle research interests include industrial
relations innovations, comparative industrial relations, and the use of replacement workers in industrial disputes.

MARK THOMPSON *(PH.D., CORNELL UNIVERSITY)* IS WILLIAM HAMILTON PROFESSOR OF
Industrial Relations in the Faculty of Commerce, University of British Columbia. His
research has appeared in major journals in Canada, the United States, and Britain, and he
has co-edited volumes on comparative industrial relations (published by the Industrial
Relations Research Association) and on public sector industrial relations in Canada (published by the IRC Press at Queen's University). He has arbitrated disputes in the public
sector for over 15 years. He is a member of the National Academy of Arbitrators, a past
president of the Canadian Industrial Relations Association, and a member of the board of
governors of the Workers' Compensation Board of British Columbia.

KENNETH WM. THORNICROFT *(LL.B., PH.D. CAND.)* IS ASSISTANT PROFESSOR OF
business law and labour relations with the Faculty of Business, University of Victoria, and
a Vancouver barrister and labour arbitrator. Professor Thornicroft is the author of over
50 journal articles and conference papers, his work appearing in the *Labor Law Journal*,
Journal of Labor Research, the *Labor Studies Journal*, *Journal of Collective
Negotiations in the Public Sector*, *Employee Relations*, the *Employee Responsibilities
and Rights Journal*, *Journal of Individual Employment Rights*, *Relations indus-
trielles/Industrial Relations*, the *Arbitration Yearbook*, and the *Canadian Bar Review*.
His major current research interests include employee rights issues, the grievance arbitration process, the relationship between "labour climate" and organizational performance, and the impact of the Canadian Charter of Rights and Freedoms on the employment relationship.

ANIL VERMA *(B. TECH, I.I.T., KANPUT (INDIA); M.B.A., UNIVERSITY OF SASKATCHEWAN;
PH.D., MASSACHUSETTS INSTITUTE OF TECHNOLOGY)* is associate professor of industrial relations and human resource management at the University of Toronto, where he holds a
joint appointment at the Faculty of Management and the Centre for Industrial Relations.
His primary research interests are in the area of management responses to unionization,
participative forms of work organization, and the contribution of human resource management policies—such as employment stabilization practices, profit/gain sharing, and
other innovations in industrial relations—to organizational effectiveness and performance.

     Professor Verma is the co-author of the following publications, in addition to arti-
cles in journals: *Industrial Relations in Canadian Industry* (with Richard P.
Chaykowski) and *Investing in People* (with Deborah Irvine). He has taught previously at
the University of Saskatchewan, the University of California (Los Angeles), and the
University of British Columbia, and he worked in the steel industry as an engineer for five
years.

PREFACE

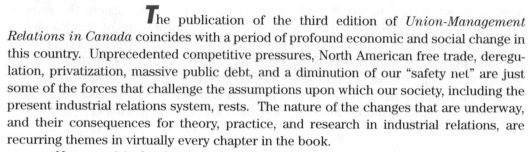

*T*he publication of the third edition of *Union-Management Relations in Canada* coincides with a period of profound economic and social change in this country. Unprecedented competitive pressures, North American free trade, deregulation, privatization, massive public debt, and a diminution of our "safety net" are just some of the forces that challenge the assumptions upon which our society, including the present industrial relations system, rests. The nature of the changes that are underway, and their consequences for theory, practice, and research in industrial relations, are recurring themes in virtually every chapter in the book.

Not surprisingly, the theme of change has produced some significant content changes for this edition. Existing chapters have been thoroughly updated and revised to reflect recent developments. A number of chapters, although bearing the same title as in the last edition, have been completely rewritten, especially where a new contributing author was involved. Two entirely new chapters have been added. The first provides an in-depth review of organized labour's response to the rapidly changing environment (Chapter 8). The second deals with employee involvement programs, describing in detail their increasing importance at the workplace level as unions and employers search for ways to deliver more productivity and a better work environment (Chapter 11).

Features that contributed to the popularity of the first two editions remain intact. The volume relies on a modified industrial relations systems model to provide a unifying framework and structure. Following this model, chapters focus on the environment of union-management relations, the major parties, the collective bargaining process, the outcomes of collective bargaining, and the nature of the relationship between unions and employers. As well, several chapters are devoted to special issues or topics (for example, international comparisons) that warrant separate attention. The result is a volume that provides comprehensive coverage of the subject matter.

The book continues to benefit from the contributions of many of the country's leading scholars and teachers of industrial relations. In a country as diverse as Canada, this ensures that the experiences in all regions of the country are reflected in the analysis, examples, and conclusions. This approach also ensures that readers are exposed to the lively mix of views and perspectives that are found within a very vibrant industrial relations community.

The text is designed to present basic introductory material and to provide a stepping-stone to a more analytic and in-depth treatment of each topic. Many of the chapters present material that is on the leading edge of research in industrial relations and, in some cases, contain analysis that is appearing in print for the first time. Most chapters provide extensive reference lists to direct the interested student to more specific information and research studies on each subject. The discussion is also aimed squarely at the practical applications of the theory, research, and statistical evidence. Industrial relations events appear daily on the evening news and in the press. Throughout the book attention is given to how the academic analysis relates to real-world problems and issues.

A book of this magnitude and collaborative effort reflects the input of numerous persons beyond the editors and contributors. We would like to express our appreciation to numerous colleagues who provided excellent suggestions for material to include in this edition. The editorial staff at Addison-Wesley was professional and well organized; in particular, we would like to thank Linda Scott for her support throughout the project. Professor Ponak would like to recognize the special contribution of the Faculty of Industrial Engineering and Management of the Technion in Haifa, Israel, where he spent his sabbatical leave while working on this book. The Lady Davis Foundation, which helped make the sabbatical possible, also is gratefully acknowledged. Professor Gunderson would like to thank the faculty, libraries, and staff of the University of Toronto Centre for Industrial Relations for their continuous support and assistance.

Morley Gunderson
Allen Ponak

CHAPTER 1

INDUSTRIAL RELATIONS

MORLEY GUNDERSON AND

ALLEN PONAK*

INDUSTRIAL RELATIONS PLAYS AN IMPORTANT PART IN EVERYDAY LIFE IN Canada. In order to help understand the practice of industrial relations and various perspectives on the study of the field, a model of industrial relations is presented in this chapter as an integrating framework. Dunlop (1958) presents an industrial relations system as composed of three actors—labour, employers, and government—interacting within market, technological, and power contexts, bound together by an ideology to establish a web of rules of the workplace. After discussing the critiques of this system, this chapter presents a modified version of the industrial relations system model. The way in which the chapters of the book follow the industrial relations systems approach is also outlined.

---

* The authors acknowledge material in this chapter that appeared in the previous edition of the textbook by Anderson, Gunderson, and Ponak (1989).

Contemporary society is characterized by rapid social, political, and economic change. The past decade has seen the creation of a free trade zone from Mexico City to Ottawa, and the general loosening of trade barriers around the world through the General Agreement on Tariffs and Trade (GATT). It has seen the collapse of the Soviet Union, the tearing down of the Berlin Wall, and the triumph of free market philosophies from Shanghai to Prague. Investment capital and multinational companies have proven both mobile and nimble. As the information highway moves from slogan to reality, we are connected by our cellular telephones, fax machines, and electronic mail. With our laptop computers and CD ROMs, our offices are with us wherever we want to take them.

These developments and many more like them exercise a profound impact on all aspects of our daily lives. In this book, we focus on the workplace and examine in particular the nature of employment relationships. Most of us work for a living or expect to once education has been completed. Many students work on a part-time basis during the school year and full time during the summer. How does the free trade agreement affect work opportunities? Do privatization and deregulation mean better jobs or worse ones? What does the accelerating pace of technological change imply for workplace training, job security, and the way in which supervisors and subordinates relate to one another? Has management developed new strategies for dealing with the expectations and insecurities of today's workers? What is the role of unions in all this—are they an archaic remnant of a bygone era or an integral participant in the changes that are underway?

An examination of our industrial relations system can help provide answers to such questions. In the broadest sense, *industrial relations* is the *study of employment relationships in industrial and post-industrial society.* While the field of industrial relations includes both unionized and non-unionized workplaces, the central focus of the field has been the unionized sector. Accordingly, this book has a heavy emphasis on union-management relations, focusing on the changes and adaptations in the thousands of workplaces governed by collective agreements.

Unions represent between 35 and 40 per cent of workers in Canada, which amounts to more than four million union members. These numbers, as substantial as they are, do not do full justice to the importance of unions in Canadian society. Union strength is concentrated in crucial industries including resources, heavy manufacturing, and telecommunications, as well as in the government sector. What happens in these industries matters. Canada's competitiveness and our standard of living are affected by the level of wages workers earn, the ease with which workplace innovations can be introduced, the degree to which employees and unions are partners in the enterprise rather than adversaries, and the amount of full-time regular jobs these industries create.

The unionized sector also has an impact on the nonunion part of our economy. Unions have traditionally led the way for the entire economy with respect to diverse employee benefits such as dental insurance and pension plans. The labour movement was one of the earliest and strongest supporters of universal medical care. Union advocacy has been instrumental in the development of general employment law applicable to all workers that provides, among other things, notice requirements in the event of layoff, premium payment for overtime, paid holidays and vacations, time off for maternity, and the right to refuse unsafe work. Union ideas about due process, typically incorporated in grievance procedures culminating in arbitration, are finding an increasingly receptive audience among major non-unionized organizations.

More explicit spillover from the union sector can be found where companies practice a union substitution strategy. Under this approach, gains made by unionized workers to whom nonunion employees can easily compare themselves are passed on to the nonunion workers; for example, nonunion Dofasco Steel closely monitors the collective agreements at Stelco, its unionized crosstown competitor, to ensure that its employees receive equal or better wages, hours, and conditions. The wages and benefits of nonunion white-collar workers of many manufacturing organizations are driven by the collective bargaining results of the blue-collar workforce. In this way, union impact spreads well beyond the direct union membership, affecting large numbers of nonunion employees.

Unions are important also because they can go on strike. The impact of strikes has been hotly debated, but not at issue is the fact that Canada has one of the highest strike rates in the world. Over the years Canadians have endured numerous postal shutdowns, the disruption of grain shipments, hospital strikes, and major work stoppages in our construction, forestry, and mining industries. We have even been deprived of professional baseball and our national religion—NHL hockey. In an increasingly sophisticated and competitive world, our reputation for an adversarial industrial relations system may be costing our country investment, customers, and markets. This is another way in which the unionized sector has an impact on all of us.

The unionized sector also holds many positive lessons. Employees most often join unions not so much in pursuit of better wages (though this may be an important factor), but in the desire for dignity and respect in their working lives. Not surprisingly, job security, fairness of opportunity, and protection against arbitrary treatment are integral components of most union contracts. Today's highly educated employee also does not care to "leave her brains at the door" when reporting to work, but wants some meaningful role in the way she does her job. Some of the most innovative employee-involvement programs have been pioneered in the unionized work places of Shell Canada in Sarnia, Cardinal River Coal in Jasper, and Canadian Airlines. Thus, knowing why workers join unions, what priorities unions pursue, and the successful strategies for meaningful worker input can provide a great deal of practical information about industrial democracy and employee motivation, two crucial ingredients in our future competitiveness.

Despite the importance of industrial relations to society, most people are not well informed about it. In the next section, several basic characteristics of the field are reviewed and the concept of an industrial relations system is introduced. This is followed by an examination of five perspectives that have been applied to its study. The chapter concludes with an overview of the Canadian industrial relations system and an outline of the chapter contents of the book.

INDUSTRIAL RELATIONS AS AN INTERDISCIPLINARY FIELD

In order to study industrial relations, it is important to understand not only the nature of the employment relationship but also the wide range of factors that influence that relationship. Thus, while the role of unions and collective bargaining in employment remains the central focus, the field also encompasses many other elements. These other elements include the role of human resource policies developed by employers; the scope of employment-related legislation enacted by the federal and provincial governments; the impact of the labour market in establishing the terms and conditions of employment for individuals across occupations, industries, and regions; the consequences of social and power relationships in the workplace; and the nature of global economic and political changes.

Given the wide range of issues related to the employment relationship, it is not surprising that industrial relations problems have been studied by economists, political scientists, sociologists, psychologists, lawyers, and historians, among others. Each discipline has selected certain problems to study, often to the exclusion of other features of the system. Economists have been interested in how the supply of and demand for labour interact in alternative market structures to determine wages, wage structures, employment, and unemployment. Emphasis is placed on the effects of unions on the wage determination process and the role of labour market variables on the decision-making behaviour of individuals, unions, and firms. Political scientists have contributed to our understanding of the internal dynamics of unions and the role of unions in the political process in both the public and private sectors. Industrial sociologists have focused on the behaviour of work groups and on the role and determinants of conflict in organizations and society. The dynamics of bargaining behaviour and the effects of wage payment systems on individual behaviour have been examined by psychologists. Legal scholars and historians have been interested in the development of the labour movement and of the legal, regulatory, and historical framework within which industrial relations has been conducted.

Most industrial relations problems, however, cannot be fully understood by adopting the theory and methods of a single discipline. For that reason industrial relations research has often drawn from several disciplines in an attempt to explain a particular issue or problem. For example, efforts to gauge the impact of unions on the productivity of firms have combined the methodology of econometrics with the theories of political science, sociology, and organizational behaviour. In this way it has been possible to weigh the negative monopoly effects of unions against their positive stabilizing role (Freeman and Medoff 1984). Attempts to understand why employee involvement programs succeed or fail have drawn from the fields of law, human resource management, psychology, and industrial engineering (Kaufman and Kleiner 1993). One of the main strengths of industrial relations has been its interdisciplinary focus.

But bringing together many disciplines has its drawbacks. The use of theory and methods from separate disciplines has made it difficult to reach agreement on a unified theoretical framework for industrial relations itself. In fact, even the desirability of such a theory has been debated for fear that it might diminish the field's traditional orientation towards practical problems by creating pressure for conformity to certain pre-ordained theoretical models. Research in the fields of organizational behaviour and economics have been criticized on such grounds (Brief and Dukerich 1991).

In the absence of a generally accepted core theory of industrial relations, reliance has been placed on input-output models to help integrate the constituent elements of the field. The most important and well known was developed by John Dunlop in 1958 in his book titled *Industrial Relations Systems*.

Dunlop's Industrial Relations System

In Dunlop's model the industrial relations system is characterized as an "analytical subsystem of an industrial society on the same logical plane as an economic system" (p. 5). The system comprises three sets of actors—government, employees and their associations, and employers and their associations—who are bound together by a common ideology. Their interactions produce the main output of the industrial relations system, a "web of rules" of the workplace and the work community. The actors exist within the technical, market, and power contexts of the system, which are viewed as the determinants of the web of rules, each context having a selective impact on a subset of the rules (for example, the market context has an impact on compensation).

The Web of Rules. The central proposition of Dunlop's theory is that the industrial relations system produces a set of rules and regulations that governs the employment relationship. The web of rules defines the rights and responsibilities of the actors in the system towards one another. The rules may be either substantive or procedural. Substantive rules include the outcomes of the system, such as wages and pay supplements, employee benefits, and working conditions. Procedural rules, on the other hand, include those arrangements between the actors that determine the ways in which substantive rules are to be made and applied as well as the methods for resolving conflicts about existing rules. The procedures for collective bargaining, grievances, and promotion, transfer, or layoff are all considered procedural rules. Thus, substantive and procedural rules combine to define the expected behaviour of each of the actors in the industrial relations system.

The Actors. Dunlop views three groups as the major parties to the industrial relations system: the government, employers and their associations, and employees and their associations. The actors determine the web of rules of the system. The web of rules can be a result of unilateral decisions of employers or governments or a result of negotiations between individuals and/or unions and employers and/or employer and industry associations. The government can be viewed as an actor in the system in two different roles: as a regulator, establishing both substantive and procedural rules by enacting legislation (for example, collective bargaining and minimum wage laws); and as a participant, either as an employer in the public sector or as a guardian of the public interest, intervening and interacting with employers and employees to determine the outcomes of the system.

The Contexts of Industrial Relations.   In Dunlop's model the type of substantive and procedural rules, as well as the degree to which they are more or less favourable to one set of actors, largely depends upon the nature of the context in which the parties interact. The market, technical, and power contexts of the industrial relations system may shift the balance of power between the parties.

The market context includes the nature of the labour and product markets facing the firm or industry. Dunlop indicates that unions will attempt to expand to control the supply of labour and to cover the total product market of the firm in order to increase their bargaining power with the employer. The market context is also viewed as particularly important in shaping the compensation package offered to employees.

The technical context of industrial relations refers to the extent to which employees or unions occupy a strategic position in the technical system of the organization or industry. The more control the union has over the technology, the greater the opportunity it has to shape the web of rules in its favour because of its greater control over the operations of the firm. For example, maintenance workers in production technologies are essential to the continuing production of goods and thus are in a strong position to establish rules favourable to themselves.

The power context reflects the relative power that the various actors have accumulated because of their status in society. The more power residing with a particular actor by virtue of its relative status, the more likely it is that the web of rules will be weighted in its direction. In some situations, the government is the major party shaping the web of rules; in other instances, the employers or employees dominate. Like each of the other contexts, power relationships may change over time, creating the potential for changes in the web of rules.

The Role of Ideology.   The stability of the industrial relations system depends on whether the actors share a common ideology. In North America, for example, the values underlying capitalism and business-oriented unionism provide the basis for a collective bargaining system that accepts that conflicts of interest between employers and employees can be resolved by private contract of the terms and conditions of employment. In an industrial relations system in which a common ideology does not exist, the actors are unlikely to be able to establish procedural rules to govern the relationship, and substantive rules may need to be unilaterally imposed.

Criticisms of the Industrial Relations Systems Model

There has been much debate in industrial relations about the strengths and weaknesses of Dunlop's model (Blain 1970; Singh 1976; Adams 1983; Craig 1988; Meltz 1993). The most common criticism is that it is only a taxonomy or classification scheme, leading to descriptive rather than explanatory research (Wood et al. 1975). Although the components of the system are identified—context, actors, rules, and ideology—the linkages between them are, in large part, left unspecified. Thus the model fails to provide a basis for the kinds of testable hypotheses that are necessary for empirical research (Blain 1970). As a result, the various researchers who have relied on the industrial relations systems model have specified different, and sometimes conflicting, relationships between the same two sets of variables.

Problems of the definition and treatment of rules have been a second source of debate. While the industrial relations community immediately accepted the concept of a web of rules of the workplace, the distinction between substantive and procedural rules has been a source of confusion (Wood et al. 1975). Although the theory is that actors in the system can establish both types of rules, some procedural rules are established by unilateral action of the government (for example, collective bargaining legislation) while others can be determined by the employer (for example, appeals procedures) or jointly between labour and management (for example, grievance procedures). The theory also fails to identify the conditions under which these different types of procedural rules are likely to have much impact on the type and comprehensiveness of the substantive rules.

Third, the model may underestimate the role of conflict in the system. Most industrial relations theorists adopt the position that an inherent conflict of interests exists between employers and employees in any society (Dahrendorf 1959; Barbash 1984). Although the nature of the ideology binding together the actors may shape the level and type of conflict that is acceptable within the system, its relevance is not discussed. Consequently, some writers discuss conflict as an output of the industrial relations system, examining strike activity in particular, while others focus on the role of conflict as a mediator between the procedural and substantive rules. Again, the lack of specificity in the treatment of conflict and ideology has created confusion in attempts to test the industrial relations systems model.

Despite these criticisms, Dunlop's industrial relations system remains the point of departure for much discussion, analysis, and research in industrial relations, especially in North America. It is a useful tool for organizing knowledge and determining the elements that fall within the boundaries of what is usually thought of as industrial relations (Godard 1994). Researchers looking for answers to practical, pressing problems, rather than elegant theoretical explanations, continue to find Dunlop's framework an attractive vehicle for structuring their analyses (Adams 1993a). The model has served as an important framework for comparing the industrial relations practices of one country with another (Hills 1993), for organizing courses and textbooks in industrial relations, and for teaching the subject (Adams 1993b). It has also been a foundation upon which many subsequent theories have been based, often as extensions or modifications designed to meet the criticisms of the basic systems approach (Meltz 1993).

Modified Version of the Industrial Relations System Model

There have been many proposals for alternatives to Dunlop's initial framework. Craig (1967) took the model out of structural terms and represented it in a more conventional systems approach, making feedback within the system explicit. Strategic choice theory questioned the premise of a shared ideology and posited that industrial relations are acted out at three distinct levels in the organization, as outlined in more detail later in this chapter (Kochan, Katz, and McKersie 1986). Meltz (1993) provided a framework that attempted to integrate the work of several different models, including Dunlop's and strategic choice, into an all-encompassing framework.

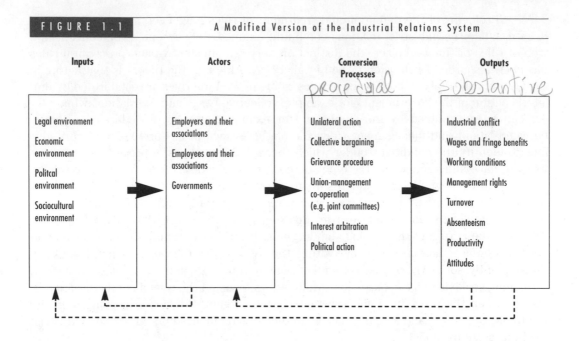

FIGURE 1.1   A Modified Version of the Industrial Relations System

For the purposes of this book, we have modified the industrial relations systems approach on the basis of continuing developments in the study and practice of industrial relations. The model is set out in Figure 1.1 and most closely resembles a model developed by Alton Craig (1988). It shows a series of sequential relationships, starting with inputs and moving through actors and conversion processes to outputs. The characteristics of the inputs and actors have both direct and indirect effects (dotted lines) on the conversion mechanisms and outputs of the system. Therefore, in thinking about the industrial relations system, it is important to consider the way in which its components interact to shape the outputs.

This model has several advantages over Dunlop's original version. First, it recognizes a wide range of inputs to industrial relations beyond the market, technological, and power contexts of the system. Industrial relations is not viewed as an isolated subsystem; rather, the identification of inputs stresses the direct importance of the economic, legal, political, and sociocultural systems in shaping the actors, their interactions, and the outputs of the system.

Second, the modified framework recognizes that the determination of the outputs of the system, including the web of rules, may result from various forms of action: unilateral action on the part of any of the actors; bilateral action (as in bargaining, grievance processing, labour-management co-operative mechanisms, day-to-day decisions at the workplace, interest arbitration, or political action by management or the union); or tripartite involvement on some issues. As a result, it is vital to conceptualize the industrial relations system as operating on several levels with the web of rules being shaped at the level of the firm, industry, sector, and societal level. Moreover, outputs produced at one level inevitably influence those produced at another.

Third, by distinguishing more clearly between procedural rules (conversion mechanisms) and substantive rules (outputs), the framework demands a recognition that the web of rules includes not only wages, benefits, and working conditions, but also all the other outputs of the conversion mechanisms. Such outputs may include changes in legislation, productivity, industrial conflict, industrial accidents, turnover, absenteeism, and employee attitudes.

Finally, the framework's feedback mechanisms indicate that it is important to see the system as dynamic rather than static. That is, outputs at one level (individual, firm, industry, sector, or society) or in one time period are likely to become inputs for another level or for another time period. For example, political action that succeeds in effecting a change in collective bargaining legislation (output) will produce a change in the legal environment (an input) from that time forward. Thus, many of the environmental conditions examined as constraints in a static view of the industrial relations system may, in fact, be seen as under the partial control of the actors when a dynamic perspective is adopted.

Although the model in Figure 1.1 addresses some of the criticisms of Dunlop's industrial relations systems model, it does not solve all of them. Most important, it does not provide directly testable hypotheses. Each of the sets of conceptual variables—inputs, actors, conversion mechanisms, outputs—contains a vast number of dimensions that can be identified, measured, and related to variables within the same conceptual set or with variables in other sets. However, as Heneman (1969) notes, every partial system is rooted in a larger system, and every experimenter must bridge the two by demonstrating common variables. In other words, the onus is placed on the researcher to identify the appropriate level of analysis, the perspective to be taken, and the variables considered important in explaining the dependent variable(s) of interest.

PERSPECTIVES ON THE STUDY OF INDUSTRIAL RELATIONS

The decisions made by researchers in this regard, for example, choosing the variables to study and the level of analysis, often will reflect their underlying value systems. Given the interdisciplinary nature of industrial relations and the absence of a central integrating theory, it is not surprising that industrial relations problems have been investigated from a number of different, and at times competing, perspectives.

Moreover, these perspectives have often reflected basic attitudes about the role and place of unions in society. From the time that the first unions were formed in the 1700s, substantial opposition to their existence emerged from employers and, at times, the state. For example, the British Combination Acts of 1799 declared unions to be a conspiracy in restraint of trade, made union activity illegal, and permitted the imprisonment of union leaders. These harsh laws were rooted in social and political values that feared any gatherings of working people in the recent aftermath of the French Revolution, and saw unions as tampering with the natural social order, which was to be determined by "survival of the fittest." While today's values are different, there is still a strong residue of suspicion regarding the role of unions; on the other hand, there is also a tradition, based partly on the Marxist response to worker repression, that harbours deep mistrust about the free market system and the motives of employers.

In studying industrial relations, it is important, therefore, to understand the different perspectives that have been developed and utilized in the field. Five common perspectives, that together represent a good cross-section of views, are discussed below: institutional, neoclassical, human resources management, strategic-choice, and political economy. Despite some overlap, each of these five approaches has its own assumptions, questions of interest, and ways of analyzing industrial relations issues.

Institutional Perspective

The institutional approach to the study of industrial relations has traditionally been *the* most central to teaching and practice in the field. As one of the oldest approaches to the study of industrial relations, it developed in the late nineteenth and early twentieth centuries (Commons 1934; Perlman 1928) as a response to the classical economic view of unions as a disruption in the marketplace. Institutional economists disagreed with this view of unions, proposing instead that the system of industrial relations requires a degree of balance between the interests of employers and employees in order to function.

According to the institutional perspective, individual workers have little or no power to resist the demands of large employers and, therefore, need a mechanism to counter the unilateral power of employers. Unions provide such a counterbalance to employer power and are therefore endorsed along with public policy to protect the rights of unions and employees. The institutional perspective accepts that some degree of conflict is inevitable between unions and employers and encourages processes like collective bargaining as effective mechanisms for resolving those conflicts (Barbash 1984).

The institutional perspective has led to research on unions and collective bargaining, public policy, strikes and dispute procedures and, to a lesser extent, management. Research is marked by attempts to understand the full range of factors that might influence the issue or problem being studied. Industrial relations systems models, either Dunlop's or its extensions, are often utilized, especially for comprehensive case analyses of particular situations. A typical institutional study includes an in-depth description of the parties—union, management, government—the situation (including the historical and legal conditions), and the particular problem at issue. The information used for the analysis includes interviews, company and union documents, and any historical or legal information that bears on the problem. This perspective has provided, in particular, a good understanding of the origins of labour organizations and the conditions under which we should expect their formation, the structure and process of collective bargaining, and the nature and content of collective agreements.

Neoclassical Perspective

Since the institutional perspective developed partially in response to classical economic thought, it is no surprise that the neoclassical perspective of industrial relations differs substantially from the institutional one. This perspective stresses the importance of market forces in setting the terms and conditions of employment in both union and nonunion situations. Unions are viewed as a constraint in the labour market, influencing wages and employment either directly through bargaining over these outcomes, or indirectly through influencing the supply of, or demand for, labour. The use of strike tactics and other exercises of power by unions further distorts the efficient operations of the market, leading to an inefficient allocation of resources. (The methodology for measuring those effects, and evidence on the magnitude of the effects, are discussed in Gunderson and Riddell 1994, p.403.)

Labour economists, following the neoclassical approach, have been particularly interested in the wage determination process and the effect of unions on the level and structure of wages. Sophisticated models have been developed to measure the impact of unions after controlling for the effect of the supply and demand for labour and conditions in the economy (say, inflation rates) that might affect wages. Similar models have been applied to the study of strikes in an effort to understand economic factors related to strike activity. At the individual level, neoclassical economists argue that wage rates are primarily a function of a person's investment in human capital through education, training, and experience. The neoclassical perspective has had an important influence on the study of industrial relations, in particular by shedding light on the movement of wages, the origins and shape of union-nonunion wage differences, and the economic predictors of strike activity. It has also encouraged the use of better specified models and more sophisticated analytical methods.

Beginning in the 1980s, increased emphasis was placed on the actual role of unions as institutions, and the importance of the union role in providing a "voice" to employees (Freeman and Medoff 1984). Subsequently, a substantial number of studies examined the effect of unions on productivity, finding in many cases a positive effect on firm productivity that at least partially offset increases in labour costs and other union-induced market interference. Thus, the neoclassical perspective while still concerned with market distortions caused by union activity, is incorporating some aspects of the institutional perspective of unions into its models. The basic tools of economics have also increasingly been applied to understand the emergence and survival of various institutional features of labour markets, such as seniority rules, mandatory retirement, overtime premiums, subcontracting, temporary-help agencies, compensation schemes and unions themselves (Gunderson 1988).

Human Resource Management Perspective

Another longstanding tradition with respect to the employment relationship is the belief that management has the capacity to understand the needs of workers and to implement programs that will produce satisfied and productive workers. An underlying assumption of the human resource management perspective is that there is no inherent conflict of interests between employees and management. Although the interests of the two groups may diverge in the short run, they can be made compatible since both parties need an efficient and profitable organization to survive. Only a profitable firm has a surplus to share with its employees in the form of high compensation and can afford to provide good working conditions and job security. This perspective sees a limited role for unions; good management techniques can create a workplace in which unions are unnecessary.

This perspective originated with the work of Fredrick W. Taylor (1911). He believed that by breaking down jobs into simple, understandable movements and by providing appropriate training, workers could become more productive. The employees would share in that increase if they were paid on a piecework basis for their level of productivity. The perspective was expanded by the Human Relations School of Elton Mayo and his colleagues. In a lengthy study (1924-32) of the work environment of employees in Western Electric Company's Hawthorne plant, Mayo (1933) found, as expected, that productivity went up as attention was paid to lighting, rest breaks, and other working conditions. However, productivity also went up when the lighting was *reduced*. It was concluded that the most important factor in raising the productivity was the attention being paid to the needs of the workers. Therefore, it was recommended that management pay much more attention to the social needs and social setting of its employees if it was interested in higher levels of productivity.

Although the actual experiments and results of the Hawthorne research have been criticized, it did start a tradition of concern for supervision and leadership focusing on both task accomplishment and social support for the employees. The field of organizational behaviour developed from this tradition. Since the 1950s, various techniques have been designed to obtain congruence between the goals of the organization and the needs of the employees. The long list has included suggestion systems, people-oriented leadership, quality circles, team production, employee-involvement programs, goal-setting systems of performance appraisal, internal communication programs, a consistent organizational culture, cafeteria-style benefit plans, and employee profit-sharing plans.

While many of these techniques were developed to foster a positive work environment for employees, an often unstated objective of such practices is the maintenance of a union-free workplace. Co-operative work innovations and work restructuring have been used, along with training, career development programs, individual pay plans, and corporate communication programs, to show employees that there is no need for union representation. Some firms have implemented formal grievance and appeal systems to substitute for union voice mechanisms.

There has been little systematic research in Canada of whether these approaches actually reduce the prospects of unionism. In fact, the human resource management perspective on industrial relations has generally not focused a great deal of attention on the question of the role of unions. This reflects underlying values that 1) deny that there is an inherent conflict of interest between employees and employers, and 2) assume that properly managed employees will have no need for unions. Much of the research is accordingly focused on the techniques of sound human resource management practices without a consideration of the role, place, or impact of unions. Nevertheless, the human resource management perspective has been a theoretical and empirical source of ideas and variables for industrial relations scholars. This is particularly true for scholars examining the question of why employees join or do not join unions and for those evaluating various employee involvement programs. This perspective has also increased in importance as the nonunion sector has grown in many industrialized countries, in part due to advances in human resource practices.

Strategic Choice Perspective

The application of strategic choice theory in industrial relations is a recent development, most closely identified with the work of Thomas Kochan and his colleagues (Kochan, McKersie, and Capelli 1984; Kochan, Katz, and McKersie 1986). Its basic premise is that the actors in the industrial relations system act strategically in order to advance their objectives, making choices that are carried out through concerted actions over a period of time. The theory of strategic choice was developed inductively, by analyzing the changes that had occurred in US industrial relations since the Second World War. While meant to be applicable to all three actors in the industrial relations system, the development of the theory and most of the work to date has focused on management.

Strategic choice theory emphasizes the relationship among organizational goals, industrial relations objectives, and the range of choices for achieving these objectives. An organization acts strategically when it recognizes the nature of these interrelationships and then adopts a course of action that produces consistency among organizational goals, industrial relations objectives, and behaviour. For example, a firm wishing to increase production and reposition itself as a low-cost producer (business goals) would build a new plant in a low-wage rural area, rather than expand production at an existing unionized facility (course of action among a range of choices). This would enhance its ability to reduce the degree of unionization of its overall work force and to lower its labour costs (industrial relations objectives). Strategic choice theory further emphasizes the importance of the economic, social, and political environments for creating continual pressure for an adaptation of goals and behaviour. Thus, the theory is a dynamic one, explicitly highlighting change.

The strategic choice framework also distinguishes three levels of industrial relations activity. The top level is the executive level at which the main business goals and values of an organization are set. The middle level is the functional level where industrial relations activities are conducted by professional staff (for example, collective bargaining; development of a substance abuse policy). In most companies, the industrial relations and human resource departments would operate at this level. Overall industrial relations objectives would be set at the top level but would be influenced by the expert knowledge of the middle level. The third level is the workplace level at which the product (or service) of the organization is produced. At this level, employees and front line supervisors interact and give practical effect to the work rules, compensation levels, communication systems, and decision-making methods devised at higher levels of the organization. Effective strategies are those that are consistent and in harmony across all three organizational levels (Chaykowski and Verma 1992).

Despite its focus on management as the initiator of change in the industrial relations system, the strategic choice perspective shares important underlying assumptions with the institutional perspective. It recognizes that inherent conflicts of interest exist between employees and employers and accepts unions and collective bargaining as legitimate and valuable mechanisms through which employees may pursue their interests (Kochan and Katz 1988). In these assumptions, strategic choice differs from the human resource management and neoclassical perspectives.

There are important differences, however, between the strategic choice and institutional perspectives. Whereas the institutional perspective places collective bargaining at the centre of the industrial relations system, strategic choice views the collective bargaining process as only one among several alternatives available to employees for achieving their goals. As a result, much greater attention is given to nonunion alternatives, to the array of potential choices, and to the reasons why employees and employers make certain choices in pursuing their respective goals. Indeed, while the institutional perspective implicitly assumes that labour, management, and government are bound together in a common ideology that supports unions and collective bargaining, strategic choice does not adopt this premise. Under the strategic choice approach, the absence of a shared ideology widens the array of choices, such as a union avoidance policy, from among which actions can be taken. The strategic choice perspective also focuses much greater theoretical attention on the top decision-making level of organizations because it is at this level that the crucial direction of an organization is set. There is less interest in the middle or functional level whose task is to help translate business goals into sound industrial relations objectives and practices. The institutional perspective, in contrast, has devoted most of its work to this middle level and to the institutions and processes that take place within it (such as negotiations and dispute resolution procedures).

In a relatively brief period, strategic choice theory has made significant and innovative research contributions, particularly with respect to management, the industrial relations actor largely ignored by a generation of researchers. By focusing on senior organizational levels and the dynamics of change, it has created new ways of examining industrial relations developments. In the future, the strategic choice perspective will be applied to the study of union and government activities. As well, because the perspective was developed in the United States, researchers are now testing the applicability of its assumptions to Canada (see Chapter 5 in this volume; Chaykowski and Verma 1992).

Political Economy Perspective

Despite a long tradition in Europe, the application of political economy to the study of industrial relations has only recently been made in Canada. Interest in Canada in this perspective has been greatly influenced by a new generation of industrial relations scholars, many of whom have trained in England, especially at the University of Warwick. Previously, most researchers had received their graduate education in the United States, where the institutional perspective is strongly emphasized.

Political economy can be defined as "an approach to industrial relations that attempts to foster a more critically-oriented, sociological understanding of industrial relations and that places emphasis on the interconnections between industrial relations and broader issues of economy and society" (Godard 1994, p. 518). Industrial relations are seen as much more than a set of economic choices and exchanges. Power is viewed as a crucial dimension, as is inherent conflict, which has been created by the great inequality between the social, economic, and political power of employees and unions on the one hand and that of employers on the other. In contrast to the institutional perspective, the political economy perspective does not consider collective bargaining capable of permanently regulating this conflict or rectifying the basic power imbalance. Governments, far from playing a neutral role, are seen as supporting employer interests.

These assumptions have produced a body of research that differs from that associated with the other perspectives. More attention is paid to structural inequalities in the workplace, with particular concern about women and minorities. Political economy also focuses on the labour process, since it is informed by a belief that "employers as buyers of units of labour can only purchase time from individuals and their availability for work, not work itself, nor work effort, nor motivation" (Littler 1993, p. 310). Thus, researchers examine informal work processes and the adjustments, adaptations, and conflicts of individual workers; to do so they frequently use the tools of industrial sociology. At the macro level, broader trends in terms of political ideology, class, and occupational structure are explored. Regulation theory has been applied to explain how changes in technology, management practices, and employment systems have contributed to the decline of union density in the United States and a number of other advanced industrial countries (Littler 1993).

The role of organized labour in the micro setting of the workplace and at the macro level of society as a whole also is of central interest to political economists. Labour is analyzed in three different ways: unions as institutions, labour as part of the labour process, and organized labour as a broad social movement (see Chapter 8). Contrary to the strategic choice perspective, political economists are sceptical that the concept of strategic choice, developed out of the experience of private sector corporations, can be applied to unions without substantial modifications to take into account their nature as political and social organizations. Indeed, they are also not comfortable with an analysis of any social institutions that relies on interpretation based on assumptions of strict economic rationality.

The development of a political economy perspective within the study of Canadian industrial relations has been important, not only for enlivening the intellectual debate about the field but for addressing issues ignored by others or for reaching different conclusions about familiar problems. New work on a number of subjects includes: how women are studied in industrial relations (Forrest 1993), the role of the state with respect to union rights (Panitch and Swartz 1993), and the nature of grievance arbitration as a control mechanism (Haiven 1991). A textbook for a wide student audience has been written from a political economy perspective (Godard 1994). Thus, while the institutional perspective will likely continue as the dominant approach to teaching and research in the field of industrial relations in Canada, political economy is establishing itself as a significant alternative.

From the preceding review of the various perspectives, it should be evident that underlying values and assumptions have an important effect on the study of industrial relations. The types of questions that are seen as important, the variables that are likely to be identified as determinants of industrial relations outcomes, and the methodological approach are all likely to be influenced by the industrial relations perspective of the researcher or teacher. Moreover, the central role to be played by unions and collective bargaining, long viewed as fundamental, is not automatically accepted in some of the perspectives.

Students should be aware of these types of differences in their own examination of industrial relations. The majority of chapters in this textbook reflect the institutional perspective, and the book follows a modified industrial relations system model to organize the material, itself identified with an institutional approach. However, other perspectives, most notably political economy, can also be found (e.g., Chapter 8). In analyzing and discussing the material, it is important to recognize the perspective from which it is being presented.

OUTLINE OF THE BOOK

This book follows the modified industrial relations systems framework set out earlier in Figure 1.1. Examined in turn are the environmental inputs, the main actors, the conversion processes, and the outputs, as well as some special sectors.

Part I focuses on the environment of industrial relations. Chapter 2 covers the important characteristics of the labour market and its impact on other aspects of the industrial relations system. A variety of topics are covered including the changing nature of labour supply, the development of part-time and nonstandard work, the effect of global competition and free trade, and the persistence of unemployment. Chapter 3 reviews the legal environment of union-management interaction: the origins of the system, the policy assumptions, and current legislation on collective bargaining. The manner in which public policy supports unionism and collective bargaining receives particular attention. Chapter 4 broadens the scope. Industrial relations practices are strongly affected by the provincial and federal legislation that governs the employment relationship of all employees, whether unionized or not. The legislative approach is outlined for such issues as minimum wages, occupational health and safety, equal employment opportunities, discrimination, and working conditions. Together these three chapters should provide the student with a basic understanding of the current economic, social, and legal environments shaping industrial relations in Canada. The material should also help show how the environment can influence the strategies of union and management, the nature of the bargaining and grievance processes, and ultimately the outcomes of the industrial relations system.

Part II focuses on two of the main actors in the industrial relations system: employers and unions. Chapter 5, relying on new, previously unpublished interview data, reviews managerial practices in large, unionized private sector organizations. The theoretical literature on management's industrial relations strategy is presented and then compared to actual practice over a range of activities including basic approaches to unions, the relationship between business strategy and industrial relations strategy, the centralization of decision making, and the strategy behind setting wages. As well, the industrial relations strategies of Canadian firms are compared to those of American and other foreign companies.

The next three chapters focus on Canadian unions—their past, present, and future. Chapter 6 provides an account of the development of Canada's labour movement and indicates how history plays an important role in helping to determine what happens today and what may be possible in the future. Chapter 7 addresses contemporary events. The current size and structure of Canada's unions are detailed, including a discussion of why workers join unions. Prospects for future growth are assessed, especially given the changes in the labour market and other aspects of Canadian society. The theme of change and the future of Canada's labour movement is continued in Chapter 8. The pressures on the post-Second World War industrial relations framework are charted and then union responses, actual and potential, are set out.

While the four chapters in the second section of the book provide in-depth information on the characteristics of two of the major actors in the industrial relations system, this section does not formally discuss government, the third actor in the system. The government plays a dual role in industrial relations: it is a regulator through its power to pass legislation, and it is an employer of several million public employees. Its role as regulator is explored in Chapters 3 and 4, which consider the legal environment. The role of government as an employer is discussed in Chapter 15, which reviews collective bargaining in the public sector.

Part III focuses on three major conversion processes in the union-management relationship: collective bargaining, grievance resolution, and employee involvement in workplace decision making. These processes translate (or convert) the goals of the actors (which have been shaped by the environment) into a specific set of outcomes or substantive rules of the employment relationship. They represent the main vehicles used for maintaining the ongoing union-management relationship. Chapter 9 examines collective bargaining, historically the most central conversion process in Canadian industrial relations. The nature of the process, in particular the way in which negotiations must balance compromise and conflict, is discussed from a theoretical and practical perspective. As well, new negotiation techniques and bargaining structure are reviewed.

Chapter 10 provides a description of the characteristics and functioning of the grievance and arbitration processes. Grievances are alleged violations of the collective agreement which, under Canadian labour law, must be resolved by a neutral arbitrator if the parties themselves are unable to achieve a settlement. Strikes and lockouts are illegal while the collective agreement is in force. In Chapter 11, developments with respect to employee involvement are examined. Employee involvement (sometimes called worker participation) programs grew substantially in the 1980s as companies, unions, and employees sought ways to improve both productivity and the quality of the work experience. The chapter reviews the forces behind the interest in employee involvement, discusses the different types of programs that are part of employee involvement, and analyzes the practical issues that help determine program success or failure.

Part IV focuses on the outcomes of the industrial relations system. The section begins in Chapter 12 with an examination of the impact of unions and collective bargaining on wages, benefits, productivity, and the management of the firm. Particular attention is paid to union-nonunion differences and to the reasons why unions usually raise wages and benefits and often have a small but positive effect on productivity. Chapter 13 provides an in-depth description of the contents of a typical collective agreement. Also called the union contract, the collective agreement is the principle document that results from the collective bargaining process. This chapter presents examples of the actual contractual provisions that are established to govern the union-management relationship and explains the importance of various aspects of these provisions. Chapter 14 looks at another type of outcome of our industrial relations system—work stoppages. Canada has one of the highest rates of strike activity among industrialized countries. The chapter examines the incidence and duration of strikes in Canada and the main factors contributing to strike activity. It also discusses the consequences of strikes.

The last section of the book, Part V, examines industrial relations in two special sectors and then compares industrial relations in Canada to the experiences of other countries. Chapter 15 is devoted to the public sector, the most highly unionized part of the economy. Issues that are explored include differences between public and private sector industrial relations practices, the nature of government as employer, and the public policy debate over strikes by public employees. Chapter 16 focuses on the province of Quebec, where language and cultural traditions have produced a number of unique industrial relations approaches. The chapter reviews developments in Quebec, allowing students to compare Quebec's system with practices in the rest of the country. Finally, no treatment of industrial relations would be complete without comparisons of our system with those of other countries. In Chapter 17, various dimensions of Canada's industrial relations systems are examined alongside those of other countries, especially the United States, Europe, and Japan. The chapter makes possible an assessment of Canada's performance in an international context.

The final chapter of the book provides a summary of the Canadian industrial relations system as well as a look ahead, attempting to predict those changes in the system that will be most important in the future.

Q U E S T I O N S

1. Compare the industrial relations system proposed by Dunlop with the system outlined in Figure 1.1.

2. What is the "web of rules"? Why is it an important concept in industrial relations theory?

3. Who are the actors in the industrial relations system? Describe their roles.

4. Choose an industry with which you are familiar. Using the industrial relations system concept, describe labour relations in that industry.

5. Examine your own values and assumptions with respect to unions and management. Which perspective best describes how you view the field of industrial relations? Which perspective is least descriptive of your own perspective?

6. Choose a major problem or issue with respect to union-management relations (for example, the level of work stoppages, gender discrimination, the impact of free trade, or unions' effects on productivity). Indicate how this issue or problem might be studied from each of the five major perspectives identified in the chapter.

7. Discuss the possibility that each of the five different perspectives analyzed in this chapter have had different degrees of relevance over different time periods, depending in part on the issues that were most relevant to each period. If this is the case, which perspective is currently most relevant?

REFERENCES

ADAMS, R. 1983. "Competing Paradigms in Industrial Relations." *Relations industrielles/Industrial Relations* 38: 508-529.

———. 1993a. "Understanding, Constructing, and Teaching Industrial Relations Theory." In R. Adams and N. Meltz, eds., *Industrial Relations Theory.* Metuchen, NJ: IMLR Press/Rutgers University.

———. 1993b. " 'All Aspects of People at Work': Unity and Division in the Study of Labor and Labor Management." In R. Adams and N. Meltz, eds., *Industrial Relations Theory.* Metuchen NJ: IMLR Press/Rutgers University.

ANDERSON, J.C., M. GUNDERSON, and A. PONAK. 1989. "Frameworks for the Study of Industrial Relations." In J. Anderson, M. Gunderson, A. Ponak, eds., *Union-Management Relations in Canada, 2nd edition.* Don Mills ON: Addison Wesley.

BARBASH, J. 1984. *The Elements of Industrial Relations.* Madison, WI: University of Wisconsin Press.

BLAIN, A.N.J. 1970. "Industrial Relations Theory: A Critical Review." *British Journal of Industrial Relations* 8: 389-407.

BRIEF, A., and J. DUKERICH. 1991. "Theory in Organizational Behavior: Can it be Useful?" In L. Cummings and B. Staw, eds., *Research in Organizational Behavior Vol. 13.* Greenwich CT: JAI Press.

CHAYKOWSKI, R., and A. VERMA. 1992. *Industrial Relations in Canadian Industry.* Toronto: Dryden.

COMMONS, J.R. 1934. *Institutional Economics: Its Place in Political Economy.* New York: Macmillan.

CRAIG, A. 1967. "A Model for the Analysis of Industrial Relations Systems." *Proceedings of the Annual Meeting of the Canadian Political Science Association.* Ottawa: CPSA.

———. 1988. "Mainstream Industrial Relations in Canada." In G. Hebert, H. Jain, and N. Meltz, eds., *The State of the Art of Industrial Relations.* Kingston and Toronto: Queen's University Industrial Relations Centre and University of Toronto Centre for Industrial Relations.

DAHRENDORF, R. 1959. *Class and Class Conflict in Industrial Society.* London: Routledge.

DUNLOP, J.T. 1958. *Industrial Relations Systems.* New York: Holt.

FORREST, A. 1993. "Women and Industrial Relations Theory: No Room in the Discourse." *Relations industrielles/Industrial Relations* 48: 409-440.

FREEMAN, R.B., and J.L. MEDOFF. 1984. *What Do Unions Do?* New York: Basic Books.

GODARD, J. 1994. *Industrial Relations: The Economy and Society.* Toronto: McGraw-Hill Ryerson.

GUNDERSON, M. 1988. "Labour Economics and Industrial Relations." In G. Hebert, H. Jain, and N. Meltz, eds., *The State of the Art in Industrial Relations.* Kingston and Toronto: Queen's University Industrial Relations Centre and University of Toronto Centre for Industrial Relations.

GUNDERSON, M., and W.C. RIDDELL. 1993. *Labour Market Economics: Theory, Evidence and Policy in Canada.* Toronto: McGraw-Hill.

HAIVEN, L. 1991. "Hegemony and the Workplace: The Role of Arbitration." In L. Haiven, S. McBride, and J. Shields, eds., *Regulating Labour: The State, Neo-Conservatism, and Industrial Relations.* Toronto: Garamond Press.

HENEMAN, H. C., Jr. 1969. "Toward a General Conceptual System of Industrial Relations: How Do We Get There?" In G. Somers, ed., *Essays in Industrial Relations Theory.* Ames: Iowa State University Press.

HILLS, S. 1993. "Integrating Industrial Relations and the Social Sciences." In R. Adams and N. Meltz, eds., *Industrial Relations Theory.* Metuchen NJ: IMLR Press/Rutgers University.

KAUFMAN, B., and M. KLEINER, eds. 1993. *Employee Representation: Alternatives and Future Directions.* Madison WI: Industrial Relations Research Association.

KOCHAN, T., and H. KATZ. 1988. *Collective Bargaining and Industrial Relations, 2nd edition.* Homewood IL: Irwin.

KOCHAN, T., H. KATZ, and R. McKERSIE. 1986. *The Transformation of American Industrial Relations.* New York: Basic Books.

KOCHAN, T., R. McKERSIE, and P. CAPPELLI. 1984. "Strategic Choice and Industrial Relations Theory." *Industrial Relations* 23: 16-39.

LITTLER, C. 1993 "Industrial Relations Theory: A Political Economy Perspective." In R. Adams and N. Meltz, eds., *Industrial Relations Theory.* Metuchen NJ: IMLR Press/Rutgers University.

MAYO, E. 1933. *Human Problems of an Industrial Civilization.* New York: Macmillan.

MELTZ, N. 1993. "Industrial Relations Systems as a Framework for Organizing Contributions to Industrial Relations Theory." In R. Adams and N. Meltz, eds., *Industrial Relations Theory.* Metuchen NJ: IMLR Press/Rutgers University.

PANITCH, L., and D. SWARTZ. 1993. *The Assault on Trade Union Freedoms.* Toronto: Garamond Press.

PERLMAN, S. 1928. *A Theory of the Labor Movement.* New York: Macmillan.

SINGH. R. 1976. "Systems Theory in the Study of Industrial Relations: Time for Reappraisal?" *Industrial Relations Journal* 7: 59-71.

TAYLOR. F. 1911. *The Principles of Scientific Management.* New York: Harper.

WOOD, S., A. WAGNER, E. ARMSTRONG, J. GOODMAN, and J. DAVIS. 1975. "The Industrial Relations System Concept as a Basis for Theory in Industrial Relations." *British Journal of Industrial Relations* 3: 241-308.

PART I

THE ENVIRONMENT OF UNION-MANAGEMENT RELATIONS

Employees, unions, and employers interact with one another within the context of broad external forces. The social, economic, and political environments help to shape the nature of industrial relations processes and outcomes and are in turn shaped by them. The movement of wages in collective agreements, for example, is usually affected by the rate of inflation, but the wage gains themselves can then affect subsequent inflation rates.

The following three chapters examine several of the most salient influences on Canadian industrial relations. Chapter 2 reviews the economic environment, focusing in particular on the labour market. It is obvious to even the most casual observer of labour relations that economic conditions have major consequences for the goals and activities of both unions and employers. This chapter attempts to explain why this is so, exploring the relationship between, for example, unemployment and collective bargaining results. Among the important issues addressed are trends in the labour market (for example, changes in the age structure of the labour force), education and training, job creation strategies, minimum wages, part-time work, and free trade.

Chapter 3 turns to the legal environment within which most union and management interaction occurs. Compared to many other countries, Canada has a highly legalistic industrial relations system. The chapter traces the origins of this system and the policy assumptions the current legislative regime reflects—specifically, a commitment to the right of workers to join unions of their choice free from employer interference. The discussion then presents key aspects of the law surrounding such issues as the acquisition of bargaining rights, the power of labour relations boards, the rights of employers, work stoppages, and dispute-resolution procedures. The chapter also highlights the role played by the Charter of Rights and Freedoms with respect to rights of all parties under collective bargaining law.

Chapter 4 also focuses on the law—in this case, the employment legislation that regulates both unionized and non-unionized employers. This area has developed rapidly in Canada since the late 1970s (for example, most provinces now require joint employee-management health and safety committees in unionized as well as non-unionized establishments), and its implications for human resource management in general and union-management relations in particular are now widely recognized. The chapter examines health and safety as well as work standards (for example, minimum wage levels), contracts of employment, unjust dismissal, anti-discrimination law, and worker compensation practices. Throughout the discussion, employment legislation's implications for union-management relations are addressed.

It is expected that at the conclusion of Part I, the reader will have a more complete understanding of the conditions and constraints under which workers, unions, and managers operate and will appreciate some of the implications of environmental change for our industrial relations system.

CHAPTER 2

THE ECONOMIC ENVIRONMENT

FRANK REID
AND NOAH M. MELTZ*

*C*HANGES IN THE LABOUR MARKET ENVIRONMENT AFFECT THE LIMITS *within which labour-management relations operate. Compensation levels and employment are affected by legislative and other changes governing markets. These include deregulation, privatization, increasing payroll taxes, expansion of human rights legislation, tightening of unemployment insurance provisions, and increases in the minimum wage. Industrial relations outcomes are also affected by changes emanating from the supply side of the labour market such as the aging of the population, the rising proportion of women in the labour force, and increases in the level of education and training. Changes in the overall state of the labour market, such as the movement from the boom of the late 1980s to the recession of the early 1990s, have critical effects on outcomes such as average wage settlements, strike activity, layoffs, and recruitment. The need for restructuring has been heightened by deindustrialization, by the general trend toward globalization of markets and, in particular, by Canadian participation in potentially far-reaching free trade agreements with the United States and Mexico and in the global reduction of tariffs through GATT.*

---

* The authors would like to acknowledge the assistance of Eva Hollander in preparing this chapter and the helpful comments of the general editors.

Many outputs of the industrial relations system are influenced by the labour market, one of the important inputs that constrains the various actors—labour, management, and the government. This chapter explores the impact on labour-management relations of recent changes in the Canadian labour market environment. Theses changes include legislation, demographic trends, and shifts in macroeconomic conditions. Since economic concepts are introduced only as needed to explain changes in industrial relations outcomes, labour economics topics are not covered in a systematic fashion. For an explanation of the basic labour economics framework underlying many of these issues, the reader should consult one of the standard Canadian labour economics textbooks such as Gunderson and Riddell (1993) and Gunderson's (1988) discussion of the relationship of labour economics to industrial relations.

The chapter begins with an overview of the way compensation and employment levels are determined in a competitive labour market. The theoretical notion of a perfectly competitive labour market is used as a benchmark to analyze compensation and working conditions in actual labour markets as well as to examine how these markets are affected by deregulation. The concept of the demand for labour is used in the analysis of various changes in legislation which affect labour costs, including an increase in the minimum wage, a rise in payroll taxes, the introduction of pay equity legislation, and the apparent "deindustrialization" of the economy.

Changes in labour supply that are analyzed include the long-term reduction in the standard work week and the work year, the aging of the population, the rising proportion of women in the labour force, and increases in the level of education and training. One of the prominent concerns among the actors in the industrial relations system is the issue of equity in earnings. In this chapter, we consider differentials by various factors such as occupation and education, as well as the argument that over the 1980s there has been an increase in the inequality of earnings—a trend that is sometimes referred to as the vanishing middle class and wage polarization.

The final sections of the chapter deal with the influence of changes in the macroeconomic environment on various aspects of labour-management relations, including wage settlements, strike activity, and contract duration. The causes of the cyclical and secular rise in the unemployment rate are considered along with policies to combat unemployment, such as work-sharing. We also explore the reasons for, and implications of, Canadian participation in potentially far-reaching trade agreements such as the Free Trade Agreement with the United States and NAFTA, which includes Mexico. Finally, we consider the important implications of the global reductions of tariffs through GATT.

RECRUITMENT AND COMPENSATION IN A COMPETITIVE LABOUR MARKET

In the classic textbook analysis of a competitive labour market, in which compensation and employment are determined by the interaction of supply and demand, there is very little analysis of the usual human resource functions of recruitment, selection, compensation, training, and planning. Although few, if any, Canadian labour markets fit the strict description of a competitive market, it is, nevertheless, instructive to consider the operation of the classic model. The competitive model is the basis upon which more complex models are built and, in many cases, the predictions from the simple competitive model are similar to those from the more complex models. In addition, the ideology of the competitive market is a powerful force in shaping public policy and is often used as a benchmark in judging the operation of actual labour markets.

Competitive labour markets are, by assumption, characterized by a large number of employers and employees of each type of labour so that no single employer or employee has a significant influence on the market wage rate. It is also assumed that there are no artificial barriers to entering any occupation. In a competitive market, each employer is a "wage-taker;" that is, the employer takes the market wage as given and decides how many employees to hire in order to maximize profits, given the product market conditions and the state of technology.

The supply of labour to any particular occupation (that is, the number of persons who want to work in that occupation) depends on numerous factors including the wage rate for that occupation; the required levels of skill, training, and experience; working conditions; the status of the occupation; and preferences of labour force members. For any fixed level of the other factors that affect labour supply, an increase in the wage rate for one occupation will make that occupation more attractive, resulting in an increased number of persons who want to work in that occupation.

The demand for labour, that is the number of persons in each occupational group that employers want to hire, depends on factors such as the wage rate for the occupation. Also, it is a derived demand, derived from the level of employers' production and technological considerations. For any fixed level of the other factors, a wage increase will tend to reduce the amount of labour (number of persons or the number of hours) employers wish to contract for. This reduction occurs for two reasons. First, an increase in wage costs will increase unit costs and the price of the product being produced, resulting in a drop in sales and a reduction in the derived demand for all inputs including labour. Second, for any given level of output, in the long run, employers will tend to substitute capital or other less expensive types of labour for the labour which has become relatively more expensive. The first adjustment is termed the output effect, and the second is termed the substitution effect. Both work in the same direction, leading to a reduction in the demand for labour as wages increase (i.e., labour demand curves slope downwards).

In the classic, competitive labour market model, there is a particular wage rate, known as the *equilibrium wage*, at which the supply of labour and the demand for labour are equal. At the equilibrium wage, no one would be unemployed; that is, everyone who wants to work at that wage rate would be able to find work. In other words, the labour market would clear. This simple model can be easily modified to allow for frictional unemployment due to employee turnover in a dynamic labour market. Although unfilled jobs and unemployed workers could coexist in this model, there would be no overall shortage of jobs at the equilibrium wage.

At any wage rate above the equilibrium wage, the supply of labour exceeds the demand for labour resulting in downward pressure on the wage rate. Conversely, at any wage rate below the equilibrium level, the demand for labour exceeds the supply of labour, resulting in unfilled job vacancies and upward pressure on the wage rate. Consequently, in a competitive labour market, compensation tends toward the equilibrium wage and employment where quantity of labour supplied equals the quantity demanded.

Although it may be tempting to dismiss the assumptions of the competitive model as unrealistic, a scientific model should be judged on the accuracy of its predictions, not on the descriptive realism of its assumptions. In this sense, the classic competitive model is somewhat like theoretical examples in physics. For instance, the mechanics of a pulley are sometimes studied without allowing for the influence of friction, or the speed of a falling object is calculated without factoring in air pressure. That is, these are abstract models that do not assume a completely realistic environment or "atmosphere."

Privatization and Deregulation

The ideology of the competitive market has provided the impetus for privatization and deregulation. Such policies involve decreasing the influence of government in product markets through the sale of government-owned enterprises and the deregulation of various product markets. In many industries, such as transportation and communications, deregulation has had dramatic impacts on industrial relations.

In the airline industry, for example, Air Canada has been privatized and there has been a reduction in regulation concerning routes and fares. The losses resulting from the severe competition, combined with the effects of the recession, have resulted in the elimination (or merger) of some smaller airlines (such as Wardair), and have even threatened the viability of the two large airlines. The crisis atmosphere in the industry has spawned changes in labour-management relations that would have been unthinkable in the previous regulated environment. The changes include unions offering to take wage concessions in exchange for part ownership of Canadian Airlines. However, as Fisher and Kondra (1992, 398) observe, "The changes were more evolutionary, rather than transformational in nature...[because of the] support of collective bargaining by Canadian labour law and the phasing in of deregulation in Canada." In the spring of 1995, "open skies" competition was extended to allow US carriers to operate freely in Canada and Canadian carriers to operate in the United States. At this writing, the long-term industrial relations implications of this development are unclear.

Although Canada Post has not been privatized, much of the same objective was achieved by converting it from a regular government department to a Crown corporation in 1981, with instructions to conduct its business as if it were a private corporation. It was transformed from a money-losing enterprise to a profitable one as a result. The industrial relations situation also improved considerably, although this was partly due to institutional changes such as the forced amalgamation of the Letter Carriers Union of Canada and the Canadian Union of Postal Workers.

In the telephone industry, the government's decision to allow Unitel to compete with Bell Canada in the long-distance market in Ontario and Quebec has substantially affected the industry. In the past, relatively low rates for local telephone service were cross-subsidized by relatively high rates for long-distance service. The arrival of competition in the long-distance market creates economic pressures for Bell Canada to end this cross-subsidization in order to compete more effectively in the long-distance market. The restructuring resulting from this change will likely have an important impact for industrial relations in the industry. For example, in 1994, with the union's agreement, Bell and 13,000 of its employees experimented with a mandatory four-day, 36-hour week instead of 40 hours over five days. This change was in anticipation of a need to reduce payroll costs by almost half a billion dollars. Following a surge in customer demand and voluntary retirements and attrition, the company gave these employees the option of returning to a five-day week or remaining on the shortened work schedule.

Improving Working Conditions: Legislation or the Market

In the past few years, there has been an increase in legislation designed to improve various aspects of the work environment through such diverse initiatives as regulating hazardous work conditions and placing limits on the hours that an employee can be compelled to work. Some market-oriented economists have argued, however, that if labour markets were competitive and properly functioning, such employment standards and human rights legislation would not be required. They argue that in a competitive labour market such conditions are handled through *compensating wage differentials*.

This argument flows from the assumed existence of full employment and the lack of artificial barriers to mobility between occupations in the competitive model. This in turn implies that, over a long period of time, the "net advantage" in each occupation would be equal for the marginal worker. Net advantage in each occupation refers to the overall desirability of the occupation when all factors are considered, including wages, employee benefits, working conditions, risk of injury, and the time and money needed to acquire the qualifications for the occupation. If the net advantage were greater in one occupation than in another, some employees (the marginal workers) would be induced to move from the less desirable occupation to the more desirable occupation. In a competitive labour market, the decrease in labour supply would tend to raise the wage in the less desirable occupation, and the increase in supply would reduce the wage in the more desirable occupation. The process would continue until, in the long run, the net advantage in the two occupations would be equal for the marginal worker.

The conclusion, which can be traced back to the work of Adam Smith more than 200 years ago, is that the equalization of the net advantage in each occupation in competitive labour markets results in compensating wage differentials that offset undesirable non-wage aspects of the job. For example, jobs that are dirty or dangerous or require a long period of training or unduly long hours of work would receive a higher wage, which would be just sufficient to offset these disadvantages for the marginal employee. Some of the market-oriented economists have argued that it also implies that competitive markets would produce differentials to compensate employees for jobs with undesirable working conditions such as underground mining, chemical waste disposal, or employment in funeral homes. Such a wage differential would also provide an economic incentive for employers to eliminate such undesirable working conditions, provided the cost of eliminating them is less than the cost of paying the compensating wage differential.

The Actual Operation of Labour Markets

Most labour markets differ from the perfectly competitive ideal in several important respects. First, although wage rates are influenced by economic forces, these rates generally do not adjust rapidly to equate supply and demand as predicted by the competitive model. Actual labour markets are often characterized by substantial periods of labour surpluses (unemployment) or some periods of labour shortages (job vacancies), even in the absence of institutional factors that impede adjustment such as minimum wage laws, equal pay legislation, or unions. In particular, adjustments following a reduction in demand for labour are often in terms of involuntary terminations (layoffs) rather than a reduction of the wage to the equilibrium level. Attempts to explain why wage adjustments do not clear the labour market in a satisfactory period of time have been the source of considerable controversy and will be discussed below in the context of barriers to labour market flexibility.

The second reason why actual labour markets differ from the competitive ideal is that most employers are "wage-setters" rather than "wage-takers" as assumed in the competitive model. Being a wage-taker implies that the employer can hire any desired amount of labour at the given market wage, but that at a slightly lower wage, the employer would not be able to attract any employees because they would leave to work at a competing firm offering the market wage. Typically, employers recognize that if they reduce the wage rate, there may be some reduction in the supply of labour to the firm (or an increase in turnover rates), but they will not lose their entire work force as assumed in the perfectly competitive case. In fact, survey evidence (Card 1992, 53) indicates that teenage workers would require a wage that is 26 per cent higher than their current wage to induce them to move to a similar job with a different employer in the same area. The size of this differential presumably reflects the substantial psychological and economic costs of changing employers, thus giving employers a substantial role as wage-setters.

Employers who are wage-setters rather than wage-takers are said to possess some degree of *monopsony power*, and it can be shown that, in exercising that power to maximize profits, they will pay a lower wage and employ fewer workers than an employer in a perfectly competitive labour market. The extreme case of monopsonistic power is a situation in which there is only one employer of a particular type of labour in the market, such as a school board that is the only employer of teachers in a community or a hospital that is the only employer of nurses. Such cases of pure monopsony are the polar opposite of a perfectly competitive labour market.

Employers with some degree of monopsony power can affect the amount of labour supplied to their establishments through their recruiting, promotion, and training procedures as well as through changes in their wage structure or the redesigning of the job. For example, a firm may try to reduce a persistent shortage of a particular skill by any combination of recruiting, promotion, training, or wage raises, or by redesigning the job so that its component parts could be done by others or by capital equipment.

Dual Labour Markets

The possible existence of dual or segmented labour markets also complicates the wage and employment determination process. According to dual labour market analysis, the labour market is segmented into noncompeting groups. The primary or core labour market generally consists of high-paying jobs with good working conditions, reasonable job security, and opportunities for training and advancement. The secondary or peripheral labour market consists of jobs with the opposite characteristics. In part because of these poor working conditions, workers in the secondary labour market exhibit high absenteeism and turnover and lack motivation for self-improvement. This, in turn, reduces their chances of leaving the secondary labour market. For this reason, and because of discrimination, custom, and tradition, these two labour markets remain segmented from each other, with little chance for workers to advance from the secondary to the primary labour market.

Does a Higher Wage Mean Fewer Jobs?

Many of the changes implemented or proposed in the industrial relations field increase labour costs. Examples include an increase in minimum wages, an increase in wages of female employees through pay equity legislation, an increase in payroll taxes such as Canada Pension Plan contributions and the Ontario Employer Health levy, an increase in the premium for overtime hours or a reduction of the standard work week after which the overtime premium applies, and an increase in pension benefits directly or by indexing benefits to inflation. In the context of a competitive labour market, an increase in labour costs will result in a reduction in employment since the demand curve for labour is downward sloping as discussed previously. In order to make an informed assessment of the potential employment impact of changes in labour costs, it is, however, often necessary to know by *how much* employment will be reduced in response to a given cost increase.

The concept used to measure the responsiveness of employment to labour costs is the *elasticity of demand for labour,* defined as the percentage reduction in employment in response to a one percentage increase in wages in a particular job (for a given level of wages and prices for the economy as a whole). The elasticity of demand for labour will vary depending upon the particulars of the situation. Generally, however, the percentage reduction in employment associated with a wage increase will be larger under the following circumstances:

- if the firm can easily substitute capital or other types of labour for the type of labour that has increased in cost,
- if it cannot pass the cost increase on to consumers without reducing demand for the product and hence the derived demand for labour,
- or if labour costs are a substantial portion of total costs so that the firm cannot easily absorb the cost increase.

The employment effect will also be greater the longer the time allowed for adjustments to take place.

A review of the empirical evidence by Hamermesh (1993) suggests that, on average, over a one-year time horizon, employment is reduced by about 3 per cent for each 10 per cent increase in labour costs. In situations where employment is particularly sensitive to labour costs, Hamermesh's work suggests the employment impact could be twice as large, and in situations in which employment is less sensitive to labour costs, the impact may be virtually zero. Hamermesh also finds that, on average, the cause of the employment reduction is divided roughly equally between a drop in sales due to the higher price of the output (the output effect) and the replacement of the more expensive labour by capital or other types of labour (the substitution effect).

The Canadian Labour Congress has advocated, as a means of creating jobs, increasing the premium rate for overtime work or completely banning overtime in order to force employers to cut back on it and to hire more employees. In a study for the Ontario Task Force on Hours of Work and Overtime, Robb and Robb (1987, Table 10) calculated that, ignoring the impact on the demand for labour, an increase in the overtime premium from time-and-one-half to double time would increase hourly paid employment in Ontario by 0.5 percent. By taking into account the negative impact on the demand for labour resulting from the increase in labour costs, however, the employment increase is only 0.2 percent.

The Impact on Employment of Raising the Minimum Wage

One goal of a minimum wage policy is to improve the equity of the distribution of income. In the context of a competitive labour market, the major drawback of a minimum wage policy is that, by setting a wage above the equilibrium wage, it may result in a reduction of employment for those working at the minimum wage. In the context of a monopsonistic labour market, however, it is theoretically possible for a moderate increase in the minimum wage to actually increase employment. The reason is that when an employer with monopsony power reduces employment below the competitive level, the employer not only saves the wages of the displaced employees, but also saves on the wages of all the organization's employees because those wages can be lower since the employer needs to attract fewer employees. In the case of a minimum wage, the latter savings are eliminated because the wage cannot be reduced below the legal minimum. The result is that the imposition of a minimum wage can cause an employer with monopsony power to increase employment.

A study of the impact of the minimum wage in Canada (Swidinsky 1980) indicated that teenage employment is reduced by 1.7 per cent for each 10 per cent increase in the minimum wage (relative to the average wage level). Swidinsky calculated that the unemployment rate for teenagers had increased by 1.2 percentage points as a result of the increased level and coverage of the minimum wage across Canada in the twenty-year period up to 1975. The methodology used was to include a minimum wage variable in a time-series analysis of the teenage unemployment rate using other variables (such as the adult unemployment rate) to provide a counter-factual prediction of what the teenage unemployment rate would have been in the absence of adjustments to the minimum wage.

Similar conclusions were obtained in a more recent study by Cousineau, Tessier, and Vaillancourt (1992) who predicted a substantial increase in the teenage unemployment rate as a result of the minimum wage increase announced by the Ontario government in 1990. The wage was to increase from $4.55 per hour (as of October 1987) to $6.70 per hour by January 1994.

The conventional wisdom that an increase in the minimum wage causes a reduction in employment has been challenged in some important recent work by Card (1992) and others using American data. An alternative quasi-experimental methodology was utilized in which minimum wage increases in one state were assessed by comparing employment levels to another state where the minimum wage did not rise. The second state served as a "control group." This quasi-experimental method used by Card appears to be more reliable on scientific grounds than the time-series analysis that was used in most previous research on the topic. Card found no evidence of negative employment impacts, which led him to conclude that more attention should be given to noncompetitive models of the labour market such as the monopsony model.

Deindustrialization

Deindustrialization refers to a shift of employment away from manufacturing and other goods production towards employment in the service sector. This trend is an issue of concern to trade union members and others since many of the jobs in the goods sector are higher paying unionized blue-collar jobs and many of the service sector jobs are lower paying and often nonunion.

There are three fundamental economic forces related to the demand for labour that account for the long-term decline in Canadian manufacturing employment as a per cent of total employment, evidence of which is discussed in Foot and Meltz (1985). First, as living standards have risen over time, there has been an increase in the consumption of both goods and services, but consumers' preferences for services have increased faster than their preferences for goods. Second, productivity growth has generally been higher in goods industries than service industries, implying that, even if the *consumption* of goods increased at the same rate as consumption of services, production requirements would dictate a slower growth of the employment rate in goods than in services. Third, the demand for labour in Canadian manufacturing has declined as production has shifted to Third World countries with lower wage rates and employee benefits and new capital equipment.

Foreign competition affects manufacturing more than services since services cannot be transported and traded as easily as manufactured goods. The shift to the service sector occurred primarily in the form of a shift in the production of some services and commodities from within manufacturing towards the service sector itself. This has occurred, for example, in many business services (financial, accounting, marketing), security and cleaning services, and cafeteria services. In addition to this shift towards purchasing from within the service sector itself, the demand for services has grown in general.

Within the service sector, which contains almost 70 per cent of the work force, there are enormous differences in employment trends, wage rates, and the extent of unionization. Government employment growth slowed markedly in the 1980s and 1990s after increasing in the 1960s and 1970s. Employment in transportation, storage, communications and utilities also did not keep up with the overall growth. In contrast, absolute and relative increases occurred in business services, retail trade, consumer services, and education and health. Earnings and the degree of unionization are high in utilities, transportation, storage, communications, government, and education and health, and low in wholesale and retail trade and consumer services. Earnings are high and unionization is low in business services.

The issue of deindustrialization, therefore, is more complex than simply moving from situations of extensive unionization and high wages to situations of low unionization and low wages. Even if the degree of unionization remains unchanged, the long-term trends toward the service sector will produce mixed results in terms of the implications for both unionization and wage rates.

Labour Force Participation and Hours of Work

The supply of labour to individual occupations depends on the net advantages in each occupation, as discussed above, but the supply of labour to the labour market as a whole requires a somewhat different analysis. Labour supply has both quality and quantity dimensions. The quality dimensions refer to such factors as motivation and alienation (subjects within the purview of personnel and organizational behaviour) as well as education and training (subjects that have been analyzed within the context of human capital theory).

The quantity dimensions of labour supply are numerous, basically involving the size of our population (births less deaths plus net immigration), the extent to which the population participates in labour market activities, and the hours worked by those who participate in the labour market. The economic determinants of these various components — births, net immigration, labour force participation, and hours of work—have been the subject matter of considerable research on the supply side of labour markets.

The theoretical framework used for the analysis of *employee preferences* for hours of work and labour force participation decisions is the "income-leisure choice model," which treats the purchase of "leisure" (a catchall word for all nonwork activities) the same as the purchase of any other commodity. The individual has a fixed amount of time that can be allocated to leisure or to earning income through work. The wage rate indicates the amount of goods and services that can be purchased by giving up one hour of leisure.

In the income-leisure choice model, an increase in the wage rate influences the number of hours the employee desires to work through two effects operating in opposite directions. On the one hand, a higher wage means the employee can earn more income and purchase more goods and services for each hour of leisure given up. This induces a substitution of goods for the relatively more expensive leisure. Leisure is more "expensive" because of the higher wage one forgoes by consuming it. This "substitution effect" means that at a higher wage, the employee will prefer to work longer hours. On the other hand, a higher wage means the employee is wealthier and can afford to consume more goods and services and more leisure. This "income effect" means that at a higher wage rate, the employee will want to consume more leisure, that is, work fewer hours. The empirical evidence suggests that, in general, the income and substitution effects are of roughly equal magnitude—that is, they tend to offset each other. This implies that a wage increase will normally affect desired hours of work only slightly or have no impact. For men, however, the income effect slightly dominates, so that wage increases tend to result in a slight reduction in their desired hours of work (i.e., the male labour supply schedule is slightly "backward bending"). For women, however, the substitution effect appears to dominate the income effect so that a wage increase tends to increase their desired hours of work (i.e., the female labour supply schedule is forward sloping).

The income-leisure choice model sheds light on several issues which are significant in labour-management relations. The standard work week in Canada has declined dramatically over the last century, influenced by both collective bargaining and employment standards legislation. In Canadian manufacturing, the standard work week has declined from 64 hours per week in 1870 to under 40 hours per week in the 1990s. In the postwar period the reduction has been in the form of longer vacations and more holidays, that is, a shorter work year, rather than reduced hours-per-week, in part because the fixed costs of commuting make the reductions in hours-per-week less economical than a longer vacation. The income-leisure choice model suggests that as productivity and real wage rates have increased over time, the income effect of the wage increase outweighed the substitution effect, resulting in a desire for more leisure and shorter work hours as the wage rate increased (for men but not for women, as discussed above).

The income-leisure choice model also allows us to analyze the impact on work incentives of changes in tax rates. One of the components of "supply-side economics" is the view that a cut in tax rates will raise the after-tax wage rate and significantly increase the desire to work longer hours. The most extreme version of this argument (the "Laffer curve") suggests that output will increase by so much that total tax *revenue* will actually increase as a result of a cut in tax *rates*. However, this analysis assumes that the substitution effect of a tax cut will substantially dominate the income effect, leading to increased work time—an assumption that seems at odds with the existing evidence.

The income-leisure choice framework also illustrates how various income maintenance programs (e.g., welfare, unemployment insurance) can reduce work incentives. This occurs because they both provide income and hence reduce the need to work (the income effect), and also because they often tax labour market earnings, usually implicitly by requiring the recipient to forgo all or some of the transfer payment if they work (the substitution effect).

Economic analysis also demonstrates the importance of the high opportunity cost of having children for women whose potential labour market earnings are high and hence who would forgo substantial earnings and perhaps a career by raising a family. Other things being equal, such women tend to have fewer children, and they tend to have them closer together in time so as to minimize the disruption to their labour market activities.

The Aging of the Population

The last decade has seen a continuation of fundamental changes in the demographic composition of the labour force that have important implications for union-management relations. One of these changes is that during the mid-1990s, the large baby boom generation (those born between 1947 and 1966) have moved solidly into the middle-aged group (30 to 50 years of age).

Foot and Venne (1990) argue that the movement of the baby boom generation into middle-age has created a mismatch between the typical organization structure and the demographic structure of the labour force. In the past, the rapidly growing labour force resulted in a "population pyramid" (with a younger population base and fewer persons at the apex in the older age groups). This roughly mirrored the typical pyramidal structure of most organizations (with fewer positions at the higher levels).

The population pyramid was transformed, however, as the baby boom generation was followed by the relatively small baby bust generation. The result was a mismatching in which the traditional upward career movement was blocked by a lack of senior positions for the baby boomers. Foot and Venne (1990) developed a measure that indicated that the degree of mismatch declined during the 1960s and early 1970s, but increased during the 1980s. They project the degree of mismatch is to continue to worsen during the 1990s and the first decade of the twenty-first century.

In terms of implications for human resource management, Foot and Venne suggest a change from a traditional linear career path up the traditional hierarchical organization, to a spiral path which combines both lateral and vertical movements. In certain circumstances there could even be acceptance of a lower position in the hierarchy as a result of downsizing of the organization or increased stress associated with greater competition (Meltz and Meltz 1992). Such changes would provide new challenges for employees, as well as greater emphasis on planning and retraining. Such changes may also call for complementary policies, such as increased study leaves or sabbaticals and modified compensation structures in which success is related not just to the level of the positions held in the organization, but also to their variety.

The aging of the labour force has other implications for industrial relations and human resource practices. Middle-aged workers tend to be more stable in their attachment to their employer than are younger workers. The aging of the labour force can be expected to reduce voluntary turnover, and this in turn can make unionization a more attractive option. The longer a worker intends to remain with an employer the more appealing is the investment of effort and money in forming and nurturing a union. In other words, for the greying labour force, the use of "voice" (unionization) becomes more attractive relative to the use of "exit" (quitting) as a way of improving the work environment.

As individuals approach retirement, their preferences in collective bargaining shift towards pension and related benefits and away from an emphasis on wages. There clearly can be sharp differences within a bargaining unit between younger workers with families to support, who are interested in the amount of take-home pay, and older workers who are prepared to accept a reduced take-home pay in favour of putting more money into a pension plan. Workers of different ages and family responsibilities may also place different emphasis on such factors as health and safety, medical benefits, and seniority and work-time practices including flexible worktime arrangements. Although workers of all ages are interested in job security, this is especially true of middle-aged workers.

The aging of the labour force has also been accompanied by an increasing emphasis on the issue of age discrimination in employment. In almost all Canadian jurisdictions, it is illegal to use age as a criteria in employment decisions such as hiring, promotion, or layoffs. Of course, there are typically exceptions concerning issues of public safety or where the employer can demonstrate an age restriction is a bona fide requirement of the job.

Mandatory retirement policies, by which an employer requires employees to retire at a fixed age (typically 65 years), are often interpreted as a form of age discrimination. During the early 1980s, some provinces (such as Quebec and Manitoba) prohibited mandatory retirement as constituting a form of age discrimination. Other provinces, such as Ontario, continue to permit mandatory retirement by placing a "cap" of 64 years on the age discrimination provision in the Ontario Human Rights Code. That is, the code does not apply to persons over the age of 64—an exemption that exists to allow mandatory retirements.

This cap was itself the subject of a challenge in 1986 under the Canadian Charter of Rights and Freedoms. The Charter, which applies to government legislation and to the government as an employer, takes legal precedence over other legislation since it is part of the Canadian Constitution. The plaintiff in the case charged that the cap is a form of age discrimination and therefore in violation of the Charter since the Charter prohibits age discrimination at any age. Although the Supreme Court ruled in 1990 that the cap was indeed age discrimination, the court found that it was reasonable for the Ontario government to impose such a cap because the abolition of mandatory retirement might have wide-ranging impacts on the industrial relations system. Basically, the Supreme Court decision means that the issue of whether mandatory retirement should be prohibited will not be made by the Court, but will be a political decision made by the provincial legislatures.

Increasing Importance of Women in the Labour Force

Another important demographic change is that during the last two decades, the Canadian labour force has been transformed from one which was predominantly male to one approaching an equal balance between men and women. In 1970 men constituted 66 per cent of the labour force, double the proportion of women, who constituted only 34 per cent. By 1993, the split was 55 per cent male and 45 per cent female, not far from a 50/50 ratio.

The change in the gender composition was primarily due to a sharp rise in the labour force participation rate of women, from 38 per cent in 1970 to 58 per cent in 1993. During the same period, the labour force participation rate of men declined somewhat from 78 per cent to 73 per cent. The rise in the female labour force participation rate is mainly due to a change in the participation rate of married women. In the past, women were likely to remain in the labour force only until they were married. Increasingly, women are returning to the labour force after childbearing, and their participation rate is moving upward toward that of men while male labour force participation has declined slightly.

The increased importance of women in the labour force has been accompanied by important changes in legislation governing their pay and working conditions. In terms of pay, *equal pay for equal work* legislation (which requires women to be paid the same as men if they are doing substantially the same job) was generally replaced with *pay equity* legislation. The latter requires that female-dominated jobs be paid the same as male-dominated jobs if the jobs are of *equal value,* based on a composite of skill, effort, responsibility, and working conditions. Gender-neutral job evaluation techniques are used to compare the value of jobs which might be in quite different occupations, such as a secretary and a truck driver.

Because the traditional complaints-based human rights approach was slow and relatively ineffective and tended to be applied mainly to the public sector, the Ontario government, in its 1987 Pay Equity Act, broke new ground by implementing a *proactive* approach that requires employers in *both* the public and private sectors (above a minimum size) to evaluate their jobs and to make appropriate adjustments if female-dominated jobs are found to be underpaid relative to male-dominated jobs for the same employer. Changes were to be phased in between 1990 and 1993, depending upon the size of the employer's workforce.

In terms of women's working conditions, there has been a heightened awareness of issues such as sexual harassment. Legislation defines the concept of sexual harassment broadly to include both direct behaviour (the threat of a reward or punishment on the job to induce a sexual favour) and indirect "poisoning the environment" through activities such as unwanted sexual comments, jokes, or leering. Unless they have appropriate policies, employers may be liable for harassment not only between supervisors and subordinates, but also between co-workers.

Increasing Importance of Part-time Work

By the mid-1990s, about one employee in six was working part-time, defined by Statistics Canada as working less than thirty hours per week. Part-time work has increased steadily from the mid-1950s when about one employee in twenty-five worked part-time (and when part-time work was defined by Statistics Canada as normally working less than thirty-five hours per week).

The rise in part-time work reflects several of the labour market trends already outlined. On the supply side, the rise in the labour force participation rate of women, particularly married women, resulted in an increase in the proportion of employees desiring to work part-time. Over two-thirds of part-time employees are female. Statistics Canada indicates that normally about three-quarters of part-timers work part-time voluntarily, although in recessions there is typically an increase in the amount of involuntary part-time work. On the demand side, since services cannot be stored as easily as goods, the increasing importance of the service sector in the economy resulted in an increase in the demand for part-time employees to meet peak periods of demand.

The federal government's Commission of Inquiry into Part-time Work (1983) found that the productivity of part-timers is generally equal to or higher than full-timers, although the compensation of part-timers is often substantially less than for full-timers doing the same work. To address this inequity, the Commission recommended employment standards legislation to provide equal pay for work of equal value for part-timers and full-timers, with benefits for part-timers prorated according to the number of hours worked. However, employer opposition to such recommendations is substantial. In Saskatchewan, the government introduced then withdrew legislation designed to prorate part-time benefits. Similarly the British Columbia government chose not to follow the advice of an independent employment review commission which had recommended prorated benefits for part-time employees.

Unions often strongly opposed the use of part-time workers, and there have been many strikes in which a major issue was the union's opposition to management proposals to increase the use of part-time employees. The reason for union opposition is that the poor compensation of part-timers was seen as a threat to the employment and compensation of full-time employees. As well, part-time workers are often more difficult to organize. Many employees do prefer part-time work, however, and if the compensation of part-timers is made comparable to that of full-timers, union opposition may diminish. Even in the absence of such legislation, unions have increased their efforts to organize part-time workers. This is partly the result of the increase in the number of part-time workers and partly the result of the decrease in the rate of unionization in the private sector. In addition, changes in labour legislation, such as Ontario's Bill 40 in 1992, permit bargaining units composed of both part-time and full-time workers if the union so requests.

Who Should Pay the Bill for Education and Training?

If Canada is to maintain and improve its standard of living in an era of increasing international competition many experts have advocated an increased reliance on high-skill, high value-added jobs. This requires greater emphasis on the education and training of the Canadian labour force, but there is debate over who should pay for such training. In the realm of postsecondary education, many have advocated an increase in university fees, perhaps coupled with an income-contingent repayment scheme in which students repay their fees only when they are employed in a job earning an above-average salary. In the area of on-the-job training, many have advocated a training levy on all firms who employ skilled workers to combat "poaching"—luring skilled workers from employers who have provided training to their employees.

In the economic literature, education and training are examined in terms of human capital theory. In order for an individual to undertake education and training, there has to be a compensating difference in the form of higher wages or improved working conditions to provide a return for the investment of time and money. The investment costs are both direct, in the form of tuition, fees, and books, and indirect, in terms of the earnings which are forgone while the person is in school.

In the case of both education and training, the government is heavily involved in subsidizing or completely covering the costs. While education is under provincial jurisdiction, training has been viewed as shared, or at times, solely under federal jurisdiction, because of the federal government's overall responsibility for economic matters. These divisions have led to conflicts over the administration of programs relating to the labour market. While the federal government operates a national system of employment offices (Canada Employment Centres), the Province of Quebec has established its own employment service (Quebec Manpower Centres).

In the early 1960s, programs tended to be on the basis of shared costs between the federal and provincial governments. In Ontario, for example, this funding provided the basis for the development of the system of community colleges, known as the Colleges of Applied Arts and Technology (CAATs). The Canada Department of Employment and Immigration's Canada Manpower Training Program has been a major source of funds for the CAATs (Meltz 1990). The heavy reliance on institutional as opposed to on-the-job training has been the subject of much criticism (Meltz 1990), but any redirection from institutional to on-the-job training would have to take into consideration the implications for provincial institutions like the community colleges, which depend on funds for institutional training.

In terms of labour-management relations, the jurisdictional division has led to some differences in training programs for various skills and also to some fragmentation of labour markets through barriers to mobility, especially in certain trades such as those in the construction industry in Quebec (although recently such barriers have been reduced). The implication is that the Canadian labour market is less responsive to labour market demands than it would be if there were a more unified approach to education, training, and mobility.

In the late 1970s, attention focused on skill shortages in Canada that had been compounded by the decrease in immigration. This decrease was partly associated with the rise of living standards in Europe, which made Canada a relatively less desirable place in which to relocate. In addition, the federal government had been consciously reducing immigration in order to encourage greater training in Canada to fill skill shortages from the ranks of the unemployed. This issue was examined by two federal government task forces: the Parliamentary Task Force on Employment Opportunities in the 80s, and Employment and Immigration's Task Force on Labour Market Development. With the upturn in the economy in the mid-1980s, immigration increased, although it is currently again being reduced. Government policy on education and training as well as on immigration will have a major impact on the supply of particular kinds of labour, which in turn will ultimately affect union-management relations in particular occupations and industries.

Education and training requirements can also be used as barriers to entry into particular occupations. The setting of artificially high standards can be used to reduce the supply of labour and thereby foster increases in wages and security of employment for the incumbent workers. Persons excluded by the barriers to entry may end up with lower wages and possibly less secure jobs, perhaps in the secondary labour market. The effect of such occupational licensing has been debated with respect to a number of professions and trades, including doctors, dentists, lawyers, and skilled tradespersons.

Earning Differentials and Recent Earnings Inequality

Market forces of supply and demand set the general boundaries for the employment and wage rate decisions by occupation and industry. The determination of earnings is affected both by collective bargaining and by government regulations such as minimum wages, training, and education requirements. In addition, the wage rates negotiated by one union may be emulated by others, including nonunion firms.

Empirical studies, such as those cited by Gunderson and Riddell (1993, 487) indicate that the ranking of *occupational* earnings has been fairly stable over long periods of time. Some changes have occurred, however, which are usually associated either with the decline of an industry (for example the deterioration in the relative position of the railroads) or a major change in technology (such as the huge increase in air traffic and in the earnings of airline pilots). The dispersion of earnings among occupations seems to have followed cycles of narrowing (1911-21 and 1941-51) and widening (1921-31, 1951-61, and 1961-71), with a long-run narrowing between occupations with high and low earnings.

Evidence also indicates the existence of substantial wage differentials by *industry*, beyond what appear to be required as compensating differentials to reflect variations in qualifications and working conditions. For example, "high wage" industries, such as tobacco products and petroleum manufacturing, appear to pay 20 per cent to 30 per cent above the competitive norm whereas "low wage" industries, such as accommodation and food services, tend to pay 20 per cent below the competitive norm (Gera and Grenier 1991). These interindustry differentials appear to be relatively stable over time and across countries.

A possible explanation for such interindustry wage differentials is the notion of "efficiency wages," i.e., employers in some industries may find it profitable to pay above the market clearing wage if the higher wage results in higher productivity through mechanisms such as greater work effort, improved morale, and lower turnover. Empirically, however, it is difficult to determine if the observed interindustry differentials reflect efficiency wages or other economic factors such as employees benefiting from the employers monopoly power in the product market. As discussed below in the section on Barriers to Labour Market Flexibility, efficiency wages can also result in unemployment by preventing the labour market from clearing.

Regional differentials in earnings are affected by the mix of industries and occupations as well as by differences in earnings due to purely geographical factors. Over time, the regional dispersion of wage rates has narrowed, although there have been cycles similar to those for occupations.

During the 1980s, there was an increase in the inequality of annual earnings of *individuals* in Canada, in contrast to the fairly constant degree of inequality during most of the postwar period, prompting a debate on the causes of the "vanishing middle class." Morissette, Myles, and Picot (1993) show that between 1981 and 1991 the Gini coefficient (a common measure of income inequality) rose over 10 per cent for men. For women the Gini coefficient increased during the early 1980s but dropped during the late 1980s, mainly because women employed part time or part year began to work more hours.

One of the possible explanations for increased inequality is the impact of dein-dustrialization. If earnings in the service sector are more unequal than in the goods sector, then the trend toward an increasing proportion of employment in services would increase inequality (Bluestone and Harrison 1982). This explanation has been rejected, however, on the basis of evidence from a number of studies that the impact of deindustrialization can account for no more than about one-fifth of the change in inequality. Morissette et al. (1993) also test and reject hypotheses that the change in inequality is due to the impact of the baby boom or an increase in the premium for education.

The factor that Morissette et al. find is most important in explaining the rise in the inequality of Canadian annual earnings is that fewer Canadians were working a "normal" work week (of 35 to 40 hours). In particular, there was an increase in the number of hours worked by those with high annual earnings. "Unlike the United States, where changes in earnings inequality have been largely a result of changes in the distribution of hourly wages, shifts in Canadian earnings inequality are, at the aggregate level, mainly driven by changes in the distribution of annual hours worked" (Morissette et al. 1993, 3).

Empirical evidence also indicates that there has been some increase in wage inequity or wage polarization in Canada over the 1980s and 1990s. This polarization has been less pronounced in Canada than in the United States, however, because unionization has not declined in Canada as it has in the United States (Lemieux 1993), and unions tend to reduce wage inequity. Furthermore, there has been a greater influx of more highly educated persons into the Canadian labour market (Freeman and Needles 1993), and this has served to restrain wages at the top of the wage distribution.

CHANGES IN THE MACROECONOMIC ENVIRONMENT

The overall state of the economy, known as the macroeconomic environment, significant-ly influences many aspects of union-management relations. An expanding economy, for example, leads to higher wage settlements and more strike activity; the latter also tends to increase in periods when there is uncertainty about high levels of inflation. An expanding economy may also facilitate the attaining of broader social goals such as occupational health and safety and pay equity and equal employment opportunities for women. It is also associated with a higher rate of growth of unionization and greater success for unions in certification and decertification applications at the labour relations boards.

In periods when the economy is in recession and temporary layoffs are more prevalent, provisions concerning seniority in layoff and recall assume a greater importance in both the negotiation and the administration of the collective agreement. In cases of per-manent layoffs or complete plant shutdown, negotiations concerning severance packages become more prominent. The overall state of the Canadian economy also affects the courts' interpretation of the length of "reasonable notice" required in wrongful dismissal cases under the common law—about one and one-half months more notice is required when the economy is in recession than when it is booming (McShane 1983).

Uncertainty about high rates of inflation tends to result in higher wage settlements and a greater prevalence of cost of living adjustment (COLA) clauses in collective agree-ments. Uncertainty can also lead to reduced contract duration as negotiators will be reluc-tant to commit themselves to a long-term agreement when they anticipate that conditions in the future may differ dramatically from conditions during negotiations.

The Rise in Unemployment

Since the unemployment rate is by far the most prominent measure of the state of the labour market environment, there was a great deal of concern among the actors in the industrial relations system when the Canadian unemployment rate rose to double-digit levels during the recessions of the early 1980s and early 1990s. There has also been a long-term gradual increase in the unemployment rate from an average of 6.7 per cent in the 1970s to 9.3 per cent in the 1980s and 11.2 per cent in 1993. Furthermore, whereas the Canadian unemployment rate was only slightly higher than the US unemployment rate during the 1970s, it was almost 2 percentage points higher during the 1980s (Card and Riddell 1993, 149) and over 4 percentage points higher in 1994. Before exploring the causes of this change, it is useful to examine the way in which unemployment is measured and then outline some useful categories of unemployment.

Unemployment is measured in Canada by a monthly Labour Force Survey covering about 48,000 households. Basically, individuals are defined as unemployed if they were available for work and did not have a job during the survey week and if they looked for work at any time in the four weeks preceding the survey. Unemployment is not conventionally measured by the number of persons drawing unemployment insurance (UI) benefits because many unemployed individuals are not eligible for UI benefits (e.g., new entrants to the labour force and individuals who have exhausted their benefits), and some individuals drawing UI are not looking for work (e.g., women on maternity leave).

Analytically, it is useful to distinguish deficient-demand unemployment, which refers to an overall lack of jobs in the labour market, from frictional and structural unemployment. Structural unemployment occurs when there is a mismatching of the characteristics of the unemployed persons and vacant jobs in terms of geographical location, occupation, or experience. Frictional unemployment occurs when, due to turnover and the fact that it takes time to locate a job, unemployed workers and suitable vacant jobs co-exist in the same labour market. New entrants to the labour market can also experience frictional unemployment. The distinction is important because policies to deal with deficient-demand unemployment (e.g., stimulation of the economy through monetary policy or government spending and taxation) differ from policies to deal with frictional or structural unemployment (e.g., education, training, relocation). The distinction is also important for union-management relations because the level of deficient-demand unemployment provides an indication of the overall state of the labour market and affects strike activity, wage settlements, and the other aspects of labour-management relations discussed above.

Empirically, one of the ways in which deficient-demand unemployment can be distinguished from frictional and structural unemployment is by plotting the time path of the unemployment rate against the job vacancy rate in a diagram known as the Beveridge curve. A change in deficient-demand unemployment is indicated by a *movement along* the unemployment-vacancy curve, whereas a change in frictional or structural unemployment is indicated by a *shift* of the curve.

Structural unemployment can increase as a result of demographic changes in the composition of the labour supply. For example, an increase in the proportion of women in the labour force can increase structural unemployment if employers are reluctant to hire them because of outdated stereotypes. Demographic changes can also increase frictional unemployment if a demographic group (e.g., youth) with an above-average turnover rate increases as a proportion of the labour force. Research (Wilton and Prescott 1992, 30-53;

Reid and Smith 1981) indicates that demographic changes increased structural and frictional unemployment by one to two percentage points in the 1970s. The relative contributions of these factors were reversed, however, with the greying of the labour force in the 1980s (Reid, Meltz, and Lonti 1990). Structural unemployment can also increase due to changes on the demand side of the labour market. Samson (1985) suggests such an increase occurred during the 1980s because of an increased divergence in the growth rate of different industries.

Research suggests that the liberalization of the UI program in 1972 increased frictional unemployment by about 1.5 percentage points, and the tightening of the program in the late 1970s decreased it by about 0.4 percentage points (Gunderson and Riddell 1993, 663-671; Riddell and Smith 1982; Riddell 1985). A more generous UI program could increase frictional unemployment by inducing the unemployed to spend a longer time searching for a new job than they would otherwise. Card and Riddell (1993) identify more generous provisions of Canada's UI program compared with the UI program in the United States as a factor in the huge (over four percentage points) differential in the unemployment rates in Canada and the US in the early 1990s. However, they also say that the major reasons for the differential are still unexplained.

A more generous UI program may also induce firms to make more use of temporary layoffs by, in effect, providing a subsidy to firms and industries that have unstable employment patterns. To eliminate the bias toward layoffs in the current UI system it has been suggested (e.g., by the Royal Commission on the Economic Union—" the Macdonald Commission") that UI premiums be subject to *experience rating* (Riddell 1985, 35). Under experience rating, the UI premium paid by a firm (or an industry) would be related to the amount of UI benefits drawn by employees laid off by that firm. Current reform proposals are concentrating on reducing UI for "repeaters" who constantly enter the UI rolls, often at the same time each year, reflecting the seasonal nature of the work they do (Human Resources Development Canada 1994).

By comparing the movement of the Beveridge curves in Canada and the US, Card and Riddell (1993) find that the increase in the Canadian unemployment rate relative to the US rate was due to an increase in structural/frictional unemployment in Canada rather than a higher level of deficient-demand unemployment. They conclude that "higher aggregate unemployment in Canada is not simply a consequence of lower aggregate employment. Indeed, employment-population ratios in the two countries are fairly similar and became more similar in the 1980s. Rather, individuals who are not working in Canada are more likely to be classified as unemployed" (Card and Riddell 1993, 184). They also conclude that, although the Canadian Unemployment Insurance system became more generous relative the US system, this change can account for at most 0.4 percentage points of the rise in the unemployment rate gap—most of the increase in the gap remains unexplained.

Barriers to Labour Market Flexibility

The pressure of international competition has resulted in increased calls for flexibility in the labour market. A difficult question is why the labour market, and wages in particular, respond so sluggishly to changes in economic conditions. The answer is the subject of considerable controversy.

Keynes (1936) argued that during periods of unemployment, employees are reluctant to accept wage cuts to preserve jobs because inequities would result from the reductions not being spread equally over the whole labour force. More importantly, he argued that the logic of a downward sloping demand for labour that applies to an individual labour market does not apply to the economy as a whole. Although a wage reduction in one market would reduce the real wage and increase employment in that market, an economy-wide reduction in wages would theoretically reduce the level of purchasing power and hence also reduce aggregate demand and the overall price level. This would prevent or delay the reduction in real wages (Keynes 1936, 269).

Another explanation, given in the context of *efficiency wage models,* is that wage reductions may reduce employee morale and productivity. This argument suggests that it may not be sensible for employers to force wage reductions during periods of unemployment, even if they have the power to do so. Another explanation for the failure of the labour market to clear is that employers in both union and nonunion establishments have an understanding or an *implicit contract* with their employees in which they agree not to reduce wages during economic downturns. The purpose of implicit contracts is to insure risk-averse workers against wage fluctuations in exchange for a slightly lower average wage over the business cycle or to prevent quits by experienced workers in whom the employer has an investment in terms of training.

Even though wage rigidity may lead to unemployment, workers may opt for such a policy, if the cost of unemployment is offset somewhat by publicly supported unemployment insurance, or if it falls on workers (e.g., youth) who may have little say in the voting mechanism of unions. Workers may also prefer that aggregate demand shocks be absorbed by employment rather than wage reductions because the former is also costly to the employer, and thereby deters the employer from "bluffing" about the true state of the demand shock. The apparent insensitivity of wages to labour market conditions has also been attributed to the existence of *staggered long-term collective agreements.* In Canada, such agreements are about two years' duration on average. Collective agreements typically specify a series of wage increases over the life of the agreement; these increases reflect labour market conditions at the time the agreement was negotiated rather than conditions at the time the increases take effect. Because of staggered expiry dates and the fact that negotiations are influenced by contracts in force while they take place, lags in the adjustment process can be significantly longer than the duration of the typical contract.

Some economists have suggested that the wage system could be made more flexible and macroeconomic performance be enhanced by the use of bonuses paid through profit-sharing or gain-sharing plans. Gain-sharing plans (e.g., the Scanlon Plan) are based on cost savings or increased production relative to a base period. Profit-sharing is based on increased profits. Gain-sharing plans are more closely related to employee effort than profit-sharing plans because profits can be affected by a wide variety of external developments that are not subject to employee control. Profit-sharing and gain-sharing plans have long been advocated as a means of improving productivity but, more recently, potential benefits for macroeconomic performance also have been suggested. Since bonuses paid are not built into base salary, they increase flexibility in the total compensation package. Profit-sharing is more effective than gain-sharing in enhancing macroeconomic flexibility because profits tend to increase in booms and decrease in recessions, but, for the same reason, gain-sharing is more effective than profit-sharing in enhancing employee effort and productivity.

The Decline in Average Wage Settlements

In the mid-1970s, just prior to the introduction of wage controls, average wage settlements were approximately 15 to 18 per cent. By the early 1990s, average wage settlements had diminished to less than two per cent, the lowest level in decades. What accounts for this dramatic change?

Empirical work on the determinants of the overall aggregate rate of wage change, known as the *Phillips Curve,* has established two basic propositions:

1. for any given level of expected inflation, wage settlements are high when the rate of deficient-demand unemployment rate is low(i.e., when the labour market is in a boom); and
2. for any given state of labour market conditions, wage settlements fully reflect changes in the expected inflation rate (Wilton and Prescott 1992, 444-448; Riddell and Smith 1982).

The reduction in wage settlements between the 1970s and the early 1990s reflects these two basic factors. First, actual and expected inflation in the mid-1970s was over 10 per cent but had declined to almost zero in the early 1990s. Second, the labour market environment was booming in the mid-1970s (the job vacancy rate was at its highest level in 20 years), but by the 1990s the unemployment rate was at double-digit levels.

When the labour market is in overall balance, the overall supply of labour equals the overall demand for labour, and the economy will experience frictional and structural unemployment but not deficient-demand unemployment. The amount of frictional and structural unemployment at this position is also known as either the "natural unemployment rate" or by the more neutral term, the "nonaccelerating inflation rate of unemployment" (NAIRU). The latter name reflects the idea that at such an overall equilibrium position, there would be no labour market pressure for the rate of wage or price change to either increase or decrease.

If the economy is at the NAIRU and is stimulated, for example, by an increased rate of growth of the money supply, the effect in the short run is to reduce the unemployment rate and increase wage settlements. Higher wage settlements are reflected in a higher inflation rate, however, and it can be demonstrated using economic analysis that, in the long run, when expectations about inflation have adjusted to the new higher rate, the economy will return to its original level of unemployment (the NAIRU) and the rate of wage change and inflation will be consistent with the new higher rate of growth of the money supply. Thus, in the short run, reduced unemployment can be "traded off" against higher inflation, but in the long run, such a trade-off is not possible.

If, conversely, the government attempts to reduce inflation by reducing the rate of growth of the money supply, the short-run impact will be an increase in unemployment above the NAIRU, a reduction in wage settlements, and eventually a reduction in inflation. When the lower actual inflation rate is fully reflected in a lower expected inflation rate, the economy can return to its original level of unemployment.

The way in which expectations about inflation are formed plays a crucial role in the adjustment process and has been the subject of considerable debate in the macroeconomics literature. To the extent that labour market participants can accurately foresee the impact of changes in government monetary policy, as suggested by the "rational expectations hypothesis," the short-run adjustment period will be reduced. Unfortunately, evidence suggests that the recession experienced during the "short-run" transition to a lower inflation rate can result in several years of severe unemployment, as revealed in the recessions of the early 1980s and 1990s.

Wage Controls

Because of the severe recession that can result when restrictive monetary policy is used to fight inflation, governments have experimented with wage and price controls to lower inflation rates. In the context of an individual, competitive labour market, forcing the wage below the equilibrium wage using legislated controls would result in a shortage of workers and would be followed by a "wage bubble" when the controls were removed and the wage rose to its equilibrium level. The same would be true for the overall economy if such "disequilibrium controls" were used to force a rate of wage and price change on the economy that was inconsistent with underlying factors such as the rate of growth of the money supply. Controls however, can be used to *complement* a restrictive monetary policy by imposing a rate of change of wages and prices that is *consistent* with the new lower rate of growth of the money supply. Such "equilibrium controls" do not result in shortages while they are in effect, nor in a wage bubble when they are removed. They simply move the economy to the new lower inflation equilibrium with a less severe rise in unemployment than if a restrictive monetary policy were used alone.

The Anti-Inflation Board (AIB) program was an economy-wide three-year wage and profit controls program introduced in October 1975. Wage increases at all private sector firms with five-hundred or more employees, and increases for all public sector employees required approval by the AIB. Guidelines for wage increases in the three years of the program were reduced successively from 10 per cent to 8 per cent to 6 percent. Although the AIB program did not fully achieve its targets for inflation and wage settlements, research indicates that it was partially successful. Wage settlements and inflation were about 2 to 4 per cent lower during the AIB period than they would have been in the absence of controls (Wilton and Prescott 1992, 486-493; Riddell and Smith 1982). There is no evidence of any "wage bubble" following the termination of the AIB nor any evidence of significant shortages or misallocation of resources during the AIB period.

Controls on public sector employees have been applied at various times since the AIB. The motivation for these controls, however, is the government's desire to restrain its expenditure and reduce the size of the government deficit rather than to reduce inflation. Public sector controls are dealt with in more length in Chapter 15 in this volume, which focuses on collective bargaining in the public sector.

Reducing Work Time to Create Jobs

An alternative set of policies that are intended to reduce unemployment and that have important implications for labour-management relations are policies to create or preserve jobs through reductions in work time. Such policies include restricting overtime work, using unemployment insurance funds to provide short-time compensation (STC) to employees on reduced work weeks, and giving employees a legal entitlement to unpaid voluntary leaves. Since restricting overtime work has been discussed above in the context of the demand for labour, the discussion in this section focuses on the latter two alternatives.

Since January 1982, the Canadian UI system has included an STC program in which employees at establishments that have reduced weekly hours to prevent layoffs receive UI payments to partially compensate for the reduction in work time (Reid and Meltz, 1984). For example, if a firm avoided a layoff of 20 per cent of its employees by reducing the work week from five days to four days, the employees would receive UI (at close to 60 per cent of their earnings) for the one day per week they are not working. In this example, the employees would receive 80 per cent of their normal weekly earnings as wages for the four days they worked plus 12 per cent (i.e., .60 x 20 per cent) of their weekly earnings as UI benefits on the fifth day, for a total income equal to 92 per cent of their normal weekly earnings. They also receive an extra day of leisure each week. The STC program proved to be popular, not only with junior employees who were threatened with layoffs, but also with the vast majority of senior employees who valued the extra day of leisure obtained with only a small reduction in weekly income.

From the employer viewpoint, the same number of hours of labour are paid under STC as under the layoff alternative—in the example, five employees working four days per week instead of four employees working five days per week. Expenditures on certain employee benefits such as medical insurance premiums that are "quasi-fixed costs" (meaning they are a fixed amount per employee rather than a fixed amount per hour of labour) are increased because more employees are retained on the payroll. On the other hand, STC saves the firm the cost of training replacements for laid-off employees who find jobs elsewhere and are not available for recall when the firm returns to full production. STC was found, on average, to be cheaper than the layoff alternative, and most employers involved in the STC program were pleased with it.

From the government viewpoint, expenditure on UI is basically the same under STC as under the layoff alternative since five employees draw UI one day per week instead of one employee drawing benefits five days per week. There was an increase in UI costs under the STC program, however, due to the waiving of the two-week waiting period (Employment and Immigration Canada 1993). This cost increase could be eliminated, however, through minor changes to the program which would not seriously harm it (Reid and Meltz 1984). Most importantly, STC is a much more equitable method of dealing with a reduced demand for labour than the layoff alternative.

Canadian survey evidence on employee preferences for work reductions (cited in Reid 1987) indicate that over one-quarter of full-time employees would *prefer* to reduce their work time with a proportionate reduction in pay. About 20 per cent of employees would prefer increased unpaid annual vacation (generally one or two weeks) and 18 per cent indicated they would prefer a shorter work week (generally one day per week). It seems anomalous that so many employees are involuntarily working more than their preferred hours, at the same time as so many other people are involuntarily unemployed. Jobs could be created for unemployed workers and the quality of life of current full-time employees could be improved by giving employees an *entitlement* to voluntary work time reductions in employment standards legislation. To begin to address this problem, the Ontario Task Force on Hours of Work and Overtime (1987, 132) recommended that the Ontario Employment Standards Act be revised to provide employees, with 10 years or more of service, the *right* to one week of voluntary unpaid leave each year, and employees within four years of retirement, an entitlement of up to four weeks of voluntary annual unpaid leave. A similar right to five days of voluntary unpaid leave each year, linked to the care and health of immediate family members, was recommended by the recent federal Advisory Group on Working Time and the Distribution of Work (Donner 1994).

Labour Market Implications of Free-Trade

One of the most significant changes in the economic environment in the early 1990s has been the increasing international competition resulting from a series of trade agreements. The bilateral Free Trade Agreement (FTA) with the United States, which took effect in 1989, was followed by the trilateral North American Free Trade Agreement (NAFTA) with the United States and Mexico, which took effect in January 1994. In 1994, in a new round of negotiations under the General Agreement on Trade and Tariffs (GATT), Canada also agreed to a reduction of tariffs in its trade with the global economy, including countries such as India, Brazil, Turkey, Indonesia, and Malaysia.

A question of great concern to many Canadians is how Canada can be expected to compete against countries with much lower wage costs and employment standards? For example, countries such as Mexico and Brazil have average hourly compensation costs which are less than one-fifth the cost in Canada (data cited in Gunderson and Riddell 1993, 217). The answer is that unit labour costs (dollars/unit) are determined by compensation (dollars/hour) divided by productivity (units/hour). If low wages generally reflect low productivity, then unit costs of production are not necessarily lower in low-wage countries. Indeed, some of Canada's toughest competition internationally comes from high-productivity countries such as Germany and Sweden, which have compensation costs about one-third higher than Canada. The concern is, however, that many of the low-wage countries are moving up the productivity spectrum and becoming low-wage, high-productivity countries.

Why have Canada (and most other countries) moved toward free trade in the last few years? The basic argument in favour of free trade is that by allowing production to be located where it is most efficient, costs can be reduced and in the long run citizens of all countries can potentially benefit from an increase in their real income. Increased efficiency arises from *comparative advantage* (which takes advantage of geographical differences in relative ability to produce goods) and *economies of scale* (which take advantage of longer production runs to utilize mass production techniques).

The estimated size of the increase in real income resulting from trade liberalization, was however, quite modest. For example, following a review of empirical studies, the Royal Commission on the Economic Union (1985, 331) indicated that real incomes of Canadians could be increased from 3 to 5 per cent on average by free trade with the United States. The benefits could be larger if free trade prevented a reduction in Canadian incomes resulting from protectionist trade restrictions that otherwise may have been imposed by the United States. By removing tariff and other trade barriers, free trade may also lead to a dissipation of inefficient market structures, regulatory regimes, and work practices that require protection from the forces of competition in order to survive. These dynamic gains from trade can enhance the conventional static gains arising from cheaper imports and increased exports.

Critics of free trade point out that the reallocation of labour and capital to achieve the more efficient outcome involves a substantial economic dislocation in the short-run. If increased efficiency is to be attained, some industries and firms will be put out of business and others will expand. In the short-run, layoffs, plant shutdowns, and a rise in structural unemployment are likely to result. Although these adjustment costs can be mitigated by adjustment policies to facilitate relocation and training (and the benefits of free trade provide the means for such compensation), it is unlikely that there will be complete compensation to the firms and workers bearing the costs of the adjustment.

Equally important, critics have suggested that free trade may lead to a "harmonization" of tax policies, employment standards, and labour relations legislation. This may occur if higher-cost countries like the United States threaten to put countervailing duties on Canadian exports that are perceived to be "subsidized" by such tax or legislative policies. Canada lies between European countries and the United States in the extent to which the government rather than individual employers and employees are responsible for the costs of health care, pensions, and other social welfare benefits. For the individual employer in Canada, this means that they have lower costs of production vis-à-vis the United States since major employers in the United States usually pay more toward health care and pensions than in Canada. As a result, these components of labour costs are lower in Canada than the United States. This factor has often been cited as giving an advantage to Canadian automobile plants. On the other hand, these benefits are financed out of taxes more in Canada, where tax costs are higher. Critics of free trade are concerned that Canada will ultimately be pressured into conforming to American standards in social policies, tax policies, and policies concerning union-management relations.

The same concern is expressed when Canada trades with low-wage countries like Mexico, which also have lower labour standards. The concern here is that plants will relocate, and capital will flow into such countries given their lower labour costs. To stem this loss of business and the associated jobs, Canadian governments may be pressured to lower their labour standards until they are more in line with those that prevail in the low-cost countries. Whether this will lead to the dissipation of lower standards and regulations, or simply put pressure on excessive regulations for which the benefits do not exceed the cost is an interesting question that merits additional analysis.

Although Canada has now had several years' experience under the FTA, measuring the actual impact of the agreement is difficult because the changes are being phased in over a number of years, and because the impacts have been confounded with the effects of other developments such as the implementation of the GST, the recession of the early 1990s, and exchange rate fluctuations. There does not yet appear to be a dismantling of Canadian employment law to harmonize with that in the United States. Indeed, in some jurisdictions, such as Ontario, employment law has become more progressive through such initiatives as pay equity, employment equity, and the prohibition of replacement workers during strikes. Ongoing assessment of the impacts of Canada's various trade arrangements will no doubt be an important topic of future research.

CONCLUSION

In analyzing the interrelationship between labour economics and industrial relations, Gunderson (1988) has identified two important linkages. The first link is the impact of the economic environment as a constraint on the behaviour of the industrial relations actors. The second link is the recent effort in the labour economics literature to explain the reasons for the existence of certain labour market institutional phenomena, rather than simply to take them as given and analyze their impact.

A number of examples have been discussed in this chapter illustrating the important constraints which the economic environment places on the behaviour of the industrial relations actors. These range from the impact of an increase in the minimum wage, to the effect of the changing age and gender composition of the labour force, to the impact of recessions and free trade. The range of issues covered is by no means exhaustive, but our hope is that it gives some insight into the diverse and important impacts that changes in the economic environment have had, and will continue to have, on the Canadian industrial relations system.

The recent research in labour economics attempting to explain the existence of institutional features, rather than just trying to analyze their impact, is also very promising. For example, traditionally, labour economists have attempted to measure the impact of unions on compensation, but more recent research has attempted to explain why unions exist in some workplaces and not others. Such explanations are of great interest in themselves, but they are also necessary if we wish to accurately measure the union impact on compensation or other areas. This is especially true when union and nonunion workplaces differ systematically but in ways not easy to calculate. Similarly, labour economists have attempted to explain changes in standard hours specified in employment standards legislation and the existence of mandatory retirement provisions in private employment contracts. Since these initiatives are leading labour economists to formulate theories about topics that are not traditionally "economic," there is great potential for economists to benefit from the institutional knowledge and multidisciplinary perspective of industrial relations scholars. The potential synergy between the two areas bodes well for future research on topics of great importance to both fields.

QUESTIONS

1. Explain each of the following terms: *compensating wage differentials; equilibrium wage; wage taker; dual labour market.*

2. Discuss why actual labour markets differ from the competitive ideal.

3. Explain why economic theory predicts that the imposition of minimum wage rates will reduce employment. In light of this expectation, what are the possible explanations for Card's (1992) finding that the raising of the minimum had no negative effect on employment?

4. Describe the different types of unemployment that researchers have identified, and discuss why the distinctions are important for purposes of public policy.

5. Describe the income-leisure choice model and explain how it can be used to shed light on significant issues in labour-management relations.

6. Discuss how the anticipated aging of the labour force will affect both industrial relations and human resource management practices.

7. The continuing high level of unemployment in Canada has prompted proposals that the available work be spread more evenly among members of the labour force, a practice that is called worksharing. Discuss the pros and cons of following this proposal and encouraging a large increase in worksharing.

8. Outline the recent trends in the industrial structure of employment in Canada. Discuss the implications for union-management relations.

REFERENCES

BLUESTONE, B., and B. HARRISON. 1982. *The Deindustrialization of America*, NY: Basic Books.

CARD, D., 1992. "Do Minimum Wages Reduce Employment? A Case Study of California, 1987-89." *Industrial and Labor Relations Review* 46 (1): 38-54.

CARD, D. and W. C. RIDDELL. 1993. "A Comparative Analysis of Unemployment in Canada and the United States." In D. Card and R. B. Freeman, eds., *Small Differences that Matter: Labor Markets and Income Maintenance in Canada and the United States*. Chicago: University of Chicago Press, 149-189.

COMMISSION OF INQUIRY INTO PART-TIME WORK. 1983. *Part-Time Work in Canada*. Ottawa: Labour Canada.

COUSINEAU, J. M., D. TESSIER, and F. VAILLANCOURT. 1992. "The Impact of the Ontarian Minimum Wage on the Unemployment of Women and the Young in Ontario: A Note." *Relations industrielles/Industrial Relations* 47 (3): 559-566.

DONNER, A. 1994. Chairperson: *Report on the Advisory Group on Working Time and the Distribution of Work*. Ottawa: Human Resources Development Canada.

EMPLOYMENT AND IMMIGRATION CANADA. 1993 *Work Sharing Evaluation: Final Report, March 1993*. Ottawa: Employment and Immigration Canada, Strategic Policy and Planning.

FISHER, E.G., and A. KONDRA. 1992. "Canada's Airlines: Recent Turbulence and Changing Flight Plans." In R. P. Chaykowski and A. Verma, eds, *Industrial Relations in Canadian Industry*. Toronto: Dryden, A Division of Holt, Rinehart and Winston of Canada, 358-404.

FOOT, D. K., and N. M. MELTZ. 1985. *Canadian Occupational Projections: An Analysis of the Economic Determinants, 1961-1981*. Hull, Quebec: Employment and Immigration Canada.

FOOT, D. K., and R. A. VENNE. 1990. "Population, Pyramids and Promotional Prospects." *Canadian Public Policy* 16, no. (4): 387-398.

FREEMAN, R., and K. NEEDLES. 1993. "Skill Differentials in Canada in an Era of Rising Labour Market Inequality." In D. Card and R. Freeman, eds, *Small Differences that Matter: Labour Markets and Income Maintenance in Canada and the United States*. Chicago: University of Chicago Press, 45-68.

GERA, S., and G. GRENIER. 1991. "Interindustry Wage Differentials and Efficiency Wages: Some Canadian Evidence." In S. Gera, ed, *Canadian Unemployment*. Ottawa: Economic Council of Canada, 129-38.

GUNDERSON, M. 1988. "Labour Economics and Industrial Relations" In G. Hébert, H. C. Jain and N. M. Meltz, eds, *The State of the Art in Industrial Relations*, Kingston, Ontario: Queen's University, Industrial Relations Centre and Centre for Industrial Relations, University of Toronto, 45-72.

GUNDERSON, M., and W. C. RIDDELL. 1993. *Labour Market Economics, Theory, Evidence and Policy in Canada*. Toronto: McGraw-Hill Ryerson.

HAMERMESH, D. 1993. *Labor Demand*. Princeton, N.J.: Princeton University Press.

HUMAN RESOURCES DEVELOPMENT CANADA. 1994. *Improving Social Security in Canada: A Discussion*. Ottawa: Supply and Services.

KEYNES, J. M. [1936] 1967. *The General Theory of Employment, Interest and Money*. London: Macmillan.

LEMIEUX, T. 1993. "Unions and Wage Inequality in Canada and the United States." In D. Card and R. Freeman, eds, *Small Differences that Matter: Labor Markets and Income Maintenance in Canada and the United States*. Chicago: University of Chicago Press, 69-108.

McSHANE, S. L. 1983. "Reasonable Notice Criteria in Common Law Wrongful Dismissal Cases." *Industrial Relations/Relations Industrielles* 38 (3): 618-633.

MELTZ, R. L., and N. M. MELTZ. 1992. *Taking Charge: Career Planning for Canadian Workers*. Toronto: Captus Press and Iguana & Associates.

MELTZ, N. M. 1990. "The Evolution of Worker Training: The Canadian Experience." In L. A. Ferman, M. Hoyman, J. Cutcher-Gershenfeld, and E. J. Savoie, eds, *New Developments in Worker Training: A Legacy for the 1990s*. Industrial Relations Research Association Series. Madison, WI: University of Wisconsin, 283-307.

MORISSETTE, R., J. MYLES, and G. PICOT. 1993. *What is Happening to Earnings Inequality in Canada?* Ottawa: Statistics Canada.

ONTARIO TASK FORCE ON HOURS OF WORK AND OVERTIME. 1987. *Working Times*. Toronto: Queen's Printer.

REID, F. 1987. *Hours of Work and Overtime Policies to Reduce Unemployment*. Background Report to the Ontario Task Force on the Hours of Work and Overtime. Toronto: Queen's Printer.

REID, F. and N. M. Meltz. 1984. "Canada's STC: A Comparison with the California Version." In R. MaCoy and M. Morand, eds, *Short-Time Compensation: A Formula for Work Sharing*. New York: Pergamon Press, 106-119.

REID, F., N. M. MELTZ, and Z. LONTI. 1990. "Regional Imbalance and Shifts in the Unemployment-vacancy Relationship." Presented at the North American Economics and Finance Association Annual Meeting. Washington, D.C.

REID, F. and D. A. SMITH. 1981. "The Impact of Demographic Changes on Unemployment." *Canadian Public Policy* 7, (2): 348-51.

RIDDELL, W. C., ed. 1985. *Work and Pay: the Canadian Labour Market.* Vol. 17 of the Research Studies of the Royal Commission on the Economic Union. Toronto: University of Toronto Press.

RIDDELL, W. C. and P. SMITH. 1982. "Expected Inflation and Wage Changes in Canada, 1967-81." *Canadian Journal of Economics* 15 (3): 377-394.

ROBB, A. L. and R. E. ROBB. 1987. *The Prospects for Creating Jobs by Reducing Hours of Work in Ontario.* Background Report to the Ontario Task Force on Hours of Work and Overtime. Toronto: Queen's Printer.

ROYAL COMMISSION ON THE ECONOMIC UNION. 1985. *Report.* Ottawa: Queen's Printer.

SAMSON, L. 1985. "A Study of the Impact of Sectoral Shifts on Aggregate Unemployment in Canada." *Canadian Journal of Economics* 18 (3): 518-30.

SWIDINSKY, R. 1980. "Minimum Wages and Teenage Unemployment." *Canadian Journal of Economics.* 13 (February): 158-171.

WILTON, D. A. and D. M. PRESCOTT. 1992. *Macroeconomics: Theory and Policy in Canada, Third Edition.* Don Mills, Ontario: Addison-Wesley.

CHAPTER 3

COLLECTIVE BARGAINING LEGISLATION

DONALD D. CARTER

CANADIAN COLLECTIVE BARGAINING LEGISLATION EXERCISES AN IMPORTANT influence over union-management relations in Canada. These collective bargaining laws closely regulate the formation of the collective bargaining relationship, govern the conduct and timing of bargaining, place restrictions on economic conflict, and even go so far as to mandate certain terms of the collective agreement. Some of the more important provisions of these laws prohibit employers from interfering with union organizing activities, require them to bargain in good faith with unions once they acquire bargaining rights, and in some Canadian jurisdictions prohibit employers from replacing striking workers. At the same time Canadian labour laws place substantial restrictions on union strike activity and other forms of economic action as well as requiring the union to represent fairly the members of the bargaining unit.

The administration of Canadian collective bargaining legislation is largely left to labour relations boards. These administrative tribunals exercise the broad powers given to them by collective bargaining legislation, playing an important role in the application of this legislation. In the exercise of their statutory powers, labour relations boards regulate both management and union activity, at times restraining certain forms of employer interference with union organizing and bargaining activity and at other times restricting the untimely use of economic sanctions by trade unions.

An important constitutional restraint now influences Canada's collective bargaining laws. Since 1982, any provincial or federal law must be read and applied in the light of the Charter of Rights and Freedoms. The Charter sets out overriding constitutional standards against which the legitimacy of legislation must be measured. Somewhat surprisingly, despite a number of important constitutional challenges, the Charter has not fundamentally altered Canadian collective bargaining laws, either to enhance union activity or to curb union activity. As a result, Canada's bargaining laws continue to be shaped by legislative amendments rather than through judicial challenges. Indeed an important feature of Canada's labour law system is the frequent legislative amendment of collective bargaining laws.

THE INFLUENCE OF LEGISLATION

Union-management relations in Canada continue to be influenced heavily by legal regulation. Labour laws in the federal jurisdiction and each of the ten provinces confine collective bargaining within a tight statutory framework. These laws, although initially modelled on the United States' Wagner Act, in many ways now go further in regulating collective bargaining than does American legislation (Weiler 1980).

There has been considerable debate about the virtues of legislative intervention on this scale. It has been argued that such a tight legal framework leaves insufficient room for the natural operation of free collective bargaining. People who take this stand usually focus on the way legislative restrictions limit recourse to the use of such economic sanctions as strikes, picketing, and lockouts. The concern is that a detailed legislative framework gives the government too prominent a role in what should be a private system of conflict resolution. Neither unions nor management, however, have consistently adopted this position, and there has been a noticeable tendency for each to seek further legislation when it is to their advantage. This ambivalence on the part of both management and unions towards government intervention has meant that, if anything, the pace of legislative activity has increased in recent years.

This increase in the regulation of union-management relations may also be part of a general trend towards a more regulated society. Collective bargaining is now an established institution of Canadian society, and its exercise has major social and economic implications. This fact has led many to conclude that union-management relations are too important to be left exclusively in the hands of management and labour and to argue that the public interest must also be considered. The concept of a public interest is usually vaguely defined, but it is often alluded to in those situations in which the general public, rather than the parties themselves, seems to be bearing the brunt of economic sanctions or in which it appears that collective bargaining is contributing to an inflationary spiral. In such situations, the industrial relations system is often perceived to be malfunctioning, and a frequent response is to call for more regulation through the legislative process.

Legislation in Canada has had both a direct and an indirect effect on union-management relations. Statutes that establish and define the collective bargaining structure within which unions and management must operate have a very direct effect upon Canadian industrial relations. As well as this body of collective bargaining law, however, there exists a wide array of other legislation that affects union-management relations in a more indirect manner. Statutes dealing with minimum standards of employment, worker health and safety, human rights, compensation for work injuries, unemployment insurance, and pensions (many of which are discussed in Chapter 4) all have some influence on the conduct of union-management relations, even though they also apply to those employees (and their employers) who have not embraced collective bargaining. This chapter deals only with the structure of collective bargaining law since both employment law and social security law, although important, have a somewhat different and less direct impact on union-management relations than does collective bargaining legislation.

THE CONSTITUTIONAL DIVISION OF LEGISLATIVE AUTHORITY

The regulation of union-management relations in Canada is divided among eleven different jurisdictions—ten provincial and one federal. The Canadian Constitution has been interpreted by the courts as giving the provinces the greater share of legislative jurisdiction over labour relations. The federal government's jurisdiction has been restricted to undertakings falling within its specific legislative authority and, incidentally, to conduct falling within its criminal law powers. Federal legislative power has been permitted to extend beyond these boundaries only in time of national emergency. Thus, the Canadian constitutional situation differs markedly from that of the United States, where the federal government's labour relations jurisdiction is much more extensive than that of the state governments (Arthurs, Carter, Fudge, Glasbeek, and Trudeau, 1993).

The constitutional division of legislative authority in Canada places most private sector employees under the labour laws of the province within which they work. Workers employed in manufacturing, mining (except uranium), forest products industries, construction, service industries, local transportation, and the provincial and local government sectors all fall within provincial jurisdiction. The predominance of provincial labour law in Canada means that the workplace relations of roughly 90 per cent of its private sector workforce are provincially regulated.

The ten provincial systems of labour law have much in common but there are also some important differences. Collective bargaining laws in the ten provinces at their inception all owed a heavy debt to the American Wagner Act. Frequent revisions of these collective bargaining laws, however, have now resulted in some significant variations among provinces. The most distinctive of these provincial systems can be found in Quebec (discussed in more detail in Chapter 16), reflecting the important social and linguistic differences between that province and the rest of Canada.

The federal government's labour relations jurisdiction covers a relatively small percentage of private sector employees, but these include workers in a number of particularly important areas of the economy. All air, rail, shipping, and trucking operations having either an interprovincial or international character fall within the federal jurisdiction, as do broadcasting enterprises, banks, uranium mines, and grain elevators. As for the public sector, all federal public servants fall within federal jurisdiction but are covered by a different collective bargaining statute than employees falling within the federal private sector. Strikes by such federal government employees as air traffic controllers and postal workers have had a significant impact in Canada. The same can be said of strikes by certain employees in the federal private sector, such as stevedores and airline and railway employees. The impact of labour disputes in the federal jurisdiction means that this jurisdiction is much more important than a simple count of employees covered by federal labour legislation would indicate.

Difficulties can arise in drawing the line between federal and provincial jurisdiction over labour relations. A business may not fall squarely within the definition of a federal undertaking but may still have some functional relationship to it. Since constitutional problems most frequently arise when a trade union is applying to a labour relations board for bargaining rights, many of these issues are resolved initially by labour boards, subject to possible review in the courts. The line between provincial and federal jurisdiction is not always clear. For example, it was held that a private trucking firm under contract to Canada Post to collect mail came under federal jurisdiction, even though it was involved in local operations that would otherwise have brought it within provincial jurisdiction. On the other hand, it was held that persons employed in a parking garage operated under contract to the federal government at Toronto's Pearson International Airport fell within the jurisdiction of Ontario.

Other difficulties can arise with the constitutional division of legislative authority. Industries, such as trucking, that have both local and interprovincial or international components may bargain as an entire industry, bringing into play both provincial and federal labour laws. As well, large employers operating local undertakings in more than one provincial jurisdiction may agree to national negotiations even though they are still governed by provincial labour legislation. Both the meatpacking industry and the elevator industry have undertaken this kind of national negotiations despite problems caused by the concurrency of provincial laws. Fortunately, many of these problems have been worked out by co-operation among agencies of the governments involved.

One advantage of the Canadian system of divided legislative authority is that it has encouraged individual Canadian jurisdictions to develop some innovative variations to their collective bargaining laws. The collective bargaining regime that the federal government enacted a few years after the end of the Second World War was intended to be a model for the provinces to follow. In the beginning the provinces did borrow heavily from this model, but over the years they have increasingly followed their own legislative paths in response to local political pressures. This tendency has led individual jurisdictions to introduce some important variations to their collective bargaining laws. The general intent of these amendments has been to strengthen the position of trade unions at both the organizational and negotiation stages of the collective bargaining process.

Indeed, if one examines labour legislation in Canada over the past forty years, one can see a clear progression of amendments that have created an increasingly favourable legal environment for trade unions and collective bargaining. Just as interesting is the fact that labour law reform in Canada tends to be contagious and that, while some jurisdictions may lag behind for a while, no Canadian jurisdiction remains far outside the prevailing pattern for very long. Labour law reform in Canada, moreover, has occurred frequently and these frequent overhauls mean that our Canadian collective bargaining laws have diverged significantly from the American model upon which they were originally based.

Canadian constitutional law was altered radically in 1982 by the adoption of the Canadian Charter of Rights and Freedoms. Canadian courts can now overrule either federal or provincial legislation if it is inconsistent with the guarantees of fundamental rights and freedoms found in the Charter. These guarantees include freedom of conscience and religion; freedom of thought, belief, opinion, and expression; freedom of association; due process under the law; and equality before and under the law. The effect of the Charter is to entrench these values, and although the Charter's standards are still subject to "such reasonable limits prescribed by law as can be demonstrably justified in a free and democratic society," the Supreme Court of Canada has already indicated that the onus rests upon those who seek to limit these fundamental values.

The Charter of Rights has thus greatly expanded the role of Canadian courts. Before its adoption, the federal and provincial legislatures had ultimate legislative authority within their respective jurisdictions, and the constitutional role of the courts was only to ensure that the legislative boundaries between the federal and provincial governments were observed. The Charter now gives courts the authority to overrule legislation, enhancing judicial authority at the expense of the elected Canadian legislatures.

The Supreme Court of Canada has already considered some Charter-based challenges to existing labour legislation. That court has made it clear that collective bargaining and strike activity, and even the acquisition of bargaining rights by a trade union, are not protected from legislative encroachment by the Charter's guarantee of freedom of association. Picketing activity also appears to attract little Charter protection, since the Supreme Court of Canada has held that the Charter does not apply when an employer is seeking to prohibit picketing by an action in the courts.

Trade unions, therefore, have received little comfort from the Charter. Clearly the Supreme Court of Canada has rejected any notion that union activities are imbued with any special constitutional status. For unions, however, an equally important issue was whether the Supreme Court might apply the Charter so as to erode existing union rights.

This issue came to a head in a landmark case involving the constitutionality of a union security arrangement found in a collective agreement between a union and Ontario's community colleges (*Lavigne v. Ontario Public Service Employees Union* (1991), 91 C.L.L.C. para. 14,029). Under this arrangement all members of the bargaining unit, regardless of whether they were union members, had union dues deducted from their pay by the employer and remitted to the union. The issue before the Supreme Court of Canada was whether the use of such dues by the union for its political activities was inconsistent with the Charter's guarantees of freedom of association and freedom of expression.

In this case the Court had to deal with three important legal issues. The threshold issue was whether the union security arrangement set out in the collective agreement between the union and the community colleges could be considered to be a form of government action since it is only government actions that are regulated by the Charter. If the union security arrangement could be characterized as a form of government action, the Court was then faced with the second issue of whether this arrangement was inconsistent with the Charter's guarantees of freedom of association and expression. Even if such an arrangement were found to be inconsistent with the Charter's guarantees, however, the Court was still required to address a third question of whether the arrangement could be considered a justifiable and reasonable limit on these guarantees.

In this important case the Supreme Court of Canada held that, even though the union security arrangement was created by a collective agreement, the compulsory collection of union dues by a government agency involved sufficient government action to attract the Charter. Four of the seven justices, however, held that the union security arrangement was not inconsistent with the Charter's guarantee of freedom of association and all seven held that it could be considered a reasonable limit on the Charter's guarantees. This decision, therefore, made it clear that union security arrangements would not be eroded by the Charter's guarantees of individual rights.

Charter litigation to this date indicates that the judiciary has been reluctant to use the Charter to alter established collective bargaining laws. So far the Charter has neither enhanced nor curbed trade union power. What this means is that in the 1990s labour law reform is back in the hands of the politicians. We must look to Canadian legislatures, rather than to the courts, for any substantial alteration of our existing collective bargaining laws.

A further constitutional consideration also affects the distribution of legislative power over labour relations. The Canadian Constitution prevents provincial governments from establishing courts or other agencies with the same kinds of powers as those of the superior courts appointed by the federal government. In other words, no province can establish its own system of courts to compete with federally appointed courts. This constitutional restriction has given rise to the question of the legitimacy of the labour relations boards established by the provinces to administer their collective bargaining laws. These boards have been given a wide remedial mandate that includes requiring reinstatement and compensation of employees discharged in breach of collective bargaining legislation and issuing cease-and-desist orders to restrain strikes and lockouts. Some people have suggested that the provincially appointed boards are acting like superior courts. It has been held, however, that the labour boards' exercise of their powers is qualitatively different from the exercise of somewhat similar powers by superior courts because the labour board powers are exercised in a labour relations context. So long as the labour boards exercise their powers in a manner necessitated by their labour relations functions, it appears that they will not be regarded as encroaching on the traditional powers of a superior court.

THE LOOSENING OF EARLY RESTRICTIONS ON EMPLOYEE ORGANIZATION

Many Canadian collective bargaining statutes now contain a preamble expressly stating that it is in the public interest to encourage the practice and procedure of collective bargaining. The Canadian legal structure has not always been so favourably disposed towards collective bargaining. At the time of Confederation there existed in Canada a number of legal restrictions to employee organization. The common law crime of conspiracy (two or more individuals' consorting for illegal purposes) could be applied to trade union organizers, making them subject to criminal prosecution. Some of the new provinces also had separate legislation effectively prohibiting collective bargaining activity. In addition, because trade unions were regarded as operating in restraint of trade (by interfering with the normal course of business transactions through such actions as strikes), they were refused access to the courts and were thus unable to enforce any rights that they might otherwise have had.

Not until the early 1870s was there some loosening of these restrictions when the arrests and prosecutions that followed the Toronto printers' strike gave rise to public demand for labour law reform. This demand may also have been encouraged by the fact that reform legislation had recently been enacted by the British Parliament. The Canadian Trades Union Act of 1872 declared that the purposes of a trade union were not to be considered unlawful merely because they might also be in restraint of trade. At the time, the Criminal Law Amendment Act legalized peaceful strikes and picketing. A few years later, in 1875 and 1876, legislation amended the definition of "criminal conspiracy" to apply only to trade combinations involving acts expressly punishable by law.

By the end of the nineteenth century, most of the legal restrictions on trade union activity had disappeared. At this point, the law relating to conspiracies in restraint of trade clearly excluded from its scope combinations of employees acting for their own reasonable protection—an exclusion still found in current Canadian competition legislation. Although trade unions were still not completely free of legal fetters, especially court-imposed restrictions on picketing, it can safely be said that many of the earlier restrictions had disappeared by the beginning of the twentieth century.

CONCILIATION LEGISLATION

The loosening of legal restrictions did not leave a legal vacuum for long. As trade union influence gradually increased, it soon became apparent that labour-management disputes were becoming more common in such key areas as railways, mining, and public utilities. Before the end of the nineteenth century, some provinces had already legislated to provide mediation or arbitration procedures on a voluntary basis. The requirement of joint consent meant, however, that recourse to such procedures was infrequent since this type of third party intervention was usually not in the interests of the stronger party.

Federal legislation providing dispute-resolution machinery, still essentially voluntary in nature, made its first appearance in 1900. The Dominion Conciliation Act allowed the federal minister of labour to appoint a conciliation board, either at the request of one of the parties or on the minister's own initiative. This procedure was essentially an exercise in factfinding where the board would investigate the dispute and make specific recommendations that would be published. It was assumed that if the public were made aware of labour disputes by means of a report from a board composed of representatives of the two parties and an independent chairperson, resulting public pressure would push the disputants to settle their differences. This factfinding procedure reappeared in a later federal statute, the Railway Disputes Act of 1903, but this law, like the 1900 statute, did not require either party to use the conciliation board. In 1906, these two conciliation statutes were consolidated into a single Conciliation and Labour Act.

A much more important legislative event occurred in 1907, following a difficult strike by western miners in the previous year. The enactment of the Industrial Disputes Investigation Act of 1907 made the conciliation board procedure compulsory for the first time and prohibited the parties from resorting to economic sanctions until the board had completed its investigation and its report was released to the public. The application of the Industrial Disputes Investigation Act was later confined strictly to federal undertakings (as a result of a landmark constitutional decision in 1925, *Toronto Electric Commissioners v. Snider*), but most provincial jurisdictions subsequently adopted the conciliation board procedure, as it became one of the early hallmarks of the Canadian labour law system.

Despite this early prominence, the conciliation board has enjoyed only mixed success in Canada. For one thing, the influence of public opinion on labour disputes is unpredictable, since publicity may harden bargaining positions just as much as it may soften them. The procedure itself usually takes a considerable period of time, and the postponement of the use of economic sanctions until the factfinding exercise is completed may actually frustrate the collective bargaining process. These disadvantages have caused conciliation boards to fall out of favour, except in the case of public sector disputes. Factfinding by tripartite conciliation boards has been largely replaced by mediation conducted by a single conciliation officer. Recourse to this form of mediation is a precondition to the use of economic sanctions in some Canadian jurisdictions.

The conciliation officer is usually a full-time government employee whose function is to act as a channel of communication in labour disputes. The process contemplates that the parties will be brought together through the persuasive efforts of the conciliation officer, rather than by the influence of public opinion. Instead of a public inquiry and public report, the conciliation officer relies on private discussions, usually conducted with each party separately. No public report is prepared, and specific recommendations are made only if they would encourage settlement of the dispute.

THE EVOLUTION OF A LEGISLATIVE FRAMEWORK FOR UNION RECOGNITION

Conciliation legislation was not the complete answer to the problems plaguing Canadian labour relations in the first half of the twentieth century. Canada was becoming an industrialized nation and union membership was on the upswing, making substantial gains during periods of economic prosperity and full employment. During the depression years of the 1930s, however, union membership declined and working conditions deteriorated as the pendulum of economic power swung in favour of employers, whose economic strength could be asserted in many ways to thwart union-organizing efforts. Employees sympathetic to a union could be dismissed at will, and new employees could be hired on what was referred to as a "yellow dog contract"—one that included the condition that they not join a trade union. Even if a majority of employees had already organized a trade union, employers could still refuse to recognize it either by continuing to deal directly with the employees or by entering into a "sweetheart" arrangement with a rival company union. At times, employer opposition went even further since violence and intimidation on the part of both employers and unions were not uncommon during this period. The basic problem was one of union recognition—a matter not dealt with by conciliation legislation.

The Wagner Act Model

This problem of union recognition was addressed first by legislators in the United States. In 1935, the National Labor Relations Act (usually called the Wagner Act) was enacted by the US Congress. This statute expressly recognized the right of employees to organize and bargain collectively with their employer. It also prohibited certain types of employer activities interfering with those rights (often called unfair labour practices). These activities included intimidation or coercion of employees to stop them from joining a union, employer support of a management-dominated company union, and unilateral changes by management in the terms of conditions of employment (for example, promises of increased wages). Employers were also required to recognize unions representing their employees and to negotiate in good faith with these unions. Just as important, this legislative scheme was to be administered by a new administrative agency, the National Labor Relations Board, rather than by the courts (which at that time did not enjoy a reputation for being favourably disposed towards collective bargaining). The legal structure created by the Wagner Act later became the basic model for the present system of Canadian labour relations law.

Certain provisions of the Wagner Act were borrowed by various Canadian jurisdictions between 1937 and 1942, but no jurisdiction, either provincial or federal, provided a complete code governing union recognition or established an administrative agency to apply such a code during that period. With the outbreak of the Second World War and the consequent shortage of workers, union organization became easier, and trade union membership grew significantly despite the lack of legal support. Pressure began to build for more comprehensive collective bargaining legislation.

The Ontario Labour Court

In 1943, Ontario took the next legislative step and introduced a collective bargaining statute along the lines of the Wagner Act, the only difference being that the administration of the statute was given to a division of the provincial supreme court, instead of to an administrative tribunal. The tenure of the Ontario Labour Court, as it was called, lasted only ten months. During that period, it performed functions similar to those now carried out by the labour boards—assessing the legitimacy of trade unions, describing appropriate bargaining units, and determining whether trade unions enjoyed the support of the employees in the bargaining unit.

The Labour Court dealt with some large and important applications for bargaining rights, but it never gained widespread acceptance with organized labour. Trade unions resented the requirement that they be represented by lawyers before the court and disliked the fact that they had no representation on the court itself. Labour's criticisms, and the need to establish a joint federal-provincial structure for the administration of collective bargaining legislation during wartime, led to the displacement of the Labour Court by an administrative tribunal.

PC 1003

In 1944, the federal government, exercising the powers of the War Measures Act, established a collective bargaining code containing all the elements of the Wagner Act model, including an administrative tribunal to administer the code. The Wartime Labour Relations Regulations (PC 1003) embraced a long list of industries considered essential for the war effort and extended federal collective bargaining law over most areas of economic activity in Canada. The regulations established the Wartime Labour Relations Board, a tribunal with primary responsibility for the administration and application of these laws. Provision was made for the establishment of local (provincial) boards, although matters of policy remained the responsibility of the federal board. At the same time the provinces, except for Quebec and Saskatchewan, suspended their own collective bargaining legislation, making the federal order applicable to an even wider range of economic activity.

The impact of the federal labour relations regulation cannot be overstated. At one stroke, it brought most economic activity in Canada within a single, comprehensive system of collective bargaining law.

Postwar Legislation

The end of the war brought a return to a divided responsibility for labour relations as the provinces began to reclaim their jurisdiction. By this time, however, the Wagner model had become firmly established throughout Canada. Anticipating the repeal of the wartime regulations, the federal government enacted a collective bargaining statute in 1948 containing the same basic elements as the wartime scheme. This statute was intended to be a model code to be followed by the provinces in order to provide some uniformity of labour legislation throughout Canada. Most provinces enacted substantially similar legislation at about the same time, reinforcing the pattern that had been established by the federal government. Despite this common beginning, the different Canadian collective bargaining systems began to develop some interesting mutations in the years that followed.

The Growth of Public Sector Legislation

For many years, collective bargaining legislation in Canada was directed towards employees in the private sector, and there was little enthusiasm for extending bargaining rights to the public sector. Indeed, public employees themselves did not appear to be inclined to embrace collective bargaining, perhaps because of its blue-collar connotations or because the general public at that time still regarded collective bargaining by government workers as inappropriate. Attitudes began to change by the 1960s. Government had increased in size, and unionism began to look increasingly attractive to public employees as they watched unionized private sector workers obtain substantial gains in wages and fringe benefits.

The watershed came in 1967 with the enactment of the Public Service Staff Relations Act (PSSRA)—a statute creating a new and distinct collective bargaining structure for employees of the federal government. The provinces soon followed with their own legislative structures for public sector collective bargaining. Some provinces borrowed the PSSRA model, but others took a different route, refusing to extend the right to strike to public employees and, instead, providing for compulsory arbitration of bargaining disputes. By the middle of the 1970s, public sector collective bargaining had become firmly established throughout Canada.

In recent years, trade union growth in Canada has occurred primarily in the public sector, and unions representing public employees now rank among the largest labour organizations in the country. (The public sector legal framework is discussed in more detail in Chapter 15.)

SOME DISTINCTIVE FEATURES OF CANADIAN COLLECTIVE BARGAINING LEGISLATION

Canadian collective bargaining legislation, although owing a substantial debt to the US Wagner Act, possesses its own distinguishing characteristics.

The Certification Process

A distinctive feature of Canadian collective bargaining legislation is that it provides a relatively simple procedure by which trade unions can acquire collective bargaining rights. A union applies to a labour board, and if it establishes that it represents a majority of a particular group of employees, it receives a certificate giving it exclusive bargaining rights for all employees in that bargaining unit. This procedure, called *certification*, is the principal method by which trade unions acquire bargaining rights in Canada.

The usual method by which trade unions establish their representative character for certification is through simple evidence of membership, as given, for example, by the "signing of cards." Nova Scotia and Alberta require an employee vote, but elsewhere in Canada such a vote is a secondary procedure for establishing representativeness; it is used by the labour boards only if there is some doubt about the reliability of the membership evidence submitted by a union. For example, in Ontario the board need not direct a vote if the union can show that more than 55 per cent of the employees in the bargaining unit are members (Adams 1993).

Extensive Restrictions on Strike Action

Canadian collective bargaining legislation severely curtails the use of economic sanctions. Strikes for the purpose of gaining recognition are expressly prohibited, as are strikes during the life of a collective agreement. Even if the parties are bargaining for a collective agreement, the right to strike is postponed in most Canadian jurisdictions until they have exhausted specified dispute settlement procedures, usually conciliation but sometimes a strike vote as well. Because these procedures have been made a precondition to the use of economic sanctions, they have often been regarded as indirect restrictions on the right to strike and lockout. Indeed, some would argue that the restrictive aspect of these procedures tends to impair their usefulness in resolving conflict.

Compulsory Grievance Arbitration

The complete restriction on strikes and lockouts during the life of the collective agreement has necessitated establishing some alternative mechanism for resolving disputes relating to the interpretation and administration of the collective agreement. As a result, Canadian collective bargaining legislation requires that collective agreements include a procedure for final and binding resolution of any unresolved disputes arising under that agreement.

Unlike the United States, where such procedures are completely a matter of negotiation between the parties, Canada assigns a public element to grievance resolution. The parties may fashion their own grievance procedures, but they are not free to dispense with such machinery since it is expressly mandated by legislation.

The fact that grievance arbitration has been made a mandatory feature of our collective bargaining system means that in Canada there has always been a public aspect to the process. Canadian legislatures have never regarded grievance arbitration as the exclusive preserve of the parties and, at times, have intervened to alter the basic legislative framework underlying the process. One of the best examples of such interventions is the 1979 amendments to Ontario's labour relations legislation which imposed on the existing grievance arbitration process a new procedure for expedited arbitration. Under this procedure, either party to the collective agreement, instead of following the procedures under the collective agreement for the selection of an arbitrator, can ask the minister of labour to refer the grievance to a single arbitrator who must then begin to hear the matter within very strict time limits. (See Chapter 10 for a full discussion of grievance procedures and arbitration.)

Recognition of the Right to Union Security

Canadian labour legislation expressly recognizes the legitimacy of arrangements that a union negotiates for its own financial security. Legislation permits unions to bargain for such arrangements as the closed shop (the requirement that a person be a member of the union before being hired), the union shop (the requirement that a person join the union on being employed), and the dues shop or Rand formula (the requirement that a person pay union dues—but not necessarily join the union—as a condition of employment). Some Canadian jurisdictions go even further by making the Rand formula mandatory, while others require the employer to collect dues on behalf of the union when so authorized by the employee. This approach contrasts sharply with that taken in some American jurisdictions, where "right-to-work" laws have restricted union security arrangements.

Extensive Protection of the Striking Worker

Three Canadian jurisdictions—British Columbia, Ontario and Quebec—place restrictions on the employer's ability to replace striking workers during the course of a labour dispute. Quebec, in 1977, was the first jurisdiction to enact these restrictions and Ontario and British Columbia enacted somewhat similar provisions in 1993. Ontario and Quebec, however, not only prohibit the use of workers from outside the striking bargaining unit, but also prohibit bargaining unit members who may prefer to work during the strike from doing so. British Columbia, on the other hand, only prohibits the use of workers from outside the bargaining unit, although the effectiveness of picket lines in that jurisdiction makes it unlikely that bargaining unit members would attempt to work during a strike. These so called "anti-scab" laws not only protect the jobs of striking workers but they also serve to enhance trade union bargaining power by making it very difficult for an employer to continue operations during a strike. In all three of these jurisdictions, despite these "anti-scab" laws, legislative provision has been made for essential services to be provided during a strike.

Anti-scab legislation is not the only form of legislative protection for striking workers. A majority of Canadian jurisdictions have legislated procedures for striking workers to be reinstated in their former jobs once they decide to return to work. Manitoba has gone one step further by also prohibiting the hiring of permanent replacement workers. Even in the absence of such legislative provisions, some Canadian labour boards have regarded an employer's refusal to reinstate striking workers by displacing replacement workers as an unfair labour practice. These Canadian labour laws, giving strikers a right to reclaim their jobs, stand in contrast to American labour laws that permit the permanent replacement of striking workers.

ADMINISTRATION OF COLLECTIVE BARGAINING LEGISLATION IN CANADA

No account of Canadian collective bargaining legislation is complete without mention of the institutions responsible for administering these laws. The primary legal institution is an administrative tribunal commonly known as the labour relations board. (An *administrative tribunal* is a public agency created by statute but having some independence from the executive branch of government.) Two other institutions, grievance arbitration, and the courts, also have important roles to play.

Labour Relations Boards

As administrative tribunals, labour relations boards derive their authority from the very collective bargaining legislation that they administer. These statutes not only impose rights and obligations on trade unions and employers but also provide the structure and procedure for the assertion of these rights.

Each of the eleven Canadian jurisdictions has established its own structure for administering its collective bargaining laws. The usual one is the labour relations board, although an important variation of this structure can be found in Quebec.

Labour relations boards, although they generally report to the government through the ministry or department of labour, are regarded as having some autonomy from that ministry. They are, as a rule, tripartite, being composed of independent chairpersons, representatives of trade unions, and representatives of employers appointed for either a fixed term (sometimes set out in the statute) or at the pleasure of the government. In the larger, more industrialized jurisdictions, the appointments are usually full time; in the smaller jurisdictions part-time appointments are more prevalent. Labour boards employ support staffs of civil servants to carry out their administrative function.

The functions performed by labour boards are both administrative and adjudicative. In carrying out the latter, labour boards bear some resemblance to the courts. The chairperson presiding over hearings makes evidential and procedural rules, and reasons are usually provided for any decision of significance. Board procedures are, however, marked by greater informality and are generally more expeditious than those of the courts. There is no requirement that the parties be represented at a hearing by a lawyer.

The presence of board members representing the two sides of the collective bargaining process is another characteristic of labour boards that distinguishes them from the courts (one exception is the federal board where the members do not have a representative role). The appointment of board members occurs only after consultation with either major employer organizations or the major trade union associations, as the case may be. These representative board members are experienced labour relations practitioners who bring to the boards an expertise that is applied in the decision-making process. The board members maintain regular contact with labour and management groups to ensure that they do not lose touch with their respective constituencies.

The presence of representative members serves to make board decisions more acceptable in the labour relations community, but it also means that labour boards are far less removed from particular disputes than any court would be. This lack of distance is generally regarded as acceptable, partly because the presence of both union and employer members on a board means that biases can be offset. The representative role of the board members can, however, cause problems if a party to a hearing has no association with the major interest groups represented. (This situation can occur when a labour board is faced with the dispute between rival trade unions, one a member of a major trade union association and the other outside it, or when a dissident employee complains about the conduct of both the union and the employer.)

Labour boards were established initially for the purpose of administering the statutory procedures for the acquisition, transfer, and termination of bargaining rights. Applications for bargaining rights and complaints relating to employer and union conduct during the organization of employees constituted the bulk of their caseload. Once the board established a collective bargaining relationship, any matters arising from that relationship were left to be resolved in other forms. Strikes, picketing, and, to a lesser extent, the conduct of the parties at the bargaining table were dealt with by the courts, while disputes relating to the interpretation of collective agreements were referred to ad hoc boards of arbitration.

Trade union bargaining rights still form the core of labour boards' jurisdiction, but these boards now deal with other aspects of labour-management relations. Since the 1970s, the powers of labour boards, particularly their remedial powers, have been expanded by express legislative provisions. Most boards can now issue directives restraining illegal strikes and lockouts and determine whether bargaining conduct is inconsistent with the statutory duty to bargain in good faith. A few boards also have the authority to arbitrate first-agreement bargaining disputes. This expansion of the jurisdiction of labour boards has quite clearly increased both their visibility and their importance.

The primary function of labour boards, however, is still to grant or withdraw bargaining rights, applying criteria either found in the legislation or developed through the boards' own decision-making process. To this end, the board must deal with issues such as the eligibility of employees to bargain collectively, the eligibility of unions to represent employees, the appropriateness of the collective bargaining constituency, and the legitimacy of evidence of union membership. On all of these issues there now exists a comprehensive body of labour board decisions interpreting the standards established in the legislation.

Unfair labour practices also form an important component of labour board jurisdiction. Collective bargaining laws place restrictions on both employer and union conduct;

employer conduct in particular is watched carefully by labour boards when unions are organizing. The extensive labour board jurisprudence dealing with employer conduct at this stage of the collective bargaining process reflects the fact that a significant number of employers are still tempted to resort to unlawful methods to resist union organization. Labour boards do not allow employers much latitude at this stage of the collective bargaining process because the economic vulnerability of unorganized employees makes them especially susceptible to employer influences. As a result, employer conduct that might otherwise be considered acceptable may be regarded in a quite different light by a labour board if its effect is to interfere with the employees' organization of a union.

Of particular concern to labour boards are statements made by employers while unions are organizing. Close attention is paid not only to the content of such statements but also to the context in which they are made. Labour boards are particularly suspicious of statements made to employees who, because they have been compelled (either directly or indirectly) to listen to such statements, are considered to be a captive audience.

To distinguish legitimate employer conduct from an unlawful and unfair labour practice, boards frequently look to motive. Employer conduct tainted by antiunion animus constitutes an unfair practice, and labour boards now have substantial authority to remedy such conduct. Employers that unlawfully interfere with union organization face the possibility of having to pay large damage awards to the union while still having that union certified as the bargaining agent. Some Canadian jurisdictions have even legislated a reverse onus of proof, requiring the employer to disprove antiunion animus.

An important component of labour board jurisdiction is the administration of the duty to bargain in good faith. Collective bargaining legislation requires both employers and unions to bargain in good faith and make every reasonable effort to reach a collective agreement. In giving meaning to this duty Canadian labour boards have tended to place greater emphasis on the manner in which negotiations are conducted rather than upon the content of the bargaining proposals themselves. This tendency reflects an understandable reluctance on the part of labour boards to interfere with the economic forces that are an integral part of any labour-management negotiation. As a result, labour boards have been reluctant to use the duty to bargain in good faith to redress an imbalance of economic power. On the other hand, this duty has been applied where the union's status as exclusive bargaining agent has been undermined by the employer dealing directly with employees or another union, and where there has been a breakdown in the process of communication at the bargaining table. As well, labour boards may look at the content of a bargaining proposal where that proposal is itself illegal or inconsistent with the scheme of the legislation. For example, employer demands to restrict the scope of the union's bargaining unit have been considered to be illegal demands and in breach of the duty to bargain in good faith.

Particular mention should be made of the extent to which union conduct is regulated by labour boards. Not only does the duty to bargain in good faith apply to unions as well as employers, but the timing of union strike activity is regulated closely by Canadian labour boards. Just as important, however, is the duty of fair representation that requires a union to represent all employees within the bargaining unit, whether they are union members or not, in a manner that is not arbitrary, discriminatory, or tainted by bad faith. This duty of fair representation applies to a union both when it is negotiating a collective agreement on behalf of the bargaining unit and when it is later administering that collective agreement. The union has the exclusive authority to decide whether to take the individual grievances of bargaining unit members to arbitration, but that authority is still subject to the duty of fair representation.

In applying the duty of fair representation, labour boards have given considerable latitude to union conduct at the bargaining table, recognizing that the union needs this latitude to prioritize the conflicting claims of different interest groups within the bargaining unit. Much closer scrutiny, however, is given to the union's role of administering the collective agreement. Here labour boards are conscious of the fact that an individual member of the bargaining unit can only claim rights established under the collective agreement through the union carrying a grievance on that individual's behalf.

Labour boards possess considerable statutory power to remedy violations of collective bargaining legislation. The discretionary aspect of this remedial power offers the boards a wide scope for applying their special expertise in fashioning remedies appropriate to the situations with which they are faced. At times, labour boards may refuse to grant any remedy at all if this response appears to be justified by the particular situation.

Labour board remedies are not only discretionary but also have a significant accommodative aspect. In many jurisdictions, before the hearing of a disputed matter, a labour relations officer is appointed by the board to settle the matter. If accommodation is reached, as it is in a high percentage of cases, the matter is never heard by the board. This active accommodative role of labour boards is another significant feature that distinguishes them from courts.

Another aspect of this accommodative approach is that boards sometimes refuse to issue an order if the conduct in question has been discontinued by the time of the hearing. The Ontario board, for example, has clearly articulated that it will not issue a directive or declaration in respect of illegal strike or lockout action if that action ceases before the hearing, unless there has been a pattern of such conduct, there is a likelihood of further occurrences, or the particular matter has more general implications.

As the accommodative aspect of the labour boards' remedial powers has assumed greater importance, there has been a decline in the use of criminal prosecutions to deal with labour relations problems. Although many collective bargaining statutes still make any contravention of their provisions a criminal offence, such prosecutions are now quite rare. Usually, they cannot be undertaken without the consent of the labour relations board—making prosecution a two-step procedure that is slow and costly. Moreover, consent to prosecute may not be forthcoming since the labour boards have come to regard prosecution as a secondary remedial route. Studies indicate that very few prosecutions are pursued even when consent to prosecute is granted (Swan and Swinton 1983).

Damages are another remedy within the discretion of the labour boards. A damage award, although intended primarily to compensate the party injured by a violation of the collective bargaining statute, has a punitive aspect since the award must be paid by the party contravening the legislation. The amount of damages reflects the extent of the loss incurred and not the seriousness of the conduct causing it. This means that damages awarded to the injured party can exceed the amount that might be levied by a fine if the matter had been made the subject of a prosecution. Most damage awards imposed by labour boards are in respect of loss of income suffered by employees who have been discriminated against in their employment because of trade union activity. However, labour boards have awarded damages to trade unions when serious contraventions of the legislation have interfered with their right to represent employees. In these cases, labour boards have ordered that a trade union be "made whole" for its organizational expenses flowing from the breach of the collective bargaining statute.

Despite the labour boards' broad remedial mandates, damages flowing from illegal strikes are usually sought through the grievance arbitration process.

Grievance Arbitration

Grievance arbitrators, although not directly involved in the application and administration of labour legislation, play a very important role in the administration of collective agreements. Where the parties are unable to resolve their differences through the grievance procedure, arbitrators are selected on an ad hoc basis to deal only with the particular dispute arising from the collective agreement. Once that dispute has been resolved the arbitrator's jurisdiction is exhausted, and if a new dispute should arise and remain unresolved, the parties must once again choose an arbitrator.

Grievance arbitration can take the form of a three-person board or a single arbitrator. The tripartite board, comprised of a union nominee, employer nominee, and independent chairperson, was at one time the more common form of grievance arbitration. More recently, however, the single arbitrator has become more popular, since this form of grievance arbitration is often regarded as being more expeditious and less costly.

Grievance arbitration should not be confused with interest arbitration. Interest arbitration, which is more frequently used in the public sector, requires the arbitrator to resolve the bargaining dispute by determining wages and working conditions and in effect writing the collective agreement for the parties. Grievance arbitration, however, only requires the arbitrator to resolve disputes arising from the administration and application of the collective agreement itself.

The Courts and Judicial Review

The role of the judiciary in the Canadian collective bargaining structure should not be overlooked. Except for Ontario's brief experiment with a labour court, the federally appointed judges of the superior courts have never directly administered Canadian collective bargaining legislation. Nevertheless, superior courts play a prominent role in labour relations law because of their general jurisdiction to administer civil and criminal law, their power to review the decisions of labour boards and grievance arbitrators, and their role as the ultimate interpreter of the Canadian Constitution. Provincially appointed courts (provincial criminal courts) also have a role in dealing with breaches of collective bargaining legislation, although such prosecutions usually require labour board consent.

Until recently, the courts appeared to be playing an increasingly less prominent and less controversial role in the Canadian industrial relations system. The expansion of labour boards' jurisdiction meant that they had assumed some of the jurisdiction once exercised by the courts, especially in respect to strikes and picketing. Moreover, legislatures had enacted specific provisions confining the role of the courts, and the courts themselves appeared to be exercising increasing restraint when reviewing decisions of labour tribunals. The courts could only nullify the decision of a labour board when the board had exceeded its statutory jurisdiction. Excess of jurisdiction, according to the courts, was limited to those circumstances where a board's decision could be regarded as "patently unreasonable."

As noted above, this balance between the legislature and the judiciary has been altered by the introduction of the Charter of Rights and Freedoms. Issues that were once regarded as labour relations issues can now be recast as constitutional issues by reference to the Charter and taken to the courts. Since the courts are the ultimate arbiters of such constitutional issues, they could strike down existing collective bargaining laws and in the process reshape Canada's industrial relations system. As we have noted, however, Canadian courts have been reluctant to use the Charter to reshape Canada's collective bargaining laws.

Summary

Canadian labour legislation has created a tight statutory structure regulating almost every aspect of union-management relations. Although that legal structure owes much to the model of the US Wagner Act, some significant differences distinguish the Canadian system of collective bargaining law from the American. Compulsory conciliation procedures have found much greater favour in Canada than in the United States, and the right to strike is more closely confined by statute in Canada. On the other hand, Canadian legislation provides a much less cumbersome certification procedure and goes further in recognizing the legitimacy of union security provisions. Canadian legislators, moreover, have gone further than their American counterparts in extending collective bargaining rights to public sector employees.

The primary responsibility for the administration of Canadian collective bargaining legislation lies with the labour boards. These administrative tribunals now have jurisdiction over most aspects of the collective bargaining relationship. The resolution of grievances arising from collective agreements, however, is still largely the responsibility of grievance arbitrators selected by the parties on an ad hoc basis. More recently, the Charter of Rights and Freedoms has given the courts more authority to review Canadian collective bargaining laws, but so far Canadian judges have been reluctant to use the Charter to alter these laws.

In fact, recent legislative amendments in two important provincial jurisdictions, British Columbia and Ontario, have had a far greater impact on Canada's collective bargaining than has the Charter. These amendments have strengthened the position of trade unions in the collective bargaining process by enhancing their ability to organize employees and by prohibiting the use of replacement workers during a strike. British Columbia has now repealed its requirement for a certification vote, replacing it with the less onerous procedure of having a union establish employee support through signed membership cards. Ontario's labour relations statute now provides union organizers with access to private property to which the public normally has access and permits picketing in these areas. Both jurisdictions have enacted "anti-scab" laws that clearly alter the existing balance of bargaining power between unions and management.

Whether this trend in labour law reform will continue is uncertain. Canada's participation in the North American Free Trade Agreement may create economic and political pressures to roll back our labour laws so that Canada can compete more effectively with the United States and Mexico. Nevertheless, at the present time, it is clear that from a trade union perspective Canada has one of the most progressive systems of collective bargaining laws in the world.

QUESTIONS

1. Discuss the implications of the increasing regulation of the Canadian industrial relations system.

2. Explain the constitutional division of legislative authority over labour relations in Canada.

3. Describe the evolution of Canadian collective bargaining law since Confederation.

4. What are the significant differences between Canadian collective bargaining laws and their US counterparts? Explain.

5. Distinguish the functions performed by grievance arbitrators from those performed by labour relations boards.

6. Explain how labour boards differ from courts.

7. Which is the better method of determining union membership support—an employee certification vote or a count of union membership cards? Explain.

8. What has been the impact of the Charter of Rights and Freedoms upon Canadian collective bargaining law?

9. What are the pros and cons of greater harmonization or uniformity of labour laws across the different Canadian jurisdictions?

10. What are the advantages/disadvantages of labour boards versus courts for the administration of collective bargaining laws?

REFERENCES

ADAMS, G.W. 1993. *Canadian Labour Law.* Aurora, Ont: Canada Law Book.

ARTHURS, H.W., D.D. CARTER, J. FUDGE, H.J. GLASBEEK, and G. TRUDEAU. 1993. *Labour Law and Industrial Relations in Canada,* 4th ed. Markham: Butterworths.

LABOUR LAW CASEBOOK GROUP. 1991. *Labour Laws: Cases, Materials and Commentary,* 5th ed. Kingston, Ont: Industrial Relations Centre, Queen's University.

SWAN, K.P., and K.E. SWINTON, eds. 1983. *Studies in Labour Law.* Toronto: Butterworths.

WEILER, P.C. 1980. *Reconcilable Differences: New Directions in Canadian Labour Law Reform.* Agincourt, Ont: Carswell.

CHAPTER 4

EMPLOYMENT LEGISLATION

DAVID MCPHILLIPS AND

GEOFFREY ENGLAND

THIS CHAPTER DEALS WITH THE BASIC LAWS GOVERNING THE EMPLOYMENT of all workers, union and nonunion, in Canada. These laws, which exist aside from those offered under collective bargaining regimes, have been created by specific statute and at common law. It is a body of law that affords protection to employees in such fundamental areas as minimum work standards, employment contracts at common law, human rights, and health and safety in the workplace. Important aspects of this protection are reviewed here, and comparisons are drawn, where appropriate, with the protection provided under collective agreements.

Whether a workplace is unionized or not, fundamental conflicts will develop over many workplace issues. Some of these conflicts can appropriately be addressed by the introduction of laws setting out acceptable standards. Employment legislation is designed to provide basic standards covering all workers, nonunionized as well as unionized. It deals with subjects as diverse as minimum wages, mass layoff notice, and chemical toxicity limits. This is particularly critical in situations where employees may lack effective bargaining power as is frequently the case in the absence of trade union representation. Approximately one-third of the Canadian work force is unionized, but even the collective agreements that are in place do not address all aspects of the employment relationship. The importance of employment legislation for employees in general and for industrial relations is now widely recognized:

> Growing awareness of limitations on the scope and effectiveness of collective bargaining has brought a growing realization that direct, substantive legislative intervention is often the only answer. Such intervention ... is becoming more pervasive and more fully elaborated. Even for employment relations covered by collective bargaining, the legal rights and obligations of the parties can no longer be adequately understood without a grasp of the impact of employment standards legislation, anti-discrimination legislation, health and safety legislation, and the like. (Labour Law Casebook Group 1986, 1)

Although Canadian jurisdictions vary in the specific rights conferred on employees, the overall approach is reasonably uniform. As with collective bargaining legislation, sections 91 and 92 of the Constitution Act, 1981 (adopting the British North America Act, 1967) divide responsibility for employment law between the federal and provincial governments. Federal employment laws such as part III of the Canada Labour Code (relating to the employment standards), the Canadian Human Rights Act, and part V of the Canada Labour Code (labour-management relations) apply to employees of airlines and railroads, banks, the postal service, the federal public sector, and communications firms (about 10 per cent of the work force). Provincial laws of a similar character apply to the 90 per cent of employees not covered by federal legislation.

Before most employment laws can be applied, a court, labour board, employment standards board, or human rights tribunal must determine that an individual is an employee as opposed to an independent contractor, apprentice, agent, or partner.[1] (In the latter cases, the parties are governed by the relevant laws of contract, agency, or partnership, respectively.) A number of tests have been developed to determine who is an employee. For example, the control test examines the power of selection, the payment of wages, the right to control the method of doing the work and the right of suspension or dismissal.[2] Because more protection is afforded an employee than ordinary contracting parties, the courts, boards, and other tribunals tend to interpret "employee" as broadly as possible.[3]

This chapter reviews the laws affecting the employment relationship. The first part outlines the work standards legislation contained in the various jurisdictions. The next part reviews the statutes and common law rules related to individual employment contracts. Human rights legislation pertaining to employment is covered in the third part, and the fourth deals with occupational health and safety.

WORK STANDARDS LEGISLATION

Each jurisdiction sets out minimum standards of work that apply to all employees. These "floors of rights" are contained either in one statute (for example, an employment standards act) or in a series of separate statutes (for example, holiday act, hours of work act) and are intended to set the threshold of rights for all workers, both union and nonunion. (In some jurisdictions, collective agreements are permitted that have less than minimum standards in one area but exceed them in others.) There is a growing emphasis on employment standards in Canada due to a number of diverse factors including the decline of unionization in some industries, mass layoffs resulting from industrial restructuring, and plant closures. Major revisions in the existing legislation have been proposed or adopted recently in British Columbia, Saskatchewan, and Ontario. However, there are some who feel that the strengthening of employment standards will be too costly and lead to greater inflexibility at a time of increased deregulation, global competition, and threats of plant relocation to other countries. Indeed, in the future, there may have to be a harmonization of employment standards between countries, particularly those who enter into trade agreements such as NAFTA.

Turning to the present, it should be noted that in many jurisdictions, employment standards acts or parts of them do not apply to certain groups of employees. In some cases, the acts do not apply to entire industries such as farming, fishing, and domestic employment (although section 15 of the Charter of Rights and Freedom may eventually result in these exclusions being ruled unconstitutional). Furthermore, the legislation will often not cover individuals who are part-timers, subcontractors, contingent workers, home workers or those on fixed-term contracts. Even within industries that are covered, the legislation may not apply to all employees for all matters; for example, overtime provisions may not apply to managers.

The areas covered in the employment standards legislation of the various jurisdictions generally include:

1. *Wage protection.* Wage protection provisions deal with such issues as when wages are to be paid, the requirement for a statement of wages, the employer's right to make deductions from earnings, assignments of wages and, in the event of nonpayment, the right of the employee to attach property or sue the directors of the employer.
2. *Hours of work.* Such issues as the daily or weekly maximum hours of work before overtime must be paid, the rate of overtime pay, requirements for lunch or coffee breaks, rules regarding split shifts, minimum call-in periods, and minimum consecutive hours free from work are generally covered.
3. *Annual vacation.* Each jurisdiction sets out a minimum annual vacation entitlement (for example, two weeks during each year worked and three weeks after five years) and states when the vacation becomes due. The provisions also set out vacation pay rates.
4. *Statutory holidays.* The legislation sets out the minimum number of statutory holidays (Christmas Day, Labour Day, and so on) to which the employee is entitled.

5. *Minimum wages.* The acts or accompanying regulations set out a minimum wage that must be paid to all employees. Some jurisdictions specify separate rates for adults and for younger workers (those under seventeen or eighteen years of age).

6. *Maternity leave.* The protections include the right to a paid or unpaid leave for a specific period of time—usually seventeen or eighteen weeks—during pregnancy and following the birth of a child. The provisions also deal with the timing of the leave and the security rights of the employee on her return to work.

7. *Termination.* Each jurisdiction sets out a minimum notice period to which most employees are entitled before termination. These notice requirements may not apply if the employee was recently hired or if the employer can prove just cause (such as theft) for termination. In most jurisdictions, the requirement is one of *notice*, so the employer can insist that the employee work during the notice period, although the employer often terminates the employee immediately by paying the wages that would be owed for the notice period. Each jurisdiction has its own formula for establishing minimum standards of notice. A typical requirement would be for a three-month eligibility period after which an employee is entitled to one week's notice. After a further period, the notice required will rise with length of service with a typical maximum of eight weeks' notice. The federal statute requires a combination of a short notice period (two weeks) and then severance pay for employees who have worked for at least twelve months. Most jurisdictions also have special notice requirements for "mass" layoffs involving, in most cases, fifty or more employees.

8. *Miscellaneous.* Because the area of work standards is constantly evolving, provisions differ among the various jurisdictions in Canada. Other areas of coverage include paternity or family leave, adoption leave, clothing or special apparel payments, child employment laws, minimum age levels for employment, bereavement leave, sick leave, and maximum board and lodging charges.

INDIVIDUAL CONTRACTS OF EMPLOYMENT

Beside the statutory provisions, other protections and obligations are imposed through the existence of an individual employment contract that every employee has with his or her employer. The terms of the employment agreement can arise in any of three ways: by implication through operation of the law; by implication by the past practice of the parties; or by express agreement of the parties. Most often, the parties do not explicitly agree to, or even discuss, most of the terms of the employment contract. Nevertheless, because express terms prevail over implied terms, it is wise for the parties to reduce as much as possible to express agreement, particularly in written form.

Implied Terms by Operation of Law

Employee.   Important implied terms of any employment contract establish that the employee is under an obligation to work, to not be absent unreasonably, to obey lawful and safe orders, to avoid serious misconduct (which may include dishonesty,[4] impropriety, drunkenness, insolence, and insubordination), to perform in a competent and careful manner (that is, to exercise skill and care), and to account for all property and money he or she receives on the employer's behalf (for a general discussion, see Christie 1993, 447-504). It has also been held that the employer has the implied right to run the business and to expect the employee to follow instructions.[5]

Each employment contract contains an implied term that the employee will serve honestly and faithfully. Further, at senior levels the employment relationship is a fiduciary one, which requires good faith, fidelity, and the avoidance of a conflict of interest.[6] This may include the duty to disclose improper conduct by fellow employees,[7] and to not disseminate confidential information.[8] Similarly, the solicitation of customers by employees while employed is a breach of the duty; solicitation after leaving employment is normally permitted unless the individual was in a senior position, in which case the fiduciary duty may well continue.[9]

The common law also requires an employee to give notice of intent to quit employment[10] (see, generally, Levitt 1985, 267-69). In practice, however, this issue of "wrongful resignation" is rarely litigated. The length of the required notice period is relatively insignificant for most employees; moreover, it may be difficult for an employer to prove damages,[11] particularly in view of the requirement to mitigate. The cost of litigation is a further disincentive.

Employer.   The obligations of the employer include paying the employee (at or above the minimum wage) and paying over gratuities.[12] The most significant implied term in an employment contract, however, is the obligation on the employer to give reasonable notice to the employee in the case of dismissal without just cause.[13] If such notice (or pay in lieu thereof) is provided, there is arguably no breach of the employment contract, and the contract lawfully terminates at the expiration of the notice period or on payment of severance money in lieu thereof. This implied term is a relatively recent addition to the common law, having replaced the nineteenth-century presumption of yearly hiring. Even today, if the employment contract is for a specific term, as is the case with, say, most professional sport coaches, no such implication of reasonable notice of termination arises, and the contract must be paid in full.[14] Further, the implied term of giving reasonable notice does not arise in cases of an employee's voluntary resignation,[15] frustration of the contract (which occurs when a contract cannot be performed because of some event beyond the parties' control—for example, a fire),[16] retirement,[17] or temporary layoff.[18]

In alleged cases of dismissal, the court has to decide three questions:

1. *Was there an express or constructive dismissal?* An "express dismissal" is an oral or written communication to the effect that the employee is being terminated. A "constructive dismissal" exists where actions by the employer can be construed as the equivalent of a dismissal. Whenever the employer unilaterally changes a fundamental term of the employment contract, such as salary level, job responsibilities, level of status or prestige, fringe benefits, or hours of work,[19] the employee may treat the contract as having been repudiated by the employer and seek the available legal remedies.

Some recent decisions hold, however, that *minor* changes to the terms of the employment agreements do not constitute a fundamental change; in these cases, the alteration has to be accepted by the employee. These cases hold that an employer must be allowed a certain degree of latitude with respect to minor changes to the employee's job functions,[20] particularly where an employee was not hired initially to fill a particular senior function.[21]

2. *If there was a dismissal, did the employer have just cause?* Once the fact of dismissal has been established, the employer must show, on the balance of probability, that just cause to terminate without reasonable notice existed. The question is not whether there was a reasonable business explanation for the changes but rather whether there was a proper legal basis to terminate the individual's employment without a reasonable warning. Economic reasons or reorganization of the operations do not constitute just cause,[22] but misconduct, including off-duty behaviour, dishonesty, and disobedience may provide cause, depending on the particular circumstances.[23] Excessive absenteeism (either culpable or nonculpable)[24] and incompetence[25] may similarly be held to amount to cause. Further, a breach of any implied terms, such as violations of conflict of interest requirements[26] or a refusal to accept geographical transfers,[27] may permit the employer to terminate the employee without notice. It is also important that the employer not have condoned or forgiven the grounds (a situation that would likely be judged the case if the employer asserted incompetence shortly after giving the employee a merit increase).

3. *If there was no just cause, what is the appropriate remedy for the employee?* In cases where just cause has not been proven, the employee is entitled to reasonable notice of dismissal. It must be emphasized that the employee has no right to retain a job; unlike a collective agreement, the common law does not bestow job security. Reinstatement is not available at common law, and the courts have thus far refused to order this remedy on the ground that it is impractical to reinstate employees, particularly those in senior positions.

Additionally, the common law requirement is for notice—that is, a warning period—rather than severance pay. In practice, for reasons of employee morale, confidentiality, and productivity, employers often terminate the employee instantly and remit wages and benefits to cover the notice period, but there is no legal requirement to do so. Although the required notice period is subject to the minimum legislative guidelines already outlined, the courts have held that common law principles require notice periods exceeding the minimum statutory limits in cases of middle and upper management positions and in some cases even for blue- or white-collar workers with long seniority. The length of the notice period likely to be required is a function of both the length of time required to obtain similar employment and a reward for past service. These are determined by reference to such factors as the employee's age, total length of service, level of responsibility, length of service in the particular position, level of education, and the availability of similar employment.[28] (See also Levitt 1985, 137-45, where seventy-six separate factors are mentioned.) It is clear from the jurisprudence that there is no fixed formula to determine the appropriate notice period in each case, which makes predictions as to legal outcomes very difficult for both the employer and the discharged employee. As a general guideline, however, often notice periods will be calculated on roughly the basis of one month (or slightly less) for each year of service, subject to being raised or lowered depending on the age of the individual, the level of management, and the availability of work for a person with his or her expertise. The cases indicate that as a practical matter, eighteen to twenty-four months is the upper range of notice periods granted by the courts.

The payment covering the notice period includes not only wages but also the fringe benefits that would have been bestowed on the employee. Since such benefits normally exceed 25 per cent of salary, the dollar amount involved under the express or implied terms of the contract is often significant.

Also potentially affecting any monetary payment awarded by the courts is whether the employee attempted to find another job following his or her termination. An employee entitled to notice has a duty to mitigate or lessen the damages by seeking other substantially similar employment.[29] It should be noted, however, that the burden of proof is on the employer to prove that the employee has not done so.[30]

Another issue that may arise is whether the discharged employee can obtain punitive damages or damages for intangible loss such as mental distress, or, in cases of people in the public arena,[31] loss of reputation. The Supreme Court of Canada has indicated that such damages are inappropriate in breach of contract cases,[32] but there have been deviations from this position.[33] The highest award of this nature in Canada to date was in *Pilato* v *Hamilton Place*, in which the Ontario court awarded $25,000 damages for mental suffering and a further $25,000 in punitive damages.[34]

Employers must be extremely careful, therefore, how and under what circumstances they discharge employees. A risk of increased damage exists if the discharge is done in a manner that can be characterized as malicious, vindictive, or harsh (other descriptions used by the courts include abrupt, humiliating, irresponsible, callous, wanton, and reckless) or if totally false and serious allegations of cause (for example, theft) are asserted. In those instances, the court may either award damages for intangible loss or significantly increase the required notice period without even separately identifying the amount as punitive damages.

The issue of "near cause" has occasionally arisen. This phrase refers to a situation in which the employer's evidence falls short of establishing just cause, but there is some evidence that the employee may be partially at fault (for example, some level of incompetence can be demonstrated). Although some decisions have held that the existence of near cause reduces the notice period, higher courts have rejected that notion.[35]

A significant development in the area of employment law has been the evolution of a form of job security for nonmanagerial employees with some seniority who do not belong to a bargaining unit. Common in Europe, though not in the United States, such legislation exists in the federal jurisdiction, Quebec, and Nova Scotia (England 1978, 472). Under part III, section 240 of the Canada Labour Code, for example, a terminated non-management employee who is not a member of a bargaining unit and has at least twelve months' service may have access to a process of adjudication similar to arbitration under a collective agreement. The adjudicator's remedies include the power to reinstate the employee into his or her previous position. The reinstatement power is discretionary, rather than mandatory, so an adjudicator is free to award damages in lieu of reinstatement where it is felt reinstatement would not be appropriate.[36] Studies have indicated that adjudicators tend to follow the same approach as arbitrators in reviewing discipline imposed by management, although at least one author has questioned the wisdom of that approach.[37]

Implied Terms by Past Practice

The conduct or past practice of the parties may also be used to decide what terms govern the employment relationship:

> The court does not apply the principles of contract law as though in a vacuum, but reviews the history of the relations between the parties in its entirety so as to arrive at a rational solution in each particular case. The relationship of master and servant in the modern corporate world cannot be determined as though that relationship consisted of a single contract with fixed terms and conditions.[38]

In *Durrant* v *Westeel-Rosco Ltd*,[39] the practice of previous executive transfers was held to be indicative of the continuing intent of the parties. It has been said, however, that any imposition of such implied terms for the benefit of the employer must be based on an interpretation that comes within the "bounds of reason."[40]

Express Terms

General Rules. Employer and employee are free to agree to express terms that will govern their employment relationship. These agreements, which will prevail over any implied terms, can be either written or oral, although the content of an oral agreement is often difficult to prove.

Both parties must be aware of all terms of the relationship; therefore, express terms that are buried in lengthy contracts or employment manuals may not be enforceable.[41] Although the courts can refuse to enforce terms that have not been voluntarily agreed to, they will, in all likelihood, uphold the application of employment clauses provided that the parties are at arm's length and there has been no coercion or improper influence of any kind on the employee to accept.[42] Only rarely have the courts rejected contacts on the basis that there was no real chance to negotiate the contents of the agreement.[43]

Litigation has also arisen in situations in which a term included in an employment agreement has "expired" either because of the passage of time or through fundamental changes in the employee's job responsibilities. For example, notice of termination terms have been held to apply no longer if significant time has passed since the employee entered into the employment contract.[44] The employment contract also faces a considerably increased risk of invalidation if the duties of the employee have changed significantly since the time that contract was executed.[45]

Provisions in employment contracts may also be struck down on the grounds that the terms of the agreement were harsh and unconscionable at the time of the making of the contract. The issue appears to have arisen primarily in cases relating to the imposition of oppressive notice periods.[46]

Finally, the terms of the contract must not violate the provisions of statutes or be contrary to public policy. For example, an employment contract may not call for less notice than that required under the applicable minimum employment standards legislation.

Specific Provisions. Express terms may deal with such basic provisions as the date of commencement of employment, salary, the period of probation, and fringe benefits. Employers may also include special terms dealing with cause for termination. A frequent inclusion by the employer is a term expressly limiting the notice period. Such a clause must be a reasonable pre-estimate of damages, not a penalty clause.[47] Further, the clause must have been brought to the attention of the employee and continue to remain in effect.[48]

Employers frequently attempt to protect their competitive position by inserting specific conflict-of-interest clauses restricting an employee's ability to deal with, for example, confidential information, use of company facilities, or assignment of inventions. A restrictive covenant is a clause by which an employer attempts to limit an employee's ability to compete with the employer or work for a competitor after the employment relationship has ended. The basic rule is that such a clause is presumptively void as being against public policy; the burden is on the employer to demonstrate that it should be enforced. To do so, the employer must demonstrate that there is a proprietary interest to be protected[49] (for example, trade secrets or confidential information), that the clause to protect that interest is reasonable in terms of length of time, geography, and nature of the restriction,[50] and that the provision does not offend the public interest.[51]

Collective Agreements versus Individual Contracts of Employment

Employees who are covered by a collective agreement must use the recources available under that contract. Thus, they are not able to sue for wrongful dismissal in the courts but must pursue their claims through the grievance procedure (ultimately leading to arbitration).[52] They have the benefit of a provision in collective agreements, imposed by labour codes, that prohibits discharge or discipline without just cause. Through the grievance procedure, a wrongfully dismissed employee is able to seek reinstatement (and lost wages) and thereby retain his or her job. Slightly more than half of terminated employees covered by a union contract are, in fact, reinstated, frequently with some back pay.

On the other hand, employers traditionally have been able to terminate nonunionized employees, either by establishing just cause or arbitrarily discharging the employee and giving proper notice. Two new trends have evolved, however. First, courts have significantly increased the common law notice periods so that long-term employees have been awarded twelve to twenty-four months' pay. This has undoubtedly served to curb the frequency of arbitrary dismissals. Second, the introduction of statutory rights of reinstatement for nonunionized employees (i.e., in the federal jurisdiction, Quebec, and Nova Scotia) has broadened the concept of job security beyond the trade union sector, although the qualification periods are still substantial. Nevertheless, it is clear that the vast majority of employees have far more job protection under a collective agreement than under individual contracts of employment.

HUMAN RIGHTS LEGISLATION

Each Canadian jurisdiction has passed specific legislation to deal with discrimination. Human rights legislation is designed to prevent discrimination against individuals on the basis of membership in specific groups. The growing heterogeneity of the workplace, including the growth in the labour force participation of women, the rise of ethnic diversity and the emphasis on integrating disabled persons has resulted in tremendous pressure to expand and enforce anti-discrimination legislation in a number of areas.

Statutes identify those groups that are expressly protected. Differences exist among human rights jurisdictions, but a typical list includes age, sex, race, colour, creed, religion, ancestry, place of origin, marital status, family status, spousal occupation, sexual orientation, mental or physical disability, physical stature, and criminal convictions unrelated to the employment. Organizations of a fraternal, philanthropic, or educational nature are generally exempted from the statutes. Although legislation deals with the prevention of discrimination in many areas (including, for example, housing and public services), this chapter focuses only on those restrictions relating to employment practices.

Enforcement of such an act generally begins with a complaint to a human rights commission or council. Most jurisdictions provide for ultimate determination of unsettled cases through a board of enquiry appointed by the minister of the department responsible for the human rights legislation. Appeals from decisions of this board can generally be made to the courts.

Two Supreme Court of Canada decisions—*Bhinder* v *CNR* and *O'Malley* v *Simpson Sears*[53]—have made it clear that liability does not depend on an employer's wilful intent to discriminate. Therefore, besides prohibiting intentional, direct discrimination, the acts cover systemic, or indirect, discrimination that has prohibited consequences (for example, height restrictions that indirectly discriminate against women).

The remedial sections of the human rights legislation are of particular significance. Human rights boards have the power of rectification. They can, for example, order reinstatement of individuals who have been fired and require the hiring of individuals who have been refused employment. Boards may also award monetary damages (for example, back wages) and order costs to be paid by the losing party. Punitive damages can also be awarded in cases where the discrimination is malevolent and intentional and where deterrence is a major goal (for example, in cases of repeated sexual harassment).

Finally, there are affirmative action remedies. In *Action Travail* v *CNR*, the human rights tribunal ordered that of every four new blue-collar workers hired by Canadian National Railways, one must be a woman until women represented 13 per cent of the employees in blue-collar jobs. The decision was overturned by the Federal Court of Appeal but was reinstated by the Supreme Court of Canada.[54]

Hiring Process

Statutes generally prohibit discrimination in the area of job advertising, application forms and interviews. Employers are prohibited from using non-neutral terms that would discourage people of certain groups (for example, people of a certain age, religion, sex, or marital status) from even applying for certain jobs. Where there are prohibitions concerning application forms and interviews, the mere asking of a question concerning a prohibited factor is a breach of the legislation. In those jurisdictions without such express protection, a complainant must demonstrate that the answer to the offending question was actually the reason for the refusal to hire.

The legislation attempts to dissuade employers from acquiring information concerning factors that should not form the basis for a hiring decision. Much of this information may be relevant once the person is hired (for example, age may affect the premiums an employee pays under a group insurance plan), but it should be obtained only after employment begins.

Equal Pay

Besides generally prohibiting discriminatory conditions of work, human rights legislation singles out pay discrimination between the sexes. The average female employee in Canada receives approximately 70 per cent of the pay of the average male. The source of the difference has been widely debated, but some of the gap (usually under 5 per cent being attributed to this factor) results from outright pay discrimination (different pay for the same or substantially similar jobs) and some from occupational segregation (the clustering of women in so-called women's jobs, such as secretarial work, child care, nursing, and waitressing). Early legislation required that equal pay be given for identical jobs. To prevent slightly different job descriptions from being given to men and women, most jurisdictions have now adopted the requirement of equal pay for "substantially similar work." The basis for that comparison is the skill, effort, and responsibility required in the similar positions.[55]

Even with legislation of this nature, the gap in earnings remains. One solution would be to avoid occupational segregation, but there is little likelihood that will occur in the near future, although affirmative action and employment equity legislation are beginning to address the problem. As a result, a movement has arisen to attempt to ensure that traditionally female jobs are paid the same as traditionally male jobs of the same value. This approach is known as "equal pay for work of equal value" or "pay equity" in Canada, and "comparable worth" in the United States.

Most Canadian jurisdictions have adopted some form of pay equity legislation,[56] although it is usually initiated only on the basis of a complaint. Furthermore, its application has been limited mainly to the public sector. In Newfoundland and British Columbia, formal legislation has not been passed, but the governments have committed themselves to its implementation in the public sector through the collective bargaining process. Only Alberta and Saskatchewan do not have pay equity legislation or a government commitment to implement pay equity for their own employees. Ontario, however, is the one province to have it apply to both the private and public sector and to not simply rely on complaints for its application. Opponents of pay equity claim it does not address the problem of occupational segregation, that it is unworkable on any large scale, that it does not permit the free market to operate, and that it may prove too costly to the economy. Advocates often reply that it may at least narrow the gap (by paying groups such as nurses more money), that the supposedly free market was designed and is operated by men, and that although implementing the principle of equal value will be difficult, it is not impossible, and that failure to do so is a denial of social justice.

Conditions of Employment

Human rights acts contain provisions that prevent employers from refusing to hire, or having different terms of employment, based on the prohibited factors. An employer can, however, justify a discriminatory action with the defence of business necessity. Most of the statutes expressly contain a provision expressly permitting discrimination for a "bona fide occupational qualification" (BFOQ). The Supreme Court has now indicated that in the case of systemic discrimination there is also a duty placed on the employer to accommodate short of undue hardship.[57] In *Renaud* v *South Okanagan School District*, the Court stated that "more than mere negligible effort is required to satisfy the duty to accommodate ... the extent to which the discriminator must go to accommodate is limited by the words 'reasonable' and 'short of undue hardship.'"[58]

In practice, the precise obligations under the duty to accommodate will vary with the particular circumstances of each case. For example, it might require an employer to modify an existing job to eliminate any lifting requirements, thereby enabling an employee with a back injury to continue to work. Or an employer may be required to provide a modified work schedule to an employee whose religion prohibits work on certain days of the week. The practical significance of such terms as "undue hardship" and "reasonable" accommodation is still being clarified, often case by case.

The number of cases dealing with various types of discrimination is now very large. The following provide illustrations of the issues that arise and of how human rights tribunals attempt to resolve them. *Bhinder* v *CNR*[59] concerned a requirement of the railway that its maintenance electricians wear hard hats. One of the employees, Bhinder, was a Sikh, who was required by his religion to wear a turban. The Supreme Court of Canada held that, although the railway's policy amounted to discrimination on the basis of religion, the rule had been adopted for genuine business reasons and was a reasonable measure in reducing the risk of injury to employees.

Cases involving discrimination on the basis of sex provide the most frequent type of complaint. The decisions address issues such as restrictive hiring practices where, if there is differential treatment, it must be shown that the rationale was truly bona fide and not based on subjective perception of what constitutes a "female" or "male" job.[60] Size requirements[61] have been held to discriminate systemically against women and thus must be supported by evidence that they are legitimate criteria.

Another case involved Rosann Cashin, a Canadian Broadcasting Corporation reporter in Newfoundland who did not have her contract renewed because her husband had been named a director of PetroCanada. Both the original tribunal and the appeal tribunal found that this behaviour constituted discrimination but disagreed on the merits of the BFOQ defence put forward by the CBC. The original panel found that a bona fide occupational qualification was not established:

> A perception that a reporter lacks objectivity, if it exists, may be based on factors which have no bearing on the reporter's actual objectivity. ... For example, if it could be proved that audiences in Newfoundland perceive female reporters to be dishonest or lacking in objectivity, I am not convinced that there would be sufficient jurisdiction for failing to hire female reporters, in the absence of evidence that female reporters were in fact dishonest or lacking in objectivity.

> If it can be said that a perception of lack of objectivity exists without basis, and that the reporter's work has not fallen from his usual high standard, how can it be said that the perception is reasonably necessary to the performance of the job if the job performance remains of high standard? Quite simply, the requirement does not relate to the work if the work is objective, fair, accurate, and balanced. This leads me to the conclusion that the perceived objectivity requirement has not met the objective requirement of the BFOQ test.[62]

The appeal tribunal disagreed, observing:

> When one considers the very high profile and public image of Richard Cashin in Newfoundland, particularly in relation to two of the most important resources of that province and the fact that his wife is a CBC broadcaster reporting on that very subject matter ... we are therefore of the view that perception of objectivity is a valid BFOQ both in the general sense and when applied to the particular circumstances of the complaint.[63]

The Federal Court of Appeal, however, reversed the appeal tribunal in May 1988 and reinstated the findings of the original board. Leave for the CBC to appeal to the Supreme Court of Canada was denied.

Sex discrimination also includes discrimination related to pregnancy. In 1989, the Supreme Court of Canada in *Brooks* v *Canada Safeway*[64] revised its previous position set down in *Bliss* v *A-G Canada*[65] and has now indicated that discrimination against pregnant individuals constitutes sex discrimination against women. Thus, sick leave policies that routinely excluded pregnancy-related illness have had to be re-written to end this form of discrimination.

Human rights legislation also regulates harassment. Discussions of harassment generally focus on sexual harassment, but other elements, such as social or religious harassment, may be involved. The Supreme Court in *Janzen and Govereau* v *Platy Enterprises and Tommy Grammas*[66] held that even if a particular statute does not include harassment as a separate heading, it still is covered under the prohibitions against discrimination on the basis of sex, race, religion, etc. Many jurisdictions, however, do include a separate provision dealing with harassment. For example, the Canada Human Rights Code provides that "it is discriminatory practice ... to harass an individual on a prohibited ground of discrimination" (section 13.1). Because employers have been held liable for acts of their employees[67] in this area, employers find it prudent to implement formal policies dealing with sexual harassment in the workplace.

The adoption of affirmative action and employment equity programs is expressly permitted by human rights codes and the Charter of Rights and Freedoms. These programs are intended to foster employment equity for groups previously discriminated against by ensuring such actions as pay adjustments, hiring quotas, and promotion standards for the disadvantaged group. In 1987, the federal government introduced the Employment Equity Act, which requires federally regulated employers with more than 100 employees to implement employment equity and to collect and annually file data, by designated group, on rate of pay, occupational distribution, and pay levels for women, visible minorities, aboriginal people, and the physically handicapped. Rather than imposing an explicit quota system, the legislation requires each program to contain "an effective enforcement mechanism," the design of which has been left to the employer. Further, as a matter of policy, the federal government, through the Federal Contractors' Program, will require compliance from all organizations employing 100 or more employees that gain federal government contracts worth more than $200,000. This program extends significantly the employment equity net.

The Charter of Rights and Freedoms

The Charter of Rights and Freedoms sets out a number of rights with which federal and provincial legislation must comply. For example, there are Charter protections for such rights as freedom of speech, religion, and association. The Charter also has a direct impact on human rights legislation through the equality provision:

> Section 15.(1) Every individual is equal before and under the law and has the right to the equal protection and equal benefit of the law without discrimination and, in particular, without discrimination based on race, national, or ethnic origin, colour, religion, sex, or mental or physical disability.

> (2) Subsection (1) does not preclude any law, program or activity that has as its object the amelioration of conditions of disadvantaged individuals or groups including those that are disadvantaged because of race, national or ethnic origin, colour, religion, sex, age, or mental or physical disability.

The rights conferred by this and other sections of the Charter are, however, subject to section 1:

> The Canadian Charter of Rights and Freedoms guarantees the rights and freedoms set out in it subject only to such reasonable limits prescribed by law as can be demonstrably justified in a free and democratic society.

The extent of the courts' willingness to interpret the prescribed rights broadly and its inclination to use the section 1 limitation will be a major factor in the long-run impact of the Charter.

The Courts have indicated that if a government attempts to restrict freedoms guaranteed by the Charter, there will be a significant requirement placed on the government to demonstrate why the restriction is necessary. The Supreme Court has indicated that it will consider whether the reduction imposed is rationally connected to the government's objection, whether the Charter rights were restricted as little as possible, whether the proportionality between the effects of the measures and the objectives which have been set out is reasonable, and whether there were other measures available to the government to achieve its objective.[68]

An example of the application of the Charter can be found in two mandatory retirement cases [1990] 3 S.C.R. 229, 76 P.L.R. (4th) 545 (S.C.C.). The mandatory retirement policies were challenged at the University of Guelph and the University of British Columbia by individuals employed at those institutions. The Supreme Court held that mandatory retirement policies constituted age discrimination, but also held under section 1 that such a restriction was a reasonable limitation in the case of universities.

Bargaining Unit Employees

Human rights legislation directly applies to all employees, both union and nonunion. Members of bargaining units, however, have added protection from discrimination. First, most of the human rights codes apply explicitly to organizations, such as trade unions and employer organizations. Trade unions are thus prohibited from discriminating and could themselves be the subjects of human rights complaints. Second, most of the labour codes contain provisions imposing on a trade union a duty of fair representation. As a result, a union cannot behave in a manner that can be characterized as bad faith, arbitrary, or discriminatory. If it does, a complaint can be filed successfully with the labour board. Third, collective agreements often contain clauses explicitly or implicitly adopting human rights principles. Discrimination on the part of an employer can then be addressed directly through the grievance process, rather than through the human rights councils.

OCCUPATIONAL HEALTH AND SAFETY

Canada's record of industrial accidents and diseases is among the worst among advanced industrial countries.[69] The number of accidents resulting in lost work on a nationwide basis rose from 479,558 in 1982 to 620,979 in 1989, although this had fallen to 455,659 in 1992.[70] The preponderance of accidents occur in a few industries, especially fishing, followed by forestry, mining, construction, transportation, public administration, agriculture, and manufacturing.[71] In addition, account must be taken of persons who have contracted a disease from exposure to dangerous chemicals, such as carcinogens, asbestos, and isocanytes, and whose symptoms may not appear for many years. It has been estimated that, in Ontario alone, 700 persons die every year from work-related cancer.[72]

Prevention of Workplace Accidents and Diseases

In all Canadian jurisdictions,[73] the goal of prevention is pursued primarily by a combination of the "external system," wherein defined standards for health and safety are established by statutory regulation, and the "internal system," wherein joint management-labour committees, or safety representatives, assume certain responsibilities for promoting health and safety at the workplace. Workers' compensation legislation, which is primarily responsible for compensating injured and sick workers, also has a preventative role in that it generally imposes more onerous financial levies on employers with poor safety records.

The External System.   The external system establishes two kinds of legal duty. The first compels employers to comply with detailed health and safety standards in the workplace, and the second imposes on employers and employees a general "performance duty" of promoting health and safety.

All provinces have a plethora of legislation, normally enacted in the form of regulations made pursuant to an enabling statute, establishing highly detailed safety rules, often geared to the circumstances of particular industries and occupations. These regulations have reference to the work process, permissible materials and chemicals, the manufacture and use of equipment, on-site facilities such as medical care, toilets and water, the worker's duty to undergo periodic medical examinations, the qualification needed to work in the industry or trade, and notification of hazards. The legislation and regulations are normally based on the recommendations of advisory agencies that have researched the health hazards connected with particular industries and occupations or with the use of particular chemicals, materials, and machinery. The Ontario Smoking in the Workplace Act,[74] enacted in 1989, is unique in prohibiting smoking in an "enclosed space," although the employer has the discretion to allow smoking in a designated zone, provided that this accounts for no more than 25 per cent of the total floor area of the enclosed space. However, the employer must make "reasonable efforts to accommodate" a worker's request to work in a place separate from a designated smoking zone. Criticisms of this "standard setting" legislation include: it is too slow to respond to the rapid developments of hazard - control technology; it cannot handle the unique facets of particular work processes, which are best known by the parties "on the spot" at the workplace level; and governments, in fixing risk standards, have tended to be overly conservative with the result that workers have had to bear an unacceptably high level of risk.[75]

In addition, the external system seeks to make all parties in the workplace take the initiative by means of statutory performance duties. Although there are variations between the provinces, the Nova Scotia Occupational Health and Safety Act[76] is typical in requiring the employer to "take every precaution that is reasonable to .... ensure the health and safety of persons at or near the workplace." Because the employer exercises ultimate control over the labour process, the Act imposes additional specific duties on the employer: to provide the requisite information and training in health and safety; to supervise the workforce to ensure that managers and employees are complying with health and safety requirements in the legislation and in the firm's rulebook; to ensure that machinery and equipment is being used and maintained properly; to ensure that protective devices and clothing are being maintained and used properly; to notify workers of workplace hazards; and to cooperate with joint health and safety committees, or with safety representatives in the plant, and with government health and safety officers. Furthermore, every worker is obliged to "take every reasonable precaution in the circumstances to protect his own health and safety and that of other persons at or near the workplace" and to "co-operate" with the employer, with his workmates and with the joint health and safety committee, the safety representative and government health and safety officers in order to protect his own and others' health and safety. The worker is also required to use protective equipment and clothing and to report hazards to the employer. Significantly, most provinces impose equivalent duties on non-employee, "independent contractors" operating at the worksite. Some provinces impose a duty on the principal contractor of a construction or other project to ensure that sub-employers on the worksite comply with their statutory obligations respecting health and safety, recognizing that the principal contractor exercises ultimate control over the project. Similarly, some provinces have recognized the appropriateness of making the owner of certain workplaces responsible for ensuring that the health and safety facilities required by the legislation are in place. For example, the owner of a shopping mall is responsible for the air quality and safe entry and egress from the mall. Finally, the Nova Scotia act adopts the common approach of requiring suppliers to ensure that the materials, tools, and equipment they provide are safe to use and that the hazard notification requirements for these products are honoured. (These regulations are described below.)

The foregoing performance duties do not create strict liability; they simply require that reasonable measures be taken. In determining reasonableness, a balance is struck between the magnitude of harm, the probability of an injury occurring, and the cost and inconvenience to the employer and other persons on the worksite of eradicating the potential hazard.[77] Thus the legislation implicitly accepts a certain level of accidents and injuries to workers.

The Internal Responsibility System.   Although an effective external system is necessary for the promotion of health and safety, all provinces have recognized that it must be buttressed by an effective internal system wherein labour and management, at the level of the workplace, assume responsibility for dealing with their own unique circumstances.[78] Moreover, an effective internal system is less costly to the public purse than a state-financed external system.

The goals of the internal responsibility system in the workplace are: to identify actual and potential hazards; to monitor the adequacy of pre-existing health and safety laws and procedures; to encourage co-operative self-compliance on the part of all members of the workplace; to investigate accidents and injuries that occur; and to formulate proposals for improving health and safety. The three pillars of the internal responsibility system are: the presence of a joint worker-management health and safety committee; the right of individuals to refuse unsafe work; and the right of employees to be informed of what constitutes a workplace hazard and how to avoid it. These have been labelled, respectively, the right to representation, the right to refuse, and the right to know. Because the parties in industry have not established these features by voluntary methods,[79] all provinces have enacted legislation to secure them. Although there are important differences of details among these statutes, they share several common elements.

First, in all provinces except Alberta and Prince Edward Island, employers hiring a defined minimum number of employees, usually twenty, are compelled to establish a joint health and safety committee comprised of equal numbers of workers and managers. In Alberta and P.E.I., the establishment of such committees is at the discretion of the executive branch of government, creating the risk of political interference. Arguably, the "twenty employee" trigger is too high. For example, in Nova Scotia it is estimated that only about ten per cent of workplaces in the province are required to have a committee.[80] In workplaces below the trigger, the legislation typically requires the establishment of worker safety representatives who perform roughly similar functions to those of a committee. The presence of a joint committee has been shown to result in dramatic reductions in injuries.[81]

The functions and powers of joint committees are defined by the provincial legislation; the parties are free to expand but not to abridge the statutory minimum requirements. Typically, a committee can receive, investigate and attempt to resolve health and safety complaints from workers and managers; conduct routine inspections of the plant and health and safety audits; participate with government officers in the latter's inspections and investigations, usually at the officer's discretion; consult with the employer and outside agencies in the development and monitoring of health and safety measures; develop and deliver educational programs; and maintain health and safety records. Committee members commonly must be paid their regular wages for committee work performed during working hours. But the legislation frequently does not address the situation where the committee has to meet outside of a particular member's working hours, for example, in shift work situations where not all committee members finish work simultaneously.

In all provinces except Ontario, the joint committees are empowered only to make recommendations to management. The legislation does not authorize them to decide unilaterally that the workplace organization, materials, or equipment are unsafe and to compel management to follow their directives. At most, the legislation requires that management co-operate with the work of the committees. Typically, the committee's only power is the ability to call a government inspector, who can then apply a stop-work order or other directive to make the workplace safe or even recommend prosecution. Not surprisingly, therefore, one recent study found that the factor most determining the effectiveness of joint committees was a supportive attitude on the part of senior management.[82] In order to give the committees stronger "teeth," the Ontario[83] legislation was amended in 1990 to authorize the issuance of a legally binding stop-work order by joint agreement of the certified worker and manager representatives on the health and safety committee. Furthermore, in workplaces where a government-appointed adjudicator has determined that this joint stop-work procedure will not adequately protect the health and safety of workers, the adjudicator can authorize the certified worker representative on the health and safety committee to issue *unilateral* orders to stop dangerous work. This represents a trail-blazing development in Canadian health and safety legislation.

Other weaknesses[84] of the joint committee system are that the training of health and safety committee members, on both employer and worker sides, is inadequate; that the degree of communication between government health and safety agencies and plant committees, and even between employer and worker representatives on committees, is inadequate; and that compliance with the statutory requirements is unduly low—a general concern with all facets of health and safety legislation. (This last aspect will be discussed in more detail later in this chapter.) In 1990, Ontario responded by creating a Workplace Health and Safety Agency, jointly controlled by labour and management to oversee education and training in health and safety. At least one employee member and one management member of every health and safety committee must receive training and "certification" to a level designated by the agency. Other provinces are doubtlessly monitoring closely the performance of the Ontario innovations in improving health and safety.

The right to refuse to perform dangerous work without fear of reprisal is obviously crucial to an effective internal responsibility system.[85] At common law, nonunionized employees are implicitly entitled under the contract of employment to refuse to obey orders that they "honestly" and "reasonably" believe to be unsafe,[86] but the absence of compulsory reinstatement and "make whole" compensation remedies at common law render this right illusory. The unionized employee enjoys the equivalent right implicitly under the collective agreement.[87] The health and safety legislation in all provinces entrenches the right to refuse in a roughly equivalent form, save in Alberta and Newfoundland where the requirement that there be an "imminent" danger appears to narrow protection to threats of an immediate rather than long-term impact on the worker.[88] The requirement of honesty means that the worker must be genuinely concerned with health and safety and not refuse work for some ulterior purpose.[89] The "reasonableness" requirement means that an average employee in similar circumstances—and these circumstances include any physical ailment of the refuser, such as a bad back or a heart condition—would conclude that an unacceptable degree of risk exists.[90] It follows that even if an assignment is subsequently proven to be safe, the refusal will nonetheless have been legally justifiable so long as it was "reasonable" at the time.

The procedure for exercising the statutory right to refuse varies between the provinces, but usually the first step is for the worker to report the danger to management and for management to investigate the matter, usually in conjunction with the health and safety committee or with a worker safety representative. If the problem cannot be resolved internally to the satisfaction of the employer and the worker, an investigation by a government health and safety officer ensues. The latter can either uphold the refusal or not and, where appropriate, can order that the work be rendered safe by the employer within a specified time. If either side is unhappy with the officer's determination, there is normally a right to appeal to an outside neutral party such as the labour relations board or a government adjudicator. The legislation commonly prohibits employers from penalizing workers who have exercised the right to refuse or any other right under the statute. If any part of the employer's motive in penalizing the worker relates to a health and safety matter—frequently called a "health and safety *animus*"—the action is unlawful and the worker can obtain reinstatement and monetary compensation from the appropriate government tribunal charged with hearing such complaints. Despite this protection, the vast majority of refusals occur in unionized organizations, probably because nonunionized employees are either ignorant of, or too afraid to exercise their legal rights.[91]

Both unionized and nonunionized employees face the possibility of loss of pay if there is no work available for them as a result of their ceasing to perform unsafe work. Neither the collective agreement nor the employment contract implicitly requires the employer to make work available to the employee; express provision must be made for this. However, the health and safety legislation in some[92] but not all provinces guarantees the employee's regular wages in this situation.

The right of workers to be notified of health and safety hazards is established not only as part of the general "performance" duty under the health and safety legislation, but also, and more importantly, as part of the Workplace Hazardous Materials Information System (WHMIS). This is a national system for hazardous material identification and handling created as a result of extensive consultation between federal and provincial governments in the 1980s and contained in provincial WHMIS statutes based on the model established by federal legislation.[93] The system has four main components. First, suppliers of designated "controlled products" are compelled to provide "labels" and "material safety data sheets" to employers which describe, amongst other things, the chemical identity of the product and the chemical composition of any ingredients reasonably believed by the supplier to be harmful. Suppliers must also describe safe handling procedures, risk descriptions and the hazard symbol as per the designated hazard classification under the statutory regulations. This information is made available to employees. Second, employers are bound to make an assessment, according to the format required by the regulations, of whether or not any biological or chemical agent that is produced in the workplace is hazardous and to notify the workforce accordingly. Third, employers must provide workers and supervisors with a copy of the regulations. Fourth, a manufacturer can appeal to the federal Hazardous Materials Information Review Commission to exempt the disclosure of confidential business information, but even exempted information must be provided to a doctor upon request in a medical emergency, or to government officials administering safety laws.

Enforcement.   Any law is only as good as its enforcement machinery. Unfortunately, disobedience to health and safety legislation is widespread. The legislation contains a blend of conciliatory and coercive enforcement techniques for, respectively, the unwitting and the wilful violators. Enforcement is handled by government health and safety inspectors who investigate worksites either routinely or when alerted by a complaint or an accident report. Officers can issue stop-work orders that require an employer to render the job safe within a specified time before work will be allowed to recommence. Such orders can be appealed, depending on the jurisdiction, either to a higher authority within the government health and safety bureaucracy or to an outside neutral party, with the courts only becoming involved if a principle of law is at issue. The legislation gives inspectors the authority to enter premises at reasonable times and to conduct an effective investigation. A common criticism[94] is that inspectorates are too inadequately staffed to ensure sufficiently regular visitations, so that renegade employers run little risk of being caught. This is especially true where there is no union at the worksite to police the legislation, since nonunionized workers are notoriously reluctant to report incidents. Also inspectors are often reluctant to issue stop-work orders in matters of a policy nature, or in those involving sensitive managerial prerogatives or potentially costly capital expenditures. In such cases, they tend either to confirm the status quo or to defer to their department superiors.[95]

Although inspectors will attempt to obtain voluntary settlements through mediation wherever possible, they can recommend that offenders be prosecuted. There are two models for prosecution in Canada.[96] The first and most common is to prosecute offenders in the regular criminal courts. As Brown indicates, this has the advantage of increasing the deterrence effect because of the social stigma attached to criminalization. But this approach also has important disadvantages that include: the high cost and delays of criminal proceedings; the lack of expertise of the judiciary in specialized health and safety matters; and the difficulty of winning convictions under the criminal law. This difficulty arises especially from the "burden of proof" provision, which requires that guilt be established "beyond a reasonable doubt," and from the evidentiary rule that excludes evidence of prior convictions from being adduced in order to establish guilt. Because of these disadvantages, prosecutions are more likely to be brought when an accident has already occurred and a conviction is therefore "winnable" rather than when only a risk of possible injury exists but nobody has yet been harmed.

The second, "administrative" model of prosecution, currently in place in British Columbia and the United States, empowers the health and safety department responsible for investigating violations—in BC the Workers' Compensation Board—to impose a penalty on offenders, with a right to appeal to a higher authority being provided within the department. In BC this would be the Appeal Division of the WCB. As Brown (1992) shows, this administrative model offers significant advantages when compared to criminal prosecution. Cost savings occur and there is a greater likelihood of securing convictions. This is because the civil standard of proof, which requires only a "balance of probabilities" to determine guilt and allows prior convictions to be submitted as evidence, is less rigorous than the standard in criminal cases. Also there is a greater likelihood of penalties being levied where a risk of injury exists but no accident has occurred. Brown argues that an ideal model would combine administrative penalties for run-of-the-mill violations with criminal prosecution held in reserve for the most serious offenders. Nevertheless, criminal prosecution remains the enforcement model of choice in most Canadian jurisdictions.

Prosecution is relatively rare, generally being reserved for situations where an accident or the risk thereof is fatal or critical, where the employer is flagrantly and deliberately flaunting the law, where the employer has a past history of violations, or where the employer obstructs inspectors in carrying out their duties. The employer generally can escape liability by showing that it exercised "due diligence" in avoiding the accident.[97] The level of fines has always been criticized as too low, but penalties are now increasing in most provinces, with Ontario taking the lead in 1989 with dramatic increases. For example,[98] in Ontario the average penalty rose from $3,200 in 1987/88 to $5,626 in 1990/91; total penalties rose from less than $1 million to more than $2 million in the same period; and there were no cases of fines exceeding $25,000 in 1989/90 but there were seventeen such cases in the following year, with four fines exceeding $100,000. Nevertheless, in each category Ontario still lags behind the administrative model in British Columbia. Technically, convicted offenders can face imprisonment under the health and safety legislation but this has occurred in only a handful of cases, usually where the person has demonstrated a total contempt for the system. In addition,[99] criminal law charges such as murder and manslaughter could be arraigned against employers who knowingly or recklessly cause injury to their workers.

Compensating Workplace Accidents and Diseases

The principal method for compensating victims who have been disabled by an accident or a disease "arising out of and in the course of employment" is workers' compensation legislation.[100] Under this legislation, the employee does not face the frequently daunting task of proving negligence on the employer's part in common law litigation. In return, however, the employee is precluded from pursuing a common law action against the employer. The courts have held that the bar on common law actions does not violate a worker's constitutional rights under the Charter of Rights and Freedoms, at least so long as the statutory benefits remain reasonably commensurate to those available at common law.[101] Arguably, the possibility of huge common law damages awards might deter employers from evading their health and safety responsibilities, and for this reason giving the worker the choice of pursuing the most favourable of either a statutory claim or a civil action would make sense.

Not all workers are covered by the legislation—domestics, homeworkers, and casuals are typical exclusions, inviting a possible claim that their right to "equality" under section 15 of the Charter has been violated.[102] Neither are all accidents and diseases covered, only those arising "out of and in the course of employment." This often involves difficult questions of causation, especially with diseases whose symptoms may not become apparent until years after contraction and which cannot obviously be attributed to a particular facet of the work process as opposed to the worker's personal lifestyle. Many claims are lost on this ground. Even an otherwise compensable injury may be exempted if it results in the loss of less than one day's pay, or if it is solely attributable to the worker's wilful misconduct, unless the injury results in death or serious disablement.

The legislation contains detailed provisions on the amount of compensation, with four main categories of benefits being recognized: death benefits; temporary total disability benefits; temporary partial disability benefits; and permanent disability benefits. A ceiling is commonly fixed on the total amount of compensation at either 90 per cent or 75 per cent of the worker's pay over a specified period, depending on the jurisdiction; and this is made subject to an overall maximum of recoverable compensation, presumably in order to discourage malingerers.

The workers' compensation schemes are administered in each province by a statutory tribunal, the workers' compensation board. Typically, the procedure begins with an adjudicator. The majority of claims are approved at this level. In many provinces, the adjudicator remits claims felt to be unmeritorious to an internal review group composed of senior workers' compensation adjudicators. The claim is then adjudicated by the board. In some provinces, the board's decision can be appealed to an arm of the workers' compensation board. Elsewhere, appeals are heard by an independent tribunal not connected with the board. The claimant is not required to pay for an appeal. The civil courts are limited to reviewing workers' compensation board and outside tribunal decisions on the grounds of jurisdictional error and breach of natural justice. The boards and tribunals are given exclusive jurisdiction to determine all issues of law and fact arising under the legislation.

The revenues for the workers' compensation system derive from a levy on employers assessed according to the nature of the industry and the size of the employer's wage bill. The amounts vary according to the accident and disease rate in particular industries, so that employers in high risk industries pay more than those in safer ones. Because this "collective" approach allows comparatively unsafe employers to take a free ride at the expense of the majority of safe employers in the industry, most provinces have complemented it with a rating system wherein a single employer's premium can be reduced or increased according to that employer's own safety record. Ontario and Saskatchewan[103] have an additional disincentive aimed at particularly unsafe workplaces, providing for the imposition of a penalty assessment of 100 per cent of an employer's annual premium if that employer's safety violations exceed significantly the group average. Ontario[104] has gone even further under its "Workwell" scheme, which empowers the Workers' Compensation Board to levy special penalties of up to 75 per cent of the firm's annual premium or $100,000 (whichever is less) on an employer whose safety performance *in the future* will *likely* be unsatisfactory. This likelihood is determined on the basis of an evaluation of the present health and safety system by a WCB officer. Individualized experience rating has been criticized for encouraging employers to contest more workers' compensation claims than they would otherwise do and to pressure sick employees to stay on the job instead of filing a claim, thereby thwarting the compensation and rehabilitation of the worker.[105] Empirically, it has not yet been established whether or not individualized experienced ratings reduce accident and disease rates.

In most provinces, an employee who has been away from work on workers' compensation is not entitled under the legislation to claim reinstatement in his or her former position when he or she is fit to resume work.[106] This seems odd when a worker who has been dismissed by reason of pregnancy or physical or mental disability in breach of the human rights legislation can be reinstated. In Ontario since 1989, however, the employer is required by section 54 of the Workers' Compensation Act to reinstate an injured employee who is "medically able to perform the essential duties" of the job held by him or her prior to the injury. If the employee is unable to perform the latter duties but is "medically able to perform suitable work," the employer must offer the employee the "first opportunity to accept suitable employment that may become available with the employer." In order to facilitate re-employment, the employer must "accommodate the work place to the needs of a worker who is impaired as a result of the injury to the extent that the accommodation does not cause the employer undue hardship." A special Reinstatement Branch of the WCB is established to mediate and adjudicate the foregoing provisions.

In sum, the present statutory machinery for preventing accidents and diseases in the workplace and for compensating the victims still suffers from many flaws. The toll in human suffering and the economic wastage caused by accidents and diseases at work remain very high. This makes health and safety one of the foremost challenges to management, labour, and governments in the years ahead.

CONCLUSION

The expansion of laws to protect employees has been dramatic in the last twenty-five years. Employment standards, human rights, common law developments, and health and safety protections have all been introduced and reinforced to ensure that employees are treated in a fairer and more humane manner. Undoubtedly, the next two decades will see further expansion of these laws. However, serious problems and questions are readily apparent:

(1) Many, if not most, employees are unaware of their rights. (2) There can be fear of reprisal by the employer should the employees pursue their rights. (3) Many of the agencies responsible for the enforcement of the laws are inadequately staffed, and hence the laws are not effectively policed. (4) The remedies provided are often inadequate to deter potential violations.

Trade unions have a role to play in overcoming these problems. Many of the rights discussed in this chapter were originally pioneered by trade unions, and they have a continuing interest not only in extending the horizons of employment legislation but also in the effective administration and enforcement of existing laws. Unions are able to ensure that members of the bargaining unit know their rights under both the general law and the collective agreement. Furthermore, unions provide a vehicle to enforce those rights and to protect employees from employer's reprisals. Finally, potent remedies can be negotiated into collective agreements to encourage compliance with employment terms.

QUESTIONS

1. Are minimum employment standards needed in an advanced society such as Canada's?

2. Why does the law not allow the courts to reinstate employees who have been dismissed without just cause at common law? Why do arbitrators have that power?

3. Should an economic recession be grounds for just cause for dismissal? How should it affect the length of notice?

4. To what extent should discrimination on the basis of the occupation of one's spouse be permitted?

5. What are the problems in the implementation of the principle of equal pay for work of equal value?

6. What effect does employment legislation have on the development of trade unions and collective bargaining?

7. Why is it necessary to legislate an internal responsibility system as a complement to the external system in order to improve workplace health and safety?

8. In what ways could the present system of worker's compensation be improved?

9. Should collective agreements be allowed to "opt out" of certain employment standards provisions, perhaps in return for other benefits?

10. What are the pros and cons of harmonization or uniformity of employment standards across the different jurisdictions in Canada?

11. If employment law generally takes precedence over collective agreements' provisions, why do collective agreements sometimes repeat the legislative requirement?

REFERENCES

BRODY, B., P. ROHANN, and L. ROMPRÉ. 1985. "Les Accidents industriels au Canada: le portait d'une decennie." *Relations industrielles/Industrial Relations* 40: 545-66.

BROWN, R.M. 1982. "Canadian Occupational Health and Safety Legislation." *Osgoode Hall Law Journal* 20.

———. 1983. "The Right To Refuse Unsafe Work." *University of British Columbia Law Review* 17: 1-34.

BRYCE, G., and P. MANGA. 1985. "The Effectiveness of Health and Safety Committees." *Relations industrielles/Industrial Relations* 40: 257-83.

CCH CANADIAN. 1987. *Master Labour Guide.* Don Mills, Ont: CCH.

CHRISTIE, I.M., G.J. ENGLAND, and B. COTTER. 1993. *Employment Law in Canada.* 2nd ed. Toronto: Butterworths.

DIGBY, C., and W.C. RIDDELL. 1986. "Occupational Health and Safety in Canada." In W.C. Riddell, ed, *Canadian Labour Relations.* Toronto: University of Toronto Press.

EDEN, G., *Relations industrielles/Industrial Relations,* 48, 1: 163-180.

ENGLAND, G. 1978. "Recent Developments in Wrongful Dismissal Laws and Some Policies for Reform." *Alberta Law Review* 16: 470-520.

FISHER, E.G., and I.F. IVANKOVITCH. 1985. "Alberta's Occupational Health and Safety Amendment Act, 1983." *Relations industrielles/Industrial Relations* 40: 115-39.

FRIDMAN, G.H.L. 1963. *The Modern Law of Employment.* London: Stevens and Sons.

GEORGE, K. 1985. "Les comités de santé et de sécurité du travail: table de concentration ou de negociation?" *Relations industrielles/Industrial Relations* 40: 512-28.

GLASBEEK, H., and S. ROWLAND. 1979. "Are Injuring and Killing at Work Crimes?" *Osgoode Hall Law Journal* 17: 506-94.

ISON, T.G. 1983. *Workmen's Compensation in Canada.* Toronto: Butterworths.

LABOUR CANADA. 1981. *Sexual Equality in the Workplace.* Conference proceedings. Ottawa: Labour Canada.

LABOUR LAW CASEBOOK GROUP. 1986. *Labour Law: Cases, Materials and Commentary.* 4th ed. Kingston, Ont: Industrial Relations Centre, Queen's University.

LESLIE, G. 1981-82. "The Statutory Right To Refuse Unsafe Work: A Comparison of Saskatchewan, Ontario and the Federal Jurisdictions." *Saskatchewan Law Review* 46: 235-70.

LEVITT, H. 1985. *The Law of Dismissal in Canada.* Aurora, Ont: Canada Law Book.

PALMER, E.E. 1982. *Collective Agreement Arbitration in Canada.* 2nd ed. Toronto: Butterworths.

PONAK, A. 1987. "Discharge Arbitration and Reinstatement in the Province of Alberta." *The Arbitration Journal* 42(2): 39-46.

SASS, R. 1985. "The Labour Process and Health: An Alternative Conception to Occupational Health and Safety." *Windsor Yearbook of Access to Justice* 5: 352-67.

SWAN, K.P., and K.E. SWINTON, eds. 1983. *Studies in Labour Law.* Toronto: Butterworths.

SWINTON, K. 1983. "Enforcement of Occupational Health and Safety: The Role of the Internal Responsibility System." In K. Swan and K. Swinton, eds, *Studies in Labour Law.* Toronto: Butterworths.

TUCKER, E. 1986. "The Persistence of Market Regulation of Occupational Health and Safety: The Stillbirth of Voluntarism." In G. England, ed, *Essays in Labour Relations Law.* Don Mills, Ont: CCH.

UNITED STATES. 1979. *Basic Patterns in Union Contracts.* 9th ed. Washington, DC: Bureau of National Affairs.

WEILER, P.C. 1980. *Reshaping Worker's Compensation For Ontario.* Ad hoc report to the Ontario Ministry of Labour. Toronto.

————. 1983. *Protecting the Worker from Disability: Challenges for the Eighties.* Ad hoc report to the Ontario Ministry of Labour. Toronto.

END NOTES

1   *Carter* v *Bell,* (1936) 1 DLR 438; *Seamone* v *Bochner,* (1951) 1 DLR 777; *Cranbrook and District Hospitals, Selkirk College,* [1975] 1 CLRBR 42; *Martin-Baker Ltd* v *Canadian Flight Ltd,* [1955] 2 All ER 72.

2   *Short* v *Henderson,* [1946] SC (HL) 24.

3   *Montreal* v *Montreal Locomotive Works Ltd,* (1947) 1 DLR 161; *Mayer* v *J. Conrad Lavigne Ltd,* (1980) 27 OR 129; *Cooperation Insurance Association* v *Kearney,* (1964) 48 DLR (2d) 1; *Stevenson, Jordon & Harrison Ltd* v *MacDonald,* (1952) 1 TLR 101.

4   *Pliniussen* v *University of Western Ontario,* (1983) 2 CCEL 1 (Ont Co Ct).

5   *Tall and Tall Air Ltd* v *Deconinck and Corporation 5 Ltd,* (1983) 51 NBR (2d) 55 (CA).

6   *Mid-Western News Agency Ltd* v *Vanpinxteren et al,* (1975) 62 DLR (3d) 555 (Sask QB); *Sheather* v *Associates Financial Services Ltd et al,* (1979) 15 BCLR 265 (SCBC); *Empey* v *Coastal Towing Company Ltd,* [1977] 1 WWR 673 (SCBC); *Pre-Cam Exploration & Development Ltd et al* v *McTavish et al,* (1966) SCR 551.

7   *Swain* v *West (Butchers), Ltd,* [1936] 3 All ER 261 (CA). *In Tyrrell* v *Alltrans Express Ltd,* (1976) 66 DLR (3d) 181 (SCBC), no such duty was found.

8   *Tasco Telephone Answering Exchange Ltd* v *Ellerbeck,* (1966) 57 DLR (2d) 500 (SCBC); *Schauenburg Industries Ltd, et al* v *Borowski et al,* (1979) 25 OR (2d) 737 (Ont HC).

9   *Alberts* v *Mountjoy,* (1977) 79 DLR (3d) 108 (Ont HC); *Canadian Aero Service Ltd* v *O'Malley et al,* [1974] 1 SCR 592; *Rajput* v *Menu Foods Ltd,* (1984) 5 CCEL 22 (Ont HC).

10   *Forest Automation Ltd* v *RMS Industrial Control,* SCBC, unreported, May 24, 1978; *Payzu Ltd* v *Hannaford,* (1918) 2 KB 248.

11   *In H.L. Weiss Forwarding Ltd* v *Omnus et al,* (1972) 5 CPR (2d) 142 (Ont HC), aff'd (no recorded reasons, Ont CA), (1976) 1 SCR 776, Moorehouse, J. awarded damages against an employee who quit without notice on the basis of the salary to which the employee would have been entitled during the period of notice. It is our opinion that this view is incorrect since it has no relevance to the actual loss suffered by the employer.

12   *Shabinsky* v *Horwitz et al,* (1971) 32 DLR (3d) 318 (Ont HC).

13   *Doyle* v *London Life Insurance Company,* BCCA, unreported, Dec 5, 1985, Vancouver Registry no CA 002277.

14   *Philip* v *Expo 86 Corp,* (1986) 13 CCEL 147; *Riddell* v *City of Vancouver,* (1985) 5 CCEL 55, upheld on appeal; *Hawkins* v *The Queen in Right of Ontario,* (1985) 8 CCEL 183 (Ont HC).

15   *Re Gillingham and Metropolitan Board of Commissioners of Police,* 26 OR (2d) 77; *Sui* v *Westcoast Transmission,* (1985) 7 CCEL 281 (SCBC); *Head* v *Ontario Provincial Police Force,* unreported, Oct 14, 1981 (Ont CA).

16   *Zalesko* v *99 Truck Parts,* (1986) 8 CCEL 201; *Yeager* v *Hastings,* (1985) 5 CCEL 226; *Lockhart* v *Chrysler,* (1985) 7 CCEL 247.

17   Bell Canada v Office and Professional Employees International Union, [1974] SCR 335, 37 DLR (3d) 561.

18   Greene v Chrysler Canada Ltd, (1985) 7 CCEL 166 (SCBC), upheld, (1985) 7 CCEL 175 (BCCA).

19   *O'Grady* v *ICBC,* (1975) 63 DLR (3d) 370; *Burton* v *MacMillan Bloedel,* [1976] 4 WWR 267; *Baker* v *Burns Foods,* 74 DLR (3d) 762; *Lesiuk* v *BC Forest Products Ltd,* (1984) 56 BCLR 216; *Pearl* v *Pacific Enercon Inc,* (1985) 7 CCEL 252.

20   *Lynch* v *Richmond Plymouth Chrysler Ltd,* unreported, May 13, 1985, Vancouver Registry no C825918, (SCBC); *Reber* v *Lloyds Bank International Canada,* (1985) 61 BCLR 361 (CA); *Patterson* v *The Queen in the Right of British Columbia et al,* (1985) 8 CCEL 213 (SCBC); *Longman* v *Federal Business Development Bank,* (1982) 36 BCLR 115 (SCBC); *Pullen* v *John C. Preston Ltd,* (1985) 7 CCEL 91 (Ont HC) at 96; *Canadian Bechtel Ltd* v *Mallenkopf,* (1983) 1 CCEL 95 (Ont CA) at 98.

21 *Longman* v *Federal Development Bank*, (1982) 36 BCLR 115 (SCBC) at 124; see also *Reber* v *Lloyds Bank International Canada*, supra note 20.

22 *O'Grady* v *ICBC*, *Burton* v *MacMillan Bloedel*, and *Baker* v *Burns Foods*, supra note 19.

23 *Pliniussen* v *University of Western Ontario*, (1984) 2 CCEL 1; *Tyrrell* v *Alltrans Express Ltd* 66 DLR (3d) 81; *Ennis* v *ICBC*, (1986) 13 CCEL 25; *Himmelman* v *King's Edgehill School*, (1985) 7 CCEL 16; *Bechard* v *Chrysler Canada Ltd*, (1979) 1098 DLR (3d) 577.

24 *Cardinas* v *Canada Dry Ltd*, (1986) 10 CCEL 1 (Ont DC); *Zelisko* v *99 Truck Parts* and *Yeager* v *Hastings*, supra note 16.

25 *Roscoe* v *McGavin*, (1984) 2 CCEL 287; *Anderson* v *Pirelli Cables Inc*, (1985) 5 CCEL 287; *Matheson* v *Matheson International Trucks Ltd*, (1985) 4 CCEL 271; *Manning* v *Surrey Memorial Hospital Society*, (1975) 54 DLR (3d) 312.

26 *Alberts* v *Mountjoy*, supra note 9; *Wells* v *Newfoundland and Labrador Nurses' Union*, SC Nfld, Dec 13, 1985, unreported.

27 *Durrant* v *Westeel Rosco Ltd*, (1978) 7 BCLR 14; *Lloyd* v *Canadian Bechtel Ltd*, BCCA, Nov 15, 1976, unreported; *Page* v *Jim Pattison*, [1982] 5 WWR 107.

28 *Bardal* v *Globe and Mail Ltd*, [1960] 24 DLR 140; *Gillespie* v *Bulkley Forest Industries Ltd*, [1974] 50 DLR 316; *Lockhart* v *Chrysler Canada Ltd*, (1984) 7 CCEL 43.

29 *Campbell* v *MacMillan Bloedel*, [1978] 2 WWR 686; *Thomson* v *Bechtel Canada Ltd*, (1984) 3 CCEL 16, (Ont HC).

30 *Red Deer College* v *Michaels*, (1975) 57 DLR (3d) 386, [1976] 2 SCR 324.

31 *Racine* v *CJRC Radio Capitale Ltd*, [1977] 2 ACWS 366; *Burmeister* v *Regina Multicultural Council*, (1986) 8 CCEL 144.

32 *Vorvis* v *ICBC 25* CCEL 81 (SCC); see also *Addis* v *Gramaphone*, [1909] AC 488; *Ansari* v *BC Hydro*, (1986) 13 CCEL 238 (SCBC).

33 *Lockhart* v *Chrysler Canada Ltd*, (1984) CCEL 43; *Misovic* v *Acres Dairy McKee Ltd*, (1985) 7 CCEL 163 (Ont CA).

34 *Pilato* v *Hamilton Place Convention Centre*, (1984) 3 CCEL 241 (Ont HC).

35 *Smith* v *Dawson Memorial Hospital*, (1978), 29 NSR (2d) 277, 45 APR 277 (NSTD); *Housepian* v *Work Wear Corporation of Canada*, (1981) 33 OR (2d) 575 (Ont Co Ct); *Steinicke* v *Manning Ltd*, (1984) 4 WWR 491, 55 BCLR 320, (1984) 4 CCEL 294; *Page* v *Jim Pattison Industries Ltd*, [1984] 4 WWR 481, (1984) 4 CCEL 283.

36 *Gulf Canada Products* v *Griffiths*, (1984) 3 CCEL 140.

37 Eden, Genevieve, *Relations Industrielles*, Vol. 48, No. 1, pp. 163-180.

38 *Campbell* v *MacMillan Bloedel Ltd*, [1978] 2 WWR 686 at 691 (SCBC).

39 Supra note 29.

40 *Rose* v *Shell Canada*, (1985) 7 CCEL 234 (SCBC).

41 *Campbell* v *MacMillan Bloedel Ltd*, supra note 39; *Mathe* v *Klohn Leonoff Ltd*, (1983) 20 ACWS (2d) 517; *Re Maritime Medical Care Inc and McLaughlin et al*, (1979) 103 DLR (3d) 159; *Chisholm* v *W.H. Bosley & Company Ltd*, (1980) 5 ACWS (2d) 358.

42 *Jobber* v *Addressograph Multigraph of Canada Ltd*, (1983) 1 CCEL 87 (Ont CA); *Matthewson* v *Aiton Power Ltd*, (1984) 3 CCEL 69 (Ont Co Ct), reversed on appeal, (1985) 8 CCEL 312 (Ont CA); *Lloyds Bank Ltd* v *Bundy* [1975] QB 326 (CA).

43 *Allison* v *Amoco Production Company*, [1975] 5 WWR 501 (Alta SC); *Nardocchio* v *Canadian Imperial Bank of Commerce*, (1979) 41 NSR (2d) (NSSC).

44 *Allison* v *Amoco Production Company*, supra note 44; *Wallace* v *Toronto-Dominion Bank*, (1983) 41 OR (2d) 161, leave to appeal denied, (1983) 52 NR 157.

45 *Lyonde* v *Canadian Acceptance Corporation Ltd*, (1984) 3 CCEL 220.

46 *Allison* v *Amoco Production Company*, supra note 44; *Matthewson* v *Aiton Power Ltd*, supra note 43; *Elsley* v *J.G. Collins Insurance Agencies Ltd*, [1978] 2 SCR 916.

47 *Matthewson* v *Aiton Power Ltd*, supra note 43; *Maxwell* v *Gibson Drugs Ltd et al*, [1979] 103 DLR (3d) 433 (SCBC).

48   *Lyonde* v *Canadian Acceptance Corp,* (1984) 3 CCEL 220; *Wallace* v *Toronto Dominion Bank,* supra note 45.

49   *Canadian Aero Service Ltd* v *O'Malley et al,* supra note 9; *Saltman Engineering Ltd* v *Campbell Engineering Company Ltd,* [1963] 3 A11 ER 413.

50   *Nelson Burns & Company* v *Grantham Industries Ltd,* [1983] 42 OR (2d) 705, 150 DLR (3d) 692; *Bassman* v *Deloitte Haskins and Sells of Canada,* (1984) 4 DLR (3d) 558 (Ont HC); *Creditel of Canada* v *Faultless et al,* 81 DLR (2d) 567.

51   *Green* v *Stanton,* (1969) 1 WWR 415; *Baker* v *Lintott,* (1980) 141 DLR 571.

52   *St. Anne-Nackawic Pulp & Paper Company Ltd* v *Canadian Paper Workers Union, Local 219,* (1986) 28 DLR (4th) 1 (SCC).

53   *Bhinder* v *CNR,* (1986) 9 CCEL 135; *O'Malley* v *Simpson-Sears,* (1986) 9 CCEL 185.

54   (1984) 5 CHRR at D/2327 [Aug 22, 1984]; (1985) 6 CHRR at D/2908 [July 16, 1985]; Supreme Court of Canada, June 1987, unreported.

55   *Re Attorney General for Alberta and Gares, et al,* 67 DLR (3d) 635; *University of Regina,* Sask Court of Queen's Bench, Oct 28, 1975, unreported; *Davies, Hickford and Toews and District of Abbotsford,* BC Board of Inquiry, Feb 1977, unreported; *Jane Bublish* v *Sask Union of Nurses,* (1983) 4 CHRR at D/1269.

56   Gunderson, Morley, "Gender Discrimination and Pay Equity Legislation," in *Aspects of Labour Economics: Essays in Honour of John Venderkamp* ed. L. Christofides, K. Grant and R. Swidinsky (Toronto: University of Toronto Press, in press).

57   *Central Alberta Dairy Pool* v *Alberta Human Rights Commission et al,* 33 CCEL 1 (SCC); *Renaud* v *Board of School Trustees, School District No. 23 (Central Okanagan) and CUPE et al,* (1992) SCJ No. 75.

58   Supra note 58, at p. 7.

59   Supra note 55.

60   *Foster* v *BC Forest Products Ltd,* BC Human Rights Board of Inquiry, April, 1979, unreported; *Colfer* v *Ottawa Board of Commissioners of Police,* Ontario Human Rights Board of Inquiry, Jan 12, 1979, unreported.

61   *Bell and Korczak* v *Lades and the Flaming Steer Steakhouse,* (1980) 1 CHRR D/155.

62   *Cashin* v *CBC,* (1986) 7 CHRR D/3203 [Nov 25, 1985], at para 25676-7.

63   Ibid, (1987) 8 CHRR D/3699 [Jan 23, 1987], at para 29281.

64   *Brooks* v *Canada Safeway* 26 CCEL 1 (SCC).

65   *Bliss* v *A.6 Canada* (1979) 1 SCR. 183 (SCC).

66   [1987] 1 WWR 355 (SCC).

67   *Robichaud* v *Canadian Armed Forces,* Supreme Court of Canada, July 29, 1987, unreported.

68   *R* v *Oakes,* 19 CRR 308 (SCC)

69   For the data, see D. Digby and W. Riddell, "Occupational Health and Safety in Canada," in W. Craig Ridell ed., *Canadian Labour Relations* (Toronto: University of Toronto Press, 1986), pp. 286-288; P. Brody, P. Rohan and L. Rompre, "Les accidents industriels au Canada: le portrait d'une decennie" (1985) 40 Re. Ind. 545.

70   Statistics Canada, "Work Injuries 1990-1992" (Ottawa: Statistics Canada Cat. No. 72-208) p. 43.

71   C. Hagger-Guenette, "Work Injuries in Canada, 1982-86" (1988), 66 Employment Earnings and Hours 219; R. Wilson and J. Chase, "Comparison of Industrial Risks" (1983), 4 Occupational Health in Ontario 59, esp. p. 61.

72   P.C. Weiler, "Protecting the Worker from Disability: Challenges for the Eighties" (Toronto: Ontario Ministry of Labour, 1983) pp. 20-23.

73   For the details of the law see Canadian Employment, Safety and Health Guide, Vols. 1, 2, and 3 (Don Mills: CCH Canadian Ltd., loose-leaf).

74   S.O. 1989, c. 48, now R.S.O. 1990, c. M 45.

75   E. Tucker, "The Persistence of Market Regulation of Occupational Health and Safety: The Stillbirth of Voluntarism" in G. England (ed.) "Essays in Labour Relations Law" (Don Mills CCH Canadian, 1983) 219, at p. 237; Ontario Advisory Council on Occupational Health and Safety, Fifth Annual Report, Vol. 1 (Toronto: Ministry of Supply and Services, 1983) pp. 23-28.

76 RSNS 1989 c. 320.

77 *Latimer* v *A.E.C.,* (1953) AC 643 (CA of UK), a case arising at common law, illustrates the balancing process applied under the legislation.

78 See generally K. Swinton, "Enforcement of Occupational Health and Safety: The Role of the Internal Responsibility System" in K. Swan and K. Swinton, eds., *Studies in Labour Law* (Toronto: Butterworths, 1983) 143.

79 The weaknesses of labour market methods for protecting the non-unionized worker are examined in Weiler, at pp. 90-94 supra, note 72. The limitations of collective bargaining are examined in K. Swinton, "Regulating Occupational Health and Safety Worker Participation Through Collective Bargaining and Legislation" in G. England, ed., *Essays in Collective Bargaining and Industrial Democracy* (Don Mills: CCH Canadian, 1983) 43.

80 Nova Scotia Occupational Health and Safety Advisory Council Discussion Paper, Oct. 20, 1993, p. 10.

81 For the Canadian experience see K.I. George, "Les comités de santé it de securité du travail," (1985), 40 Rel. Ind. 512; G. Bryce and P. Manga, "The Effectiveness of Health and Safety Committees" (1985), 40 Rel. Ind. 257. The USA studies to the same effect are reviewed in P.C. Weiler, at pp. 108-110, supra, note 4.

82 G. Bryce and P. Manga, "The Effectiveness of Health and Safety Committees" (1985), 40 Rel. Ind. 257.é

83 Occupational Health and Safety Act, RSO 1990, CO 1 (as am.).

84 See generally Ontario Advisory Council on Occupational Health and Occupational Safety, Ninth Annual Report "Toronto: Ministry of Supply and Services, (1987) esp. pp. 49-57.

85 R. Brown, "The Right to Refuse Unsafe Work" (1983), 17 UBC L. Rev. 1.

86 *Ottoman Band* v *Chakarian,* (1930) AC 277 (HL).

87 D. Brown and D. Beatty, "Canadian Labour Arbitration," 3rd ed., (Aurora: Canada Law Book, 1990, loose leaf) para. 7: 3621.

88 *Timpauer* v *Air Canada* (1986), 11 CCEL 81, at p. 90 (FCA).

89 A work refusal for an ulterior purpose will be grounds for discipline, e.g., *Canadian Pacific Forest Products Ltd.* v *International Woodworkers of America (Canada) Local 1085,* (1992), 6 COHSC 32 (BC Arbitration Bd., Kelleher), and if undertaken collectively in order to extract employment concessions from the employer will constitute a strike under the collective bargaining legislation.

90 See I. Christies, G. England and B. Cotter, *Employment Law in Canada* (Toronto: Butterworths, 2nd ed., 1993) at pp. 345-349.

91 Tucker, at p. 235, supra, note 75.

92 E.g., Nova Scotia Occupational Health and Safety Act s. 22(4).

93 See C. Moser and P. Simon, *Hazardous Products: Canada's WHMIS Laws* (Don Mills: CCH Canadian, 2nd ed., 1989).

94 Tucker, at pp. 243-44, supra, note 75.

95 Tucker, at p. 243, supra, note 75.

96 R. Brown, "Administrative and Criminal Penalties in the Enforcement of Occupational Health and Safety Legislation" (1992), 30 Osgoode Hall LJ 691.

97 *R.* v *Ellis Don,* (1991), 34 CCEL 130 (Ont CA), rev. (1992), 84 DLR (4th) 161 (SCC)

98 Brown, at pp. 713-15, supra, note 26. For the Alberta experience with increasing penalties, see E.G. Fisher and I.F. Ivankovich, "Alberta's Occupational Health and Safety Amendment Act, 1983" (1985) 40 Rel. Ind. 115, at 128.

99 H. Glasbeek and S. Rowland, "Are Injury and Killing at Work Crimes?" (1979) 17 Osgoode Hall LJ.

100 See generally T.G. Ison, *Workers' Compensation in Canada* (Toronto: Butterworths, 2nd. ed., 1989), and the more critical analysis by P.C. Weiler, "Reshaping Workers' Compensation for Ontario: A Report Submitted to Robert G. Elgie, MD, Minister of Labour" (Toronto: Ministry of Government Services, 1980).

101 *Reference re Sections 32 and 34 of the Workers' Compensation Act* (1986), 61 Nfld & PEIR 147 (Nfld SC); affd. 67 Nfld & PEIR 16 (Nfld CA); affd. 76 Nfld & PEIR 181 (SCC).

102 The employees would have to belong to a group protected under s.15 so as to ground a complaint of "systemic discrimination," as described earlier in this chapter.

103 Ontario Workers' Compensation Act RSO 1990 c. W 11 s. 103 (8); Saskatchewan Workers' Compensation Act SS. 1979, c. W-17.1 s. 123.

104 Workers' Compensation Act s. 103 (4).

105 T. Ison, "The Significance of Experience Rating" (1986) 24 Osgoode Hall LJ 723.

106 Weiler is critical of this position, at pp. 110-13 and 125, supra, note 30.

PART II
THE ACTORS
IN THE
INDUSTRIAL
RELATIONS SYSTEM

The chapters in this section of the book focus on unions and management, the two primary participants in the industrial relations system. Unions and management, of course, are not the only actors. The role of government, as legislator and as employer, is pervasive throughout the system, and independent neutrals, such as arbitrators, also play an important part. But it is unions and employers that have the lead roles in Canadian industrial relations. They are the impelling forces, and accordingly this section concentrates on their goals, activities, and strategies. (Independent neutrals are dealt with in Chapters 10 and 14, while government's role is discussed in Chapters 3, 4, and 15.)

The role of management in industrial relations has traditionally been cast in reactive terms. It is unions that are seen as the initiators, with employers responding, often defensively, to various union thrusts. Because of broad economic and political trends, this situation began to change in the 1980s, and now it is often employers who are viewed as the driving force in reshaping industrial relations. Chapter 5 discusses the approaches companies are taking with respect to relationships with their unions. It also assesses the degree to which real changes are in fact occurring. Drawing on extensive interviews in large unionized firms, the author concludes that managers have by and large accepted the presence of unions within their organizations and have attempted to achieve business goals through the collective bargaining process. The approach in Canada is contrasted to the strategy of employers in the United States who have been much more likely to attempt to eliminate unions from their enterprises.

The next three chapters examine the past, present, and future of the Canadian labour movement. Perhaps more than most other institutions in our society, unions are creatures of their accumulated past experience, partly because they are social organizations as well as economic ones. Understanding the past thus helps make sense of the present. Chapter 6 attempts to place Canadian union history in perspective, showing how, for example, the labour movement's relationship with the New Democratic Party is only the most recent of its many attempts to ensure enduring political strength. The discussion also reviews the many internal schisms within the labour movement—it is not always "solidarity forever"—and assesses the close, and at times acrimonious, relationship between American and Canadian unions.

Chapter 7 presents a comprehensive assessment of organized labour in Canada as the twentieth century draws to a close. Its size, growth prospects, and problems are examined within a framework that designates unions as specialized organizations with their own culture, goals, and procedures. The complexities of union structure are explained, and an analysis is provided of unions as democratic organizations led by elected officials. The relative strength of Canadian labour is contrasted to the precarious position of the union movement in the United States.

The final chapter in this section, Chapter 8, focuses on macro-level societal changes and the implications of these changes for organized labour. Written from a political economy perspective, the chapter explores how, and in what ways, the globalization of work, new technologies, and other forces of change have transformed the modern workplace. The challenges faced by unions, and the need for innovative solutions on the part of organized labour, are analyzed along with a discussion of new union strategies that have already been adopted.

Overall, the four chapters in this part of the book should provide the reader with the background necessary to understand how each of the major actors has been defined by historical, political, economic, and cultural influences and to assess the actors' mutual interaction as it is described later in the text.

CHAPTER 5

THE MANAGEMENT OF INDUSTRIAL RELATIONS

M ARK T HOMPSON *

*I*NDUSTRIAL RELATIONS SCHOLARS TRADITIONALLY HAVE NEGLECTED THE *role of management in their field. The array of information and materials on the labour movement and the role of government in Canadian industrial relations is extensive and studied widely. Yet little attention has been paid to the third actor in industrial relations—the employer. This omission is now being remedied, spurred in part by developments in the 1980s and 1990s, which focused attention on management's role as a proactive force in industrial relations. This chapter will provide a broad overview of the industrial relations policies and practices of Canadian companies, relying heavily on unpublished data collected between 1988 and 1993.*

* The research in this chapter was funded by a grant from the Social Sciences and Humanities Research Council. Michael Piczak and Louise Verschelden provided valuable assistance in completing interviews. The author is solely responsible for the views expressed.

Managers are engaged in a multitude of tasks, many of which are not accessible to outsiders. Business leaders seldom debate their strategies openly, at least in part because this knowledge might aid competitors. Few business publications discuss industrial relations, especially its conflictual aspects. Management statements on industrial relations tend to be general and positive, dominated by sentiments such as "People are our most important asset" or "We need to build more positive relations with our unions." By contrast, firms that deliberately tolerate high turnover among employees, pay wages below industry norms, or seek confrontation with their unions seldom state these objectives publicly. Sometimes, their policies come close to violating the law, so they have a strong interest in avoiding public statements.

Compared with management, sources of information on labour are much more available. Labour unions are political organizations dedicated to the basic task of representing workers. Their newsletters and magazines are distributed widely and their conventions are often open to the public. Elected union officials are usually articulate about the goals and programs of their organizations. The media report convention debates on union policies. Information on governments is similarly available. Any citizen can easily examine legislation, and changes are discussed widely. Administrative decisions on labour law are published and easily available.

In addition to accessibility, the history of industrial relations in Canada and other developed countries since the Second World War has also contributed to relative inattention to the role of management. In the era after the war, the economy expanded steadily and demand for labour was high. During this time, management was seen as reacting to labour's initiatives. Employers generally resisted the organization of unions in their firms. When labour was successful in winning certification, management tended to resist bargaining demands almost automatically, even when experienced negotiators realized that concessions were necessary. In some provinces, employers asked the government for restrictive legislation when they found labour's pressures at the bargaining table too strong to resist. Few innovations in employee relations originated from the initiative of management.

Since the recession of the 1980s, the course of post-war labour relations has reversed in many respects. Periods of high unemployment and low economic growth strengthen the position of employers compared with workers and unions (Streeck 1987). Employers have taken the initiative at the bargaining table, demanding roll-backs of contract provisions, wage freezes, lump-sum payments instead of wage increases, and more flexible work practices. While these initiatives have not always been successful, unions have been placed on the defensive. In addition, employers have triggered changes in established bargaining structures, generally to decentralize bargaining. The meat-packing industry, for instance, had a system of industry-wide bargaining dating from the 1940s that employers dismantled in the 1980s (Novek 1989). Organized labour had limited success in resisting these measures. High unemployment rates, job growth in the hard-to-organize small business and service sectors, and government policies favouring greater reliance on the market, all weakened labour's position. Union growth in the private sector has slowed dramatically, and in several industries membership has declined. Labour militancy, as measured by the number and extent of strikes, has fallen significantly (see Chapter 14).

In an increasingly market-driven economic climate, many Canadian firms found themselves to be high-cost producers compared with their foreign competitors. In addition to reducing overhead costs, eliminating less-profitable operations, and refocusing their business strategies, many companies looked for a competitive advantage in their management of human resources. Senior managers proclaimed the need to integrate human resource strategies with the firm's general business strategy; they were no longer merely reacting to labour's initiatives.

These developments alone would have focused greater attention on the role of management in industrial relations. However, foreign examples of managerial policies were also influential. In the United States, the combination of a weakened labour movement, relaxed enforcement of laws protecting collective bargaining, and strong managerial initiatives caused the "transformation" of American industrial relations (Kochan, Katz, and McKersie 1986). The British government of Prime Minister Margaret Thatcher adopted policies to weaken the labour movement and encouraged employers to take advantage of their new bargaining power. In Australia, the Labor Party Government of Prime Minister Hawke embarked on a program to improve productivity by reforming industrial relations within a framework of labour-management cooperation. New Zealand deregulated labour relations, dismantling a century-old industrial relations system based on arbitration.

The example of American management is, of course, the most influential in Canada. Data gathered there suggest that industrial relations strategies and outcomes are increasingly linked to general business strategy (Kochan, Capelli, and McKersie 1984). Thus, management can organize its industrial relations in much the same way as other functional areas such as marketing, production, and finance. Strategic choice theory, applied to industrial relations, suggested that management had the capacity to alter the fundamental nature of labour-management relations in a firm (Kochan, Katz, and McKersie 1986). Several prominent firms exercised "strategic choice" to change the nature of their relationship with their unions, in a few cases eliminating them completely. Unions were forced to reduce the levels of wages or fringe benefits in their collective agreements ("concession bargaining"). Many firms closed unionized operations in the northern and eastern states, where labour is strong, and opened new facilities in the south and southwest, where it is easier to avoid unionization completely. The strategic choice model challenged the traditional reactive position of employers. It suggested strongly that management could take the initiative in dealing with labour.

There are several reasons to question the application of the strategic choice model, as it operated in the United States, to Canada. As Chapter 7 of this volume shows, the Canadian labour movement fared better in the 1980s and 1990s than its American counterpart. While union density fell considerably in the United States, it remained stable in Canada. Canadian unions resisted many employer demands for concessions and mounted several large strikes to support major principles in bargaining. This power of resistance in Canadian unions suggests that employers here may not have the same relative bargaining power as in US corporations. Is it then possible to integrate industrial relations strategies with overall business strategy?

This chapter will first examine industrial relations strategies in Canadian companies. It will then describe the place of industrial relations in these firms and examine the links between industrial relations and major business decisions. It will conclude with an overview of industrial relations initiatives Canadian firms have undertaken in recent years.

The major source of data is a sample of 106 major Canadian firms in the private sector that engage in collective bargaining in a substantial way. Through interviews conducted by this author, senior industrial relations executives provided information on many aspects of industrial relations in their firms. The firms ranged in size from 950 to 57,000 employees. Their total employment was 971,000. A total of 66 per cent of the sample was Canadian-owned; another 20 per cent was controlled by US firms, while the remaining 14 per cent fell under other foreign ownership. More than 50 per cent of the firms were in manufacturing, with the remainder spread across other sectors. Except for manufacturing, no single sector accounted for over 10 per cent of the sample. To complement information drawn from the sample, the chapter also will refer to published sources.

BUSINESS STRATEGY AND INDUSTRIAL RELATIONS STRATEGY

Business strategy is often viewed as a cycle with several components (Thompson and Strickland 1989). The process is continuous, and individual elements may take place over a period of several years.

- The first stage in the cycle is the development of a concept of the business and a vision of where the organization should be headed. Often the question is posed: "What business are we in?" or "What business should we be in?"
- The second stage of a strategy cycle is to translate the organizational mission into specific performance objectives. The business and its subsidiary units must have targets, such as market share, against which to measure their performance.
- The third stage is the development of strategies to achieve the performance objectives for the business, and for its components and functional areas (including industrial relations).
- The fourth stage is the implementation of the strategy, i.e., using the strategies to achieve the performance targets.
- The final stage of the strategy cycle is the evaluation of performance, which normally sets in motion the reformulation of at least part of the cycle.

For strategic choice theorists, industrial relations strategies should be a part of business strategy on the same basis as marketing, production, or finance. Industrial relations would play a minor role in developing the concept of a business, but it does lend itself to specific performance objectives. For example, a performance objective might be the reduction of labour costs by 10 per cent. The development of a strategy for achieving that objective might involve decreases in the number of employees, the successful introduction of technological change, reductions in overtime worked, or cuts in wages and benefit levels (Anderson 1989). A firm emphasizing product quality or reliability should focus its industrial relations strategy on employing highly qualified workers, maintaining labour peace, and fostering high commitment to corporate goals in the labour force. If a company could operate with low-skilled labour, then a low-wage policy with little attention to training might be appropriate. Labour unrest would then take the form of higher turnover.

When industrial relations strategies do not coincide with business strategies, the consequences can be grave. Several air carriers in the United States were successful in negotiating "two-tier" wage structures as a strategy for cost reduction. Under this system, starting wages for newly hired employees were considerably lower than the pay of employees hired before the system took effect. Unions reluctantly agreed to these reductions, partly because the persons most directly affected were not yet employees and thus had no voice in the decision. However, the result of this arrangement was that employees with the same qualifications doing the same work could receive very different salaries, based on slight differences in length of service. This situation bred discontent among airline workers and affected the quality of service customers received. After a short life, most two-tier wage systems disappeared. Heeding these lessons, Canadian airlines avoided two-tier wage scales, although they did negotiate reductions in the starting wages for some occupations.

Constraints on Strategy

Despite these examples of linkages between business and industrial relations strategies, integration can be difficult. The theory of integration of the two strategies is built on several assumptions, some not stated or even understood by both parties. Managers are presumed to have considerable latitude in changing the nature of industrial relations in their firms, for instance by reducing labour costs quickly. These assumptions may be valid for the United States, where the labour movement is weak in many sectors, but it is not obvious that management has such freedom in Canada. Many Canadian industrial relations executives referred to major strikes as turning points for industrial relations in their firms. Some of these disputes caused management to re-examine its position and promoted improvements in labour relations. Other stoppages had the effect of limiting management's actions by proving that unions could successfully resist employer initiatives.

Legal considerations also influence industrial relations strategies. Labour relations statutes constrain employer tactics designed to resist unionization or to eliminate unions where they exist. Both parties are obligated to negotiate in good faith and make every reasonable effort to reach agreement. Such agreements are legally binding, and the law in most jurisdictions requires that they provide for arbitration as the final step of a grievance procedure. Thus, many management initiatives in areas covered by collective agreements are subject to challenge through these grievance procedures, further limiting an employer's options (Anderson 1989).

Legislation imposes other constraints on management. Unionized firms are not free to negotiate directly with their employees to implement a strategy. By law, employers have almost no voice in their employees' choice of a union. Some firms can evade the law by favouring one union over another, but that process generally carries high risks. Nor can management close an operation and move the work elsewhere without incurring liabilities, which may include retention of the union and collective agreement.

Management's freedom of action is always limited to some extent by the desire and ability of its unions to resist employer initiatives. Even nonunion firms could have problems with a strategy that works to the disadvantage of the employees. Their employees could join a union to resist reductions in their wages and conditions of work, especially in industries or regions where unionism is well entrenched. Unionized firms following the strategy cycle have to work within the limits their collective agreements impose because these contracts can only be altered with the consent of the employees whom they cover. The most obvious example would be the problems a firm might face trying to reduce wage levels or to displace workers with a new technology that would enable it to adopt a low-price strategy. This firm should expect its workers to resist these moves vigorously. Depending on the relative bargaining power of the parties, the unionized labour force might thwart management's plans completely. On the other hand, unions differ in their willingness to co-operate with management plans. Some have accepted job losses or a reduction in their contractual rights to gain rights to participate in joint committees to plan changes in the employer's organization.

The constraints on management action do not mean that employers are not free to act independently to establish an industrial relations strategy. A major factor in determining the ability of an employer to act strategically is the relative bargaining power of the parties. In the 1990s, the balance of power at the bargaining table clearly has shifted toward management. High rates of unemployment, a decline in labour militancy, plant closures, deregulation, and free trade agreements with the United States and Mexico, all have combined to increase the ability of employers to resist union pressures and to obtain their objectives in collective bargaining. Conservative governments in most regions of the country have further added to this advantage. Changes in labour law enacted in British Columbia and Alberta in the late 1980s had the express purpose of weakening labour's bargaining position.

There are many examples of Canadian firms that have changed their fundamental approach to industrial relations—from confrontation to co-operation or from acceptance of unionism to resistance. One large, capital-intensive resource firm experienced bitter strikes at both of its major operations (located in different regions) in the same year. These stoppages, which included sabotage and minor violence, cost the company heavily. The firm maintained operations at a reduced level by using supervisors, an action that antagonized strikers and led to violence. After the stoppages ended, senior management concluded that it had provoked the strikes by making excessive demands on its two unions, and that a more patient and cooperative approach was necessary. Within a few years, labour relations at both sites had become quite peaceful, aided also by a change of leaders in one of the two unions with which the firm dealt.

Another illustration is a transportation firm which concluded that unionization of its employees was helpful, since most of its customers were unionized and their employees might resist dealing with nonunion workers. But the company consciously sought to limit the size of the units represented by individual unions and preferred to avoid dealing with the major union in its industry. Instead there was a mixture of independent unions, smaller transportation unions and unions that represented its customers' workers. Bargaining generally has been peaceful, and no stoppage can damage the company in a major way. Two large manufacturing firms in the same industry followed opposite strategies to deal with fluctuations in production. To introduce a new product, one built new plants under an agreement with its union for automatic recognition. As demand shifted to the new product, however, existing operations had to be closed, putting thousands of employees out of work. This firm's competitor avoided building new plants, preferring to retool older facilities. Management required its employees to work overtime when demand for the product was high. During shifts in demand, overtime work fell sharply, but layoffs were rare.

ELEMENTS OF AN INDUSTRIAL RELATIONS STRATEGY

Within the limitations on management's freedom of action, common elements of a firm's industrial relations strategy can be discerned. The first element is the employer's view on the unionization of its employees, both in terms of existing relationships with labour and the organization of new units; in other words, will a company resist unionization of unorganized plants, try to remove unions where they exist, or follow a more accommodating strategy? A second element relates to compensation and how wages and employee benefits compare with those for other firms. Some firms are leaders in the labour market and presumably find that this position enables them to hire more selectively, avoid labour strife, and retain their labour force. Others prefer a lower wage bill and choose to accept turnover and labour unrest. Third, a firm must decide how it will conduct its affairs in the workplace, i.e., the extent to which it seeks to encourage cooperation with the union instead of attempting to bypass the union by communicating directly with employees.

Dealing with Unions

Few Canadian companies have a clearly articulated industrial relations strategy on their view of unions. Instead their approach to dealing with unions is part of the "corporate culture," i.e., a set of values shared by management about this subject. However, it is possible to identify four general strategies that apply to most companies:

1. The "union acceptance" strategy means that the company accepts the inevitability of unionism and collective bargaining for some or all of its operations. These companies may prefer not to have unions, but remain neutral when a union attempts to organize one of their nonunion operations. Within the framework of collective bargaining, the company seeks to negotiate the most favourable settlements possible.

2. The "union resistance" strategy exists in partially unionized firms that seek to limit the spread of unions to the unorganized parts of their work force, although they accept the legitimacy of their existing unions. They normally oppose union organizing campaigns within their organizations vigorously. On the other hand, they may negotiate with their unions in a nonconfrontational style.

3. A third strategy can be called "union removal." The basic goal of companies using this strategy is to eliminate unions where they exist in their operations. These employers resist negotiating any collective agreements that give unionized employees better conditions than have been provided for nonunion workers. They do this to emphasize the minimum role a union can play. They engage in extensive and continuing campaigns to discourage union activity among their nonunion workers and resist any attempt by unions to organize their employees.

4. Companies that are not unionized but fear that a union may gain a foothold in their organizations may follow a "union substitution/avoidance" strategy. They establish their own forms of representation, designed to make their employees regard unions as unnecessary or inferior to management-sponsored bodies.

To determine the relative importance of these strategies, senior industrial executives were asked the following question:

Which statement(s) best describes your company's overall labour relations policies?:

Concentrate on negotiating the best possible collective agreements;
Concentrate on limiting the influence or spread of unions; or
Concentrate on removing unions where they exist.

As Table 5.1 shows, most companies in the sample followed the union acceptance strategy; the next most popular was the union resistance strategy. None had the removal of unions as their primary strategy, although a few did include that strategy for some locations. Firms with multiple strategies appeared willing to accept unions in some or most of their operations, but wanted to limit or remove particular unions elsewhere. Because the sample was limited to firms with a significant degree of unionization, there were no examples of the union substitution/avoidance strategy, although a few companies followed that strategy at nonunion locations.

TABLE 5.1   Overall Industrial Relations Policy

Policy	Per Cent of Sample
Concentrate on negotiating the best possible collective agreements	70.8
Concentrate on limiting the influence or spread of unions	9.4
Concentrate on removing unions where they exist	0
Multiple answers	18.9
Best collective agreement and limit influence or spread of unions	13.3
Limit influence or spread of unions and remove incumbent unions	2.8
Best collective agreement and remove incumbent unions	0
All three policies	2.8
No policy/no answer	0.9

Nevertheless, few Canadian companies are enthusiastic about unions. When asked to "describe your company's policy toward unionization of new plants or installations," 71 per cent of the companies preferred not to have a union or opposed unionization actively during an organizing campaign (Table 5.2). However, the most common answer to this question was: "We try to manage well enough to make a union unnecessary, but we respect our employees' choice if they select one." It is noteworthy that most companies *do not* oppose unionization actively, in contrast to the United States, where employers vigorously resist union organizing campaigns (Weiler 1982).

If US and Canadian policies differ, which path do American companies operating in Canada follow? It is frequently assumed that American companies retain their industrial relations policies when they operate in Canada. The presence of US-based international unions, which represent over one-third of all Canadian union members, strengthens this assumption. In fact, there is little indication that the aggressive antiunion practices so popular in the United States are imported into Canada.

TABLE 5.2   Policy Toward Unionization of New Plants or Installations

Policy	Per Cent of Sample
Prefer to be nonunion, but accept employees' choice/remain neutral	36.8
Actively oppose unionization	34.0
Recognition/certification of new units automatic	4.7
Accept/prefer a union	5.7
Nonunion status is an unrealistic/impossible policy	2.8
No recent experience with new plants	2.8
No policy/answer	10.4
Other	2.8

Tables 5.3 and 5.4 show that there is very little difference in industrial relations policies based on ownership. Most industrial relations executives of foreign-owned firms reported that their head offices had little or no influence on their activities. Management at the foreign headquarters wanted to be informed of major events, such as strikes, but seldom dictated policies or practices in their Canadian affiliate. The manager of one American-owned firm that is almost entirely nonunion in the United States but about 35 per cent unionized in Canada, declared, "We play by the rules where we operate. In the United States, there are no rules. Here rules exist, and we follow them."

Responses to the questions about overall industrial relations policies were also broken down by the industrial sector of the firm and the province where the headquarters is located. Again there were few differences except for the oil industry, which clearly resists unions more than firms in other sectors and also dominates the companies in the sample from Alberta.

TABLE 5.3   Overall Industrial Relations Policy by Nationality of Company
(Per Cent of National Sample)

Policy	Canada	US	UK	Other
Negotiate best agreements	65.7	76.2	100.0	77.8
Limit influence/spread of unions	11.4	4.8	0	11.1
Remove unions	0	0	0	0
Multiple	21.4	19.0	0	11.1
Best agreement and limit unions	13.0	19.0	0	11.1
Limit influence and remove unions	4.2	0	0	0
Best agreement and remove unions	0	0	0	0
Best agreement, limit influence and remove	4.2	0	0	0
No policy/no answer	1.4	0	0	0

TABLE 5.4   Policy Toward Unionization of New Plants or Installations by Nationality of Company
(Per Cent of National Sample)

Policy	Nationality of Company			
	Canada	US	UK	Other Foreign
Prefer to be nonunion but accept employees' choice/remain neutral	35.7	33.3	50.0	44.4
Actively oppose unionization	34.3	33.3	33.3	33.3
Recognition/certification of new units is automatic	2.9	9.5	—	11.1
Accept/prefer a union	8.6	—	—	—
Nonunion status is an unrealistic/impossible policy	2.9	—	—	11.1
No recent experience with new plants	2.9	4.8	—	—
No policy/answer	10.0	14.3	16.7	—
Other	2.9	4.8	—	—

While none of the large unionized companies surveyed for this chapter had a union removal strategy, there is evidence of this strategy in other firms. Aided by the small size of individual branches and high turnover of union supporters, chartered banks had such a strategy from 1979 to 1983 (Brody et al. 1993). The Canadian Imperial Bank of Commerce had set the tone of industrial relations for its employees when it engaged in a massive propaganda campaign against unionism. The Canada Labour Relations Board found the employer had committed so many unfair labour practices that the president of the bank was required to write a letter to each employee apologizing and expressing the bank's willingness to abide by the law. Despite such measures, less than one quarter of all unions certified in chartered banks survived (Brody et al. 1993). In the early 1980s, unions certified six branches of Eaton's Department Store. In Ontario, the company refused to negotiate a first collective agreement after a six-month strike. After the Manitoba Labour Relations Board imposed a first contract for a Brandon branch, the company dismissed half of the employees and demanded concessions from the union. By the end of the decade, these bargaining units too had decertified (Palmer, 1992).

While data on the extent of union substitution policies are not readily available, a handful of published accounts describe this strategy. The petroleum industry has several examples of these policies. Imperial Oil has relied upon "joint industrial councils (JICs)" as part of a general strategy to discourage unionization since 1919. Other elements include slightly higher wage scales and generous employee benefits (which are not negotiated with unions at any locations). JICs were introduced into the Canadian oil industry through the influence of William Lyon MacKenzie King, Canada's first minister of labour and later prime minister. The councils consist of equal numbers of managers (selected) and employees (elected by their peers) who meet regularly to discuss health and safety, recreation, production issues, and occasional grievances (Taras 1994a).

Petro Canada has "Employee Management Advisory Committees" (EMACs) at several of its operations. These joint committees meet semiannually to discuss grievances and production issues. Employees receive an information booklet outlining the structure and the powers of the EMAC and containing several other provisions commonly found in collective agreements, with the notable exceptions of seniority rights, promotion criteria, job security, and a formal grievance procedure.

About 30 per cent of employees in the petroleum industry are covered by formal nonunion representation schemes. Despite this substantial presence, the policy has draw-backs. Systems such as JICs consume a great deal of management time and open the employer to minor employee pressure tactics. Imperial Oil unilaterally cancelled one JIC, and its workers cancelled another at a second location. At Petro Canada, at least one EMAC was the basis of a successful union certification (Taras 1994a).

Since the 1930s, Dofasco, a steel producer located in Hamilton, Ontario, has had a human resources strategy designed to prevent unionization by the United Steelworkers, which had organized the other major steel producers in Hamilton and elsewhere. Dofasco does not have a formal mechanism for soliciting employees' views. However, it matches the wage rates negotiated by the United Steelworkers and adds a profit-sharing plan. In addition, it sponsors social events and recreational activities for its employees. There is a concerted effort to foster a sense of community among employees (Storey 1983).

These examples of union substitution strategies, combined with survey results of unionized firms, convincingly demonstrate that Canadian companies prefer to operate without a union. An equally significant conclusion is that most large companies do not oppose union organization vigorously, allowing employees to decide whether they want union representation. Once a union is certified, most employers seek to negotiate the best collective agreement possible. For large Canadian employers experienced in collective bargaining, the dominant strategy for dealing with unions is union acceptance.

Relative Compensation

All employers must be aware of labour market realities when selecting compensation levels for their employees. Firms whose wages fall below normal levels for the region in which they operate can expect to experience high turnover, employee dissatisfaction, and difficulties in recruiting. For some companies, the savings realized by holding wage costs down offset the disadvantages, especially when the labour force is unskilled. High-wage strategies offer the opposite benefits and costs. High-wage firms are preferred employers in many localities, so they have no difficulty in recruiting staff with strong qualifications. Turnover usually is low, although employee dissatisfaction can still be a problem if other elements of the employment relationship are deficient.

Unionized employers have difficulty pursuing a low-wage strategy, and even nonunion employers in an industry where unions operate also face problems with this policy. Nonetheless, low-wage firms do exist with and without unions. Where unions are present, workers can easily compare wages, and union members expect their unions to negotiate better compensation. Overall in Canada, union members tend to receive wages that are 10 to 25 per cent higher than nonunion members in similar circumstances, although there can be considerable variation in the experience of specific work groups (see Chapter 12). Apart from their bargaining power, unions bring information on wage levels in other firms to their members' attention, thereby introducing additional market pressures into corporate wage determination.

TABLE 5.5   Comparison for Wages and Employee Benefits

Comparison Group	Per Cent of Sample
Other firms, in the same industry/sector	76.5
Other firms in the same industry/region	13.7
Other firms in the same region	6.9
None/other	2.9

Unsurprisingly, compensation issues are important to managers. In a 1980 survey, Canadian industrial relations managers were asked to rank the importance of bargaining issues on a scale of 1 to 4, with 1 being the least important. Ninety-five per cent of the respondents ranked wage levels as either 3 or 4 in importance, and 73 per cent also ranked wage administration (skill differentials, incentive pay, etc.) as a 3 or 4 in importance. For other compensation issues, the results were similar—between 60 and 75 per cent of the respondents ranked them with 3 or 4 (Godard and Kochan 1982).

In the current survey of unionized companies, senior industrial relations executives were asked with which other firms they compared their wages and employee benefits (Table 5.5). Except in rare cases when wage levels may determine the ability of a company to operate successfully, management decisions on appropriate wage rates are based on a combination of the firm's cost structure and the wages other firms pay in the same industry, especially their product market competitors. Wage levels in local or regional labour markets are far less important.

Because large firms in this sample were deliberately over-represented, one would expect their wages to be above average for all firms in Canada (Gunderson and Riddell 1993). Table 5.6 shows that 40 per cent of the firms believe that their compensation is higher than the average for their relevant comparison group in the same industry or region. Previous surveys have found a high degree of satisfaction among unionized employers with collectively bargained wage rates (Godard and Kochan 1982), suggesting that large unionized employers are content to be at or above the average for their industry. Except in rare circumstances, bargaining objectives do not attempt to reduce wages below the levels of domestic competition. Indeed, private sector wage roll-backs have never been a big part of Canadian industrial relations.

TABLE 5.6   Wages and Employee Benefits Relative to Comparison Group

Comparison	Per Cent of Sample
Above average	34.6
Above average/average	5.8
Average	54.8
Average/below average	2.9
Below average	1.9

Workplace Change

If unionized Canadian firms have decided not to alter the fundamental nature of their relationships with unions and are at least resigned to a high wage strategy, what other responses have they made to an increasingly competitive environment? Previous research has shown that almost half of unionized firms engage in some form of employee participation or consultation, although safety programs are often required by law. Quality and performance-related programs also are popular (Betcherman et al. 1994b; Smith 1993). Profit-sharing is less often used by unionized companies (Betcherman, et al. 1994a).

Research reported here, based on interviews, revealed some of the same patterns, although differences in definitions prevent direct comparisons of studies. When managers were asked in an open-ended question what initiatives they had taken to improve labour relations and productivity, the most common response was that they had taken steps to improve communications with their unions and their employees (35 per cent). The subject matter of communications with unions tended to be the operations and financial statistics of the firm. Deliberate efforts were made to steer discussions away from industrial relations issues (e.g., grievances, potential collective bargaining demands). Line management rather than industrial relations staff typically represented the employer. A common format was regular meetings with union officials to discuss production matters, such as the volume or quality of production. Often employers presented financial reports for the firm. Union representatives had the opportunity to comment or ask questions, but management saw these meetings as forums for providing information, not as a form of consultation. These sessions enabled management to exchange views with its unions and to discuss issues of mutual concern without at the same time yielding any of its authority to make decisions on matters not covered by the collective agreement. There is no evidence that unions have become involved in strategic decisions by management through these meetings (Wagar 1994).

The focus on production and financial issues was necessary because the purpose of improved communications with unions and employees was clearly to encourage an appreciation by union leaders and their members of the financial, competitive, and production issues that the employer was facing. Employers believed that they would enjoy a more co-operative bargaining relationship and a smoother acceptance of changes in their operations if unions understood the reasons for their decisions and the pressures the firm faced. Not all of these programs had a long history, but employers almost universally regarded them as successful.

In addition to improving communications, another common employer initiative encourages employees to take more responsibility for improving productivity and product quality. About 20 per cent of all employers in the sample instituted formal programs to improve quality. These programs have several names, "quality circles," "total quality management," or "quality improvement" systems. While these programs differ in many important details, they all include the involvement of teams of employees, supervisors, facilitators, and technical advisers to make specific improvements in the quality of the product or service for which they are responsible.

A successful quality improvement program in a container company is illustrative. The company has a high volume operation, with many thousands of units produced each day. The containers are shipped to customers who process food, beverages, home cleaning products, and other goods. The filling of the containers by the company's customers is also a high-volume operation. If a container breaks on the production line, the cost to the customer from the interruption in production, cleanup, and damage to equipment can be considerable, as much as $20,000 per incident. The company already had a high-quality product—there were only two to three breaks per 10,000 containers, but the quality improvement program reduced the figure to one break per 100,000 units, better than the American competition. As part of the program, the company also reduced the number of quality inspectors. The company's objective was to lower the rate to a single break for each 200,000 units. A quality improvement program involved bargaining-unit members, supervisors, and engineers, who were all invited to suggest changes to the production process to achieve quality targets.

Employee-involvement programs were another management plan to change the workplace. These programs, found in 20 per cent of the companies surveyed, are designed to solicit employee suggestions on production issues, work schedules, and other workplace problems (see Chapter 11). These usually involve "mixed" teams of employees (union members) and supervisors. Unions usually are wary of employee-involvement programs, which are initiated and fundamentally controlled by management. They see these forms of consultation as a threat to their role as the exclusive representative of employees in the workplace. Unions also fear that an unstated purpose of these activities is to undermine the attachment of workers to their union. Employers in the sample reported that opposition tends to be strongest at the national level of labour organizations. Local unions, particularly when they see that their plant or operation is having competitive difficulties, are usually more receptive. It is not uncommon, however, for unions to withhold support for these endeavours, without opposing them formally. In private conversations, some employers have tacitly admitted that they expect employee-involvement programs to weaken the militancy of their workers, so labour's concerns may be justified.

The increased use of communication with labour and greater reliance on employee involvement developed together with a substantial degree of union-management consultation, much of which has existed for some time. Managers were asked if their organizations engaged in consultation with their unions in the following areas: production, employee assistance (counselling for employees with personal problems), technological change, safety and health, and profit-sharing. Over 90 per cent of all firms in the sample engaged in consultation on safety and health. However, in most Canadian jurisdictions, firms with more than 10 employees are required to establish safety and health committees, so the responses to this question were affected by legal requirements. There are no such requirements for consultation on production issues, but 73 per cent of all firms had such programs. Slightly fewer, 67 per cent, consulted with their unions on technological change, and 62 per cent had joint employee assistance programs. In the matter of profit-sharing, on the other hand, consultation was not common; only 11 per cent of the companies reported that they consulted with their unions on profit-sharing.

In summary, the most common labour relations responses of Canadian employers to increased competitive pressures was to co-operate with unions and seek assistance from their workers. It is noteworthy that in adopting these strategies, most employers rejected other, more confrontational approaches. Only two companies stated that they chose to confront their union or to regain management rights that were constrained by the collective agreement. Examples of "concession bargaining," i.e., demanding reductions in the terms and conditions of employment contained in collective agreements, also were rare. A handful of firms stated that they relied on changes to their collective agreements to improve productivity, and several companies in the sample reported that they had traded new clauses in collective agreements for job security or other benefits to workers. However, large unionized Canadian companies clearly chose co-operation over confrontation.

INDUSTRIAL RELATIONS AND MANAGEMENT DECISIONS

This discussion of the industrial relations strategies of large Canadian companies does not address directly the question of the possible linkages between a firm's business policy and its industrial relations policy. Most respondents treated industrial relations policies as isolated from other business decisions. However, there were linkages of industrial relations to specific corporate decisions. The impact of industrial relations on various corporate decisions are summarized in Table 5.7.

TABLE 5.7   Impact of Labour Relations on Corporate Decisions (Per Cent of Sample)

Policy/Impact	No Impact	Considered but Not Significant	Important/Dominant Factor
Investment in new plants	24	25	51
Adoption of new technology	31	40	29
Choosing site for new plant	35	27	38
Purchase of components, supplies, etc.	51	31	18
Re-organization of company	36	31	33

It is clear that industrial relations can be a significant factor in the decision whether to invest in a new plant, rather than in an existing plant. Several aspects of industrial relations may affect this decision, including the current industrial relations climate in the plant, the provisions of the collective agreement there, and the attitude of the union representing workers. Plants where industrial relations are perceived to be poor are clearly at a disadvantage in attracting new investment from their corporate owners. However, this conclusion should be seen in conjunction with the finding that in a quarter of the companies, labour matters had no impact on such investment decisions.

Thirty-eight per cent of the companies reported that labour relations were an important or a dominant factor in the decision of where to locate a plant. Slightly less, 35 per cent, stated that industrial relations had no impact on the choice of a plant site, and 27 per cent suggested that it was not a significant factor (Table 5.7). This fact is surprising in some respects, because there are frequent public statements from business about the importance of the industrial relations climate. When changes in labour law are debated, private sector firms often threaten to leave the province if government policies are too prolabour. It appears that such policies have more effect on decisions to invest in existing installations than on decisions to locate a new plant. Why would this apparent contradiction exist? For some firms, location decisions are relatively obvious. Resource companies normally have to locate where a particular resource exists, and retail firms must be close to their markets. Manufacturing firms in particular may have the option of locating in different areas. Several firms reported that they had deliberately chosen to build new plants away from existing facilities to avoid coverage by a collective agreement that they regarded as too restrictive. By contrast, one major manufacturing firm has a corporate policy of rebuilding existing facilities rather than closing them and building new plants elsewhere. The firm accepts that its union will be less accommodating in changing the collective agreement at an existing plant than it might be at a new site, but wishes to avoid the damage to morale and the costs of closing a complete plant or even a major production facility within a plant.

The impact of collective bargaining and unionism on technological change has been discussed frequently, usually to determine the impact of unionization on the adoption of new technology. A survey of 216 Canadian firms in the mid-1980s found that the presence of unions was not a significant factor in determining the rate of technological change, but did affect the way in which these changes took place (Betcherman 1991). These results are mirrored in the present survey. Most companies said that the decision to adopt new technology was not affected by industrial relations factors. Less than one-third of unionized firms stated that labour relations was an important consideration with respect to the introduction of new technology. Decisions with respect to company re-organization and acquisition of components and supplies also were largely unaffected by industrial relations (Table 5.7). These findings are again consistent with previous surveys (Betcherman et al. 1994a).

Given the low impact of industrial relations on key business decisions, there is little support for the proposition that integration is occurring between industrial relations policies and business strategies. While the bargaining power of unions may make a difference in operational decisions, unions remain marginal to the formulation of strategic decisions. The only real exception lies with respect to the new investment in existing plants where a poor industrial relations climate can discourage investment. Yet even here, only half of large unionized firms considered industrial relations to be an important factor. Whether the separation of industrial relations and business strategy can persist is another question. As companies in Canada continue to face strong competitive pressures, they may find that traditional modes of decision making that exclude industrial relations considerations are no longer adequate.

MANAGEMENT PROCESSES

The responsibility for ensuring that industrial relations strategies are translated into practice is divided among industrial relations staff, human resource departments, and line managers. Managers of large unionized firms emphasized the importance of the collective bargaining process in meeting corporate objectives. Three major managerial functions in a system of collective bargaining are: (1) preparation for bargaining, (2) the conduct of bargaining, and (3) contract administration. The resources and talents necessary for each of these functions can vary considerably.

Preparation for Bargaining

Ideally, preparation for bargaining should be an ongoing, year-round process. In practice, however, many organizations seem to wait until several months before the expiry of a collective agreement before beginning active preparation. Typically, there are five elements in preparations for bargaining: (1) monitoring industry and regional settlements; (2) monitoring union developments; (3) monitoring worker attitudes; (4) conducting background research for bargaining; and (5) developing negotiating proposals (Godard and Kochan 1982).

As indicated above, most firms compare their wages and fringe benefits to other companies in the same industry, and secondarily to firms in the same region. There are a variety of sources for such information—industry associations, private publications, government surveys, and private surveys. Given this array of information, which normally is not expensive to obtain, most firms can base their bargaining strategies on an extensive knowledge of settlements their competitors in product and labour markets have reached.

Monitoring of union developments is done informally. Industrial relations staff often deal with union representatives on at least a weekly basis, and from these meetings they learn of the union's activities in other bargaining units, the internal politics of the local or national union, convention resolutions and other news. Nearly all unions publish periodicals for their members, and managers frequently subscribe to these or receive copies as a courtesy. These publications are particularly useful for their discussions of settlements and union bargaining objectives.

Monitoring of worker attitudes also is generally informal. Firms without unions or that follow strategies of union removal or union substitution, often use written surveys to measure employees' views on a variety of subjects. For instance, a large employer in the service sector has unions at a majority of its locations, but strongly resists any union organizing campaigns at new sites and existing nonunion sites. It commissions attitude surveys from time to time in its nonunion establishments to guide its human resource policies. Few firms would conduct such surveys among their unionized employees. Unions would resent such efforts to bypass their procedures for learning members' wishes, and surveys might infringe upon a union's legal rights as an exclusive bargaining agent. Thus, line managers and industrial relations managers attempt to stay abreast of employee morale and problems as part of their daily contacts with the unionized labour force. The subjects of grievances are a useful source of information, as are discussions raised in union-management committees.

Background research for bargaining occurs in the months before the commencement of negotiations. Industrial relations staff are responsible for generating proposals the employer may present to the union in negotiations as well as responses to issues the union is expected to raise. There are varying degrees of formality in this process. Some firms have elaborate systems for obtaining the views of supervisors and managers, while others rely on information provided as part of other labour relations functions. Employer staff estimate the costs of possible union demands as well as any management proposals. If there are troublesome areas in the collective agreement, alternate language must be prepared for discussion in bargaining.

When the background research is complete, the industrial relations staff must obtain approval from senior management for a bargaining position, commonly known as a "mandate." This approval generally comes from corporate managers. These are major decisions for any employer and are carefully weighed. The costs of union and management positions must be presented, together with an estimate of the final settlement range. The impact of a settlement at one location on other bargaining relationships must be considered. Central control of mandates enables employers to manage their labour costs as part of the general budgetary process of the organization. In general, management negotiators are given considerable latitude to settle within their mandate, but must seek permission from corporate officers if they believe that they must exceed the mandate to obtain a settlement.

Conduct of Bargaining and Contract Administration

Bargaining is conducted according to the principles explained in Chapter 9 of this volume. A member of the industrial relations staff normally is the principal spokesperson for the employer, supported by one or more other industrial relations staff, representatives of line management, and perhaps a financial analyst. Generally, ratification of settlements takes place at the same level of the organization where the mandate was approved. On the other hand, higher levels of authority are often involved when a threat to go on strike is made. The consequences of a stoppage are sufficiently important that the highest levels of management authority are at least informed before a decision is made to reject a union proposal that is backed by a credible strike threat.

Chapter 10 of this volume describes the process of contract administration. Survey respondents reported that local management is primarily responsible for this function, including decisions to take a dispute to arbitration. Line managers may be advised by industrial relations staff reporting to them or by managers at higher levels of the organization. Firms also rely upon outside lawyers to advise them in arbitration matters and to present their cases.

THE SIZE AND STRUCTURE OF INDUSTRIAL RELATIONS STAFF

Decisions to sign a collective agreement or take a strike can have broad implications for the firm—there may be costs in the millions of dollars and relations with customers and suppliers can be affected, as can the morale of the labour force, the authority and flexibility of line management, and the firm's relations with government. Successful industrial relations can improve efficiency, raise profits, and generally contribute to the well-being of an organization.

Because many industrial relations processes can be highly technical and complex, organizations must assign technically competent staff to assist line management and to conduct many specialized functions. The work load of industrial relations staff can be highly variable. By law, collective agreements must have a duration of at least one year, and many agreements are renegotiated once every two or three years. In the periods leading up to the renewal of collective agreements, the demands on industrial relations staff are great, but the work load diminishes considerably after negotiations end. Thus, it is impractical to employ large staffs for collective bargaining when the workload during slack periods may not justify their presence. Although contract administration is an ongoing process, the concentration of this activity at the level of the plant or work site under the direction of line management limits the contribution of staff specialists (Godard and Kochan 1982).

A common mechanism for dealing with the availability of industrial relations expertise is to combine industrial relations and human resources management staff functions. While industrial relations personnel primarily support collective bargaining, the human resources staff deal with nonunion workers. They also deal with aspects of the employment relationship for unionized workers not covered by the collective agreement. In several cases, the department where these two functions are located also is responsible for occupational safety and health.

To explain the role of industrial relations staff within Canadian companies, respondents provided data on the number of staff at each level of the organization. (In practice, it proved impossible to isolate persons who performed only industrial relations functions, since many combined industrial relations with other activities.) The picture that emerges is one of extensive variation. One firm reported that it had 96 persons employed in industrial relations functions, while two others with the same number of employees had 12 and 22 industrial relations staff respectively. Apart from the extremes, one would expect the number of staff to be related to the number of employees. Table 5.8 shows that the ratio of staff to employees varied greatly. Such factors as the number of bargaining units, their dispersion, and industry characteristics were all important determinants of the number of industrial relations staff. In addition, firms with headquarters in the English-speaking provinces and large operations in Quebec often maintain parallel industrial relations staffs for the two language groups. Quebec law requires that most industrial relations functions be carried out in French, so unilingual Anglophones are not able to operate there, especially in such functions as measuring the attitude of the work force or advising managers on the disposition of grievances. Companies with headquarters in Montreal relied on the corporate staff to manage industrial relations in both languages.

These data suggest that industrial relations is not purely a staff function. Managers in most levels of firms have responsibility for industrial relations activities. The dominant pattern is for line managers to carry out industrial relations activities, supported by relatively small staffs.

TABLE 5.8   Ratio of Employees to Industrial Relations Staff

Employees per Staff Person	Per Cent of Companies
Under 200 to 1	22
201 - 400 to 1	17
401 - 600 to 1	24
Over 600 to 1	37
Average for sample	497 to 1

CENTRALIZATION OF AUTHORITY

Decentralization is an important theme in Canadian industrial relations. Legislation is highly fragmented, with the provinces exercising primary jurisdiction over industrial relations. Independent labour relations boards interpret provincial and federal legislation according to their own standards. The diversity of the economy and local labour market conditions is another element of decentralization that affects industrial relations. Bargaining structures in Canada are among the most decentralized in the world. Only 6 per cent of the firms in this survey negotiated through employers' associations, for instance, and most private sector firms negotiate on a plant-by-plant basis. On the labour side, no national or regional body has a formal role in collective bargaining. In many industries, several unions represent individual bargaining units, normally with little co-ordination among them (see Chapter 9).

These environmental conditions might lead to decentralized management structures for industrial relations. Regional bargaining patterns would complicate centralized control over collective bargaining outcomes. Legislative differences make the co-ordination of bargaining difficult. Decisions in the area of contract administration are typically in the hands of local management.

Conversely, organization theory predicts centralized control over industrial relations. Decisions on industrial relations matters can be extremely significant to employers, and the industrial relations environment is turbulent and unpredictable. Some decisions may require rapid responses by management. All these conditions normally lead to centralized decision making in other areas of management (Thompson and Foley 1991). The theory of strategic choice rests on the assumption that senior management can impose significant changes in corporate policies concerning industrial relations. This assumption obviously implies a high degree of centralization (Kochan, Katz, and McKersie 1986). On the other hand, when decision criteria are vague and professional expertise is important (conditions found in Canadian industrial relations), decision structures are likely to be less centralized (Connors 1992).

Thus, reasons exist for both centralized control and decentralized decision making in industrial relations. To find out which factors are more influential, three aspects of management decision making were analyzed:

1. the degree to which senior managers report that they control industrial relations decisions;
2. the degree to which senior managers control the formulation of industrial relations policies; and
3. the relative size of industrial relations staffs at various levels of the organization.

The most obvious measure of centralization is where the final authority for specific industrial relations decisions lies. Senior executives were asked, "At what level is there final authority to decide the following issues?" for wages, fringe benefits, contract language, contract settlement terms, strikes, grievances, and initiatives to improve industrial relations. Four choices were available: corporate, meaning the Canadian (or foreign) headquarters; divisional, if the company was organized on a product basis; regional, if region was the basis of organization; and plant, i.e., the actual worksite.

TABLE 5.9   Responsibility for Industrial Relations Decisions (Percentage Replies)

Issue	Corporate	Shared Authority	Division	Region (Group)	Plant
Wages	64.5	21.5	7.5	5.6	0
Employee benefits	64.5	21.5	6.5	4.7	0
Contract language	36	39	9	5	11
Contract settlement terms	55.7	24.5	4.7	3.8	3.8
To take a strike	72.0	23.4	2.8	1.9	0
To settle/arbitrate a grievance	20	30	18	9	23
Initiatives to improve labour relations	9	61	9	4	18

Table 5.9 illustrates that authority to make collective bargaining decisions—to determine wages and fringe benefits and to take a strike—is highly centralized. The picture is different for the decisions involving contract administration—settling grievances or going to arbitration—where authority is widely dispersed among different levels of the organization. Few organizations had regional or group structures, so there were not many examples of authority resting with this level. Occasionally, the authority for a decision was shared between two levels, typically the corporate and the operating division, i.e., the level immediately below corporate. Several of the companies belonged to employer associations. These organizations normally determine mandates for bargaining and settle disputes based on the votes of their members, so corporation and association were combined.

A second measure of centralization is policy formulation. Although few companies had written industrial relations policies, most had unwritten policies on which managers could rely. It is possible that policies formally approved at the corporate level were really the ratification of decisions made at lower levels of the management hierarchy. Respondents were asked to rate the degree of corporate involvement at different levels of their organizations in policy decisions, ranging from not being involved at all to having direct responsibility for the decision.

The data in Table 5.10 reinforce the previous information on the centralization of authority. Even in areas where corporate managers do not have operational responsibility,

TABLE 5.10   Corporate Involvement in Industrial Relations Policies (Per Cent of Sample)

Policy/Involvement	Directly Responsible	Participate with Other Units	Approves Decisions Routinely	Involved Occasionally	Not Involved at All	No Policy
Unionization	53.5	18.2	1.0	5.1	4.0	18.2
Union avoidance	45.2	19.4	3.2	5.4	4.3	22.6
Research for bargaining	49.5	18.9	2.1	11.6	8.4	9.5
Advising negotiating team	62.8	14.9	4.3	5.3	6.4	6.4
Approving draft agreements	55.3	17.0	4.3	10.6	7.4	5.3
Monitoring labour relations	54.8	18.3	4.3	8.6	5.4	8.6
Settlement of grievances/arbitration	32.6	19.1	6.7	16.9	13.5	11.2

for instance in the monitoring of labour relations, they do have a significant role in the formulation of the policies under which lower-level managers will operate.

The location of industrial relations staff is also a measure of the degree of the centralization of decisions. The degree of staff concentration in a specialized area should show the distribution of influence over both policy and operational decisions. Table 5.11 shows that a high proportion of industrial relations staff is found in the corporate or division levels of Canadian companies, strengthening the conclusion that industrial relations issues are handled at the corporate level. Less than half the staff is located at the plant level, where collective bargaining, grievance meetings, and supervisor training actually take place.

TABLE 5.11   Location of Industrial Relations Staff

Level	Per Cent of Staff
Corporate	33.5
Division	15.8
Group	8.6
Plant	42.1

The results of this survey indicate a high degree of centralization of authority for key industrial relations decisions and policies, especially decisions connected with collective bargaining. It appears that the importance of these decisions, their complexity, political character, and the uncertainty of the business environment outweigh the decentralizing tendencies of the Canadian industrial relations system.

CONCLUSIONS

Management will be the focus of attention in industrial relations for the remainder of the 1990s, and knowledge of policies and practices will increase during that time. The theoretical linkages of industrial relations strategies with business strategies appear to be difficult, but possible under favourable circumstances. Firms that have adopted industrial relations strategies tied to their business strategies are very satisfied with the results. As employers become more sophisticated about the possibilities of this approach, more examples should appear. At present industrial relations considerations influence few business decisions heavily. It is not clear whether this situation reflects the relative ignorance among many senior managers of industrial relations considerations, the importance of other factors (such as access to the market or raw materials costs), or the confidence of senior management that they can operate successfully within the general context of Canadian industrial relations.

The hard-line approach of American employers toward their unions and employees has little acceptance in Canada, although most Canadian employers would prefer not to have a union. However, in large, partially unionized firms, they respect their employees' choice of a union and work to maximize their position within the framework of collective bargaining.

Large firms are resigned to paying above-average wages and employee benefits, and they accept that collective bargaining raises their visibility in the labour market.

In the face of stronger competitive pressures in the 1980s and 1990s, unionized firms have emphasized communication with their unions and a reliance on existing arrangements for union-management consultation to prove to their unions and employees the economic realities of product markets and to solve operational problems jointly. Labour-management consultation is especially common on the subjects of occupational health and safety, production problems, employee assistance, and technological change. Authority for bargaining decisions is highly centralized, despite decentralized bargaining structures and the shift of responsibility toward line management for some industrial relations processes.

In many respects, the unionized segments of the Canadian economy have performed well without having to remove or severely weaken either the unions or the collective bargaining process. Many unionized companies compete successfully in international markets. Productivity and product quality are high. Public policy has played a minor role in the recent initiatives of Canadian employers. But market pressures, fed by international competition, free trade agreements, changing technology, and deregulation will continue to challenge existing strategies and practices.

QUESTIONS

1. How can business strategy apply to industrial relations?

2. Distinguish among the broad strategies of union acceptance, union resistance, union removal, and union substitution/avoidance.

3. What are some of the industrial relations issues facing a firm wishing to pursue a low wage strategy of compensation?

4. What are some employer initiatives to improve productivity and industrial relations in the workplace?

5. Discuss the main elements in an employer's preparation for bargaining.

6. What factors would lead to the decentralization of authority for management industrial relations decisions? What factors lead to centralization of authority?

REFERENCES

ANDERSON, J. C. 1989. "The Strategic Management of Industrial Relations." In J. C. Anderson, M. Gunderson and A. Ponak, eds, *Union-Management Relations in Canada*, 2nd ed. Toronto: Addison-Wesley.

BETCHERMAN, G., K. McMULLEN, N. LECKIE, and C. CARON. 1994a. *The Canadian Workplace in Transition*. Kingston, Ont.: IRC Press.

BETCHERMAN, G., N. LECKIE, and A. VERMA 1994b. "HRM Innovations in Canada: Evidence from Establishment Surveys." School of Industrial Relations/Industrial Relations Centre, Queen's University at Kingston.

BETCHERMAN, G. 1991. "The effect of unions on the innovative behaviour of firms in Canada." *Industrial Relations Journal*, 22 (2): 142-151.

BRODY, B., K. SEAVER, and T. TREMBLAY. 1993. "The Deunionization of Canadian Banks." In T. S. Kuttner, ed, *The Industrial Relations System: Future Trends and Developments. Proceedings of the XXIXth Conference of the Canadian Industrial Relations Association*. Fredericton, NB: CIRA, 1: 381-396.

CHAYKOWSKI, R., and A. VERMA, eds. 1992. *Industrial Relations in Canadian Industry*. Toronto: Dryden Press.

CONNORS, P. 1992. "Decision Making Participation Patterns: The Role of Organizational Context." *Academy of Management Journal*, 35 (1): 218-231.

GODARD, J. H., and T. A. KOCHAN. 1982. "Canadian Management Under Collective Bargaining: Policies, Processes, Structure, and Effectiveness." In J. C. Anderson and M. Gunderson, eds, *Union-Management Relations in Canada*. Toronto: Addison-Wesley.

GUNDERSON, M., and W. C. RIDDELL. 1993. *Labour Market Economics: Theory, Evidence and Policy in Canada*, 3rd ed. Toronto: McGraw-Hill Ryerson.

KOCHAN, T. A., H. C. KATZ, and R. B. McKERSIE. 1986. *The Transformation of American Industrial Relations*. New York: Basic Books.

KOCHAN, T. A., P. CAPELLI, and R. McKERSIE. 1984. "Strategic Choice and Industrial Relations Theory." *Industrial Relations*, 23: 16-39.

NOVEK, J. 1989. "Peripheralizing Core Labour Markets? The Case of the Canadian Meat Packing Industry." *Work, Employment & Society*, 3 (2), 17-37.

PALMER, B. D. 1992. *Working Class Experience: Rethinking the History of Canadian Labour, 1800-1991*. Toronto: McClelland & Stewart.

SMITH, A. E. 1993. "Canadian Industrial Relations in Transition." *Relations industrielles/Industrial Relations* 48, (4): 641-660

STOREY, R. 1983. "Unionization Versus Corporate Welfare: The Dofasco Way." *Labour/Le Travailleur (*Fall): 7-42.

STREECK, W. 1987. "The Uncertainties of Management in the Management of Uncertainty: Employers, Labor Relations and Industrial Adjustment in the 1980s." *Work, Employment and Society* 1 (3): 281-308.

TARAS, D. G. 1994a. "Impact of Industrial Relations Strategies on Selected Human Resource Practices in a Partially Unionized Industry: The Canadian Petroleum Sector." Unpublished PhD dissertation, University of Calgary.

TARAS, D. G. 1994b. "Tracing the Transborder Flow of a Nonunion Employee Representation Plan." Administrative Sciences Association of Canada Annual Conference.

THOMPSON, A. A., and A. J. STRICKLAND III. 1989. *Strategy Formulation and Implementation: Tasks of the General Manager*, 3rd ed. Homewood, IL: Irwin.

THOMPSON, M., and J. FOLEY. 1991. "Centralization of Management Authority in Canadian Industrial Relations." *Women and Industrial Relations; Proceedings of the 28th Annual Meeting of the Canadian Industrial Relations Association*, Donald Carter, Ed. (Quebec: CIRA), pp. 475-484.

WAGAR, T. H. 1994. *Human Resource Management Practices and Organizational Performance: Evidence from Atlantic Canada.* Kingston, Ont.: IRC Press, Industrial Relations Centre, Queen's University.

WEILER, P. 1982. "Promises to Keep: Securing Workers' Right to Self-Organization under the NLRA." *Harvard Law Review, 96:* 1,769-1,827.

CHAPTER 6

THE HISTORY OF THE CANADIAN LABOUR MOVEMENT

DESMOND MORTON

Unions in Canada have been shaped by history. Like unions everywhere, they are products of political, economic, and social circumstances. Their three phases of development—from craft through industrial to public service unionism—have been responses to stages in the Canadian economy and to the willingness of governments and legislatures to respect the right of workers to organize.

Union effectiveness also depends on the state of the labour market. In Canada, labour's economic weakness has often led to increased political involvement. Bargaining and political action have proved to be mutually supportive activities.

International unions, a unique feature of Canada's labour history, emerged naturally from the integration of the North American labour market. The erection of barriers on human movement, even as trade barriers were declining, cut into the logic of international unionism and has led to its recent dramatic decline.

The past is a player in industrial relations. We got here from there through evolving institutions, practices, and values. With us on the journey came souvenirs of past victories and defeats, old betrayals, and recollected heroism. The details of such battles as the Winnipeg General Strike or the struggles of Cape Breton miners may be recalled fuzzily or inaccurately, but their potency as inspiration is undiluted.

Canadian historians of labour are engrossed by the issues of nationalism, political action, and union structure. Did the triumph of international unionism in 1902 delay the emergence of a radical, mass-based Canadian labour movement? Has the commitment to political action outside the traditional parties characterized Canadian unionism or merely divided it? Has the acceptance of parliamentary politics and a legalistic structure of industrial relations given Canadian unionism legitimate influence or eroded its revolutionary potential? Such might-have-beens of history are more than intriguing diversions; they reflect choices made, challenged, and sometimes reversed over more than a century of Canadian labour's evolution. They matter still.

FORMATIVE YEARS

Individuals and Groups

Industrial relations reflect a conflict between groups and individual interests. North America offered a paradise to the individual: freedom from custom, a promise of cheap land, the myth that anyone could make a fortune. Backbreaking labour in the woods or in canal- or railway-building was a means to ultimate ownership of a farm or business or the status of contractor. To accept the permanent status of a hired person was to fail the challenge of the new country (Baldwin 1972; Fingard 1974; Morton 1990).

Yet circumstances cried out for co-operation and organization. Without neighbourly support, pioneer life was unendurable. Immigrants needed communal associations such as the St George's Society or the Orange Order for help in finding work and for support in illness and bereavement. Workers in the same trade collected funds to meet the cost of sickness, funerals, or unemployment. Trades organized to accompany members on their final journey. "We Bury Our Dead" boasted Quebec's Ship-Labourers' Benevolent Society (Cooper 1949). We know most about early unions from accounts of the processions, picnics, and banquets they organized to heighten their members' self-esteem and pleasure. "United to Support, Not Combined to Injure" proclaimed Canada's oldest surviving local union, the Toronto Typographers (Forsey 1982; Zerker 1981).

Only scarcity or special skills allowed workers more than a subsistence wage. Skills were scarce in nineteenth-century Canada, and so was labour when immigration lagged behind a cyclical boom. "People of the same trade," noted Adam Smith, "seldom meet together, even for merriment or diversion, but the conversation ends in some conspiracy against the public or in some contrivance to raise prices." Workers, even when united for benevolent ends, fulfilled Smith's expectation. Politely worded newspaper advertisements sometimes notified employers of the new rate for printers or carpenters. Saint John ship-labourers, claims E.A. Forsey (1982), "ruled the port with a rod of iron," setting their rates and quitting work in a body to attend any member's funeral. Toronto printers fought and generally won a struggle for their rate: 33 cents per thousand ems of handset type (Zerker 1981). Coopers, moulders, and glass-blowers set their own pace. Glass-blowers insisted on a "Blue Monday" to recover from the weekend, with a promise to "Give her Hell" on Tuesday and the rest of the week (Kealey 1980; Morton 1990; Palmer 1979).

Early Unions

Common law and colonial statutes agreed with Adam Smith: union rate-setting was conspiracy in restraint of trade. A strike challenged a master's authority over his servants. An employee who left his master's service without permission could go to prison. If such laws were only rarely enforced, perhaps it was because they were not necessary. Early labour organizations in Canada were tiny, local, and even scant. Except at moments of provocation, Canadians were law-abiding. Changes came in the mid-nineteenth century. H.A. Pentland (1981) argues that after 1850 a modern industrial economy began to emerge in Canada, made possible by canals and particularly by railways. Certainly railways added to labour mobility and made it year-round. Workers soon had personal experience of wage rates and working conditions in Boston, New York, and Chicago. Mobility made locally based unionism ineffective (Forsey 1982).

As usual, the institution emerged to fit the times. "New Model" unionism, represented by the Amalgamated Society of Engineers (ASE) in Great Britain and by such American imitations as the Moulders' Union, emerged in the 1850s with high dues, strong centralized leadership, and a goal of organizing an entire craft. Both established branches or locals in Canada. Skilled tradesmen on the Grand Trunk Railway brought ASE connections with them from England. In 1863, William Sylvis toured Canada to add locals to his Moulders' Union. Typographers, carpenters, painters, coopers, the shoemakers of the Knights of St Crispin, and other craft organizations had Canadian affiliates by 1870. "New Model" unionism was craft-based, protecting better-paid workers from the perennial fear of dilution, replacement, or technological obsolescence. For thirty years, the Moulders' Union fought employers for the right to hire their own "bucks" (helpers). How else could they keep moulders in scarce supply? (Forsey 1982; Kealey 1973a; Langdon 1973; Morton 1990; Palmer 1979)

Workers could also identify common concerns. The anticonspiracy law threatened all unions. Mass immigration undermined wages. The narrow, property-based franchise excluded workingmen from political power and assaulted their self-respect. A city-wide trades assembly or "labour union" was a platform for ambitious leaders or for politicians currying favour (Forsey 1982; Langdon 1973).

The Nine-Hour Movement

The Confederation era combined high hopes and unusual prosperity, at least in central Canada. The atmosphere encouraged union leaders in Toronto, Hamilton, and Montreal, as well as smaller centres, to create central organizations. In 1872, Hamilton's John Ryan proposed that such organization make a co-ordinated bid for a nine-hour day. The scheme was too ambitious. In Hamilton, employers fought back. Toronto printers jumped the gun and struck their old enemy, George Brown of the *Globe*. In turn, Brown charged the strike leaders with conspiracy, and the nine-hour movement was forgotten in the excitement. Happy to embarrass his leading Liberal antagonist, Sir John A. Macdonald, the Tory prime minister, adapted British Liberal legislation and gave Canada the Trade Unions Act, legalizing union activity. The legality, however, was meagre, and the act was matched by another law making most strike activity a criminal offence (Battye 1979; Ostry 1960; Palmer 1983; Zerker 1981).

Though the nine-hour movement failed, it inspired Toronto labour leaders in 1873 to summon delegates to form a Canadian Labour Union (CLU). The cost of travel limited representation to Ontario, but the CLU's debates presaged union concerns for a century to come: the need to organize, the problems of apprenticeship, the dangers from mass immigration, and the novel proposition that workers should have their own members of Parliament. Such concerns were premature. Although the CLU could boast legislative achievements—repeal of the harsh Master and Servants' Act in 1877, for one—it perished with many other labour organizations during the depression of the 1870s. Such union leaders as survived were drawn into campaigning for or against the Conservatives' panacea for a restored prosperity, the National Policy of high tariffs to protect domestic manufacturing (Forsey 1982; Morton 1990; Ostry 1960).

The Knights of Labour

Craft unions revived slowly in the 1880s, but their progress was overshadowed by the influx of a new kind of organization, the Holy and Noble Order of the Knights of Labour. Founded in Philadelphia in 1868 as a secret society, the Knights grew slowly until 1879 when new leaders persuaded the Order to dilute its principles and abandon its tight rules of secrecy. With the North American economy in full recovery, the timing was ideal. So was the Knights' mixture of radical idealism and practical caution. The Knights preached the fundamental worth of a "co-operative commonwealth." Unlike craft unions, the Knights opened their assemblies without distinction of race, sex, or skill, excluding only lawyers, bankers, and tavern keepers. At the same time, organizers and lecturers preached patience, moderation, and the need for thorough education in the Order's principles. Strikes were considered a desperate last resort; far better for unhappy workers to create their own co-operative industries (Forsey 1982; Kealey and Palmer 1982; Morton 1990; Palmer 1983).

The first Knights entered Canada as early as 1875. "Mixed assemblies" for workers of all trades were ideal for Canadian towns too small to support a local of carpenters or moulders. The Knights profited from whatever industrial boom the National Policy fostered; they also benefited from the revulsion at harsh working conditions, frequent accidents, and the exploitation of female and child workers. Canadians in the mid-1880s had a surprising appetite for radical talk. Assemblies of Knights were formed from Halifax to Victoria. In Montreal, the Knights used pressure from the Vatican to overcome the hostility of the local Catholic hierarchy. As the Chevaliers du Travail, they became a force in French Canada (Desrosiers and Héroux 1973; Kealey 1980; Kealey and Palmer 1982; Morton 1990; Palmer 1983).

The Knights' passion for education generated newspapers, lecturers, and Canada's first social critic with an international reputation, T. Phillips Thompson. Liberals and Conservatives respected labour's apparent strength, adopting the first factory safety legislation in Ontario in 1886 and in Quebec in 1887, extending the franchise, and choosing a few Knights as candidates. A federal royal commission investigated the relations of capital and labour. Even if its recommendations were ignored, it provided contemporaries (and historians) with evidence of industrial conditions, such as the beatings administered by a Montreal cigarmaker to his young workers or the debt-ridden circumstances of Cape Breton miners. By 1894, Labour Day (the first Monday in September) had become a statutory holiday in recognition of the Knights' most basic proposition: the dignity of labour (Hann 1976; Kealey 1973a; Kealey and Palmer 1982; Morton 1990; Palmer 1983).

The order sank, however, as quickly as it had risen. In fact, its thousands of members rarely stayed long. In Canada, it never had more than 20,000 members at any one time, but as many as 100,000 men and women may have belonged at some point or other. The flood of members could never be indoctrinated with the Knights' principles. Instead, they struck employers or were locked out, and when defeat soon followed, craft union leaders were confirmed in their suspicions that the unskilled could not be organized and the "industrial" union was misconceived. In larger cities such as Hamilton, political activity led to shattering disputes. Personal rivalry and the perennial conflict between purity and pragmatism undermined the Knights and the wider organizations they influenced. In the United States more than in Canada, employers exploited differences between the Knights and the other craft unions, organized after 1886 in the American Federation of Labour (AFL). By the 1890s, the Knights were defunct in the United States and a fading remnant in Canada (Desrosiers and Héroux 1973; Forsey 1982; Kealey and Palmer 1982; Palmer 1979).

Trades and Labour

The AFL president, Sam Gompers, drew two lessons from the Knights: partisan politics and "dual unionism" (two unions organizing the same industry) were fatal to a sound labour organization. Canadians tried to find a compromise. In 1883 and again in 1886, the Toronto Trades and Labour Council summoned a "national" congress. From 1886, the Trades and Labour Congress of Canada (TLC) would meet annually as "the Parliament of Canadian Labour," passing policies and promoting them as best it could in Ottawa and the provincial capitals. Delegates called for shorter hours of work, enforcement of factory acts, control of European immigration, and an absolute ban on Oriental immigrants. Restricting the labour market was justified as the workers' counterpart to the tariff. Unionists also sought free education for children and exclusion of women from dangerous factory and mining jobs. Humanitarianism would shrink the labour market. The TLC also wanted the Senate abolished and the franchise extended, and it proposed such democratic innovations as proportional representation and the use of referenda (Forsey 1982; Morton 1990).

From the first, TLC leaders promoted their policies by lobbying governments in what they soon dubbed "cap in hand" sessions. Frustration led some of them to call for direct labour representation; the tiny clutch of unionists elected between 1887 and 1900 as Conservatives or Liberals proved so ineffective that the alternative of a "labour" party and program became more persuasive. Still, unionism in the 1890s was mainly talk. A renewed depression reduced the remaining Knights' assemblies to paper organizations and left even hardened craft unions struggling to protect their members and their cherished funds (Forsey 1982; Morton 1990; Robin 1968).

Hinterland Unions

Despite the young TLC's claim to be a national body, it spoke only for central Canada. Locals of craft unions could be found from Halifax (and St John's in the separate Dominion of Newfoundland) to Victoria, but they had little impact on the resource industries, which under the National Policy, were expected to feed the factories of central Canada.

Coal mining, vital to running the new railways and factories and to heating the homes of prairie settlers, involved skilled and dangerous work, but the miners were isolated and at the mercy of operators. James Dunsmuir, developer of Vancouver Island coal mines, could count on the Royal Navy and the militia to protect strikebreakers. When white labour failed him, Dunsmuir recruited Chinese. Anger at scabs joined racism as a factor in anti-Oriental prejudice among British Columbia workers (Bowen 1982; Morton 1990; Phillips 1967; Robin 1968).

In Nova Scotia, there was no Dunsmuir, the Orient was too remote to supply labour, and most mining companies were small. That helped the Provincial Workmen's Association (PWA), founded by miners in 1879, to survive bitter strikes, employer resistance, and the corrosive rivalry between Cape Breton and the mainland. In Halifax, the PWA obtained major legislative gains in mine safety, education, and working conditions. Its nemesis was the Dominion Coal Company, a conglomerate that bought up small operators, tamed the PWA, and reduced it to a dutiful dependent surviving on dues collected by the employer (Canadian Labour Congress 1976; McKay 1986).

GROWTH AND DIVISION

From 1873 to 1896, Canada had experienced substantial economic expansion despite a pervading atmosphere of hard times. In 1896, a change of government coincided with a dramatic improvement in the market for Canada's natural products. The new Liberal government of Wilfrid Laurier found itself floating on a wave of prosperity. Factories expanded. The west, painfully opened by the Conservatives, now received hosts of settlers. A single transcontinental railway was not enough; by 1914, Canada had three (Avery 1979; Morton 1990).

Canadian workers shared the mood but not the benefits. Seeking to gain a share, they found an ally in Sam Gompers's AFL, which was in the full flood of an organizing drive in the United States. Worried that US corporations would turn to cheap, unorganized Canadian labour, Gompers commissioned a Hamilton carpenter and socialist, John Flett, as a full-time AFL organizer. Flett's whirlwind campaign from 1898 to 1900 left a host of new union locals from Charlottetown to Windsor. In many communities today, the history of unionism dates from Flett's visit. Part-time AFL organizers added to his total (Babcock 1975; Forsey 1982; Palmer 1979; 1983).

The Berlin Convention

Employers, politicians, and rival unionists objected to the AFL invasion. Ralph Smith, the first British Columbian president of the TLC and a Liberal-Labour MP, wanted a Canadian Federation of Labour, equal to and independent from the AFL. The issue was addressed at the TLC's 1902 convention in Berlin (now Kitchener, Ontario). Flett had urged his young locals to affiliate. Older delegates were angry that some of Smith's supporters represented defunct unions. Even his Nanaimo union denied him credentials. In the showdown, Smith was defeated (Babcock 1975; Forsey 1982).

The Berlin meeting affected only a few thousand unionists. The TLC and its conventions had never been taken very seriously. The 1902 decision, however, was historic. Henceforth, craft unions with headquarters in the United States ("international unions") would dominate the TLC. The Knights and other Canadian unions "dual" to AFL organizations were forced to found their own "national" organization called the National Trades and Labour Congress (soon changed to the Canadian Federation of Labour). It was a feeble alternative, but as a rival to the TLC, it gave Canada most of the problems of "dual unionism." Meanwhile employers mustered nationalist arguments against AFL-style unionism.

A later generation of historians would dismiss the Berlin decision as the result of American meddling. Yet the fact remains that Canadian unionists ran the Berlin convention and made choices that seemed logical. They wanted to share a North American standard of living. In time, of course, employers came to tolerate Gompers's brand of unionism, which offered stability and moderation in contract negotiations and a cautious reformism in the political arena (Babcock 1975; Forsey 1982; Heron 1984; Morton 1990; Palmer 1979).

Radical Internationals

Moderation was not the philosophy of all international unions. Gompers's bitter enemies, the Western Federation of Miners (WFM), invaded British Columbia's hard-rock mining industry. The radical United Brotherhood of Railroad Employees tried to organize the Canadian Pacific Railway. Later, the Industrial Workers of the World (IWW) waged free-speech fights in Edmonton, Victoria, and other western cities. It also recruited supporters among construction crews, loggers, and the "bunkhouse men" who developed the western Canadian infrastructure. An AFL affiliate, the United Mineworkers (UMW), built locals in Alberta coal mines, but it was checkmated in a year-long struggle to oust the Provincial Workmen's Association in Nova Scotia in 1909/10 and in an even more brutal struggle to bring any kind of unionism to Vancouver Island in 1913/14 (Avery 1979; MacEwan 1976; McCormack 1978; Phillips 1967).

The years just before 1914 saw some of the most violent and extensive strikes in Canadian history. Thousands of troops and police had to guard docks and factories, coal mines and streetcars while employers used strikebreakers to tame unions. Canadian business echoed the contemporary American fashion for scientific management, labour-saving devices, and frontal assaults on the right to organize. Unions in Toronto, Hamilton, and other major cities suffered serious setbacks. They responded with a new political militancy. In union halls, speakers passionately debated whether unions, with their moderate demands, would delay the revolution. Socialists, radicals, and straight "labourists" had different prescriptions, but the power and the obvious injustices of Canadian capitalism furnished a common target (Heron and Palmer 1977; Heron 1984; Piva 1979; Robin 1968).

Mackenzie King and the IDI Act

Labour turbulence demanded a political response. In 1900, Laurier's government created a tiny Department of Labour, in part to oversee arbitration of railway labour disputes. William Lyon Mackenzie King became editor of the new *Labour Gazette*, beginning a public career dedicated, by his own account, to the service of the underprivileged and the Liberal party. King was a fussy bachelor and a careerist; he was also a brilliant mediator with a strong belief that publicity could be a useful ally in pushing opponents into a settlement. King soon became the government's all-purpose industrial peacemaker. In the process, he found that some employers and most union radicals were unreasonable. He also failed to see why the issue of union recognition could ever justify a strike (Craven 1981; Dawson 1958; Ferns and Ostry 1975; Whittaker 1977).

In 1907, after a prolonged Alberta coal strike had brought prairie residents to the verge of freezing, King embodied his hard-earned wisdom in the Industrial Disputes Investigation (IDI) Act. The IDI Act met a demand urged for years by the TLC: government investigation of industrial disputes. The act gave weak unions a chance to face an employer and state their case in a period when strikes were usually hopeless. However, as American unions had learned, an arrangement that gave employers time to continue operations, stockpile product, train strikebreakers, and victimize union activists left workers at a serious disadvantage. The AFL's efforts to warn the TLC largely failed; for the time being, labour joined the chorus of praise for King and his new law. On the strength of his achievement, King entered Parliament in 1908 and soon became minister of labour. When he was defeated in 1911, he founded a new career helping the Rockefeller family with its labour problems. King's ingenuity led him to advocate "employee representation plans" as a substitute for "unreasonable" unions. Ironically, this Canadian invention became better know in the 1920s as "the American Plan" (Craven 1981; Dawson 1958; Ferns and Ostry 1975).

The First World War

By 1913, the Laurier boom had burst. The two newest transcontinental railways skidded towards bankruptcy and threatened to take the rest of Canada's economy with them. By 1914, the jobless outnumbered the 170,000 union members. Although the TLC had condemned the war as a capitalist plot, when it came in August, unionists enlisted or joined employers in a clamour for war contracts. By 1916, a brand-new munitions industry struggled to meet the wartime appetite for artillery shells. The new Imperial Munitions Board faced such a labour shortage that it had to dream up ingenious ways to entice women into its factories. Wages equal to men's were promised, although seldom delivered. When Ottawa attempted to finance the war effort by borrowing and increasing the money supply, prices almost doubled. So did wages, though more slowly and only for workers with bargaining power (Morton 1990; Thompson 1978).

Unionism had always been strong in metal manufacturing; in the munitions industry, membership soared, particularly in the International Association of Machinists (IAM). Unionism also spread to the civil service, to the employees of the burgeoning telephone companies, even to police forces. The IDI Act, extended to all war industries, encouraged organization even as it curbed strikes. By 1917, unionists had a fresh grievance; not only had Ottawa introduced conscription without consulting the TLC leadership, but it had also ignored the British and American example of bringing labour into the nation's councils. One response—offering labour candidates in the 1917 election—proved a humiliating failure. Not one was elected. Militants had another strategy. Some had long been convinced that the general strike could be labour's decisive weapon. In the summer of 1918, Winnipeg workers gave the idea a modest tryout; in a few days, with backing from sympathetic citizens, civic employees won the right to organize (Bercuson 1974; Siemiatckyi 1978; Thompson 1978).

Union leaders in the west had usually been more radical than their eastern counterparts. By the end of the war in 1918, they were full of fight. When the TLC met in Quebec City that year, however, eastern moderates prevailed. Radical wartime leaders were defeated, and Tom Moore, a Niagara Falls carpenter, began a presidency that would last almost without interruption until 1943. Indignant westerners agreed to meet in Calgary in March 1919 to plot a counterattack. Some were more ambitious. The Calgary meeting launched plans for a wholesale western secession from the TLC to form One Big Union (OBU) free of craft jurisdictional barriers, business union values, and eastern moderation (Bercuson 1974; 1978; McCormack 1978).

The Winnipeg General Strike

Plans for the OBU were still taking shape when Winnipeg members of the IAM decided on a second general strike, this time to force recognition from their employers. The tactic fitted the mood of Winnipeg's working men and women. At 11:00 on May 15, 1919, between 25,000 and 30,000 Winnipeggers walked out—twice as many as even held union cards (Bercuson 1974; McNaught and Bercuson 1974).

This time, neither citizens nor government were tolerant. The war was over, Europe was in turmoil, and politicians and property owners alike were terrified by claims that Russia's Bolshevik revolution would spread. When the strike committee authorized provision of essential services to prevent charges of strikebreaking, it was promptly denounced for usurping government authority. War veterans ignored union appeals for calm and demonstrated in the streets for (and against) the strike. Penniless workers trickled back to work. The government fired striking postal workers; the city dismissed unionized policemen. The railway unions ordered members back to work on pain of losing their union-run pensions. In predawn raids on June 17, police seized real and presumed strike leaders. When strikers and their families gathered to protest, mounted police charged down Main Street and special constables followed. A few days after Bloody Saturday, on June 26, the strike ended (Bercuson 1974; McNaught and Bercuson 1974).

After a brief, heady start in the wake of the strike, the One Big Union idea died too. As a bargaining strategy, the general strike was discredited, and the OBU had little else to offer. In much of postwar Canada, labour turned to conventional politics. In 1921, north-end Winnipeg sent J.S. Woodsworth to Parliament. A pacifist clergyman, he had been arrested for editing the strike newspaper. In Nova Scotia, Ontario, Manitoba, Alberta, and British Columbia, labour won more provincial seats than ever before. In Ontario and Alberta, labour members joined farmers to form governments. A few cautious reforms followed; on the whole, however, the farmers' predilection for low taxes, cheap government, and the prohibition of liquor made alliances fragile and unproductive (Bercuson 1978; Robin 1968).

Labour in the 1920s

Postwar Canadian labour was almost as conservative as the farmers. Wartime membership evaporated. The OBU schism confirmed the moderates' control of the TLC. Divisions and disillusionment with postwar provincial alliances confirmed Gompers's old warnings against political action. Instead of threatening Liberals or Conservatives, TLC leaders now preferred to lobby for influence and favours (Robin 1968).

The OBU was not the only split. In 1921, the TLC's biggest Canadian affiliate, The Canadian Brotherhood of Railroad Employees (CBRE), was denounced as a dual union by the AFL's Brotherhood of Railroad and Steamship Clerks (BRSC) and forced out of the TLC. Aaron Mosher, the CBRE's leader, swept up the fragments of national unionism left over from the 1902 Berlin decision and, in 1926, formed the aggressively nationalist All-Canadian Congress of Labour (ACCL) (Logan 1948; Morton 1990). In Quebec, the Catholic hierarchy had been trying to build a confessional union movement since 1900; at first their efforts had borne little fruit, but the war and the conscription crisis gave the movement a powerful impetus. In 1921, the Catholic *syndicats* (unions) formed a central organization, the Confédération des travailleurs catholiques du Canada (CTCC), and added a new aspect to the discordant voice of Canadian Labour (Latham 1930; Rouillard 1981). A Canadian Communist party was also formed in 1921. Its early policy of trying to dominate craft unions and TLC conventions by boring from within led to failure and frequent expulsions. In 1927, Moscow ordered a new policy of "parallel unionism." When an attempt to capture Mosher's new organization failed, the Communists founded the Workers' Unity League (WUL) (Avakumovic 1975; Liversedge 1973; Robin 1968; Rodney 1968).

A labour movement fragmented among craft, Catholic, nationalist, and revolutionary organizations had little influence on government or employers. In Nova Scotia, the United Mineworkers had finally supplanted the PWA in 1917, but it soon fell victim to internal divisions, ruthless wage-cutting by absentee owners, and a series of strikes that reduced Cape Breton miners to literal starvation by 1926. Later, miners would claim that they had defied a boast by the local manager that they could not "stand the gaff." At the time, there was more misery than defiance (Liversedge 1973; MacEwan 1976).

Not only unions fragmented in the 1920s. In 1926 the Judicial Committee of the Privy Council decided, in the Snider case, that labour relations were in the constitutional domain of the provinces, not Ottawa. Rival systems soon emerged (Liversedge 1973).

The Great Depression

Beginning in 1928 with a largely unsold wheat crop, Canada's resource-based economy unravelled in the face of a world-wide depression. Few Canadians were unaffected, though the worst impact fell on the young, on the unskilled, and on westerners. Considering the extent of the disaster, union membership proved surprisingly robust, falling by only one-eighth, from 319,000 in 1929 to 281,000 in 1935 (see Figure 7.1). Initially, wage rates fell more slowly than prices. For the TLC and most of its rivals, the Great Depression was no time to organize. The exception was the WUL. At Estevan, Saskatchewan; at Stratford, Ontario; at Flin Flon, Manitoba; at Noranda, Quebec; and at Blubber Bay, British Columbia, its efforts ended in bloodshed and defeat, but the setbacks added to Canada's sparse tradition of class struggle. Among miners and lumber workers and especially among newer immigrants from eastern Europe, the WUL won occasional victories. Communists also organized the unemployed and the "Royal Twenty-Centers," the wretchedly paid inmates of government relief camps (Abella 1974; Avakumovic 1975; Dumas 1975; Liversedge 1973).

The Great Depression inspired some Canadians to hunt for remedies. Enthusiasts explored technocracy, monetary schemes, and religious salvation. Socialists, reformers, agrarian radicals, and the remnants of local labour parties met in Calgary in 1932 and in Regina in 1933 to create the Co-operative Commonwealth Federation (CCF). Its leader was Winnipeg's Labour MP, J.S. Woodsworth. Organized labour was cool. The presence of Aaron Mosher at the CCF's Calgary meeting was excuse enough for the TLC to reject the new party (Young 1969). Most Canadians, made nervous and conservative by the crisis, preferred leaders, such as Duff Pattullo of British Columbia and Mitch Hepburn of Ontario, who mixed a populist concern for "the little guy" with support for old-fashioned values (McKenty 1967).

| FIGURE 6.1 | Union Members as a Percentage of All Nonagricultural Workers, Canada, 1917–1993 |

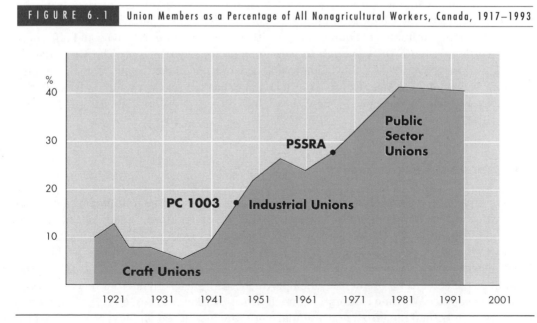

In the spring of 1933, Communists sent unemployed workers on what became known as the "On-to-Ottawa" trek. On July 1, it ended in bloodshed at Regina. Voters sympathized with the men, not with their leaders (Avakumovic 1975). With the slogan "King or Chaos," the Liberals easily defeated the depression-era government of R.B. Bennett (Liversedge 1973; Morton 1990; and Bullen 1984).

INDUSTRIAL UNIONS

The CIO in Canada

In 1935, a series of distant events affected Canadian labour. Moscow ordered its followers to join existing labour organizations to fight the rising menace of fascism. Canada's Communists obediently dissolved the WUL. In Washington, the Wagner Act became law. American labour could now turn to a National Labor Relations Board to force obdurate employers to recognize a democratically chosen union. The new law, plus ingenuity and courage, allowed organizers to crack open the huge industrial plants and mills that had defied unionization for sixty years. Organizing committees, ignoring old barriers of craft and trade, appropriated the image of a popular president in their campaigns. Franklin Delano Roosevelt, they claimed, would want workers to sign a card. In an angry split from the reactionary, craft-dominated AFL, the new unions and some older allies formed the Congress of Industrial Organizations (CIO) in 1937 (Abella 1973; MacDowell 1978).

In Canada news of organizing victories in Akron, Flint, and Pittsburgh made the CIO sound like magic. In the spring of 1937, workers at the big General Motors plant in Oshawa, near Toronto, signed up in the CIO's United Auto Workers and demanded a contract. Resistance came less from the company than from Ontario Premier Hepburn, who was convinced that the CIO was a Communist conspiracy bent on paralyzing the province's industry and its profitable gold mines. Faced with a strike, a penniless CIO could offer only brave words and bluff—just enough to win a compromise settlement. The CIO drive in Canada was largely stifled. A slowly improving economy, however, revived labour militancy, from Valleyfield, Quebec, where a Catholic union battled textile manufacturers, to the Great Lakes, where seamen formed their first effective union (Abella 1973; 1974; Kaplan 1987).

The Second World War

Canada entered the Second World War in September 1939, although its impact hit home only with the Nazi blitzkrieg in the spring of 1940. War again lifted Canada out of an economic depression. In 1939, one worker in six was unemployed; by 1941 the labour shortage was so acute that Ottawa imposed selective service on men and women. A burst of inflation was curbed by price controls, wages frozen at 1925-29 levels, high taxes, and the premiums collected for a brand new unemployment insurance scheme that no one in 1941 actually needed. Wartime orders-in-council froze workers in essential occupations, removed able-bodied men from nonessential employment, curbed employers' rights to hire and fire, and limited employees' rights to quit or switch jobs.

A fragmented labour movement met the war in fragmented ways. The TLC leaders stayed close to Mackenzie King and his labour minister, Humphrey Mitchell. Communist unionists, on Moscow's orders, tried to disrupt the war effort, but when Hitler invaded the Soviet Union in 1941, they switched sides and demanded a no-strike pledge. Members of the CCF backed the war effort but also saw it as a time to make union and political gains. As thousand of workers joined war industries to produce ships, guns, radios, radar sets, and most of the British Army's vehicles, union gains were possible. The CIO unions found the opportunity they had lost in 1937, but craft unions too joined the organizing rush, forgetting jurisdictional principles in the process. By 1944, Canada had 744,000 union members, twice the 1939 total (Abella 1973; Avakumovic 1975; Copp 1976; MacDowell 1978; 1983; Morton 1990; Young 1969).

The National War Labour Order

The war years posed problems for unions. Fragmentation increased in 1939 when the TLC, at AFL insistence, expelled its CIO affiliates. They promptly joined Mosher's organization to form the Canadian Congress of Labour (CCL). The result was a sixteen-year rivalry, political division, and ultimately, much raiding. Neither was labour benefited by the hostility of King's powerful minister of munitions, C.D. Howe. He and the dollar-a-year executives who managed the wartime economy and employers such as H.G. Hilton of the Steel Company of Canada had no intention of allowing "a war for freedom" to be won by unions. In 1941/2, a midwinter strike taught the gold miners at Kirkland Lake, Ontario, that they would get no help from the government even when employers behaved unfairly. And when unions were formed, they were bound by wartime wage controls (MacDowell 1978; 1983; Webber 1985).

In 1943, with the war's outcome no longer in doubt, some unions rebelled. In January, the United Steelworkers struck for 55 cents an hour. Howe fumed, but the government gave in. Jailed workers could hardly pour steel. More strikes followed, until 1943 came close to 1919 as a year of labour conflict (see Figure 6.2). The prime minister turned to the National War Labour Board. Its chairman, Judge C.P. McTague, had seen the injustice at Kirkland Lake. His report was clear: Canada needed an equivalent to the United States' Wagner Act to avoid strikes over the basic right to organize (MacDowell 1978; 1982).

For King, convinced of the perfection of his IDI Act, the advice was painful. It was also painfully clear that workers were deserting the Liberals for a growing CCF. In 1943, the CCF had narrowly missed victory in Ontario; months later it led both older parties in the polls and won formal endorsement from the Canadian Congress of Labour. The message was clear: King moved his party to the left. In 1944, Liberals endorsed family allowances, promised universal health and hospital insurance, and guaranteed to deliver "high and stable levels of employment" in postwar Canada. For labour, King approved PC 1003, the National War Labour Order, in February 1944. As McTague had urged, Canadian workers would have clear rules to govern the definition of bargaining units, the certification and recognition of units, and the enforcement of fair labour practices, at least while the war lasted. PC 1003 also included the IDI Act principles of a cooling-off period and

FIGURE 6.2   Percentage of Estimated Total Working Time Lost from Strikes and Lockouts, Canada, 1913–1993

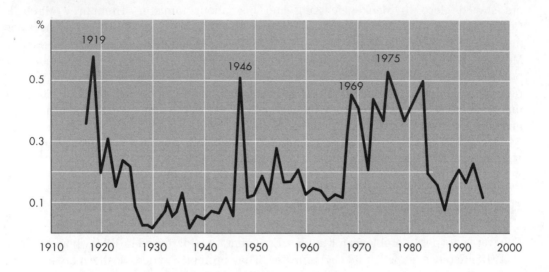

investigation, if only to reassure King. Translated into a federal statute in 1948 and adapted and modified by all ten provinces (see Chapter 3), the 1944 regulation became the unintended foundation of modern Canadian industrial relations (MacDowell 1978; Pickersgill 1977; Young 1969).

The Rand Formula

When peace returned in 1945, union gains were in jeopardy. Many Canadians feared a return to the Depression. Employers included unions among the wartime burdens they hoped to escape.

A union might be certified, but its effectiveness depended on financial backing. In the fall of 1945, the United Auto Workers struck the Ford Motor Company to win a guaranteed checkoff of dues from every employee. A long struggle, made famous by a mass car blockade of the factory, ended in arbitration. Justice Ivan Rand scolded the union for its tactics but conceded that its representation benefited every worker in the plant. Every worker there must pay dues, he ruled, though no one should be forced to join the union. The Rand formula ("agency shop") became a basis for union security in Canada (Jantzi 1978; Morton 1990; Moulton 1974).

Postwar Strikes

Instead of falling into postwar depression, Canada entered a boom. People spent wartime savings to satisfy fifteen years of yearning for homes, cars, refrigerators, and even kitchen tables. When the young industrial unions co-ordinated their 1946 bargaining strategy, they faced employers who could sell anything they could find workers to produce. Certainly, business fought union demands. So did King's government, narrowly re-elected in 1945, but a booming economy made resistance painful. British Columbia woodworkers, Great Lakes sailors, textile workers at Valleyfield, Quebec, and steelworkers at Hamilton and Sault Ste Marie, Ontario, and Sydney, Nova Scotia, helped make 1946 one of Canada's most costly years for strikes (1919 and 1976 were comparable—see Figure 7.2). The rubber industry lost 800,000 days of production. More strikes followed in 1947. Not all the labour struggles were victorious. Cape Breton and Namaimo miners and Nova Scotia fishermen lost bitter battles (Abella 1973; Copp 1976; Frank 1983; Morton 1990).

Yet the postwar strikes saw little of the violence and desperation of earlier labour struggles. Even at Hamilton, where Stelco's mill was blockaded for weeks, a veteran labour mayor and a well-managed police force cooled tensions. Strikes were long, but settlements were realistic compromises. Communist, CCF, and nonpartisan unions differed little in their bargaining tactics or their results. By 1948 it was clear that unions had become as normal in Canadian manufacturing as they had been in construction and on the railways. Their members would share the postwar prosperity (Jantzi 1978; Morton 1990; Palmer 1983).

Labour's Cold War

Bargaining strategies temporarily hid the bitter political rivalries in the postwar labour movement. Communists and CCFers had battled ever since the 1930s. C.H. Millard, driven from the Oshawa local he had led in 1937, rebuilt the Steelworkers in Canada as a pillar of the CCF. Communists used their influence to nullify the CCL endorsement of the CCF. In 1945, opportune alliances between Liberals and Communists undermined CCF hopes of victory in working-class constituencies. Long before the Cold War made anticommunism fashionable, Millard and other CCF unionists were bent on driving Communists from power in the labour movement (Abella 1972; Horowitz 1968; Young 1969).

Aided by developing suspicion of the Communists and by the Communists' own misjudgment, CCFers and nonpartisan allies ended Communist influence in the CCL and its affiliates by 1950. In the TLC, the Communist issue focused on the Canadian Seamen's Union (CSU). At first, TLC leaders defended the Communist-run union, even after Pat Sullivan, its president and a TLC secretary-treasurer, publicly confessed that the union had called strikes to support Soviet policy. Finally, brutal pressure from the AFL and exasperation at CSU tactics led the TLC president, Percy Bengough, to change sides. With help from Ottawa and the shipping companies, who turned a blind eye to illegal and gangster tactics, the AFL's Seafarers' International Union (SIU) wiped out the Canadian union (Abella 1973; Jantzi 1978; Sullivan 1955).

What had begun as a struggle between democratic socialists and Communists was caught up in the cold war. Some Communist-run unions, notably the United Electrical Workers (UEW) and the United Fishermen and Allied Workers (UFAW) survived expulsion to rejoin the Canadian Labour Congress in 1972. Others dissolved into anti-Communist unions. In the process, many of the differences between TLC and CCL affiliates faded. Wartime organizing had already blurred distinctions between craft and industrial principles. Industrial unions, such as the UAW, had to deal separately with skilled trades groups; the IAM, a craft union, signed up thousands of unskilled workers. From 1940, both congresses were dominated by international unions. Both had eliminated Communist influences, endorsed Canada's commitment to the North Atlantic Treaty Organization (NATO), and accepted the potential and limits of free collective bargaining in a mixed economy. Both congresses pledged themselves to reunion of what American pressure had split asunder in 1939. Only the CCL's link to the CCF and the personal antipathy of two old men, Bengough and Mosher, now kept the two groups apart (Abella 1973; Copp 1980; Finkelman and Goldenberg 1983; Horowitz 1968).

The Asbestos Strike

If the TLC and CCL would reunite, Quebec's CTCC might join them. In 1949, a long, violent strike at Asbestos pitted the Catholic unions against the conservative, nationalist regime of Maurice Duplessis. Neither side gained much in the outcome, but a key segment of Quebec labour and intellectual opinion, represented by Jean Marchand and Pierre Elliot Trudeau, had broken with the old clerical nationalism of French Canada. The split was deepened when a Catholic union struck Dupuis Frères, a Quebec-owned department store. Like other Canadians, the Québécois wanted their share of prosperity, and their own nationalist labour organization was sharing the struggle. At Asbestos and elsewhere, unions could make common cause (Isbester 1971; Rouillard 1981; Trudeau 1974). (See Chapter 16.)

The Canadian Labour Congress

In the 1950s, union solidarity made sense. As membership totals had stabilized, unions were spending money raiding rivals instead of organizing the unorganized. With 350,000 members to the TLC's 522,000 in 1952, the CCL was not likely to catch up. Its drive to organize T. Eaton Company workers had ended in failure (Sufrin 1982). When Newfoundland joined Confederation in 1949, its few thousand union members were split between the congresses; neither could organize the new province (Hattenhauer, nd). Bengough's successor, Claude Jodoin, a Montrealer with experience in the textile unions, would be acceptable to the CCL and perhaps also to the Catholic confederation. Mosher's retirement, after an embarrassing quarrel in his own union, also cleared the decks. More important, unionists came to realize that progress in Canada depended on peace between the AFL and the CIO. In 1956, only weeks after the American organizations had united as the AFL-CIO, the Canadian Labour Congress (CLC) met at Toronto for its merger convention.

The biggest potential stumbling block, political action, was cautiously deferred to the CLC's second convention. By then, the federal CCF had been annihilated by John Diefenbaker's 1958 Conservative triumph. Over the grumbling of their rank and file, CCF leaders agreed to work with the Canadian Labour Congress to build a new party for labour, the CCF, and the "liberally minded." Three years of persuasion, organization, and education, helped by a serious recession and the conspicuous failures of the Diefenbaker government, built to a climax in August 1961, with the founding convention of the New

Democratic Party (NDP). Voters had a fresh-looking alternative, committed to full employment, medicare and hostility to nuclear weapons. The leader, Tommy Douglas, could remind labour audiences that, as premier of Saskatchewan, he had given his rural province the most advanced labour legislation in Canada. With the NDP launched, its CLC backers slipped discreetly away to renew lobbying contacts with whatever party held power. The NDP was left to find money and backers among old CCFers, new labour supporters, and a sceptical electorate (Horowitz 1968; Morton 1990; Young 1969).

UNIONS AND GOVERNMENTS

Union Setbacks

The high hopes of the merger movement were not realized. As Germany and Japan returned to world competition, Canada's postwar advantage quickly faded. Diefenbaker's electoral victories drew on a conservative, antiunion mood. The prestige of the new CLC could not stop Quebec's Duplessis from crushing an illegal strike at Murdochville in 1957 or Newfoundland's Joey Smallwood from decertifying the International Woodworkers of America (IWA) in the midst of a violent 1959 loggers' strike. The CLC could not even stop an affiliate, the Carpenters, from accepting Smallwood's invitation to take over the IWA's jurisdiction (Hattenhauer, nd; Kwavnick 1971). By 1960 Quebec's Catholic unions made it clear that merger was not for them. Instead, under Jean Marchand, they abandoned the last traces of confessionalism and emerged as the militant, nationalist Confédération des syndicats nationaux (CSN) or, in English, Confederation of National Trade Unions (CNTU). The decision was a portent of Quebec's future. (See Chapter 16.)

The Canadian Labour Congress suffered from other setbacks. Unions in Canada had prided themselves on their freedom from gangsterism. An ugly exception was the SIU. Its leader, Hal Banks, applied to rival unions the same brutal tactics that had beaten the CSU. Only in 1960 did the CLC expel the Seafarers, and then it had to plead for government help to end Banks's reign of terror. A royal commission reported seventy-five instances of violence and wondered pointedly why Canadian labour leaders had not complained earlier (Kaplan 1987; Kwavnick 1971).

Political action was another disappointment. In 1962, the NDP won only nineteen federal seats, and it fell to eighteen seats in 1963. Even after the party's electoral support climbed to 18 per cent in 1965, its parliamentary strength hovered at twenty seats, far short of the founding convention's hopes. Old CCFers blamed the trade union link; most CLC affiliates ignored labour's chosen party. In British Columbia, where the NDP made its biggest gains, a Social Credit government banned union financial contributions. In Ottawa, the NDP link allowed the Conservative government of John Diefenbaker to ignore CLC nominees for government appointments (Horowitz 1968; Kwavnick 1971; Morton 1990).

The best argument for merger in 1956 had been the need to organize, a problem that grew increasingly more difficult. In an antiunion climate, governments made certification harder. An Ontario legislature committee confessed in 1958 that its major concern in labour-management relations was "the preservation of public peace and the protection of the individual worker against oppression" (quoted in Morton 1990, 247). Oppression meant unions. Employers learned to drag out certification procedures. At Murdochville, copper miners had struck illegally only after waiting five years for recognition. Union membership grew slowly, but the share of potential membership fell sharply from 33.3 per cent of the labour force in 1956 to only 29.4 per cent in 1964 (Gérin-Lajoie 1982; Morton 1990).

If adding members seemed difficult in the early 1960s, losing them was easy. Technological change threatened entire occupations. Two desperate strikes could not save the Brotherhood of Locomotive Firemen from diesel engines. Toronto's typographers, members of Canada's oldest union, struck in 1964 against technological changes in the city's three newspapers. They lost. In 1965, even the most cautious of unions, the locomotive engineers, risked members' jobs to protest runthroughs made possible by new equipment. After investigation, Mr. Justice Samuel Freedman condemned an illegal strike but he also challenged the inviolability of a signed contract. Even during the life of a collective agreement, he argued, unions should be able to negotiate about the impact of technological change (Laxer 1976; Stewart 1976; Zerker 1981).

Freedman's proposal joined a host of demands that unions presented to governments in the 1960s. Organizers wanted changes to certification rules so that abstainers would not automatically be counted as having voted no. The CNTU demanded that Ottawa break up nation-wide bargaining units that favoured its CLC rivals. In Ontario and British Columbia, unionists went to jail for defying ex parte injunctions granted to employers. Lester Pearson's minority Liberal government, elected in 1963, faced a host of problems in Canada's industrial relations system (Morton 1990).

Public Sector Unionism

High on the list of labour problems in 1963 was the challenge of civil service unionism. The problem was not new. Unions had existed in the post office since 1891. In 1944, Saskatchewan's new CCF government had given provincial employees the right to bargain and strike. But those cases were exceptions. Traditionally, civil servants traded low pay for security, pensions, and—in the public mind—easy workloads. By the 1960s, those advantages were gone. Private sector workers had won similar fringe benefits, and prosperity guaranteed job security. In the Diefenbaker years, efforts to balance the budget forced repeated postponement of civil service wage increases. By 1963, Liberals, Tories, and New Democrats all promised to allow free collective bargaining for federal employees. In 1964, as part of its quiet revolution, Quebec set the pace by allowing its employees the right to strike (Finkelman and Goldenberg 1983; Morton 1990; Rouillard 1981).

In 1967, Parliament adopted the Public Service Staff Relations Act (PSSRA). Following the familiar pattern of Canadian labour relations legislation, it created an independent board to run the machinery. Less traditionally, the PSSRA allowed bargaining units to opt for compulsory arbitration or the right to strike. The weak and divided civil service federations buried old quarrels and merged as the Public Service Alliance of Canada.

Across Canada, most provincial governments followed Ottawa's example, though several provinces denied their workers the right to strike. Merger of rival TLC and CCL unions in a single Canadian Union of Public Employees (CUPE) coincided with a dramatic increase in public spending on education, health, and social services. Like civil servants, public sector employees were ready to be organized. By the early 1970s, CUPE had become the largest union in Canada. In many provinces, nurses and teachers abandoned old professional restraints and embraced militant bargaining and strike action. From facing stagnant or falling membership at the outset of the 1960s, unionism in Canada had entered its fastest period of growth since the Second World War (Finkelman and Goldenberg 1983; Morton 1990).

The Woods Task Force

In 1966, union militancy reached a peak with a wave of wildcat strikes, frequent rejections of negotiated settlements by unions' rank and file, the first national railway strike since 1960, and the first of a series of postal strikes. At Montreal, where the rush to complete Expo 67 allowed construction trades to extract record wages, the normally passive longshoremen closed the port until their demands were met. When St Lawrence Seaway workers threatened to follow suit, negotiators bought peace with a 30 per cent wage raise. Amidst a storm of criticism, the Liberal government of Lester Pearson bundled up its labour relations problems and handed them to a task force headed by H.D. Woods, a professor at McGill University (Cross 1974; Morton 1990).

By the time Woods reported, Canada had a majority government and a new prime minister. Pierre Elliott Trudeau had backed the Asbestos strikers in 1949, voted NDP in 1963, and joined the Liberal government in 1965 in tandem with his friend Jean Marchand of the CNTU. But if unionists expected an ally, they found Trudeau enigmatic and unpredictable, strangely cold to the pragmatic and material concerns of ordinary workers. They were bewildered by Trudeau's about-faces—from pledging "no more free stuff" in 1968 to transforming unemployment insurance into a vast income maintenance plan in 1972; from denouncing wage controls in 1974 to imposing them in 1975 (Laxer 1976; Morton 1990; Stewart 1976).

Unions and Nationalism

One Trudeau stand was unchanging: a disdain for emotional nationalism in Canada or in his native Quebec. Many Canadians felt otherwise. Canadian opinion-leaders condemned US policy in Vietnam and American investment in Canada. Unions with American headquarters were easy targets for right-wing and left-wing nationalists. Within the CLC, the growth of Canadian-based public service unions ended the old dominance of the internationals. In 1972, the CLC surrendered to a CUPE-led campaign for autonomy guidelines for Canadian districts of internationals. It also granted its Quebec Federation of Labour (QFL) greater autonomy and financial resources (Crispo 1967; Morton 1990).

Pressure on the internationals was heightened by the annual publication of statistics under the new Corporations and Labour Unions Returns Act, which exaggerated the money Canadians sent to the United States and understated what they got back. Since many Canadian districts actually represented a financial drain on parent unions, many internationals were persuaded to grant autonomy and even friendly separation. The Communication Workers of Canada and the Canadian Paperworkers Union were two that led the way from international affiliation to full independence. By 1979, the historic dominance of international unions in the Canadian movement had ended; for the first time, nationally based unions represented a majority of organized workers, and the trend continued steadily into the 1980s.

In Quebec in the 1970s, unions became vehicles of revolutionary protest for intellectuals and young people angry at English-speaking dominance of the provincial economy and at a Liberal government that opposed independence. The 1972 common front of the CNTU, the Quebec Federation of Labour, and the teachers' union set out to bargain for the province's public employees. Months of fiery speeches, demonstrations, and strikes gave the image, if not the substance, of a civil war against Robert Bourassa's Liberal government. The tactics failed, union leaders were briefly jailed, and Bourassa swept the 1973 election. Labour unity shattered in a violent jurisdictional struggle at the giant James Bay hydroelectric development. Canadian Labour Congress affiliates in the QFL joined Quebec nationalists to work for the Parti Québécois victory of November 15, 1976 (Laxer 1976; Palmer 1983; Rouillard 1981).

Inflation and Protest

For most Canadians, inflation, unemployment, and the disappearance of long-established industries outweighed nationalism as a preoccupation for the 1970s. Blame could be distributed among the Trudeau government, the world oil cartel, and multinational corporations, but unions were also handy scapegoats.

The Woods Task Force had generally praised Canada's industrial relations system in 1969. The right to organize was strengthened by a new federal labour code in 1971 and by legislation in the three western provinces won by the New Democrats between 1969 and 1972. Technological change could now be negotiated more easily; union members gained a voice in matters of occupational health and safety; and industrial democracy became part of the rhetoric of, if rarely the practice in, labour relations. Such reforms did nothing to curb inflation, driven to double digits by a host of factors ranging from the decline of the US dollar to Ottawa's decision in 1974 to index both taxes and expenditures and to finance the growing gap by borrowing. To defend members' incomes at the end of long, pre-inflationary contracts, many unions went on strike. A public inclined to judge causes by the noise they made could believe that wage demands fuelled inflation, not the reverse (Cross 1974; Morton 1990; Stewart 1976).

In 1974, Trudeau won a fresh majority by ridiculing Tory proposals for a temporary wage and price freeze; on Thanksgiving Day 1975, his government proclaimed sweeping controls to curb inflation. Among the targets of the new Anti-Inflation Board (AIB) was union bargaining power. Most unions fought back. The CLC co-ordinated court challenges and protest rallies; its national Day of Protest on the anniversary of controls kept a million union members home from work. Some union insiders, predicting a long period of government controls, devised an ingenious case for tripartite government-labour-management controls of the economy, with an all-powerful CLC playing all the cards for working people. Such schemes were forgotten in 1978 when controls, with all their anomalies and distortions, were lifted. The labour movement emerged to fight for catch-up in an economic setting of plant shutdowns, mass layoffs, and the highest unemployment rate since 1939 (Canadian Labour Congress 1976; Morton 1990; Palmer 1983).

Politics and Divisions

As it had before in hard times, the labour movement tightened its belt, fought some desperate holding actions—notably against INCO at Sudbury, Ontario, in 1978/9—and remembered that it was a political as well as an economic force. Under a new, more pugnacious president, Dennis McDermott, the CLC set out to help its neglected political partner, the New Democratic Party. Labour support had brought more money to the NDP than the CCF had ever received, but no more than a quarter of union members or their families voted for the party and many of them had defected in 1974, dropping the NDP to a mere 15 per cent of the popular vote. The CLC's anti-AIB campaign showed the futility of extraparliamentary politics; a "parallel campaign" in 1979 and again in 1980 sought to develop an NDP-union voting bloc. The campaign helped Ed Broadbent, an autoworker's son from Oshawa, to lead the NDP back to its old plateau of support, but it was the Conservatives and then the Liberals under a reinvigorated Pierre Elliott Trudeau who won the elections. Local results confirmed that most unionists again had ignored their leaders' political guidance (Morton 1986; 1990; Roberts and Bullen 1984).

RECESSION AND CHANGE

The Canadian Federation of Labour

Politics and nationalism strained the unity of the CLC. The traditional construction trades had never felt comfortable with the Congress's responses to either concern. They were internationals in the Gompers tradition, indifferent to the NDP and suspicious of the earnest, well-educated ideologues who so often spoke for the new public sector unions. A persistent grievance was the CLC practice of allowing rank-and-file delegates at its conventions. AFL-CIO meetings were restricted almost wholly to union officials.

A sharper complaint arose from Quebec legislation designed to prevent the violent union rivalry in the construction industry that had exploded at James Bay in 1974. When the QFL organized its own construction union and won jurisdiction, the building trades demanded that the CLC discipline its affiliate. With Canada threatened by separatism, the Congress refused to give Quebec a fresh grievance. The upshot, in March 1981, was a formal breach between the CLC and some of its most vulnerable and conservative affiliates. Two years later, most of the defectors united in the Canadian Federation of Labour (CFL), bound by strict Gompers principles of business unionism and political neutrality (Morton 1990). (For a comparison of the various federations' membership in recent years, see Figure 6.3.)

Recession in the 1980s

The schisms and splits were sadly reminiscent of the 1930s. So were the economic conditions of the early 1980s. Unemployment, persistently high in the 1970s, reached 1.3 million in 1983. A world that had painfully adjusted to two massive oil-price increases now discovered that a price collapse could also be a disaster as huge investments in exploration and energy substitution went sour. Markets for most of Canada's resources collapsed and thousands of jobs vanished.

The crisis for labour hit earlier in the United States. Lacking Canada's public sector unionization of the 1960s, American unions represented only 18 per cent of the work force in 1984, compared to 40 per cent in Canada. The slide of American economic development to the southwest forced US unions to organize in a hostile environment in the face of antiunion legislation. Canadian unionists could only wonder when that climate would spread north. In 1986, Bob White, McDermott's articulate young successor at the head of the United Auto Workers in Canada, forced the issue of autonomy for his union, to insulate it from an atmosphere of contract concessions and compromises. White's Canadian Auto Workers' Union (CAW) contrasted with the United Steelworkers, whose bright Canadian leader, Lynn Williams, took his ideas and talent to Pittsburgh to become international president of the huge but troubled union in 1983 (Lipset 1986; Morton 1990).

Recovery, when it came in the mid-1980s, brought higher profits, inflation, and an acceleration of technological change long before unemployment figures were seriously affected. When new jobs appeared, they were in the ill-paid and unorganized retail, financial and service sectors. Campaigns to organize bank employees and the retail giant, Eaton's, failed, as they had before, in the face of employer opposition and resistance to a first agreement. A violent Montreal strike persuaded Quebec to ban the use of strikebreakers, but not for ten years did another province, Ontario, follow suit. Ottawa's refusal

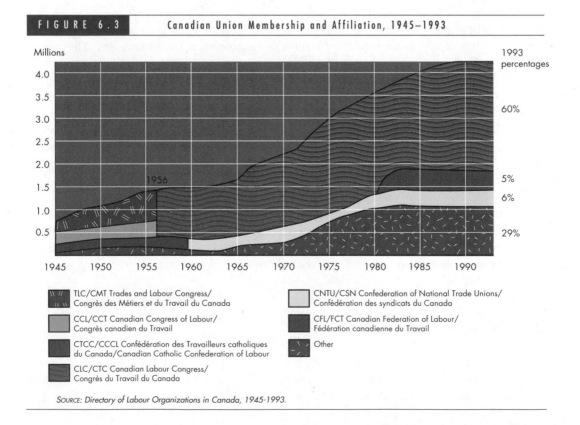

| FIGURE 6.3 | Canadian Union Membership and Affiliation, 1945–1993 |

TLC/CMT Trades and Labour Congress/ Congrès des Métiers et du Travail du Canada

CCL/CCT Canadian Congress of Labour/ Congrès canadien du Travail

CTCC/CCCL Confédération des Travailleurs catholiques du Canada/Canadian Catholic Confederation of Labour

CLC/CTC Canadian Labour Congress/ Congrès du Travail du Canada

CNTU/CSN Confederation of National Trade Unions/ Confédération des syndicats du Canada

CFL/FCT Canadian Federation of Labour/ Fédération canadienne du Travail

Other

SOURCE: *Directory of Labour Organizations in Canada, 1945-1993.*

contributed to a tragic crime in Yellowknife in 1992, when nine strikebreaking miners perished in a bombing incident. Ontario's NDP government also made it easier for workers to choose a union, though a renewed brutal recession gave few workers much incentive.

Public sector workers found that what Parliament and legislatures gave, they could also take away. In 1982, the Trudeau government imposed a policy of "6 and 5" per cent wage guidelines on all the employees it could control, and most other provinces adopted their own forms of public-sector wage control (Finkelman and Goldenberg, 1983). In June 1983, after British Columbia's Social Credit government imposed drastic cuts on its public sector, labour, teachers, the elderly and other victims created a "solidarity" movement that came close to a general strike. Solidarity dissolved after union leaders, recognizing the limits of their popularity, settled for a compromise (Palmer 1986). In 1984 exasperated voters reduced the Liberals to forty federal seats. Brian Mulroney's Conservatives swept to power, and the NDP was lucky to keep its traditional one-fifth of the vote.

Public-sector unionism was a factor in 1984: the public resented even six per cent pay increases in mid-recession. Driven to frequent strikes in their mismanaged enterprise, postal workers became national symbols of mindless union militancy (White 1990). Because the government had the power and could re-write the rules, mature bargaining relations were slower to develop in the public sector than they had been when unions and businesses had had to negotiate in a fixed framework of laws. The Mulroney government did nothing overt to undermine a labour relations regime in which the prime minister had spent his professional career but had made no friends either.

Free Trade and Recession

The worst setback for Canada's unions in the 1980s—the negotiation of the Canada-US Free Trade Agreement, followed four years later by its extension to Mexico—might have come from either Liberals or Tories. On both sides of the border, business leaders talked of creating a level playing field, and one of the biggest bumps on the Canadian side was a strong labour movement, well established in resource and manufacturing industries. Whether it was free trade or a coincident recession, more than 300,000 well-paid manufacturing jobs vanished in Ontario alone between 1990 and 1993; most were unionized. Across Canada unemployment climbed to 1982 levels, but the collapse of long-established industries often left middle-aged, middle-class workers hunting hopelessly for a job. In the early 1980s, unions had proudly resisted concessions on wages and working rules; there was not much room for such pride in the 1990s. Only the automotive sector, protected by the 1965 Auto Trade pact, could keep its old gains and add a few new ones.

The backlash to free trade and a renewed recession helped Bob Rae and the NDP form Ontario's first pro-labour government on September 8, 1990. A year later, the NDP was back in power in British Columbia and Saskatchewan too. While the NDP governments delivered on promises of employment and pay equity and industrial relations reforms, recession finance put them on a collision course with the public-sector unions that increasingly dominated Canada's labour movement. Having tried to spend his way out of the first year of recession, Ontario's Bob Rae found his deficit soaring from $3 billion to $18 billion in two years. Faced with a credit squeeze, plunging tax revenues, and a greater share of the costs of welfare and health, Rae cut costs, raised taxes and cut public-sector wages in the name of a "social contract." Ideally the social contract was a socialist solution that protected jobs, shared sacrifice, and offered workers an opportunity of a greater say in their workplace. In practice, unions were outraged that "their" government had opened valid contracts in mid-term. Urged by public-sector affiliates, the Ontario Federation of Labour withdrew support from Rae's government and blamed him for the NDP's dismal showing in the 1992 federal election. Elsewhere, as in Ontario, NDP governments wrestled with tough times and tough measures, but their erstwhile union backers showed no desire to share the responsibility or the pain.

Vulnerable and Adaptable

In the mid-1990s, Canada's unions looked more vulnerable than they had in decades. The industrial sectors they had dominated—resources and manufacturing—were in decline. Huge government deficits and demands for down-sizing and privatization threatened the public-sector institutions where the union movement had found its main growth since the 1950s. Repudiation of the NDP by voters and by the labour movement's own leaders left labour without political allies or leverage.

Yet unions had always survived by transforming themselves, and the forces of change were as strong as ever. The millions of women who joined the workforce in the 1970s had changed unions in the 1980s. Unions had taken up the new issues of day care, maternity leave, and pay equity and they had accepted women leaders (Briskin and Yanz 1984). In 1986, Shirley Carr won the presidency of the CLC. An aging workforce and some shocking corporate raids on employee pension funds persuaded unions that they must be involved in pension management. The environmental movement helped unions establish new expectations for workplace health and safety and a new consciousness that employment and the environment were not at odds.

In a conservative, pro-business climate of opinion, it is easy to find critics of unions. Still, most Canadians agree that unions have brought benefits to their members and that unions should and will grow. Much that has made Canada a humane and civilized society has come from the social vision of its labour movement.

QUESTIONS

1. What were the principles of the "New Model" unionism? Why did they succeed in nineteenth-century Britain, the United States, and Canada?

2. Why did labour seek to establish central organizations, in Canada? What obstacles did they have to overcome?

3. "Boundaries were made by the bosses." Assess the impact of American unionism on the development of a trade union movement in Canada.

4. American labour history has to deal with the contribution of "great men" such as Samuel Gompers and John L. Lewis. Comment on the contribution of similar figures in Canadian labour history or explain their absence.

5. What was the contribution of William Lyon Mackenzie King to the practice of industrial relations in Canada?

6. Assess the political and legal circumstances that contributed to the emergence of (a) craft unions, (b) industrial unions, *or* (c) public service unions.

7. Unions in Canada differed from American unions by helping to establish a democratic socialist party in 1961. In the light of the experience in both countries, was the Canadian policy wiser than the American?

8. In 1976, the Canadian Labour Congress endorsed the concept of "social corporatism." Assess the significance of corporatist ideas on the philosophy of industrial relations in Canada.

9. Quebec has been said to be "une province qui n'est pas comme les autres." How far does its distinctiveness extend to the labour movement? What elements are similar to the rest of Canada?

10. Time lost through strikes reached record levels in 1919, 1946, and 1976. Has there been a pattern in the rise and fall of labour militancy in Canada?

REFERENCES

ABELLA, I. 1973. *Nationalism, Communism and Canadian Labour.* Toronto: University of Toronto Press.

———. 1974. *On Strike: Six Key Labour Struggles in Canada, 1919-1949.* Toronto: James Lewis and Samuel.

AVAKUMOVIC, I. 1975. *The Communist Party in Canada: A History.* Toronto: McClelland & Stewart.

AVERY, D. 1979. *Dangerous Foreigners: European Immigrant Workers and Labour Radicalism in Canada, 1896-1932.* Toronto: McClelland & Stewart.

BABCOCK, R. 1975. *Gompers in Canada: A Study in American Continentalism before the First World War.* Toronto: University of Toronto Press.

BATTYE, J. 1979. "The Nine-Hour Pioneers: The Genesis of the Canadian Labour Movement." *Labour/Le Travailleur:* 4: 25-56.

BERCUSON, D. 1974. *Confrontation in Winnipeg: Labour, Industrial Relations and the General Strike.* Montreal: McGill-Queen's University Press.

———. 1978. *Fools and Wise Men: The Rise and Fall of the One Big Union.* Toronto: McGraw-Hill Ryerson.

BOWEN, L. 1982. *Boss Whistle: The Coal Miners of Vancouver Island Remember.* Lantzville, BC: Oolichan Books.

BRADWIN, E. 1972. *The Bunkhouse Man.* Toronto: University of Toronto Press.

BRISKIN, L., and L. YANZ. 1984. *Union Sisters: Women in the Labour Movement.* Toronto: Women's Press.

CANADIAN LABOUR CONGRESS. 1976. *Labour's Manifesto for Canada.* Ottawa: CLC.

COOPER, J.I. 1949. "The Quebec Ship-Labourers' Benevolent Society." *Canadian Historical Review 30* (4): 336-43.

COPP, J. 1974. *The Anatomy of Poverty: The Condition of the Working Class in Montreal, 1897-1929.* Toronto: McClelland & Stewart.

———. 1976. *Industrial Unionism in Kitchener.* Elora, Ont: Cumnock Press.

————. 1980. *The IEU in Canada*. Elora, Ont: Cumnock Press.

CRAVEN, P. 1981. *"An Impartial Umpire:" Industrial Relations and the Canadian State*. Toronto: University of Toronto Press.

CRISPO, J. 1967. *International Unionism: A Study of Canadian-American Relations*. Toronto: McGraw-Hill Ryerson.

CROSS, M.S., ed. 1974. *The Workingman in the Nineteenth Century*. Toronto: Oxford University Press.

DAWSON, R.M. 1958. *William Lyon Mackenzie King: A Political Biography*. Vol 1. Toronto: University of Toronto Press.

DESROSIERS, P. and D. HÉROUX. 1973. *Le Travailleur québécois et le Syndicalisme*. Montréal: Les Presses de l'Université du Québec.

DUMAS, E. 1975. *The Bitter Thirties in Quebec*. Montreal: Black Rose.

FERNS, H.S., and B. OSTRY. 1975. *The Age of Mackenzie King*. Toronto: James Lorimer.

FINGARD, J. 1974. "The Winter's Tale: Contours of Pre-Industrial Poverty in British America. 1815-1860." *Historical Papers* 1974: 65-94. Canadian Historical Association. Ottawa:

FINKELMAN, J., and S.B. GOLDENBERG. 1983. *Collective Bargaining in the Public Service. The Federal Experience in Canada*. 2 vols. Montreal: Institute for Research on Public Policy.

FORSEY, E. 1982. *Trade Unions in Canada, 1812-1902*. Toronto: University of Toronto Press.

FRANK, J.A. 1983. "The 'Ingredients' in Violent Labour Conflict, Patterns in Four Case Studies." *Labour/Le Travailleur* 12(Fall): 87-112.

GÉRIN-LAJOIE, J. 1982. *Les métallos (1936-1981)*. Montreal: Boréal-Express.

HANN, R. 1976. "Brainworkers and the Knights of Labour." In G. Kealey and P.Warrian, eds, *Essays in Canadian Working Class History*. Toronto: McClelland & Stewart.

HATTENHAUER, R.J. n.d. *A Brief History of Newfoundland*. St. John's: Queen's Printer.

HERON, C. 1984. "Labourism and the Canadian Working Class." *Labour/Le Travail* 13(Spring): 45-75.

HERON, C. and B. PALMER. 1977. "Through the Prism of the Strike." *Canadian Historical Review* 58(4): 423-57.

HOROWITZ, G. 1968. *Canadian Labour in Politics*. Toronto: University of Toronto Press.

ISBESTER, F. 1971. "Quebec Labour in Perspective." In R. Miller and F. Isbester, eds, *Canadian Labour in Transition*. Scarborough, Ont: Prentice-Hall.

JANTZI, D. 1978. "The Ford and Stelco Strikes." In R. Laxer, ed, *Union Organization and Strikes*. Toronto: University of Toronto Press.

KAPLAN, W. 1987. *Everything That Floats: Pat Sullivan, Hal Banks and the Seamen's Unions of Canada*. Toronto: University of Toronto Press.

KEALEY, K.G. 1973a. "Artisans Respond to Industrialism: Shoemakers, Shoe Factories and the Knights of St. Crispin in Toronto." Historical Papers, 1973, pp 137-57. Canadian Historical Association. Ottawa.

————, ed. *1973b. Canada Investigates Industrialism*. Toronto: University of Toronto Press.

————.1980. *Toronto Workers Respond to Industrial Capitalism*. Toronto: University of Toronto Press.

KEALEY, K.G., and B. PALMER. 1982. *Dreaming of What Might Be: The Knights of Labour in Ontario, 1880-1900*. Cambridge: Cambridge University Press.

KWAVNICK, D. 1971. *Organized Labour and Pressure Group Policies: The Canadian Labour Congress, 1956-1968*. Montreal: McGill-Queen's University Press.

LABOUR CANADA. Various issues. *Strikes and Lockouts in Canada*.

LANGDON, S. 1973. "The Emergence of the Canadian Working-Class Movement, 1845-1875." *Journal of Canadian Studies*. 7(2-3); 3-13, 8-25.

LATHAM, A.B. 1930. *The Catholic and National Labour Unions of Canada*. Toronto: University of Toronto Press.

LAXER, J. 1976. *Canada's Unions*. Toronto: McClelland & Stewart.

LIPSET, S.M., ed., 1986. *Unions in Transition: Entering the Second Century.* San Francisco: Institute for Contemporary Studies.

LIVERSEDGE, R. 1973. *Recollections of the On-to-Ottawa Trek.* Toronto: McClelland & Stewart.

LOGAN, H.A. 1948. *Trade Unions in Canada.* Toronto: Macmillan.

McCORMACK, R. 1978. *Reformers, Rebels, and Revolutionaries: The Western Canadian Radical Movement, 1899-1919.* Toronto: University of Toronto Press.

MacDOWELL, L.S. 1978. "The Formation of the Canadian Industrial Relations System during World War Two." *Labour/Le Travailleur* 3: 175-96.

———. 1982. "The 1943 Steel Strike Against Wartime Wage Controls." *Labour/Le Travailleur.* 10(Autumn): 65-85.

———. 1983. *Remember Kirkland Lake: The Gold Miners' Strike of 1941-2.* Toronto: University of Toronto Press.

MacEWEN, P. 1976. *Miners and Steelworkers of Cape Breton.* Toronto: Samuel, Stevens & Hakkert.

McKAY, I.S. 1986. "By Wisdom, Wile or War: The Provincial Workman's Association and the Struggle for Working-Class Independence in Nova Scotia." *Labour/Le Travailleur* 18(Fall): 13-62.

McKENTY, N. 1967. *Mitch Hepburn.* Toronto: McClelland & Stewart.

McNAUGHT, K., and D. BERCUSON. 1974. *The Winnipeg Strike 1919.* Toronto: Longman.

MAKI. D., and K. STRAND. 1984. "The Determinants of Strike Activity: An Interindustry Analysis." *Relations industrielles/Industrial Relations.* 39: 77-91.

MORTON. D. 1990. *Working People: An Illustrated History of the Canadian Labour Movement.* Toronto: Summerhill Press/St. Johns: Breakwater Books.

———. 1986. *The New Democrats, 1961-1986. The Politics of Change.* Toronto: Copp-Clark Pitman.

MOULTON, D. 1974. "Windsor, 1945." In I. Abella, ed, *On Strike: Six Key Labour Struggles in Canada, 1919-1949.* James, Lewis & Samuel.

OSTRY, B. 1960. "Conservatives, Liberals and Labour in the 1870s." *Canadian Historical Review* 41(2): 93-127.

PALMER, B. 1979. *A Culture in Conflict: Skilled Workers and Industrial Capitalism in Hamilton, Ontario, 1860-1914.* Montreal: McGill-Queen's University Press.

———. 1983. *Working Class Experience: The Rise and Reconstitution of Canadian Labour, 1860-1980.* Toronto: Butterworths.

———. 1986. "The Rise and Fall of British Columbia Solidarity." In B. Palmer, ed, *The Character of the Class Struggle: Essays in Canadian Working-Class History.* Toronto: McClelland & Stewart.

PANITCH, L., and D. SWARTZ. 1984. "Towards Permanent Exceptionalism: Coercion and Consent in Canadian Industrial Relations." *Labour/Le Travailleur* 13(Spring): 133-57.

PENTLAND, H. 1981. *Labour and Capital in Canada, 1650-1800.* Toronto: James Lorimer.

PHILLIPS, P. 1967. *No Power Greater: A Century of Labour in BC.* Vancouver: BC Federation of Labour.

PICKERSGILL, J. 1980. *The Mackenzie King Record.* Vol 1. Toronto: University of Toronto Press.

PIVA, M. 1979. *The Condition of the Working Class in Toronto, 1900-1921.* Ottawa: University of Ottawa Press.

RIDDELL, W.C. 1986. *Labour-Management Cooperation in Canada.* Toronto: University of Toronto Press.

ROBERTS, W., and J. BULLEN. 1984. "A Heritage of Hope and Struggle: Workers, Unions and Politics in Canada, 1936-1986." In M. Cross and G. Kealey, eds, *Modern Canada, 1930-1980s.* Vol 5, *Readings in Canadian Social History.* Toronto: McClelland & Stewart.

ROBIN, M. 1968. *Radical Politics and Canadian Labour, 1880-1930.* Kingston, Ontario: Centre for Industrial Relations, Queen's University.

RODNEY, W. 1968. *Soldiers of the International: A History of the Communist Party of Canada, 1919-1929.* Toronto: University of Toronto Press.

ROUILLARD, J. 1979. *Les Syndicats nationaux au Québec de 1900 é 1938.* Québec: Presse de l'Université Laval.

———. 1981. *Histoire de la CSN.* Montreal: Boréal-Express.

SIEMIATCKYI, M. 1978. "Munitions and Labour Militancy: The 1916 Hamilton Machinists' Strike." *Labour/Le Travailleur* 3: 131-52.

STEWART, W. 1976. *Strike.* Toronto: McClelland & Stewart.

SURFIN, E. 1982. *The Eaton Drive: The Campaign To Organize Canada's Largest Department Store, 1948-1952.* Toronto: Fitzhenry & Whiteside.

SULLIVAN, J.A. 1955. *Red Sails on the Great Lakes.* Toronto: Macmillan.

THOMPSPON, J. 1978. *The Harvests of War: The Prairie West, 1914-1918.* Toronto: McClelland & Stewart.

TRUDEAU, P., ed. 1974. *The Asbestos Strike.* Toronto: James Lorimer.

WEBBER, J. "The Malaise of Compulsory Conciliation: Strike Prevention in Canada during World War II." *Labour/Le Travailleur* 15(Spring): 57-85.

WHITE, J. 1990. *Mail and Female: Women and the Canadian Union of Postal Workers.* Toronto: Thompson Educational Press.

WHITAKER, R. 1977. "The Liberal Corporatist Ideas of Mackenzie King." *Labour/Le Travailleur* 2: 1997.

YOUNG, W. 1969. *The Anatomy of a Party: The National CCF.* Toronto: Toronto University Press.

ZERKER, S. 1981. *The Rise and Fall of the Toronto Typographers Union, 1832-1972: A Case Study of Foreign Domination.* Toronto: University of Toronto Press.

UNIONS: MEMBERSHIP, STRUCTURES, AND ACTIONS

G R E G O R   M U R R A Y *

*T*HE REPRESENTATION OF WORKERS BY UNIONS IS A MAJOR FEATURE OF *industrial relations. This chapter considers the basic characteristics of trade union representation in Canada and explores the challenges faced by labour unions as they seek to adapt to the changing political economy of industrial relations. After surveying trends in union growth and changes in the composition of union membership, it focuses on why individuals join unions. The chapter gives an overview of the main components of union structure, the types of affiliations that link these different components, and the impact of economic restructuring on them. It also explores the problems and potential of union democracy. Finally, there is an examination of different types of union actions, be they political or economic, within or beyond the workplace.*

* This chapter draws on material that has been gathered over the past several years with the financial support of the Social Science and Humanities Research Council of Canada, the Fonds pour la formation de chercheurs et l'aide à la recherche of Quebec, and the Confédération des syndicats nationaux. The author wishes to thank the many trade unionists who have assisted in the gathering and the interpretation of the data.

At the beginning of 1994, there were approximately 4.1 million union members in Canada distributed among 16,965 local unions. These unions represented roughly 29.2 per cent of all people active in the labour market (employed or unemployed), and 37.5 per cent of nonagricultural paid workers (excluding the self-employed and the unemployed). They negotiated the terms and conditions of employment of roughly 40 per cent of paid workers and undoubtedly exerted considerable influence on the employment conditions of many other workers. Union representatives were, moreover, present in a wide variety of public and private bodies in Canada concerned with labour market and social questions, ranging from health and safety at work to pay equity, training, and economic adjustment. Labour unions are undoubtedly one of the most important social actors in the Canadian labour market, and students and practitioners of labour–management relations require a thorough understanding of union organizations and their actions.

This chapter attempts to achieve that objective while highlighting both the great diversity that characterizes unions in Canada and the nature of the changes that they are currently experiencing. The first part concerns the different dimensions of union membership: growth trends, comparisons with other national experiences, distribution of union members, why people join unions, and pressures on union membership. The second part of the chapter looks successively at the structure of unions and their internal governance. The final part of the chapter concerns union actions, be they economic, such as collective bargaining and work place reorganization, or political, such as support for political parties or positions on social issues.

UNION MEMBERSHIP

Trends in Membership Growth

Faced with a variety of significant structural adjustments over the last two decades, unions have represented a diminishing proportion of the labour force in many of the industrialized Western economies. The recent history of Canadian trade unionism, then, is somewhat of an anomaly, particularly when compared with the fortunes of the neighbouring US labour movement. While the number of union members in the United States has diminished in both absolute and relative terms over the past two decades, falling from 20.9 million in 1970 to 16.7 million in 1990, the Canadian union movement has experienced a steady but gradual growth in aggregate union membership: from 2.2 million in 1971 to 3.4 million in 1981 to 4.0 million in 1991 (see Table 7.1). Although aggregate union membership has remained relatively stable through the 1990s, reaching 4.1 million in 1994, its growth during the 1980s was particularly remarkable given that labour movements in so many other countries experienced absolute membership declines over the same period (see OECD 1991). But this stability belies significant changes in the composition of union membership to which we will return in later sections of this chapter.

TABLE 7.1   Union Membership in Canada, 1911–1994

Year	Membership (thousands)	Membership as Percentage of Nonagricultural Paid Workers	Year	Membership (thousands)	Membership as Percentage of Nonagricultural Paid Workers
1911	133	—	1981	3487	36.7
1916	160	—	1982	3617	37.0
1921	313	16.0	1983	3563	37.9
1926	275	12.0	1984	3651	38.8
1931	311	15.3	1985	3666	38.1
1936	323	16.2	1986	3730	37.7
1941	462	18.0	1987	3782	37.0
1946	832	27.9	1988	3841	36.5
1951	1029	28.4	1989	3944	36.2
1956	1352	33.3	1990	4031	36.2
1961	1447	31.6	1991	4068	36.3
1966	1736	30.7	1992	4089	37.4
1971	2231	32.4	1993	4071	37.6
1976	3042	36.9	1994	4078	37.5

NOTE: Data on union membership for the years 1911 to1946 are as of December 31. Thereafter, they refer to January 1 of each year.
SOURCES: For 1911 to 1966, Dion (1986); for 1971 to 1994, Labour Canada (1994).

There are a variety of ways of measuring union membership and relative union presence. There are also several sources of such information that depend on different methods of data collection and reporting periods (see Kumar 1988). This chapter draws on the three principal sources of information on union membership. Human Resources Development Canada, formerly known as Labour Canada, publishes a biennial directory of labour organizations that includes an annual survey of union membership (Labour Canada). Statistics Canada conducts a detailed survey of union organizations that is usually published two to three years after the reporting period (CALURA). Statistics Canada also conducts a detailed household survey of individual experience in the labour market that provides information on the characteristics of individual union members (LMAS). Some provincial ministries of labour also produce data on provincial union movements based on either the analysis of collective agreements concluded within their jurisdiction or surveys of unions operating in their province.

Thus union membership figures will vary according to the type of measure and the source of the data. Readers should be aware that this is also the case in this chapter. The key distinction in measuring union membership is between absolute levels of union membership, how many individuals unions represent, and relative levels of union membership, the proportion of workers that they represent.

The absolute measure of union membership poses at least three problems. First, the principal surveys generally exclude small independent local organizations, and they sometimes exclude professional groupings, such as police and firefighters' associations, that perform union functions. Second, it is necessary to distinguish between union membership and collective bargaining coverage. The former refers to the number of individuals who are members of a union, the latter to all those persons whose terms and conditions of employment are determined by a union through the process of collective bargaining and who may or may not be a member of a union. In 1990, for example, in addition to the estimated 3.96 million union members, there were another 536,000 persons covered by a collective agreement (LMAS 1991). Third, there are potential problems with union reporting. Not all unions have sophisticated systems for keeping track of their membership, the level of which can fluctuate considerably during the course of a year. Moreover, some unions might either under- or over-report their membership, in order to increase their importance or, alternatively, reduce their financial obligations in affiliation fees.

The relative measure of union membership, union density, expresses the proportion of the labour force that is unionized. If expressed as a proportion of the total civilian labour force, which includes all of those persons who were either employed, including the self-employed, or seeking employment, then the rate of unionization tends to be lower than if expressed as the proportion of nonagricultural paid workers. Union density is most typically expressed in terms of this latter measure because it facilitates comparisons between countries with varying degrees of industrialization, and because it is a more accurate gauge of potential union membership. However, it is still not entirely accurate as a measure of potential union membership since most legal jurisdictions in Canada do not permit the unionization of certain categories of paid employees, such as managers and other supervisory personnel. At the beginning of 1994, it was estimated that 37.5 per cent of paid nonagricultural workers were members of a union (see Table 7.1). The rate of collective bargaining coverage, including those workers whose terms and conditions of employment were negotiated by a union but who were not themselves union members, tends to be several percentage points higher. At the end of 1990, for instance, the rate of collective bargaining coverage was estimated to be 37.2 per cent of employed paid workers, while union density was measured at 32.8 per cent (LMAS 1991).

Absolute membership figures reflect the relative health of unions, especially in terms of dues income and levels of organizing. Measures of relative union membership are especially useful for understanding the importance of unions in different industries and occupations. These two types of measures should be understood as complements because they express different aspects of union membership activity (Bain and Price 1983, 4). For instance, as is sometimes the case during downturns in economic activity, union density might actually increase while union membership declines or remains stable. Thus, while absolute union membership in Canada remained fairly stable between 1991 and 1994, relative density as a percentage of nonagricultural paid workers increased from 36.3 per cent to 37.5 per cent because of shrinking employment levels in the context of weak economic growth.

To compare Canadian union growth with that of other industrialized economies, only the German union movement, among the Group of Seven largest industrial economies (G-7), for example, demonstrates a comparable stability over the last decade. The aggregate membership performance of Canadian trade unions contrasts markedly with the more significant declines in union membership in countries such as France, Japan, the United Kingdom, and the United States (OECD 1991; Murray 1994).

Trade union membership by province reflects these national trends (see Table 7.2). In absolute terms, union membership in all provinces increased significantly over the last two decades. There are, however, significant differences in the levels of union density from one province to another. At one end of the scale, Newfoundland consistently exhibits the highest union density (53.3 per cent), followed by Quebec (40.6 per cent) and British Columbia (38.7 per cent). Alberta has the lowest level of union density (26.4 per cent) followed by Nova Scotia (31 per cent) and Ontario (31.9 per cent).

TABLE 7.2   Union Density by Province, 1991

Province	Union Density (%)	Province	Union Density (%)
Newfoundland	53.3	Ontario	31.9
Prince Edward Island	33.2	Manitoba	37.1
Nova Scotia	31.0	Saskatchewan	32.9
New Brunswick	36.8	Alberta	26.4
Quebec	40.6	British Columbia	38.7

NOTE: Union density is calculated on the basis of union membership and the number of paid workers in December 1991 excluding pensioners, the unemployed, and members in the Territories.

SOURCE: CALURA, 1993, 25.

There are three explanations for these differences. First, differing industrial structures account for some of the variation. Employment in Newfoundland, for example, is concentrated in a number of industries that are traditionally strongly unionized. Second, the expansion and contraction of different regional labour markets also play a role. Whereas aggregate union growth in Quebec and Ontario has been comparable over the last decade, union density has increased in Quebec but remained fairly stable in Ontario. That has occurred because the Ontario labour market has expanded much more rapidly, and aggregate membership growth has only just kept pace with the expansion of employment. Finally, there are also important differences in community attitudes to unionism that, despite initial differences in industrial structure, spill over into other sectors when people consider the acceptability of unionism as a way of regulating employment relations. The rate of unionization in large metropolitan areas varies greatly, from roughly 60 per cent in the Quebec City and Chicoutimi-Jonquière areas in 1991 to only 27.1 per cent in Calgary (CALURA). While industrial structure clearly explains some of these variations, differences in community attitudes about the benefits of unionism also play a role. (For a study of this phenomenon in the cases of Edmonton and Winnipeg, see Krahn and Lowe 1984.)

Canadian versus US Union Membership

The contrasting fortunes of trade unions in Canada and the United States over the last two decades have sparked considerable research on the increasing divergence in the fortunes of the two labour movements (Kumar 1993; Riddell 1993).

Table 7.3 gives an overview of the evolution of union membership in the two countries. Whereas they displayed similar patterns of growth throughout the first half of this century, they began to diverge sharply in the mid-1960s. The relative degree of unionization in Canada is now twice that of the United States. Moreover, there is a substantial differential in the rate of unionization in all sectors.

TABLE 7.3   Union Membership and Density in Canada and the United States

| Year | CANADA | | UNITED STATES | |
	Membership (thousands)	Percentage of Nonagricultural Paid Workers	Membership (thousands)	Percentage of Nonagricultural Paid Workers
1946	832	24.2	12,254	30.4
1951	1,029	30.2	15,139	31.7
1956	1,352	33.6	16,446	31.4
1961	1,447	30.6	15,401	28.5
1966	1,736	30.7	18,922	29.6
1971	2,231	32.4	20,711	29.1
1976	3,042	36.9	22,153	27.9
1981	3,487	36.7	20,647	22.6
1986	3,730	37.7	16,975	17.1
1991	4,068	36.3	16,568	15.3
1992	4,089	37.4	16,390	15.1

SOURCE: Kumar, 1993, 12–13.

The explanation of this divergence relates to both demand and supply factors. On the demand side, it appears that there is a greater demand for union representation in Canada, particularly in the private sector. On the supply side, there is considerable evidence that Canadian workers have, for a variety of reasons, easier access to unionization. Many US scholars and trade union leaders point to contrasting public policies as one of the principal differences in the relative fortunes of Canadian and US labour unions. They argue that the revival of trade union fortunes in the United States is contingent on securing substantial changes in public policy (Weiler 1984; Block 1993). It has also been suggested that

Canadian unions have been more innovative (Murray 1991; Kumar 1993), pursued new organizing with more vigour than their counterparts in the United States (Rose and Chaison 1990), achieved political change and favourable public policy more effectively (Bruce 1989), and pursued a broader social agenda over a longer period (Piore 1983; Robinson 1993).

Minority views in this debate should nonetheless be noted. Troy (1992), in particular, has argued that the divergence between the US and Canadian union movements has been greatly exaggerated by the failure to take account of the greater size of the public sector in Canada, and that, in fact, the union movements in both private sectors are in decline. Although it is difficult to disentangle fully this effect, Riddell (1993, 133) has estimated that only 7 per cent of the gap between US and Canadian unionization rates is accounted for by the greater proportion of the Canadian workforce in the public sector.

While not contesting the extent of divergence between the two countries, some authors suggest that, in the context of increasing continental economic integration, there will be increasing pressures on Canada's favourable legislative climate for unions (Belous 1989; Robinson 1994). Canadian labour might then suffer a decline in membership fortunes comparable to that of the union movement in the United States. It has also been argued, however, that the kinds of cohesive labour relations associated with high levels of union density in many small nations, for example, in the Scandanavian economies, can actually be a source of competitive advantage (see Freeman 1990).

Distribution of Union Membership

Union membership is not evenly distributed throughout the economy. There are significant variations by sociodemographic characteristics, industry, occupation, firm size, and employment status.

A first source of variation is by sex (see Table 7.4). The rate of unionization of women has tended to be less than that of men. Roughly 29.5 per cent of women, as opposed to 35.7 per cent of men, were union members in 1990 (LMAS 1991). In the following year, there were 1.58 million women union members in Canada, constituting 40.7 per cent of union members (CALURA 1993). This represents a significant change over the last three decades. In 1962, women constituted only 16.4 per cent of all union members. This percentage increased to 23.5 per cent in 1971 and 31 per cent in 1981 (Arrowsmith 1992, 67). Moreover, while male union membership has grown very slowly over the last decade, female union membership has increased substantially. For example, from 1981 to 1991, male union membership increased by only 5.7 per cent, and actually declined between 1989 and 1991, while female union membership increased by 61.6 per cent (calculated from CALURA 1993 and 1983). Thus, underlying a relative stability in union membership over the last several years is an increasing feminization of the union movement that has significant implications for the changing character of unions in Canada (see White 1993; Briskin and McDermott 1993).

TABLE 7.4 Union Membership and Collective Bargaining Coverage by Sex, Age, Employment Status, and Establishment Size, 1990

	Percentage Union Membership	Percentage Collective Bargaining Coverage
Sex		
Male	35.7	40.2
Female	29.5	34.0
Age		
16–24 years	14.9	19.3
25–34 years	32.1	36.7
35–44 years	39.4	43.8
45–54 years	44.1	48.4
55–69 years	40.1	44.6
Employment Status		
Part time	22.9	27.2
Full time	35.3	39.8
Establishment Size		
Less than 20 employees	8.3	10.2
20–99 employees	22.9	26.9
100–499 employees	42.3	47.5
500 or more employees	49.4	55.4
Total	32.8	37.2

NOTE: Estimates calculated from unpublished data provided by a survey of individual's labour market activity during 1990. For each job held, respondents indicated whether they were a union member and if their terms and conditions of employment were determined by a collective agreement. These estimates concern the last paid job held by each respondent in 1990.

SOURCE: LMAS, 1991.

There are also considerable variations in the degree of unionization by industry (see Table 7.5). According to Statistics Canada figures for 1991 (CALURA 1993), civil servants in public administration are, by far, the most unionized industry group (77.9 per cent). They are followed by industries characterized either by a degree of public ownership (transport and communications, 55.2 per cent) or public regulation (construction, 64.2 per cent). While many of the service industries remain little unionized (accommodation, food, and beverage, for instance, with only an 8.2 per cent level of unionization), education and health services, which are primarily offered in the public sector, have unionization rates of 75.3 and 50.9 per cent respectively. Together, the education and health sectors account for almost one-third of all union members in Canada.

TABLE 7.5 Union Density by Industry, 1991

Industry	Membership	Union Density (%)
Agriculture	2,438	1.7
Forestry	29,418	65.4
Fishing and trapping	6,072	41.9
Mines, quarries, oil wells	45,309	28.4
Manufacturing	636,287	36.2
Construction	338,139	64.2
Transportation, communication, other utilities	473,524	55.2
Wholesale and retail trade	231,180	11.6
Finance	21,201	4.2
Business services	20,530	3.7
Educational services	657,168	75.3
Health services	576,603	50.9
Accommodation, food, beverage	59,316	8.2
Other services	81,330	14.2
Public administration	644,762	77.9
Total	3,829,322	35.1

NOTE: Union density is calculated on the basis of union membership and the number of paid workers in December 1991 excluding pensioners, the unemployed, and members in the Territories.

SOURCE: CALURA, 1993, 24.

Manufacturing, which has traditionally been highly unionized, has experienced both an absolute decline in union membership and a relative decline in union density over the last decade, falling from 44.3 per cent in 1982 to 36.2 per cent in 1991. Indeed, the most significant change in union composition over the past two decades has been the declining proportion of union members in manufacturing and the increased proportion of public sector workers in the union movement. For example, 38.9 per cent of union members came from manufacturing in 1966 as opposed to only 16.6 per cent in 1991. The public services (health, education, and public administration) accounted for 49.1 per cent of union members in Canada in 1991 (CALURA 1993).

The least unionized industries include those that have been growing most quickly. Thus, only 11.6 per cent of those working in wholesale and retail trade are unionized, and the rate of unionization falls to 4.2 per cent in the finance sector. It should be emphasized that the degree of unionization in these two sectors has increased steadily over the past two decades, but the overall degree of unionization remains extremely weak. This poses a significant challenge for the labour movement because its areas of relative strength seem to be those that are now either in decline (manufacturing, primary industries) or growing more slowly (the public sector). As the employment structure continues to shift towards the private services, the future of the Canadian union movement, in many ways, hinges on its ability to negotiate this change.

In this regard, it is worth noting some regional differences in the degree of unionization of the private services, as measured by collective bargaining coverage (LMAS 1991). For example, in two areas of strong employment growth, trade and financial services, the union movements in Quebec (20.8 per cent and 19.9 per cent) and British Columbia (19.5 per cent and 14.5 per cent) have been more successful in the unionization of such private services than has the Ontario union movement (11.4 per cent and 8.23 per cent respectively).

These sectoral differences in the degree of unionization of industries are also apparent by occupational category. There are much higher percentages of union members in some occupations than others. Traditional jobs involving skills in manufacturing, construction, and transport tend to be highly unionized. Unions also have a significant presence among professional and technical job categories. For example, 49.3 per cent of professional and scientific employees are unionized. This high degree of unionization reflects the high concentrations of such employees in areas of sector employment such as health and education. By contrast, only 9.3 per cent of sales employees, 17.4 per cent of managerial employees, and 26.7 per cent of office employees are members of a union (LMAS 1991).

The distribution of union members by firm size is also highly variable (see Table 7.4). The overall level of collective bargaining coverage was 37.2 per cent of paid workers in 1990 (LMAS 1991). This figure was only 10.2 per cent for firms with less than twenty employers, 26.9 per cent for establishments with twenty to one hundred employees, 47.5 per cent for establishments with between one hundred and five hundred employees, and 55.4 per cent for establishments with more than five hundred employees. Fully 79.6 per cent of workers covered by a collective agreement worked in firms of one hundred or more employees, even though only 55.7 per cent of paid employees worked in such firms. It is well known that unions have a more difficult time securing their presence in smaller firms, and this is reflected in the data on the distribution of collective bargaining coverage by firm size.

Employment status also exerts an effect on the degree of unionization since full-time workers (those working more than 30 hours per week) tend to be more unionized than are part-time workers. Collective bargaining coverage for full-time workers was 39.8 per cent in 1990 as opposed to 27.2 per cent for part-time workers (Table 7.4). This differential constitutes a challenge for Canadian trade unions because there continues to be a more rapid expansion of part-time employment than full-time employment and of contingent or atypical jobs, such as short-term contracts, as opposed to full-time, permanent jobs.

Union Joining

Why do some workers join unions and others do not? A first distinction should be made here between the propensity of an individual to join (the demand for union representation) and his or her opportunity to do so (the supply of union representation). Propensity refers to the individual preference, whereas opportunity concerns the context in which those preferences are exercised.

In terms of their propensity to unionize, individuals have many different images of unions, and these have an effect on their interest in being a union member. At the most general level, unions elicit a high degree of support. While the extent of this support varies over time in relation to particular current events, when asked by polling organizations such as Gallup whether unions are a "good thing" or a "bad thing," the majority of Canadians tend to respond that they are a "good thing." There are, however, regional variations in these attitudes. For example, people in the Maritimes, Quebec, and British Columbia have tended to express stronger support for unions than do people in Ontario and the Prairie provinces (Rouillard 1991, 285). These findings are consistent with similar types of research in the United States (Commission on the Future of Worker–Management Relations 1994, 63). The instrumentality of unions is also fairly widely accepted, since most workers perceive an advantage to being a union member, though some also think unions are too powerful. Moreover, there appears to be a widespread appreciation of the role of unions in protecting workers from arbitrary employer behaviour in the workplace.

Yet, in terms of individual propensity, it is clear that not all workers want to be union members. Most of the North American research on attitudes to union representation indicates a clear division between unionized and nonunionized workers. The majority of nonunion members would appear to wish to remain so. Estimates of the desire of nonunionized employees to join a union tend to be fairly stable. For example, 32 per cent of nonunion respondents to a Canadian Federation of Labour survey indicated that they were likely or somewhat likely to want to join a union or a professional association (Verma and Bergeron 1991, 390). Similarly, Bergeron (1994, 779), in a study of nonunionized workers in private services in Toronto and Montreal, found that 39.6 per cent of his sample were likely to want to unionize. These Canadian findings resemble those of similar American surveys from 1977 to 1991, which have recorded from 38.6 per cent to 35.2 per cent of nonunion respondents expressing a desire to unionize (Farber and Krueger 1993, 114).

By the same token, the majority of union members seem to be quite satisfied with their status (Gallagher and Strauss 1991, 145). This apparently common-sense division is not entirely satisfactory because job seekers do not usually have a choice of jobs between unionized and nonunionized workplaces; individuals take jobs that are available irrespective of union status. This leads to two observations. First, socialization into the job would appear to be quite important. Second, it requires a particular set of circumstances for individuals to cross the threshold from union to nonunion.

There is considerable literature on why nonunion employees chose to unionize. This is particularly true in the United States where, because certification elections rather than the simple signing of cards are the rule rather than the exception, there is much interest in explaining voting intentions and behaviour. Barling, Fullagar, and Kelloway (1992, 69) point to three factors that appear to be of greatest significance in the propensity to unionize: job dissatisfaction, general union attitudes, and perceived union instrumentality. Thus, persons who are dissatisfied with their jobs are more likely to want to unionize. This is generally the case in terms of extrinsic factors such as working conditions and pay (low pay, dissatisfaction with one's pay, or perceived inequities). Dissatisfaction with the intrinsic aspects of work, such as relative levels of participation in decision making, can also increase the propensity to unionize in some organizational contexts (Barling et al. 1992, 52). Those who perceive unions as being too powerful or undemocratic are less likely to want to unionize. Those who believe that unions are likely to improve their working conditions are more likely to unionize.

Although some authors point to sociodemographic differences in attitudes to unions, most studies discount their importance (Barling et al. 1992, 35). Other authors add factors such as the impact of family and community socialization on general union attitudes and the presence of fairly cohesive work groups (Bergeron 1994). Social and institutional factors clearly play an important role in the taming of the union image, for once individuals are unionized they are more likely to have positive attitudes towards the union as an institution.

Whatever the propensity of individuals to join a union may be, there remains the question of their real opportunity to do so. The overall economic context, the types of industries and jobs in which people work, prevailing public policies, the degree of employer opposition, and union strategies and resources invested in organizing, all will have an impact on the accessability of unionism. Canadian public policy, in particular, has generally been fairly supportive of unionization and, in contrast to the United States, deliberately affords the employer little opportunity to be involved in what is regarded as the exercise of an employee right to choose to be represented by a union. Partly for this reason, Riddell (1993) estimates that whereas only 44 per cent of Americans who want to be unionized are in unions, fully 76 per cent of Canadians who wish to do so are in fact in unions. There are, of course, many ways of influencing the decision to unionize, and, until their employees are actually unionized, most employers continue to be opposed to unionization. Thereafter, it is more likely that the priority becomes how to have a constructive working relationship (see Thompson 1993 and Chapter 5).

Pressures on Union Membership

If Canadian unions have performed fairly well over the last decade relative to other labour movements, the pressures operating on them are nonetheless very intense. The Canadian union movement is increasingly under challenge because the employment areas in which it has traditionally been most representative, particularly manufacturing and public administration, are shrinking, while the areas in which it is less representative, particularly private services, are the most important sources of employment growth. Between 1967 and 1988, employment growth in the goods sector of the Canadian economy (primary, manufacturing, and construction) was limited to 0.9 per cent per annum, whereas service sector growth (both public and private) was 3.2 per cent annually (Economic Council of Canada 1990). Although union growth has largely kept pace with the growth in public service employment, this is not the case with the private services sector, which is of particular importance since public service employment growth is stagnating while private services continue to expand. The challenge is clear because the rate of unionization in the private services in 1990 was only 10.5 per cent (LMAS 1991).

Yet there is considerable evidence that the Canadian union movement has proved to be highly adaptable and fairly inventive over the last decade. Several indicators point in this direction: the overall growth in aggregate union membership, continuing high levels of recruitment activity, the entry of women into the labour market, and a certain success in obtaining changes in provincial labour laws that facilitate new recruitment.

However, changes in employment structure continue to exert a significant impact on union structures; these structures are explored further in the next section.

UNION STRUCTURE

Components of Union Structure

Union structure might be envisaged as being made up of several basic building blocks: the certification unit, the local union, the national or international union, the central labour body or congress, and affiliations to international labour organizations by any one of these other levels of union structure.

The cornerstone of all union structures in Canada is the *certification unit* or *appropriate bargaining unit*. This is the defined group of workers for which a labour board or other similar administrative body grants exclusive bargaining rights to a designated agent, after a majority of those workers have indicated support for union representation. In the Ontario legislation, for example, this is defined as "a unit of employees appropriate for collective bargaining, whether it is an employer unit or plant unit or a subdivision of both" (Cornish and Spinks 1994, 159).

Bargaining units in Canada are generally quite small and bargaining is highly decentralized. With the notable exception of the public sector, the norm is the negotiation of a single agreement between an employer and a union for a single site. Even among those most likely to deviate from this norm (i.e., agreements covering 500 employees or more), 80 per cent of these agreements in 1990 involved a single union and a single employer, 11 per cent involved more than one union and a single employer, 9 per cent involved a single union and more than one employer, and only 1 per cent involved more than one employer and more than one union (see Chapter 9 and Kumar et al 1991, 223). The focus of union activity is generally at the level of the certification unit and, unlike in many European countries characterized by national level bargaining, Canadian union structure is highly decentralized with fairly weak vertical integration between different hierarchical levels of union organization.

This decentralization is further exacerbated by the division of powers over labour matters within the Canadian federation. Roughly 10 per cent of Canadian workers fall under federal jurisdiction. Their representative arrangements are governed by the federal government's legislative framework. The other 90 per cent are subject to the different provincial jurisdictions whose labour codes may vary considerably (Royal Commission 1985, vol. 2, 672).

Despite this decentralization, the certification unit is most frequently also part of a larger union structure. At the local level, a *union local* may be made up of one or more such certification units. Union locals in industries such as construction are typically made up of multiple certification units. In large manufacturing establishments, on the other hand, the local union generally consists of a single certification unit. Local unions have their own form of governance with statutes, rules of procedure, and periodic elections. There were nearly 17,000 such local unions in Canada at the beginning of 1994 (see Table 7.6).

TABLE 7.6   Union Membership by Congress Affiliation, 1994

	Locals	Membership	Percentage of Membership
Canadian Labour Congress (CLC)	9,366	2,480,153	60.8
Confédération des syndicats nationaux (CSN-CNTU)	2,234	258,675	6.3
Canadian Federation of Labour (CFL)	418	200,446	4.9
AFL–CIO only	29	18,217	0.4
Centrale de l'enseignement du Québec (CEQ)	310	106,609	2.6
Centrale des syndicats démocratiques (CSD)	108	58,507	1.4
Confederation of Canadian Unions (CCU)	53	20,698	0.5
Canadian National Federation of Independent Unions (CNFIU)	12	2,072	0.1
Unaffiliated international unions	28	9,492	0.2
Unaffiliated national unions	4,097	791,235	19.4
Independent local organizations	310	131,883	3.2
Total	16,965	4,077,987	100.0

SOURCE: Labour Canada, 1994, xiv.

Some locals are highly autonomous. Indeed, there are many independent local unions in Canada that have no other form of affiliation. Approximately 3.2 per cent of union members belong to such locals. Typical examples would include the McGill University Physical Plant Employees Association, the Calgary Police Association, and the Coca-Cola Bottling Employees Association in Victoria (Labour Canada 1992).

Whatever their degree of autonomy, most local unions are part of a larger structure. A union local is typically chartered by a *national* or *international union organization* from which it receives its name and its statutes. For example, Local 444 of the National Automobile, Aerospace and Agricultural Implement Workers Union of Canada, better known as the Canadian Auto Workers Union (CAW), organizes Chrysler employees in Windsor. It is a constituent unit of the national union and is governed in accordance with its constitution.

National and international unions organize and charter locals in the industries or professions defined by their constitutions or policies. This is known as a union's jurisdiction. For example, the United Steelworkers of America has traditionally organized workers in mining, metal transformation, and some areas of manufacturing across North America. The United Brotherhood of Carpenters and Joiners of America has organized carpenters in the building trades. The Canadian Union of Postal Workers has organized workers of Canada Post. As we will see below, such jurisdictions are increasingly being altered by changes in industrial structure and the consequent strategies pursued by unions to diversify their membership base. There were 911 national and international unions operating in Canada at the beginning of 1994 (Labour Canada 1994, xv). Among these, the sixteen largest (those totalling more than 50,000 members) accounted for 54.4 per cent of all union members in Canada (see Table 7.7).

TABLE 7.7   Largest Unions in Canada and their Affiliations, 1994

		Number (thousands)	Membership As % of Total Union Membership
1.	Canadian Union of Public Employees — CUPE (CLC)	409.8	10.1
2.	National Union of Public and General Employees — NUPGE (CLC)	307.6	7.5
3.	United Food and Commercial Workers International Union — UFCW (AFL–CIO/CLC)	175.0	4.3
4.	National Automobile, Aerospace and Agricultural Implement Workers Union of Canada — CAW (CLC)	170.0	4.2
5.	Public Service Alliance of Canada — PSAC (CLC)	167.8	4.1
6.	United Steelworkers of America — USWA (AFL–CIO/CLC)	161.2	4.0
7.	Communications, Energy and Paperworkers Union — CEP (CLC)	149.0	3.7
8.	International Brotherhood of Teamsters — (AFL–CIO/CLC)	95.0	2.3
9.	Fédération des affaires sociales — FAS (CSN)	94.7	2.3
10.	Service Employees International Union — SEIU (AFL–CIO/CLC)	80.0	2.0
11.	Fédération des enseignantes et enseignants des commissions scolaires — FEECS (CEQ)	75.0	1.8
12.	International Brotherhood of Electrical Workers — IBEW (AFL–CIO/CFL)	67.3	1.7
13.	United Brotherhood of Carpenters and Joiners of America — (AFL–CIO/CLC)	56.0	1.4
14.	International Association of Machinists and Aerospace Workers — IAM (AFL–CIO/CLC)	55.1	1.4
15.	Laborers' International Union of North America — LIUNA (AFL–CIO/CLC)	54.8	1.3
16.	Canadian Union of Postal Workers — CUPW (CLC)	51.0	1.3
17.	Ontario Nurses' Association — ONA (Independant)	50.2	1.2
	Total of the largest unions (50,000 or more members)	2,219.5	54.4
	Smaller unions (fewer than 50,000 members)	1,858.5	45.6
	Total of all unions	4,078.0	100.0

SOURCE: Labour Canada, 1994, xvi–xx.

Most, but not all, of these unions are, in turn, affiliated with *central labour bodies* or *congresses*. For instance, the Canadian Autoworkers Union, a national union, is affiliated to the Canadian Labour Congress. Similarly, the United Brotherhood of Carpenters and Joiners of America, an international union, is affiliated with the AFL-CIO in the United States and with the Canadian Labour Congress in Canada.

These central labour bodies have both a national presence and, in the case of the Canadian Labour Congress, a significant provincial and territorial presence in the form of twelve *provincial and territorial federations of labour*. For example, the Quebec, Ontario, and Yukon Federations of Labour organize congress affiliates in those particular provinces and represent union interests at the provincial government level. In Quebec there are also several autonomous central labour bodies or confederations, notably the Confédération des syndicats nationaux (CSN) and the Centrale de l'enseignement du Québec (CEQ).

Labour congresses or confederations are also present at district or regional levels. In the case of CLC affiliates, 121 *local labour councils* coordinate the activities of congress locals in a particular district, for example the Sudbury and District Labour Council or the Halifax–Dartmouth and District Labour Council. In Quebec, the Conseils centraux play a similar role for CSN affiliates.

These central labour bodies, as well as many of the national and international unions affiliated with them, generally maintain *international affiliations*. For example, the Canadian Labour Congress is affiliated with the International Confederation of Free Trade Unions, a grouping of 152 affiliates in 108 countries (Labour Canada 1992, 219). National and international unions are also affiliated with various international labour federations. For example, many of the public sector unions in Canada, such as the National Union of Public and General Employees (NUPGE), are affiliated with the Public Services International. International labour linkages are becoming increasingly important. For instance, national union leaders now coordinate their own meeting to coincide with the G-7 summit meeting of the seven largest industrial nations. International labour federations have also sought to play a more active role in international labour solidarity issues affecting particular industries.

The next sections focus in more detail on the three most important levels of union structure: labour congresses, national and international union organizations, and union locals.

Central Labour Congresses

The Canadian Labour Congress is the principal central labour congress in Canada. It represented 2.48 million members at the beginning of 1994, approximately 61 per cent of union members in Canada. There were ninety national and international unions affiliated with the CLC. They pay affiliation fees to the CLC on a per member basis. The CLC also has a very small number of directly chartered locals but the major form of affiliation is still through national and international labour organizations. It is such organizations and not the CLC or its provincial federations of labour that provide the bulk of direct services to members. Although the Canadian Labour Congress did experiment with recruitment in the financial sector in the 1970s, labour congresses generally do not negotiate for their members, nor do they recruit new members. That is the role of their affiliated organizations.

Labour congresses thus focus on representational and policy-making activities in the social, economic, and political spheres. For example, CLC representatives participate in a number of national and international bodies to deal with issues such as training, unemployment insurance, and social policy on behalf of its members. Representatives of provincial federations of labour do likewise at the provincial level. Only the Quebec Federation of Labour, whose distinct status within the Congress was first recognized in 1974 and further clarified at the 1994 CLC convention, tends to assume other roles normally reserved for affiliates, such as the co-ordination of sectoral bargaining in the Quebec public sector and construction industry.

Affiliated unions zealously maintain their autonomy, and the CLC has very weak formal authority over the activities of its affiliates. Given this weak vertical integration and the congress's relative lack of financial resources, co-ordination between the congress and its principal affiliates depends more on consensus building on policy issues and on persuading the affiliates to commit resources to particular campaigns. However, because of increasing conflicts between affiliates over jurisdictional issues, the CLC has in recent years bolstered its disciplinary powers over individual affiliates, thereby limiting the possibility for a local union to switch its allegiance from one national or international union to another. This was, in particular, the result of a bitter dispute in the Maritimes between the United Food and Commercial Workers Union (UFCW) and the Canadian Auto Workers (CAW) over the decision of many certification units in the fishing industry to transfer their allegiance from the former to the latter. However, there have been many other examples of inter-union conflicts over jurisdictional issues.

The CLC is governed by an executive council that is elected by delegates from local unions to its biennial convention. The president, two vice-presidents, and the secretary-treasurer hold full-time positions. Robert White, who had previously been president of a major affiliate, the Canadian Auto Workers Union, was elected president in 1992. The other members of the CLC executive are generally the senior officers of the major affiliated unions. A certain number of these positions are reserved for women union leaders and representatives of visible minorities. The executive and its various subcommittees meet at regular intervals between biennial congresses to determine the best ways to implement CLC policy.

The Confédération des syndicats nationaux (CSN) is the second largest labour congress. Formerly a confessional or Catholic union movement, but fully secular since the early 1960s, its membership is located almost exclusively in Quebec. As a rule, and unlike many CLC affiliates in other provinces, certification is vested exclusively in the local union (Verge and Murray 1991, 62). Union locals then affiliate directly to the CSN as well as to one of its eight industrial or sectoral federations and to one of its regional councils (Conseils centraux). That means that local unions are free to re-affiliate with other labour centrals should they be dissatisfied with their representation or services. In the public sector, in particular, there is considerable movement back and forth between different central affiliations at the beginning of each bargaining round. The CSN represents approximately 2,200 local unions and 250,000 members. Like the CLC, it is administered by a number of full-time executive officers who are elected at a biennial congress. Its industrial federations do likewise. Unlike the CLC, but like some of the labour congresses in continental Europe, the degree of vertical and horizontal integration of locals within the CSN is highly developed, with meetings bringing together different affiliates at regular intervals (see Chapter 16).

The Canadian union movement has become increasingly fragmented over the last several decades. In contrast to the 1960s and 1970s, when the CLC could claim to represent nearly 75 per cent of all union members in Canada, it now represents 60.8 per cent (see Table 7.6). This change is not the result of a decline in the overall affiliated membership of the CLC but rather it reflects three factors: (1) continued increases in membership of nonaffiliated unions, particularly those representing professionals in the health and education sector; (2) a modification in the reporting requirements of Statistics Canada (see CALURA) which, on paper at least, "increased" the number of unaffiliated union members; and (3) the breakaway of a number of US-based affiliated unions, especially in the construction trades, from the Canadian Labour Congress in 1982, to form the Canadian Federation of Labour (CFL).

The creation of the Canadian Federation of Labour represents a more conservative approach to union political involvement and social change than the CLC has developed over the last several decades. The Canadian Federation of Labour represents roughly 200,000 members from 418 local unions, many of which are affiliated with large international unions in the construction trades such as the International Brotherhood of Electrical Workers, the United Association of Journeymen and Apprentices of the Plumbing and Pipe Fitting Industry of the United States and Canada, and the International Union of Operating Engineers. Although there were increasing tensions between the varying philosophies of these particular unions and some of the public sector unions in the CLC, the specific impetus for the creation of the CFL arose from a jurisdictional dispute in the Quebec construction industry in which the FTQ, the provincial component of the CLC, had set up a rival umbrella body for construction workers in the province of Quebec (Rose 1983).

Other labour congresses in Canada include the Centrale de l'enseignement du Québec (CEQ), a confederation of Quebec public sector unions located primarily but not exclusively in the field of education; the Centrale des syndicats démocratiques (CSD), a small grouping of Quebec unions that broke away from the CSN in the early 1970s; and the Confederation of Canadian Unions (CCU), a loose grouping of independent local Canadian unions with a specific nationalist perspective (Table 7.6).

National and International Unions

In terms of the organization of resources and the development of strategies, national and international unions are undoubtedly the most significant organizational level. It is generally at this level that major decisions about approaches to bargaining, recruitment, and political activity are made. As befits the decentralization of the Canadian labour movement, national and international unions in Canada are highly diverse in their structures and policies.

Table 7.7 lists those unions with more than 50,000 members at the beginning of 1994 as well as their affiliations with central labour congresses. By far the largest is the Canadian Union of Public Employees (CUPE) with roughly 410,000 members in a wide variety of public sector occupations in municipal employment, public and private transport, and the health and education sectors. Such a union is a complex organization with a national office, provincial and often district offices, a national executive board and several full-time executive officers, hundreds of employees including support staff, a wide range of specialists at its Ottawa headquarters, and a large number of field staff.

The National Union of Public and General Employees (NUPGE) is the second largest union in Canada. Unlike some of the other large national and international unions that provide the bulk of the services to their members, it is, in fact, a federation of highly autonomous provincial government employees unions. The Public Service Alliance of Canada (PSAC) is the fifth largest union and represents federal government employees. The United Food and Commercial Workers Unions and the United Steelworkers of America are the largest international unions in Canada. Both organize primarily in the private sector. The Canadian Autoworkers (CAW) is the largest national union in the private sector.

By international standards, one of the more peculiar features of Canadian unionism has been the interpenetration of Canadian and American union structures. Indeed, among the industrialized economies, only in Ireland and Britain are union structures linked in this way. Because of the high degree of integration of the two economies, the two major phases of union development in the United States, craft and industrial unionism, spilled over the northern US border, and a large proportion of Canadian union members have belonged to such "international" unions. An important trend has been the relative decline in the importance of international or American unionism. At the beginning of 1994, 29.5 per cent of union members in Canada belonged to unions whose headquarters were based in the United States (Labour Canada 1994). This represents a complete reversal in the importance of international unionism in Canada, since only twenty-five years earlier, in 1969, 65 per cent of union members in Canada belonged to international unions.

National unions have been growing much faster than international unions, particularly because of the spread of unionization in the public sector, where almost all union members belong to national unions. There have also been some significant splits from parent US unions. One of the most visible separations was that of the Canadian Auto Workers union, which in 1985 split from the United Auto Workers. This move towards greater Canadian autonomy has also occurred in other industries, notably in communications and paper in the 1970s and in the breweries and woodworking in the 1980s.

The move to greater Canadian autonomy has not always resulted in secession by Canadian members within US-based unions. There has been a growing movement towards more self-governance by the Canadian members of international unions (Thompson and Blum 1983). From the early 1970s, the Canadian Labour Congress adopted a set of minimum standards for the governance of Canadian union members by Canadians. These included provisions on the election of Canadian officers by Canadians, the right to determine policies that deal with national affairs and to speak for their unions in Canada, separate affiliations with international union bodies, and freedom from constitutional or policy constraints to participate fully in the Canadian community.

International unions remain a significant feature of Canadian union structure. Of the seventeen largest unions listed in Table 7.7, eight are international unions and nine are national unions. As workers strive to construct cross-border alliances to deal with common problems in the context of the internationalization of production, not only are many forms of international unionism likely to endure, but new forms will also probably emerge.

Unions have a wide variety of internal structures that tend to reflect the evolution of particular visions of territorial, occupational, and industrial solidarities as well as administrative arrangements for providing services to members. The great historical conflict was, of course, between craft unionism, which favoured occupational solidarities, and industrial unionism, which sought to organize workers on the basis of industries. Most unions continue to be based on either an occupational or an industrial principle. While the Canadian Airline Pilots Association organizes only airline pilots within the airline industry, the former Paperworkers Union of Canada organized most salaried workers within the paper industry. For most unions, however, these organizing jurisdictions have become increasingly blurred over time. Changes in the sectoral distribution of employment have had profound implications on these organizing principles. A significant modification in union structure is thus under way.

First, many previously single industry unions are involved in mergers. In 1992, for example, three major industrial unions, the Canadian Paperworkers Union, the Communications and Electrical Workers of Canada, and the Energy, Chemical Workers Union, merged to create a single new union, the Communications, Energy and

Paperworkers Union of Canada (CEP). The Canadian Auto Workers have also been extremely active, merging successively in the 1990s with the Canadian Association of Industrial, Mechanical and Allied Workers; the United Electrical, Radio and Machine Workers of Canada; the Marconi Employees' Union; the Canadian Division Brotherhood of Railway Carmen; the Canadian Textile and Chemical Union; and the Canadian Brotherhood of Railway, Transport and General Workers.

Second, many of the industrial unions in the manufacturing sector have been faced with declining membership and diminished opportunities for new recruitment activity in their traditional jurisdictions. This has prompted some unions to diversify their areas of recruitment. One of the more striking examples of this phenomenon is that of the Steelworkers Union, which is increasingly involved in recruitment in the service sector. This trend accelerated throughout the 1980s as the Steelworkers, seeking to compensate for significant membership loss in traditional areas of strength such as mining and manufacturing, began organizing among security guards and hotel and restaurant workers. It was further bolstered in 1993 when the Canadian members of the Retail, Wholesale and Department Store Union joined the Steelworkers. In addition, public sector unions have begun to recruit in the private sector. What was formerly called the National Union of Provincial Government Employees is now known as the National Union of Public and General Employees (NUPGE) in order to reflect better this change in vocation. One of its component unions, the BC Government Employees Union, which was greatly affected by the successive waves of privatization of public services implemented by Social Credit governments in British Columbia, was particularly active in recruiting members outside of the civil service. Many private and public sector unions in previously well-defined sectors have made selective incursions into other areas, either to compensate for membership loss elsewhere or to respond to changes in the organization of production that are likely to affect the employment conditions of existing membership.

Thus, industrial unionism is slowly giving way to new varieties of general unionism. In the past, there were a few unions that organized in a wide variety of sectors. Such *general unions* were based on neither craft nor industrial jurisdictions. For example, the International Brotherhood of Teamsters, though concentrated in trucking and warehousing, organized in almost any sector and grew to be one of the largest unions in North America. The search for appropriate union structures that can take root in the new service sector is likely to accelerate this transformation of industrial and craft unions into modified forms of general unionism over the coming decade.

At the same time, there is a reaction to this trend in terms of the importance of different occupational groupings both within and between unions. In particular, it should be noted that there are a large number of unaffiliated national unions. These unions typically represent professional groups in the public sector such as teachers and nurses. They have traditionally opted not to affiliate with a central labour body such as the Canadian Labour Congress because they have been wary of the political associations. But, in an era in which the jurisdictional lines have become increasingly muddled, the clearer professional focus of some of these unions has proved to be an impetus for growth. Such has been the case, for example, of the nurses union in Quebec, but there are also an increasing number of professional associations representing other health care professionals in many provinces.

Union Locals

The decentralization of Canadian union structure means that many local unions have a high degree of autonomy. Local unions tend to reflect either their craft or industrial union servicing traditions, though pressures on existing union structures are contributing to the emergence of other hybrid local models.

The craft tradition tends towards a very autonomous local union that organizes a large number of certification units on a regional basis. All dues are paid to that local. It generally has a full-time president who employs business agents to carry out the basic servicing activities of the union. The local union is affiliated with a national or international union to which it pays dues on a pro rata basis. The degree of centralization is therefore fairly weak, and financial control is more typically vested at the local level. With the growing demands on union services centrally, unions organized along this model have added centralized services, but their ability to do so in an effective manner is limited by both the autonomy of local unions and their weak financial capacity at the central level.

The industrial tradition is more centralized. The local union traditionally, but not exclusively, consisted of one certification unit. Local unions had part-time presidents, who did not draw their salary from the union, and the locals were serviced by a cadre of full-time officials employed by the national or international union. Dues were paid by members to the national or international union. Some portion of these dues, in conformity with the prevailing constitutional provisions of the organization, were then allocated to the local union. The proportion of dues accruing to the local level varied considerably by industry and organization. The central union body or the head office generally developed specialized services that were delivered through field staff. The steelworkers and the autoworkers are both good examples of this tradition.

Many of the new public sector unions tended to adopt some variation of the industrial union model. Most evolved from government employee staff associations whose high degree of centralization reflected their employer's structure. While public sector unions might organize a broad range of employees for a particular government employer, their internal organization, unlike that of industrial unions, is sometimes based on professional category rather than location or administrative unit. They have tended to develop expert services at the head office and have fairly weak structures locally. Decentralization of government services and, in some regions, privatization are exerting increasing pressures, however, on this distribution of responsibilities.

There is considerable pressure on all of these models because of changes in industrial structure. Some models appear to be better suited to the new exigencies of the service economy than do others. The changing organization of the firm and larger trends in the labour market have also had a marked, if highly differential, impact on the structures and strategies of local unions. Most notably, the declining size of existing bargaining units and the small size of many new certifications have prompted some unions to amalgamate different certifications into larger, composite locals.

This is particularly evident in many of the older unions that are characterized by a craft structure and that have traditionally organized a multiplicity of units within a single local and built their servicing structures around this type of arrangement. In the case of the United Food and Commercial Workers Union, for example, there are new hybrid models where local unions still maintain a high degree of autonomy, but there is also a tendency to increase the presence of full-time officials paid by the national union to carry out some of the basic services and to be involved in policy coordination.

The local structures of "industrial model" unions, such as the United Steelworkers of America, are also undergoing significant change (see Murray forthcoming). With the infusion of smaller certification units, particularly in the private services, the Steelworkers Union has gradually altered its local structures, with the average number of certifications per local increasing. This represents a conscious organizing and servicing strategy designed to better meet the needs of new membership groups in both the service sector and in small manufacturing units. Indeed, it has aimed to create union locals that are better able to adjust to the small size of the new units typically being organized. It also has sought to achieve a viable servicing strategy in terms of the relative cost of reaching a multiplicity of small units and providing access to basic services. The union has done this at times by training full-time lay representatives rather than professional business agents or servicing staff. The increased importance of amalgamated locals naturally pushes unions organized on the industrial model towards greater decentralization in the distribution of services as local unions assume new responsibilities and local officers change their roles.

Services and Dues

Canadian unions face increasing demands from their members to provide a wide range of sophisticated services. Basic services start, of course, with the negotiation and application of a collective agreement in a particular workplace. While such a service might be provided by a lay official such as a local union president or a shop steward or by a full-time official working either for the national or the local union, larger certification units generally require increasingly complex back-up services, such as research and legal services. The wider the range of issues dealt with in the collective agreement, the more complex is the range of services required. Thus, in recent years, most unions have added health and safety, pension, and pay equity specialists. There is also an increasing demand for information and advice on company finances, work reorganization, new technologies, and environmental regulations. Many unions also seek to provide some supplementary services. Unions began, of course, as mutual insurance societies to provide benefits to craft workers in times of hardship. Strike pay and supplementary health and insurance schemes are examples of such benefits. Some unions have expanded into other types of individual services such as legal, financial, counselling, and employment advice to members. Other unions have sought to develop collective instruments, such as investment funds, in order to safeguard and promote employment in particular workplaces.

Whereas most unions used to charge dues on a flat rate basis, they switched to a percentage basis during the inflationary period of the 1970s. Union dues are typically 1 to 2 per cent of salary. For example, the monthly dues of Steelworker members are established by the international constitution at 1.3 per cent of total salary with provisos for minimum and maximum contributions. The constitution also indicates the percentage distribution of this revenue between different levels of the union. Thus, both the local union and the international union receive 44 per cent of dues, 7 per cent goes to the strike fund, and smaller amounts are allocated to education (1 per cent), political action (1 per cent) and organizing (3 per cent). Unions with more decentralized traditions, such as the United Food and Commercial Workers Union, have more variable arrangements, since the local union is free to fix its own level of dues from which it then must pay per capita affiliation fees, often on a flat rate basis, to other levels of the union.

Yet, as the demand and need for services increases, there is a decreased capacity to pay for them. In particular, structural changes in the labour market have resulted in reduced real dues income per member as overall income has remained static with new members often either working part time or earning less in the general service occupations (Murray 1991). This has increased the pressure on union services and led to a certain rethinking of the role of full-time staff in some unions, especially of the relative division of labour between staff and activists and the role of education and self-empowerment in the provision of services by activists. Once again, this has potentially profound cultural ramifications for the way that people think about their organizations, though it is altogether less clear that widespread changes have actually taken place. Indeed, there would appear to be some scope for a larger debate about the nature of union democracy and how this is to be reflected in the creation of new structures and the provision of services.

Union Governance and Democracy

The union as an organization is characterized by a certain ambiguity, for it is both collective and democratic. It is necessarily collective because its power is derived from its capacity to co-ordinate the actions of its members in order to achieve a common objective, for example, the negotiation of a pension plan. If a union is to exercise a degree of power for its members, it invariably exercises a degree of power over them (Hyman 1975, 65). Craft unions were traditionally illustrative of this point because their power vis-à-vis the employer depended on their control of entry into the trade and their disciplinary powers over those exercising the trade (Clegg 1976, 30).

Unions are also democratic organizations with constitutions that ensure the protection of individual members and guarantee the right of members to participate in the selection and application of policies and to choose their leaders. The power of the collective over the individual is thus limited by the democratic character of the union as well as by certain legislative and Charter of Rights provisions regarding union elections and strike votes, the ratification of collective agreements, the duty of fair representation, and the observance of principles of natural justice.

Even if the possibility of participating in the economic life of their workplace and their country is an important motive for workers becoming union members, it is probably safe to say that the primary objective of most union members is not to enjoy the experience of democracy. Rather, the democratic character of the union is a way of controlling the pursuit of collective goals. Moreover, the attainment of such goals invariably depends on the willingness of individual members to forego individual prerogatives in favour of democratically agreed-upon collective objectives. The dilemma for union democracy, therefore, is the choice between a stable leadership and efficient organization, on the one hand, and the right of opposition with all of the attendant risks of fragmentation and disorder (Hemmingway 1978, 2).

This tension between collectivism and democracy is central to the union organization and affects much of its internal life. Drawing on what a famous observer of life in voluntary organizations labelled the "iron law of oligarchy" (Michels 1962), a pessimistic vision of union democracy suggests that, sooner or later, leadership ends up being concentrated in the hands of a small elite that is not easily removed from power. Such a concentration of power can, of course, lead to abuse. The image of certain union bosses connected to underworld racketeering in the United States readily springs to mind, but there have also been such abuses in Canada (see, for example, Kaplan 1987 on the case of the International Seafarers Union in the 1950s and 1960s). More typically, full-time officials in many unions exercise a tremendous influence on policy outcomes and application.

A more optimistic vision suggests that unions are constantly subject to democratic renewal (Hyman 1971). Union leaders cannot ignore the real and democratic limits of their power. While such limits are formally part of the governance of the union, they are also highly practical. The constant possibility of election defeat, the potential emergence of organized opposition within the union, the obligation for union officials to account for their actions, and, ultimately, the need to mobilize union members in the pursuit of certain objectives and maintain a degree of satisfaction about the attainment of these objectives are all factors that limit the power of union leadership. Most union leaderships are preoccupied by the problem of ensuring membership participation. Many have altered their internal structures to facilitate membership participation, especially that of women and visible minorities, and to respond better to their needs. Drawing on the traditions of their former parent union in the United States, the CAW constitution provides for a type of ombudsperson procedure, where a board made up of impartial individuals from outside the union will hear any membership complaint about improper internal procedures.

There are several possibilities available for membership participation within the union. The most typical form of participation involves membership input on collective bargaining. Members are asked for input on the objectives of particular bargaining rounds; they can participate in meetings that frame these objectives; the law generally obliges them to ratify formally any decision to strike or to accept a collective agreement. This aspect of union life generally stimulates high levels of participation.

Members can also take on other tasks related to the life of the collective agreement or the representation of union members within the establishment. Stewards or workplace representatives are concerned with the application of the collective agreement and the expression of grievances. Workplace health and safety representatives are specifically concerned with this aspect of union work. Increasingly, there are other new channels for membership participation and activism on issues such as pay equity and training.

Members also play a role in the administration of the union. The most typical form of participation involves attendance at local union meetings, even if most observers agree that, outside the most intense periods of collective bargaining, the rate of membership attendance at such meetings remains very low. Union members also elect their local leaders. The local union must also be represented at other decision-making bodies within union structures. While the number and level of such bodies varies from one union to another, the final decision-making authority in almost all unions is some form of convention or congress to which local unions send voting delegates on the basis of their membership. The frequency of such conventions can vary from one to five years or more. Most unions elect their leadership at such conventions, a form of indirect membership elections.

Some unions, notably the Steelworkers, elect their leaders by direct membership postal ballot.

In between conventions, most unions provide for other decision-making bodies to deliberate on the implementation of policy. Sometimes, this involves a small number of full-time executive members elected at a convention or otherwise. Sometimes, it involves some form of representative council at which most major locals or territorial or professional groupings would be present. Some unions, for example the Autoworkers, have both an executive and a quarterly council meeting to which all locals are requested to send delegates. Many unions also have regional structures that might duplicate these arrangements. In particular, this is the case with the Quebec sections of many national and international unions. Over the past two decades, they have developed forms of self-governance that recognize the "distinct" character of their Quebec membership within the larger union structure. Local unions also send delegates, in principle at least, to the conventions of their national and provincial central labour bodies.

The degree of membership participation in the administration of the union tends to be less than that in the bargaining activities of the union. Most unions nonetheless depend almost entirely on the activism of their members to ensure their daily operations. The dynamism and influence of a union ultimately depend on the participation of the membership. Most unions invest heavily in membership education in order to train members to administer their organizations. They also seek to ensure that members do participate and to solve the perpetual participation problems that seem to characterize most voluntary organizations. The possibility of renewing the democratic life of the union is also, of course, a guarantee of its democratic character. As for individual union members, the scope available to them to participate in the democratic life of their unions can be a training ground for the experience of democracy in the larger society as well as an occasion for developing their own abilities. Many union activists speak glowingly of the tremendous influence that union participation has had on their personal development and of how it has enriched their understanding of society.

Challenges for Union Structure and Governance

There are a number of common structural adjustments taking place in Canadian unions to reflect the changes in membership composition, the movements in corporate structure, the rise of new identities at work, and the real problems of organizing new groups of workers into unions.

With women participating in the labour force in growing numbers, unions have had to focus on ensuring that women enjoy a more active role in organized labour. The unionization of the public sector brought large numbers of women members into the ranks of unions. Moreover, the growth of private service sector employment suggests there is an even greater potential for union membership growth among women in the future. However, many women members have charged that unions do not reflect their concerns or accommodate their needs by allowing them to participate in official roles within their unions. Thus, through the 1970s and 1980s, there has been a continuing debate as women have sought to introduce issues such as sexual harassment, child care, maternity leave, affirmative action, and pay equity to union agendas. Debate has also surrounded attempts to ensure that women were adequately represented in elected positions and the different structures of their unions, and attempts to eliminate barriers to active participation in the life of the union (see Briskin and McDermott 1993, 5). Indeed, women's groups and the feminist movement more generally have been a major source of renewal for many unions, and some union leaderships, for example that of CUPE, are now beginning to reflect their formative experience in union women's committees and in coalition activity with other feminist groups.

The relative success of women in this endeavour has served as an example to other groups, such as visible minorities, to claim equivalent recognition within the political channels of their unions. Thus, many unions have adopted a variety of affirmative action measures to ensure the greater participation of different membership groups. Special internal structures based on specific identities, such as gender, ethnicity, or sexual orientation, have also provided a focus for new types of activism. Union leaderships, such as in the Steelworkers, are increasingly confronted with the cultural implications of the changing composition of their union's membership, not least in order to avoid potential backlash from traditional sectors of the union where there may be some nostalgia for an older industrial structure.

At the local level, the rise of the composite or amalgamated local has been a response to the importance of smaller unit size in both manufacturing and services. At other levels, there is the question of how to achieve effective co-ordinating mechanisms in an effort to organize the new groups into viable structures and make links between core and peripheral workers. This is an enduring problem in a large number of unions. Thus, the challenge of fostering participation and giving a sense of ownership to the various groups in their organizations will continue to be a major preoccupation for unions attempting to achieve structural adjustments at different levels of their organizations.

UNION ACTION

Nature of Union Action

The choice traditionally available to a union is between economic and political action. If its objectives were defined largely in terms of the improvement of the terms and conditions of employment of its members, a union might rely exclusively on collective bargaining and, ultimately, on recourse to sanctions such as a strike. Alternatively, it might employ various forms of political action, be it through lobbying, the creation of a political party, or even a mass movement, to pursue the same objectives. Moreover, a union might define its objectives more widely, seeking to represent its members, not only as wage earners but also as citizens (see Murray and Verge 1994). Indeed, central union bodies often aspire to be the voice for all workers.

Why do particular union movements emphasize one type of action rather than another? Many explanations point to the way in which the formative period of the trade union movement in a particular country leaves an imprint on choices of union action. In particular, did workers already enjoy universal suffrage and was the labour market characterized by shortages or an excess supply of unskilled labour? If a particular country's labour movement played a key role in obtaining the vote, for men at least, it was likely to continue this political role. If there was a shortage of unskilled labour in that country, then the labour movement would generally rely on economic action or collective bargaining. However, if an excess supply of unskilled labour existed, that meant that political action was more likely to improve the lot of the vast majority of unionized workers. In North America, where labour shortages were common and the right to vote came independently of the formation of the labour movement, early unions were typically characterized by the label "bread and butter" unionism since they tended to concentrate their action in the realm of collective bargaining.

The creation of industrial unions was characterized by a period of political ferment leading to the formal obligation on the part of employers to recognize unions where a majority of workers favoured such representation. The consolidation of our current industrial relations regime in the immediate aftermath of the post–Second World War period, however, tended to emphasize the narrow economic or industrial character of union representation to the detriment of a broader civic or sociopolitical role (see Giles forthcoming). Increasingly, the union movement tends to rely on some combination of both economic and political methods. This can be clearly seen over the last decade. Not only have Canadian unions become more involved in various forms of political action, but they have sought to develop new mechanisms for talking with employers outside of the traditional collective bargaining framework. While many of the current debates, be they about workers' participation, pay equity, or training, continue to be concentrated at the level of the firm, there is an increasing tendency to broaden the range of union concerns and to intervene at a variety of levels beyond the firm, such as the sectoral, regional, provincial, national, and even international levels.

Collective Bargaining

The classic method of union action is, of course, collective bargaining, a subject that is treated in some detail elsewhere in this volume (see Chapter 9). It should be emphasized, however, that Canadian unions have long pursued a strategy of wage militancy. Indeed, even during the recession of the early 1980s, the CLC adopted a "no concessions" policy.

Unions are currently faced with important shifts in corporate strategy and organization that place traditional collective bargaining under severe pressure. At root here is the social reorganization of production at the workplace, which is particularly evident in the use of new production systems and the reorganization of internal labour markets in the firm. This results in what might be seen as a dual, and sometimes contradictory, process of *integration* and *differentiation*. (This section draws on Murray 1992.)

Integration refers to the ideological reconstruction of the workplace around new production systems and management techniques that seek to mobilize employee enthusiasm and knowledge to achieve greater productivity and competitiveness (Wells 1993). At one end of the continuum, this might be perceived as yet another management fad in a never-ending cycle of participative initiatives. Alternatively, it might be considered a complete reconstruction of the social system of the enterprise, and can, indeed, seek to integrate (or exclude) certain forms of participation and workers' representative mechanisms into the very culture of the firm. This can involve a range of new managerial practices including total quality management, quality circles, different modes of remuneration, and new forms of participation in the firm. Whatever its orientation, and it certainly varies greatly from one firm to another, this integrative process opens up a range of strategic questions for union organizations.

At the same time, often within the very same firms, there is also a process of differentiation whereby firms seek to attain new levels of "flexibility" by transforming traditional full-time, secure jobs into other categories of employment. These can include part-time, contractual, temporary, or subcontracted work. Also, the firm can identify different profit centres and can reorganize production and services into smaller, more highly differentiated units or forego employment relations altogether in favour of outside contractors. Another aspect of differentiation is the creation of specialist employee categories that function outside traditional promotion and wage systems. This multiplication of internal labour markets cuts across traditional lines of union solidarity since relationships between workers and their wages and working conditions are entirely redefined. Some employers, in particular, have sought to disconnect or reorganize traditional wage comparisons between firms and units through this same philosophy of differentiation. In the retail food sector, for example, there have been numerous franchising activities that result either in de-unionization or increased differentiation between contracts. Moreover, this is far from being a strictly private sector phenomenon. Public agencies have sought to emulate differentiation strategies both in the organization of services and in the wages and conditions of their direct employees or their contracted workers.

Pattern bargaining, the co-ordination of bargaining objectives and tactics within a particular sector, previously tended to alleviate the effects of this decentralization. The kinds of comparative linkages previously associated with such patterns are increasingly difficult to maintain in more competitive product markets, however. There are various new union strategies to deal with these developments. Unions have been seeking to build broader-based bargaining structures to obtain greater bargaining power and to create viable servicing structures. In terms of bargaining agenda, in addition to traditional and ever-present concerns over job security and remuneration, unions have made some effort to enlarge their bargaining strategies to reflect the changed political economy and the preoccupations of new groups in the labour market. Thus, there has been a widening of traditional concerns to encompass issues such as pay equity and child care.

Workplace Reorganization

There is currently considerable debate within the labour movement over the challenge of workplace reorganization. The new "co-operative" union strategies that focus almost exclusively within the individual firm to the detriment of larger labour market solidarities are a particular source of contention. Some unions, be they at the local level or at provincial or sectoral levels, are, by the nature of their own histories and the product markets of the firms in which they exist, clearly tempted by the appeal of enduring, co-operative, strife-free relationships with their employers. This kind of new "enterprise" unionism is currently being promoted in a number of countries. Moreover, the threat of unemployment in an era of economic restructuring and global competition pushes many local and national union leaders towards more collaborative relationships with their employers.

However, the real vulnerability of the Canadian economy and some of the inherent contradictions of the new workplace mean that the promise of this type of unionism is often difficult to maintain. This applies not only at the level of the enterprise, where performance does not always meet promise, but also outside the immediate universe of the firm, where a growing group of workers are defined by their "exclusion from" rather than by their "inclusion in" such a co-operative paradigm. Many unions have sought to construct different forms of "partnership" to protect employment on a company-by-company and, occasionally, even on a sectoral basis. Such agreements, however, often significantly restrict a local union's chances for greater solidarity with other unions in the same sector.

Most unions have developed some kind of policy response to change in the workplace. Some, such as the Communications, Energy and Paperworkers Union of Canada (CEP) and the Confédération des syndicats nationaux (CSN), have actively promoted a co-operative approach to change in the workplace. Others, notably the CAW, have advocated a more critical approach. Most unions, however, are in agreement in assessing "involvement in work reorganization as part of the broader strategy of social and economic change" (Kumar 1993b, 28–29).

Hitherto at least, the effect of workplace reorganization on the union as an institution has not been that dramatic (Betcherman et al. 1994; Godard 1994). However, many observers see longer-term implications, be they positive or negative, for the future role of the union (Bourque and Rioux 1994; Rinehart et al. 1994). In particular, they argue that the previous model of union action in the workplace, indeed the entire logic underlying most collective agreements, was predicated on a certain form of work organization that many describe as "Taylorist." (This refers to an extensive and scientific division of labour in which most production jobs are characterized by a narrow range of predefined tasks, standardized procedures, and close supervision.) The recasting of this form of work organization, they say, has quite profound implications for the way that the union operates (Bélanger and Murray 1994). Most analysts agree that unions now have little choice but to be involved in the reorganization of the workplaces where they are present. The challenge, then, is how to maintain a significant role, indeed to consolidate their institutional autonomy in an expanded realm of intervention within the workplace. They must do this in order to ensure the protection of their members while at the same time enlarging the scope for worker participation and choice.

Economic Restructuring beyond the Workplace

In the context of current socioeconomic transformations both within and beyond the firm, representation beyond the firm is increasingly important. We are now witnessing the creation of consultative and representative forums and institutions to deal with issues such as training, sectoral adjustment, productivity, pay equity, and regional economic development. At the national level, the labour movement has traditionally played some role in the administration of certain labour market social programs such as unemployment insurance. For example, one of the four representatives on the Employment and Immigration Commission, which is responsible for the system of unemployment insurance, is only appointed after consultations with the labour movement. The CLC's relations with the federal government deteriorated considerably, however, during the 1970s when wage controls were imposed.

The severity of the recession in the early 1980s prompted many union leaders to seek to diversify union action in the economic sphere. Labour has come to define the representation of economic interests more widely and the government, to a limited degree at least, has come to recognize the legitimacy of such representation. One of the most visible initiatives was the creation of the Canadian Labour Market and Productivity Centre (CLMPC) in 1984 to promote more and better quality jobs. This tripartite body has twelve labour representatives (nine from the CLC and three from the CFL). Moreover, it has actively promoted labour participation in a wide variety of sectoral initiatives designed to restructure the workplace and modernize industries (CLMPC 1992).

At the instigation of the CLMPC, the Canadian Labour Force Development Board was created in 1991. This body, which is responsible for establishing overall priorities for labour force training, includes eight labour representatives. There has also been a proliferation of sectoral initiatives to deal with issues of restructuring and training in particular industries. One of the best known of these is the Canadian Steel Trade and Employment Conference (CSTEC), a bipartite union–employer body that deals with trade and employment adjustment questions in the steel industry. There are currently several other sectoral training initiatives such as in auto parts and communications. Moreover, this multiplication of consultative bodies concerned with economic restructuring and involving participation by union representatives has, to varying degrees, been replicated at provincial level. The Premier's Council on Economic Renewal in Ontario is an example in this regard.

Another type of economic action concerns new labour vehicles for effecting economic change and protecting jobs. The Quebec Federation of Labour was a pioneer in the creation of its Solidarity Fund in 1984. Operating as a registered retirement savings plan (RRSP), this fund is designed to channel worker investment into the safeguarding and creation of jobs, primarily through risk capital (see Fournier 1991). This fund benefits from both federal and provincial government tax credits. The Canadian Federation of Labour has also created a highly successful Working Ventures capital fund with similar objectives. Several other provincial governments have also granted special tax recognition to such funds.

Political Action

Political action concerns the defence of the worker both as a wage earner and as a citizen. The importance of political activities as a dimension of union action was confirmed by a 1991 Supreme Court of Canada decision (*Lavigne* v. *Ontario Public Service Employees Union* (1991) 81 D.L.R. (4th) 545 (S.C.C.)). When a member of the Ontario Public Service Employees Union challenged the right of his union to use his compulsory union dues for purposes other than collective bargaining, the court ruled that political activity was a legitimate extension of collective bargaining.

Unions exhibit varying attitudes to the role of the market and the need for social change. On the one hand, many union leaders are content to continue in the tradition of "bread and butter" unionism. This *business unionism* broadly accepts the operative assumptions of the market place and seeks to get the best deal possible for its members within these limits. On the other hand, many union leaders express a more critical view of the workings of the market and argue for the need to promote social and political change as an integral part of union activity. Such *social unionism* plays an increasingly important role in the analysis of economic restructuring advanced by unions in Canada (Pupo and White 1994). Union political involvement varies from no political activity at all to pressure group activity that seeks to influence the parliamentary or governmental process, direct partisan political action in favour of a particular political party, and coalition activity designed to work with other social groups towards common objectives.

The Canadian Federation of Labour is a good example of a union central that rejects partisan political activity. As stated by its president, "the CFL is committed to an approach based on principle and strong representation, but not on partisanship" (McCambly 1988). Similarly, although it is involved in a wide variety of political activities, the statutes of the Confédération des syndicats nationaux in Quebec expressly forbid it to support a particular political party. Most of the nonaffiliated unions and many public sector unions are also expressly nonpartisan. They have, though, been increasingly involved in a variety of political activities as increasingly severe restraints have been placed on their ability to bargain collectively (see Panitch and Swartz 1993).

In contrast, many CLC affiliates have long maintained a close relationship with the New Democratic Party of Canada and its predecessor the Co-operative Commonwealth Federation. Moreover, from the election of 1979, the CLC became increasingly allied with the NDP. Indeed, with the creation of the Canadian Federation of Labour at the beginning of the 1980s, the departure of some of the more conservative, business-oriented unions from the CLC no doubt facilitated this process. This special relationship has translated into active and financial support. Many, but not all, CLC affiliates are organically linked to the NDP. The NDP constitution provides for both individual and affiliated membership. Affiliated membership is available to organizations such as trade unions, farm groups, co-operatives, and women's organizations, and the cost of affiliated membership is generally at a lesser rate than individual membership. Affiliated organizations and, in practice, trade unions are directly represented on the different decision-making bodies of the NDP. Leaders of affiliated organizations such as the CAW and the USWA participate actively in debates about policy and the selection of leaders.

Both its distance from government at the federal level and the experience of government at the provincial level have put strains on the relationship between labour and the NDP that are not unlike the problems observed between labour parties and union movements in many other countries. The poor showing of the NDP in the 1993 federal election led some union leaders to query whether a strong identification with the NDP was really an asset for the representation of their members' interests. The recent experience of the NDP government in Ontario and its implementation of social contract legislation provides a good illustration of some of the tensions inherent in the relationship between organized labour and the NDP. The scars caused by this particular episode, in which the government suspended free collective bargaining and enacted wage restraint legislation in the Ontario public sector, has caused many public sector unions and some private sector unions, such as the Canadian Autoworkers, to refuse to support this particular government. Nor are such strains unique to the NDP. Similar tensions were observed between Quebec labour unions and the Parti Québécois government of the 1970s and the early 1980s. It would be surprising if similar tensions were not to arise during the mandate of the Parti Québécois government of the 1990s.

Unions in Canada have been increasingly involved in a variety of other kinds of political activity, most notably in coalitions with other groups, as they have sought to influence the outcome of public debates on a range of issues. Faced with the question of how to project the new labour market developments and the preoccupations of their new membership into the larger political and social arena, unions have been forced to effect broader coalitions with other social groups.

Most important have been the successive debates on the free trade agreement with the United States and the North American Free Trade Agreement (NAFTA). During these debates, Canadian unions worked with many other social groups against the free trade treaties (see Robinson 1994). Similarly, some unions have increasingly shared platforms with other groups on questions such as the environment, equal rights, and international solidarity. A number of unions have also created special funds to assist their work in this domain. The Steelworkers Union, in particular, created its Humanity Fund to assist international development projects. Similarly, the CAW's social justice fund is designed to promote worthy projects both in Canada and abroad. Many unions have, of course, long maintained an active civic and community role in philanthropic work such as the United Way or other special charitable causes. To cite but one of many examples, the United Food and Commercial Workers Union invests considerable organizational resources in an annual fund-raising campaign for research on leukemia.

CONCLUSION

This chapter has sought to portray the changing character of unions in Canada. Unions are obliged to come to terms with market changes, but the extent and the direction of adaptation is quite different from one union to another.

These changes have been made in a context of relative success—a veritable Canadian "exceptionalism." Not only has union membership increased in Canada in almost every year since the 1960s, but the labour movement has sought, however imperfectly, to adapt to the major environmental changes of the 1990s: integration of part-time workers, integration of women, changing structural dynamics of the labour movement, and the expression of the identities of at least some of the new labour market groups.

These developments presage a change to new union forms that take account of the broader trends in the economy and society. Just as we can now look back on the decline of craft unionism as the passing of an exclusive but effective organizational form, so too can we increasingly discern the limits of the industrial union model. This latter was closely associated with the creation of the Congress of Industrial Organizations (CIO) in the United States in the 1930s and was widely diffused in Canada in the years of post-war industrial expansion. The model was premised on the protection of its particular membership, primarily male, mass-production workers, through the elaboration of workplace- or company-level collective agreements. These agreements regulated in detail some aspects of the job, while leaving broader questions of work organization in the realm of managerial prerogative. The jurisdiction of the industrial union model was restricted to particular industries and its organizational form was focused on particular units, generally one agreement per local, with external solidarities being extended only as far as pattern bargaining required some kind of linkage with other units.

The real importance of the new service sector, the significance of workplace reorganization, the changes in union membership and practices, and the continuing mutations of previous organizational forms all point towards the emergence of new forms of union organization. The future of Canadian unions very much depends on the emergence of these new models, their appeal to an increasingly heterogeneous workforce, and their success in dealing with the problems encountered by workers in their workplaces and beyond.

QUESTIONS

1. Discuss the different measures of union membership and the strengths and weaknesses of each.

2. Discuss the growing divergence in union density between Canada and the United States. Is it likely to continue?

3. Describe the sectoral differences in the degree of unionization by industry in Canada and the challenges that these pose for unions.

4. Why do some workers join unions and others do not?

5. How would you explain the basic structural choices that a potential union member has in regard to the type of union he or she might join?

6. What is the impact of changes in the larger economy on the definition of union jurisdictions?

7. What are the different possibilities for a union member to participate in the life of the union? Is the union inevitably an oligarchy?

8. Discuss the different ways that Canadian unions have responded to economic restructuring and workplace reorganization.

9. Why do unions become involved in political activity? Discuss the relative merits of a partisan as opposed to a nonpartisan approach to such political activity.

REFERENCES

ARROWSMITH, J. D. 1992. *Canada's Trade Unions: An Information Manual*. Kingston: Industrial Relations Centre, Queen's University.

BAIN, G.S., and R. PRICE. 1983. "Union Growth: Dimensions, Determinants, and Destiny." In G.S. Bain, ed, *Industrial Relations in Great Britain*. Oxford: Basil Blackwell, 3–34.

BARLING, J., C. FULLAGAR, and E.K. KELLOWAY. 1992. *The Union and Its Members: A Psychological Approach*. New York: Oxford University Press.

BÉLANGER, J., and G. MURRAY. 1994. "Unions and Economic Restructuring." *Relations industrielles/Industrial Relations* 49: 648–656.

BELOUS, R.S. 1989. "The Impact of the US Canadian Free Trade Agreement on Labour Management Relations: Facing New Pressures." In G. Laflamme, G. Murray, J. Bélanger and G. Ferland, eds, *Flexibility and Labour Markets in Canada and the United States*. Geneva: International Institute for Labour Studies, 261–274.

BERGERON, J.-G. 1994. "Les facteurs explicatifs de la propension à se syndiquer dans les services privés." *Relations industrielles/Industrial Relations* 49: 776–793.

BETCHERMAN, G., K. McMULLEN, N. LECKIE, and C. CARON. 1994. *The Canadian Workplace in Transition*. Kingston: IRC Press.

BLOCK, R. 1993. "Unionization, Collective Bargaining and Legal Institutions in the United States and Canada." *Queen's Papers in Industrial Relations* 1993, no. 4. Kingston: Industrial Relations Centre, Queen's University.

BOURQUE, R., and C. RIOUX. 1994. "Tendances récentes de la négociation collective dans l'industrie du papier au Québec." *Relations industrielles/Industrial Relations* 49: 730–749.

BRISKIN, L., and P. McDERMOTT, eds. 1993. *Women Challenging Unions: Feminism, Democracy and Militancy*. Toronto: University of Toronto Press.

BRUCE, P.G. 1989. "Political Parties and Labor Legislation in Canada and the US." *Industrial Relations* 28: 115–141.

CALURA. Various years. Statistics Canada. Catalogue 71-202. *Annual Report of the Minister of Industry, Science and Technology under the Corporations and Labour Unions Returns Act Part II — Labour unions*. Ottawa: Minister of Industry, Science and Technology.

CLEGG, H.A. 1976. *Trade Unionism under Collective Bargaining*. Oxford: Basil Blackwell.

CLMPC (CANADIAN LABOUR MARKET AND PRODUCTIVITY CENTRE). 1992. "The Role of Business–Labour Sectoral Initiatives in Economic Restructuring." *Quarterly Labour Market Productivity Review* No. 1–2: 26–38.

COMMISSION ON THE FUTURE OF WORKER–MANAGEMENT RELATIONS. 1994. *Fact-Finding Report*. Washington: US Department of Labor and US Department of Commerce.

CORNISH, M., and L. SPINKS. 1994. *Organizing Unions*. Toronto: Second Story Press.

DION, G. 1986. *Dictionnaire canadien des relations du travail*, 2ᵉ édition. Québec: Presses de l'Université Laval.

ECONOMIC COUNCIL OF CANADA. 1990. *Good Jobs Bad Jobs*. Ottawa: Economic Council of Canada.

FARBER, H.S., and A.B. KRUEGER. 1993. "Union Membership in the United States: The Decline Continues." In B.E. Kaufman and M. Kleiner, eds, *Employee Representation: Alternatives and Future Directions*. Madison, WI: Industrial Relations Research Association, 105–134.

FOURNIER, L. 1991. *Solidarité Inc.: Un nouveau syndicalisme créateur d'emplois*. Montréal: Éditions Québec/Amérique.

FREEMAN, R.B. 1990. "Canada and the World Labour Market to the Year 2000." In K. Newton, T. Schweitzer, and J. Voyer, eds, *Perspective 2000*. Ottawa: Supply and Services Canada, 187–198.

GALLAGHER, D.G., and G. STRAUSS. 1991. "Union Membership Attitudes and Participation." In G. Strauss, D.G. Gallagher, and J. Fiorito, eds, *The State of the Unions*. Madison, WI, Industrial Relations Research Association, 139–174.

GILES, A. Forthcoming. "The Political Economy of the Postwar Settlement: The State and Industrial Relations in Comparative–Historical Perspective." In A. Giles and G. Murray, eds, *Critical Political Economy and Canadian Industrial Relations*.

GODARD, J. 1994. "Labour and Employee Relations in the Canadian Private Sector: Report to Participants in the LERS Surveys." October 1994, mimeo.

HEMMINGWAY, J. 1978. *Conflict and Democracy*. Oxford: Clarendon Press.

HYMAN, R. 1971. *Marxism and the Sociology of Trade Unionism*. London: Pluto Press.

HYMAN, R. 1975. *Industrial Relations*. London: Macmillan.

KAPLAN W. 1987. *Everything That Floats*. Toronto: University of Toronto Press.

KRAHN, H., and G.S. LOWE. 1984. "Community Influences on Attitudes Towards Unions." *Relations industrielles/Industrial Relations* 39: 93–113.

KUMAR, P. 1988. "Estimates of Unionism and Collective Bargaining Coverage in Canada." *Relations industrielles/Industrial Relations* 43: 757–779.

KUMAR, P. 1993. *From Uniformity to Divergence: Industrial Relations in Canada and the United States*. Kingston: Queen's University, IRC Press.

KUMAR, P. 1993b. "Candian Labour's Response to Work Reorganization." *Queen's Papers in Industrial Relations* 1993, no. 6: 32p.

KUMAR, P., D. ARROWSMITH, and M.L. COATES. 1991. *Canadian Labour Relations: An Information Manual*. Kingston: Industrial Relations Centre, Queen's University.

LABOUR CANADA, BUREAU OF LABOUR INFORMATION. Various years. *Directory of Labour Organizations in Canada*. Ottawa: Minister of Supply and Services Canada.

LMAS *(Labour Market Activity Survey)*. 1991. Ottawa: Statistics Canada. Catalogue MDF-3853b.

McCAMBLY, J. 1988. "The CFL Approach: Replacing Labor Confrontation by Participation." *Canadian Speeches* 2: 7–11.

MICHELS, R. 1962. *Political Parties*. New York: Collier Books, first published 1911.

MURRAY, G. 1991. "Exceptionalisme canadien? L'évolution récente du syndicalisme au Canada." *La Revue de l'IRES* 7: 81–105.

MURRAY, G. 1992. "Union Culture and Organizational Change in Ontario and Quebec." In C. Leys and M. Mendell, eds, *Culture and Social Change*. Montreal: Black Rose Books, 39–61.

MURRAY, G. 1994. "Structure and Identity: The Impact of Union Structure in Comparative Perspective." *Employee Relations* 16, no. 2: 24–40.

MURRAY, G. Forthcoming. "The Political Economy of Trade Unionism: Restructuring and Organizational Adjustment in Industrial Trade Unions." In A. Giles and G. Murray, eds, *Critical Political Economy and Canadian Industrial Relations*.

MURRAY, G., and P. VERGE. 1993. "Transformation de l'entreprise et représentation syndicale." *Relations industrielles/Industrial Relations* 48: 3–55.

MURRAY, G., and P. VERGE. 1994. "La représentation syndicale au-delà de l'entreprise." *Les Cahiers de droit* 35: 419–466.

OECD. 1991. "Trends in Trade Union Membership." *Employment Outlook* (July).

PANITCH, L., and D. SWARTZ. 1993. *The Assault on Trade Union Freedoms*. Toronto: Garamond Press.

PIORE, M. 1983. "Can the American Labor Movement Survive Re-Gomperization?" In B.D. Dennis, ed, *Proceedings of the Thirty-Fifth Annual Meeting*. Madison: Industrial Relations Research Association, 30–39.

PUPO, N., and J. WHITE. 1994. "Union Leaders and the Economic Crisis: Responses to Restructuring." *Relations industrielles/Industrial Relations* 49: 821–845.

RIDDELL, W.C. 1993. "Unionization in Canada and the United States: A Tale of Two Countries." In D. Card and R.B. Freeman, eds, *Small Differences That Matter: Labor Markets and Income Maintenance in Canada and the United States*. Chicago: The University of Chicago Press, 109–148.

RINEHART, J., C. HUXLEY, and D. ROBERTSON. 1994. "Worker Commitment and Labour Management Relations under Lean Production at CAMI." *Relations industrielles/Industrial Relations* 49: 750–775.

ROBINSON, I. 1993. "Economistic Unionism in Crisis: The Origins, Consequences, and Prospects of Divergence in Labour-Movement Characteristics." In J. Jenson and R. Mahon, eds, *The Challenge of Restructuring: North American Labor Movements Respond*. Philadelphia: Temple University Press, 19–47.

ROBINSON, I. 1994. "NAFTA, Social Unionism, and Labour Movement Power in Canada and the United States." *Relations industrielles/Industrial Relations* 49: 657–695.

ROSE, J.B. 1983. "Somes Notes on the Building Trades–Canadian Labour Congress Dispute" *Industrial Relations* 22: 87–93.

ROSE, J.B., and G.N. CHAISON. 1990. "New Measures of Union Organizing in the United States and Canada." *Industrial Relations* 29: 457–468.

ROUILLARD, J. 1991. "Le syndicalisme dans l'opinion publique au Canada." *Relations industrielles/Industrial Relations* 46: 277–305.

ROYAL COMMISSION ON THE ECONOMIC UNION AND DEVELOPMENT PROSPECTS FOR CANADA. 1985. *Report*. 3 vols. Ottawa: Minister of Supply and Services Canada.

THOMPSON, M. 1993. "Convergence in International Unionism, etc.: The Case of Canada and the USA. Comment." *British Journal of Industrial Relations* 31: 299–303.

THOMPSON, M., and A.A. BLUM. 1983. "International Unionism in Canada: The Move to Local Control." *Industrial Relations* 22: 71–86.

TROY, L. 1992. "Convergence in International Unionism, etc.: The Case of Canada and the USA." *British Journal of Industrial Relations* 30: 1–43.

VERGE, P., and G. MURRAY. 1991. *Le droit et les syndicats*. Sainte-Foy: Presses de l'Université Laval.

VERMA, A., and J.-G. BERGERON. 1991."Canadian Workers' Preference for Unionization: Some Recent Evidence." In D. Carter, ed, *Women and Industrial Relations: Proceedings of the 28th Conference of the Canadian Industrial Relations Association*. Quebec: Canadian Industrial Relations Association, 389–399.

WEILER, P. 1984. "Striking a New Balance: Freedom of Contract and the Prospects for Union Representation." *Harvard Law Review* 98: 351–420.

WELLS, D. 1993. "Are Strong Unions Compatible with the New Model of Human Resource Management?" *Relations industrielles/Industrial Relations* 48: 56–85.

WHITE, J. 1993. *Sisters and Solidarity: Women and Unions in Canada*. Toronto: Thompson Educational Publishing, Inc.

CHAPTER 8

LABOUR STRATEGIES IN THE NEW SOCIAL ORDER: A POLITICAL ECONOMY PERSPECTIVE

CARLA LIPSIG-MUMMÉ[*]

SOMETIME BETWEEN THE END OF THE 1970S AND THE EARLY 1990S, a complex series of economic and political changes put an end to the economic growth patterns and labour relationships of the post Second World War era. That former pattern of labour relations has been called "the postwar settlement," or the Wagner Act model. But from the 1970s on, there occurred repeated recessions, stubbornly high unemployment, a stagnation in economic growth, the acceleration of global integration of corporate ownership and production, and the widespread desire of governments of all political stripes to retreat from state ownership and regulation of the labour market. All of these factors changed the environment for labour relations in Canada and other high-wage, industrialized countries fundamentally, perhaps irrevocably. After a generation of deepening and broadening worker security, the pendulum began to swing backward during the 1970s and 1980s, undoing many of the gains that unions had obtained for their members and for unorganized workers during the welfare state era, and creating a climate of insecurity, unemployment, and uncertain futures for young Canadians.

[*] The author wishes to thank Kai Lai for research assistance, and Gerry Hunnius for reading and advising on revisions. In addition, the financial support of SSHRC is gratefully acknowledged.

This transformation of the social and economic climate led many researchers to question the effectiveness of the Wagner Act model for regulating the labour market and to examine the ways in which employers and unions developed and pursued their strategic repositioning. It also produced widespread criticism of the state for abdicating its role in establishing and maintaining fair working conditions and access to unionization in a fragmenting labour market.

In North America, (as in Europe), continental economic integration (through the Free Trade Agreement (FTA) between Canada and the United States and then the North American Free Trade Agreement (NAFTA) between Canada, the US and Mexico led to the rapid shifting of manufacturing jobs from high-wage economies (such as Canada) to the lower-wage economies (such as Mexico) in which workers were less protected by legislation and free unionism (Grinspun and Cameron 1993; Middlebrook 1991; Shaiken 1990). The de-industrialization of high-wage economies was accompanied by a new managerial militancy, by garage-and-basement re-industrialization in the manufacturing and data-processing sectors, and by the innovative use of technology. It was also accompanied by the flourishing of smaller-scale, more difficult to regulate manufacturing and service production and by the proliferation of contracting out and subcontracting arrangements. The decentralization of employer responsibility and the growth of small business increased the dangers to employee health and safety, to employment security, to protection against discrimination, to maintenance of minimum wages and standards, and to the ability of both unions and the state to enforce decent working conditions (Drache and Glasbeek 1992; Fudge 1991b).

THE POLITICAL ECONOMY OF LABOUR RELATIONS

In this New Social Order, each of the principal institutional actors in labour relations—unions and their members, private sector corporations, and the diverse levels of government—have had to reposition strategically. How well have they managed? What has been the process by which actors within each group have reassessed their needs and their capacities? How can the events and the actors' responses best be assessed?

The basic and radical changes in the environment for labour relations and in the strategic options for actors have led to questions about the ability of contemporary labour relations theory to explain the rapid changes taking place. As a result, an alternative theoretical approach has evolved that has come to be known as the "political economy" of labour relations.

Political Economy's Critique of Mainstream Industrial Relations

Three underlying assumptions of mainstream industrial relations have come in for critical re-examination by political economists:

1. *The notion of labour relations as a system that tends towards equilibrium.* Mainstream labour relations theorists present the interaction between labour, management, and the state as a cooperative system that sets rules for regulating work relations. Political economists, in contrast, believe that each of the parties represents fundamentally different interests. Disagreement is as common, if not more so, than agreement over desired outcomes, social priorities, and the best methods for achieving the outcomes. Since political economists see the relationships that structure the world of work as concerned with power—complex and volatile, marked by competition, conflict, and sometimes by collaboration—the idea that equilibrium is the natural state of the relationship seems to them naive (Hyman 1989a). Equilibrium, they believe, negates the idea of change and imposes a false image of stability and rational evolution on what is actually a very unstable relationship. They also point out that conflict is inherent in a system that places actors with very different objectives in opposition to each other, and that it serves no purpose to imagine that conflict can be "managed" or "institutionalized" in such a way that the system can remain in balance.

2. *Level playing fields and the neutrality of the state.* Mainstream labour relations theory sees labour law and government policy since the 1940s as levelling out the inherent inequalities of power between unions and management. This approach also assumes that the state acts as a neutral umpire rather than as the representative of particular social groups. Political economists, on the other hand, are considerably more cynical. A number of important recent studies have been devoted to showing the built-in inequalities of labour law with respect to gender, race, employment status, and age (Fudge 1991a, 1991b). They demonstrate, through historical research, the ways in which labour legislation concerning the certification of unions, and the setting of limits to their scope of action, has not been neutral at all (Cornish and Spink 1994; Armstrong and Armstrong 1994; Cook, Lorwin, and Daniels 1984). Phrases like "the institutionalization of conflict" and "the domestication of union militancy" reveal the focus of this research. Where the state is concerned, recent political economy studies in Canada have underlined the state's double role, both as employer and as articulator of the policies of the political party in power (Panitch and Swartz 1988). In particular, they have looked at public sector employment as a kind of "contested terrain" where the state chooses policies of regulation of its own employees for three reasons: to advance its own political vision; to respond to the interest groups outside the government to which it is indebted; and to set an example for the private sector. In terms of the relative power of management and labour, political economists have studied particular strikes and analyzed management policy and strategy for research, development, and investment decisions to demonstrate that profound inequalities of power continue to exist between capital and labour (Wells 1986).

3. *Labour and management as rational actors.* There is an influential trend within mainstream labour relations theory that presents unions and management as actors who choose their strategies rationally and act only after evaluating all relevant costs and benefits. Political economists, in contrast, consider this an artificial construct that distorts the history and procedures of strategic decision making by oversimplification. Although they are interested in the strategic choice analysis that some American authors have been applying to private enterprise, political economists note that it does not work well with unions. They point to the role that organizational memory, cultures of militancy, styles of leadership, and inter-union rivalry play in unions, and argue that when strategies are chosen and acted upon, rational decision making is not a relevant concept. Therefore, the notion of strategic choice as it has been developed to explain corporate behaviour is only marginally explanatory when applied to unions (Fells 1989; Lipsig-Mummé 1987).

The Focus of Political Economy

There are also silences or blank spaces in mainstream industrial relations theory, which in the eyes of political economists render it unable to adequately explain an economic world that is in the process of breakdown and messy transition. Among these blanks, the most important are

1. the lack of research on gender and race in the world of work;
2. the relative paucity of research on the labour process, that is, on the competition for control of how and by whom work is carried out in the workplace, and with what division of power between managers, workers, and intermediary groups;
3. the "under-researching" of government policy and politics and the way they impact on the broader environment of labour relations;
4. the unwillingness to acknowledge the roles of ideology and class in shaping the behaviour of labour, management, and government;
5. the lack of research on workers as subjects and actors; and
6. the tendency to present collective bargaining as the primary or only way in which the competition to control the world of work is played out.

As well as having these silences, mainstream labour relations uses a different research methodology than that employed by political economists. Political economy perceives the mainstream study of labour relations in North America to be heavily influenced by economic modelling, econometrics, behavioural psychology, and human resource management, often attempting to emulate the controlled experiments of the natural sciences. Political economy, in contrast, has been influenced more by the fields of sociology, law, economics, political science and history. Methodologically, political economy insists that it is a social science and that social interactions can never be richly or adequately explained by reference to research methods drawn from laboratory situations and the controlled behaviour of specimens. Political economists study their research subjects in historical and sometimes international context. They are fascinated by the idea of letting participants— most often workers—speak for themselves. And they have returned unions to centre stage as actors and subjects, rather than mere objects confined to reaction.

Concepts of Labour

When political economists talk about *labour* they mean three things. "Labour" refers to *trade unions,* those legally constituted organizations which workers have mandated to negotiate the terms of their working lives. The "trade union movement" is the sum of unions operating within a given geographical territory. Political economists have been interested in a wide range of topics concerning labour organizations. These topics include how unions were formed in the past and how they are formed in the present, trade union structure, internal democracy and styles of leadership, cultures of militancy, and the crystallization of bargaining priorities (Burawoy 1985; Heron 1989; Kealey and Warrian 1976).

Labour also refers to *the labour process,* or the process of production; that is, the work that people put into creating goods or services, the technological organization of that work, and the social organization of the production process (Rinehart 1987). In important ways, what one labours at defines one's place in society. Political economists, strongly influenced by social history and sociology, have dissected the "contested terrain" of the workplace. To do this, they have analyzed the conflict over the control of work, which is embodied in formal and informal workplace rules. They have also analyzed employer strategies for extracting greater productivity and "domesticating conflict" (such as the creation of work teams, participative management, and profit sharing); differences between the sexes over the setting of and reaction to workplace rules; and international comparisons of worker reaction to the labour process (Burawoy 1985).

Finally, labour refers to *a social movement*—the labour movement, which brings working people together not just to negotiate for their wages, hours, and conditions of work, but also to organize to lessen injustice and inequality in society. The labour movement often includes a political party as well as trade unions, and often seeks to make coalitions with other social justice groups in society. Political economists have studied the limits and possibilities of trade union political action, the ways in which unions organize to pressure for social justice issues, and the differences and similarities in labour's political activities in a number of countries. Most recently, political economists have been interested in the union movement's attempts to work more closely with social justice groups. They have asked what this means for labour's historic role as leader of social justice crusades and whether the turn towards coalitions will reverse the qualitative decline of labour's power or dilute its identity (Lipsig-Mummé, 1993). (However, there is remarkably little analysis of the disintegration at the federal level of the NDP, labour's political party in English Canada, or of the remarkable capacity of the Parti Québécois to obtain labour's support without becoming a labour party.)

These definitions set the terms for the discussion of labour strategies to which this chapter is devoted. We will be asking, as a central question, how labour has responded to the major changes in the environment, especially the managerial and technologically driven changes that have occurred in the labour process since the late 1970s. We will also examine the quite widespread unwillingness or ineffectiveness of Canadian provincial and federal governments to modernize employment protection for their citizens. In other words, we will focus on the question of whether labour, in both its trade union and social movement dimensions, has successfully repositioned itself in response to the New Social Order.

THE POSTWAR SETTLEMENT

During the Second World War, the federal government used its wartime powers to pass bill PC1003, an act that was to transform labour-management relations in the private sector, and influence public sector labour relations in Canada, for the next fifty years. PC1003, and the labour codes that were enacted subsequently by the provinces and the federal government after the war had ended, was Keynesian in inspiration and based on the American Wagner Act, which had been introduced as part of the New Deal in the United States, and which defined a new and far more interventionist role for the state in the economy. Within this vision, trade unions were recognized as legitimate institutions for worker representation, although they were seen as junior partners in economic and social development.

In Canada, PC1003 regulated private sector collective bargaining, and was linked both to the enactment of a series of laws regulating labour relations in other sectors and to a series of social programs. It was enacted partly as a result of the shift within Canadian political thinking towards Keynesianism, or the logic of the welfare state, and partly because there was a considerable and well-grounded fear of industrial militancy during the war years.

PC1003 and the Postwar Web of Labour Legislation

PC1003 was meant to give workers the right to form and join unions without being forced to resort to industrial warfare to get those unions recognized. It created an administrative framework for regulating not only the formation of unions, but also the process and content of collective bargaining and the defusing of labour-management conflict in the private sector. Enshrining a state-administered process by which a union would be recognized as sole bargaining agent for a group of workers if it could prove support by a majority, the law also articulated management's duty to bargain, the centrality of collective bargaining and of the signed contract, the importance of seniority as a method of determining rights among workers, the importance of the grievance procedure, and the limits of responsible conflict. At the same time as it enshrined the notion of adversarial labour-management relations, it embedded the practice of collective bargaining in an institutional framework aimed at keeping conflict within well-defined limits.

While it would be difficult to overestimate the importance of PC1003, it is equally important to note that it was only one strand in a web of legal regulations developed in the twenty years after the Second World War and aimed at creating Canada's regulatory system for labour relations in the era of the welfare state. While the labour codes derived from PC1003 are the central elements of this system, a web of labour relations regulation is formed by other laws. These include older laws such as the common law contract of employment and the minimum standards regulations, and more contemporary ones such as the Rand formula, the public sector collective bargaining laws, the human rights laws as well as, in some provinces, separate laws governing labour relations in the construction sector. This complex of legal regulation formed a roughly integrated whole that was characteristic of the welfare state era in Canada.

Quebec is the exception to this evolution, in three ways. First, Quebec's Wagner-Act-like labour code was passed in 1943, but it was honoured more in the breach than the observance by the highly personalized Duplessis government until 1959. The numerous high-profile occasions when Duplessis intervened personally to suppress workers' right to strike, underscored the contradictions crystallizing in the Quebec modernization process and testified to the ability of the executive to subvert the legislative arm of government (Harvey 1980). Second, post-Wagner modernization of Quebec's labour code began early in the late 1970s, and has continued in a piecemeal fashion through the 1990s. Third, Quebec has maintained, since the 1930s, two additional, separate streams of labour legislation, corporatist in inspiration, which regulate the working conditions of a considerable number of workers. The first of these, known as the "decree" system, or the system for the juridical extension of collective agreements, was developed in the depths of the Depression to "take wages out of competition" and to set threshold wages for workers in industrial and service sectors dominated by small-scale, unstable, low-profit businesses, such as garments, hairdressing, auto repair (Bernier 1993). The second stream of corporatist labour regulation in Quebec is the Corporations Act, which regulates the activities of all professional corporations (many more professions are regulated by corporation in Quebec than in English Canada), and has served as a springboard to the unionization of these professionals. The most notable examples here are professionals in the health and education sectors.

In addition to civilizing the process of union formation, PC1003 and its postwar successor laws institutionalized union action and transformed the culture of union militancy. They defined under what circumstances, at what time of the year, and with what instruments of pressure, industrial conflict could occur. Spontaneous walkouts and strikes, called before the union was granted recognition by the state, were outlawed. The laws determined who could become a union member and who could not. They discouraged workers from joining unions in workplaces where the union might not gain bargaining rights in the short term, thus making the organizing of workers in these workplaces unviable for unions. The laws also prohibited strikes during the life of a collective agreement, and gave the state the right to decide when and under what conditions a union could speak for its members. For example, they contained the requirement that a union be granted legal recognition by the state before it could act as bargaining agent for its members, limitations on when and under what circumstances strikes became legal, and requirements for a membership vote in some jurisdictions before a strike could be considered legal. The laws also gave to the state the determining voice in union structure and the structure of collective bargaining (e.g. through the certification process).

As application of the laws proceeded during the 1950s, 1960s, and 1970s, it became evident that the pattern of union certification by the state had created a system of decentralized bargaining in Canada. The certification process led to an unnecessary and counterproductive proliferation of too small unions competing within the same sectors.(The health sector is one of the most extreme examples of this today.) In a very real way, the price that workers and their unions paid for legal regulation of the union-formation process was the opening of a door to the involvement of the state within the union. A central, but little discussed aspect of PC1003 is the fact that the accreditation process weakened the direct relationship between union and membership: it meant that unions were granted the right to speak for their members by the state, not directly by their members. And union structure adapted to the structure of state accreditation, which by the 1990s has become a major factor in labour's weakness and strategic paralysis.

Deepening and Broadening Worker Security

The development of a mature welfare state in the postwar period, the return to economic prosperity, and the continued growth of trade unionism led to a postwar period of deepening and broadening worker security (Lipsig-Mummé 1987). Full employment, or at least full employment for males, was a goal shared by all actors in the labour relations system. By "deepening," we mean the extension of security for workers in the workplace, in their life outside work, and in their situation beyond the employment relationship. This goal is based on the belief that worker security needs to be "secured" more inclusively than simply in the workplace during a worker's years of active employment. In this sense deepening can be considered a process that added layers of protection throughout the welfare state era in two broad ways: first, by extending and anchoring the rights of workers to form unions and to allow them to act effectively; and second, by extending the social safety net and workers' access to it. Some of the most important aspects of the "deepening of worker protection" are the gaining of the right to organize and the dues checkoff, the enactment of unemployment insurance, workers' compensation, the Canada Pension Plan, medicare, free basic education, protection against unjust dismissal, protection against discrimination, parental leave, and health and safety protective legislation. What was the impetus for the several layers of government to deepen worker protection? Partly it derived from the Keynesian idea that well-protected, educated, healthy workers represented by unions would participate more fully in the building of national prosperity through increased consumption. Part of the impetus, however, came from the pressures placed on government by a growing and feisty union movement, which sought to extend the protections it had obtained in collective bargaining to all workers, unionized or not.

The second dimension of extending worker security in the settlement after the Second World War is called "broadening." By broadening worker security we mean extending the rights mentioned above to growing numbers and groups of workers and basing this extension on the belief that rights available to some should be available to all. This occurred through extending unionization to larger numbers of workers. In 1946, 27.9 per cent of paid nonagricultural workers were union members; in 1992, that figure was 37.4 per cent. Broadening also occurred through the expansion of the definitions of persons eligible to be covered by other pieces of social and labour legislation. It can be argued that one objective in the broadening of worker security has been to reduce the segmentation of the labour market and open up the boundaries that have spelled divergent career opportunities for male and female workers, public and private employees, full-time and part-time workers.

But the broadening of worker security did not occur evenly. The web of law regulating labour relations in English Canada was not without internal contradiction and tension. Different laws applied to some groups but not to all, creating a "separate but not necessarily equal" access to union protection for workers in different employment situations. In the first instance, labour legislation encouraged the growth of unionization and its spread to (mainly male) workers throughout the core and primary industries via the vehicle of collective bargaining. In short order, these workers gained coverage by the other employment-related and social-safety-net programs. It proved more difficult, however, for the majority of women workers to gain coverage by collective bargaining and related legislation, since women have historically been clustered in the under-unionized services and in part-time employment. In contrast to men, who have historically held full-time jobs and been overwhelmingly represented in the sectors to which the collective bargaining laws applied, women workers have tended to work under the minimum standards statutes. This has happened for three reasons: because of the precarious nature of women's employment contract; because of the absence or lack of dynamism of unions in their firms or sectors; and because of the often spurious legal fiction that they were self-employed, as in the case of industrial homeworkers. (Regardless of what else has changed in women's employment patterns, at the beginning of the 1990s two-thirds of working women were still clustered in service, clerical, and sales occupations.) After being encouraged to take up paid labour in the manufacturing sector during the Second World War, and after having been forced out of this labour market when the soldiers returned to claim "their" jobs, women re-entered the labour force during the 1950s and 1960s through part-time employment in the private, and then the public, sectors.

In the public sector, rapid growth in employment during the 1960s resulted in bringing more women into the wage labour force. Rapid unionization followed the rapid growth in the numbers employed, and today public sector unionism represents the largest body of unionized women workers. In the private sector, however, the broadening of worker security was largely a failure. Private services have been growing steadily since the Depression, and today represent one out of two Canadian jobs as well as the most dynamic source of new job creation. This sector, however, remains the least unionized, with the largest number of part-time employees and the greatest wage disparity between full-time and part-time or part-year employees. Women form the overwhelming majority of workers in the private service sector.

The uneven broadening of worker security divided workers along other lines as well. Direct and indirect employees of the several levels of government work under public sector labour legislation and essential services laws that restrict their right to strike considerably more than is the case for private sector workers. This has forced public employees to define their forms of action in very different ways from private sector workers.

In other words, when we look at the progress in broadening worker security during the years of postwar settlement after the Second World War, what we see is legislative reinforcement of a segmented labour market, with different groups of workers (distinguished by gender, race, and sector of employment) regulated by different labour law provisions, and enjoying differential access to the employment-based programs. In particular, male and female workers, workers employed in manufacturing and those employed by the state, full-time workers and part-time or otherwise precariously employed workers, have followed different tracks throughout their working lives.

THE BREAKDOWN OF THE POSTWAR SETTLEMENT AND THE THIRD INDUSTRIAL REVOLUTION

From the early 1970s onwards, economic and political changes effectively terminated the postwar settlement, although the process was protracted and an understanding of what was happening was slow to crystallize. The breakdown of the postwar labour relations system occurred in two stages, the first stretching from the early 1970s to the mid-1980s, and the second from the mid-1980s to the present. We may characterize the period as a whole as the Third Industrial Revolution, from which a New Social Order is emerging.

The complex of economic changes that developed out of the oil crises of the early 1970s led to a decade of economic stagnation, inflation, accelerated corporate mergers and bankruptcies, high unemployment and government helplessness (Haiven et al 1991). It also triggered a new managerial militancy that had a number of results and took several forms. Chief among these was the belief, espoused by management in enterprises of all sizes, that obtaining flexibility in production arrangements was crucial. The presence of strong unions was seen as impeding restructuring in the workplace and as acting in the political arena as a too-effective guardian of a too-costly welfare state. Undermining employment security and replacing it with "flexible" work arrangements thus became a principal strategy in the repositioning of enterprises during these decades. By the mid-1980s it was becoming clear that management was withdrawing its support for Keynesianism, rejecting the legitimacy of the welfare-state organization of society, and targeting unions as the major obstacles to the modernization of the Canadian economy and the ability of Canadian corporations to reposition in the post-protectionist global markets.

The breakdown of the compact that had defined trade unionism's role in Canadian civil society did not happen all at once, nor were unions quick to understand its dimensions. But it underscored the need for trade unions to define new strategies in the face of what was emerging as a New Social Order. More specifically, the messy problems of the 1970s and 1980s called upon unions to develop new strategies for:

1.   organizing a rapidly changing working class,
2.   maintaining political leverage over the formation of economic and social policy, and
3.   gaining some voice in the introduction of new forms of technology and work organization.

The tenacity of these problems even after inflation subsided led many observers to question whether Wagner Act labour regulation was not outmoded.

The First Stage of Economic Restructuring

The first stage developed out of the series of shocks produced by the oil crises of the early 1970s and stretched, in most Canadian regions, to the early 1980s. This stage was characterized by the emergence of tenaciously high unemployment; a decline in numbers of manufacturing jobs and a proliferation of low-wage, precarious employment in the private services industry; the massive re-entry, and subsequent ghettoization of women in the labour market and the decline in male labour force participation; the introduction of new information-processing technology as a managerial strategy for intensifying the organization of work and weakening the employment contract; the plateauing and then the cutting back of public sector employment; and the emergence of what was to become a chronic fiscal crisis in the welfare state and a preoccupation with the deficit. The impact of these developments was magnified by the continuous freeing of the business community from government regulation and control. Faced with these combined pressures, welfare states such as the United Kingdom, the United States, and Canada came by the 1980s to be governed by political parties that questioned the basic philosophy of organizing society as a welfare state. Over the decade of the 1980s, these governments would succeed in terminating the postwar settlement in labour relations either by radically changing the legal framework under which unions and employers competed (as in the United Kingdom), or by a de facto hollowing out of the regulations that had protected access to unionization, thus making them not only useless, but sometimes dangerous to worker organization (as in the United States.) Other countries, like France and Australia, elected labour or socialist governments in the mid-1980s, which inherited almost a decade of economic breakdown and confusion, and which chose to protect the survival of the welfare state by reducing it to minimal dimensions. In these countries, union rights were in the main protected and sometimes modernized, but the state encouraged changes in the structure of employment, training, and the role of managers. These governments had a very mixed track record, testifying to the enormous contradictions facing the labour movement and its political allies when it comes to power in a time of profound capitalist economic restructuring.

The fiscal crisis of the welfare state was created by the intensification of contradictory pressures. On the one hand, the pressures for economic support came both from the growing number of unemployed and from private enterprise seeking government grants so as not to cut jobs or move production elsewhere. On the other hand, state revenues began dropping in the 1970s and continued dropping as a result of the rising number of unemployed, so there was less money with which to support needy corporations or individuals. As James O'Connor (1972) so presciently noted, the emergence of a chronic fiscal crisis for welfare states was both cause and effect of the political and economic changes that underwrote it.

In other words, the first wave of economic restructuring struck the Canadian labour movement, but also unions in Europe and the United States, as an essentially economic and only secondarily socio-political, phenomenon. Caught off balance, slow to recognize the magnitude and interdependence of the changes taking place, the labour movement suffered both quantitative and qualitative decline. In quantitative terms, unions lost membership, and real wages and the social wage declined. Government measures were either explicitly anti-union, inadequate in terms of the scale of modernization necessary, or implemented changes that were effective in the short term but impossible for the union to implement over the long term. Qualitatively, unions found their influence, social authority, and political power in decline, not only with the public at large, but with their own members as well. In other words, loss of authority and influence was at least partly the result of quantitative decline. Furthermore, quantitative and qualitative decline came to heighten centrifugal pressures within organized labour, leading sometimes to a weakening of the national peak council (i.e., labour confederations such as the CLC), and sometimes to a breakdown in solidarity between unions organizing in the goods-producing and service-producing sectors. A further symptom of the decline of union power was widespread organizational soul-searching concerning the internal sources of union cohesion and the problem of reinvigorating member militancy. The need for a new union strategy, or strategic repositioning, began to be felt acutely everywhere in the high-wage economies by the end of the first stage of globalization.

The Second Wave of Economic Restructuring

We are now aware that the political economy of world capitalism changed more definitively during the second wave of restructuring than it did during the first. The second wave of economic restructuring gathered strength during the mid- to late-1980s and eventually gave form to the New Social Order. It introduced four new elements that were to be of crucial importance to union movements in all the high-wage countries:

1.   trade liberalization and the formation of regional trading blocs;
2.   the weakening of national governments;
3.   the coming of age of corporate strategic innovation as a major factor that reshaped the job market, the social organization of production, and the parameters of trade union action; and
4.   the disappearance of full-time secure jobs as the typical form of employment and the establishment of precarious employment as the norm rather than the exception.

By the early 1990s, the formation of the three trading blocs in Europe, North America, and Asia; the expansionist urges of Japan, the United States and some countries within the European Union; and the supranational integration of large corporations with their investment and plant-locating decisions increasingly driven by global concerns, each contributed to a generalized weakening of national governments. In Canada, the United Kingdom, France, and elsewhere, the centrifugal pressures forcing these nations to forge international economic links intensified longstanding domestic pressures. These were often expressed as a rejection of the legitimacy of the national government through secessionist movements or pressure for increased regional autonomy. Combined with the reduction of protectionism, the development of managed trade zones, common currencies, and more open labour and product markets, these pressures resulted in the evisceration of many states' ability or willingness to maintain the standards of life and work for their citizens that had long been associated with the welfare state. These combined forces also put unbearable pressures on trade unions, whose strategies for more than a century had been based on the assumption that the organized politics in the national arena was the proper forum for their struggle to influence the state.

In addition, by accelerating the integration of continental or pan-continental labour markets between unequal national partners, as in North America, the trading blocs contributed to the re-emergence of metropolis-periphery relations. (The concept of metropolis-periphery relationships between two or more national economies refers to the capacity of the stronger country to restructure the weaker so as to serve the needs of the stronger, all the while sapping the capacity of the weaker to establish its own healthy pattern of economic development.)

In Canada, for example, the accelerated loss of jobs in the industrial and service sectors, at least partly because of the Free Trade Agreement with the United States, contributed significantly to the widespread perception by citizens that their government was helpless and without vision. This, in turn, created a "legitimation crisis," best symbolized by the results of the 1993 federal elections. In North America, as continental economic integration has proceeded, the national governments of the junior partners, Canada and Mexico, have increasingly exercised less real control over the economic and social life of their citizens. The locus of economic decision making has shifted to the United States. How realistic is it for unions in Canada then, to continue to focus on influencing Canadian federal policy in order to defend their gains and extend economic and social democracy? And if the welfare state of the junior partner no longer serves as an effective arena for political action, what will take its place?

In addition to the macro-political changes which were stimulated by the increased global integration of multinational corporations, the Canadian labour market has suffered a profound transformation—almost a revolution—that has not yet run its course. Prior to the 1980s, the postwar labour market was characterized by high male labour force participation rates and growing female participation rates, by the pre-eminence of full-time secure employment and the presence of a small precarious-employment sector, and by growing unionization and average-sized firms that made it possible for unions to organize. In contrast, the labour market of the later 1980s came to be characterized by de-industrialization and the proliferation of under-regulated service industry jobs, the spread and feminization of poverty, the unfettered growth of precarious employment, the weakening of the state's ability to set and enforce minimum labour standards, the legitimation within union ranks of managerial strategies that previously would have been rejected as union-busting, and the unravelling of the traditional ties between unions and social democratic parties. In Quebec in the 1980s and in Ontario, British Columbia, and Saskatchewan in the 1990s, unions played a crucial role in electing labour or labour-friendly parties, only to find that once elected, "their" parties distanced themselves from their earlier, close relationships with the unions. In three of the four provinces (Quebec, Ontario, British Columbia), the labour-friendly party in power typically pursued a two-track strategy towards the unions. This consisted of modernizing labour law and strengthening enforcement provisions for the manufacturing and primary industries, while cutting into the conditions of work and bases of union power for their own employees in the public sector.

At the same time as Canada was drawn into the early stages of continental economic integration through the FTA and then through NAFTA, the full creativity of new employer strategies for managing labour began to be felt (in some industries, such as autos, these new strategies had penetrated earlier). Regardless of the size of the enterprise, regardless of whether it operated in the public or private sector or targeted a domestic or international market, by the last third of the 1980s employers in all sectors identified the reduction of labour costs as essential to "corporate repositioning" in "the newly competitive, global marketplace."

Over the past decade, employers have gone about reducing labour costs in a number of the following ways, depending on the locus of their production and sales. All of the following are considered to contribute to employer flexibility:

1. the introduction of new technologies that need fewer workers, intensify work for those still employed, may increase surveillance, and can permit the geographic dispersal of the labour force;
2. the laying off or retiring of a portion of the existing labour force, intensifying work for those remaining, or "downsizing" the volume of production;
3. the transferring of production to low-wage, "newly industrializing economies" in Southeast Asia or Latin America, homeworkers within Canada, or through contracting and subcontracting out. In each case, the manufacturers put several levels of legal distance between themselves and the workers who produce their product or service. At each level, some of the ancillary costs associated with the production of the good or service are hived off—to the contractor or to the worker. In this case, the fate of the garment industry in Canada may serve as an early warning for other industries: through a combination of the transfer of production to low-wage countries, the use of contractors and homeworkers, the loss of tariff protection and the exemption of homeworkers from the labour code, that industry has virtually gone underground in Canada, impossible to regulate by the state or to organize by unions;
4. the introduction of various forms of participative management and inter-worker competition (Quality of Working Life (QWL) teams), which are thought to increase worker productivity by increasing the quantity and quality of what is produced, but which also weaken union presence in the workplace and divide union locals from each other. Notable here is the policy of automobile manufacturers to force their plants to compete against each other to obtain the contract for the production of a particular model;
5. the focusing of job creation on part-time, cyclical, on-call, own-account employment, which may not be paid fringe benefits and which is difficult to unionize, thus transforming full-time secure jobs into precarious or casual ones and favouring two-tier hiring in unionized environments;
6. punitive disinvestment, that is, the pursuit by multi-plant enterprises of a policy of channelling new investment (in new technologies) towards their nonunion units, while allowing the unionized units to stagnate, becoming therefore uncompetitive;
7. increasing the political pressure on sympathetic parties or the various levels of government to reduce or abolish payroll-related taxes; and
8. weakening or marginalizing unions by some combination of the above, undermining seniority in unionized workplaces; keeping unions out of new worksites.

"Job shedding," "downsizing," "trimming the fat," and "lean production" continued from the 1980s to the 1990s, and they are all continuing today, when it has become clear that any recovery, when it comes, will be jobless. Male labour force participation declined from 74 per cent in 1975 to 67 per cent in 1991. Female labour force participation continued to climb to a record high of 58.6 per cent but, in partial contrast to the 1960s, women entered the labour force through the bad jobs: part-time, casual, cyclical, on-call and without benefits or job security. Women had always tended to enter the job market through the part-time door; what is new in the 1990s is the spread of precarious employment to all economic sectors and an increasing number of occupations. However, as precarious employment continues to proliferate, with almost twice as many part-time as full-time jobs created, women's unemployment rate has fallen below that of men.

The labour market of the New Social Order, therefore, bears little resemblance to the labour market of the postwar settlement era that was created by PC1003. We may summarize the emerging labour market by reference to its three most prominent aspects:

1. *The privatization of services.* As public sector employment declines as a share of total Canadian employment, the private services emerge as the largest sector and the most dynamic creator of part-time, insecure, casual employment;
2. *The feminization of employment opportunities.* As increasing numbers of new jobs are created they take on the image of women's traditional form of work: part-time, and without the benefit of unions or job security.
3. *The spread of precarious employment.* Homeworking, telework, part-time or part-year employment, cyclical, commission or on-call employment are all being adapted to clerical, sales, and manufacturing employment. Few full-time, secure jobs are being created, and employers are opting to create "flexible" positions that will be difficult to unionize, will not force them to pay benefits, and will allow them to avoid payroll-related taxes.

All of these developments pose particular and demanding challenges to Canadian unions.

THE TWO CANADIAN LABOUR MOVEMENTS

When we ask how Canadian trade unions are reacting to the leaner, meaner climate for advancing workers' interests, it is important to remember that there are not one but two Canadian trade union movements.

A trade union movement embraces all unions operating within certain geographic boundaries, regardless of size or affiliation. It is relatively easy to identify the Canadian, or English Canadian, labour movement: it is composed of the Canadian Labour Congress (CLC) and its affiliates; the Confederation of Canadian Unions (CCU) and its affiliates; the Canadian Federation of Labour (CFL) and its affiliates; independent unions such as teachers' associations and nurses' unions; a scattering of organizations representing miners, aluminum workers, and others. But within Quebec another, separate trade union movement exists, composed of the affiliates of the centrales, such as the Confédération des syndicats nationaux (CSN), the Centrale de l'enseignement du Québec (CEQ), the Confédération des syndicats democratiques (CSD), the Fédération des infirmiers et infirmières du Québec (FIIQ), a numerically important group of independents, and the CLC's Quebec affiliate, the Fédération des travailleurs et travailleuses du Québec (FTQ). What makes the Quebec trade union movement a separate entity? First, is the consciousness of its collective identity and a shared language and history. Second, is the focusing by the centrales on competition and collaboration with each other. Third, is the priority all Quebec unions give to lobbying the provincial rather than the federal government. Fourth, is the preference for developing projects on a Quebec rather than a Canadian scale, in both the domestic and international arenas. Fifth, there is a profound commitment to Quebec, rather than Canadian, nationalism.

To say that there is a distinct Quebec trade union movement that marches to its own drum is not to deny the links that Quebec unions have with English Canadian and US labour organizations. These links are necessary, but often, as is the case with the FTQ, fraught with contradictions and tensions. This leads to some strange alliances: for example the Métallos, the Quebec branch of the United Steelworkers of America, maintains closer links with Pittsburgh than it does with the Steelworkers in English Canada. The Quebec affiliates of the large pan-Canadian public sector unions in the FTQ often work more closely with each other than they do with their "parent" unions in English Canada.

We can find comparable examples in English Canada. Few English-speaking Canadians would deny that "a" Canadian union movement exists, but several of the largest Canadian unions are only regional branches of their "parent" US unions: the United Steelworkers, the United Food and Commercial Workers, the International Brotherhood of Teamsters, for example. They, too, are Janus-faced: they develop projects, alliances, and lobby government with other Canadian unions, but they live a second life, as Canadian regions of US unions. There is no doubt, however, that over the past fifteen years the pan-Canadian identity has become more important than the international for almost all Canadian unions.

Major Ideological Currents

When we ask about trade union response, then, we must ask the question twice: once for the Canadian union movement, and once for the Quebec. But both movements have been decisively influenced by three major ideological currents originating outside Canada, as well as numerous other currents which had minor, regionally specific, or transient influence. To an important degree, ideology and the internal structure of union democracy are linked.

Catholic Corporatist Unionism

Catholic corporatist unionism developed within the Catholic Church in Europe as a bulwark against communism, socialism and the absorption of catholic workers into non-religious unions. It came to Quebec, Belgium, France, Portugal and other Catholic societies at the beginning of the twentieth century, with some minor impact among European immigrants to the rest of Canada and in the U.S. By the mid-1930s it had become the numerically most important form of trade unionism in Quebec, as well as the most conservative. But by the mid-1960s, when Quebec was in the throes of the telescoped modernization process known as the Quiet Revolution, the historically Catholic and corporatist union confederations, the CSN and the CEQ, deconfessionalized (broke ties with the Catholic Church) and moved rapidly towards a form of libertarian socialism, composed of a complex amalgam of influences. (In this, they paralleled the changes in the French Confédération française du travail, also a formerly Catholic union confederation (Lipsig-

Mummé 1980)). These Quebec centrales, or union confederations, were for fifteen years in the 1960s and 1970s a fertile battlefield where post-Catholic unionism worked out its new definition of libertarian socialism by debating and struggling with the proponents of syndicalism and the various Marxist-Leninist and Trotskyist groups that had so much influence on Quebec's social life during those years (FTQ 1972; CSN 1972; CEQ 1972). In these debates, the formerly Catholic, conservative and corporatist union confederations articulated the most radical vision of capitalism as a source of injustice and misery, and of labour as a source of sweeping and creative social change, that has been put forth in Canada since the great organizing years of the 1940s. (And if one listened closely, echoes of the revolutionary syndicalism of the vanished One Big Union, and of the anti-capitalist utopianism of the long-absorbed Knights of Labour, could be heard in those debates as well.) In ways that have not yet been adequately studied, these Quebec debates also influenced the worldview of unions in English Canada during the 1970s.

Gomperism, or craft-based business unionism (named after Samuel Gompers, president of the American Federation of Labor), characterized labour organization during the First Industrial Revolution and became the most important, U.S.-oriented force in Canadian labour from the beginning to the middle of the twentieth century. Over that period, it acted effectively to marginalize autonomous Canadian unionism, making the Trades and Labour Congress, the largest Canadian labour confederation, effectively a pawn of the US labour movement. The Gomperist craft unions in Canada today remain those most closely linked to, and subordinate to, their US parent unions. Many, but not all, split from the CLC to form the Canadian Federation of Labour.

Reutherism, or industrially based social justice unionism (after Walter Reuther, first president of the United Autoworkers and symbol of industrial unionism in the United States), drew its strength from the assembly line workers of the Second Industrial Revolution, the industries we today call the smokestack industries. Combining inclusive industrial forms of solidarity with solid political organizing, it grew rapidly in Canada after the Great Depression, and by the time of the formation of the Canadian Labour Congress in the mid-1950s had become the most typical form of Canadian unionism, both in its structure and in its values and priorities.

Ideology and New Forms of Union Representation

Beginning in the late 1960s and through the 1980s, unions from the Reutherist tradition in English Canada led the way in gaining autonomy from their US union parent organizations. In Quebec they took the lead in negotiating increasing independence for the Fédération des travailleurs/ses du Québec from the CLC. And it is these unions that also redefined and invigorated the notion of social justice unionism and sectorally based representation in Canadian terms, while the unions from which they sprang in the United States suffered terminally from the impact of concession bargaining and their lack of political voice. In Canada, these unions, descendants of the great organizing strikes of the 1930s and 1940s in the auto, steel, rubber, and textile industries, insisted on the definition of labour as a social movement and on the importance of creating an effective political voice for labour in parliamentary politics. In coupling this renewed social unionism to Canadian nationalism from the late 1960s onward, they provided the newly formed public sector unions with a useful starting point from which to define progressive unionism in their work situations. The public sector unions, growing rapidly from the mid-1960s through the 1980s, moved painfully, unevenly, and in some cases incompletely from their self-definition as professional or staff associations to a self-definition as workers' organizations belonging to the labour movement. Today they form the largest sectoral grouping within the Canadian labour movement, and they are in the forefront of the Third Industrial Revolution, which is based on information-processing technologies. The public sectors unions have emerged as the unlikely inheritors of a social justice unionism that sprang from the assembly line and the smokestack industries. Moreover, some public sector unions are adapting the tenets of social justice unionism to their particular sectoral and occupational needs and have begun to create union structures, organizing strategies, and new forms of solidarity tailored to the identity of their members.

The interaction between these three ideologies played out differently in Quebec and English Canada. In Quebec, all three competed with each other, influenced each other, and have retained credibility to the present day. Gomperism, the plain and simple unionism of the skilled craft worker, has been reborn in the professional unionism of teachers and nurses, while Reutherism, or social justice unionism, defines the ideology of the industrial unions, but one fused with a kind of utopian syndicalism to influence both action and discourse of the unskilled and semiskilled worker in the public services. In English Canada, in contrast, Catholic corporatist unionism was never widespread and in any event was a spent force by the 1920s; and the question of national versus US affiliation has almost obscured the debate between industrial and craft unionism, that is between Gomperism and Reutherism.

THE UNRAVELLING OF THE POSTWAR SETTLEMENT

For both the English Canadian and the Quebec movements, however, the years of the postwar settlement (starting only in 1960 in Quebec) allowed inter-sectoral and inter-organizational solidarity to flourish, and unions in very different fields had the luxury of defining their common cause and of supporting each others' causes. But the unravelling of the postwar settlement exacerbated the divergence of priorities within the labour movement, a divergence that had always been dangerously close to the surface. During the second stage of economic restructuring, the working class and its unions in both English Canada and Quebec suffered from two important fissures—a divide between the union and nonunion populations, and a debate within the labour movement over strategies.

The Union - Non-Union Divide

On the one hand, the divide grew between the unionized and non-unionized populations. The welfare state was increasingly unwilling to protect the non-unionized, and as their standard of living slipped, they came to see trade unionists as a too-well protected labour aristocracy. Throughout the period of the postwar settlement, the deepening and broadening of worker security through the expansion of employment and social programs and the spread of collective bargaining had encouraged unorganized and unemployed workers to see unions as a possible instrument for bettering their individual situations. As unemployment grew during the 1970s and then remained tenaciously high, unions and their members offered an easy target for bitterness and blame. Some unions in the late 1980s and early 1990s undertook the difficult task of repositioning themselves vis-à-vis those outside their ranks, creating committees of unemployed workers and committees to organize young workers. But until it became clear that the recovery would be jobless, and unemployment would remain high, unions generally avoided the more difficult problem of redistributing the available work. In this regard, the Canadian Auto Workers in 1993 were pioneers in convincing their members in an Ontario local to forego overtime to create additional jobs. In Quebec, the question of sharing the shrinking pool of jobs more widely has been on the union agenda in the CSN, CEQ, and among some FTQ unions since 1990. (For a discussion of some relevant job creation strategies, see Lipsig-Mummé 1993b.)

However, the political implications of the redefinition of union members as a labour aristocracy have been very different in Quebec and English Canada. In English Canada, the inchoate anger of the economically disenfranchised was cultivated by the reformist populism of the Reform Party to the detriment of the NDP. In Quebec it was focused by the longstanding community organizations, the "groupes populaires," among whom, for the first time in thirty years, a disdain for unions ("dinosaurs") was heard. The response of the community groups to the high unemployment rates of the early 1990s was to recreate a web of "self-help organizations" reminiscent of pre-Quiet Revolution parish life.

Strategic Tensions within the Labour Movement

The second fissure that appeared during the breakdown of the postwar settlement concerned internal relations within the union movement. The broadening and deepening of worker security during the postwar generation had also encouraged the collaboration amongst unions in the manufacturing and primary industries, in the public sector, and in the weakly organized private service industries. The growing fiscal crisis of the welfare state during the 1980s, however, forced a rupture in this alliance, as the needs and priorities of these three groups diverged.

In both English Canada and Quebec, manufacturing and primary sector manual workers were hit by plant closures, technological layoffs, international competition and the marginalization of the union presence in the workplace through the introduction of Japanese managerial techniques and punitive disinvestment. These workers identified the retention of manufacturing jobs, the creation of new manufacturing jobs, retraining, and the search for investors, as their urgent priorities. This embattled group, so long the bedrock of industrial unionism and organized labour in Canada and other high-wage economies, was now losing power within the labour movement because its ranks had been decimated. The role of the state became pivotal, and a debate was opened: should there be collaboration with the state and with employers in hope that this could create a lifeline in the stabilization of employment and even though it would certainly entail concessions and a distancing from militant adversarialism? Defensive accommodation, given the more palatable name of New Partnership or sectoral or meso-corporatism, and involving risky investment in shoring up unprofitable small businesses, became attractive to unions that would not have considered these measures in easier times. By 1990 the CSN in Quebec, and by 1991 the Steelworkers in Ontario, were unlikely converts to this position (CSN 1990, USWA 1992). The alternative strategy was for manufacturing unions to firm up their own ranks, reach out to coalitions with social justice groups, and attempt to seize the agenda creatively while making only those concessions that could not be avoided. Militant adversarialism, or traditional social justice unionism, worked brilliantly in the auto sector, carrying the Canadian Auto Workers through, while other unions were making concessions.

The debate between defensive accommodation and militant adversarialism has by no means been resolved, but it is the needs of workers in the manufacturing sector primarily which has made labour investment in venture capital funds, such as the Fonds de Solidarité in Quebec, and the venture capital funds of the Canadian Federation of Labour, as well as those in British Columbia and Manitoba, so popular. And it is its pressing need for new government legislation concerning worker buyouts, protection against plant closures, the implementation of training and development programs, and the defence of unemployment insurance, which have led many unions in this category to defend NDP governments even when these governments have been in open conflict with the public sector unions. In Quebec, following the disastrous confrontation between the Parti Québécois government and the public sector unions in 1982-83, the FTQ, in which private sector unions play a most important role, distanced itself from the PQ in the 1985 elections, but returned to its traditional support in 1989.

The second component of the union movement is composed of public sector workers, who face issues different from those confronting workers in the manufacturing sector. Having found that state managerial practices made a mockery of their commitment to service, they put quality of work, recognition of their professionalism, the security of the employment contract, and the right to negotiate the introduction of technological change (typified by the introduction of telework in the federal public service), at the head of their list of priorities. For state employees, partnership with their management was seen to inevitably weaken unionism. (In Quebec they formed Common Fronts to bargain together against the provincial government; in English Canada the unexpectedly successful 1991 strike by the Public Service Alliance of Canada transformed the consciousness of civil servants in general.)

The third group, private sector workers in commerce and finance, personal service, and service to business, form the segment of the labour market that accounts for one of every two Canadian jobs. This group is weakly unionized and suffers from more primitive employment conditions, reminiscent of the pre-welfare state industrial relations system of raw class conflict. It is also difficult to unionize because of the limits of the Wagner Act model, the small size of the average enterprise, and the radically effective anti-unionism of employers. Service sector unionism therefore, has as its first priority the extension and protection of the simple right to organize. But as an under-unionized sector, it has become a kind of free-fire zone to which dynamic industrial unions in the manufacturing sector, faced with the loss of jobs in their traditional jurisdictions, can turn in order to replenish their ranks. In English Canada, the big smokestack unions like the Steelworkers and the CAW are in the process of transforming themselves into general unions, and this is a measure of how important the new organizing attempts or mergers with the private service unions have been. In Quebec the historical legitimation of inter-centrale rivalry complicates the campaign to unionize this sector.

Labour and Politics

Like the NDP and the Parti Québécois, the Canadian and Quebec union movements are firm believers in Keynesianism, that is, they advocate a strongly centralized state intervening dynamically by economic regulation. But unlike the two political parties, both labour movements have been schizophrenic about their own position in relationship to a stronger state, and particularly about how to relate to "their" party when it runs the government. In English Canada, the experience of unions when the NDP has held provincial office has often been bitter and divisive, leading to a serious division between the party and goods-and-service-producing unions and contributing to the disintegration of labour's political voice in federal politics.

But for Quebec labour, the state to be reinforced is the Quebec state. After the confrontation between public sector unions and the PQ in 1982-83, the PQ distanced itself from its traditional social democracy and emerged as the party of the Quebec business class. The union centrales, which (with the exception of the CSD) are committed to Quebec independence, returned to support the transformed PQ after 1990, arguing that a national coalition was necessary to attain independence, and after that the struggle for socialism could begin. In the mid-1980s, however, a split between the PQ and unions led to the defeat of the party in 1985. The CSN and the CEQ then joined the FTQ in "concertation." This is a brand of New Partnership or sectoral corporatism that has led them to eschew the militant adversarialism which had been their trademark in the 1970s and to forge concessionary deals at the firm level in manufacturing and at the sectoral level in education and in certain parts of the health sector (CSN 1990). In both public and private sectors, the union logic was to work with the state (even with the Liberals in power) in order to build the strongest possible Quebec economy with which to begin life as a sovereign state.

To this end the centrales also distanced themselves from their former opposition to NAFTA and focused on developing sectoral relations with US and Mexican unions. They were willing to be consulted in any kind of economic planning, and they have moved towards a new analysis of the organization of work as a subject for bipartite discussion rather than contractual negotiation.

In English Canada, however, the issues have been at once more complex and more diffuse. In its role as collective bargaining agent and worker representative in negotiating the labour process—and as a social movement—the English Canadian labour movement has historically been crosscut by four tensions:

1. between integration into an "international" labour movement and the construction of an autonomous, Canadian movement;
2. between craft and industrial organizing principles;
3. between business unionism and social unionism;
4. between regional or industrial union autonomy and effectively centralized, national coordination.

When we consider these tensions in conjunction with the contemporary changes in the structure of employment, the technological bases for work organization, and managerial attitudes towards trade unionism, we may argue that the Canadian labour movement faces a series of difficult challenges if it is to strategically reposition in the New Social Order.

THE FIVE CHALLENGES FACING CANADIAN LABOUR

The Challenge to Organize the New Working Class

For the working class of the first decades of the twenty-first century, male and female labour force participation rates will equalize rapidly. The typical job will be precarious and fragmentary, offering neither security of tenure nor full-time employment. Nonstandard, atypical employment will be full-time and secure, perhaps in a small manufacturing sector, more certainly in education and the civil service. The private services will employ more than one in two Canadians, while less than 10 per cent of Canadians will be employed in producing goods. Ironically, as formerly good jobs are transformed into bad jobs, more and more education will be required, and the longing for craft identification, for the sense of artisanship, may well continue to grow among those very workers whose limited skills make it an impossible dream. Because security will be such a rare commodity, the young will be encouraged to train for skills, not professions, and will be encouraged to learn the most portable skills.

Women, workers of colour, the young, and the elderly will be more prominent in this workforce than they are today. Yet as part-time, part-year, casual employees, their needs will be different, their priorities different, their relationship to work and to the union, profoundly different from the male, full-time, goods-producing worker who typified the union member of the postwar settlement years. In order to organize the new working class, today's trade unions will have to develop tactics to reach workers for whom one job is not the centre of the universe. This will entail a modernization of organizing tactics along two tracks that build on some older, all but forgotten, approaches.

The first track is that of community unionism. When unions organize workers of several different languages, races, or ethnic origins, community unionism, developed during the nineteenth century, makes a lot of sense. The term has been used in several different ways, but we may take it as a general rubric meaning union organizing that starts from the belief that work is an integral part of community life and that the community should be involved with organizing as well as with the maintenance of labour standards. Community involvement entails developing "permeable" union structures, ones that open out to the community. It also entails the development of new representative structures in which unions and the community share.

The second track of new union organizing may well have to take into consideration the worker's longing for artisanship, the desire to be seen as a professional, which permeates all work situations, regardless of formally defined skill levels. Unions like the Service Employees International Union have discovered that tapping into and organizing around the desire for skills recognition, can be a powerful organizing tool. But more than a tool, it is a return to the earliest forms of organization. Organizing assembly line workers from the 1930s on was based on their sense of alienation and exploitation. In contrast, the earlier, nineteenth century unionizing drives appealed to skilled workers on the basis of their pride in their work. Unions may well find it useful to return to that longing for skill recognition and professionalism as they set about organizing the more highly educated, more severely deskilled, precarious working population of the twenty-first century.

Next, today's labour movement will have to revamp bargaining priorities to respond to this new group of members. Should this seem impossible or utopian, two observations are in order. First, in a number of other high-wage economies, the past ten years have led to a radical restructuring on the part of the union movement, if only because survival clearly demanded adaptation. Second, in the 1920s the union movement in Canada (and in the United States) went into decline and on the defensive, as corporate innovations in the structure of production led to the widespread introduction of the assembly line and the Second Industrial Revolution. Yet throughout that difficult decade, labour continued representing the former working class—the skilled tradesmen of the First Industrial Revolution. It was not until new unions emerged that were willing to organize the semi-skilled and the unskilled, and that developed creative new tactics to do so (among them, the sit-in), that the labour movement began to regain vitality and shift its emphasis to speaking for, and to, the new working class that was then emerging. Just such a turn-around is necessary now, at the beginning of the Third Industrial Revolution.

The Challenge to Represent Different Dreams

The radically polarized working class of the early twenty-first century, divided between the small labour aristocracy holding full-time secure jobs and the mass of workers holding precarious jobs, will have a difficult time finding common ground. Today's unions will not only continue to adapt their organizing techniques to the office and the small shop, but they will have to become considerably more multilingual than they already are. As the sense of individual identification with the working class disappears, certain of the most prized rights that trade unions won in the mid-twentieth century, like seniority and job-control unionism, will no longer be as relevant to a union movement the majority of whose members are precariously employed. In any case, these rights will be of doubtful benefit to workers without security of tenure. Furthermore, the commitment to obtaining as much work as possible for those already employed, including overtime, is already attracting powerful opposition, especially from those outside the ranks of the organized employed. Will unions choose to continue the struggle for full employment? Will they assume that high basic unemployment is here to stay and thus that job sharing should be considered? Can both strategies be pursued at the same time?

Another issue also demands attention. The rise, spread, and effectiveness of advocacy groups, especially of equity advocacy groups (based on race, gender, sexual preference, abilities, and disabilities), is a two-edged sword for labour and any other organization that works to create a broadly based solidarity. On the one hand, the crystallization of interest groups is healthy and healing; on the other, it leads to the kind of small-group individualism that makes concerted action difficult to organize and sustain. Coalitions only occasionally function as long-term, broadly based, effective social movements. Can unions and advocacy groups work together and enrich each other without blurring the essential identity and specific objectives of each partner?

The Challenge to Construct New, Effective Alliances

The dissolution of class, craft, or industrial identity, and the shift to a service economy, have already begun to affect the cohesion within unions and the relations of unions to each other. Among unions in English Canada, the principal area of competition is the under-unionized private services. In any one of a number of areas, such as nursing homes, retail trade, and hotels, between three and eight unions may be in competition for new members. It has already become urgent for the Canadian labour movement to restructure rationally, perhaps creating a smaller number of "super unions," each representing a broadly defined jurisdiction. (At present, understanding the structure of union affiliation is an exercise in industrial archaeology; new groups are added on rather than integrated into a union structure.) This would reduce the incidence of raiding and the cost of inter-union competition, and it would help the labour movement as a whole to function more effectively. In Quebec, the longstanding existence of several union centrales has the benediction of time, but not much else. There is, unfortunately, no inter-centrale adjudicating body that settles disputes or decides which union gets new members.

Another dimension of the growing search for new alliances is the issue of sectoral regroupings. The development of globalization over the past twenty years has made the creation of real, working, international links between unions on the basis of sharing the same industrial sector (telecommunications, metalworking, food processing, etc.), not only logical but necessary. It would not be utopian to suggest that since Canada is in the process of integration into a continental economic order, increasing sectoral links with unions in the United States and Mexico could make both organizing and collective bargaining more efficient.

Although this idea is logical, there are numerous obstacles. The most important is that unions in Canada, as elsewhere, are understandably nationalist rather than internationalist. Arguing for raising labour and living standards in poorer countries is often a thinly veiled ploy for keeping the jobs at home in the high-wage country. The second obstacle is political: the struggle by Canadian unions to separate from their US parent organizations is recent, and sometimes bitter. In order to create trinational union linkages based on information sharing or even joint bargaining by sector, the relationship between Canadian and US unions will have to evolve. Finally, in order to develop effective trinational sectoral alliances, the internal structure of the Canadian labour movement will have to be rationalized, so that one and not several competitive unions represent workers in a given sector.

The Challenge to Roll Back the Intensification of Work

Intensification means an increase of work for those who remain employed. It also means the loss of some degree of autonomy at work for those who remain employed, either as a result of the introduction of new technologies, or by the introduction of scientific management into sectors where it was previously absent, such as private services. Intensification can, therefore be expressed quantitatively, as an increase of the average number of hours worked, or it can be expressed qualitatively, as an increased pace of work or the loss of relative freedom at work. While it is difficult to systematically collect cross-sectoral evidence of the scope and impact of deskilling, which is a byproduct of intensification, unions act on the premise that it is occurring widely, in all sectors and most occupations. An initial response to the intensification of work would be to document evidence of where and to what degree it is occurring and to study the responses of unions.

The more difficult problem is the crafting of an integrated strategy of response, and beyond that, a strategy of union-initiated change. Canadian collective bargaining is decentralized. With thousands of collective agreements, and a too-large number of fiercely individualist, too-small unions, this challenge, like the challenge to integrate and co-ordinate new organizing drives, reveals once again the impact of the CLC's weakness as a coordinating body. Across all this fragmentation, however, the basic need to modernize labour legislation and the Wagner Act model, to compensate for fragmentation and weakness at the bargaining table, is emerging as a common theme. In other words, if labour is to respond creatively to the intensification of work and the other managerial initiatives described earlier in this chapter, it will have to do so in an integrated way. This, in turn, requires important changes in the structure of accreditation to allow unions to organize workers in small workplaces and those working part-time and part-year. Various ways of "broadening the bargaining base" are currently under discussion, such as sectoral negotiation, adapting Quebec's venerable decree system to contemporary Canada, or multi-employer accreditation (Bernier 1993). The modernization of Wagnerism seems imperative.

But is there widespread agreement on this priority? In Quebec, labouring under a somewhat modernized labour code, the principal unions in health, education, and municipal services, as well as several unions in key heavy industries, have undertaken to negotiate "changes to the organization of work" on a contract-by-contract, employer-by-employer basis, without pressing for major labour code changes. The results have been the subject of fierce debate: is a uniquely "Quebec model" of the new industrial relations emerging? It is too early to say with any certainty, but in 1994 there was concerted, visible opposition to this strategic direction within both the CEQ and the CSN.

The Challenge to Influence Social and Economic Policy

While maximizing union influence over social and economic government policy has always been an important union priority in English Canada and Quebec, the two union movements have gone about it in different ways. Historically, the influence of Quebec's post-Catholic unions has led labour to seek to influence governments from an extra-parliamentary stance, although the FTQ has always sought a party with which to develop a privileged relationship. The dominant strategy of extra-parliamentary politics has had both extremely conservative and modern syndicalist supporters. The conservative view is that a union has no business in politics, either as a lobbyist or as an interest group. The syndicalists argue that the inherent corruption of all bourgeois parliaments leads to a strategy of pressure from without: putting a quarter of a million demonstrators outside the National Assembly will do more than the election of a number of labour supporters inside. The convergence of left and right led to a surprising marginalization of labour's political voice until the mid-1980s, when the turn towards "concertation" brought all the union centrales into a more consultative relationship with government policy makers. All evidence over the past decade, however, points to the disappearance of a distinct labour voice, with unions reduced to the status of one interest group among many.

In English Canada, the typically weak labourist model has worked better when the NDP was out of power than when it gained office. In Ontario, Saskatchewan, and British Columbia, the election of the NDP has intensified internal divisions within the labour movement. One group, usually based in the private sector and in the manufacturing or primary industries, typically retains a privileged relationship with the party-become-government, supporting it in various ways and accepting the compromising of principles that all parties make when in power. Another group, however, often composed of those advocacy groups and public and para-public sector workers who have been the targets of "their" government's austerity budgets, has moved from disillusionment, to bitterness, to extra-parliamentary futility, ushering in the defeat of "their" government and its return to opposition status. While the union movement as a whole has had considerable influence over provincial governments in the setting of social policy and those areas of economic policy for which provinces are responsible during the NDP's time in power, they have never had more than sporadic influence in federal politics. Furthermore, the cost of electing the NDP at the provincial level has been union divisions, a general weakening of the labour movement, and often the ushering in of a successor government that wants to hear nothing of labour's voice. There is an obvious need, then, for the trade union movement to develop new alliances, new strategies, and new ways of influencing the setting of the social and economic agendas.

QUESTIONS

1. Define the deepening of worker security.
2. Define the broadening of worker security.
3. What factors contributed to the breakdown of worker security? When?
4. How well is the Canadian Labour Congress suited to reposition itself in the New Social Order?
5. What are the principal conflicts dividing the Canadian union movement today?
6. What are the principal challenges facing the Canadian labour movement?

REFERENCES

ADAMS, R. J. 1989. "North American Industrial Relations: Divergent Trends in Canada and the United States." *International Labour Review* 128: 47-64.

ANDERSON, P. 1970. "The Limits and Possibilities of Trade Union Action." In C. Cockburn, ed., *The Incompatibles.* London: Penguin.

ARMSTRONG, P., and H. ARMSTRONG. 1994. *The Double Ghetto: Canadian Women and Their Segregated Work,* 3rd ed. Toronto: McClelland & Stewart.

ARTHURS, H.W., D.D. CARTER, and H.J. GLASBEEK. 1981. *Labour Law and Industrial Relations in Canada.* Scarborough, Ont.: Butterworths and Co. Ltd.

BAMBER, G. J., ed. 1987. *International and Comparative Industrial Relations: A Study of Developed Market Economies.* London: Allen and Unwin.

BANKS, A., and J. METZGAR. 1989. "Participating in Management: Union Organizing on New Terrain." *Labour Research Review* vol. VII, no. 2. Chicago: Midwest Center for Labor Research.

BERGMANN, B. R. 1987. "Pay Equity: Surprising Answers to Hard Questions." *Challenge.* 30 (May/June): 207-216.

BERNIER, J. 1993. "Modernizing the Quebec Decree System." *Working Paper Series.* Centre for Research on Work and Society, York University.

BLYTON, P., A. DASMALCHIAN, and R. ADAMSON. 1987. "Developing the Concept of Industrial Relations Climate." *Journal of Industrial Relations* 29 (June): 207-216.

BOYER, R. 1987. "Labour Flexibility in Seven European Countries: A Look at Labour Management Relations." *Social and Labour Bulletin:* 13-18.

de BRESSON, C. 1987. *Understanding Technological Change.* Montreal: Black Rose Books.

BURAWOY, M. 1985. *The Politics of Production: Factory Regimes Under Capitalism and Socialism.* London: Verso.

BURNS, T.R., L.E. KARLSSON, and V. RUS, eds. 1979. *Work and Power: the Liberation of Work and the Control of Political Power.* London: Sage Publications Ltd.

CAMPBELL, D. 1989. "Multinational Labor Relations in the European Community." *ILR Report* 27 (Fall): 7-14.

CANADIAN LABOUR MARKET AND PRODUCTIVITY CENTRE, COMMITTEE ON WOMEN AND ECONOMIC RESTRUCTURING. 1994. *Women and Economic Restructuring.* Ottawa: Canadian Labour Market and Productivity Centre.

————, Economic Restructuring Committee. 1993. *Canada: Meeting the Challenge of Change: A Statement.* Ottawa: Canadian Labour Market and Productivity Centre.

CENTRALE DE L'ENSEIGNEMENT DU QUÉBEC (CEQ). 1972. *L'école au service de la classe dominante.* Québec.

CHAYKOWSKI, R. P. 1989. "Pay Equity Legislation." *Research and Current Issues Series.* no. 59. Kingston, Ont: Industrial Relations Centre, Queen's University.

COATES, M. L. 1989. "Pay and Employment Equity." *Reprint Series* no. 84. Kingston, Ont: Industrial Relations Centre, Queen's University.

CONFÉDÉRATION DES SYNDICATS NATIONAUX (CSN). 1972. *Ne comptons que sur nos propres moyens.* Montréal.

————. 1990. *Vers un nouveau partenariat.* Montréal.

COOK, A., B. LORWIN and A.K. DANIELS. 1984. *Women and Trade Unions in Eleven Industrialized Countries.* Philadelphia: Temple University Press.

CORNISH, M., and L. SPINK. 1994. *Organizing Unions.* Philadelphia: Temple University Press.

CRAVEN, P. 1978. *Technological Change and the Workforce.* Toronto: Ontario Institute for Studies in Education.

CRAYPO., C., and B. NISSEN, eds. 1993. *Grand Designs: the Impact of Corporate Strategies on Workers, Unions, and Communities.* Ithaca, New York: ILR Press.

DENIS, S., and R. DENIS. 1992. *Les syndicats face au pouvoir.* Montréal: Editions du Vermillon.

DILLON, B., and S.O. SIOCHRU. 1989. "Trade Unions and the Internal Market: The Contribution of Contemporary Theory to Strategy." *Warwick Papers in Industrial Relations* no. 28. Coventry, England: Industrial Relations Research Unit, University of Warwick.

DRACHE, D., and H. GLASBEEK. 1992. *The Changing Workplace: Reshaping Canada's Industrial Relations System.* Toronto: James Lorimer & Company.

EDWARDS, P.K., and H. SCULLION. 1982. *The Social Organization of Industrial Conflict: Control and Resistance in the Workplace.* Oxford: Basil Blackwell.

ELLIOT, C. J. 1987. *Pay Equity Handbook: A Step-by-Step Guide to Implementing Equal Pay for Work of Equal Value in Ontario.* Aurora, Ont.: Canada Law Book.

ESPING-ANDERSEN, G. 1985. *Politics Against Markets: The Social Democratic Road to Power.* Princeton, N.J.: Princeton University Press.

FÉDÉRATION DES TRAVAILLEURS ET TRAVAILLEUSES DU QUÉBEC (FTQ). 1972. *L'État rouage.* Montréal.

FELLS, R.E. 1989. "The Employment Relationship, Control and Strategic Choice in the Study of Industrial Relationships." *Labour and Industry* 2 (October): 470-492.

FLANAGAN, T. 1987. "Equal Pay for Work of Equal Value: Issues and Policies." *Canadian Public Policy* 13 (December): 435-492.

FORREST, A. 1992. "Women and Unions: Does Our Theory Fit?" *CIRA Proceedings* 333-344.

FUDGE, J., and P. McDERMOTT, eds. 1991. *Just Wages: A Feminist Assessment of Pay Equity.* Toronto: University of Toronto Press.

————. 1991. *Labour Law's Little Sister: The Employment Standards Act and the Feminization of Labour.* Ottawa, Ont: Canadian Centre for Policy Alternatives.

FULCHER, J. 1988. "On the Explanation of Industrial Relations Diversity: Labour Movements, Employers and the State in Britain and Sweden." *British Journal of Industrial Relations* 26 (July): 246-274.

GERHMANN, B.R. 1987. "The Job Market, Sex Bias, and Comparable Worth." *Public Personnel Management* 16 (Summer): 173-180.

GLADSTONE, A., ed. 1989. *Current Issues in Labour Relations: An International Perspective.* New York: Walter de Gruyter.

GORDON, D.M., R. EDWARDS, and M. REICH. 1982. *Segmented Work, Divided Workers: The Historical Transformation of Labor in the United States.* New York: Cambridge University Press.

GRINSPUN, R., and M. A. CAMERON. 1993. *The Political Economy of North American Free Trade.* Ottawa: Canadian Centre for Policy Alternatives.

HAIVEN, L., S. MCBRIDE, and J. SHIELDS, eds. 1990. *Regulating Labour: The State, Neo-Conservatism and Industrial Relations.* Toronto: Garamond Press in co-operation with the Society for Socialist Studies.

HARVEY, F. 1980. *Le mouvement ouvrier au Québec.* Montréal: Boréal.

HÉBERT, G.,. H.C. JAIN, and N. MELTZ., eds. 1989. *The State of the Art in Industrial Relations: A Project of the Canadian Industrial Relations Association.* Kingston, Ont.: Industrial Relations Centre, Queen's University.

HERON, C. 1989. *The Canadian Labour Movement: A Short History.* Toronto: J. Lorimer.

HORRIGAN, J., and A. HARRIMAN. 1988. "Comparable Worth: Public Sector Unions and Employers Provide a Model for Implementing Pay Equity." *Labor Law Journal* 39 (October): 704-711.

HYMAN, R. 1989. *The Political Economy of Industrial Relations.* London: MacMillan.

————. 1989. *Strikes,* 4th ed. Basingstoke: Macmillan Press.

————. 1985. "Labour Exclusion *and* New Patterns of Co-operation? Dualism and Division in Labour Strategies." Paper for the *Conference on Labour Exclusion or New Patterns of Co-operation,* December.

JENSON, J., E. HAGEN, and C. REDDY, eds. 1988. *Feminization of the Labour Force: Paradoxes and Promises.* Cambridge: Polity Press.

JENSON, J., R. MAHON, and M. BIENEFELD. 1993. *Production, Space, Identity.* Toronto: Canadian Scholar's Press.

KEALEY, G., and P. WARRIAN. 1976. *Essays in Canadian Working Class History.* McClelland & Stewart.

KILLINGSWORTH, M.R. 1987. "Heterogeneous Preferences, Compensation, Wage Differentials, and Comparable Worth." *Quarterly Journal of Economics* 102: 42.

KUMAR, P. 1989. "Academic Research on Labour: Strengthening Union-University Links." *Queen's Papers in Industrial Relations; 1989-90.* Kingston, Ont.: Industrial Relations Centre, Queen's University.

————. 1987. "Recent Labour-Management Relations Approaches in Canada: Will They Endure?" *Queen's Papers in Industrial Relations; 1987-9.* Kingston, Ont.: Industrial Relations Centre, Queen's University.

LA BOTZ, D. 1992. *Mask of Democracy: Labor Suppression in Mexico Today.* Boston: South End Press.

LEMIEUX, V. 1989 "How Pay Equity Legislation Came to Ontario." *Canadian Public Administration.* 32 (Summer): 274-303.

LIPSIG-MUMMÉ, C. 1993 "Organising Women in the Low Paid Trades". In P. Armstrong and P. Connolly, *Feminism in Action.* Toronto: Canadian Scholar's Press.

————. 1993 "Future Conditional: Wars of Position on the Quebec Labour Movement" in J. Jenson, R. Mahon and M. Bienefeld, *Production, Space and Identity.* Toronto: Canadian Scholar's Press.

————. 1994. "Le dilemme du socialisme démocratique dans les pays developpés." *Relations* July-August.

————. 1993. "Solidarities and Boundaries." *Social Planning Council.* .

————. 1989. "Canadian and American Unions Respond to Economic Crisis." *Journal of Industrial Relations* June.

————. 1989. "La population syndiquée." *Labour/Le travail* 23.

————. 1987. "Organizing Women in the Low-Paid Trades." *Studies in Political Economy* no. 22.

LITTLER, C.R. 1982. *The Development of the Labour Process in Capitalist Societies: A Comparative Study of the Transformation of Work Organization in Britain, Japan and the USA.* London: Heinemann Educational Books.

LOWE, G. S., and H. J. KRAHN, eds. 1984. *Working Canadians: Readings in the Sociology of Work and Industry.* Toronto: Meuthen.

MARIN, M. 1988. "Social Dialogue: Key Factor to Bringing About a Community Social Pattern: European Communities." *Social and Labour Bulletin.* 1: 5-9.

MIDDLEBROOK, K., ed. 1991. *Unions, Workers, and the State in Mexico.* San Diego: Center for US-Mexican Studies, University of California.

MIDWEST CENTER FOR LABOR RESEARCH. 1985. "Workers as Owners." *Labor Research Review* 6.

————. 1991. "Let's Get Moving! Organizing for the 90s." *Labor Research Review* 18.

MILLAR, E. 1987. *Experience in the Federal Sector.* Canadian Industrial Relations Association, 24th Annual Meeting (June): 889-894.

MILLER, D.C., and W. H. FORM. 1980. *Industrial Sociology: Work in Organizational Life,* 3rd ed. New York: Harper & Row.

MISHRA, R. 1984. *The Welfare State in Crisis: Social Thought and Social Change.* Brighton, Sussex: Wheatsheaf Books.

MOODY, K. 1988. *An Injury to All.* London: Verso.

MONTGOMERY, E., and W. WASCHER. 1987. "Race and Gender Wage Inequality in Services and Manufacturing." *Industrial Relations* 26 (Fall): 284-290.

NOBLE, D. 1984. *Forces of Production: A Social History of Industrial Automation.* New York: Knopf.

O'CONNOR, J. 1972. *The Fiscal Crisis of the State.* New York: St. Martin's.

ODHNOFF, J. 1987. "A Decade of Work Research: Tenth Anniversary of the Swedish Center for Working Life." *Economic and Industrial Democracy.* 8 (February): 131-134.

VAN OTTER, C. 1990. *Integrating Workplace Development and Social Research: The LOM program in Sweden.* Proceedings of the Forty-Second Annual Meeting, Industrial Relations Research Association (December): 282-293. Madison, WI.: University of Wisconsin.

PANITCH, L., and D. SWARTZ. 1988. *The Assault on Trade Union Freedoms: From Consent to Coercion.* Toronto: Garamond Press.

PAY EQUITY COMMISSION OF ONTARIO. 1988. *Pay Equity Implementation Series,* v. 7. Toronto.

PIORE, M.J., and C.F. SABEL. 1984. *The Second Industrial Divide: Possibilities for Prosperity.* New York: Basic Books, Inc.

RANKIN, T. 1990. *New Forms of Work Organization: The Challenge for North American Unions.* Toronto: University of Toronto Press.

REGINI, M., ed. 1992. *The Future of Labour Movements.* London: Sage Publications Ltd.

RINEHART, J. W. 1987. *The Tyranny of Work: Alienation and the Labour Process,* 2nd ed. Toronto: Harcourt Brace Janovich.

ROBB, R. E. 1987. "Equal Pay for Work of Equal Value: Issues and Policies." *Canadian Public Policy* 13 (December): 445-461.

SABEL, C. 1982. *Work and Politics: The Division of Labour in Industry.* Cambridge: Cambridge University Press.

SALVATI, M. 1989. "A Long Cycle in Industrial Relations, or Regulation Theory and Political Economy." *Labour Review of Labour Economics and Industrial Relations* 3 (Spring): 41-72.

SHETTKAT, R. *The Labor Market Dynamics of Economic Restructuring: The United States and Germany in Transition.* New York: Praeger.

SHAIKEN, H. 1984. *Work Transformed: Automation and Labor in the Computer Age.* New York: Holt, Rinehart and Winston.

———. 1990. *Mexico in the Global Economy: High Technology and Work Organization in Export Industries.* San Diego: Center for US-Mexican Studies, University of California.

SHAPIRO, D.M., and M. STELCNER. 1987. "The Persistence of the Male-Female Earnings Gap in Canada, 1970-1980; The Impact of Equal Pay Laws and Language Policies." *Canadian Public Policy* 13 (December): 462-476.

SHOSTAK, A. 1991. *Robust Unionism.* Ithaca: Cornell University Press.

TODRES, E., B. FALK, and F. WELCH. 1987. *Women's Issues and Industrial Relations: The Challenge of Pay Equity Legislation in Ontario.* Canadian Industrial Relations Association, 24th Annual Meeting (June): 67-85.

THOMPSON, P. 1983. *The Nature of Work: An Introduction to Debates on the Labour Process.* London: Macmillan.

UNITED STEELWORKERS OF AMERICA. 1991. *Empowering Workers in the Global Economy.* Toronto.

VIKLUND, B. 1988. "Industrial Relations in Sweden in the 1990s." *IRRA Series,* 41st Annual Meeting (December): 330-341.

WEBER, A. R. 1988. *Understanding Change in Industrial Relations: A Second Look.* Industrial Relations Research Association, 40th Annual Meeting. (December): 361-364.

WELLS, D. 1986. *Soft Sell: "Quality of Working Life" Programs and the Productivity Race.* Ottawa, Ont.: Canadian Centre for Policy Alternatives.

———. 1987. *Empty Promises: Quality of Working Life Programs and the Labour Movement.* New York: Monthly Review Press.

WEVER, K.R. 1988. "Industrial Relations Developments in France, West Germany, the UK and Sweden: An American assessment." *IRRA Series,* 41st Annual Meeting (December): 361-364.

WHITE, J. 1993. *Sisters and Solidarity: Women in Unions in Canada.* Toronto: Thompson Educational Publishing.

WOMACK, J., D.T. JONES, and D. ROOS. 1991. *The Machine That Changed the World: The Story of Lean Production.* New York: Harper-Collins.

ZIMBALIST, A. 1979. *Case Studies on the Labor Process.* New York: Monthly Review Press.

ZUBOFF, S. 1988. *In the Age of the Smart Machine: The Future of Work and Power.* New York: Basic Books.

PART III
CONVERSION PROCESSES IN THE INDUSTRIAL RELATIONS SYSTEM

Labour and management bring a variety of goals and expectations to the workplace. On some matters, the goals are shared; on others, the objectives of the two sides diverge sharply. Whether goals are shared or in conflict, however, mutually acceptable solutions must be devised. It is the function of the conversion processes to translate the desires of labour and management into acceptable workplace practices.

The three chapters in this section are devoted to the major conversion processes. Chapter 9 describes collective bargaining, probably the most easily recognizable industrial relations process. In collective bargaining, representatives of labour and management meet, discuss, and ultimately make decisions on a wide variety of issues of interest to both employees and the employer—issues ranging from how much and in what manner employees are to be paid, to how many hours they will work, to how promotions will be decided. The chapter begins with an analysis of bargaining structure, an especially important topic because Canada has one of the most decentralized systems in the world. The discussion then turns to process. Collective bargaining is a process of negotiation and compromise. It is also frequently a conflictual process since failure by the negotiators to agree may result in a work stoppage, which is costly to all parties. This and many other features of collective bargaining are reviewed in the discussion.

Chapter 10 turns to another type of conversion process, grievance resolution mechanisms. All labour-management contracts in Canada include procedures for settling problems that arise in interpreting and applying the provisions of the contract—problems that may range from implementation of a drug-testing program to ambiguity in the wording of the contract itself. The grievance procedure is designed to deal with these and other situations that arise while the labour-management agreement is in effect. It provides for discussion between progressively higher levels of union and management officials and, should discussion alone fail to resolve the matter, culminates in binding arbitration by an outside neutral. Chapter 10 illustrates the procedure in detail and critically evaluates its attributes and drawbacks.

The final conversion process described in this section is employee involvement (also known as worker participation), presented in Chapter 11. Increasingly, informed observers and the participants in industrial relations are recognizing the benefits that greater participation by employees in decision making can produce. Modern workplaces, whether in manufacturing or services, emphasize flexibility and quality, both of which require knowledgeable, motivated employees. Programs that provide meaningful employee decision making can ensure that the knowledge that workers possess is effectively utilized and that employees remain committed to their work. Hence the popularity of of quality circles, self-managed work teams, re-engineered work processes, and similar ideas. Chapter 11 discusses these and other forms of employee involvement and presents the special problems that can arise in unionized workplaces. Particular attention is paid to successful innovations in Canadian workplaces.

By the end of this section, the reader should have a good grasp of the different ways in which the interests of the main actors are translated to the workplace. As well, the three chapters should provide a practical sense of how such important processes as labour negotiations and grievance arbitration actually work.

THE STRUCTURE AND PROCESS OF COLLECTIVE BARGAINING

RICHARD P. CHAYKOWSKI [*]

COLLECTIVE BARGAINING IS THE MAIN PROCESS THROUGH WHICH THE wages, hours, and working conditions of unionized employees are determined. The structure and process of collective bargaining are shaped both by the approaches and objectives of the management and union negotiators and by the legal and legislative framework governing labour relations. Union and management representatives must bargain in conformity with the requirements of the law in their own jurisdiction. But within this context, the parties have significant latitude in deciding the types of issues to be negotiated, the time taken to negotiate, and the actual method or process used to reach an agreement. This chapter will cover two general areas: (1) the structure of collective bargaining between firms and unions, and (2) the factors that affect the process and outcomes of collective bargaining. The discussion will primarily address collective bargaining in the private sector; in places, though, specific mention of the public sector is made.

[*] The author appreciates the assistance of Bill Murnighan of the Ontario Labour Management Services at the Ministry of Labour in providing bargaining structure data, and of Morley Gunderson, Allen Ponak, and Caroline Weber for helpful comments.

INTRODUCTION

Collective bargaining is a decision-making process through which union and management negotiators determine the terms and conditions of employment for a specific group of unionized workers. The results of the negotiations are set down in a contract (or collective agreement) that details what the parties have decided with respect to wages, benefits, hours of work, management rights, seniority, and the myriad other matters that may be discussed during bargaining (see Chapter 13 for more on the collective agreement). When major unions and employers are involved, collective bargaining can be a high-profile process that attracts a great deal of media attention. The public may be treated to the spectre of haggard negotiators putting together late night final offers, followed by early morning "final final" offers, all conducted amidst public posturing.

The purpose of this chapter is to place the collective bargaining process into perspective in order to understand why the parties behave as they do and to appreciate the less visible processes that lie beneath the surface of negotiations. The first section considers the nature of the different types of structures under which the process of collective bargaining occurs. Some firms may bargain with only one union to obtain a collective agreement, whereas other firms may engage in collective bargaining with several different unions to obtain a separate collective agreement with each. In both cases, the process of collective bargaining involves negotiations between a management team and one or more union teams. But the question of whom management and the union represent and to whom the collective agreement applies may well differ in the two cases. Thus, an appreciation of collective bargaining involves not only an understanding of the process, but an awareness as well of the important elements of bargaining structure.

The second main area of discussion concerns the actual collective bargaining process; that is, how the parties actually engage in collective bargaining and the various approaches adopted by management and union negotiating teams. Because the objective of the negotiation process is to achieve a collective agreement, both parties will be affected in important and obvious ways by the type of settlement reached through collective bargaining. In turn, the terms of the final collective agreement (e.g., the wage increases agreed upon) are directly affected by the negotiation process itself.

THE STRUCTURE OF COLLECTIVE BARGAINING

Bargaining structure is concerned with the scope of employees and employers covered by the negotiation process. Collective bargaining is highly decentralized in Canada with negotiations most often occurring between a single employer and a single union. Unlike the situation in Europe, it is relatively rare to have a set of negotiations cover employees in many companies across an entire industry or to involve more than one union at a time. Such structures do exist, however, and can be a significant part of the bargaining environment in certain industries. For example, in construction it is not uncommon for an association of employers to negotiate one province-wide collective agreement with each union in the industry. Such arrangements remain a distinct minority.

Research has shown that structure is associated with bargaining power, the level of conflict, the type of issues that are negotiated, and the internal politics on each side of the negotiating table (Anderson 1989). It is also difficult to evaluate the bargaining process without knowing to whom the collective agreement that is being negotiated will eventually apply. The 1994–95 professional hockey lockout, an example of a multi-employer bargaining structure, is a case in point. An appreciation of this set of negotiations required an understanding that twenty-six separate employers operating in two countries were involved, each with different operating costs, financial resources, and philosophies. Thus, little progress across the bargaining table could be made until the management side resolved its internal debate about the necessity of a salary cap. In contrast, bargaining in which a single employer is involved usually has less complicated dynamics.

Practical and legal factors are largely responsible for this country's decentralized bargaining structure. Aside from the federal jurisdiction, the labour laws of each province contain enough differences to make bargaining across provincial borders very difficult. Union organizing and bargaining unit determination still occur worksite by worksite, creating a fragmented patchwork of certification arrangements. Such fragmentation is compounded when competing unions represent workers in the same industry or occupation. On an historical basis, the composition and scope of original bargaining units has reflected union attempts to organize separately craft (skilled trades) workers, production workers, and office staff at a given workplace. Labour relations boards have been reluctant to tamper with long-standing industry practices or to require that new bargaining units span more than one establishment or employer for fear of discouraging unionization. Taken together, these factors have produced one of the most decentralized bargaining systems in the world.

Bargaining Structures

Drawing from ongoing practice, six basic bargaining structures can be identified. These structures are differentiated on the basis of: (1) the number of *employers* involved (single versus multi); (2) for single employers, the number of *establishments* involved (single versus multi) where establishment is defined as a specific place of business; and (3) the number of *unions* involved (single versus multi). Each of these six structures is set out below.[1]

Single Employer — Single Establishment — Single Union

One of the most prevalent bargaining structures, this involves localized negotiations at a single place of business or workplace. Examples include Robin Hood Multi-Food and the United Food and Commercial Workers (UFCW) at its plant in Saskatoon, Carleton University and its faculty association, and Dominion Textile and most of the Quebec plants represented by the Fédération canadienne des travailleurs du textile. In some cases, this form of bargaining occurs because the employer operates at one location only, has only one unionized establishment among its various facilities, or has different unions at different locations. In other cases, plant-by-plant bargaining takes place because of the preferences of the employer or the union.

Single Employer — Multi-Establishment — Single Union

Another very widespread type of bargaining arrangement, this structure involves the negotiation of a common collective agreement across several workplaces by the same employer and union. This structure is characteristic of public service bargaining between the Public Service Alliance of Canada and the federal government; of telecommunications where, for example, New Brunswick Telephone negotiates a province-wide agreement with its technicians represented by the Communications, Energy and Paperworkers Union; and of the retail food industry where the norm is a regional contract for each of the major supermarket chains and the dominant union, usually the UFCW. This bargaining arrangement makes a great deal of sense where the employer runs an integrated operation across a number of fairly similar establishments. It is also efficient for both union and management negotiators.

Single Employer — Single Establishment — Multi-Union

This type of bargaining structure is very rare in Canadian industry. It involves a negotiating partnership between two or more different unions within the same establishment. This situation might arise, for example, if production workers represented by an industrial union negotiated together with maintenance workers represented by a craft union, or where a number of small craft unions join forces. One example of this bargaining structure can be found in the negotiations between Pacific Press of Vancouver and the Joint Council of Newspaper Unions.

Single Employer — Multi-Establishment — Multi-Union

This type of bargaining arrangement is also relatively rare, occurring most notably in the railway industry where coalitions of different operating unions negotiate as a group with each of the major rail companies. Thus, negotiations would take place across the entire company's operations and involve most of its unions. This bargaining structure is most likely to be found in industries characterized by a few very large employers and a number of small craft unions.

Multi-Employer — Multi-Establishment — Single Union

This bargaining structure involves a coalition of employers bargaining as a group with a dominant industrial or occupational union. It is a bargaining arrangement that can be found in a number of major industries including health care, intercity trucking, construction, forestry, and garment manufacturing. In Alberta, for example, a hospital employers association negotiates a province-wide agreement with registered nurses that covers close to one hundred individual hospitals. In trucking, the Teamsters negotiate a series of regional contracts with associations of transportation companies. British Columbia forestry companies have had a tradition of jointly negotiating regional contracts with the Woodworkers Union through an employer bargaining organization aptly named Forest Industrial Relations (FIR). These centralized bargaining arrangements stand in sharp contrast to the more decentralized structures that characterize most bargaining relationships in Canada.

Multi-Employer — Multi-Establishment — Multi-Union

The most centralized form of bargaining, this arrangement involves coalitions of unions and employers at a single negotiating table. It is relatively rare, being restricted almost exclusively to construction industry negotiations where it has usually been introduced only through government pressure following difficult labour disputes. This extremely centralized structure has been used at various times in Quebec, Alberta, and British Columbia (Rose 1992).

In addition to these six basic bargaining structures, variations on these structures add some additional complexity. The most important variation is found in situations where multi-establishment negotiations (either single or multi-employer) are combined with establishment-level negotiations. This has been a popular form of bargaining in automobile manufacturing, forestry, hospitals, and some provincial civil services. Under this arrangement, a master collective agreement is usually negotiated first at a central bargaining table. Following completion of the centralized bargaining, further negotiations then take place over local issues on an individual-establishment basis. In the automobile industry, however, local and master negotiations may occur simultaneously (Kumar and Meltz 1992).

Another interesting structural variation occurred in the Western Canada beer industry during the 1970s and 1980s. While bargaining was formally between single employers and a single union on a multi-establishment basis, the three major brewers (Molson, Labatts, and Carling) agreed among themselves to resist certain concessions being proposed by the union. It was feared that if one of the employers conceded to the union demands, the other two employers would have little choice but to grant the same concessions. The three companies were able to time their individual negotiations in such a way that all three collective agreements expired at the same time, and they had agreed that a strike against one company would produce an industry shutdown. This prevented the union from playing one company off against the others by threatening a strike that would jeopardize only the struck company's market share, a tactic that had proved very successful in the past. The employers' approach converted the bargaining structure, for practical purposes, from a single into a multi-employer one, greatly enhancing employer bargaining power. This example illustrates why structure can be such an important ingredient in the bargaining process.[2]

Pattern Bargaining

In addition to the employees and employers who are directly governed by a given set of negotiations, the outcome of a collective bargaining session will often exercise an indirect influence on others. Thus, any discussion of bargaining structure needs to assess not only those to whom the negotiations formally apply, but also the employees and employers who will be informally affected by the results. Pattern bargaining can be defined as a situation in which a key bargaining settlement sets the standard for other settlements. It became an important feature of Canadian industrial relations in the 1950 to 1980 period.

Arthur Ross (1948) emphasized the importance of "equitable comparisons" of collective bargaining settlements by management and unions in explaining why wage gains in one set of negotiations can influence the outcomes in another. Ross referred to the range of influence of major settlements on other negotiations—which he argued was limited in scope—as an "orbit of coercive comparison." Ross recognized the importance of market forces, the political nature of the union organization, and the structure of employer and union bargaining arrangements as important influences on the tendency to equalize wages across collective agreements:

> It is when the several locals of a single international union centralize their wage policies and consolidate their strategies, when separate industrial establishments are brought under common ownership, when the state plays an increasingly active

role in setting rates of pay, when rival unions compete with one another for jurisdiction, when related unions negotiate together for mutual protection, and when
employers organize into associations to preserve a common front that comparisons become coercive in the determination of wages. (Ross 1948, 74)

For the unions, the benefit of patterning has been to enhance their ability to "take wages
out of competition." To varying degrees, the patterning of settlements has occurred in several major industries in the primary and manufacturing sectors, such as steel, mining,
autos, and meatpacking. For example, in meatpacking the major firms and the union actually engaged in centralized or national bargaining that led to standardized wages and contract clauses (e.g., union security) for a number of years (Forrest 1989).[3]

But by the 1980s, firms were confronted by a variety of internal and external pressures, including increased competition, the rapid diffusion of advanced technologies, and
deregulation and privatization initiatives, which generated increasing diversity in business
and employment conditions across establishments (Chaykowski and Verma 1992). As
firms pressured unions to negotiate wage and working conditions that would better reflect
the increasingly unique circumstances emerging at the establishment level, pattern and
centralized bargaining in many industries broke down.

The negotiation of collective agreements in the Canadian auto industry remains an
important exception to the decline of pattern bargaining. Each of the Big Three automakers negotiates separately with the Canadian Auto Workers (CAW). But each firm negotiates a national master agreement covering major items such as wages, shift premiums, the
grievance and arbitration mechanism, and hours of work, and which covers all bargaining
units at that firm. Then, for each bargaining unit, the firm also negotiates a local agreement
that includes establishment-specific items related to issues such as seniority, layoff and
recall rules, and wage scales for the various job classifications. The CAW typically targets
one firm with which to bargain first; the settlement achieved is then intended to serve as
a pattern for negotiations with the remaining firms (Kumar and Meltz 1992).

Further Decentralization

The pressures that led to the decline of pattern bargaining had a similar impact on bargaining structure. Though Canadian collective bargaining already is concentrated at the
single-employer, single-union level, the few centralized arrangements in place came under
substantial pressure beginning in the 1980s. As a result, long-standing centralized bargaining structures in meatpacking, forestry, and textiles were either abandoned or weakened, almost always at the employer's initiative. Pressures for decentralization also
emerged in the public sector. In the early 1990s, the Alberta government created a number of regional health care boards and strongly advocated that bargaining be conducted on
a regional basis rather than provincewide, as had long been the practice.

These trends are not unique to Canada. Many other countries have experienced
pressures towards more decentralized collective bargaining though few started with the
degree of decentralization found in this country. Katz (1993, 13) offers several explanations for the broader international trend that has emerged towards the decentralization of
bargaining:

... decentralization results from shifts in bargaining power, the spread of new work organization that puts a premium on flexibility and employee participation, and a decentralization of corporate structure and diversification of worker preferences.

Katz (1993, 16–17) also suggests that international evidence supports the conclusion that the first two factors have played a role in decentralization, but that the role of the third factor is probably not substantial. This tendency towards the decentralization of bargaining is occurring in countries such as the United States, the United Kingdom, and Australia, as well as some European countries (Katz 1993). Although Canada was not considered in this study, Canadian qualitative evidence that bargaining is becoming increasingly decentralized is consistent with these international trends.

MODEL OF THE PROCESS OF COLLECTIVE BARGAINING

Once a bargaining unit has been established and a union has been certified as the exclusive representative of the employees in the unit, collective bargaining becomes the means by which the terms and conditions of the employment contract are established. Although many issues and objectives are initially brought to the negotiating table by both the union and management negotiators, the observed results of the negotiation process typically yield a set of agreed-upon outcomes that may differ quite substantially from the original objectives of either party. Figure 9.1 presents a conceptual framework of those factors that determine the outcomes of collective bargaining. This framework identifies (1) the linkages between the goals and power of the union and management, (2) the process of negotiating a contract, and (3) the outcomes of collective bargaining.

| FIGURE 9.1 | Determinants of Collective Bargaining Outcomes |

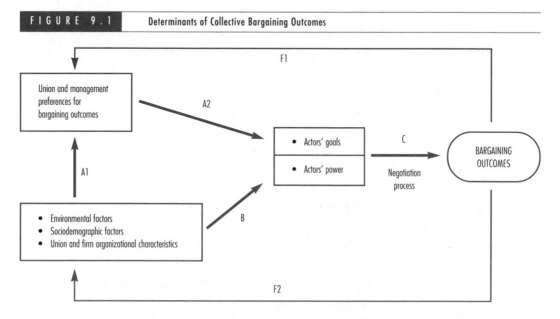

SOURCE: Chaykowski (1990, 330, Figure 1). This figure is an extension of Delaney and Sockell (1989, 571, Figure 1).

The actual *outcomes* of the process of collective bargaining are specified in the clauses of the collective bargaining agreement (see Chapter 13). The specific outcomes of collective bargaining that are determined through the negotiation process in turn depend upon the *goals* of the union and management, the *power* that the parties have to achieve their desired objectives, and the statutory requirements that may constrain the bargaining process. The bargaining goals of the union and management are determined by their respective preferences for alternative bargaining outcomes (path A2 of Figure 9.1). The preferences of the parties are in turn determined by a variety of environmental, sociodemographic and organizational characteristics (path A1 of Figure 9.1). While the relative power of the parties is also determined by various environmental, sociodemographic, and organizational characteristics (path B of Figure 9.1), it is affected by the dynamics of the negotiation process as well. The *negotiation process* (relationship C of Figure 9.1) links the goals and power of both the union and management on the one hand, and the outcomes of collective bargaining on the other hand, and accounts for why the initial objectives of the union and management tend to differ from the results achieved.

The set of factors and relationships that together determine collective bargaining outcomes is presented in Figure 9.1 in the context of a linear, static framework in order to emphasize the basic relationships at work and in order to guide the following discussion of each of the developments of the model. However, the following examination of each of the components of the model will also reveal the complex manner in which they are interrelated and how their effects may change over time.

UNION AND MANAGEMENT BARGAINING GOALS

The *goals* of management and unions may cover the full range of issues with which employees and managers may be expected to be concerned in the workplace. Both parties are typically interested in negotiating over goals in such areas as

- Wages
- Union security
  (e.g., mandatory payment of union dues)
- Employee security
  (e.g., contracting-out; seniority rules on layoffs and for promotions; severance pay benefits)
- Grievance and arbitration procedures
  (e.g., grievance process)
- Hours and days of work
  (e.g., daily and weekly hours of work; normal work-week)
- Overtime and premium pay
  (e.g., distribution of overtime among employees; rates of overtime pay)
- Level and structure of compensation
  (e.g., wage levels and the type of pay system, such as hourly wages versus piece rates versus incentive systems)

- Vacations and leaves
  (e.g., weeks of vacation; number of paid holidays; provision for education, parental, or bereavement leave)

- Allowances
  (e.g., pay for clothing, tools, moving expenses)

- Technological change
  (e.g., advance notice of the introduction of new technology; retraining)

- Health and safety
  (e.g., sick leave; disability benefits)

- Employee Benefits
  (e.g., pension benefits; life insurance; extended health benefits)

- Worker–management relationship
  (e.g., joint committees)

For a particular issue, both the union and the firm will attempt to achieve their most preferred outcomes. In some cases, the interests of management and union are likely to be directly opposed (e.g., on wages). If gains to one party in turn imply that less is available for the other, then the issue is referred to as being *distributive* in nature. For example, wage increases provide a good example of a distributive issue: all else being equal, providing more of a firm's earnings to employees as wages implies that the firm then has less resources to distribute to the stockholders or to use for other purposes. That is, greater wages will increase the well-being of employees but decrease the well-being of management and/or stockholders.

In other areas, the interests of the union and management may have significant elements in common, so that providing more of the outcome will increase the well-being of both the union and management. These types of issues are referred to as *integrative*. For example, establishing joint union–management committees to examine work reorganization that is aimed at increasing productivity could benefit both parties if they agree to share any gains in productivity between them. Alternatively, expenditures that improve workplace health and safety could benefit both workers (directly) and the firm (by lowering accident rates and thereby lowering assessments under the workers' compensation insurance program). [4]

The goals of the union and management are shaped by a variety of influences, including environmental factors, sociodemographic factors, and organizational characteristics. Environmental factors may include the state of the economy, changes in the technology of production, or recent contract settlements in comparable workplaces. Economic factors include macroeconomic influences such as inflation or changes in economic growth. Inflation is an example of a macroeconomic influence that affects union goals. In periods of rapid and prolonged inflation, the union may seek a cost-of-living adjustment clause that provides wage adjustments based upon increases in the consumer price index.

Changes in technology may affect workplace safety or ergonomics, the pace of work, job skills and training requirements, and the number of workers required. For example, a new technology that permits the same level of production with the use of fewer, but more highly skilled, workers may induce the union to bargain for severance packages for employees who are laid off as a result of the introduction of the new technology.

Alternatively, the union could seek rules governing transfer rights for displaced workers or bargain for union involvement in worker training programs.

Sociodemographic factors may include the age or gender composition of the collective bargaining unit. These workforce sociodemographic characteristics may be systematically associated with preferences for certain types of employment outcomes. Consequently, the union leadership may attempt to formulate bargaining goals that incorporate these specific preferences. For example, if the average age of a particular workforce is high, then workers may (on average) exhibit preferences for enhanced pensions or for strong seniority rules governing promotions and transfers. These preferences would probably differ noticeably from those of another workforce with a much lower average age. Alternatively, all else being equal, a workforce with a high proportion of females may (on average) express greater preferences for family-related benefits, such as maternity and paternity leaves, child-care facilities, and workplace anti-discrimination programs.

Finally, the characteristics of the firm or union can affect their respective bargaining objectives. For example, a management strategy of decentralizing authority and decision making within the organization may require new workplace organizational structures or some form of employee involvement programs (e.g., joint union–management committees or teams). Bargaining with the union may therefore involve the manner and conditions under which the union will participate in and, indeed, support the establishment of new workplace structures.[5]

It is important to note, as Figure 9.1 illustrates, that these factors and characteristics *indirectly* have an impact on the goals of the union leadership and management: each factor acts as a determinant of the preferences of the parties for various types of bargaining outcomes (relationship A1). But the preferences of the parties in turn shape the specific goals or objectives that are sought in the collective bargaining process (relationship A2).

THE CONCEPT AND ROLE OF POWER IN COLLECTIVE BARGAINING

The typical observation that two parties engaged in negotiations have unequal leverage or advantage in obtaining their preferred outcome is rooted in the intuitive notion that one party always has greater power. While power is itself not quantifiable, the concept of power can be defined, and the types of factors that give rise to power with respect to collective bargaining outcomes can be examined.

The Concept of Bargaining Power

The ability of the parties to achieve their desired outcome or objective on a given issue will depend on their relative *bargaining power*. The classic conceptual definition of bargaining power is provided by Chamberlain and Kuhn (1986) and includes both the costs associated with a disagreement and the costs that result from an agreement. Examples of the *costs of disagreement* may include: the lost production (firm's cost) and wages (employee's cost) associated with a strike or lockout; the withdrawal of labour's active co-operation with management in the workplace (firm's cost); bad publicity associated with a strike (firm's cost); and threatened plant closures (employee's cost). Examples of the *costs of agreement* could include: the direct costs of agreeing to increases in wages and benefits (firm's cost); or possible nonmonetary costs associated with agreeing to a joint participation program (a cost to the union leadership if the membership views union participation with management as "selling out") (Chamberlain and Kuhn 1986, 180–196). Using the notions of costs of agreement and disagreement, Chamberlain and Kuhn define power as

> ... the ability to secure another's agreement on one's own terms. A union's bargaining power at any point of time *is*, for example, management's willingness to agree to the union's terms. Management's willingness, in turn, depends upon the costs of disagreeing with the union terms relative to the costs of agreeing to them. (Chamberlain and Kuhn 1986, 176)

The power of a particular union (or management) in collective bargaining is clearly expected to vary over time. Variations will occur with the specific issue being negotiated and with the particular negotiating tactics used by the parties (Chamberlain and Kuhn 1986, 177–178). In the following section we examine the underlying factors that give rise to bargaining power.

The Determinants of Bargaining Power

The power of the union and management in collective bargaining depends upon a variety of environmental, sociodemographic, and organizational factors. These factors directly determine the power that the union and firm can exert in the negotiation process (refer to relationship B in Figure 9.1).

Environmental factors could include shifts in public support for workers who are on strike, modifications of the legislative framework governing labour relations, or changes in economic circumstances. Environmental influences can therefore affect not just the balance of power but also the goals of the parties.

The effect of public opinion on the relative power of the parties is probably more subtle than other environmental factors. For example, changes in public opinion may involve increased community support for striking workers, which could induce the firm to improve its bargaining offers in order to garner public favour. Consequently, union strike strategies may include publicity efforts to encourage the public to boycott the products of the firm. In the public sector, popular opinion may be especially important (see Chapter 15).

The legal environment is generally believed to be a significant determinant of union power, since legislation can require that certain items be included in the contract, or it can place limits on the behaviour or actions of the parties. Amendments to the labour relations legislation of British Columbia and Ontario in the early 1990s were generally viewed as providing increased support for unions (Carter 1993). Prohibiting the use of replacement workers during a strike strengthens the effectiveness of the union strike weapon, since the ability of management to operate its facilities during a work stoppage is now limited (see Chapter 3).

Economic conditions have a primary influence on the relative bargaining power of unions and management. In times of economic growth (an upswing in the business cycle), when the demand for products is increasing, employers will be reluctant to bear the losses associated with a strike, all else being equal. Alternatively, in periods of high unemployment, alternative employment opportunities for workers tend to be fewer so that, all else equal, the union membership may be less willing to engage in a prolonged strike. These specific examples illustrate how economic conditions can affect the willingness of the parties to bear the costs of disagreement (in the form of a work stoppage). Another related consideration is the ease with which consumers may substitute other products for the goods that cannot be supplied during a strike. For example, if Canadian steel manufacturers are struck, automakers may seek out other steel suppliers or attempt to substitute away from steel toward other materials (e.g., plastics) in the manufacturing process. In fact, strikes at the outset of the 1990s in the Canadian steel industry appear to have induced both of these effects (Verma and Weiler 1992).

During the 1980s and 1990s, broader shifts in the Canadian economic context have had a longer-term impact on the relative bargaining power of unions and firms. An intensely competitive business environment has been fostered by numerous factors: changes in foreign and domestic public policies, such as deregulation and the further strengthening of North–South trade links through the North American Free Trade Agreement; increased capital mobility and (more generally) the globalization of markets; and the rapid diffusion of advanced production technologies. These influences have created pressures on firms to reduce prices, lower the costs of production, and increase productivity. In addition, increased capital mobility and new production methods have facilitated the movement of facilities "offshore" to lower-cost regions. New technologies are more rapidly diffused and are often associated with fewer workers, new skill requirements, and new methods of organizing work. Firms have sought wage concessions or wage freezes, threatened to close facilities if unions did not co-operate with management demands, attempted to reorganize workplaces, and generally engaged in downsizing their workforces.

Confronted with these pressures, the power of many unions to enforce their demands has been reduced. Recognizing the implications of bargaining in this new environment, many unions have moderated their wage demands and sought to focus their objectives on membership concerns over employment security. Unions have also carefully considered co-operating with management in their efforts to reorganize work in order to increase productivity, although most unions have developed position papers that state the conditions necessary for their involvement.[6]

The privatization of Crown corporations (e.g., Air Canada) and the deregulation of industries (e.g., transportation and telecommunications) provide good examples of how shifts in public policies can also affect the bargaining relationship through their impact on the economic environment. The completion of the process of deregulation of the airline industry in 1988, and the privatization of Pacific Western Airlines (which later purchased Canadian Pacific to form Canadian Airlines International) in 1983 and of Air Canada in 1989, created significant competitive pressures in the industry (Fisher and Kondra 1992). Recent policy initiatives aimed at deregulating the telecommunications industry are creating similar pressures, which are most noticeable in the market for long-distance telephone services. Unions realize that long-term growth in employee compensation can no longer be readily absorbed by the rate increases once common in regulated industries.

Diverse *sociodemographic characteristics* may be associated with disparate personal preferences, and therefore bargaining preferences, among the membership. In addition, the membership may be divided in its views on whether a particular issue is sufficiently important to warrant a strike if the bargaining objective is not achieved during negotiations. Consequently, the leadership must often account for diverse preferences among its membership when formulating bargaining objectives and when assessing the extent of membership support for engaging in a strike to achieve certain bargaining outcomes.

Organizational characteristics that affect power may be broadly defined to include the type of product produced, the technology of production, or the characteristics of the union or firm (e.g., cohesiveness of the union membership, resources available to the union during a strike). If the product is one that can be stockpiled, then management can continue to sell its product during a strike, thereby generating revenues and maintaining its contractual relationships with customers. This capability would minimize the economic impact of a work stoppage on the firm. Alternatively, if the firm produces a good that cannot be stockpiled or a service (which obviously cannot be stockpiled) then a strike would clearly have an immediate impact on the firm's revenues and customer base. For example, the United Steelworkers of America engaged in a thirteen-week strike against Stelco in 1990 when negotiations broke down. This strike involved lost wages for the workers but also a significant permanent loss of customers for the firm and for the steel industry as a whole:

> The company estimated that, during the strike, roughly 5 per cent of its customer base had vanished. Some steel-consuming industrial plants had closed, and others had turned to imports. Together, the loss of these customers meant a reduction in demand of 400,000 tons for the Canadian steel industry. (Verma and Warrian 1992, 114)

The nature of the technology of production has a direct impact on the ability of management to continue operations during a strike. If the production process enables management employees to operate the facilities themselves, then the impact of a work stoppage could be minimal. For example, in a refinery that requires relatively few workers and is operated by means of control panels, supervisors and managers could maintain operations. During work stoppages in the telephone industry, supervisors have maintained a basic level of services by performing the tasks of operators. Alternatively, the technology of production may require highly specialized skills in the regular workforce; the specialized skill requirements would not permit management to perform the work of skilled workers themselves or to hire replacement workers (where allowed by labour legislation).

One of the most important internal organizational characteristics of the union is its status as a political organization. For example, the membership may be politically divided in its support for the elected union leadership, which could in turn undermine the solidarity of the union or the support provided to the leadership during the negotiating process. In practice, once a tentative agreement has been reached between the union and management negotiating teams, the membership will vote on the "package" offered by the firm. In some cases the final offer, although endorsed by the leadership, may be rejected in a vote; this would likely serve to affect both the bargaining posture and authority of leadership.

Note that while a vote that rejects a tentative package may serve to undermine confidence in the leadership and detract from their bargaining position, it may also serve to provide the leadership with a strong mandate to bargain hard for improvements. They would do so, secure in the knowledge that the membership is fully supportive and possibly prepared to endure a strike to enforce their demands, and this support would increase the power underlying the union leadership's position. Other characteristics of the union, such as the resources available, can affect its ability to maintain a work stoppage. The magnitude of the union strike fund could directly affect the length of time the membership is willing (or able) to maintain a strike action. Strike funds are accumulated through union dues and are used to provide small payments to workers while they are on strike. Payments are usually made weekly and are aimed at maintaining subsistence requirements.

Intra-organizational dynamics are also important within the firm. The management bargaining team typically serves a variety of interests among managers with different responsibilities. Also, while the union bargaining team must reconcile any settlement with the desires of the rank-and-file membership, so too must the management bargaining team reconcile the negotiated settlement with the goals and objectives of senior management. Centralized bargaining structures in particular may be prone to internal politics, since the objectives of several employers and unions (as the case may be) have to be melded into unified positions that inevitably reflect some compromise.

The various environmental, sociodemographic, and organizational characteristics that affect power operate simultaneously. The particular factors that determine the relative power of the union and management vary considerably over time, across industries, or across jurisdictions—which is why we expect the power of the parties to vary as well. Because the interrelationships among the factors that give rise to power are so complex, one cannot reasonably expect to determine, in advance, their net effect on collective bargaining. In practice, this creates a degree of uncertainty in most negotiations; thus an important element in bargaining is the gathering of information about the other side's bargaining power through the give and take of negotiations.

NEGOTIATING THE COLLECTIVE AGREEMENT: PROCESS AND INNOVATIONS

The negotiation process (relationship C of Figure 9.1) links the goals and power of the parties with the outcomes of collective bargaining. While the union and management assert their power in order to achieve their goals, the actual process of negotiating the collective agreement can assume its own dynamic, which can itself constitute an important factor in determining the eventual contract outcomes. This section begins with a discussion of the concept of a "zone of agreement," which provides insight into the basis for defining a potential agreement. This discussion is followed by a brief description of the manner in which collective bargaining proceeds when a contract requires renegotiation, including a characterization of the process and dynamics of the negotiation process, and a discussion of why disagreement, or impasses, may occur.

The Potential for Agreement in Negotiations

Most negotiations involve attempts to resolve numerous issues, many of which are typically interrelated. One of the most fundamental concerns is whether there even exists a potential basis for agreement. That is, do the *positions* of the parties create a common ground, or are the minimum positions of each party too far apart to permit any common ground? Further, can the parties change their positions on one issue (e.g., wages) during the negotiating process in reaction to changes in positions that occur regarding another issue (e.g., pension benefits)? Defining a "potential zone of agreement" provides a theoretical basis for understanding why an agreement may, or may not, occur.

For a single issue, the notion of a potential "zone of agreement" between union and management negotiators is depicted in Figure 9.2. Consider negotiations over a single issue for which the union seeks an increased value that management seeks to resist (e.g., wages). In Figure 9.2, the following reference points create a potential zone of agreement between the parties:

- The left-most point (A) represents the lowest value of wages that will induce workers to offer their services, while the right-most point (B) represents the highest level of wages possible that would still permit the firm to operate;

- UM represents the minimum wage level that the union will accept (often referred to as the union "resistance point");

- MM represents the maximum wage level that the management will offer the union (often referred to as the management "resistance point").

In the example of bargaining over wages, management may attempt to focus its bargaining strategy on achieving a specific wage level that it believes represents the best it can do (that is, the lowest wage that it can offer the union). Realistically, management prefers to offer any wage level that is less than MM in Figure 9.2. Since management prefers any wage level less than MM (Area 1 and Area 3), management will certainly prefer wage levels less than UM. However, the union will never agree to any wage offers in Area 1 (i.e., wages below UM), since this area corresponds to wages that are less than the level that is minimally acceptable to the union (UM). But management may not know that wage offers below UM (Area 1) are not acceptable to the union.

From its perspective, the union may focus on a particular wage level that it believes represents the best that can be obtained from management in negotiations (that is, the highest wage it can successfully negotiate). But the union generally prefers any wage level greater than UM (Area 2 and Area 3)—so the union will certainly prefer a wage level that is greater than MM. But management will never agree to any wage demand in Area 2 (i.e., wages above MM), since this area corresponds to wages that are greater than the maximum wage level that is acceptable to management (MM). On its part, the union may not know that wage demands that are greater than Mm (Area 2) are not acceptable to the management.

Area 3 is a *potential* zone of agreement because the union's lowest acceptable demand (point UM) is less than management's highest possible offer (point MM). The *existence* of a potential agreement zone will yield a settlement as long as the parties can bargain to some point within Area 3. However, one cannot determine in advance where within this range the parties will settle. The process of bargaining allows an exchange of offers and information that allows management and the union to learn more about their true "resistance" points; in general, it permits both parties to learn more about the range of outcomes that is acceptable to each:

> Negotiation ... is back-and-forth communication designed to reach an agreement when you and the other side have some interests that are shared and others that are opposed. (Fisher and Ury 1983, xi)

Obtaining a solution in Area 3 would be made easier if each party revealed its true resistance points; the parties will typically not do so in order to gain a strategic advantage. That is, each will attempt to "bluff," to exaggerate its true resistance point, or employ other tactics in order to obtain a solution closest to its own most preferred wage level.

FIGURE 9.2   Potential Zone of Agreement for a Single Bargaining Issue

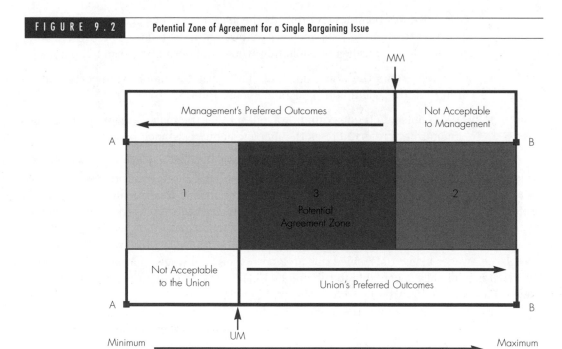

A   = lower bound of feasible wage.
B   = upper bound of feasible wage.
UM   = the lowest wage level that the union will accept.
MM   = the highest wage level that management will offer.
Area 1 = wage levels that are unacceptable to the union.
Area 2 = wage levels that are unacceptable to management.
Area 3 = potential zone of agreement because the union's minimum acceptable wage (Um) is less than management's highest offer (Mm)

SOURCE: Based on Walton and McKersie (1991, 43, Figure 2–15)

This type of bargaining dynamic assumes that management and the union are bargaining over a single issue or, if more than one issue is being negotiated, that the parties are bargaining over each issue separately. But in most cases, management and the union negotiate several issues at the same time and negotiations over one issue can affect the bargaining over the other. This means that the process of negotiating over one issue can affect the positions that the parties take regarding the other issue. As a consequence, the union and management may seek trade-offs across these two issues because the potential gains in one issue may offset what they must offer for the other issue. For example, this trade-off may be especially appealing because one party (e.g., the union) may place a greater weight on obtaining more of Issue X (e.g., health and safety) than Issue Y (e.g., vacation)—perhaps because the membership places more value on greater health and safety than on more vacation. This type of scenario, which is typical of most negotiations, helps explain why collective bargaining is such a challenging and dynamic process.

Negotiating the Collective Agreement

If a collective agreement is in effect, then near the expiration of the contract the union must give notice to the employer of its intention to bargain for a new collective agreement, after which the parties must meet within a specified period of time; the specific require-

TABLE 9.1   Statutory Requirements for Notice to Commence and Obligation to Begin Collective Bargaining

Jurisdiction	Period of Notice to Bargain (before expiry date of contract)	Obligation to Bargain (after providing notice)
Federal	Within 3 months [a]	Within 20 days [b]
Alberta	120 to 60 days [a]	Within 30 days
British Columbia	Within 4 months [c]	Within 10 days
Manitoba	90 to 30 days [b]	Within 10 days [a]
New Brunswick	90 to 30 days	Within 20 days [a]
Newfoundland	60 to 30 days [b]	Within 20 days [a]
Nova Scotia	Within 2 months	Within 20 days [a]
Ontario	Within 90 days [b]	Within 15 days [a]
PEI	Within 2 months [b]	Within 20 days [a]
Quebec	Within 90 days [b]	"Forthwith"
Saskatchewan	60 to 30 days	"Forthwith"

[a] Union and management may agree to a longer period.
[b] Union and management may agree otherwise.
[c] Notice is "deemed" given at 90 days before the contract expires.

SOURCE: Minister of Supply and Services Canada, *Industrial Relations Legislation in Canada,* 1993. Catalogue No. L31-79/1994E.

ments vary across jurisdictions (refer to Table 9.1). The union and management negotiating teams prepare their positions on each issue over which they wish to negotiate. The priority attached to each issue, as well as the target and resistance points set by the union negotiating team, typically reflect the goals and objectives of the membership. Similarly, the major issues over which management has unique concerns, as well as management positions on issues over which the union wishes to bargain, are determined in consultation with the various constituent groups within the firm.

In traditional bargaining, each team has a spokesperson. The tone of the meetings has commonly been adversarial, with the teams facing each other as "opposites." The union may present its "demands," with the management team withdrawing to examine the requests and subsequently returning to respond with an "offer" (a *position* on each issue of concern). The union will usually then withdraw from the negotiating table to examine the proposal in "caucus." Each side will caucus regularly throughout the negotiating process as each team discusses and debates the merits of the latest offer. Offers are analyzed and evaluated: the economic value of offers related to wages, pensions, holidays, severance packages for laid-off workers, or other issues with a monetary value are "costed;" the merits of offers related to issues with no readily quantifiable value (e.g., changes to promotion rules) are evaluated. This process of preparing and evaluating offers and counteroffers typically continues over many days or weeks until either all issues have been resolved or an impasse is reached.

If the parties cannot reach an agreement, then either party may request that the government appoint a conciliation officer. (In some jurisdictions, if the conciliator cannot facilitate an agreement, then the government may, but in practice rarely does, recommend that a conciliation board be appointed.) If the impasse continues and the collective agreement has expired, the union has a legal right to engage in a work stoppage and management has a legal right to lock out. Before a strike or lockout becomes legal, certain prerequisites have to be satisfied; typically these include a strike vote and strike notice. Even after a work stoppage occurs, the parties will continue their negotiations, often with the help of a government-appointed mediator. While a mediator may assist in achieving an agreement, the process of collective bargaining is affected by a diverse set of factors. These include the relative power of the parties (determined to some extent by the costs associated with a strike or lockout); the skill and personalities of the negotiators; and union and management access to information regarding the true positions of the other side.

Innovations in the Process of Bargaining

Since the issues that are subject to collective bargaining are of consequence to the parties, the process of bargaining is typically pursued strenuously and often results in strained relationships, whether or not a strike or lockout occurs. Achieving a new contract is important in itself, but the union and management also attempt to achieve a resolution to their differences that each considers workable during the term of the collective agreement. The traditional approach to improving the negotiating process, which increases the likelihood of obtaining a collective agreement without an impasse, is to engage in some form of conciliation or mediation. However, these types of third-party interventions occur in the context of traditional bargaining and tend not to alter the process. The effectiveness of these approaches are therefore constrained by the limitations associated with traditional adversarial bargaining itself.

In recent years, several approaches to improving the process of collective bargaining have been developed in order to avoid costly strikes and lockouts and to improve the quality of the relationship during the period after the negotiations are concluded. Several of these approaches include "interest-based" and "mutual gains" bargaining. The core of these approaches centres on attempting to alter both the focus of the bargaining and the behavioural approach to negotiating.

These techniques are rooted in the generic approach to bargaining referred to as *principled bargaining* (Fisher and Ury 1983).[7] This approach was developed as an alternative to traditional confrontational bargaining characterized by situations involving low levels of trust, high conflict, the use of tactics to gain an advantage, a focus on the positions that the parties bring to the negotiations, and an emphasis on win–lose outcomes. Instead of focusing on the *positions* that the parties may assume in a negotiating situation, this approach centres on the underlying *interests* of the parties (Fisher and Ury 1983). Recognizing that the interests of the parties may conflict, Fisher and Ury suggested moving away from traditional adversarial bargaining through four procedures:

- separating the personalities of the people from the problem under discussion;

- focusing on the underlying interests of the parties, and not on their bargaining positions;

- inventing options that give rise to mutual gain instead of to win–lose solutions; and

- in negotiating outcomes, developing objective criteria that involve fairness in both standards and procedures.

The bargaining concepts advanced by Fisher and Ury are general in nature, so that aspects of principled bargaining have been successfully adopted by negotiators in the process of collective bargaining. But since each individual bargaining relationship tends to be unique, these principles have in practice given rise to a variety of techniques. One of these techniques is the form of negotiating called "mutual gains" bargaining. Recent analyses of mutual gains bargaining have raised concerns about some inherent limitations to its effectiveness. For example, since the process is based primarily on behavioural principles, it may give insufficient weight either to the importance of the relative power of the parties or to the institutional context in which the parties function and conduct negotiations (Friedman 1994; Heckscher and Hall 1994). However, Friedman (1994) has provided suggestions to increase the effectiveness of current practices. These suggestions focus on minimizing barriers to increased trust, altering the roles of the parties in negotiations, and modifying power imbalances between the union and management (Friedman 1994).

There is little systematic evidence currently available regarding how extensively these "principled" approaches are used, their success, or whether their usage tends to be sustained over time. While there appears to be strong interest in these types of bargaining innovations, traditional "hard bargaining" probably remains the predominant approach. Anecdotal evidence indicates, however, that some major unions and employers are utilizing principled bargaining, including

- Petro-Canada and the Communications, Energy and Paperworkers Union (CEP),

- Bell Canada and the CEP,

- Cardinal River Coal and the United Mine Workers,

- Cominco Fertilizers (Potash Operations) and the United Steelworkers of America (USWA),

- TransAlta Utilities and the International Brotherhood of Electrical Workers, and

- Algoma Steel and the USWA.

THE OUTCOMES OF COLLECTIVE BARGAINING

Generally, the outcomes of collective bargaining include both the contractual agreement as well as impacts at the organizational (i.e., micro) level. At the organizational level, the outcomes of collective bargaining include several basic elements:

1. There are immediate contractual results of the collective bargaining process. The contractual outcomes include the terms and conditions of employment specified in the collective bargaining agreement (e.g., wage increases, benefit increases, and changes in work rules) (see Chapter 13 on the collective agreement).

2. Many aspects of the contract can have effects on the operating efficiency and functioning of the firm. In particular, changes in the collective agreement can have important consequences for compensation systems, productivity levels, and management practices (refer to Chapter 12 on union impacts).

3. The tone and dynamics of the negotiations process itself can have a substantial "spillover" impact on the ongoing relationship between employees and managers during the term of the collective agreement. Specifically, whether the negotiations can be characterized as adversarial, bitter, and highly conflictual on the one hand, or as more co-operative and positive on the other hand, can affect the level of co-operation and harmony that exists between management and employees during the day-to-day operations of the company. Naturally, problems that develop over the term of the collective agreement often set the stage for the types of issues and level of adverseness that the parties bring to the bargaining table when the contract is due for renegotiation.

Considered across firms and unions, the results of collective bargaining can also have a range of impacts on broader socioeconomic (i.e., macro-level) outcomes including aggregate economic output (through strike activity and productivity) and inflation (through wage increases).

Taken together, the interrelationships presented in the framework in Figure 9.1 describe the set of factors and processes that determine collective bargaining outcomes. But the model depicted in Figure 9.1 only conveys a *static* sense of the processes. The feedback loops (loops F1 and F2) indicate that there is also a *dynamic* element to the process over time because, as noted above, the outcomes achieved in one round of collective bargaining can in turn affect the objectives of the management and union in a subsequent round. This concept of feedback loops highlight the fact that the union–management relationship is a long-term one. The way in which collective bargaining has functioned in previous stages of the relationship affects the way collective bargaining will function in the future.

CONCLUSION

The bargaining goals and priorities of unions and firms are being continuously shaped by a variety of environmental factors. In particular, increasingly competitive economic conditions brought on by the internationalization of markets, social pressures for workplace change, and shifts in the composition of the workforce over the past twenty-five years have translated into new concerns and priorities. Both employers and unions have reacted to these pressures at the bargaining table, while governments have engaged in changes to the public policy environment.

Employers have undergone significant changes in attempting to increase productivity and reduce costs. In many cases, firms have changed organizational structures, reorganized the workplace and introduced new technologies, and altered the nature of their workforces. Organizational changes have included reductions in the number of levels in hierarchies and in the size of the workforce in order to lower the costs of production. Efforts to reorganize work and introduce new technologies have often been accompanied by changes in the number of tasks performed by employees and in employee skill levels. In addition, many firms have attempted to introduce new types of employee compensation systems (e.g., profit-sharing or lump-sum payments). Over the past decade, these changes have transformed the bargaining agenda of many employers across industries; for unions, they have raised the importance of issues related to job security, the scope of work, job descriptions and work rules, and the basis of pay. The ongoing changes have also affected bargaining structure, weakening traditional pattern bargaining arrangements and placing even more emphasis on decentralized negotiations.

Several emerging trends in the labour movement may be expected to have an important, yet somewhat complex, impact on both the structure and the process of collective bargaining in Canada. First, there has been an erosion of union membership, which has served to weaken union strength. This has been partly a result of the changes in employment patterns—including shifts away from traditional areas of union strength in heavy industry towards relatively less unionized service industries—and partly a result of the ongoing down-sizing of workforces across organizations. Many major unions have therefore begun to organize workers outside of their traditional industries (Kumar 1993). For example, the United Steelworkers has organized taxi drivers and fishery workers, the United Food and Commercial Workers has organized workers in nursing homes, the Canadian Auto Workers has organized rail workers, and the Canadian Union of Public Employees has organized workers in both the airline and longshoring industries (Chaykowski and Verma 1992, 22). In an especially contentious case, the Canadian Auto

Workers recently prevailed over the United Steelworkers for the right to represent miners at the Mine Mill local at Falconbridge Limited in Falconbridge, Ontario.

Second, there has been considerable merger activity among unions in both the private and public sectors — often among unions that might otherwise, based on their traditional composition and coverage, appear unlikely to merge (Kumar 1993). Although most mergers involve a small and a large union, a recent example of a significant merger among major unions occurred with the integration of the Communications and Electrical Workers of Canada (which is primarily in telecommunications), the Energy and Chemical Workers (organized in the energy sector) and the Paperworkers Union (traditionally in the forest products manufacturing industry) into the Communications, Energy and Paperworkers Union.

Many of these types of changes have altered the membership composition of unions and are expected to have significant long-term implications for their priorities and bargaining objectives, their power, and the breadth of their activity:

> Mergers, affiliations and realignments are considered necessary to: (a) provide greater access to resources for stepped-up organizing and for delivering more effective membership services; (b) solidify the membership base and improve bargaining strength; (c) become a countervailing force against growing corporate mergers, buy-outs and takeovers; and (d) mount effective social and political campaigns for legislative changes.... (Kumar 1993, 57)

Therefore, by revitalising their organizing efforts and seeking out advantageous merger possibilities, many unions have developed new bargaining priorities and strategies and renewed their strength at the bargaining table.

For many firms and unions, the difficult socioeconomic challenges of the past decade have translated into increasingly adversarial negotiations. Firms have often sought wage concessions, engaged in layoffs, or changed their work organization in order to reduce costs and increase productivity, while unions have struggled to protect pay levels and preserve job security. For other organizations, a major challenge has been to achieve better solutions through collective bargaining. This has in turn encouraged the parties to experiment with innovative approaches such as mutual gains bargaining. However, in the 1990s the traditional approach to collective bargaining remains the centrepiece of Canadian industrial relations.

QUESTIONS

1. Identify the major factors that can have an influence on
   a) the process of collective bargaining;
   b) the outcomes of collective bargaining.
2. Define each of the different types of collective bargaining structures.
3. What types of bargaining structures tend to be most prevalent in Canada? Explain why these types of structures predominate.

4. Indicate why pattern bargaining may be breaking down in Canada over the 1980s and 1990s. How would you document such a trend? Would you expect it to occur in both the public and private sectors?

5. Using the concepts of bargaining target and resistance points, explain how a management and union bargaining session could lead to
   a) a zone of potential agreement;
   b) a range of potential disagreement.

6. Identify an alternative method or approach to collective bargaining that management and unions may use—often in an attempt to avoid strikes and to achieve a settlement. Why might management and the union prefer one method over another?

7. Explain the difference between *positions* and *interests* in collective bargaining.

8. Analyze a recently completed labour–management contract negotiation using the model in Figure 9.1.

REFERENCES

ANDERSON, J. 1989. "The Structure of Collective Bargaining in Canada." In J. Anderson, M. Gunderson, and A. Ponak, eds, *Union–Management Relations In Canada*. 2nd ed. Don Mills: Addison-Wesley.

CARTER, D. 1993. "The Changing Face of Labour Law." Address to the Annual Spring Industrial Relations Seminar, Queen's University (May 10) mimeo.

CHAMBERLAIN, N.W., and J.W. KUHN. 1986. *Collective Bargaining*, 3rd ed. New York, NY: McGraw-Hill Book Company.

CHAYKOWSKI, R.P. 1995. "Innovation and Cooperation in Canadian Industrial Relations: Adapting to NAFTA." Paper prepared for the Canada–United States–Mexico Conference on Labor Law and Industrial Relations. Washington, DC (September 19–20, 1994).

CHAYKOWSKI, R.P., and A. VERMA. 1992. "Adjustment and Restructuring in Canadian Industrial Relations." In R. Chaykowski and A. Verma, eds, *Industrial Relations in Canadian Industry*. Toronto, ON: Holt, Rinehart and Winston.

CHAYKOWSKI, R.P. 1990. "Union and Firm Preferences for Bargaining Outcomes in the Private Sector." *Relations industrielles/Industrial Relations* 45(2): 326–355.

DELANEY, J., and D. SOCKELL. 1989. "The Mandatory–Permissive Distinction and Collective Bargaining Outcomes." *Industrial and Labor Relations Review* 42 (4): 566–583.

FISHER, E.G., and A. KONDRA. 1992. "Canada's Airlines: Recent Turbulence and Changing Flight Plans." In R. Chaykowski and A. Verma, eds, *Industrial Relations in Canadian Industry*. Toronto, ON: Holt, Rinehart and Winston.

FISHER, R., and W. URY. 1983. *Getting to Yes: Negotiating Agreement Without Giving In*. New York, NY: Penguin Books.

FORREST, A. 1989. "The Rise and Fall of National Bargaining in the Canadian Meat-Packing Industry." *Relations industrielles/Industrial Relations* 44(2): 393–406.

FRIEDMAN, R. 1994."Missing Ingredients in Mutual Gains Bargaining Theory." *Negotiation Journal* (July): 265–280.

GODARD, J. 1994 "Labour and Employee Relations in the Canadian Private Sector: Report to Participants in the LERS Surveys." October 1994, mimeo.

HECKSCHER, C., and L. HULL. 1994. "Mutual Gains and Beyond: Two Levels of Intervention." *Negotiation Journal* (July): 235–248.

KATZ, H. 1993. "The Decentralization of Collective Bargaining: A Literature Review and Comparative Analysis." *Industrial and Labor Relations Review* 47 (1): 13–22.

KUMAR, P. 1993. *From Uniformity to Divergence: Industrial Relations in Canada and the United States*. Kingston, ON: Queen's University IRC Press.

KUMAR, P., and N. MELTZ. 1992. "Industrial Relations in the Canadian Automobile Industry." In R. Chaykowski and A. Verma, eds, *Industrial Relations in Canadian Industry*. Toronto, ON: Holt, Rinehart and Winston.

LABOUR CANADA. 1993. *Industrial Relations Legislation in Canada*. Ottawa, ON: Labour Canada.

ROSE, J. 1992. "Industrial Relations in the Construction Industry in the 1980s." In R. Chaykowski and A. Verma, eds, *Industrial Relations in Canadian Industry*. Toronto, ON: Holt, Rinehart and Winston.

ROSS, A.M. 1948. *Trade Union Wage Policy*. Berkeley: University of California Press.

VERMA, A., and P. WARRIAN. 1992. "Industrial Relations in the Canadian Steel Industry." In R. Chaykowski and A. Verma, eds, *Industrial Relations in Canadian Industry*. Toronto, ON: Holt, Rinehart and Winston.

VERMA, A., and J. WEILER. 1992. "Industrial Relations in the Canadian Telephone Industry." In R. Chaykowski and A. Verma, eds, *Industrial Relations in Canadian Industry*. Toronto, ON: Holt, Rinehart and Winston.

WALTON, R.E., and R.B. McKERSIE. 1991. *A Behavioral Theory of Labor Negotiations: An Analysis of a Social Interaction System*. 2nd ed. Ithaca, NY: ILR Press.

END NOTES

1   Data that would enable a complete breakdown of the frequency of the major bargaining structures are not available. The best data set is restricted to bargaining units with more than 500 employees (see Godard 1994 Table viii), which can significantly skew the actual situation.

2   Since the late 1980s, this bargaining structure has changed, in part because of the rise of small brewers and the merger activity in the industry.

3   The three major firms included Canada Packers, Burns, and Swift. The dominant union in meatpacking was originally the United Packinghouse Workers of America, which was succeeded by the Canadian Food and Allied Workers (CFAW); the CFAW merged with the Retail Clerks International Union in 1979 to form the United Food and Commercial Workers (Forrest 1989, 394).

4   This simple example assumes that the gains from lower assessments are greater than the cost of the expenditures undertaken to improve health and safety.

5   The importance of these issues is illustrated by developments in the relationship between the Communications Workers of Canada (CWC) (which recently merged with other unions to form the Communications, Energy and Paperworkers Union) and Bell Canada. The negotiations leading to the 1991 collective agreement led to the establishment of a high-level, joint union–management taskforce aimed at producing a framework for broad-based workplace reorganization (Chaykowski 1994).

6   Each of the United Steelworkers of America, the Canadian Auto Workers, and the Communications, Energy and Paperworkers has developed a rigorous "Statement on Work Reorganization" that either specifies the conditions for union participation in employee involvement programs or guides the approach of the union to workplace change (Kumar 1993, 93).

7   This approach is thoroughly discussed in the book *Getting to Yes* by Robert Fisher and William Ury, which arose out of work done through the Harvard Negotiation Project at Harvard University. (See the References section.)

CHAPTER 10

GRIEVANCES AND THEIR RESOLUTION

KENNETH WM. THORNICROFT AND GENEVIEVE EDEN

GRIEVANCE ARBITRATION PLAYS A CENTRAL ROLE IN THE UNION-management relationship. This chapter describes the grievance arbitration process and the legislative framework within which grievances are regulated. Factors that may influence grievance initiation are discussed as well as factors that may affect grievance outcomes and arbitral remedies. Arbitrator characteristics and initiatives underway to train prospective arbitrators are reviewed. Strengths and weaknesses of traditional grievance arbitration are identified and alternatives such as expedited arbitration and grievance mediation are examined.

A standard feature of Canadian labour law is the restriction of strike activity during the term of a collective bargaining agreement. It is sometimes assumed that the quid pro quo for this legislated "no-strike" provision is the employer's undertaking not to lock out bargaining unit employees during the term of the agreement. However, the exchange is not a no-strike provision for a no-lockout provision. Rather, it is more accurate to characterize both the no-strike and no-lockout provisions as one side of the coin, with the *grievance arbitration* process as the other. Thus, midterm contractual disputes can be resolved through the grievance arbitration procedure without work stoppages.

The grievance arbitration process is a very important factor in the overall union-management relationship. Indeed, grievance activity has long been identified by industrial relations scholars as an indicator of the underlying labour climate (Connerton, Freeman, and Medoff 1979; Dastmalchian and Ng 1990; Godard 1991; Ichniowski 1986; Katz, Kochan, and Gobeille 1983; Katz, Kochan, and Weber 1985; Norsworthy and Zabala 1985; Schuster 1985). There is evidence that unresolved grievances can have a "spillover effect" leading to lower organizational efficiency and productivity and increased workplace conflict (Brett and Goldberg 1979).

A *grievance* is "an allegation, usually by an individual [employee], but sometimes by the union or management, of misinterpretation or misapplication of a collective bargaining agreement or of traditional work practices" (Doherty 1989). A collective bargaining agreement is an employment contract, and thus, to file a grievance is to allege a breach of contract. However, rather than pursuing an action for breach of contract in the civil courts (with attendant delay and expense), labour relations practitioners have adopted an alternative form of dispute resolution, namely *grievance arbitration*, as their preferred mechanism for resolving disputes about the meaning, interpretation, or application of a collective bargaining agreement.

Grievance arbitration was originally conceived as an equitable, inexpensive, and expeditious solution to the problem of contract disputes between union and management. Grievance arbitration has been lauded as an effective mechanism for improving workplace democracy and for providing employees with a meaningful voice in matters affecting their employment (Freeman and Medoff 1984). Despite such favourable comment, however, others have argued that the contemporary grievance arbitration process is in need of repair—the process is too slow, too expensive, and overly "legalistic." In light of these criticisms, both policy makers and labour relations practitioners have endeavoured to formulate alternative systems for resolving workplace disputes. In this chapter, we shall describe the modern grievance arbitration process, outline some of the criticisms of the process, and set out some of the more innovative solutions for resolving workplace disputes that are now being put into practice.

GRIEVANCE PROCEDURES IN CANADA

At the outset it is important to distinguish grievance or *rights arbitration* from *interest arbitration*. Interest arbitration is concerned with the initial determination of contract rights when the parties themselves cannot produce a negotiated settlement. Interest arbitration is usually mandated by legislation as a substitute for the use of strikes and lockouts.

It is common in the public sector, especially for police and firefighters, when the right to strike is denied, or when striking employees have been ordered back to work by ad hoc legislation (Ponak and Thompson, this volume). Rights or grievance arbitration, on the other hand, is exclusively concerned with the enforcement of rights established by a collective bargaining agreement. In essence, interest arbitration involves establishing the terms and conditions of the collective agreement (especially wages and other benefits) while grievance arbitration involves interpreting the existing agreement. In this chapter, we shall focus our discussion solely on grievance arbitration.

All Canadian jurisdictions, except Saskatchewan, have mandated in their labour laws that grievances be resolved by arbitration (Saskatchewan has proposed amendments to its Trade Union Act to mandate grievance arbitration). For example, section 57(1) of the Canada Labour Code provides as follows:

> 57(1) Every collective agreement shall contain a provision for final settlement without stoppage of work, by arbitration or otherwise, of all differences between the parties to or employees bound by the collective agreement, concerning its interpretation, application, administration or alleged contravention.

The Internal Grievance Process

Collective bargaining agreements invariably include an internal two- or three- step process in which the grievance is reviewed at successively higher levels of the organization. Of the 118 grievance procedures reviewed in Gandz (1978), the number of steps ranged from two to seven, with two-thirds of the procedures involving three steps. A typical grievance procedure is set out in Table 10.1. At the first step of the process, a grievance is filed, either orally or in writing, alleging a violation of the collective agreement. Prior to the filing of a grievance, the parties may have attempted to resolve the dispute informally. In many cases, the local union steward will draft the grievance and file it on behalf of the *grievor* (the party on whose behalf the grievance is filed—in the United States, the term *grievant* seems to be preferred).

As the grievance proceeds through the internal dispute resolution process, the matter may be considered by successively more senior management and union representatives. At any stage the grievance can be settled or withdrawn, but if the matter cannot be resolved, the final step is a hearing before a neutral arbitrator or arbitration board. If the grievance arbitration process can be likened to a pyramid, then the final step of arbitration stands at the apex. In the vast majority of cases, grievances are settled internally, thereby avoiding the expense, delay, and conflict inherent in the arbitration process. For example, in an Ontario study, Gandz (1979) found that over 98 percent of grievances were settled short of arbitration. Similar results based on US data were reported by Graham and Heshizer (1978).

The Substance of Grievances

Grievances are most often filed by the union. Although management has an equal right to file grievances when it believes that the union is not honouring the collective agreement, it rarely does so because management has the right to simply implement the contract in a manner consistent with its interpretation. If the union does not agree with management's approach, it can file a grievance.

Most union-initiated grievances are filed on behalf of individual employees and are referred to as *individual grievances*. An example would be a claim by one employee that her overtime payment was incorrectly calculated on her last paycheque. Occasionally, two or more employees may have a similar question about how the contract was carried out; in such cases, the union may attempt to address the concern of all of the aggrieved employees together and file what is called a *group grievance*. For example, it may turn out that several employees on the same shift all believe their overtime pay was calculated incorrectly in much the same fashion. A group grievance allows for the shared problem to be addressed at the same time. A third type of grievance is known as a *policy grievance*. These are grievances that affect all employees represented by the union and might include issues such as the right of management to introduce a specific type of program to monitor absenteeism, to contract out work, or to require employees to take drug tests.

Because grievances allege a contract violation, they can cover literally any issue that is contained in the collective agreement. Thus, hundreds of different subjects can be raised in the grievance process including seniority rights, pay and benefits, promotions, and layoffs. Quite frequently, grievances are filed concerning employee discipline or discharge. In discipline or discharge grievances, the onus falls on management to show that it had "just cause," not merely to discipline the employee, but to impose the actual penalty. If the employer's disciplinary actions do not clear the just cause hurdle, arbitrators will set aside (i.e., rule against) the discipline. In some cases, the discipline will be set aside in its entirety, while in others, the arbitrator may substitute a lesser penalty. For example, if the employer did not have just cause to terminate an employee even though the employee engaged in some form of misconduct, the arbitrator might set aside the discharge and substitute a two-week unpaid suspension.

If the grievance does not concern a matter of employee discipline, the onus or burden of proof lies upon the union. Arbitrators often hold the parties to different levels of proof depending on the nature of the grievance (Thornicroft 1989a). For example, in discharge cases involving allegations of theft or other criminal conduct, arbitrators will sometimes apply the normal criminal burden, namely, proof beyond a reasonable doubt. In most other cases, the normal level of proof called for in civil trials, proof on a "balance of probabilities" (sometimes referred to as the "preponderance of evidence"), will be applied.

TABLE 10.1   Typical Grievance Procedure

	Process	Comment
Step 1	Oral presentation of grievance to the supervisor within time limitations (if any) for filing grievances.	Grievance usually presented by union steward.
If grievance not settled … **Step 2**	Written presentation of the grievance to the Director of Labour Relations or the Unit Manager.	At this stage, a specialist grievance officer may act on the grievor's behalf.
If grievance not settled … **Step 3**	Grievance presented to the plant manager or most senior officer responsible for labour relations.	Often several grievances are reviewed at a single Step 3 meeting with most being settled.

If grievance not settled …
Step 4
	Matter set down for arbitration either before a single arbitrator or an Arbitration panel.
	  Arbitrator (or panel chair) may be appointed on an ad hoc basis or may be designated in the collective agreement.
		Both parties may choose to be represented by legal counsel.
		  Arbitration award is intended to result in a final and binding decision but award may be challenged by way of judicial review.

Time Limits

Very often, the collective bargaining agreement will provide for a "limitation period"—if the grievance is not filed within the time limited by the agreement, the respondent party (usually the employer) is not required to consider the matter (i.e., the grievance is not *arbitrable*). As illustrated in Table 10.2, the vast majority of collective agreements contain time limits within which grievances must be filed; nearly one-half of the agreements require grievances to be filed no later than two weeks after the matter takes place.

TABLE 10.2   Time Limits for Initiating Grievances

(Major Collective Agreements [100+ employees] British Columbia, 1991) Limitation Period	% of Agreements	% of Employees
72 hours or less	4.6	0.7
5 days	4.6	2.4
1 week	9.2	11.9
10 days	14.6	7.2
2 weeks	13.1	23.3
3 weeks	9.2	7.5
1 month	20.8	33.6
No time limit	15.4	7.3
Varies with type of grievance	1.5	0.2
Other provisions	6.9	5.9
Total %	100.0	100.0
Number	130	220,368

SOURCE: Ministry of Skills, Training and Labour, Province of British Columbia (unpublished data).

Of course, there are always strategic considerations involved in refusing to deal with a grievance that is "out of time." Will the same issue merely arise once again in another grievance? Will the unresolved conflict "spill over" into the workplace? In some agreements, the arbitrator is given authority to override contractual time limits. In British Columbia, the arbitrator is specifically authorized by section 89(e) of the Labour Relations Code to "relieve, on just and reasonable terms, against breaches of time limits or other procedural requirements set out in the collective agreement...." Similar legislative override provisions are contained in the labour laws of Manitoba, Ontario, and Quebec.

Sole Arbitrator or Board?

Once referred to arbitration, the grievance may be decided by a single arbitrator or by a tripartite arbitration board or panel. In the latter case, each party chooses one representative to a panel chaired by a neutral arbitrator (the neutral selected by the parties jointly, or failing agreement, appointed by a third party—usually the Minister of Labour or the Labour Relations Board). The neutral chair of an arbitration panel effectively becomes the decision-maker, however, because the panel need only reach a majority conclusion, not a unanimous one. In the event that neither nominee agrees with the neutral chair's decision, the chair's decision is deemed to be the final award. The proportion of arbitration awards rendered by sole arbitrators appears to vary by jurisdiction: about two-thirds in Nova Scotia between 1980 and 1986 (Gilson and Gillis 1987), in Newfoundland between 1980 and 1991 (Thornicroft 1993) and in Ontario between 1985 and 1986 (Rose 1991); approximately one-half in British Columbia during the period 1966 to 1981 (Stanton 1983); but only about one-quarter in Alberta during 1985 to 1988 (Ponak and Olson 1992).

The Union's Duty of Fair Representation

The union is usually not required to take each and every unresolved grievance to arbitration. However, in deciding either to settle or withdraw a grievance, the union must not be motivated by some improper or discriminatory purpose. Under Canadian labour law, unions have a statutory *duty of fair representation* (DFR). If a bargaining unit employee believes that he or she has been treated unfairly by the union, a complaint can be filed with the labour relations board. While DFR complaints are not uncommon, relatively few succeed. For example, in 1991 and 1992, the British Columbia Labour Relations Board received 278 DFR complaints. Of these, 14 per cent were withdrawn, 37 per cent were dismissed as unfounded, 45 per cent were resolved in favour of the union, and only 4 per cent were resolved in favour of the complainant (Industrial Relations Council, 1992). If the DFR complaint also raises a human rights issue, such as discrimination based on religion, the employee could also proceed with a separate human rights complaint and/or a civil action for damages. In 1992, the Supreme Court of Canada, in *Renaud* v *Central Okanagan School Board and CUPE*, held both the union and the employer liable for religious discrimination. The basis of the claim against the union was its failure to agree to waive the strict application of a shift schedule set out in its collective agreement so that the claimant would not, in accordance with his religion, have to work on Friday evenings.

Costs

A frequently voiced complaint about the grievance arbitration process is its cost (Berkeley 1989; Bowers et al. 1982; Rose 1986; Winter 1983). Certainly, in comparison to the costs of litigation in the civil courts, arbitration appears to be a bargain. However, the grievance arbitration process is not cost free, although there is no direct cost to grievors (unlike in the civil courts) for pursuing their rights—their costs are absorbed by their union. The usual practice is for each party to pay their own costs of investigation and representation, and to share the arbitrator's fees equally. Most arbitrators charge the parties on a per diem basis; fees can range from $500 to over $2,000 per day plus related expenses (such as hearing room rental charges). Arbitrators usually charge for the time spent in the hearing and for reviewing written submissions, conducting research, and writing their awards. Arbitrators' total fees for an arbitration where the hearing itself is concluded within a single day typically range from $2,500 to $5,000. If the parties are also paying their nominees to an arbitration board, then the hearing costs will be that much higher; even when partisan appointees are unpaid union or management employees rather than paid "independents," there are still additional overhead costs such as time away from work to attend the hearing and on-the-job preparation time.

Either party (and especially management) may retain legal counsel to present their case to the arbitrator—most lawyers charge hourly fees ranging from about $100 to over $300 per hour. A lawyer would spend about 20 hours preparing for, and appearing at, a single-day arbitration hearing. Many unions (and some firms, particularly for Step 1 and Step 2 meetings) do not retain lawyers on an ad hoc basis, utilizing instead in-house "grievance officers" to represent their members. In that instance, a fair assessment of the costs of the arbitration process should also include the grievance officer's wages and benefits as well as any other reasonable overhead charges.

Judicial Review of Grievance Arbitration Awards

Arbitrators do not have the formal authority to ensure that the parties comply with their awards. However, under Canadian labour law, an arbitration award can be filed with the provincial superior trial court and thereafter can be enforced as an ordinary court order. If a party continues to ignore the arbitrator's order after it has been filed with the court, that party risks a fine or even imprisonment for contempt of court. In light of these potential sanctions, few parties ignore an arbitration award, although the disgruntled party may seek to overturn the award, in a subsequent application for judicial review.

Most jurisdictions have attempted to limit judicial review of arbitration awards through what is known as a *privative clause*. For example, section 101 of the British Columbia Labour Relations Code provides:

> 101. Except as provided in this Part, the decision or award of an arbitration board under this Code is final and conclusive and is not open to question or review in a court on any grounds whatsoever....

Section 99 of the British Columbia Labour Relations Code gives the Labour Relations Board a limited statutory power to review an arbitration award if there was a denial of a fair hearing or if the award was contrary to established labour relations law or policy. However, even in those jurisdictions where judicial review has not been restricted by a privative clause, the courts have generally deferred to arbitrators' decisions. In general, a court will not overturn an arbitrator's award simply because the court disagrees with the result; it must be shown that the arbitrator made a clear jurisdictional error or conducted a procedurally unfair hearing (i.e., there was a breach of the so-called "rules of natural justice").

GRIEVANCE FILING BEHAVIOUR

Grievances are one mechanism that bargaining unit employees can utilize to voice their dissatisfaction with the status quo (Freeman and Medoff 1984; Rees 1991). The *grievance rate* refers to the number of grievances filed per employee in the bargaining unit. There is some evidence that lower rates are associated with more "positive" and cooperative union-management relationships (Gandz 1979; Gandz and Whitehead 1982). Low grievance rates, however, do not necessarily imply an absence of workplace dissatisfaction. A low grievance rate may result from management domination of employees or from employee fear of management reprisals for filing grievances. A high grievance rate may also result from union domination of the employment relationship (Lewin and Peterson 1988) or may reflect the institutional structure of the union. Some union constitutions provide that they must take all individual grievances to arbitration. Constitutionally, the union cannot internally vet frivolous grievances, and this could increase the filing of such grievances. High grievance rates may also result when other venues for dealing with conflict and releasing pent-up frustration are not available. This can be the case, for example, if the collective agreement comes up for renewal every three years, as opposed to every year. Hebdon (1991) provides empirical evidence based on Ontario data that prohibiting the right to strike leads to more grievances.

Grievance initiation is a complex process involving three actors—the employee, the supervisor, and the shop steward (Bemmels et al., 1991). Studies of grievance initiation behaviour have focused on individual grievor attributes such as demographic characteristics and personality traits. However, there has been no clear pattern of results; the only consistent finding across studies is that younger workers tend to file more grievances than older workers (Cappelli and Chauvin 1991; Labig and Greer 1988).

While employees have a major role in grievance initiation, the behaviour of supervisors and shop stewards may also have an influence. Bemmels (1994) found that supervisor behaviour emphasizing mutual trust and respect between the supervisor and employees, and knowledge of the collective agreement was associated with lower grievance rates, while supervisor behaviour emphasizing production or achieving organizational goals was associated with higher grievance rates. However, other studies have found the relationships to be weak and inconsistent (Labig and Greer 1988).

Lower grievance rates may occur if stewards resolve potential grievances informally, while higher rates may result if stewards try to convince employees to file more frequently (Bemmels 1994). Grievance rates also may be influenced by industry (Gideon and Peterson 1979; Bemmels 1994), the level of technology (Nelson 1979), the degree of technological change in the organization (Peach and Livernash 1974), the centralization of decision making (Weiss 1957), the availability of alternative employment (i.e., "exit") opportunities (Cappelli and Chauvin 1991), and as noted above, the general labour-management "climate." In the case of public sector employees who do not have legislated strike rights, the grievance process may serve as a "safety valve," which may lead to higher grievance rates (Hebdon, 1991).

Since early resolution of grievances is usually believed to be to the advantage of all concerned, some research has emphasized the identification of the determinants of early settlements. Early settlement (e.g., at Step 1 or 2) has been found to be more likely when there is a co-operative bargaining relationship (Turner and Robinson 1972), when first-line supervisors have more experience (Knight 1986a), when the parties learn from previous grievance outcomes (Knight 1986b), and when attorneys are *not* involved prior to the arbitration stage (Deitsch and Ditts 1986).

THE ARBITRATORS: BACKGROUND CHARACTERISTICS AND TRAINING

The arbitrator profession is largely unregulated. There is nothing in the law preventing anyone from "hanging out a shingle" and announcing their availability to arbitrate unresolved grievances. However, the reality is that relatively few individuals conduct the majority of arbitrations within any given jurisdiction. The parties are simply unwilling, in many instances, to allow inexperienced arbitrators to resolve their disputes. Furthermore, in many collective agreements, a roster of experienced arbitrators is set out and cases are assigned on a rotational basis. If the minister of labour or labour board is called upon to appoint an arbitrator, they will invariably draw a name from their own panel of experienced arbitrators.

Thus, in almost every jurisdiction there are a few arbitrators who are extremely busy, and many others who are quite underutilized. Gandz and Warrian (1977) in an Ontario study found that 76 per cent of arbitration awards in Ontario were rendered by only thirteen arbitrators. Similar levels of arbitrator concentration have been reported in Alberta (Ponak 1987), British Columbia (Eeckhout 1981), Nova Scotia (Gilson and Gillis 1987), Newfoundland (Thornicroft 1993) and in the United States (Heneman and Sandver 1983; Primeaux and Brannen 1975). However, the growing utilization of expedited arbitration (discussed in more detail later) may have the effect of reducing the parties' reliance on a small corps of arbitrators. For example, in Ontario, since the introduction of expedited arbitration in 1979, twenty arbitrators completed a training program and were added to the province's list of approved arbitrators; these newly trained arbitrators issued 20.3 per cent of the awards rendered in 1985-86. Over one-quarter of their caseloads involved non-expedited arbitrations (Rose, 1991).

Most labour relations practitioners have well-defined views about what makes a good arbitrator, and experience and good judgment are two characteristics that are likely to appear on any list of "desired attributes." In a survey of nearly 300 members of the National Academy of Arbitrators (Allen and Jennings 1988), the following attributes were listed as being most important (in descending order): personal integrity; experience, both as an arbitrator and within labour relations generally (Westerkamp and Miller, 1971); and perceived neutrality. The respondents did not believe that a legal education was particularly necessary to succeed as an arbitrator although a majority of arbitrators are lawyers.

The typical arbitrator is a relatively older male (*very* few women have as yet forged successful careers as arbitrators), university trained in law or labour relations, and experienced in labour relations as a union or management representative, labour relations board member or university professor. Most arbitrators do not work full time in the profession. In a survey involving 459 arbitrators, Bemmels (1990a) found that 7 per cent were women, 63 per cent held a law degree, the average age was nearly 56 years, and only about one-third were full-time arbitrators. Similar results have been found by Allen and Jennings (1988), Deitsch and Dilts (1989), and Heneman and Sandver (1983). Unlike professions such as law, medicine, and engineering, there is no umbrella organization that arbitrators are required to join. However, many arbitrators are members of one or more of the following organizations (all of which hold annual conventions or workshops): the National Academy of Arbitrators, the American Arbitration Association, the Society of Professionals in Dispute Resolution, the Industrial Relations Research Association, and the Canadian Industrial Relations Association.

In most jurisdictions there is little formal training provided to prospective arbitrators, although there are initiatives under way in several provinces to train new arbitrators. For example, in Newfoundland the training of arbitrators has been taken on by the tripartite (employer, union, and government) Labour-Management Co-operation Committee. This committee appoints new arbitrators to the provincial panel after they have met the following criteria: a series of personal interviews, a four-day course on arbitration practice and procedure, a comprehensive written examination, and attendance at several hearings followed by the submission of "draft" awards for review and critique by existing panel members. In Alberta, the Arbitration and Mediation Society has taken on responsibility for the training of new arbitrators. The British Columbia Labour Relations Code establishes a new Collective Agreement Arbitration Bureau that has the responsibility for recruiting and training new arbitrators.

In Ontario, the labour legislation provides for the formation of a labour management advisory committee to advise the minister of persons qualified to be added to the list of approved arbitrators from which ministerial appointments are made. The committee plays an active advisory role in the Ontario development program. Graduates of the program are frequently used for these ministerial appointments to expedited arbitration cases. Initially, in fact, newly trained arbitrators relied almost exclusively on these ministerial appointments involving expedited cases. This dependence has declined in recent years, suggesting that the new arbitrators are gaining acceptance in the field (Rose 1991).

"LEGALISM" IN GRIEVANCE ARBITRATION: BANE OR BENEFIT?

It has become fashionable in recent years to decry the creeping "legalism" of the grievance arbitration process (Allen and Jennings 1988; Berkeley 1989; Raffaele 1982). Lawyers are well entrenched in the grievance arbitration process, in most cases through the initiatives of the parties themselves. Lawyers are often selected to serve as arbitrator or arbitration panel chair. Bloom and Cavanagh (1986) found that unions preferred lawyer-arbitrators whereas management preferred arbitrators who were economists. The results of several studies, in different jurisdictions, show that most arbitrators have legal training. The proportion of arbitrators who are lawyers has been documented based on US data as being 51 per cent by Allen and Jennings (1988); nearly 75 per cent by Heneman and Sandver (1983), 63 per cent by Bemmels (1990a), and 65 per cent by Thornicroft (1989b). Canadian studies have found the proportion of arbitrators who are lawyers to be over 80 per cent in Ontario (Barnacle, 1991) and nearly 50 per cent in Newfoundland (Thornicroft 1993).

Lawyers are also involved as representatives of the parties although rarely at Steps 1 or 2 of the grievance process. In most cases, management will appoint an internal officer to represent its interests, and grievors are usually represented by the local union steward or a staff grievance officer. However, if the grievance proceeds to arbitration, the parties (and most especially management) are frequently represented by legal counsel. The proportion of arbitrations in which legal counsel was involved, and the management-union split, has been documented as 80-50 in Ontario (Barnacle 1991); 44-21 in an earlier Ontario study (Goldblatt 1974); 73-51 in the United States (American Arbitration Association 1984) and 40-10 in Newfoundland (Thornicroft 1994a). Ponak (1987) found that one or both parties were represented by legal counsel in three-quarters of his Alberta sample.

Presumably, parties retain legal counsel in order to improve their chances of success, a presumption that has not been empirically verified (Block and Stieber 1987; Thornicroft 1994b). We shall examine this issue later in this chapter. Another, more clearly demonstrated effect of lawyers' involvement in the grievance arbitration process is delay, the issue to which we now turn.

JUSTICE DELAYED, JUSTICE DENIED: DELAY IN GRIEVANCE ARBITRATION

As previously noted, grievance arbitration was originally conceived as an expeditious and inexpensive mechanism for resolving contract disputes. However, there is mounting evidence that, today, the grievance arbitration process is not particularly expeditious. In a survey of 360 union and management advocates, the union representatives identified "delays by the other side" as the most serious fault with the arbitration process (Berkeley 1989). It is not uncommon for a grievance that ultimately goes to arbitration to take more than a year to be resolved, that is, from the date of its filing to the date the arbitrator's decision is issued (though most grievances are resolved well before arbitration).

As indicated in Table 10.3, most of the delay occurs in the pre-hearing phase. Delay in getting to an arbitration hearing may be attributed to the busy schedules of lawyers and arbitrators. Although lawyers and arbitrators may be partly to blame for the delay, however, the parties are not compelled to retain a particular arbitrator or to engage legal counsel. Much of this delay in the pre-hearing phase may also be taken up in processing the grievance through the internal grievance mechanism. Certainly, this is the view of at least one commentator (Seitz 1981):

> In many relationships there are four or five grievance steps, in each of which no more takes place than had occurred in a preceding step. The union merely repeats what it said before and the employer representative merely uses a previous grievance answer as a rubber stamp. While all this transpires, to no effective purpose, the grievant waits for justice and time marches on.

Ponak and Olson (1992) found that discharge cases arising in the public (versus private) sector or heard by tripartite panels (versus sole arbitrators) took relatively longer to conclude. Stanton (1983), Barnacle (1991), and Thornicroft (1993) also found that sole arbitrators were more expeditious than tripartite panels. Despite the delay associated with tripartite panels, the parties may nonetheless desire an arbitration panel so that

TABLE 10.3:   Studies of Delay in Grievance Arbitration

Study	Jurisdiction	Time Frame	Pre-Hearing Delay	Hearing to Award	Total[a] Delay
Goldblatt (1974)	Ontario	1971-1973	212	37	256
Fricke (1976)	Alberta	1973-1975	157	46	214
Kochan and Katz (1988)	USA	1975	—	—	223
Labour Arbitration Cases	Canada	1975	—	—	283
Stanton (1983)	B.C.	1966-1981	—	—	240
Winter (1983)	Ontario	1980	258	36	301
Rose (1986)	Ontario	1983	—	48	342
F.M.C.S. (1988)	USA	1985-1987	281	64	345
Olson (1990)	Alberta	1985-1988	268	70	345L
abour Arbitration Cases	Canada	1987-1988	366	101	428
Barnacle (1991)	Ontario	1983-1986	168	—	240
Thornicroft (1993)	Newfoundland	1980-1991	146	35	181

[a]Total Delay (calendar days) may not equal sum of "Pre-Hearing Delay" and "Hearing to Award" due to missing information and multi-day hearings

SOURCE: Adapted, with additional references, from Ponak and Olson (1992).

their nominees can reinforce the parties' respective positions in closed-door sessions with the neutral chair (Veglahn 1987). Goldblatt (1974), Barnacle (1991), and Thornicroft (1994a) all identified lawyers as a significant source of delay in grievance arbitration, although this was not found in Ponak and Olson (1992).

While delay may not have a major impact in some types of cases, it is a particular concern in discharge grievances because the employee remains off the job until the grievance is resolved. If a discharged employee is ultimately reinstated one year later, the remedy may ring hollow—the employee may have found a new job and be reluctant to return to the old one or may have relocated to another province in search of work. Moreover, some studies have found an inverse relationship between delay in getting to the hearing and the probability of reinstatement (Adams 1978; Barnacle 1991). Delay in discharge cases also can adversely affect the employer since the amount of backpay, should the grievor be reinstated, increases with the passage of time.

GRIEVANCE OUTCOMES AND ARBITRAL REMEDIES

Arbitrator Characteristics

Arbitrators have wide discretion to remedy breaches of collective agreements. They need not follow precedent in their deliberations. Each case is judged on its own merits. The actual remedy ordered will, of course, depend on the nature of the grievance and can range from a simple declaratory order (e.g., management has the right to contract out equipment maintenance work), to monetary awards, to employee reinstatement orders (either uncon-ditionally or on terms, and with or without backpay). The courts have repeatedly indicat-ed that arbitration awards will not be quashed or set aside simply because the arbitrator's proposed remedy is "creative."

Although arbitrators have considerable flexibility in fashioning their awards, they may develop a tendency to "tailor" their awards so as not to unduly offend either union or management; this may be a particular problem with relatively inexperienced arbitrators (Bemmels 1991b). Since the parties themselves select their decision maker, arbitrators have an incentive to keep the "scales in balance." Arbitrators, not surprisingly, reject this view saying that they are predominantly influenced by the contract language, the past practice of the parties, principles of fairness, and precedent from other cases (Allen 1976; Jennings and Allen 1993).

Some commentators argue that arbitral outcomes are influenced by the arbitra-tors' background characteristics such as age, education and experience (Briggs and Anderson 1980; Dworkin 1974; Lawson 1981; Nelson and Curry, 1981; Primeaux and Brannen 1975; Rezler and Peterson 1978). However, several studies have found that arbi-trators' background characteristics have little or essentially no effect on the decisions they make (Fleming 1965; Heneman and Sandver 1983; Bemmels 1990a; Kauffman et al. 1994).

As noted earlier, the particpation of lawyers appears to be a source of *delay* in the arbitration process. Do lawyers also affect arbitration *outcomes*? Although Bankston (1976) found that lawyer-arbitrators held significantly different views about certain labour relations issues compared to arbitrators whose "home discipline" was economics, business, or industrial relations, the overwhelming evidence is that lawyer-arbitrators do *not* decide cases any differently than arbitrators who are not legally trained (Barnacle 1991; Bemmels 1990a/1990b; Deitsch and Dilts 1989; Heneman and Sandver 1983; Kauffman et al. 1994; Thornicroft 1994b; Thornton and Zirkel 1990).

Still others provide evidence that suggests arbitrators are influenced by personal values in their decisions (Gross 1967; Bankston 1976; Gandz and Warrian 1977). According to this view, the values held by arbitrators subtly influence various factors: their selection of relevant data, emphasis on certain evidence, acceptance of certain procedural methods, attitude toward prior arbitration awards, and literal or broad reading of the contract (Gross 1967). This view is not shared by other researchers, however, who believe that arbitrators' personal values and attitudes do not affect their awards (Ashenfelter 1987; Doeringer 1977).

Legal Representation

The efficacy of legal representation is also a matter of considerable empirical debate. Goldblatt (1974), Ponak (1987), and Wagar (1994) found that unions won comparatively more cases when they were represented by legal counsel and management was not; the reverse pattern also prevailed, suggesting that it is the "imbalance" in legal representation that is the critical factor in grievance arbitration outcomes (Dickens, Jones, Weekes, and Hart 1985; Block and Stieber 1987). Barnacle (1991, 164) did not specifically test the "imbalance" hypothesis but nevertheless suggested that "...the greater relative use of legal counsel was associated with greater 'win' rates for both parties."   Most recently, Thornicroft (1994b) found that lawyers had no impact on disciplinary grievance arbitration outcomes in Newfoundland over the period 1980 to 1992. Taken together, the empirical evidence suggests that lawyers have little, if any, impact on grievance outcomes when *each* or *neither* party is represented, but may favourably shift the odds when only *one* party is legally represented and the other is not. This implies that unions and employers could reduce their arbitration costs if they would mutually agree not to employ lawyers.

Grievor Characteristics

Researchers have also examined grievor and case characteristics in order to determine if these are systematically related to grievance outcomes. For example, Thornicroft (1989b) found that arbitrators treated grievors in alcohol cases rather more leniently than similarly situated grievors whose substance of choice was marijuana or some other nonprescription drug. Not surprisingly, and consistent with the theory of "progressive discipline" (namely, that repeated acts of misconduct should be met with increasingly more severe penalties), grievors with poor work records are less likely to succeed in arbitration compared to grievors with unblemished work histories (Barnacle 1991; Ponak 1987; Thornicroft 1989, 1994b).

A substantial body of research has also examined the impact of the grievor's gender on arbitration outcomes. Bemmels (1988a/b/c; 1990b; 1991a/b) suggests there are two competing hypotheses, given that most arbitrators are male: the "chivalry" hypothesis (which operates in favour of women) and the "evil woman" hypothesis (which operates to their detriment). The empirical evidence, summarized in Table 10.4, suggests no consensus. Ten studies have found some evidence of bias in favour of females, six found no bias in favour of either sex, and one found a bias against females. These results, however, are based solely on an analysis of arbitration *awards,* and not on the prior steps of *filing* a grievance or *referring* it to arbitration. It may be that in examining arbitrators' awards (and, by implication, arbitrators themselves), researchers are overlooking two other possible sources of bias. First, there may be a gender-based difference in grievance *filing behaviour.* Perhaps females tend to file grievances only when there is a very compelling case in their favour. If so, it would hardly be surprising to discover that a comparatively higher proportion of the grievances of females (vis-à-vis males) are sustained on arbitration. Such an observed result would, however, have little to do with a generalized arbitral predisposition in favour of women. Second, the decision to *refer* a grievance to arbitration rests, not with the individual grievor, but rather with the certified bargaining agent (hence the phrase "the union owns the grievance"). If the bargaining agent is likely to refer a grievance from a woman only if she is likely to win, it would follow that their win rates would be higher compared with male grievors. The "pro-female" bias apparently displayed at the arbitration stage would merely reflect the relative merits of females' claims by the time they got to arbitration. Only the most "meritorious" cases on the part of females would be filed and referred to arbitration. To date, these other possible sources of bias have not been examined in any rigorous empirical study.

TABLE 10.4:   Gender Effects in Grievance Arbitration

Study/Year	Data Sources	Gender Bias?
Rodgers and Helburn (1984)	37 discharge awards drawn from five southwestern U.S. chemical refineries (1975-1981)	Anti-female bias
Bigoness and DuBose (1985)	80 personnel management students	No gender bias
Dalton and Todor (1985)	294 grievances filed in a 1-year period at a single western U.S. public utility	Pro-female bias
Ponak (1987)	150 unpublished discharge arbitration awards from Alberta (1982-1984)	Pro-female bias
Block and Stieber (1987)	755 published (BNA and CCH) grievance arbitration awards (1979-1982)	No gender bias
Bemmels (1988a)	104 discharge arbitration awards from Alberta (1981-1983)	Pro-female bias
Bemmels (1988b)	633 grievance arbitration awards from British Columbia (1977-1982)	Limited evidence of pro-female bias
Bemmels (1988c)	Vols. 67-87 *Labor Arbitration Reports* (1,812 awards from 1976-1986)	Pro-female bias by male, but not female, arbitrators
Scott and Shadoan (1989)	Vols. 69-80 *Labor Arbitration Awards* (169 awards from 1969-1980)	No gender bias
Thornicroft (1989b)	Vols. 85-91 *Labor Arbitration Reports* (145 substance abuse discharge awards from 1985-1988)	Evidence of pro-female bias in drug, but not alcohol, cases
Bemmels (1990)	131 arbitrators listed in IRRA directory	No gender bias
Barnacle (1991)	821 grievance arbitration awards from Ontario (1983-1986)	Limited evidence of pro-female bias
Bemmels (1991)	Vols. 67-87 *Labor Arbitration Reports* (557 awards from 1976-1987)	Limited evidence of pro-female bias by male, but not female, arbitrators
Bemmels (1991)	230 male arbitrators listed in NAA or IRRA directory	Pro-female bias
Caudill and Oswald (1992)	re-estimate of Bemmels's 1988 Alberta data	Pro-female bias
Crow and Logan (1994)	248 arbitration awards	No gender bias
Thornicroft (1995)	350 grievance arbitration awards from Newfoundland (1980-1992)	No gender bias

ALTERNATIVES TO CONVENTIONAL GRIEVANCE ARBITRATION

As discussed earlier in this chapter, grievance arbitration was originally conceived as an expeditious, inexpensive, and relatively informal mechanism for resolving contract disputes. Over the years, serious concerns have been raised about its effectiveness in these areas. Critics argue that the system has become too slow, too expensive, and increasingly legalistic. Criticisms have been levied against the protracted hearings, the length of arbitrators' decisions and their lack of clarity, and the short supply of competent and experienced arbitrators. Against this background of high expectations and mounting criticism of traditional grievance arbitration, increased attention has been paid to alternatives such as expedited arbitration and grievance mediation.

Expedited Arbitration

While there are many variants, expedited arbitration generally involves procedures designed to reduce delay and cost in the hearing of a grievance and issuance of an award. These procedures include relying on single arbitrators rather than tripartite boards, eliminating lengthy written decisions, and scheduling several grievances for a single hearing.

There are two categories of expedited arbitration: private and statutory. Private systems are developed and operated by mutual agreement of the parties. Statutory systems exist through legislative provisions; the expedited procedure is available to the parties as an alternative to their collectively bargained grievance procedures.

One of the earliest statutory expedited arbitration systems was found in British Columbia, where section 96(1) of the Industrial Relations Act (now repealed) permitted the Industrial Relations Council to mediate and arbitrate grievances at the request of either party. Between 1981 and 1986, an average of 609 applications were received each year and an average of 69 percent were settled by mediation prior to the arbitration stage (Thompson 1992).

One of the best known statutory systems of expedited arbitration is section 46 of the Ontario Labour Relations Act. The Act provides unions and employers with a choice of procedures; grievances can either be processed through section 46 or through the conventional negotiated arbitration procedures. Section 46 gives *either* party the right to apply to the Ministry of Labour for the appointment of an arbitrator. The minister appoints a sole arbitrator who must schedule a hearing within twenty-one days of the application and is expected to issue an award within twenty-one days of the hearing. In addition, the minister may appoint a grievance settlement officer to mediate a dispute on a voluntary basis.

The scope of section 46 is broad in that it embraces all arbitral issues. Relatively straightforward issues like those involving seniority are more likely to go to expedited arbitration, although overall there is little difference between the types of grievances processed through section 46 and conventional grievance arbitration. Perhaps it is somewhat surprising, given their seriousness, that the proportion of discipline and discharge cases resolved by expedited arbitration and conventional arbitration is about the same, at approximately 34 per cent (Rose 1991).

Substantial use has been made of section 46. Statistics provided by the Ministry of Labour's Office of Arbitration indicate that expedited arbitration has grown from 19 per cent of all awards in 1980/81 to 45 per cent of the total in 1992/93 (Table 10.5). Of the total grievances received for expedited arbitration during this period, 47 per cent were settled by grievance settlement officers.

TABLE 10.5:   Expedited and Conventional Arbitration Awards, 1981/82 to 1992/93

YEAR	Expedited Awards	Conventional Awards	Expedited as a Percentage of Total Arbitration Awards
1981/82	277	1,174	19%
1982/83	440	1,182	27%
1983/84	573	1,097	34%
1984/85	517	997	34%
1985/86	621	1,122	36%
1986/87	660	1,141	37%
1987/88	665	1,136	37%
1988/89	561	866	39%
1989/90	540	824	40%
1990/91	587	745	44%
1991/92	492	730	40%
1992/93	537	655	45%
Totals	6,470	11,669	36%

SOURCE: Office of Arbitration, Ontario Ministry of Labour.

Section 46 has resulted in substantial savings in cost and time. Between 1980/81 and 1985/86, the estimated total savings of expedited arbitration over conventional arbitration was $8.6 million, of which $6.4 million was the result of grievance mediation (Rose 1991). The estimated average elapsed time between the incident and an expedited arbitration award was four months, compared with 11.5 months under conventional arbitration.

Also in Ontario, the Labour Relations Board has jurisdiction under the Labour Relations Act to resolve grievances in the construction industry through a process of grievance mediation and expedited arbitration. The available evidence indicates that this procedure provides informal, fast, and inexpensive dispute resolution (Rose 1986).

In 1985, Manitoba enacted a statutory expedited arbitration scheme similar to that in Ontario. Hearings are scheduled within 28 days and awards issued within 14 days for a discharge or suspension and within 28 days for other cases. In the first two years of the operation of the system, 70 per cent of all cases referred were settled by mediation (Rose 1989). There are no restrictions on the scope of arbitrable issues. Saskatchewan is currently in the process of amending The Trade Union Act to include provisions for an expedited arbitration process.

Private systems of mutually agreed upon expedited arbitration outside of the legislative framework are still relatively rare, in both Canada and in the United States, although there is some evidence that they are expanding in Canada.

One of the older systems is the Canadian Railway Office of Arbitration (CROA), established in 1965. It provides for a single permanent arbitrator, who typically hears five to seven cases in a day and issues a written award and rationale normally within a week. Cases are often presented by way of a written brief, and witnesses are rarely called. The majority of cases are not conducted by lawyers, and all types of issues are involved. Significant time and cost savings have been reported (Picher 1991). A grievance commissioner system was adopted in 1972 by Inco and two locals of the United Steelworkers. Two commissioners serve as permanent arbitrators and hear cases alternately on predetermined dates each month (Thompson 1992).

A privately negotiated expedited arbitration process also exists in British Columbia between the Health Labour Relations Association and the Hospital Employees Union. Features of the system include both process issues and substantive issues. Process issues include: cases scheduled monthly, hearings on location, no use of lawyers, limited use of prior case law, decisions rendered in three days and written briefly on a set form, agreed-upon experienced arbitrators, no restrictions on the type of issues, and witnesses not normally used. Substantive issues include: no precedential value to decisions, and decisions not referred to in any other proceedings. The process has proved significantly faster and less expensive than conventional arbitration (Arbogast 1991).

Also in British Columbia, the provincial government and the Government Employees' Union recently revived a system for expedited arbitration first developed in 1979, but the scope of grievances is restricted. Expedited arbitration clauses were also contained in approximately 25 per cent of all collective agreements between local school boards in BC (Thompson 1992). In longshoring in BC, instant arbitration is also used, whereby an arbitrator is on call twenty-four hours a day and responds immediately when on-the-spot decisions are required (Thompson 1992).

Grievance Mediation

Another response to the shortcomings of conventional grievance arbitration is grievance mediation. Such mediation is sometimes incorporated as a voluntary step in expedited arbitration or in conventional grievance arbitration.

In grievance mediation, a trained, third party neutral (the mediator) assists union and management representatives in reaching a voluntary settlement of their grievance. Mediators may assist in the clarification of issues and positions and initiate suggestions for possible resolution of the grievance, although they do not make final decisions. If the parties are unable to resolve the grievance, it goes to arbitration. Grievance mediation is confidential in that, unless both parties consent, nothing said or done in mediation can be used as evidence in subsequent legal proceedings. Moreover, settlements can be made without prejudice, that is, no precedent is created by the settlement to be used in any future cases.

The benefits of grievance mediation have been extolled by many researchers (House 1992; Skratek 1993; Sherman 1991). Strengths of the process are: (1) faster resolution of cases—there are no written decisions to wait for; (2) less expensive—lower cost for mediators compared to arbitrators and less time consuming; (3) less adversarial—the focus is on resolving rather than winning; and (4) more of an educational process for the parties—the experience with the skilled mediator may improve their ability to resolve grievances themselves. Indeed, the use of a more collaborative, problem-solving approach can improve the overall labour-management relationship; rather than stonewalling, the parties look for solutions (Quinn et al. 1990; Goldberg 1989). The experience in Ontario, Manitoba, and Saskatchewan under statutory reforms has shown that mediation does promote the settlement of grievance disputes and results in substantial time and cost savings.

Apart from the statutory reforms in expedited arbitration, there is little published research on the effect of grievance mediation in Canada. In the pre-hearing mediation process used by the Ontario Crown Employees' Grievance Settlement Board, approximately 70 to 80 per cent of all cases were resolved prior to the hearing stage (Fraser and Shime 1989). In the Ontario construction industry, negotiated settlements with grievance mediation were achieved in 87 per cent of the cases between 1980 and 1984 (Whitehead et al. 1988).

In the United States, voluntary grievance mediation has resulted in significant time and cost savings in the bituminous coal industry (Roberts et al. 1990; Brett and Goldberg 1979) as well as in the telephone, electric power, manufacturing, petroleum refining, retail drug, local government, secondary education, and mass transit industries (Goldberg 1989). It is estimated that, in the United States, more than two thousand grievances have been referred to mediation, and about 80 percent of those have been successfully resolved without proceeding to arbitration (Skratek 1993).

Overall, the evidence indicates that a high proportion of grievances are settled when grievance mediation is in place, although determining its net independent effect would require comparisons with settlement rates in the absence of mediation. The evidence suggests that grievance mediation results in time and cost savings and it may also improve the parties' problem-solving ability and their overall relationship. The procedure appears to offer sufficient promise to warrant its extended use and further evaluation.

CONCLUSION

Grievance arbitration plays a central role in the union-management relationship. It was originally conceived as an equitable, inexpensive, and expeditious mechanism for resolving contract disputes. This still remains true in a comparative sense. Arbitration is a much more accessible procedure to handle a discharge, for example, than is a lawsuit in the civil courts. There is no direct cost to grievors for pursuing their rights—their costs are absorbed by their union dues. A major strength of grievance arbitration is that it is under the control of the parties themselves. It has been lauded as an effective mechanism for improving workplace democracy and for providing employees with a meaningful voice in matters affecting their employment.

However, over the years, serious concerns have been raised about the effectiveness of grievance arbitration. It has been argued that the contemporary grievance arbitration process is too slow, too expensive, and overly legalistic. In light of these criticisms, both policy makers and labour relations practitioners have attempted to formulate alternative systems for resolving workplace disputes, systems such as expedited arbitration and grievance mediation.

The findings suggest that statutory expedited arbitration schemes are widely accepted by the parties, and that they promote the settlement of grievances and produce substantial time and cost savings. Although examples of private systems of expedited arbitration exist, the examples cited are the exception; furthermore, due to the lack of published data, it is difficult to obtain current information on these systems.

The available evidence on grievance mediation indicates that this procedure provides informal, fast, and inexpensive dispute resolution. It is flexible and allows the parties more control over the outcome. However, most of the published research on the effects of grievance mediation has been done in the United States; Canadian research has focused on statutory reforms. There is little published research on the effect of private systems of grievance mediation in Canada. It appears to offer sufficient promise to warrant its extended use and further evaluation.

QUESTIONS

1. To what extent can the grievance process be utilized as a mechanism for employees to "voice" their concerns about workplace issues?

2. It has been said that the grievance process is the quid pro quo for a no-strike/no-lockout clause in the collective agreement. Is this trade-off a "fair" one?

3. Some parties choose sole arbitrators while others prefer to use three-person panels. What are the pros and cons of each format?

4. What remedy does a bargaining unit employee have when the union does not take his or her unresolved grievance to arbitration?

5. What changes, if any, would you propose to the contemporary grievance arbitration process to ensure that it is a relatively quick, inexpensive, and just process?

6. How does "expedited arbitration" differ from "conventional arbitration"?

7. Do you feel that lawyers should be banned from the grievance arbitration process? Why or why not?

REFERENCES

ADAMS, G.A. 1978. *Grievance Arbitration of Discharge Cases.* Kingston, Ontario: Industrial Relations Centre, Queen's University.

ALLEN, A.D., Jr. 1976. "Procedures in Labor Arbitration: Views from Arbitrators Themselves." *Labor Studies Journal* 1: 190-202.

ALLEN, A.D., Jr., and D.F. JENNINGS. 1988. "Sounding Out the Nation's Arbitrators: An NAA Survey." *Labor Law Journal* 39: 423-431.

AMERICAN ARBITRATION ASSOCIATION. 1984. *Study Time: A Quarterly Letter of News and Comment for the AAA Arbitrator.* New York, N.Y.: American Arbitration Association.

ARBOGAST, M.W. 1991. "Resolving Issues and Improving Relationships through the Use of Expedited Arbitration." In Proceedings of the 28th Conference of the Canadian Industrial Relations Association, Kingston, Ontario: 533-542.

ASHENFELTER, O. 1987. "Arbitration and Negotiation Process: Arbitrator Behavior." *American Economic Review* 77: 342-346.

BANKSTON, E. 1976. "Value Differences Between Attorney and Economist Labor Arbitrators." In Proceedings of the 29th Annual Winter Meeting of the Industrial Relations Research Association, Madison, Wisconsin: IRRA, 151-160.

BARNACLE, P.J. 1991. *Arbitration of Discharge Grievances in Ontario: Outcomes and Reinstatement Experiences.* Kingston, Ontario: Industrial Relations Centre, Queen's University.

BEMMELS, B. 1988a. "The Effect of Grievants' Gender on Arbitrators' Decisions." *Industrial and Labor Relations Review* 41: 251-262.

———. 1988b. "Gender Effects in Discipline Arbitration: Evidence from British Columbia." *Academy of Management Journal* 31: 699-706.

———. 1988c. "Gender Effects in Discharge Arbitration." *Industrial and Labor Relations Review* 42: 63-76.

———. 1990a. "Arbitrator Characteristics and Arbitrator Decisions." *Journal of Labor Research* 11: 181-192.

———. 1990b. "The Effect of Grievants' Gender and Arbitrator Characteristics on Arbitration Decisions." *Labor Studies Journal* 15: 48-61.

———. 1991a. "Gender Effects in Grievance Arbitration." *Industrial Relations* 30: 150-162.

———. 1991b. "Attribution Theory and Discipline Arbitration." *Industrial and Labor Relations Review* 44: 548-562.

———. 1994. "The Determinants of Grievance Initiation." *Industrial and Labor Relations Review* 47: 285-301.

BEMMELS, B., Y. RESHEF, and K. STRATTON-DEVINE. 1991. "The Roles of Supervisors, Employees, and Stewards in Grievance Initiation." *Industrial and Labor Relations Review* 45: 15-30.

BERKELEY, A.E. 1989. "The Most Serious Faults in Labor-Management Arbitration Today and What Can Be Done to Remedy Them." *Labor Law Journal* 40: 728-733.

BIGONESS, W.J., and P.B. DuBOSE. 1985. "Effects of Gender on Arbitrators' Decisions." *Academy of Management Journal* 28: 485-491.

BLOCK, R.N., and J. STIEBER. 1987. "The Impact of Attorneys and Arbitrators on Arbitration Awards." *Industrial and Labor Relations Review* 40: 543-555.

BLOOM, D.E., and C.L. CAVANAGH. 1986. "An Analysis of the Selection of Arbitrators." *American Economic Review* 76: 408-422.

BOWERS, M.H., R.L. SEEBER, and L.E. STALLWORTH. 1982. "Grievance Mediation: A Route to Resolution for the Cost-Conscious 1980s." In Proceedings of the 1982 Spring Meeting of the Industrial Relations Research Association, 459-464.

BRETT, J., and S.B. GOLDBERG. 1979. "Wildcat Strikes in Bituminous Coal Mining." *Industrial and Labor Relations Review* 32: 465-483.

BRIGGS, S.S., and J.C. ANDERSON. 1980. "An Empirical Investigation of Arbitrator Acceptability." *Industrial Relations* 19: 163-174.

CAPPELLI, P. and K. CHAUVIN. 1991. "A Test of an Efficiency Model of Grievance Activity." *Industrial and Labor Relations Review* 45: 3-14.

CAUDILL, S.B., and S.L. OSWALD. 1992. "An Alternative to Bemmels's Method of Investigating Biases in Arbitration." *Industrial and Labor Relations Review* 45: 800-805.

CONNERTON, M., R.B. FREEMAN, and J.L. MEDOFF. 1979. "Productivity and Industrial Relations: The Case of U.S. Bituminous Coal." Harvard University, Department of Economics, Mimeograph.

CROW, S.M., and J.W. LOGAN. 1994. "Arbitrators' Characteristics and Decision-Making Records, Gender of Arbitrators and Grievants, and the Presence of Legal Counsel as Predictors of Arbitral Outcomes." *Employee Responsibilities and Rights Journal* 7: 169-185.

DALTON, D.R., and W.D. TODOR. 1985. "Gender and Workplace Justice: A Field Assessment." *Personnel Psychology* 38: 133-151.

DASTMALCHIAN, A., and I. NG. 1990. "Industrial Relations Climate and Grievance Outcomes." *Relations Industrielles/Industrial Relations* 45: 311-325.

DEITSCH, C., and D.A. DILTS. 1986. "Factors Affecting Pre-Arbitral Settlement of Rights Disputes: Predicting the Method of Rights Dispute Resolution." *Journal of Labor Research* 7: 69-78.

DEITSCH, C.R., and D.A. DILTS. 1989. "An Analysis of Arbitrator Characteristics and Their Effect on Decision Making in Discharge Cases." *Labor Law Journal* 40: 112-116.

DICKENS, L., M. JONES, B. WEEKES, and M. HART. 1985. *Dismissed: A Study of Unfair Dismissal and the Industrial Tribunal System.* Oxford, England: Basil Blackwell Limited.

DOERINGER, P.B. 1977. "Discussion: Value Differences between Attorney and Economist Labor Arbitrators." In Proceedings of the Twenty-Ninth Annual Meeting of the Industrial Relations Research Association, Madison, Wisconsin: IRRA, 186-189.

DOHERTY, R.E. 1989. *Industrial and Labor Relations Terms: A Glossary* (5th ed.). Ithaca, New York: ILR Press.

DWORKIN, H.J. 1974. "How Arbitrators Decide Cases." *Labor Law Journal* 25: 200-210.

EECKHOUT, T. 1981. "An Analysis of Discharge Arbitration in British Columbia." M.S. Thesis, Faculty of Commerce and Business Administration, University of British Columbia.

FEDERAL MEDIATION AND CONCILIATION SERVICE. 1988. *Annual Report.* Washington, D.C.: FMCS.

FLEMING, R.W. 1965. *The Labor Arbitration Process.* Urbana, Illinois: University of Illinois Press.

FRASER, D., and O.B. SHIME. 1989. "The Ontario Grievance Settlement Board." In Proceedings of the 26th Conference of the Canadian Industrial Relations Association, Laval, Québec, 567-578.

FREEMAN, R.B., and J.L. MEDOFF. 1984. *What Do Unions Do?* New York, New York: Basic Books, Inc.

FRICKE, J.G. 1976. An Empirical Study of the Grievance Arbitration Process in Alberta. Edmonton, Alberta: Alberta Labour.

GANDZ, J., and J.D. WHITEHEAD. 1982. "The Relationship Between Industrial Relations Climate and Grievance Initiation and Resolution." In Proceedings of the Thirty-Fourth Annual Meeting, Industrial Relations Research Association, Madison, Wisconsin: IRRA, 320-328.

GANDZ, J. 1979. "Grievance Initiation and Resolution: A Test of the Behavioural Theory." *Relations Industrielles/Industrial Relations* 34: 778-792.

GANDZ, J., and P.J. WARRIAN. 1977. "Does it Matter Who Arbitrates?—A Statistical Analysis of Arbitration Awards in Ontario," *Labour Gazette* 77: 65-75.

GANDZ, J. 1978. "Employee Grievances: Incidence and Patterns of Resolution." Ph.D. Thesis, York University, Toronto.

GIDEON, T.F., and R.B. PETERSON. 1979. "A Comparison of Alternative Grievance Procedures." *Employee Relations Law Journal* 5: 222-233.

GILSON, C.H.H., and L.P. GILLIS. 1987. "Grievance Arbitration in Nova Scotia." *Relations Industrielles/Industrial Relations* 42: 256-269.

GODARD, J. 1991. "The Progressive HRM Paradigm: A Theoretical and Empirical Re-Examination." *Relations Industrielles/Industrial Relations* 46: 378-400.

GOLDBERG, S.B. 1989. "Grievance Mediation: A Successful Alternative to Labor Arbitration." *Negotiation Journal* 5: 9-15.

GOLDBLATT, H. 1974. *Justice Delayed...The Arbitration Process.* Toronto, Ontario: Labour Council of Metropolitan Toronto.

GRAHAM, H., and B. HESHIZER. 1978. "The Effect of Contract Language on Low-Level Settlement of Grievances." *Labor Law Journal* 30: 427-432.

GROSS, J.A. 1967. "Value Judgements in the Decisions of Labor Arbitrators." *Industrial and Labor Relations Review* 21: 55-72.

HEBDON, R. 1991. "Ontario's No-Strike Laws: A Test of the Safety-Valve Hypothesis." In Proceedings of the 28th Conference of the Canadian Industrial Relations Association, Kingston, Ontario, 347-357.

HENEMAN, H.G., III, and M.H. SANDVER. 1983. "Arbitrators' Backgrounds and Behavior." *Journal of Labor Research* 4: 115-124.

HOUSE, N.C. 1992. "Grievance Mediation: AT&T's Experience." *Labor Law Journal* 43: 491-495.

ICHNIOWSKI, C. 1986. "The Effects of Grievance Activity on Productivity." *Industrial and Labor Relations Review* 40: 75-89.

INDUSTRIAL RELATIONS COUNCIL (IRC). 1992. *Annual Report.* Vancouver, BC: Labour Relations Board of British Columbia.

JENNINGS, D.F., and A.D. ALLEN, Jr. 1993. "How Arbitrators View the Process of Labor Arbitration: A Longitudinal Analysis." *Labor Studies Journal* 17: 41-50.

KATZ, H.C., T.A. KOCHAN, and K.R. GOBEILLE. 1983. "Industrial Relations Performance, Economic Performance, and QWL Programs: An Interplant Analysis." *Industrial and Labor Relations Review* 37: 3-17.

KATZ, H.C., T.A. KOCHAN, and M.R. WEBER. 1985. "Assessing the Effects of Industrial Relations Systems and Efforts to Improve the Quality of Working Life on Organizational Effectiveness." *Academy of Management Journal* 28: 509-526.

KAUFFMAN, N., D. VANLWAARDEN, and C. FLOYD. 1994. "Values and Arbitrator Selections." *Labor Law Journal* 45: 49-54.

KNIGHT, T.R. 1986a. "Correlates of Informal Grievance Resolution Among First-Line Supervisors." *Relations industrielles* 41: 281-98.

———. 1986b. "Feedback and Grievance Resolution." *Industrial and Labor Relations Review* 39: 585-98.

KOCHAN, T.A., and H. KATZ. 1988. *Collective Bargaining and Industrial Relations,* 2nd ed. Homewood, Illinois: Richard D. Irwin, Inc.

LABIG, C.E., Jr., and C.R. GREER. 1988. "Grievance Initiation: A Literature Survey and Suggestions for Future Research." *Journal of Labor Research* 9: 1-27.

LAWSON, E.W., Jr. 1981. "Arbitrator Acceptability: Factors Affecting Selection." *The Arbitration Journal* 36: 22-29.

LEWIN, D., and R.B. PETERSON, 1988. *The Modern Grievance Procedure in the United States.* Westport, Connecticut: Quorum Books.

NELSON, N.E. 1979. "Grievance Rates and Technology." *Academy of Management Journal* 22: 810-815.

NELSON, N.E., and E.M. CURRY. 1981. "Arbitral Decision Making: The Impact of Occupation, Education, Age and Experience." *Industrial Relations* 20: 312-317.

NORSWORTHY, J.R., and C.A. ZABALA. 1985. "Worker Attitudes, Worker Behavior, and Productivity in the U.S. Automobile Industry, 1959-1976." *Industrial and Labor Relations Review* 38: 544-557.

OLSON, C. 1990. "Time Delays in Grievance Arbitration." MBA Thesis, University of Calgary.

PEACH, D.A., and R.E. LIVERNASH. 1974. *Grievance Initiation and Resolution: A Study in Basic Steel.* Cambridge, Massachusetts: Harvard University Press.

PICHER, M.D. 1991. "The Canadian Railway Office of Arbitration." *Labour Arbitration Yearbook* 1: 37-54.

PONAK, A., and C. OLSON. 1992. "Time Delays in Grievance Arbitration." *Relations Industrielles/Industrial Relations* 47: 690-708.

PONAK, A. 1987. "Discharge Arbitration and Reinstatement in the Province of Alberta." *The Arbitration Journal*, 42: 39-46.

PRIMEAUX, W.J., and D.E. BRANNEN. 1975. "Why Few Arbitrators Are Deemed Acceptable." *Monthly Labor Review* 98: 27-30.

QUINN, T.J., M. ROSENBAUM, and D.S. McPHERSON. 1990. "Grievance Mediation and Grievance Negotiation Skills: Building Collaborative Relationships." *Labor Law Journal* 41: 763-769.

RAFFAELE, J.A. 1982. "Lawyers in Labor Arbitration." *The Arbitration Journal* 37: 14-23.

REES, D.I. 1991. "Grievance Procedure Strength and Teacher Quits." *Industrial and Labor Relations Review* 45: 31-43.

REZLER, J., and D. PETERSON. 1978. "Strategies of Arbitrator Selection." *Labor Arbitration Reports* 70: 1,307-1,320.

ROBERTS, M.T., R.S. WOLTERS, W.H. HOLLEY, Jr., and H.S. FIELD. 1990. "Grievance Mediation: A Management Perspective." *Arbitration Journal* 45: 15-23.

RODGERS, R.C., and I.B. HELBURN. 1984. "The Arbitrariness of Arbitrators' Decisions." In Proceedings of the 37th Annual Meeting of the Industrial Relations Research Association, Madison, Wisconsin: IRRA, 234-241.

ROSE, J.B. 1986. "Statutory Expedited Grievance Arbitration: The Case of Ontario." *The Arbitration Journal* 41: 30-45.

———. 1989. "Innovative Grievance Arbitration Systems." *Labour Relations into the 1990s.* University of Lethbridge: CCH Canadian Ltd., 64-84.

———. 1991. "The Emergence of Expedited Arbitration." *Labour Arbitration Yearbook* 1: 13-22.

SCHUSTER, M. 1985. "Models of Cooperation and Change in Union Settings." *Industrial Relations* 24: 382-394.

SCOTT, C., and E. SHADOAN. 1989. "The Effect of Gender on Arbitration Decisions." *Journal of Labor Research* 10: 429-436.

SEITZ, P. 1981. "Delay: The Asp in the Bosom of Arbitration." *The Arbitration Journal* 36: 29-35.

SHERMAN, M.R. 1991. "Streamlined Mediation: Alternative to Litigating Discharge Disputes." *Arbitration Journal* 46: 34-37.

SKRATEK, S. 1993. "Grievance Mediation: How to Make the Process Work for You." *Labor Law Journal* 44: 507-511.

STANTON, J. 1983. *Labour Arbitrations: Boon or Bane for Unions?* Vancouver, BC: Butterworth and Company.

THOMPSON, M. 1992. "Expedited Arbitration: Promise and Performance." *Labour Arbitration Yearbook* 3: 41-53.

THORNICROFT, K.W. 1989a. "Arbitrators, Social Values and the Burden of Proof in Substance Abuse Discharge Cases." *Labor Law Journal* 40: 582-593.

———. 1989b. "Arbitrators and Substance Abuse Discharge Grievances: An Empirical Assessment." *Labor Studies Journal* 14: 40-65.

————. 1991. "Patterns of Teacher Bargaining in Canada and the United States." *Labor Law Journal* 42: 779-791.

————. 1993. "Accounting for Delay in Grievance Arbitration." *Labor Law Journal* 44: 543-553.

————. 1994a. "Lawyers and Grievance Arbitration: Delay and Outcome Effects." *Labour Studies Journal* 18: 39-51.

————. 1994b. "Do Lawyers Affect Grievance Arbitration Outomes?" *Relations Industrielles/Industrial Relations* 49: 357-372.

————. 1995. "Gender Effects in Grievance Arbitration...Revisited." *Labor Studies Journal* (in press).

THORNTON, R.J., and P.A. ZIRKEL. 1990. "The Consistency and Predictability of Grievance Arbitration Awards. *Industrial Labour Relations Review* 43(2): 294-307.

TURNER, J.T., and J.W. ROBINSON. 1972. "A Pilot Study on the Validity of Grievance Settlement Rates as a Predictor of the Union-Management Relationship." *Journal of Industrial Relations* (Australia) 14: 314-22.

VEGLAHN, P.A. 1987. "Grievance Arbitration by Arbitration Boards: A Survey of the Parties." *The Arbitration Journal* 42: 47-54.

WAGAR, T.H. 1994. "The Effect of Lawyers on Non-Discipline/Discharge Arbitration Decisions." *Journal of Labor Research* 15: 283-293.

WEISS, E.C. 1957. "Relations of Personnel Statistics to Organizational Structures." *Personnel Psychology* 10: 27-42.

WESTERKAMP, P.R., and A.K. MILLER. 1971. "The Acceptability of Inexperienced Arbitrators: An Experiment." *Labor Law Journal* 22: 763-770.

WHITEHEAD, J.D., E.M. AIM, and L.A. WHITEHEAD. 1988. "Dispute Resolution in Canada: Selected Examples of Recent Innovations." In selected SPIDR Proceedings 1987-1988, New York City and Los Angeles: 200-218.

WINTER, C. 1983. *Grievance Arbitration Cost and Time,* 1980. Toronto, Ontario: Research Branch, Ontario Ministry of Labour.

CHAPTER 11

EMPLOYEE INVOLVEMENT IN THE WORKPLACE

ANIL VERMA *

*E*MPLOYEE INVOLVEMENT (EI) IN DECISION MAKING IS NOT A NEW IDEA. *Yet, despite its intuitive appeal and its compatibility with macroeconomic trends of increasing competition and workplace demands for higher quality and innovation, the diffusion and effective implementation of EI remains elusive. Employee involvement can be a significant reversal of certain Tayloristic principles on which most Canadian organizations rely. Despite the failures, EI has continued to grow in popularity, perhaps because some organizations have effectively used EI to create a more innovative and productive workplace. This chapter addresses several challenges for managers in the general context as well as in the unionized workplace.*

* The author would like to acknowledge helpful feedback from Morley Gunderson and Allen Ponak on an earlier draft of this chapter. Partial financial support from the Social Sciences and Humanities Research Council of Canada is gratefully acknowledged.

Systems of employee involvement (EI) or worker participation[1] have received much attention in the past fifteen years from practitioners and researchers alike. Although greater employee involvement on the job has been suggested since the 1950s, it was not until more recently that the idea had any significant impact on the way decisions are made within the organization. This is also true in the context of labour–management relations, where the growth of direct participation for employees signifies one of the more important changes occurring within the industrial relations system.

At one level, employee involvement can be viewed as a significant reversal of certain Tayloristic principles. Frederick Taylor believed that one of the most important principles of scientific management was the separation of roles between management and labour. Management was to devise the "best way" of doing the job, and the worker was to follow scientifically derived instructions. Taylor did not want workers to be "thinking" about the production process lest they tamper with the most efficient way of doing the job. At one point, Taylor argued that any involvement of the worker with the production process could be "fatal" to success. The idea of greater employee involvement is essentially a reversal of this aspect of Taylorism. Given the pervasive influence that Tayloristic principles have had on organizational practice since the beginning of this century, the introduction of greater employee involvement poses many challenges for managers, employees, and union leadership.

This chapter addresses five key questions that arise when considering systems of employee involvement:

1. What forms of employee involvement have emerged in practice in recent years?

2. What is the extent of diffusion of employee involvement practices across workplaces?

3. What is the effect of employee involvement systems on performance?

4. What is the effect of employee involvement on employer–employee and union–management relations?

5. What is the role, if any, of public policy in the diffusion of innovations such as employee involvement?

EMERGENT FORMS OF EMPLOYEE INVOLVEMENT

Involvement or participation in decision making can take many forms depending on the choices made in each of several dimensions of participation (Dachler and Wilpert 1978). First and foremost, there is the issue of *direct* versus *indirect* forms of participation. In forums such as collective bargaining and the legislative process, participation is through elected representatives and, hence, indirect. Participation in a work or quality team is called direct because the individual is personally involved. Direct involvement can be at the individual or the group level. Suggestion schemes, common to many companies, are examples of a mild form of involvement at the individual level. Quality circles, on the other hand, are examples of group participation.

The second dimension of participation is the *extent* to which it is allowed. Consultation is a weak form of participation because it does not imply decision-making authority. Equal say in decision making for all parties and the power to implement decisions are two examples of stronger forms of participation. Some highly participative forums may also contain a mechanism to resolve any disputes among the parties participating in decision making.

The third dimension of participation is the substantive *content* of decision making, i.e., the set of issues over which decision making is exercised. This may be limited to a single issue such as the administration of training programs or the resolution of quality problems on the job. It can also be broader in scope to include more than one set of issues. In some cases, participative forums may have an open-ended mandate to consider a broad range of workplace issues.

These dimensions help us understand different kinds of employee involvement schemes and plans. The focus of this chapter is on direct forms of employee involvement in which workers participate in groups. Thus, indirect participation and forums of individual involvement are excluded. The scope of participation considered ranges widely, from single issues to broad mandates. Two types of commonly found, group-oriented direct participation forums are discussed later in this chapter.

There are several reasons for limiting the focus to direct forms of participation at the group level. To start with, these forums are relatively new developments in the history of work organization in this century. Second, they have registered sharp growth in practice in North America over the last fifteen years.

Third, the innovation and adoption of these forms of employee participation poses important questions for industrial relations theory as well as organization theory. The Canadian system of industrial relations has relied, traditionally and almost exclusively, on indirect participation through collective bargaining and grievance procedures. How does the introduction of direct forms of participation affect relations among the actors within the industrial relations system? Is direct participation compatible with indirect participation, or does it, as is often alleged, supplant the need for indirect representation? Can quality circles take the place of unions? Direct participation, as pointed out earlier, also challenges traditional organizational structures by reversing one of the key facets of Tayloristic work organization. Although the implications of direct participation for organization theory are considered to be outside the scope of this chapter, the consequences of direct participation for organizational processes and structures will be pointed out wherever possible.

DEVELOPMENTS IN THE CANADIAN WORKPLACE

Before discussing employee involvement plans in greater detail, it is important to understand the workplace context within which these practices are being adopted. Faced with increasing competition from abroad and deregulation at home, Canadian firms have two broad options to choose from to cope with the new challenges. The first option is to lower wages to levels prevailing in the competitor economies.[2] For a variety of reasons,[3] this option is not feasible for most Canadian firms. Even if Canadian wages were cut substantially, they would still remain well above wages in most Third World countries.[4]

An alternative strategy would be to maintain higher wages but seek a comparative advantage through product innovation, quality, service, and specialization.[5] Porter (1980; 1990) calls this a differentiation strategy by which firms seek to distinguish their products from the low-cost producers. Successful differentiation requires that the firm employ technological and organizational innovation to develop new products quickly. These products must be of a high quality and come with reliable service so that they can fetch the premium price needed to support high wages. The success of this strategy depends on mobilizing a highly skilled, trained, flexible, and motivated workforce.

A Model of Workplace Policies under Conditions of Competition

A model of the workplace under conditions of increasing international competition is shown in Figure 11.1. In this model, it is argued that increased competition due to growing international trade, deregulation, privatization, and the introduction of flexible technologies (e.g., computer-based information and process technology) has brought pressures on firms to meet the market demands of low cost, high quality, and rapid innovation. The model then lists the specific characteristics of the workforce that would help firms meet these demands. Employees would have high levels of skill and training; they would feel involved with and committed to the company; they would be flexible enough to meet unexpected challenges; and they would show adaptability to shifts in demand.

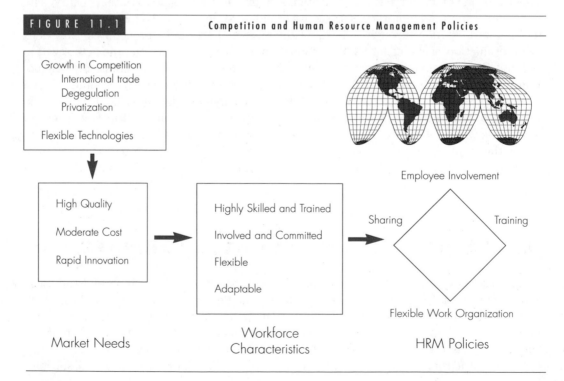

| FIGURE 11.1 | Competition and Human Resource Management Policies |

Growth in Competition
International trade
Degegulation
Privatization

Flexible Technologies

High Quality

Moderate Cost

Rapid Innovation

Market Needs

Highly Skilled and Trained

Involved and Committed

Flexible

Adaptable

Workforce Characteristics

Employee Involvement

Sharing   Training

Flexible Work Organization

HRM Policies

SOURCE: Adapted from Verma and Weiler (1994).

Traditional methods of production are Tayloristic in design and practice. Narrowly defined jobs and a strict separation of managerial and employee roles result in a semi-skilled workforce engaged in repetitive tasks. Employees are not required or encouraged to get involved in the production process. Product designs do not change frequently, and the managerial emphasis is typically on mass execution of a fairly standard and repetitive process. This production process is, therefore, under pressure to change when markets become more dynamic. Product demand, in both quality and quantity, varies more frequently, requiring more frequent changes on the shop floor. The employees, therefore, must be able to understand and comply with these changes.

Thus, under conditions of increasing competition and flexible technologies, work-forces would have to become highly skilled and trained, involved with the production process, and flexible and adaptable to shifting market conditions. The human resource management (HRM) policies and practices that will lead to the creation and maintenance of a workforce with these characteristics, it is argued, will require innovative policies in four key areas: training, employee involvement, work organization, and compensation (sharing).

Creation of a highly skilled workforce requires that firms invest more resources in *training*. The emphasis on quality and innovation within the differentiation strategy also means that firms must get their workers more involved in the production process. Hence, a greater emphasis on *employee involvement* may be expected. *Equity theory* suggests that people are motivated to seek equitable rather than maximum rewards, i.e., they think their rewards should be comparable to what other people with similar skills and experience receive. *Expectancy theory* suggests that people are motivated only when they believe that expended efforts will generate commensurate rewards. When these two theories are combined, they imply that, unless workers share in the fruits of labour, it is unlikely that they will expend maximum effort. High involvement policies and programs are unlikely to be effective unless they are complemented with a set of policies that promote *sharing*.[6] Sharing need not be confined to financial matters alone. It can also take the form of sharing information. To promote employee involvement, many organizations began, in the 1980s, to share information widely with all levels of employees. Sharing can also be extended to privileges; removal of hierarchical privileges such as preferential parking, cafeterias, and washrooms for managers can also promote the perception that workers are partners in the enterprise.

As competition forces firms to move to higher-value-added products and greater investment in skills, there will be greater pressure to move away from Tayloristic to more *flexible forms of work organization* (Gerwin and Kolodny 1992). Traditional or Tayloristic work organization requires work to be divided into small parts, which discourages broad-based training in skills. Each worker knows and performs only a very small portion of the total work; hence it is difficult to substitute one worker for another. Thus, traditional forms of work organization cannot take advantage of broader multiskill training, nor can they fit with the concept of greater employee involvement by which employees are encouraged to think of all aspects of work. Team-based work organization, in which workers have multiple skills and greater responsibility for decentralized decision making, is much more compatible with a high-value-added workplace that is competing on the basis of high quality and innovation.

To summarize, employee involvement does not occur in isolation from other human resource practices. In practice, we may expect that growth in employee involvement will be associated with more investment in training, some innovations in compensation, and more flexible forms of work organization.

The Diffusion of Employee Involvement and Other Innovations

Information on the extent of EI and other innovations in Canadian workplaces has been scant and available only sporadically (Table 11.1). The 1993 Human Resource Practices Survey (HRPS) was limited to four industries (wood products, fabricated metal products, electrical and electronic products, and business services) across 714 establishments (Betcherman et al. 1994). Another survey, the Working with Technology Survey (WWTS) was conducted in 1985 (Long 1989; Betcherman and McMullen 1986) and repeated in 1991 (Betcherman et al. 1994; Betcherman, Leckie, and Verma 1993). Although the measures used by these surveys are not all identical and, therefore, not directly comparable, results from the Canadian surveys are presented along with results from US surveys to put them in context.

As indicated in Table 11.1, some form of employee involvement was reported by 43 per cent of Canadian establishments in the HRPS Survey. Respondents were asked if the establishment had any of the popular forms of employee involvement such as quality circles, quality-of-worklife programs or total-quality-management initiatives. This figure likely overestimates the average for all sectors because of its bias towards manufacturing, where workplace innovations have generally preceded those in the service and public sectors. The survey results suggest that although employee involvement has not yet spread to a majority of Canadian establishments, its practice has established a foothold in many organizations.

Based on these figures, it is difficult to conclude that the incidence of training has been growing through the 1980s and the 1990s, although it is prevalent in a significant number of firms.[7] Statistics Canada's 1987 Human Resource Training and Development Survey found that 31 per cent of the establishments reported formal in-house training programs. The National Training Survey taken in 1991, which defined training more broadly to include both internal and external training as well as various forms of on-the-job training, found training practices prevalent in 70 per cent of establishments surveyed. Whatever the precise estimate, it is clear from these data that training as a human resource practice has also become widespread.

Flexible forms of work organization such as job rotation, job enlargement and enrichment, and self-directed work teams were reported by 15.7 to 22.5 per cent of the establishments. At least one of these practices was used in 37 per cent of the firms surveyed (Betcherman et al. 1994, 34). Variable pay practices such as gainsharing, profit-sharing, employee stock ownership plans, and pay-for-skill were reported by 6.5 to 21.6 per cent of the establishments.

Thus, both theory and empirical evidence in this section suggests that employee involvement does not stand in isolation from other complementary human resource practices in the workplace.

TABLE 11.1   Incidence of Workplace HR Practices: Canada and US (Per cent of establishments
reporting each practice)

Human Resource Practices	Canada		United States	
Reference	Betcherman et al. (1994)	Long (1989)	Osterman (1994)	Lawler et al. (1992)
Survey	HRPS Survey 1993	WWTS Survey 1985	MIT Survey 1992	GAQ Survey 1987 CEQ Survey 1990
Employee involvement	43.1 — includes quality circles, total quality management, quality-of-worklife	14.2 — quality circles 19.4 — other problem-solving groups 47.5 — WWTS 1991	78.2 — of any coverage 64.0 — covering at least 50% of the workforce	61 — 1987 QCs only 66 — 1990 QCs only 70 — 1987 } Groups other 86 — 1990 } than QCs
Training	31 — 1987 Human Resource Training and Development Survey 70 — 1991 National Training Survey		32 — off-the-job 45.1 — cross- training	
Flexible work organization				
Job rotation	22.5			
Job enlargement	21.1			
Job enrichment	21.4	21.9		60 (1987); 75 (1990)
Self-directed work teams	15.7	11.0		25 (1987); 28 (1990)
Variable pay				
Profit sharing	21.6	25.0	44.7	65 (1987); 63 (1990)
Employee stock option plans	14.1	n/a	n/a	61 (1987); 64 (1990)
Pay-for-skill	14.5	7.4	30.4	40 (1987); 51 (1990)
Gainsharing	6.5	9.7	13.7	26 (1987); 39 (1990)
Other incentive pay	6.4	n/a	n/a	Individual incentive: 87 (1987); 90 (1990) Team incentive: 59 (1990)

SOURCE: Based on studies cited.

A GENERAL THEORY OF EMPLOYEE INVOLVEMENT

At the policy level, the introduction of employee involvement has been driven, historically, by two distinct underlying philosophies. The first approach is derived from a moral, ethical, and sociocultural base. Its main precept is that greater say in decision making for those who are affected by these decisions is an ideal that is as pertinent to the workplace as it is to democratic societies. The European notion of industrial democracy and the systems of co-determination that exist in Germany and several other countries in Western Europe are good illustrations of this approach. It should be noted that most operationalizations of industrial democracy in Europe have taken the form of indirect rather than direct participation and are mandated by law.

The second approach, championed by Japanese and North American firms, derives from the utilitarian principle that practices like employee involvement are a means to other important ends such as higher quality and productivity. In this view, employee participation leads to better outcomes for all parties because it improves productivity and creates more satisfied and energized workers.

There is no single theory of why employee involvement would produce positive outcomes. Rather, a number of theories such as expectancy theory, attribution theory, and equity theory have been combined to develop models that predict the outcomes of EI (Cotton 1993). A selected number of models are reviewed here, very briefly, to show how and why positive effects of participation on productivity and affective responses such as job satisfaction may be expected.

Sashkin (1976) suggested that the psychological and cognitive effects of employee involvement are likely to produce a feeling of "ownership" of decisions among employees. In this model, EI is also seen as leading to shared norms and greater information flow. These outcomes, in turn, will lead to increased commitment, higher quality, and a higher capacity for adapting to change. Locke and Schweiger (1979) argue that employee involvement may increase productivity through two different mechanisms: cognitive effects, such as better communication and better understanding of the job, and motivational effects, such as a greater sense of "ownership" stemming from ego involvement and increased trust. In general, most motivational theories such as Maslow's need-hierarchy theory or Herzberg's two-factor theory of motivators and dissatisfiers can be tied directly or indirectly to employee involvement (Cotton 1993).

In other models, employee involvement is seen as reducing role conflict and role ambiguity (Schuler 1980). Employee involvement may also strengthen expectancy links between performance and rewards because the employee will know more about which behaviours are rewarded (Lee and Schuler 1982).

Factors leading to the adoption of EI

What causes firms to move in the direction of greater EI? Based on a number of case studies, the reasons can be classified into five categories (Verma 1990).

Crisis

External shocks like loss of profits or markets, financial crises caused by recessions, or deregulation account for the vast majority of firms that adopt greater employee involvement. In general, unless there are compelling reasons for change, people are likely to be satisfied with the status quo and will be loathe to accept innovations.

Implementation of EI involves its own costs, which can be, in general, quite high. A crisis, therefore, is a double-edged sword when it comes to introducing EI. On one hand, it provides an incentive for change, but on the other hand, it requires resources that may be scarce during a crisis. Experience seems to suggest that a crisis of moderate proportions provides the best combination of the incentive to change and the needed resources. A severe crisis, such as a firm moving rapidly towards bankruptcy, is unlikely to leave the firm with sufficient resources to invest in EI.

Crisis in the Labour–Management Relationship

In a smaller number of cases, EI adoptions take place in the aftermath of a crisis in the labour–management relationship. Some adversarial relationships keep getting more conflictual until they assume crisis proportions. At this point the parties usually introduce a number of initiatives to improve relations, and EI can be a part of that effort.

Workplace Problems

In a small number of cases, certain crises of the workplace, as opposed to crises of survival or of labour–management relationships, account for the adoption of greater employee involvement. The case of Manitoba Telephone System (MTS) and the CEP Union, discussed in Verma and Cutcher-Gershenfeld (1993) is a good illustration of this approach. EI was adopted at MTS largely in response to the need to reduce stress on the job.

Emulation

In some organizations, EI is adopted as a result of comparing themselves with the best practice in other firms. EI professionals communicate with each other through extensive networks. Word is thus passed on about cutting-edge practices from one organization to another. Some companies, especially those that benchmark themselves against their most successful competitors, adopt EI simply because they find that it has won acceptance among leading-edge firms. The introduction of EI programs in the Canadian oil industry follows this pattern (Taras and Ponak 1994).

Proactive Adoption

A few firms adopt EI because they anticipate problems that are likely to occur in the future and they want to be prepared. These organizations truly believe that EI is a better way to manage and to compete effectively. These are typically large companies or members of large conglomerates. Some illustrative examples are Boeing, Bell Canada, and Motorola.

Emergent Forms of EI

The various types of EI programs found in practice can be divided into two categories (Cutcher-Gershenfeld, Kochan, and Verma 1991). The first is characterized by its self-contained nature, that is, the participative form is accompanied by few, if any, corresponding changes in organizational structure, procedures, or other subsystems. The Japanese quality circles (QCs) are a good example of this form of participation. This narrow form is notable because it does not threaten or require a change in the traditional hierarchy of the organization. Because of their self-contained nature, such forms can be seen as an add-on feature that requires relatively little effort to implement. Perhaps for this reason, QCs became the single most popular form of employee involvement in the US in the 1980s.

The second type of employee involvement is characterized by its high degree of integration with, and impact on the rest of, the organization. Such forms require a host of changes in organizational structures and procedures. Typical examples of this type of participation are autonomous or semiautonomous work groups. In their very design, they are intended to challenge the traditional hierarchical structure of authority. Because their impact on the organization is substantial, such forms require a large investment in terms of cost and effort and, hence, are more difficult to implement. This explains, in part, why the diffusion of these forms has remained well below the first type.

The categorization above indicates that the deepest challenges are posed by the second type of EI and by the first type as it makes a transition to the second type. The choice of a particular form of EI may have important consequences in the long run even if the different forms appear nearly equivalent in their short-run impact. Later in this chapter, the forms of EI are linked to the sustainability of EI programs over time.

The Organizational Consequences of EI

There are many areas of change following implementation of EI in an organization. For the sake of brevity and focus, three areas where the impact of EI is felt most are considered below. These are also the areas where most attention is needed in the formative period during which the foundation for EI effectiveness is laid.

Training

As discussed earlier, one of the most important consequences of introducing EI is an increase in training. The traditional organization invests only a modest sum in training, and most of that is directed at management or at training in technical and functional skills. Effective implementation of EI requires that training be increased in both magnitude and in scope. Training in problem-solving and team-based skills is a must. Notably successful companies in Canada appear to be investing roughly five to seven days of training per employee per annum on an ongoing basis (Verma and Irvine 1992).

It appears that successful companies use training in the context of EI for three distinct purposes. First, the task of training is to inform employees and socialize them into appreciating both the value of their input and the organizational need to improve quality and productivity. There is ample research evidence to show that firms have been generally quite successful in raising awareness of EI and in getting employees to identify with strategic goals of the business. The second task for training is to provide employees with a set of basic skills in problem solving so that they can begin to get involved. Finally, training is used to upgrade skills continually, to disseminate information about the firm's strategic direction, and to renew interest on an ongoing basis.

First-Line Supervision

First-line supervisors are among the first managers directly affected by the introduction of EI in the organization (Klein 1988; Klein and Posey 1986). Experience shows that if EI is to be meaningful, certain changes must occur in the quality and quantity of first-line supervision. This process occurs through the gradual increase in employee problem-solving skills and through their willingness to assume more autonomy and responsibility. If the formal organization does not recognize this trend and account for it in its own plans, it is likely that the EI process will begin to lose steam.

In many organizations, the introduction of EI has been followed by a decrease in the amount of direct supervision and by redefining the role of a supervisor from that of a monitor to that of a co-ordinator and facilitator (Klein 1988). If EI is effective, workers do not need as much supervision. Also, if workers are learning problem-solving skills, they need a different kind of support. They need someone to train them, facilitate communication with other parts of the organization, help develop benchmarks, and assist with the acquisition of information. Supervisory functions are evolving in many organizations along these lines.

Information Flow

The medium- to long-term consequences of EI for the organization are in the area of information flow and access. A hierarchical organization is characterized by a protocol for information flow both horizontally and vertically. The introduction of EI creates a demand for information that severely tests the old protocol: employees at progressively lower levels of the organization have access to progressively less and less information. A new protocol for sharing information must be developed if lower-level employees have to access detailed information for problem solving on the shop floor on a regular basis.

Organizations have developed a wide variety of ways to deal with increasing demands for access to information. In some companies, employee teams include staff representatives from support departments like accounting, engineering, and maintenance. The support staff become a link between the team and other departments for access to information. Usually, however, there are not enough such personnel to staff every employee team. In many situations, it is difficult for nonmanagerial employees to request and receive technical or cost data from other departments. Yet, the need to increase the flow of information is urgent if EI is to be effective and successful.

The Effect of EI on Productivity and Satisfaction

Numerous studies have been conducted to measure the effects of participation on individual and organizational outcomes since the 1950s.[8] The results will be summarized in this section to provide an overview of the state of our knowledge about this area.

The results of more than fifty research studies demonstrate that it has not always been possible to show a direct, significant, and positive impact from EI on bottom-line measures of cost and productivity (see Table 11.2). While a majority of studies do show a positive impact, the effects frequently vary, and a number of studies have found no effect.

TABLE 11.2   Summary of Research Studies: The Effect of Employee Participation on Performance and Satisfaction

Form of Participation	Results on Performance			Results on Satisfaction		
	Positive Effect	Negative Effect	No Effect	Positive Effect	Negative Effect	No Effect
Participation in work decisions	11 studies (73%)	1 study	3 studies	4 studies (50%)	1 study	3 studies
Overall summary	Positive			Mixed		
Consultative participation	4 studies (80%)	—	1 study	3 studies (75%)	—	1 study
Overall summary	Positive			Positive		
Short-term participation	1 study (9%)	—	10 studies	2 studies	—	5 studies
Overall summary	—		No effect			No effect
Informal participation	5 studies (80%)	—	1 study	17 studies (85%)	—	3 studies
Overall summary	Positive			Positive		
Employee ownership	3 studies (100%)	—	—	4 studies (80%)	—	—
Overall summary	Positive			Positive		
Representative participation	1 study (25%)	1 study	2 studies	4 studies (50%)	2 studies	2 studies
Overall summary	—		No effect			No effect

NOTES: This table is derived from J.L. Cotton, D.A. Vollrath, K.L. Froggatt, M.I. Lengnick-Hall, and K.R. Jennings, "Employee Participation: Diverse Forms and Different Outcomes," *Academy of Management Review* 13(1), 1988, 8–22. Some simplification has been made to make the table more reader friendly. A complete list of the studies included in the table appears in the original publication.

The entries in the cells show the number of studies in that category with the percentage of all studies in that category shown in parentheses. The overall conclusion is considered positive if more than two-thirds of the studies indicate a positive finding.

The positive effects of participation are more clearly observed in the case of job satisfaction, where the evidence supports the finding of a small but positive impact. Similar results have been reported by two other reviews of studies on employee participation (Locke and Schweiger 1979; Miller and Monge 1986).

A number of case studies reported in the literature have also provided evidence of positive effects of employee participation. While these reports provide glowing testimonials for EI programs, it is harder to interpret this sort of evidence. For example, the vast majority of such reported cases involve success stories. Rarely does the case-study literature touch on cases that have failed. There are no reliable estimates of the failure rate among EI programs. However, anecdotal evidence places the attrition rate at as high as 40 per cent in the first two or three years of introduction (Rankin 1986). The high attrition rate in the 1980s may be indicative of the early stages of the learning curve for organizations. Many of the case studies are reported by those who are directly involved with the initiative, such as the managers or consultants responsible for its design and implementation. Thus, many of these studies suffer from a lack of objectivity or from the absence of rigorous scientific investigation.

There are also methodological problems in isolating the precise contribution of EI programs as distinct from effects of technology or markets or other changes that happened simultaneously with EI. As a rule, wherever positive EI impacts were reported, there were changes in technology, products, markets, processes, materials, or even manpower.

Critics of impact studies argue that precise measurement of EI programs is impossible for two reasons. First, the benefits of greater employee involvement will show up in individual as well as group activity, and few of these studies measure group outcomes such as the launch of a new product or the effective implementation of a new system. Further, some impacts of EI may be observable only when organizations go through sudden and unexpected change such as technological innovation (e.g., EI may make employees more amenable to technological change), downsizing (e.g., employees may identify more strongly with the strategic goals of the business), or the introduction of new markets or products (e.g., EI may aid in the development of a more flexible and agile organization). Most studies in the past have not measured such effects because of the problems inherent in such measurement.

Second, critics charge that measuring returns to EI in a narrow, short-term frame will hurt the very process the study is designed to measure. The EI process would be affected by the measurements because the participants would very likely experience some anxiety if they knew they were being monitored. Consequently, in many firms, managers have decided not to measure the outcomes of EI, at least in the short run.[9]

Third, in field studies, it is difficult to measure the separate and independent impact of EI because the program is often introduced along with other workplace changes and innovations.

In practice, the decision to introduce greater employee involvement is not always made contingent upon a demonstration based on hard data that the EI program will have a positive impact. Often, quantitative assessment of EI and its impact on performance is made only after the program has had some time to become absorbed, in whole or in part, into the organizational culture.

EI IN UNIONIZED ENVIRONMENTS

It is in the unionized context that EI poses the greatest challenges for all actors in the industrial relations system. Implementation of EI in a union environment is problematic because EI is an ideologically loaded intervention in the employment relationship. Employee involvement is a powerful tool that can alter the way employees relate to work, the workplace, and work relations. As discussed below, many unions fear that employee involvement is a potent socialization tool through which employers can co-opt employees into a managerial agenda and, thereby, weaken collective bargaining and the union. These fears have been fuelled in part by the growth of the nonunion sector in the US where employers have successfully resisted unionization in new nonunion plants by implementing, among other policies, greater employee involvement (Verma and Kochan 1985).

The vast majority of unionized workplaces have experienced difficulties in implementing EI, but not only for the reasons stated above. The introduction of EI requires a drastic change in the traditional labour–management relationship, which has conventionally been characterized by a separation of management and labour roles and the associated mutual distrust and adversarial bargaining.

Impediments to EI Adoption and Implementation

A number of impediments to the introduction of EI in unionized workplaces have been identified in the literature. They include difficulties associated with history, knowledge, and union involvement.

The History of Labour–Management Relations

Many of the companies that began to introduce EI in the 1980s discovered that their enthusiasm was not universally shared. Quite often unions were not nearly as excited at the prospect of introducing EI. Part of the reason lay in the history of adversarial relations that had taught each of the parties to exercise caution, if not plain mistrust, in dealing with the other side. Thus, the initial call for collaboration for mutual benefit has often been ignored because of long-standing resentments.

In cases where EI has had a more successful start, the introduction has been preceded generally by a series of activities whose intent and effect has been to build the relationship up from its adversarial past. In general, the following sequence may occur at a site where EI is being introduced:

1. Teams of employees, both from management and the union, visit other organizations where EI has proved to be successful.

2. The company invites EI experts to speak at its training sessions. Some of these sessions are attended by union and management representatives.

3. The company and the union agree to attend an off-site workshop designed especially to discuss mutual interests.

4. Union and management agree to expand the traditional bargaining agenda by removing obstacles like a large backlog of unresolved grievances.

5. Both sides agree to form a joint steering committee to oversee the design and implementation of the employee involvement program.

Where the parties do not invest in such prior relationship building, the results are generally unfavourable. In some cases, the union refuses to discuss the EI issue, forcing management either to implement it on their own or to drop the initiative altogether. In other cases, EI has a very slow start and proves ineffective despite several years of costly investments. Eventually the effort is either formally cancelled or it dies slowly through lack of interest.

The Knowledge Gap

Another impediment to effective introduction of EI lies in the imbalance of knowledge of and expertise in EI matters between labour and management. Management, in most cases, has had a head start; they began learning about the nuts and bolts of EI much earlier than their union counterparts. Management has worked closely with the behavioural scientists and other experts who developed EI concepts in the 1960s and the 1970s. Management has also had access to better resources for hiring experts and for training their own personnel in emerging organizational innovations.

Labour organizations, on the other hand, have lagged behind in educating their leaders and their membership about these concepts. This gap was more glaring in the early- and mid-1980s. Although the knowledge gap has narrowed a great deal in the 1990s, it remains an important hurdle that must be overcome if EI is to be diffused widely in the unionized sector. Lack of resources for educating labour leaders is one issue that can be addressed by pooling resources both from the company as well as from public sources. There are other issues that resources alone cannot address. Some of these are discussed in the next section.

Union Involvement

The key decisions for these firms are, first, to choose whether their union is to have any involvement, and second, to decide the extent or scope of that involvement.

Extent of Involvement. The extent of union involvement can be described in terms of the following five levels. Under *unilateral management decision making*, management makes all the decisions and there is no role for the union. Under *managerial information sharing*, management informs the union of its plans and actions, and the union may have the right to request information. This does not allow for any direct input into decision making, but it does provide additional resources (i.e., information) to the union to represent its interests through traditional channels.

Under *consultation*, management provides information and solicits union input with no promise of acting on the input. The power of decision making remains with management, who become better informed about the needs of the union as a result of the consultative process. Progressive managers would try to accommodate union needs as best as possible. Autocratic managers or militant union leaders could, however, defeat the process by making consultation irrelevant to decision making. Under *decision making by consensus*, both sides make decisions jointly but agree to rule only by consensus. Legal authority remains with management but formal authority is delegated to a joint forum. There is no dispute-resolution mechanism. In the event of a dispute that cannot be resolved, authority reverts to its traditional owner, the management.

Finally, under *joint governance*, decisions are made jointly by both sides with a dispute-resolution procedure in place in the event that the two sides cannot agree (Verma and Cutcher-Gershenfeld 1993).

Scope of Involvement. Unions can be involved in various stages of EI—these include idea, design, and implementation. In the vast majority of cases, the union is brought into the picture only at the implementation stage. This sets up a very dysfunctional dynamic between the parties right from the start. The union feels that by the time it is involved, most of the major features of the EI program have been set; consequently, it has little impact on the design. As such, the union is frequently put into the position either of agreeing to a package designed unilaterally by management experts or of rejecting the package completely.

Union Concerns about EI. Unions have articulated their concerns about EI in a variety of ways ranging from the ideological to the practical. Apart from some ideologically driven hardline opinions, most union concerns have to do with the potential impact of EI on the collective bargaining process. If union leaders perceive that EI will weaken collective bargaining and the union, they are generally opposed to it. They worry that EI may co-opt workers into a managerial agenda (i.e., improve quality and productivity) to such an extent that workers will begin to see the union as irrelevant to their welfare. Unions also worry that some employers will use EI meetings to promote antiunion sentiments among workers to the point that they will be ready to decertify their union.

Case evidence strongly suggests that EI does have the potential to thwart union interests (Verma and Kochan 1985). But there is no evidence to indicate that this potential is innate to EI or that it is inherent in EI's dynamic as an organizational process. Rather, the evidence suggests that, like any other instrument, EI can be used for a variety of purposes, both functional and dysfunctional. Examples of such effects are discussed later in this section.

A variety of motivations underlie union leaders' concerns about employee involvement programs. The most important of these is that EI programs socialize workers with pro-company and possibly antiunion views. Not all employers use EI as a forum to reinforce antiunionism, but almost all programs do conduct training and provide information on a firm's competitive position and on the need to improve productivity and upgrade technology. Some studies have found that EI has a positive effect on the extent to which workers identify with company goals (Lischeron and Wall 1975; Verma and McKersie 1987). This positive influence is termed a *program effect* (Verma 1989).

A second concern for unions is the possibility that EI programs attract workers with antiunion views. In other words, EI programs result in a sorting of workers by their affinity to the union—pro-union workers stay away while workers less active in the union tend to volunteer for participation in the program. This has been called the *selection effect* (Verma 1989).

Empirical studies suggest that a union's own involvement may determine whether the program and selection effects are positive or negative. Where unions support EI programs, the program effect is positive and the selection effect zero or absent (Verma 1989; Thacker and Fields 1987). On the other hand, when a union is not involved in EI, there is evidence of a negative selection effect, i.e., workers less active in the union are more likely to volunteer for EI (Verma and McKersie 1987). These results suggest that by withdrawing from EI efforts, unions may be creating a self-fulfilling prophecy, i.e, lack of union involvement may create the very effects unions fear most.

The extent to which union fears may be justified also depends on management's intent. EI can be used to undermine as well as reinforce and reform the labour–management relationship. One research study that monitored EI developments in companies like Boeing, Cummins Engine, General Motors, Xerox, Western Airlines, Alcoa, Budd, Boise Cascade, and Goodyear over a number of years, found that EI tended to reinforce collective bargaining in cases where its principles were used to address external shocks such as restructuring due to recessions and other crises (Cutcher-Gershenfeld, Kochan, and Verma 1991). On the other hand, in cases where EI principles were suspended or bypassed during these critical incidents, EI tended either to disappear or to undermine the collective bargaining process.

The Consequences of Noninvolvement of Unions. As indicated in the preceding discussion on the extent of union involvement in EI, management faces a series of choices when it comes to its relations with the union. The most important question is whether to involve the union at all. Before answering this question, management must consider very carefully the implications of implementing EI without any involvement on the part of the union.

It is not uncommon to find managers who believe that they can "go it alone" on the issue of implementing EI. This is natural given the EI expertise that management can usually marshal on its own. Moreover, many managers feel that EI is largely a bilateral matter between themselves and their employees and that the union as a third party has no role, expertise, or contribution to make. Research shows that noninvolvement of unions in the EI process can lead to a number of problems that managers must anticipate (Verma and McKersie 1987).

First, lack of union involvement may be viewed by some employees as an ambiguous signal. Most employees trust the union more than they do management to safeguard their interests. They may wonder why the union is not saying anything about EI, a program that appears to have such great impact on their jobs. This potentially disruptive effect, while discernible in some surveys, is clearly not a great threat, at least in the short term (Verma 1989). But the lack of union involvement can also be viewed as a missed opportunity for management to marshal union support in making EI more effective. Unions can carry some appeals more effectively to workers than can management. Thus, there is a positive potential that must not be forgotten in making these decisions.

Second, if the union chooses to oppose the EI program, it can very effectively compromise the program's impact on the workers. Unions have threatened and carried out anti-EI campaigns with some success. At BC Tel, the union opposed quality circles. To make its opposition effective, the union conducted an education campaign that turned workers against quality circles. Other unions, including the United Steelworkers and the Communications Workers of America, have stated that if they were not given active roles in implementing EI, they would carry out campaigns against EI programs.

An active opposition campaign by the union sends confusing signals to workers. They become unsure whom they should believe—union leaders or managers? Employee surveys at many companies, including Boeing and Xerox, have documented a schism that develops among workers when they hear these conflicting messages about EI (Verma and McKersie 1985; Cutcher-Gershenfeld 1988). Those who are active in the union tend to view EI in negative terms, while those who are less interested in (or opposed to) the union tend to view EI in positive terms. Clearly, these divisions do not bode well for a successful EI effort.

Should management decide to get the union involved, it would have to make choices about the extent and scope of union involvement. There is not a great deal of systematic research on the pros and cons of different choices that managers make in this regard. There is, however, much case and anecdotal evidence. Many of these studies suggest that the general rule of thumb is to get the union involved as early in the process as possible, perhaps at the idea stage. The evidence also points to an active rather than passive union role as the key to effectiveness.

Canadian Unions and Direct Participation

When Canadian firms began to introduce direct participation processes such as quality circles and work teams, a number of unions saw these forums as an employer ploy to gain the upper hand in industrial relations. Several unions warned of the dangers of direct participation forums and urged workers to oppose these managerial initiatives. Notable among the warnings were statements by the Canadian Auto Workers, the Canadian Paperworkers Union (1990), and the labour federations in Ontario and British Columbia. Many other unions, such the International Woodworkers of America and the Canadian Labour Congress, issued statements of caution and provided guidelines on the conditions under which a union could get involved in such efforts.

By the end of the 1980s, a number of other unions had developed their expertise in such matters and they had begun to join hands with a small number of companies in exploring and implementing worker participation in the context of workplace reorganization. Notable among these unions were the Communications Workers of Canada (later the Communications, Energy and Paperworkers), who adopted a policy at their annual convention in 1992, and the United Steelworkers of America, who held a major policy conference on restructuring in 1991. Both these statements endorsed the idea of proactive union involvement in introducing innovations such as direct worker participation through joint efforts with management.

It is possible that the lack of enthusiasm for EI programs on the part of some unions has slowed down the diffusion of EI in workplaces represented by these unions. However, it would be misleading to suggest that the examples of union opposition cited above have completely blocked the adoption of EI in those jurisdictions. In the decentralized Canadian industrial relations system, since the power to sign collective agreements rests with union locals rather than with union centrals, a number of workplaces have adopted EI programs despite formal union policy statements critical of them. For example, the CAMI auto assembly plant in Ontario, a joint venture between General Motors and Suzuki, has adopted a team-based production system in agreement with its local of the Canadian Auto Workers.

Joint Governance

At the opposite end of the spectrum from noninvolvement of unions is the process of joint governance. Under joint governance, union and management leaders bear *joint* responsibility for making decisions, i.e., both sides share decision-making power. Although joint governance is not very common yet in North America, there is a small but growing number of such arrangements (Verma and Cutcher-Gershenfeld 1993).

Since joint governance is the ultimate step in union involvement, it poses the greatest problems and subsumes many of the issues of lower levels of involvement. Traditionally and legally, the authority for decision making has always resided primarily with management. It seems remarkable that any manager would give up this authority willingly. It seems equally remarkable that elected union leaders would agree to join management in making day-to-day decisions. Yet, for some parties, the benefits of joint governance apparently outweigh the costs.

Joint governance is both a radical departure from the conventional decision-making process and also a gradual extension of the principle of EI. It challenges traditional labour and management roles, but it also builds on the long tradition of labour–management committees. It creates a forum for creative co-operation, but it also formalizes power in decision making so that each side can maintain its independence. In these and other ways, joint governance creates unique opportunities for innovative problem solving where other methods may fail.

What are its consequences for the parties? What factors persuade the parties to enter into joint governance? Once introduced, what impact does joint governance have on the organization? What makes joint governance effective as a decision-making process? While a full discussion of these issues is beyond the scope of this chapter, the following propositions, based on case evidence, are offered, based largely on Verma and Cutcher-Gershenfeld (1993). It is argued that some parties entering into joint governance are often pushed into it by events, while others enter believing that joint governance is integral to an effective labour–management relationship. The internal dynamic of joint governance is driven by the simultaneous opportunity for both co-operation and conflict. The parties have equal freedom and power to raise disputes or to develop solutions. Once implemented, joint governance requires that both direct and indirect participation be used in the workplace; that substantive rules be replaced by procedural ones; and that management and the union exchange skills, i.e., that management learn some political skills while the union must learn some business skills.

Propositions on the Antecedents of Joint Governance

1. Some degree of "crisis" cajoles the parties into joint governance. But joint governance is unlikely, as a volunteer effort, if the degree of "crisis" is too low or too high.

2. Some degree of relationship building (informal or formal) through advisory joint programs is a necessary, but not sufficient, condition for joint governance.

Propositions on the Internal Dynamics of Joint Governance

3. Under joint governance, the surfacing and resolution of conflict is a necessary condition for effective (and far-reaching) co-operation. In the absence of effective conflict resolution, co-operation will be undercut.

4. Under joint governance, the identification and pursuit of common interests is a necessary condition for effective (and comprehensive) dispute resolution. In the absence of meaningful co-operation, conflicts will escalate out of control.

Propositions on the Consequences of Joint Governance

5. Without direct participation, representative forms of participation will have limited impact on workplace outcomes; without representative forms of participation, direct forms of participation will create new tensions in the employment relationship.

6. Joint governance will promote procedural rule making as parties get used to joint decision making. This will gradually reduce the emphasis and reliance on substantive rules.

7. Joint governance will steer the union—a political institution—to build administrative competence at the shop floor and at higher levels; similarly, it will steer the management—a hierarchical institution—to build political competence at the shop floor and at higher levels.

Despite many potential advantages, joint governance remains limited in its diffusion in Canadian, US, and other industrial relations systems. As with any change process, the evolution of joint governance faces many hurdles—institutional, political, and attitudinal. The small number of joint governance arrangements that have evolved over the last dozen years or so provides a useful window on their feasibility and utility. From these early experiments we need to learn more about conditions that facilitate these arrangements and their consequences for the parties.

THE SUSTAINABILITY OF EMPLOYEE INVOLVEMENT PROGRAMS

The practice of employee involvement has seen many innovations and, some would say, fads over the past fifteen years. In the 1970s, the quality-of-worklife (QWL) movement was very strong, and under its banner a number of significant EI programs were launched. In the 1980s, quality circles (QCs) became very popular. The 1990s have seen a major growth in total-quality-management (TQM) programs. Employee involvement is the underlying idea behind all these programs. The shifting sands of management fads and fashions raise a fundamental question about employee involvement: what factors sustain such innovations over time?

Although there are very few empirical studies of the sustainability issue based on large random samples, the case-study literature suggests a number of generalizations that can provide useful guidelines for future research and practice. First, as discussed earlier in the section on the organizational consequences of employee involvement, sustainability is facilitated by access to information and communication within the organization and by corresponding changes in training and work organization. Second, a number of theorists have argued that, in unionized organizations, the support and co-operation of the union would enhance the effectiveness and sustainability of the EI process (Kochan, Katz, and Mower 1984).

Further, as discussed earlier in the section on emergent types of EI, there is a link between sustainability and the type of EI: the narrow, self-contained type modelled on Japanese-style quality circles, or the integrated form evident in the autonomous work groups. The first type appears easier to introduce because its implementation requires relatively minor changes in the organization. However, it is harder to sustain (at least in the North American setting), given its narrow scope. The second type is harder to implement given all the changes that need to be made, but easier to sustain because of its wide scope (Lawler and Mohrman 1985). There is some empirical support for these propositions in the case-study literature (Cutcher-Gershenfeld, Kochan, and Verma 1991).

A key area for the long-term success of employee involvement in any organization, but especially a unionized one, is the issue of employment security under EI and its consequences for collective bargaining and labour–management relations in general. Since concerns over job security are fundamental to employee interests, it is only natural for employees to wonder about the effect of EI programs that seek to improve the productivity and quality of their own jobs. Few people would be willing parties to eliminating their own jobs. Hence, EI programs must create an implicit, if not explicit, guarantee that participants in the program will not become victims of their own success. In some organizations, such as Xerox and Saturn, explicit employment guarantees have been made within the context of employee involvement. In others, implicit guarantees often accompany successful implementation.

In several documented cases, the loss of employment through major layoffs has often derailed EI programs. In firms such as Budd, Cummins Engine, and more recently, US West, large-scale layoffs have led to a deterioration of labour–management co-operation, to a cancellation of the program, or to both. This is not to say that EI programs cannot be sustained in firms that are going through external shocks like downsizing, restructuring, or market upheavals. In a small number of cases, when the EI process was used to inform people about important business decisions, even when the decisions had negative outcomes for employees, the trauma positively reinforced the EI process. At Xerox when key business decisions such as subcontracting and location of a new plant were made through the EI process, that process was reinforced. On the other hand, when key decisions bypass the EI process, the effect is to undermine employee involvement.

THE ROLE OF PUBLIC POLICY

One view of the role of public policy in the area of workplace change such as employee involvement is that the government should be noninterventional, i.e., the parties should be left to handle it on their own. In that case, the cost to the parties of failing to address the needs of the market through the introduction of EI may be high. Some firms would go out of business or be taken over by a management that would impose harsh measures to adjust to market needs. Many would argue that this is the way the market does and should work, i.e., firms and unions unable or unwilling to adjust to market changes pay the price by going out of business. In this view, public policy has no significant role to play in the process of adjustment. It must allow labour and management either to respond to changes or to let market forces take their toll on inefficient enterprises.

Alternately, the government may take a more interventionist approach to restructuring in industrial relations. In this approach, certain inflexibilities are seen as inherent in the system of collective bargaining. It follows then that collective bargaining left to the parties may not produce consistent results in adopting innovations such as EI. The government may intervene in a variety of ways to "help" the parties arrive at agreements that introduce innovations such as EI for the sake of preserving jobs and improving productivity (Verma and Weiler 1994).

As discussed earlier, innovations such as EI appear to suffer from a "legitimacy gap," i.e., there is no consensus between labour and management on what innovations such as teams, contingent pay, or greater worker involvement can do for the restructured workplace (Verma 1990). Hence, there is a need to create a common knowledge base that will lend credibility to certain innovations. Perhaps these innovations need to be redesigned by joint labour–management teams before they will become useful. Until a common approach to innovations is developed, it is likely that Canadian workplaces will adopt much-needed innovations only at a very slow pace.

A second element of public policy response comes from the recognition that collective bargaining takes place in an institutional, political, and historical context that often makes it difficult to negotiate any large-scale changes in the workplace. In other words, left to itself, collective bargaining is unlikely to embrace substantial changes. In practice, crises of various sorts, financial or conflictual, provide the most common incentive for large-scale change. Public policy, therefore, must either rely on crises to facilitate change or else facilitate change in other ways.

Public Policy Responses in Canada

A variety of public policy responses have been aimed at workplace change and innovations in the 1980s and 1990s: institutional support for innovations; the amendment of labour codes to facilitate the adoption of innovations; and government intervention to "catalyze" agreements among the parties.

Notable among institutions created to support workplace innovations is the Canadian Labour Market and Productivity Centre (CLMPC). It was established in 1984 to facilitate a mutual-interest agenda at the national level. This is a federally funded research centre run by a joint board of labour and management representatives. Training is another area for joint initiatives at federal and provincial levels. At the national level, the federal government has created the Canadian Labour Force Development Board (CLFDB), a labour–management board that advises the government on training policy. In 1992 the Ontario government announced the formation of the Ontario Training and Adjustment Board (OTAB), which is to formulate policy and administer training funds. The government has gradually moved all training-related programs from various ministries to OTAB.

In addition, sector-specific labour–management councils to address training needs have been created by the federal government. The Canadian Steel Trade and Employment Council (CSTEC) in the steel industry and the Sectoral Skills Council for the electrical and electronics industry are two good examples.

In the early 1990s, the Ontario government also investigated, but has not implemented, an experimental program that would use neutral third parties to facilitate the change process at the enterprise level. This could take place either within the context of a bargaining round or outside it. The assumption is that the parties may need the assistance of neutrals who are skilled at consensus building and also have a good knowledge of innovations such as EI.

Government as "Catalyst" in the Change Process

Another element of policy response to the change process is one in which the government acts as a direct catalyst instead of as a co-ordinator as in the services described above. Because government resources are considerable, there are several ways in which the process of providing an impetus for innovation can be implemented: legislation can be used to encourage certain behaviours; meetings of the two sides can be convened with specific agendas for innovation; and the government can act as a model employer by leading the way in demonstrating the efficacy of certain kinds of innovations such as EI.

Governments in both Ontario and British Columbia amended their labour relations acts in the early 1990s to strengthen collective bargaining and to encourage workplace reform. There are two approaches that can be used to encourage the parties to consult with each other and to make decisions jointly in the workplace. Section 53 of the BC labour relations act and section 44.1 of the Ontario act provide for a joint consultation process that can be invoked by either party. Provision for a joint consultation committee must be included in every collective agreement, failing which the law can be invoked to provide such a committee. Joint consultation can begin with commencement of bargaining but must also be available during the term of the agreement. The objective of consultation is to "promote the co-operative resolution of workplace issues, to respond and adapt to changes in the economy, to foster the development of work-related skills and to promote workplace productivity." Lastly, the parties can jointly request the mediation services of the government to appoint a facilitator to assist in developing a more co-operative relationship.

An alternate approach, contained in section 54 in British Columbia and in section 41.1 in Ontario, is to facilitate joint decision making in the area of workplace change. An earlier version of the BC labour code provided for joint decision making in the event of technological change (sections 74 and 76). The new section 54 in British Columbia broadens the scope from technological change to any kind of workplace change ("a measure, policy, practice or change that affects the terms, conditions or security of employment of a significant number of employees"). It requires that an adjustment plan for the change must be arrived at jointly. It thus provides for a process that is similar to that found in Germany under the works council statutes. This is a considerable departure from the early Wagner Act model, which results in narrow definitions of what is "bargainable" in the United States (Verma and Meltz 1994).

Another policy approach is for the government to facilitate discussions aimed at introducing change. In a typical case, a minister of the government may convene a meeting of the leading unions and employers in an industry or may engage in trilateral negotiations with a company and its union (Verma and Meltz 1994). This approach has produced a number of agreements in Quebec in the last few years that have introduced varying degrees of EI to the workplace (Bourque and Vallée 1994).

Lastly, the government can initiate change by acting as a model employer. This can be seen in two recent innovations in the health sectors in Ontario and British Columbia. In Ontario, a Liberal government mandated positions for nurses on hospital Fiscal Advisory Committees in 1990 by an order-in-council. In the BC Health Care sector, a "social contract" was negotiated on an industry-wide, province-wide basis by the government, management, and three unions in 1993. It allows for broad input by workers and unions in policy formulation and implementation. It is, as yet, too early to assess the full impact of these innovations.

LOOKING BEYOND: THE FUTURE FOR EI

Direct forms of employee participation have established a presence in the Canadian workplace since the late 1970s. Although the idea of greater say for workers has been accepted in principle, its implementation continues to be fraught with ambiguity and uncertainty. Battles, both ideological and tactical, continue to be fought about the scope, the extent, and the form that participation is to take within the organization.

Despite the intuitive appeal of the idea of employee involvement, its diffusion and effective implementation is far from assured. EI requires each party to the employment relationship to alter its traditional stance towards the other party. As noted earlier, joint governance may provide one way to accommodate the conflict between managers wanting to have some control over operations and employees wanting to have some say in decisions that affect them. Even as managers and union leaders grapple with ways to implement EI effectively, there is no doubt that workers' expectations will continue to move in step with changing norms within free and democratic societies. Competitive pressures from the marketplace for better quality and greater product innovation are also unlikely to ease in the future. The net result will be to force both managers and union leaders to devise better ways of implementing greater employee involvement as an integral part of work and workplace relations.

QUESTIONS

1. What advantages and disadvantages do EI systems offer over purely Tayloristic forms of work organization?
2. Debate the proposition that EI should be implemented *only* if it improves productivity and efficiency.
3. What are the limits of EI in decision making? In other words, identify situations where direct EI should be limited by design.
4. Identify key organizational and external factors that will make an organization more likely to adopt greater EI.
5. Identify individual, group, organizational, and external factors that cause many EI programs to fail.
6. Is EI more or less likely to be adopted in a unionized organization? Why?
7. Do EI programs have the potential to destabilize labour–management relations? Give reasons. How can managers make EI a positive intervention in labour–management relations?
8. Debate the proposition that EI is a decentralized, workplace issue in which public policy (i.e., the government) has no role to play.
9. Discuss the role of various management levels and functions in the successful implementation of EI: top management, middle management, first-line managers, HR/IR managers, line managers.
10. Given increasing globalization of product markets, what is the prognosis for diffusion of EI over the next ten years? Discuss.

REFERENCES

BETCHERMAN, G., and K. McMULLEN. 1986. *Working With Technology: A Survey of Automation in Canada*. Ottawa: Ministry of Supply and Services.

BETCHERMAN, G., K. McMULLEN, N. LECKIE, and C. CARON. 1994. *The Canadian Workplace in Transition*. Kingston, ON: IRC Press.

BOURQUE, R., and G. VALLÉE 1994. "Contrats sociaux: ententes de partenariat ou ententes de longue durée? Inventaire et analyse juridique." *Info ressources humaines*. Québec: Association des professionels du Québec.

CANADIAN AUTO WORKERS (CAW). No date. *CAW Statement on the Reorganization of Work.*

CANADIAN LABOUR CONGRESS (CLC). No date. *A Trade Union QWL Agenda.*

CANADIAN PAPERWORKERS UNION (CPU). 1990. "The Team Concept and the Restructuring of the Workplace." *CPU Journal* 10(2).

COMMUNICATIONS WORKERS OF CANADA (CWC). 1992. *Prosperity and Progress: CWC's Vision for Shaping the Future*, 9th Annual Convention, June 15–19 1992.

COTTON, J. L. 1993. *Employee Involvement.* Newbury Park, CA: Sage.

COTTON, J.L., D.A. VOLLRATH, K.L. FROGGATT, M.L. LENGNICK-HALL, and K. R. JENNINGS. 1988. "Employee Participation: Diverse Forms and Different Outcomes." *Academy of Management Review* 13(1): 8–22.

CUTCHER-GERSHENFELD, J. 1988. *Tracing a Transformation in Industrial Relations: The Case of Xerox Corporation and the Amalgamated Clothing and Textile Workers Union.* Washington, DC: Bureau of Labor-Management Relations and Cooperative Programs, U.S. Department of Labor (BLMR 123).

CUTCHER-GERSHENFELD, J., T. A. KOCHAN, and A. VERMA. 1991. "Recent Developments in US Employee Involvement Initiatives: Erosion or Transformation", in D. Sockell, D. Lewin and D. Lipsky, eds, *Advances in Industrial and Labor Relations*, vol. 5, JAI Press: 1–31.

DACHLER, P. H., and B. WILPERT. 1978. "Conceptual Dimensions and Boundaries of Participation in Organizations: A Critical Evaluation." *Administrative Science Quarterly* 23(1): 1–39.

GERWIN, D., and H. KOLODNY. 1992. *Management of Advanced Manufacturing Technology.* New York: John Wiley & Sons.

ILO (International Labour Organization). 1993. *Yearbook of Labour Statistics.* Geneva: ILO.

KLEIN, J.A. 1988. *The Changing Role of First-Line Supervisors and Middle Managers.* Washington, DC: Bureau of Labor-Management Relations and Cooperative Programs, U.S. Department of Labor (BLMR 126).

KLEIN, J.A., and P.A. POSEY. 1986. "A Good Supervisor Is a Good Supervisor Anywhere". *Harvard Business Review*, November-December.

KOCHAN, T.A., H.C. KATZ, and N. MOWER. 1984. *Worker-Participation and American Unions: Threat or Opportunity?* Kalamazoo, MI: Upjohn.

LAWLER, E.E., and S.A. MOHRMAN. 1985. "Quality Circles after the Fad." *Harvard Business Review* 63(1): 64–71.

LAWLER, E.E., S.A. MOHRMAN, and G.E. LEDFORD. 1992. *Employee Involvement and Total Quality Management.* San Francisco: Jossey Bass.

LEE, C., and R.S. SCHULER. 1982. "A Constructive Replication and Extension of a Role and Expectancy Perception Model of Participation in Decision-Making". *Journal of Occupational Psychology* 55: 109–118.

LISCHERON, J.A., and T.D. WALL. 1975. "Employee Participation — An Experimental Field Study." *Human Relations* 28: 863–84.

LOCKE, E.A., and D.M. SCHWEIGER. 1979. "Participation in Decision-Making: One More Look." In B.M. Staw, ed, *Research in Organizational Behavior*, vol. 1. Greenwich, CT: JAI Press.

LONG, R.J. 1989. "Patterns of Workplace Innovations in Canada". *Relations industrielles/Industrial Relations*, 44(4): 805–825.

MILLER, K.I., and P.R. MONGE. 1986. "Participation, Satisfaction, and Productivity: A Meta-Analytic Review." *Academy of Management Journal* 29(4): 727–753.

OSTERMAN, P. 1994. "How Common Is Workplace Transformation and Who Adopts It?" *Industrial and Labor Relations Review* 47(2): 173–188.

PORTER, M.E. 1980. *Competitive Strategy.* New York: Macmillan.

———. 1990. *The Competitive Advantage of Nations.* New York: Macmillan.

RANKIN, T. 1986. "Integrating QWL and Collective Bargaining." *Worklife Review* 5(3).

SASHKIN, M. 1976. "Changing Towards Participative Management Approaches: A Model and Methods." *Academy of Management Review* 1(3): 75–86.

SCHULER, R.S. 1980. "A Role and Expectancy Perception Model of Participation in Decision-Making." *Academy of Management Journal* 23: 331–340.

TARAS, D. and A. PONAK. In press. "Petro-Canada: A Model of the Union Cooperation Strategy within the Canadian Petroleum Industry." In A. Verma and R.P. Chaykowski, eds, *From Contract to Commitment: Employment Relations at the Firm-Level in Canada.* Kingston, ON: IRC Press.

THACKER, J.W. and M.W. FIELDS. 1987. "Union Involvement in Quality-of-Worklife Efforts: A Longitudinal Investigation." *Personnel Psychology* 40: 97–111.

UNITED STEELWORKERS OF AMERICA (Canada). 1991. *Empowering Workers in the Global Economy, A Labour Agenda for the 1990s.* Papers prepared for a conference in Toronto, October 22–23,

VERMA, A. 1989. "Joint Participation Programs: Self-Help or Suicide for Labor?" *Industrial Relations* 28(3): 401–410.

———. 1990. *The Prospects for Innovation in Canadian Industrial Relations in the 1990s.* Ottawa: Canadian Federation of Labour and World Trade Centres in Canada Joint Committee on Labour Market Adjustment.

VERMA, A., and J. CUTCHER-GERSHENFELD. 1993. "Joint Governance in the Workplace: Beyond Union–Management Cooperation and Worker Participation". In B.E. Kaufman and M.M. Kleiner, eds, *Employee Representation: Alternatives and Future Directions.* Madison, WI: Industrial Relations Research Association: 197–234.

VERMA, A., and D. IRVINE. 1992. *Investing in People: The Key to Canada's Growth and Prosperity.* Toronto: Information Technology Association of Canada.

VERMA, A., and T.A. KOCHAN. 1985. "The Growth and Nature of the Nonunion Sector Within a Firm." In T.A. Kochan, ed, *Challenges and Choices Facing American Labor.* Cambridge, Ma: M.I.T. Press: 89–118.

VERMA, A., and R.B. McKERSIE. 1987. "Employee Involvement Programs: The Implications of Non-involvement by Unions." *Industrial and Labor Relations Review* 40(4): 556–568.

VERMA, A., and N.M. MELTZ. 1994. "Canadian Developments in Industrial Relations and Implications for the U.S." Paper presented to *Conference on Labor Relations Institutions and Economic Performance, Work and Technology Institute*, March 14-15, Washington, D.C.

VERMA, A., and J.P. WEILER. 1994. *Understanding Change in Canadian Industrial Relations: Firm-level Choices and Responses.* Kingston, ON: IRC Press.

WAGNER, J.A. 1994. "Participation's Effects on Performance and Satisfaction: A Reconsideration of Research Evidence." *Academy of Management Review* 19(2): 312–330.

E N D   N O T E S

1   Throughout this chapter the terms employee involvement, worker participation, and employee participation will be used interchangeably.

2   While any firm could benefit from lower wages, the greatest advantage would accrue to those firms that were labour intensive or to those that faced competition from low-wage countries or both.

3   Making deep cuts in wages is a difficult objective given the pluralist and democratic nature of Canadian society. Sometimes when deep wage cuts can be achieved it is only at the substantial social cost of work stoppages, violence, and suspension (even if temporary) of the democratic rights of workers. Also, a low-wage strategy can reduce the purchasing power necessary to sustain demand for goods and services.

4   In 1992, manufacturing wages in Mexico were only 12.9 per cent of Canadian wages, in China 1.6 per cent, and in South Korea 48 per cent (ILO 1993).

5   Despite its wide appeal to many Canadian industries, the differentiation strategy may be limited in its applicability to some low-value-added industries. This may be true in industries with, among other factors, simple and mature technology and labour costs that account for a high percentage of the total cost. In such cases, the only course may be to reduce wages, a strategy that may not be feasible. Canada may simply not be able to retain those industries.

6   Sharing can be operationalized in practice in a variety of ways. Sharing profits or gains with workers according to a preset formula is one way of conveying to workers that they will get an equitable return on their efforts. Employee ownership is yet another method that has gained some currency in recent years.

7   Establishment surveys of training, in general, do not ask about the extent of coverage, i.e., two establishments, one with 100 per cent of its employees covered and another with only 10 per cent of its employees under training, would be counted similarly. Thus, caution in interpreting such data is advised.

8   Reviews of many of these studies can be found in Locke and Schweiger (1979); Miller and Monge (1986); Cotton, Vollrath, Froggatt, Lengnick-Hall, and Jennings (1988); Cotton (1993); and Wagner (1994).

9   Measurement of outcomes such as costs and productivity should not be confused with general assessment and evaluation of the EI program. In fact, many of the firms that do not collect data on costs and output relating to EI do conduct employee surveys and focus groups to get subjective feedback from the employees on the EI program.

PART IV

THE OUTCOMES OF THE INDUSTRIAL RELATIONS SYSTEM

The various conversion processes (collective bargaining, for example) discussed in the previous section produce a number of outcomes. The major ones are recorded in the labour-management contract (the collective agreement) as well as in other documents such as letters of understanding. Such agreements, in turn, have consequences for productivity, employee morale, workforce size, and a host of other organizational characteristics.

Chapter 12 focuses on the impact of unions. The extensive literature on compensation is reviewed, with particular emphasis on why unionized workers usually earn more money than their nonunion counterparts. The discussion then focuses on some of the less easily quantified aspects of union impact—the effect of unions on productivity and on management practices. It is clear that unions have a substantial impact on management practices, since the collective agreement introduces a host of rules to which management must adhere. Whether such rules result in more efficiency or less efficiency is not as clear. Studies on this subject have come to contrary conclusions, some showing that unionization increases productivity, others finding no change or a negative impact. One likely source for this variation, discussed in the chapter, lies in management's strategic response to the union.

On a day-to-day basis, union impact is exercised through the collective agreement, a document that specifies the terms and conditions of employment for the workforce. It is signed by both the union and the employer and is binding for a fixed duration. Just before its expiry, it is renegotiated for another fixed period of time. The contents of the collective agreement, its importance in the day-to-day working lives of employees, and the practical implications for managers are described in Chapter 13.

Sometimes the conversion processes do not lead directly to an agreement, and overt conflict between the union and employer occurs. Most often such conflict takes the form of a work stoppage. Strikes and lockouts constitute another outcome of our industrial relations system, and, as readers will discover, Canada has one of the highest rates of time lost from such stoppages among all industrialized countries. Chapter 14 details Canada's strike experience, beginning with a discussion of the various ways that work stoppages can be recorded and measured. Further perspective is provided by a breakdown of strikes and lockouts by time period, geographic region, industry, and type of dispute. Although strike rates in Canada are high by international standards, there is considerable variation within the country across provinces and especially industries. Further, approximately nine out of ten negotiations are settled without a stoppage. The discussion focuses on reasons for such variation, reviewing economic and noneconomic factors associated with strike activity, as well as the consequences of strikes. This section has obvious policy implications, because knowing why strikes occur is a necessary first step towards reducing their incidence and duration. Although some strikes are unavoidable (and perhaps even desirable), the discussion provides insights into how some might be prevented.

On completion of this section, the reader should understand the consequences of unionism and collective bargaining for employees, employers, and the public. He or she should now have a fairly clear appreciation of the actors, the forces that influence them, and the nature and results of their interactions. The way in which the various parts of the industrial relations system fit together should also be increasingly apparent.

UNION IMPACT ON COMPENSATION, PRODUCTIVITY, AND MANAGEMENT OF THE ORGANIZATION

MORLEY GUNDERSON AND
DOUGLAS HYATT

THE IMPACT OF UNIONS ON COMPENSATION PROVIDES AN EXCELLENT example of an area in which our understanding can be furthered by a judicious blend of industrial relations with knowledge from another discipline—in this case, economics. This theme is portrayed throughout the chapter as it moves from a discussion of union goals and power to the methods used by unions for attaining their objectives to the actual impact of unions on wages, wage structures, fringe benefits, productivity, and the management of the organization itself.

Few topics in labour market analysis have received as much attention as the impact that unions have on the way in which companies operate. Particular attention has been focused on the way unions affect wages and benefits, on the impact unions have on how an organization is managed, and on the consequences unions have for productivity. From studies on the subject, a consensus has emerged on some questions, limited agreement on many, and fundamental disagreement on others. The purpose of this chapter is to outline the extent of our knowledge of the impact of unions, highlighting the points of agreement and disagreement. Special emphasis is given to placing the issue of union impact on compensation (which has traditionally been the major focus of analysis by economists and econometricians) within a broader industrial relations perspective. This approach is particularly important if we want to gain a better understanding of the many factors (such as the bargaining structure) that influence the way unions affect wages and other important outcomes of the industrial relations system.

No attempt is made to review the literature exhaustively. For example, Lewis (1986a) contains a review of approximately 200 studies of the union impact on wages alone, and Gunderson and Riddell (1993) review 11 Canadian studies of the wage impact. Rather, the chapter focuses on existing reviews of various aspects of the literature, including methodology, Canadian studies, and those union impact studies that have special interest to students of industrial relations.

The goals of unions are discussed first, followed by an analysis of the determinants of union power and the methods whereby unions achieve their goals. Problems in measuring union impact are explained. Finally the empirical evidence regarding union impact on wages and wage structures, fringe benefits, working conditions, productivity, and the management of the organization itself are discussed.

UNION GOALS

Although the focus of most of the economic analysis of unions is on their impact on compensation, it is important to put the union impact into a broader perspective. Workers join unions as much to ensure a modicum of job security and due process at the workplace as for the economic objective of higher compensation. Hence, the grievance procedure and contract provisions on such matters as seniority and dismissal are often as important as, if not more important than, compensation objectives. In addition, as a first step in attaining its central objectives, a union must succeed in being recognized as the sole bargaining agent for the workers it represents.

Even when the focus is only on the compensation goal, unions may not have a clear single objective. To say that unions seek only to maximize the wages of their members does not take into consideration the adverse employment effect that can result from such a policy. Unions are concerned about the employment prospects of both union and nonunion workers. A goal of maximizing the wage bill (wages times employment) of union members recognizes both the wage and employment objectives of unions, as well as the possible trade-off between the two. However, this objective could also imply that unions would be willing to lower their wage below the nonunion wage simply to increase employment and thus the wage bill of union members. On the other hand, a goal of maximizing the wage bill could suggest that equal weight is given to the wage and employment component of the wage bill objective.

It appears more reasonable to assume that although unions care about both the wages and employability of their members, these objectives are in fact given different weights. The balancing of these objectives is likely to depend upon the voting power of the union members affected. For example, current union members may support higher wage gains at the expense of the recruitment of fewer new employees. Such potential new recruits have no vote on current union policies and therefore no way to affect the wage/employment trade-off. Thus, unions may favour wage gains to the point at which such gains affect the employability of existing union members. Moreover, to the extent that union policies reflect the preferences of the median union voter (i.e., longer-term employees), new employees may have little say in union decisions. In such circumstances, a reduction in the workforce will result in the layoff of newer workers rather than in a reduction in hours or wages of average union members. It may also result in "two-tier" wage contracts, whereby the wages of incumbent workers—the "insiders" or voting members—are protected, but the wages of new recruits are at a lower level.

If the possibility of mass layoffs, or of a plant closing, becomes a viable threat, then even the job security of the median union voter may be threatened. In this situation, the union may agree to wage cuts or other forms of concession bargaining to preserve jobs. Unions may also accept hours reductions, early retirement, or other forms of worksharing to avoid layoffs.

The relative weights that unions attach to the various components of their overall goals also depend upon other factors. For example, unions may be reluctant to take wage cuts even if doing so would preserve employment opportunities. This may reflect the fact that the job losses are likely to be concentrated among probationary workers, casual employees, outside contractors, or less senior union members who represent a minority of votes. It may also reflect the fact that there is no guarantee that concession bargaining on the part of unions will lead to job security anyway (unless that is specifically part of the bargain). As well, the cost of layoffs may be mitigated by unemployment insurance, while wage concessions or hours reductions are not supported by such insurance. Unions also may be reluctant to give wage concessions simply because the firm says it cannot pay; union willingness to do so would give the firm an incentive to bluff about its ability to pay. Faced with a firm arguing an inability to pay, a union may compel it to lay off workers because layoffs are also costly to the firm (e.g., through the possible loss of trained employees) as well as to workers, whereas wage concessions are costly only to workers. This logic may explain, in part, the paradox that adverse demand shocks usually lead to layoffs rather than small wage concessions, even when workers are risk-averse.

The objectives of unions are further complicated by the various internal union tradeoffs among union members and between union leaders and the rank-and-file. Different groups within the union often have different preferences—and different degrees of political power to effect them. Older workers may prefer generous pensions while younger workers may prefer higher wages; women may prefer job flexibility while men prefer a fixed schedule; married workers may prefer dental and medical plans while single workers prefer longer vacations. To the extent that unions reflect the wishes of the median union voter, society may properly be concerned that the preferences of younger workers or minorities are not reflected adequately.

Differences between union leaders and the rank-and-file membership can also affect union goals. At times, union leaders are accused of being too much like management; at other times, they are accused of being too radical and politically active. The political survival of elected union officials depends on their ability to reflect the wishes of their members. Consequently, they will always try to gauge the intensity of the preferences (and the political power) of their constituent groups. Strikes may be a means to this end. Strikes may also be used by union leaders to scale down the expectations of some members who might otherwise accuse the leadership of selling out too early.

UNION POWER

Internal Power

The power of a union to fulfil its goals depends, in part, on a consensus within the union with respect to those goals. This agreement must come from the various groups within the union, from the leadership and the rank-and-file members, and from other unions and affiliated bodies. Jurisdictional disputes, rank-and-file discontent with union leadership, and rivalry within the membership can all dissipate the energies of the union and prevent it from marshalling its power.

External Power and Elasticity of Demand for Labour

A union's power to realize its wage demands depends not only on its internal strength but also on the particular objective circumstances it faces. Many of these factors can be summarized under the rubric of the elasticity of demand for union labour. In general, according to the Hicks-Marshall laws of derived demand, the demand for union labour is inelastic and hence wage increases are not dampened by a large adverse employment effect if: (1) there are few good substitute products for those produced by union labour; (2) it is technologically or institutionally difficult to substitute other inputs in the production process (i.e., capital, energy, materials or other, perhaps non-union, types of labour) for union labour; (3) the supply of substitute inputs is inelastic; and (4) the cost of union labour is a small proportion of the total cost of production.

Substitute Products.   If there are few good substitutes for the products or services produced by unionized labour, union wage cost increases may be passed on to the consumer in the form of price increases without a substantial reduction in the demand for those products and, therefore, without a fall in the derived demand for union labour. This case may occur, for example, if a tariff or import quota protects the product from foreign competition, if the product is advertised through the union label, or if the whole industry is organized so as to prevent the substitution of nonunion-made products for union-made products.

In declining industries, for example, there may be very little threat of new entry from non-union firms. In such circumstances, unions may engage in an "end-game" strategy whereby they demand high wage increases in spite of the declining demand because they know that the lower paying non-union firms are not likely to enter the industry, given that it is in decline (Lawrence and Lawrence 1985). In such circumstances, unions may be able to garner a larger *share* of profits, even though overall profits are declining.

There are two important implications stemming from the link between the elasticity of the product demand curve and the elasticity of the labour demand curve. First, the demand for union labour will be more inelastic in the short term than over the longer term. In the longer term, products or services that are better substitutes for those produced by union labour may become available due to the introduction of new products or to increased foreign competition as a result of reductions in tariffs and the elimination of import quotas under a free trade agreement. As a result, the demand for the product becomes more elastic over time and, since the demand for labour is derived from the demand for the product being produced, the demand for union labour will also become more elastic over time. Thus, it may become more and more difficult for union wage increases to be passed on through higher prices without a noticeably adverse effect on employment.

The second important implication is that for any particular industry, a single firm's demand for labour will be more elastic than the demand for labour by the industry as a whole. This is because each firm's output will generally be a reasonably good substitute for the output of other firms in the industry. Thus, if a single firm in the industry raised the price of its product as a result of an increase in union wages, the demand for the single firm's output would fall dramatically, and hence employment at that firm would also fall. However, if all firms in the industry increased their prices, then it would become more difficult for consumers to find close substitutes. It is for this reason that unions prefer to organize as many firms within an industry as possible in order to prevent the substitution of nonunion-made products for union-made products.

Difficulty in Using Substitute Inputs. If there are few good substitute inputs for union labour, or if it is technologically or institutionally difficult to substitute other factors of production for union labour, then unions can obtain wage increases with less worry about substitutes being used for unionized labour. Hence, unions are very concerned about technological change and alternative processes that represent a substitution of capital for union labour. This is evidenced by their concern over computerized technology and their desire to have collective agreements re-opened if major technological change occurs. Restrictive work practices ("featherbedding" rules) are also designed, in part, to prevent the substitution of other inputs for union labour. Professional associations also try to control the substitution of less highly trained workers for professionals.

Another possible substitute for union labour is nonunion labour. Firms may try to use such labour by contracting out or by assigning work to probationary workers or supervisory personnel who are not in the bargaining unit. Obviously, unions try to control the use of such nonunion labour, in part through union security provisions whereby unions do the hiring (hiring halls) or whereby all persons in the bargaining unit are required to join the union as a condition of employment (union shop) or to pay union dues (agency shop or use of the Rand formula).

In the public sector, where the right to strike is granted, certain "essential service" employees can be "designated" as not having the right to strike, and this can severely weaken the power of the union. For this reason, unions will generally try to minimize the number of such designated employees.

To the extent that a reserve of low-wage labour in the economy is also a threat to union labour, unions may support full-employment policies, income maintenance programs, and restrictive immigration policies to reduce the reserve. If the size of the low-wage labour pool cannot itself be controlled, unions at least want to make that pool of labour more expensive. To do this they may support wage-fixing policies (minimum wages, equal pay, "fair" wages on government contracts, and wage-extension decrees) as well as labour-standards programs that make the use of such nonunion labour more expensive. This is not the only reason for union support of these policies, but it may be one reason.

Supply of Substitute Inputs is Inelastic.   An increase in wages will cause employers to substitute cheaper inputs for more expensive union labour. As the demand for substitute inputs increases, so will the price of these substitutes, thereby diminishing the firm's incentive to substitute away from union labour. Stated differently, the more inelastic the supply of substitute inputs, the more inelastic will be the demand for union labour.

Labour Cost Portion.   In general, if the costs of unionized labour are a small proportion of the total costs of a firm, the firm can more easily absorb union wage increases; the resultant cost increases simply do not matter much relative to the total cost picture of the firm. This may be the case, for example, for certain skilled craft workers and small professional groups, and for capital-intensive industries. It may, in part, explain the reluctance of these groups to merge with larger groups within whose wage demands their own demands would be subsumed.

Noncompetitive Markets

The degree of competition prevailing in the environment affects the power of unions and hence their ability to win gains for their members. Noncompetitive situations can prevail in the product market and in the labour market, with both situations affecting the power of unions.

Monopoly in the Product Market.   Conventional wisdom suggests that a firm that has a monopoly in the product market has a greater ability to pay out of monopoly profits, and that unions can garner high wage increases in such circumstances. In addition, if the firm is a regulated monopoly, it may be concerned about its public image and hence willing to "buy" good labour relations by paying high wages; it may also feel that it can obtain permission to pass any wage increase on to the public in the form of rate increases.

These arguments are plausible, but they do not necessarily imply that unions can get larger wage increases when product markets are noncompetitive or monopolistic in the extreme. Monopolies may have a greater ability to pay, but they may also have a greater ability to resist union wage demands. They may use their monopoly profits to resist unionization or to set up structures (for example, using capital equipment or extensive nonunion supervision) that weaken the power of unions or that enable employers to withstand a lengthy and costly strike. If rate increases are calculated on the capital base, monopolists have an added incentive to expand that base at the expense of labour costs. In essence, the impact of monopoly on the ability of the union to win wage increases is theoretically ambiguous. Empirically, however, the dramatic decline in union wages that has occurred under deregulation suggests that unions in the regulated sectors are able to appropriate some monopoly profits and that union wage gains are higher in noncompetitive product markets.

Public Sector Employees. There is a presumption that unions in the public sector can become quite powerful because their employers are not subject to a competitive profit constraint. In essence, says the theory, the political constraint in the public sector is not as binding as the profit constraint in the private sector. Union wage increases can be passed on to taxpayers, who must have the essential services and cannot buy them elsewhere, who are often ill-informed about the "tax price" of public services, and who exercise their democratic prerogatives only occasionally by voting on a package of issues of which the wage costs of services may be only a small part. Of real concern is the possibility that public sector employers may try to save on current wage costs by granting liberal compensation to be paid by future taxpayers, possibly when another political party is in power. Such deferred wages can come in the form of regular seniority-based wage increases, liberal retirement pensions, or job security.

Although these arguments do suggest that public sector unions should be quite powerful, there are also forces—usually more subtle ones—working in the opposite direction. Taxpayers are scrutinizing government with increasing severity, and they may sympathize more with employers, forgetting that it takes two sides to create a dispute. Politicians may seek to curb inflation by moderating public sector wage settlements, and they may even prolong or foster strikes to gain the media exposure that is crucial to their prominence. Employers in the public sector, unlike those in the private sector, do not usually lose their (tax) revenues during a strike.

The prominence of wage controls that were adopted by various provincial governments in the 1980s shows how willing governments have become to apply restraints on their public sector employees in the hope that this practice will spill over into the private sector. The recent practice of a number of provincial governments of requiring their employees to take unpaid leave days (e.g., under Ontario's Social Contract Act, 1993) highlights what may be the new method of public sector cost containment in the 1990s. Clearly, unions in the public sector can be subject to political pressures that restrain their power, even to the extent of suspending collective bargaining.

When they have the right to strike, public sector unions themselves may find it difficult to exert pressure if their members are reluctant to withhold essential services or if their right to strike is circumscribed by limitations such as the requirement to have designated workers who do not have the right-to-strike. In essence, the power of unions in the public sector relative to the private sector is theoretically ambiguous. Hence, the differential impact of unions in the private and public sector is ultimately an empirical proposition. (The evidence to support this proposition is discussed later in the chapter.)

Monopsony. Noncompetitive conditions also prevail in labour markets that are dominated by a single employer—termed a *monopsonist* to indicate that the firm is a monopolistic buyer of labour. Such a firm is so large relative to the size of the local labour market that it has to raise wages to attract additional workers; conversely, it does not lose all of its work force if it lowers wages. A monopsonist is extremely sensitive about raising wages to attract additional workers because it knows it will have to pay these higher rates to its existing work force in order to maintain internal equity of the wage structure. This fact serves to depress wages paid by the monopsonist relative to what it would pay if it were a competitive buyer of labour.

Monopsonists are ripe for union organizing because union wage increases, at least within a certain range, can actually lead to their hiring more labour. This paradoxical result occurs because when faced with a fixed union wage that they must pay to all their workers, monopsonists are no longer constrained in their hiring decisions by the fact that they have to raise wages to attract additional workers; all workers are paid the union rate for each job. Thus, the wage demands of unions, at least for a range of wage increases, are not constrained by the possibility of reduced employment opportunities. Clearly, these circumstances afford room for considerable bargaining in that there is a range of wage increases that the monopsonist can absorb. With so much to gain and lose, one would expect a high degree of conflict in organizing and in bargaining—an observation that seems borne out in the isolated one-industry towns that characterize monopsony.

METHODS OF ACHIEVING COMPENSATION GOALS

Given unions' various objectives and sources of power, they use a variety of methods—some direct, others indirect—to achieve their compensation goals. The direct methods usually have to do with the setting of union wage rates; the indirect methods usually involve changing the conditions and power relationships under which collective bargaining takes place. Different unions may follow different methods, and the same union may change its methods over time as objective circumstances (the economy, legislation) change. The main methods through which unions achieve their compensation goals are collective bargaining and interest arbitration, restricting the labour supply, altering the demand for union labour, wage fixing in the nonunion sector, and altering the bargaining environment, process, and structure.

Collective Bargaining and Interest Arbitration

Collective bargaining is the most direct and the most common way for unions to influence the compensation of their members. Because the collective agreement, by law, has to cover all members of the bargaining unit, the rates it specifies must also apply to nonunion members of the bargaining unit. The ultimate sanction of the union, if it is allowed, is the strike; however, other sanctions, such as work to rule (following exactly the requirements of the contract, company policy, or law to the detriment of productivity), abuse of the grievance procedure, and even sabotage are possible.

Industrial unions tend to use direct determination of compensation through the collective bargaining process. In competitive markets, they are constrained by the factors, discussed in the previous section, that influence the elasticity of demand for their labour, and hence the extent to which union wage increases are likely to be countered by reductions in the firm's overall work force.

Where the right to strike is not allowed, as in many parts of the public sector, interest arbitration is usually used to determine the terms of a new collective agreement. Arbitrators use various criteria including comparability with the private sector, prevailing community rates, ability to pay, productivity, cost-of-living changes, minimum required living standards, and the need to recruit and retain a viable work force.

Restricting Labour Supply

Craft unions and professional associations often try to affect their compensation indirectly through control of the labour supply. Craft unions use such methods as the hiring hall, apprenticeship ratios, and high union dues, and possibly even discrimination. By restricting the labour supply to the trade, the union pushes wages higher than they would be in the absence of the restriction.

Professional associations behave much like craft unions in attempting to restrict the supply of labour to their profession. This ability to do so may be quite powerful, as in the case of self-licensing professions, such as medicine or law, where only people who obtain the licence may practise. Or it may be less powerful, as in the case of certified professions, where others can practise but only those who are certified can use the requisite title. In the latter case, substitutes are possible, but they may be imperfect substitutes in the sense that uncertified workers cannot use the professionally designated title.

The power of occupational self-licensing is usually granted to a profession by law ostensibly to protect the public vis-a-vis services that they may have to have, that are often complicated to evaluate, that are infrequently purchased, and that involve severe adverse consequences if improperly provided. Because the provision of the services is so complicated, only members of the profession itself are deemed capable of deciding how they should best be provided; hence, the profession is given the power to regulate itself. Thus, the self-regulating professions have achieved the unique position of determining not only the demand for their services (only they can tell their clients how much of their services to purchase) but also, through self-licensing, the supply. Under such circumstances, there is a possibility that professional groups may try to artificially raise their members' compensation by increasing the demand for or reducing the supply of their services. This potential is even greater if third parties or public revenues are used to pay for the service.

Devices that professional groups can use to control the supply of labour to an occupation include setting the entry and exit rates for professional schools; requiring training for new entrants; establishing requirements with respect to residence or citizenship; and constraining the extent to which paraprofessionals can perform the service. Policies that pass the cost of these restrictions on to new entrants to the profession are particularly attractive to incumbent professionals (who are the ones who decide on the requirements) because the latter group can appropriate the benefits of the higher compensation, while the new professionals bear many of the costs. Hence, one can expect increasingly stringent training requirements with "grandparent" clauses stating that incumbents do not have to meet them. Once the new professionals become incumbent professionals, they may tend to impose even further requirements. The potential for costly overqualification is obvious.

Altering Demand for Union Labour

Unions can also increase the wages of their members by increasing the demand for union labour and by making that demand more inelastic so that pressure for union wage increases is not dampened by the threat of employment cuts. From our previous discussion of the determinants of the elasticity of demand for labour, we know that unions may do this through contract provisions regarding technological change, contracting out, and restrictive work practices, as well as through supportive advertising (for example, the union label). At the political level, unions may also oppose free trade and extensive immigration, and they may support income-maintenance programs and aggregate demand policies that will reduce the pool of low-wage or unemployed labour.

Wage Fixing in the Nonunion Sector

In an indirect attempt to alter the demand for union labour, unions may also support wage-fixing policies that will raise the wages of nonunion labour, thereby reducing the substitution of such labour for union labour. The main elements of wage-fixing legislation are the minimum wage, equal pay legislation, fair wages on government contracts, and wage extension by decree.

Unions have to walk a fine line in supporting such legislation, however, because it can clearly be used as a substitute for unionization: if legislation can take care of workers, the need for unions may be reduced. It is ironic, in fact, that much wage-fixing legislation originated with the hidden objective of reducing the need for unions. Over time, however, unions have been able to turn such legislation to their own ends to reduce nonunion competition.

Altering the Bargaining Environment, Process, and Structure

In an even more indirect fashion, unions may try to affect their compensation gains by altering the environment, process, and structure in which collective bargaining takes place. Especially in times of wage controls, unions can be expected to bargain for changes in their bargaining environment or structure that will enhance their future wage gains; with current wage increases restricted, they may well trade off current wages for future wages. In fact, as a quid pro quo for acceptance of wage restraints, governments may give the labour movement a political concession that will enhance the unions' future bargaining position.

Environment.   Changes in labour relations legislation can obviously alter relative bargaining strengths. For example, union power rises if legislation requires nonunion workers in the bargaining unit to pay union dues or prohibits the use of replacement workers during a work stoppage. Having aspects of health and safety and minimum labour standards covered by legislation enables unions to concentrate their bargaining on other factors. The overall economic environment can also affect union bargaining power; one reason unions support full-employment policies is so that employers do not always have a pool of low-wage labour as a potential substitute for union labour.

Unions may also try to alter the distribution of power relationships in society as a whole. This attempt is regarded as especially important by people who believe that wages are determined not only by the human-capital characteristics of workers (as emphasized by neoclassical economists) and by the characteristics of jobs (as emphasized by the dual and segmented labour market theorists), but also by the power relationships in society which determine relative shares of income for the various groups. Attempts by unions to obtain a social contract or tripartitism can be regarded as attempts to alter the overall power relationship within which collective bargaining takes place.

Process. Unions may also try to alter the process of collective bargaining in a manner conducive to meeting their objectives. Changing some aspects of the process holds the potential for mutual gain; this is the case, for example, with respect to continuous bargaining, joint committees, and productivity bargaining. Other elements of the process, however, benefit one party more than the other; in such circumstances, one expects change only in return for other concessions. This could be the case, for example, with respect to contract expiration dates or the use of third parties.

Structure. The structure of bargaining—in particular the degree of centralization of the bargaining and negotiating units—can have an obvious effect on bargaining outcomes. To a large extent, the structure is imposed by labour relations boards in their determination of appropriate bargaining units. In Canada, the result has traditionally been decentralized units, in part because requiring more centralized units would effectively preclude some organizing drives. The structure is essentially malleable, however, and can be affected by such factors as union mergers, the merging or breaking away of bargaining units, and accreditation of employers' associations. The structure is also affected by collective bargaining; the setting of common expiration dates on contracts, for example, effectively dictates a form of centralized bargaining. A degree of centralization also results from "pattern bargaining" (a specific contract sets the pattern for related sectors) and from interest arbitration if certain wage awards set a precedent. The "decree system" in the province of Quebec (mutually agreed-upon rates are extended throughout the industry) is also effectively a form of centralized bargaining.

Although the structure and, in particular, the degree of centralization can have an impact on bargaining outcomes, there is no consensus on the expected direction of the impact. Centralized structures may give unions monopoly power, increasing their threat by enabling them to shut down a whole sector. Such unions are also protected from multiplant employers' shifting of production to other operations in the event of a strike. Moreover, employers may be more willing to make concessions in centralized systems because a uniform wage increase for all employers in a given product market does not give any one of them a competitive advantage. On the other hand, with greater union power comes greater responsibility. Unions that bargain centrally are under considerable public and government pressure to consider the national interest, especially in times of wage and price restraints. In addition, centralized bargaining can prevent a single union from disrupting a whole sector by shutting down the weakest link. Centralized employer structures may also enable employers to behave as monopsonists, paying a lower wage because they dominate the labour market.

Thus, in theory, the degree of centralization can have an indeterminate impact on bargaining outcomes. Unfortunately, the limited empirical evidence that exists (reviewed in Davies 1986, 242-45) is not always in agreement, although most studies suggest that the union impact on wages is greater in decentralized rather than centralized structures.

SOME PROBLEMS IN ASCERTAINING THE UNION IMPACT

Attempts to quantify the impact of unions have met with numerous estimation problems. The most important are those of separating cause and effect and of controlling for quality differences.

Separating Cause and Effect

Conventional wisdom suggests that causality runs in the direction of unions' causing higher wages in the union sector. There are reasons, however, to suggest that causality may also operate in the other direction—that is, that unions are more likely to be formed in situations in which high wages already exist. In such circumstances, estimation procedures that do not account for this reverse causality may erroneously credit unions with creating a union-nonunion wage differential. Simultaneous-equation estimation procedures are required to account for this reverse causality.

There are numerous possible rationales for the hypothesis that high wages "cause" unionization, as well as vice versa. Ashenfelter and Johnson (1972)—who were the first to deal formally with the simultaneity problem—argue that unionization may be more likely to arise in high-wage sectors because they are easier to organize and because the higher wages may enable workers in such sectors to afford to buy more of everything, including union services.

The "exit-voice" theory advanced by Hirschman (1970) can also be used to explain the causality from high wages to unionization. Hirschman argues that the traditional mechanism of economists—competition, or the threat of "exit"—is neither the preferred nor an available device in all markets. There are situations in which exit is precluded or in which it is preferable to try to improve the situation not by leaving or threatening to leave but rather by utilizing various forms of "voice." In fact, where exit is precluded or difficult, voice becomes a more important device for improving the situation.

For example, some firms may pay high wages (sometimes termed "efficiency wages") to reduce turnover, to have a large queue of applicants, or to improve morale and "buy" employee commitment. Workers in these firms are reluctant to leave because of the high wages—that is, exit is reduced. And since exit is reduced, they turn to voice as the mechanism to improve their situation. Unions can be thought of as the institutional embodiment of voice—the means by which workers attempt to have a say in their work environment (Freeman 1976, Freeman and Medoff 1979; 1984). The causality in such a situation runs from high wages (and hence reduced exit) to unionization (as the form of voice).

An appealing element of this perspective is that it reconciles the views of industrial relations analysts, who emphasize the importance of the union in achieving due process and job security at the workplace, with the views of economists, who emphasize the wage impact of unions. Unions are associated both with higher wages for their members and with job security and due process at the workplace.

Quality Differences

Another problem in measuring the pure wage impact of unions occurs because quality differences between union and nonunion workers are likely if union workers have a wage advantage over nonunion workers. Firms that pay the higher union wage rate are likely to have a longer queue of applicants than firms that pay the lower nonunion rate; this difference will occur whether unions cause the higher wage rate or are a result of it. Given the longer queue, unionized firms can be more selective than nonunionized firms in their hiring and recruiting procedures, thereby obtaining higher-quality workers with more education, training, and experience, as well as more of such typically unobserved characteristics as motivation. Of course, firms in this situation may try to increase job assignments (for example, by increasing the pace of work); however, unions may try to resist such adjustments lest they offset the union wage impact itself.

In these circumstances, it is extremely important for an analyst who is measuring the pure impact of unions on wages to control for differences in the characteristics of workers and job assignments. Otherwise the "omitted variables" may upwardly bias the amount of the union impact (the union-nonunion wage differential will reflect better-quality workers and perhaps more complex job assignments in the union sector). The bias could also work in the opposite direction, if, for example, it is more difficult for employers to dismiss poorer-quality workers in the union sector or if poorer-quality workers try to sort themselves into the more secure union jobs.

Measurement Techniques and Data

The vast majority of studies of the union impact have focused on measuring the union-nonunion wage differential, since wages are more readily observed than other industrial relations outcomes. To be able to attribute the union-nonunion wage differential purely to the impact of unions, it is necessary to control for other wage-determining factors, including the characteristics of the workers (e.g., education, experience, gender) and the characteristics of the jobs (e.g., occupation, industry, region). As indicated previously, it is extremely important to control for these factors since, faced with a union wage increase, employers try to be more selective in their hiring decisions and may try to change the nature of job assignments.

The impact of these factors is usually controlled through the use of multiple-regression analysis, which indicates the effect on wages of each explanatory variable, including a measure of unionization, while holding the other wage-determining factors constant. The regression equation is often estimated on cross-sections of aggregate or macro data relating wages in an industry, city, or state to the proportion of the industry, city, or state that is unionized. Comprehensive reviews of these macro studies are contained in Lewis (1963) for US studies prior to 1963 and in Lewis (1983) for studies after 1962.

In more recent years, with the availability of micro data sets that have the individual worker as the unit of observation, a large number of econometric studies have estimated the union impact by comparing the wages of union and nonunion workers (or establishments), after controlling for the effect of various observable and unobservable determinants of earnings. These and other micro cross-section studies, using the individual worker or establishment as the unit of observation, are reviewed in Lewis (1986a; 1986b). Controlling for the effect of unobservable factors is important because, as discussed previously, workers may sort themselves or be sorted into the union and nonunion sectors on the basis of both observable characteristics (such as education and experience) and conventionally unobserved characteristics (such as motivation or risk aversion). In essence, unionization is an endogenous variable, and union workers may be a select subsample in terms of both observed and unobserved characteristics.

Controlling for differences between union and nonunion workers in their observed characteristics is straightforward; it involves including control variables, such as education and experience, in the estimated earnings equations. Controlling for the conventionally unobserved differences (termed "unobserved heterogeneity") is more difficult. Essentially, it involves estimating an equation of the determinants of whether the worker is a union member and using this information to construct an artificial variable that basically controls for the sample selection bias that otherwise may occur because of unobserved differences. This artificial control variable is then included in the earnings equations to get an estimate of the pure union impact after controlling for the effects of both observed differences (represented by conventional control variables) and unobserved differences (represented by this artificially constructed control variable) between union and nonunion workers.

The simultaneous-equation procedure that jointly estimates earnings as a function of union status and union status as a function of earnings and other factors (that is, treats union status as endogenous) is the subject matter of considerable recent econometric research (for example, with US data, Duncan and Leigh 1980; Lee 1978; and with Canadian data, Kumar and Stengos 1985; Robinson and Tomes 1984; and Simpson 1985).

An alternative procedure to control for conventionally unobserved differences between union and nonunion workers is to use panel or longitudinal data that follow the same individuals over time. The analyst makes the reasonable assumption that the conventional unobserved factors (for example, motivation) remain constant for each individual. The union impact is identified when these individuals change their union status over time (US studies using longitudinal data include Mellow 1981; Mincer 1983; Moore and Raisian 1983; and Jakubson 1991; Canadian studies include Grant, Swidinsky, and Vanderkamp 1987; Robinson 1989; and Swidinsky and Kupferschmidt 1991). Freeman (1984) reviews the methodological problems with such studies. Unfortunately, this methodology gives rise to problems of its own since only a small sample of individuals change their union status, and when they do so, it is often under unusual circumstances and other factors are also often changing, thereby making it difficult to disentangle a pure union impact. It has generally been the case that estimates of the union impact obtained from longitudinal data are smaller than those obtained from cross-sectional data. Robinson (1989) suggests that the differences between cross-sectional and longitudinal estimates may be due to unobserved heterogeneity not accounted for in longitudinal studies, and errors in determining whether or not an individual is a union member at different points in time. The latter measurement error problem tends to create a greater bias in the estimates of the union impact on longitudinal data than those based on cross-sectional data.

UNION IMPACT ON COMPENSATION AND PRODUCTIVITY

In varying degrees, the numerous empirical studies of the impact of unions attempt to account for the measurement problems just discussed. Unions can affect various aspects of compensation, including wages and wage structures, nonunion wages, fringe benefits, and productivity. Reviews of this evidence are contained in Gunderson and Riddell (1993) and Lewis (1963; 1986a; 1986b).

Impact on Wages and Wage Structures

The early macro studies based an aggregate data (reviewed in Lewis 1963) estimated union-nonunion wage differentials of 10 to 15 per cent. More recent estimates, based on micro data on individual workers and often utilizing simultaneous-equation techniques to account for reverse causality and unobserved quality differences, tend to find somewhat higher estimates, often in the range of 20 to 30 per cent. There is much more variability in the latter estimates, reflecting the fact that simultaneous-equation procedures are often sensitive to the specification of the relationship and to the techniques for controlling for unobserved quality differences. More recent estimates based on longitudinal or panel data sets tend to find smaller union wage effects, usually in the neighbourhood of 10 per cent. These differences reflect the real difficulties of sorting out cause and effect and of controlling for the myriad of observed and unobserved differences between union and nonunion workers.

The union impact on wages tends to be larger in recessions and smaller at the peak of the business cycle, reflecting the fact that union wages are less sensitive to economic fluctuations than are nonunion wages (in part because union workers have long-term wage contracts). There is also some evidence that, in the United States, the union-nonunion wage differential grew in the 1970s.

The union impact is higher for blue-collar and less skilled workers than for white-collar and more skilled workers. Generally, union workers tend to get a "flat" union premium, but that amount declines with productivity-related characteristics such as experience, education, and skill. This phenomenon gives rise to union wage profiles that are higher but flatter than nonunion wage profiles with respect to such factors as age, experience, and education. This finding is consistent with the view of unions as institutions that blunt the impact of market forces by gaining a constant increase for members, but having their wages increase less than the wages of nonunion workers for increments in productivity-related characteristics.

Thus, with respect to the overall dispersion of wages, unions exert two opposing effects. They narrow wage differentials that reflect such factors as skill, education, and experience; however, they widen the overall dispersion by creating a new source of dispersion—the union-nonunion wage differential. There is some evidence that the equalizing effect dominates, so that unions tend to reduce the overall dispersion of wages (Belman and Heywood 1990; Freeman 1980a; Hyclack 1980; Meng 1990; Quan 1984).

The union-nonunion wage gap tends to be similar for men and women, based on US data (almost 50 studies reviewed in Lewis 1986). However, based on Canadian data, Doiron and Riddell (1992) find the union wage impact to be larger for females than for males, but that females benefit less from unions because they are less likely to be covered by a collective agreement. They find that these opposing effects offset each other, so that overall unions neither increase nor decrease the male-female wage gap.

Somewhat surprisingly, the empirical evidence suggests that the union impact tends to be smaller in the public than private sector, although there is considerable diversity in this result (reviews are contained in Freeman 1986; Lewin, Horton, and Kuhn 1979; and Mitchell 1983, all based on US data; Robinson and Tomes 1984; Simpson 1985; and Riddell 1992, based on Canadian data).

Impact on Nonunion Wages

Unions can affect the wages of nonunion workers through a variety of mechanisms. To the extent that unionized wage increases reduce employment opportunities in the unionized sector, the excess supply of labour from that sector should serve to depress wages in the nonunion sector. This effect may, however, be mitigated if unions are able to "featherbed" (require the use of excess amounts of labour in the union sector).

On the demand side, the demand for nonunion labour—and hence the nonunion wage—is affected in an indeterminate manner by an increase in the wages of union workers. The demand for nonunion labour may increase to the extent that nonunion labour is substituted for the now more expensive union labour. Unions will certainly resist such a substitution, but it still occurs in a number of ways—for example, through contracting-out, using nonunion supervisors, or even relocating production to a nonunion sector. In addition, output demand may shift from the products produced by the more expensive union sector to those produced in the cheaper nonunion sector. (This effect may be minimized if the whole sector can be organized). On the other hand, the demand for some nonunion labour may decrease to the extent that it is complementary to (i.e., works in tandem with) union labour or to such an extent that firms reduce their scale of output (in the extreme, perhaps even closing down) in response to the higher union labour cost; in such circumstances firms may employ less of both union and nonunion labour.

Other forces are at work institutionally whereby nonunion wages are affected by unionization. As discussed previously, unions can affect nonunion wages by supporting wage-fixing legislation, which applies mainly to the nonunion sector. In addition, nonunion firms may raise their wages to avoid the threat of becoming unionized. In the extreme, they may pay wages in excess of the going union wage rate to avoid what they regard as other costs associated with becoming unionized, notably interference with managerial prerogatives (Taras 1994). Nonunion firms may also be compelled to raise their wages so as to compete with unionized firms for a given work force or to restore traditional wage relativities that existed before unionization. The last argument, however, ignores the fact that nonunion firms should not have to worry about recruiting problems or restoring traditional wage patterns because they will have a supply influx of workers who cannot get jobs in the high-wage union sector (in essence, market forces suggest that their recruiting problems are lessened and that there is reduced pressure to maintain a traditional wage pattern).

Clearly, unions affect the wages of nonunion workers through a variety of institutional, market, and legislative forces. Since these forces do not all work in the same direction, it is not possible to state theoretically the expected impact of unions on the wages of nonunion workers; one must appeal to the empirical evidence. In his earlier work, Lewis (1963, 194) concluded that unionism has probably lowered the wages of nonunion workers but by a small amount—less than 3 or 4 per cent. Kahn (1978; 1980) finds that nonunion wages are generally decreased by unionism but that the overall average effect masks considerable variability, with some groups, such as nonunion white men, receiving a large wage increase from unionism.

Impact on Employee Benefits

Empirical evidence (Freeman 1981; Ichniowski 1980) indicates that unions increase the employee benefits of their members even more than they increase their wages. This may occur for a variety of reasons.

To the extent that unionization makes workers better off, they can afford to buy more of everything, including employee benefits; this will be especially important if they enter the higher tax brackets and employee benefits are not taxed. In addition, unions, being a political institution of "voice" (Freeman 1976; Freeman and Medoff 1979; 1984), can be expected to represent the wishes of the average worker (more specifically, the median voting member) as opposed to the marginal worker, whose interest is most likely to be represented by the mechanism of exit or mobility. Since the average worker is more likely than the marginal worker to be older, with seniority and with a family, the collective preferences are more likely to favour employee benefits, especially pensions and life, accident, and health insurance.

Employee benefits, as a form of deferred compensation, may also be more prevalent in unionized establishments than in nonunion ones (for Canadian evidence see Swidinsky and Kupferschmidt 1991). Employers may prefer deferred wages as compensation because they provide a threat that can be used to ensure effort from their employees. The threat is the possibility of dismissal and therefore the loss of deferred wages. Deferred wages can also provide employees with an interest in the financial solvency of the firm. In addition, deferred compensation reduces turnover since employees who quit would lose some or all of their deferred wages (for example, pension and vacation rights). Employees may willingly accept a deferred wage if they are given a sufficiently high wage to compensate for some of it being deferred (and hence its receipt being uncertain), or if they are provided with sufficient guarantees that the employer will ultimately pay. Such guarantees are more likely when they are provided in a collective agreement, which, for example, prevents arbitrary dismissal and reinforces the legal obligation to provide the promised payments. In essence, unionization makes the payment of fringe benefits in the form of deferred wages a feasible compensation scheme. Hence one can expect such employee benefits to be associated with unionization.

Impact on Productivity

Although recognized for a long time by industrial relations analysts (Slichter, Healy, and Livernash 1960), the potential positive impact of unions on various aspects of productivity has only recently been analyzed and quantified by labour economists (Brown and Medoff 1978; Clark 1980; Freeman and Medoff 1979; 1984; and others comprehensively reviewed in Belman 1992). As Freeman and Medoff indicate, there are two dominant views of trade unions. The monopoly view regards unions as creating economic inefficiency by raising wages above the competitive norm, by inducing strikes, and by requiring featherbedding work rules that compel the employer to use inefficient amounts of union labour. An alternative view is that unions have positive effects on productivity by reducing turnover, "shocking" management into more efficient practices, improving morale and cooperation among workers, providing information about the collective preferences of workers, and improving communications between labour and management.

As indicated throughout this chapter, the preponderance of empirical literature on the impact of unions has focused on the extent to which unions raise wages above the competitive wage that otherwise would prevail. That unions do this would not be denied by trade unionists; in fact, one of the avowed purposes of the union movement is "to take labour out of the market." To the extent that the wage impact exists, however, it will lead to inefficiencies since management will use excessive amounts of capital and nonunion labour relative to higher-priced union labour. Management will also utilize excessively high-quality union labour. Rees (1963) estimates that these inefficiencies led to an output loss of approximately 0.14 per cent of gross national product (GNP) in the United States in 1957; De Fina (1983) puts it at about 0.1 per cent of GNP.

Despite the frequent focus on the wage impact of unions, there is growing literature on their more positive impact on various aspects of productivity. These studies examine the direct effects on productivity after controlling for the fact that the union wage premium results in an indirect productivity increase by inducing firms to substitute capital for labour and by enabling them to hire more productive workers.

Specifically, unions have been found to lower quit rates (Blau and Kahn 1983; Freeman 1980b; Leigh 1979, all using US data; Swidinsky 1992 using Canadian data), to increase tenure with the firm (Addison and Castro 1987), and to raise productivity or output per worker (studies reviewed in Freeman and Medoff 1984; Belman 1992; and Gunderson and Riddell 1993). There is not universal agreement in the latter area, however, and the results are often sensitive to the type of data used and the specification of the output equation (see, for example, Mitchell and Stone 1992 and Maki 1983, which are based on Canadian data). There is also conflicting evidence on the effects of unions on productivity in the public sector, although most studies show unions there to have had no net effect, either positive or negative (such studies are reviewed in Freeman 1986, 62).

Some analysts also offer evidence that unionized environments have more strenuous work conditions than nonunionized ones, with, for example, a structured work setting, inflexible hours, and a faster work pace. This may reflect the fact that unionism is more likely to occur in response to such working conditions or that some employers are able to respond to the union wage advantage by changing the conditions of work, partly to take advantage of a higher-quality work force. Without claiming to be able to disentangle the true relationship between cause and effect, Duncan and Stafford (1980) estimate that about two-fifths of the union-nonunion wage differential reflects a compensating wage for these more demanding working conditions. Kalachek and Raines (1980) find that employers are able to offset some of the union wage cost increase by more stringent hiring standards, notably with respect to the education qualifications of their workers.

The labour relations climate in the workplace can also influence the productivity of union workers. A good union-management relationship can amplify the productivity-enhancing effects of unions, especially through information sharing and a focus in bargaining on mutual gains rather than on rules that control the behaviours of the parties. Conversely, a poor industrial relations climate can exacerbate the negative impacts on productivity. A number of studies have found negative productivity effects where labour relations are generally bad, as evidenced for example by a large number of grievances (Belman 1992; Ichniowski 1986; Kochan, Katz, and Mower 1985; Read 1982), by strikes (Maki 1983; Bemmels 1987), and by "wildcat" strikes (Flaherty 1987).

Impact on Profitability

Although these productivity-inducing effects probably offset some of the wage cost increases resulting from unionism, they are unlikely to offset all of them. If they did, one would expect to see managers, or at least shareholders, welcoming unions—a phenomenon rarely observed (except in cases of "company unions" that management controls). At least some union wage gains must represent real gains to union workers and real costs to employers, otherwise one would not see workers organizing or employers resisting unionization. This is also evidenced by the fact that union firms tend to be less profitable than nonunion firms (Maki and Meredeth 1986, based on Canadian data; Becker and Olson 1989; 1992; Hirsch 1991; Belman 1992; and Voos and Mishel 1986; all based on US data).

UNION IMPACT ON MANAGEMENT OF THE ORGANIZATION

As discussed previously, the importance of unions for many employees is not so much in the wage and fringe benefits they can achieve as in their ensuring a modicum of job security and due process at the workplace. In achieving these ends, unions can also have a substantial impact on the way management runs the organization—restricting the otherwise unfettered rights of management (within the law) to run the firm in what could be an arbitrary or even capricious manner with respect to employees. This result may occur as a byproduct of the way in which unions try to achieve their compensation objectives, or it may be pursued by unions as an end in itself.

Mechanisms For Affecting Management of the Organization

Unions have injected a degree of due process and hence have affected the management of the organization in a variety of ways. The most obvious mechanisms are specific provisions (e.g., seniority) in the collective agreement as well as the grievance procedure for interpreting and breathing life into the agreement. Unions have also been instrumental in encouraging and at times helping to enforce legislative employment standards, which regulate such factors as minimum wages, pay and employment equity, hours of work and overtime, paid vacations and holidays, maternity leave, and employee termination. They can also be involved in joint union-management committees (most noticeably on health and safety), and union representatives may even be on the board of directors of the company.

Legislative Assistance

Legislative initiatives have often helped unions achieve due process and circumscribe the otherwise unfettered rights of management in the employment relationship. This aid has taken a variety of forms: the legal obligation to recognize a certified union as the workers' exclusive bargaining agent and to bargain in good faith; the legal recognition of collective agreements and of the grievance procedure with its own jurisprudence; and the establishment of employment standards and health and safety legislation that effectively give government backing and enforcement to a number of issues over which unions might otherwise have to negotiate. On many issues, legislative initiatives have used the existing machinery of collective bargaining and the union's communications network to provide effective enforcement. Such is the case, for example, in the health and safety area (with the use of joint committees as part of the "internal responsibility" system) and in pay equity (with unions to be involved in job-evaluation procedures and in the allocation of awards pertaining to equal pay for work of equal value).

Examples of Impact on Management of the Organization

Given their emphasis on the rights and well-being of workers, unions' effects on the management of the organization have been on those dimensions of managerial decision making that impinge most directly on the workforce. Many of these are discussed in Kaufman and Kaufman (1987, 342), who conclude, "Union firms in our sample are significantly more likely to have grievance procedures, job-posting systems, and other restrictions that limit management's prerogative in promotion, classification and job assignment."

At the hiring stage, the union impact is usually negligible; this lack of effect normally extends for a brief probationary period, when managerial discretion is largely unfettered. The exception is the situation in which unions have negotiated union security clauses involving a "closed shop" (only union members can be hired). This is often coupled with the union's running a "hiring hall" (the union acts as the employment agency, having the exclusive right to refer employees to the firm). These forms of union security provisions are rare, however, existing mainly in some areas of construction and longshoring.

After the hiring and probationary period, the union impact becomes more prominent. Almost invariably, collective agreements contain clauses requiring "just cause" for discipline and discharge; situations involving these clauses are the most common source of grievance arbitration cases. Seniority provisions regulating managerial discretion in matters such as promotion, transfer, layoff, and recall are also very common in collective agreements as well as a common source of grievance arbitration cases.

This is not to say that the use of seniority necessarily leads to undesirable outcomes. Seniority is almost always used as a criterion in combination with some measure of ability and/or qualification. Thus, the use of seniority may well constrain employers, but it may also force them to measure ability more conscientiously and generally to ensure fairness in the decision-making process. Hence, better outcomes may result.

Restrictions on contracting-out are also prevalent in collective agreements, in part because employers can undercut the power of a union by contracting out certain jobs to the nonunion sector. This issue is currently highly contentious; management wants the right to contract out as part of its increased drive for flexibility, and unions fear the loss of union jobs, especially in the current climate of down-sizing. Policy makers also have some concern that contracting-out may be used as a way of getting around legislative intervention in such areas as employment standards and equal pay legislation. Often the subcontracting goes to the self-employed individuals or to small firms, where the legislation is more difficult to enforce.

Regulations on job assignment (who can do what work) can also restrict managerial discretion. The extreme form of these rules often involved featherbedding practices such as the requirement that containers be unloaded and reloaded at ports or that a fireman be maintained on diesel engines. These requirements were usually introduced at times of dramatic technological change (e.g., containerization of shipping, conversion from steam locomotives to diesel engines) in order to preserve the jobs of incumbent workers. Eventually, there was strong pressure to bargain them away, often in return for guarantees of job security or for guarantees that work force reductions would occur through voluntary transfers, quits, or retirements.

Other restrictions on managerial discretion include the right to refuse overtime, and requirements for advance notice or transfer rights in the case of plant closings or technological change. In most circumstances, however, these restrictions are not prominent features of collective agreements; they are more often introduced by legislation.

Some Unintended Side-Effects

In some instances, union practices that restrict managerial discretion can have unintended side-effects. For example, seniority provisions can be an obstacle to attempts to achieve pay and employment opportunities that are equal for men and women since women tend to accumulate less seniority (especially if they leave the labour market for child-raising). They can also be an obstacle in accommodating the needs of disabled persons at the workplace. Requirements for specific ratios of apprentices to journeymen can inhibit firms from expanding their training to meet certain shortages. Prohibitions on the use of part-time labour can inhibit employers from reducing overtime and sharing the available work. Requirements for severance pay and advance notice and concern over unfair or unjust dismissal cases can make employers reluctant to hire new workers who might eventually have to be laid off.

Unfortunately, it is exceedingly difficult to disentangle fact from fiction in this area. Contract regulations undoubtedly may have such side-effects; however, they also provide employers with a convenient excuse for not hiring more minorities, engaging in more training or worksharing, or recruiting. If regulations are truly barriers, they can be negotiated away, and unions will be under more pressure to do so if they impede social progress in such matters as equal pay and equal employment opportunity, training, worksharing, and unemployment reduction.

Restrictions in the Public Sector

The previous discussion suggested that in the private sector, union restrictions on managerial discretion are largely limited to matters, such as seniority, discipline, and discharge, that have direct implications for the job security of and due process for union workers. In general, there are few attempts to limit managerial authority over other matters. In many parts of the public sector, however, unions try to bargain over broader issues and may thereby encroach on managerial authority. Such encroachment is especially the case with restrictions imposed by professionals (many of which are particular to professionals and do not apply to nonprofessionals in the public service).

In some instances, civil service regulations severely reduce the scope of bargaining, thereby preventing the parties from bargaining over some items that are exclusively under the authority of management. In other cases, the regulations preclude bargaining over wages, a prohibition that may encourage the parties to bargain over nonwage items, some of which may involve managerial decisions. Also, the professionalization of many kinds of employees in the public sector means that these employees invariably want more of a say in the management of the organization, and they often possess the expertise to make such decisions.

The limited empirical evidence available in this area tends to suggest that public sector unions do have a considerable impact on the management of the organization. Teachers, for example, often bargain over class size and pupil/teacher ratios (Hall and Carroll 1973; Woodbury 1985), motivated both by educational quality and employment protection. In fact, Goldschmidt and Stuart (1986) list a wide array of nonwage items that teachers typically bargain over, including curriculum content, class sizes, placement of suspended students, and the selection and transferring of students. They conclude that these items usually put severe constraints on the ability of school districts to adapt to changing circumstances. On the other hand, in a study of the US federal civil service, Beyer, Trice, and Hunt (1980) find that when a union is present and articulates its position, supervisors tend to be more aware of and use policies to deal with equal employment opportunities as well as employee problems with alcoholism.

CONCLUSION

There is probably no single statement about the impact of unions that can be made with absolute certainty—not even concerning the question of whether unions have any impact on the compensation of their members. For every generalization, there are at least some studies that disagree. Perhaps this should not be surprising, given the large number of studies based on different methodologies and data sets and given the subtle complexities of what, on the surface, appears to be a relatively simple measurement problem.

Nevertheless, the variety of studies provides us with some generalizations that are more robust than others. It appears that unions have had a positive impact on the compensation of their members and a slight negative impact on the wages of nonunion workers. The union impact is largest for blue-collar and less skilled workers. In fact, union workers tend to get a flat wage premium, but then receive relatively low returns for increases in such factors as skill, education, and experience. Overall, unions have probably reduced wage disparities and had a larger impact on employee benefits than wages. The union premium is similar for men and women, although some Canadian evidence suggests it is larger for females. Women, however, tend to be less unionized and receive fewer benefits of unionism for that reason.

Some avenues of recent research have highlighted the complexities that are involved in the relationship between unions and compensation. Unionism may be a result of, as well as a cause of, high wages, and union workers may differ from nonunion workers in terms of unobserved, as well as observed, characteristics. Also, unionized establishments may adjust to costly union wage increases by raising their hiring standards and altering their work conditions. Unions may also have a beneficial impact on productivity, which may offset some of the wage cost increase associated with unionization, albeit unionization does reduce profitability.

Unions reduce managerial discretion through provisions in collective agreements, through the grievance procedure, and through support of legislative regulation of the work environment. Although intervention is limited at the hiring and probationary stages, it later becomes substantial through seniority provisions and requirements for "just cause" in cases of discipline and discharge. Other regulations pertain to contracting-out, job assignments, and, to a lesser degree, safety, worktime practices, plant closings, and technological change (the latter issues are more often the subject matter of legislation than of collective bargaining).

Public sector employees, mainly professionals, have done more direct bargaining than private sector workers over what might be perceived as managerial issues. This likely reflects a combination of professional concern over these issues and a realization that they can be an important way of affecting working conditions and job security.

This decade will be an interesting one for analyzing the impact of unions on a variety of outcomes—wages, job security, fringe benefits, productivity, and managerial discretion. Unions are clearly on the defensive in the United States, and this situation is likely to affect Canadian unions, especially given the spread of foreign competition, deregulation, and freer trade. In these circumstances, employers are likely to want more managerial discretion and flexibility, and unions are likely to seek more job security and better fringe benefits, such as generous retirement pensions (in part as a worksharing device). However, this conflict also provides the opportunity for the parties to deal creatively with challenges stemming from the dramatic changes in the Canadian industrial relations system and its environment.

Global competition, trade liberalization and the greater international flow of capital are likely to have a profound impact on union goals and strategies, and ultimately on wage and other outcomes. Unions may simply not be able to continue wage premiums of 20 per cent because this higher labour cost will lead to more imports of lower-priced foreign-produced goods. As well, employers may locate their plants in countries where labour costs are not as high.

In essence, it is difficult for unions to "take labour out of competition" now that the labour market is international. Labour will be under pressure to adopt more international strategies. It will also have to focus less on wages and other outcomes that impose costs on employers and more on ensuring due process and "voice" mechanisms that may be less costly to employers. There will also be more emphasis on labour-management co-operation and on reducing adversarial bargaining. Unions will also likely have to direct more of their efforts toward the political level to influence governments into increasing the "social wage." It is clear that the next few years pose some interesting and important challenges and opportunities for unions.

QUESTIONS

1. Discuss unions' various goals, and indicate their implications for wages, fringe benefits, and wage structures.

2. "The power of unions depends on the economic environment in which unions operate." Discuss.

3. Discuss the determinants of the elasticity of demand for union labour in both the construction industry and the public sector, indicating what this should imply about the ability of unions to achieve wage gains in those sectors.

4. "Unions can have no long-run impact on wages because if they did then union-ized firms would go out of business." Discuss.

5. Discuss the impact of unions on the wages of nonunion workers.

6. Discuss how unionized firms may adjust their hiring standards and working con-ditions when faced with unions. What does this imply about the measured union-nonunion wage differential?

7. Discuss the mechanisms whereby unionism may be a response to high wages as well as a cause of high wages. What does this imply about the measured union-nonunion wage differential?

8. Why may fringe benefits be a preferred form of compensation for union mem-bers even more than for nonunion members?

9. Discuss the mechanisms whereby unions can affect productivity. What does this imply about the costs to the firm that result from unionization?

10. "The study of unionization represents a fertile ground for the judicious blending of a knowledge of institutional industrial relations, economic analysis, and sta-tistical techniques." Discuss, specifically highlighting the strengths and weak-nesses of each of these areas.

11. Discuss the various ways in which unions may affect managerial discretion in running the organization. Is such union impact greater in the public or the pri-vate sector?

12. What effects would you expect global competition and trade liberalization to have on the impact of unions?

REFERENCES

ADDISON, J., and A. CASTRO. 1987. "The Importance of Lifetime Jobs: Differences Between Union and Nonunion Workers." *Industrial and Labor Relations Review* 40: 393-405.

ASHENFELTER, O., and G. JOHNSON. 1972. "Unionism, Relative Wages and Labour Quality in US Manufacturing Industries." *International Economic Review* 13: 488-507.

BECKER, B., and C. OLSON. 1989. "Unionism and Shareholder Interests." *Industrial and Labor Relations Review* 42: 246-62.

———. 1992. "Unions and Firm Profits." *Industrial Relations* 31: 395-415.

BELMAN, D. 1992. "Unions, the Quality of Labour Relations, and Firm Performance." In L. Mishel and P. Voos, eds., *Unions and Economic Competitiveness.* Armonk, New York: M.E. Sharp, Inc.

BELMAN, D., and J. HEYWOOD. 1990. "Union Membership, Union Organization, and the Dispersion of Wages." *Review of Economics and Statistics* 72: 148-53.

BEMMELS, B. 1987. "How Unions Affect Productivity in Manufacturing Plants." *Industrial and Labor Relations Review* 40: 241-253.

BEYER, J.M., H.M. TRICE, and R.E. HUNT. 1980. "The Impact of Federal Sector Unions on Supervisors' Use of Personnel Policies." *Industrial and Labor Relations Review* 33: 212–31.

BLAU, F.D., and L.M. KAHN. 1983. "Unionism, Seniority, and Turnover." *Industrial Relations* 22: 362-73.

BROWN, C., and J. MEDOFF. 1978. "Trade Unions in the Production Process." *Journal of Political Economy* 86: 355-78.

CLARK, K. 1980. "The Impact of Unionization on Productivity: A Case Study." *Industrial and Labor Relations Review* 33: 451-69.

DAVIES, R.J. 1986. "The Structure of Collective Bargaining in Canada." In W.C. Riddell, ed., *Canadian Labour Relations.* Toronto: University of Toronto Press.

DEFINA, R.H. 1983. "Unions, Relative Wages, and Economic Efficiency." *Journal of Labor Economics* 1: 408-92.

DOIRON, D., and W. RIDDELL. 1994. "The Impact of Unionization on Male-Female Earnings Differentials in Canada." *Journal of Human Resources* 29: 504-34.

DUNCAN, G., and D. LEIGH. 1980. "Wage Determination in the Union and Nonunion Sectors: A Sample Selectivity Approach." *Industrial and Labor Relations Review* 34: 24-34.

DUNCAN, G., and F. STAFFORD. 1980. "Do Union Members Receive Compensating Wages Differentials?" *American Economic Review* 70: 335-71.

FLAHERTY, S. 1987. "Strike Activity, Worker Militancy, and Productivity Change in Manufacturing: 1961-1981." *Industrial and Labor Relations Review* 40: 585-600.

FREEMAN, R. 1976. "Individual Mobility and Union Voice in the Labor Market." *American Economic Review Proceedings* 66: 361-68.

———. 1980a. "Unionism and the Dispersion of Wages." *Industrial and Labor Relations Review* 34: 3-23.

———. 1980b. "The Effect of Unionism on Worker Attachment to Firms." *Journal of Labor Research* 1: 29-62.

———. 1981. "The Effect of Unionism on Fringe Benefits." *Industrial and Labor Relations Review* 34: 489-509.

———. "Longitudinal Analysis of the Effects of Trade Unions." *Journal of Labor Economics* 2: 1-26.

———. 1986. "Unionism Comes to the Public Sector." *Journal of Economic Literature* 24: 41-86.

FREEMAN, R., and J. MEDOFF. 1979. "The Two Faces of Unionism." *The Public Interest* 7: 6993.

———. 1984. *What Do Unions Do?* New York: Basic Books.

GOLDSCHMIDT, S.M., and L.E. STUART. 1986. "The Extent and Impact of Educational Policy Bargaining." *Industrial and Labor Relations Review* 39: 350-60.

GRANT, E.K., R. SWIDINSKY, and J. VANDERKAMP. 1987. "Canadian Union-Non-Union Wage Differentials." *Industrial and Labor Relations Review* 41: 93-107.

GUNDERSON, M., and W.C. RIDDELL. 1993. Labour Market Economics: *Theory, Evidence and Policy in Canada,* 3rd edition. Toronto: McGraw-Hill.

HALL, W., and N. CARROLL. 1973. "The Effects of Teachers' Organizations on Salaries and Class Size." *Industrial and Labor Relations Review* 26: 834-41.

HIRSCH, B. 1991. "Union Coverage and Profitability Among US Firms." *Review of Economics and Statistics* 73: 69-77.

HIRSCHMAN, A. 1970. *Exit, Voice and Loyalty.* Cambridge, Mass.: Harvard University Press.

HYCLACK, T. 1980. "Unions and Income Inequality." *Industrial Relations* 19: 212-15.

ICHNIOWSKI, C. 1980. "Economic Effects of the Firefighters' Union." *Industrial and Labor Relations Review* 33: 198-211.

———. 1986. "The Effects of Grievance Activity on Productivity." *Industrial and Labor Relations Review* 40: 75-89.

JAKUBSON, G. 1991. "Estimation and Testing of the Union Wage Effect Using Panel Data." *Review of Economic Studies* 58: 971-91.

KAHN, L. 1978. "The Effect of Unions on the Earnings of Non-Union Workers." *Industrial and Labor Relations Review* 31: 205-216.

———. 1980. "Union Spillover Effects on Unorganized Labor Markets." *Journal of Human Resources* 15: 87-98.

KALACHEK, E., and F. RAINES. 1980. "Trade Unions and Hiring Standards." *Journal of Labor Research* 1: 63-76.

KAUFMAN, R.S., and R.T. KAUFMAN. 1987. "Union Effects on Productivity, Personnel Practices, and Survival in the Automotive Parts Industry." *Journal of Labor Research* 8: 333-50.

KOCHAN, T., H. KATZ, and N. MOWER. 1985. "Worker Participation and American Unions." In T. Kochan, ed., *Challenges and Choices Facing American Unions.* Cambridge: MIT Press.

KUMAR, P., and T. STENGOS. 1985. "Measuring The Union Relative Wage Impact: A Methodological Note." *Canadian Journal of Economics* 18: 182-89.

LAWRENCE C., and R. LAWRENCE. 1985. "Manufacturing Wage Dispersion: An End Game Interpretation." *Brookings Papers on Economic Activity* 1: 47-106.

LEE, LUNG-FEI. 1978. "Unionism and Wage Rates: A Simultaneous Equations Model with Qualitative and Limited Dependent Variables." *International Economic Review* 19: 415-34.

LEIGH, D. 1979. "Unions and Nonwage Racial Discrimination." *Industrial and Labor Relations Review* 32: 439-50.

LEWIN, D., R. HORTON, and J. KUHN. 1979. *Collective Bargaining and Manpower Utilization in Big City Governments.* New York: Universe Books.

LEWIS, H.G. 1963. *Unionism and Relative Wages in the United States.* Chicago: University of Chicago Press.

———. 1983. "Union Relative Wage Effects: A Survey of Macro Estimates." *Journal of Labor Economics* 1: 1-27.

———. 1986a. *Union Relative Wage Effects: A Survey.* Chicago: University of Chicago Press.

———. 1986b. "Union Relative Wage Effects." In O. Ashenfelter and R. Layard, eds., *Handbook of Labor Economics.* Vol. 1. New York: Elsevier Science Publishers.

MAKI, D.R., 1983. "Trade Unions and Productivity: Conventional Estimates." *Relations industrielles/Industrial Relations* 38: 211-25.

MAKI, D., and L. MEREDITH. 1986. "The Effect of Unions on Profitability: Canadian Evidence." *Relations industrielles/ Industrial Relations* 41: 54-68.

MELLOW, W. 1981. "Unionism and Wages: A Longitudinal Analysis." *Review of Economics and Statistics* 63: 43-52.

MENG, R. 1990. "Union Effects on Wage Dispersion in Canadian Industry." *Economic Letters* 32: 399-403.

MINCER, J. 1983. "Union Effects: Wages, Turnover and Job Training." In J.D. Reid, Jr., ed., *New Approaches to Labor Unions.* Greenwich, CT: JAI Press.

MITCHELL, D. 1983. "Unions and Wages in the Public Sector: A Review of Recent Evidence." *Journal of Collective Negotiations in the Public Sector* 12: 337-53.

MITCHELL, M., and J. STONE 1992. "Union Effects on Productivity: Evidence From Western US Sawmills." *Industrial and Labor Relations Review* 46: 135-145.

MOORE, W., and J. RAISIAN. 1983. "The Level and Growth of Union/Non-Union Relative Wage Effects, 1967-1977." *Journal of Labor Research* 4: 65-80.

QUAN, N. 1984. "Unionism and the Size Distribution of Earnings." *Industrial Relations* 24: 270-77.

READ, L. 1982. "Canada Post: A Case Study in the Correlation of Collective Will and Productivity." In D.J. Daly, ed., *Research on Productivity of Relevance to Canada.* Ottawa: Social Science Federation of Canada.

REES, A. 1963. "The Effect of Unions on Resource Allocation." *Journal of Law and Economics* 6: 69-78.

RIDDELL, W. 1993. "Unionization in Canada and the United States: A Tale of Two Countries." In D. Card and R. Freeman, eds., *US and Canadian Labour Markets.* Chicago: University of Chicago Press.

ROBINSON, C. 1989. "The Joint Determination of Union Status and Union Wage Effects: Some Tests of Alternative Models." *Journal of Political Economy* 97: 639-67.

ROBINSON, C., and N. TOMES. 1984. "Union Wage Differentials in the Public and Private Sectors: A Simultaneous Equations Specification." *Journal of Labor Economics* 2: 106-27.

SIMPSON, W. 1985. "The Impact of Unions on the Structure of Canadian Wages: An Empirical Study with Micro Data." *Canadian Journal of Economics* 18: 164-81.

SLICHTER, S., J. HEALY, and R. LIVERNASH. 1960. *The Impact of Collective Bargaining on Management.* Washington: Brookings Institution.

SWIDINSKY, R. 1992. "Unionism and the Job Attachment of Canadian Workers." *Relations industrielles/Industrial Relations* 47: 729-751.

SWIDINSKY, R., and M. KUPFERSCHMIDT. 1991. "Longitudinal Estimates of the Union Effects on Wages, Wage Dispersion and Pension Fringe Benefits." *Relations industrielles/Industrial Relations* 46: 819-838.

TARAS, D. 1994. "Impact of Industrial Relations Strategies on Selected Human Resources Practices in a Partially Unionized Industry: The Canadian Petroleum Sector." Ph.D. dissertation, Faculty of Management, University of Calgary.

VOOS, P., and L. MISHEL. 1986. "The Union Impact on Profits: Evidence from Industry Price-Cost Margin Data." *Journal of Labor Economics* 4: 105-33.

WOODBURY, S. 1985. "The Scope of Bargaining Outcomes in Public Schools." *Industrial and Labor Relations Review* 38: 195-210.

CHAPTER 13

THE COLLECTIVE AGREEMENT

ANTHONY GILES AND
AKIVAH STARKMAN *

THIS CHAPTER EXAMINES THE MAJOR TYPES OF PROVISIONS FOUND IN collective agreements in Canada. These provisions are discussed under four broad headings: the control of conflict and the union-management relationship; the wage-effort bargain; the control of jobs; and the control of work behaviour and the work environment. The chapter also discusses those economic developments in the 1980s and 1990s which have had a major impact on the contents of collective agreements.

* The authors acknowledge material in this chapter that appeared in the previous edition of the textbook by Anderson, Gunderson, and Ponak (1989).

  Unless otherwise noted, the statistics cited in the chapter were provided by the Bureau of Labour Information, Human Resources Development Canada. These statistics cover all bargaining units in Canada with 500 or more employees.

The mass media usually focuses attention on the most dramatic activities of unions and employers—midnight negotiations, nation-wide strikes, picket line incidents, and the like. Less well understood is the tangible result of all the sound and fury that accompanies negotiations—the collective agreement that regulates the daily relationships between workers, unions, and employers. For unionized workers, "the agreement" (or "the contract") is an important factor shaping their work lives; stewards, elected union officers, and paid union officials spend much of their time ensuring that management lives up to its side of the agreement; supervisors and human resource managers closely monitor the application of the agreement; and labour arbitrators settle grievances over the interpretation of provisions in the agreement. In short, for those involved in industrial relations on a day-to-day basis, the collective agreement is a matter of vital concern.

THE DEVELOPMENT AND FUNCTIONS OF THE COLLECTIVE AGREEMENT

In 1901, when Local 713 of the Carpenters' Union reached an agreement with contractors in Niagara Falls, the contract contained only eight brief clauses:

1. The rate of wages for journeymen carpenters and joiners shall be 25 cents per hour.
2. The hours of work shall be nine (9) hours per day.
3. The rate of pay for legal holidays and overtime shall be time and one-half, except for mill hands.
4. No union man shall take any kind of lump work or sub-contract from a carpenter-contractor.
5. If a contractor applies to the union for men and the union cannot supply them, the contractor can hire any men he likes at any rate of wages, but these men must be discharged before any union man is laid off.
6. Planing mill proprietors shall be bound by these promises only as far as they apply to carpenters and bench hands.
7. Pay days shall be on Saturdays, and the contractor shall pay the men their wages on the job where they are working.
8. The agreement shall go into effect on May 1, 1901, and shall continue for one year. (Curtis 1966, 3)

Although the issues covered by this agreement still figure prominently in union-management relations, most modern collective agreements run much longer, are more complex, and cover a wider range of issues than did the typical agreement of the era before the Second World War. In fact, collective agreements in this country (and the United States) are also longer, more detailed, and broader than are contracts in most other advanced capitalist societies. These distinctive characteristics of Canadian collective agreements emerged as one component of a broader restructuring of industrial relations in the 1940s (MacDowell 1978; Drache and Glasbeek 1992).

The early craft unions, like the Carpenters', were often able to defend their interests by exercising control over the supply of skilled labour and instituting a variety of work rules. However, the unskilled and semiskilled workers who flocked into industrial unions in the 1930s and 1940s were in a different position:

> Unlike the craft union, the industrial union has a heterogeneous membership that has had no uniform work-experience to establish customary rules and conditions of employment.... These members have no customary entitlement to a particular job, or to a particular kind of work, or to promotion, or transfer, or retention in case of work-shortage. Consequently, they look to a union to define their rights, to make the rules that will govern their employment, and to enforce the arrangements made.
>
> Furthermore, in response to the demands of their members for greater security in every sense of the word, industrial unions have extended bargaining into areas which did not concern the crafts, [such as] hospitalization benefits, medical care, accident benefits, lay-off allowances, pensions, etc. (Curtis 1966, 5-6)

The rise of industrial unionism, then, prompted workers to concentrate on obtaining their goals through negotiations with individual employers. In addition, the political weakness of the Canadian labour movement led unions to look to the negotiating process as a means of advancing members' interests. They could not act like unions in many European countries, where government legislation played a more important role in regulating the employment relationship.

Even more important than the nature of unionism, however, were the strategies and policies pursued by employers and the government, particularly those adopted in response to the industrial and political unrest of the 1940s. Paradoxically, the fierce resistance of Canadian employers to their employees' attempts to unionize was (and, to a degree, still is) a major cause of the growth of detailed collective agreements. Once required to negotiate with their employees through unions, most employers tend to seek ways to restrict the workplace activities of unions, to reduce the number of issues subject to union influence, and to adhere to collective agreements in a narrowly legalistic manner (Adams 1977, 41).

This strategy of deflecting the impact of unions has been abetted by state policy and by the way collective agreements have come to be interpreted by arbitrators. Since 1944, most jurisdictions in Canada have required collective agreements to be binding for periods of no less than one year, and have banned work stoppages during the life of the agreement. Thus, unlike countries where agreements can be renegotiated whenever one side or the other feels some change is warranted or where problems that arise during the life of the agreement can be negotiated, Canadian union negotiators must strive for collective agreements that are comprehensive and detailed. Moreover, because most arbitrators hold that management retains authority over any matter not explicitly mentioned in the collective agreement, unions are compelled to channel their concerns into the negotiating process, rather than deal with management more informally. Last, because grievance arbitration (the approved method of resolving disputes during the term of the agreement) is so legalistic, contract language has to be drafted with great care.

Collective agreements have also been influenced by legal developments in another way. General labour statutes, human rights legislation, occupational health and safety acts, and employment standards laws all set out a number of requirements that must be adhered to in the collective agreement. For example, it is illegal to discriminate against employees on a number of specific grounds including age, sex, religion, and disability; in most provinces joint safety committees must be established; employees must be provided a day off with pay on certain statutory holidays; and strikes and lockouts are illegal during the term of the collective agreement.

For the most part, the parties have attempted to incorporate such legal requirements explicitly into the collective agreement, even though the absence of these provisions would not negate their effect (i.e., even if a contract had no antidiscrimination clause, it would still be illegal to discriminate). There are several reasons for including these types of legal requirements in the collective agreement. First, the contract provisions are a good way of educating those bound by the contract, employees and management alike, about some of their legal obligations. Second, through negotiation the parties are able to specify the manner in which the legal requirements might be made to best fit their specific needs (e.g., the composition of a safety committee or what happens in situations in which some employees must work on a statutory holiday). Third, by including certain legal requirements in the collective agreement, the subject matter becomes subject to the grievance procedure, which might be advantageous in terms of time and cost compared to a human rights tribunal or the courts.

For all these reasons, the collective agreement plays a central role in Canadian labour-management relations. Still, it must not be forgotten that labour-management relations in the workplace are not fully regulated by formal agreements. In nonunionized settings, of course, employment relations are governed by the individual contract of employment and employment legislation. Although some nonunionized organizations follow employment policies that are closely modelled on collective agreements, often in an attempt to dissuade their employees from unionizing, individual employees in such workplaces are usually powerless to win improvements in their terms and conditions of employment in the face of employer recalcitrance. Indeed, at their heart, collective agreements reflect a transformation of this relationship into one of collective regulation of employment.

Even in unionized workplaces, however, much of the interaction between workers, their stewards, and managers takes place without any reference to the existing collective agreement. In some cases, it involves deliberate evasion of the terms of the contract. In others, collectively negotiated rules or procedures mean little to the actual balance of influence between a particular work group and its supervisor. Yet, even where issues, problems, and disputes are not closely connected to the terms and conditions specified in the collective agreement, the agreement is part of the background of the daily struggles and interactions in the workplace, and thus it shapes the relationships and perceptions of the participants.

As we saw above, lengthy and complex collective agreements emerged as a key element in the post-Second World War system of Canadian industrial relations. Since the early 1980s, however, this system has been subjected to considerable pressures: intensified global competition fuelled by declining barriers to the flow of goods, service and investment across national borders; rapid technological innovations, notably in the fields of communications, computer systems, and robotics; major changes in the structure of labour markets, including a relative shift away from manufacturing and towards services; a proliferation of new, more precarious forms of employment; an aging workforce; a steady increase in female labour force participation; a persistently high level of unemployment; increasing attention to individual rights as reflected in the Charter of Rights and Freedoms and human rights legislation in general; public sector financial difficulties; and a more conservative political climate (Chaykowski and Verma 1992; Drache and Glasbeek 1992).

The resulting pressures have heightened tensions in industrial relations and have prompted employers, governments, and unions to develop new strategies. High on the agenda of employers are the issues of labour costs, labour force and organizational flexibility, and productivity. These concerns have translated into demands by employers for a variety of fundamental changes in collective agreements. In some cases, employers have demanded concessions from workers and unions, particularly with respect to wages and benefit packages. More often, significant changes in existing practices have been proposed, ranging from new forms of work organization to restructuring of remuneration and job classification systems.

To a certain extent, the labour movement has been put on the defensive by these developments. Thus, a major preoccupation of unions has been the preservation of past gains and the strengthening of collective agreement provisions with respect to job security. In addition, however, unions have brought new issues to the bargaining table. Some of these concerns constitute a direct response to employer strategies, as in the case of union demands for greater involvement in new forms of work organization. In other cases, unions have sought to introduce collective agreement provisions which respond to the changing composition of their actual and potential membership and increased social concern with the rights of particular groups.

Although some of these issues and tensions have been taken up outside the area of collective bargaining, many have been the focus of negotiations between unions and employers. The extent to which collective agreements in Canada are changing to reflect these new approaches will therefore be a central theme of the examination of the contents of collective agreements in this chapter.

THE COLLECTIVE AGREEMENT: AN OVERVIEW

Anyone who leafs through a collective agreement for the first time finds a bewildering array of clauses, subclauses, appendices, schedules, letters of intent, and other sections, many with mysteriously phrased names. Collective agreements are sometimes so complex and legalistic that workers and supervisors barely understand their contents and need to rely on experienced shop stewards, union business agents, and specialized managers. (In fact, one test of the effectiveness of a collective agreement in regulating relationships at the workplace is how familiar workers and supervisors are with its contents. If the union has a strong presence, it is not unusual to see workers keeping a copy of the agreement close at hand and referring to it extensively during arguments with management.) For the student of collective agreements, matters are made worse by the fact that the thousands of collective agreements in effect in Canada at any one time differ from each other quite substantially. After all, each agreement is the product of a unique negotiating relationship, and each is amended many times as the two sides renegotiate the terms and conditions of employment.

Nevertheless, most collective agreements have some basic similarities, as well as a common structure that underlies their many complexities and outward variations. Like most legal contracts, collective agreements are divided into articles (also called sections or clauses), which are usually further divided into subclauses. Almost all collective agreements begin with an article explaining the purpose of the agreement. If the agreement is complex, a list of definitions may also appear near the beginning of the document. Most agreements then include a number of clauses that define and regulate the relationship between the union and the employer—clauses setting out the definition of the bargaining unit, outlining management rights and union security, establishing a grievance arbitration procedure, and so on. The second major group of articles that appears in the collective agreement is often those specifying hours of work and details of pay. Here one finds articles that define the normal length of the work day, rules about overtime, rights to time off with and without pay, wage schedules covering different classifications of employees, various wage premiums (such as shift bonuses) and other matters that together constitute what is called the wage-effort bargain.

A third group of articles in collective agreements contain clauses on how the organization's internal labour market and production system will be operated. For example, agreements often include rules governing how promotions are to be made, how technological changes are to be instituted, how layoffs are to be handled, and so on. Although articles dealing with these matters are not necessarily grouped together in the agreement, they have in common the function of controlling individual and group rights with respect to the allocation of tasks and job opportunities.

The fourth group of clauses typically found in agreements (again not necessarily all in one place) is those that set out conditions with respect to the work environment (such as safety rules) and work behaviour (for example, rules on discipline).

Usually the collective agreement concludes with a clause that specifies the duration of the agreement, followed by the signatures of the employer and union representatives. Many agreements also include appendices containing details of particular arrangements considered too lengthy or complex to include in the body of the agreement (such as wage schedules). Lastly, attached to some agreements are letters of understanding, memoranda of agreement, or other supplementary documents; depending on the wording, these may be considered part of the agreement, or they may be unenforceable promises made by one side or the other.

The remainder of this chapter discusses the four main groups of articles just outlined. Because it would be impossible to discuss every conceivable type of clause in each of the four categories, the emphasis is on types of clauses that are common, generally significant, or of special contemporary relevance.

THE UNION-MANAGEMENT RELATIONSHIP AND THE CONTROL OF CONFLICT

Inherent in the very idea of a collective agreement is the existence of a relationship between an employer and a group of employees acting collectively through a union. Thus, an agreement does more than set the price of labour; it establishes a relationship between the employer and union, a process that normally entails conflict over the division of authority and definition of rights and responsibilities. In practice, the contours of the union-management relationship are defined by three central features of collective agreements: the extent to which joint decision making replaces unilateral managerial authority; the status and role accorded to the union; and the manner in which disagreements and disputes that arise during the life of the agreement are handled.

Management Rights

The phrase "management rights" refers to management's prerogative to make decisions and to take actions to manage the organization. A typical example of a management rights clause in a collective agreement is:

> The Union acknowledges that it is the exclusive function of the Company, subject always to the provisions of the Agreement, to hire, promote, demote, transfer, suspend, discharge or otherwise discipline. . . . The Union also acknowledges that the Company has certain other rights prominent among which, but by no means wholly inclusive, are the rights to decide the number and location of its plants, their machines and tool equipment, the products to be manufactured, the method of manufacture, the schedules of products and the general control and direction of the business of the Company. It is further recognized by the Union that the Company may from time to time apply rules and regulations to be observed by the employees so as to assure proper direction and discipline and safety for the working forces.

Management rights clauses vary in their specificity, but almost all collective agreements do contain such clauses.

Even with some management rights spelled out in the agreement, there is the question of who has authority over those issues not mentioned in the contract. One way in which management attempts to settle this issue is by insisting on the inclusion of a clause designed to restrict union involvement to those subjects explicitly defined in the agreement (Young 1975, 173), such as the following:

> All the functions, rights, powers and authority which the Employer has not abridged, delegated or modified by the Agreement are recognized by the Union as being retained by the Employer.

If such a clause is not included in the agreement, management can rely on another tool to limit the involvement of workers and their unions—the residual rights theory. This theory is based on the assertion that all the rights and privileges that employers exercised before unionization must be considered to be reserved to them afterwards except for those specifically limited by the collective agreement.

The implications of the residual rights doctrine are exemplified in the case of the Russelsteel company, which employed three truck drivers to operate vehicles leased from another firm. When Russelsteel entered into a contract with a different firm for the supply of both drivers and trucks, the truck drivers were offered a choice of joining the new contractor or staying with Russelsteel as warehouse labourers at a reduced rate of pay. The truck drivers and their union argued that the recognition clause in the agreement was an implicit limitation on management's ability to subcontract. The arbitrator rejected this argument, saying that because the collective agreement did not explicitly prevent subcontracting, management enjoyed the unfettered right to contract out (*Re Russelsteel Ltd.* v *United Steelworkers* (1966), 17 LAC 253 (Arthurs)). The case was not an isolated one: "There is almost total consensus in the arbitration process in Ontario," writes Weiler, "that unions must negotiate limitations on such functions [shift scheduling, subcontracting, relocation, changes in work arrangements, and so on] before arbitration boards can enforce them" (*Re International Brotherhood of Boilermakers etc and Howden & Parsons (Canada) Ltd* (1970) 21 LAC 177 (Weiler)).

This view has been challenged not only by labour leaders but also by some industrial relations scholars and arbitrators, for both philosophical and practical reasons. For instance, in the 1958 Falconbridge case, Bora Laskin, later Chief Justice of the Supreme Court of Canada, argued that the advent of collective bargaining fundamentally altered the relationship between labour and management by putting them on an equal footing. According to this view, a contract is the only basis of their understanding with each other, a basis from which neither party can be permitted to depart or renege. Therefore, any "future concerns" not dealt with in the collective agreement should be dealt with in the spirit of the agreement itself and with a view to the climate of collective bargaining. This climate is to be ascertained by examining "elements of policy, statutory and otherwise, of which the collective agreement is an expression" (*Re Sudbury Mine, Mill and Smelter Workers, Local 598, and Falconbridge Nickel Mines Ltd* (1958) 8 LAC 276 (Laskin)). Thus, Laskin rejected the notion that previously acquired management powers could be validly imported into the contractual situation and thenceforth dignified as residual rights.

Other critics of the residual rights doctrine rely implicitly on the "implied obligations doctrine" to support their position. For example, on the philosophical side, it is argued that:

> Labor always had many inherent rights such as the right to strike . . . the right to organize . . . the right to a fair share of the Company's income . . . the right to safe, healthful working conditions. . . . Failure of management to recognize such rights does not indicate they did not exist. . . . Both parties have rights to stability and protection from unbargained changes in wages, hours, and working conditions. . . . The right to direct, where it involves wages, hours, or working conditions is a procedural right. It does not imply some right over and above labor's right. (Goldberg 1985, 312-13)

From a practical point of view, Killingsworth (1969) argues that management's right to assert discretion over any subject is not simply a question of legal niceties but is instead a function of its ability to exercise power over its employees. To argue the reserved rights doctrine as a principle without considering the nature of the power relationship is of little value.

The criticisms of the residual rights theory have not prevailed, however, and managerial authority over issues and decisions not specifically governed by the collective agreement remains largely unimpaired. The major exceptions are cases where it can be shown that a management decision was motivated by antiunion considerations (such as plant relocations designed to allow the company to operate without a union) or if it can be shown that management acted in bad faith or in a discriminatory manner (Fisher and Sherwood 1984). There are, of course, numerous legislative limitations on the employment policies followed by employers, ranging from minimum employment standards to federal and provincial charters of rights (Hébert 1992). By and large, however, the reluctance of arbitrators to limit management rights has severely restricted the role that workers and their unions can play in the functioning of the organization. Moreover, by granting authority to management over any issue not explicitly included in the collective agreement, supporters of the residual rights doctrine have created a situation in which unions are considered trespassers on managerial prerogatives, instead of having an equal claim to a role in the management of the organization.

Union Rights and Security

When a union becomes the certified bargaining agent for a group of employees, it is said to have been "recognized" by the employer. Most collective agreements contain a clause (often simply repeating the certifying agency's definition of the bargaining unit) making this recognition explicit and defining which employees are members of the unit. Certain categories of employees are commonly excluded from the bargaining unit. Such exclusions sometimes reflect the pattern of authority in the organization; frequently excluded, for example, are supervisors, security personnel, and employees who have access to confidential information regarding labour relations. In other cases, however, exclusions are rooted in the structure of the organization's internal labour market. The most significant case is the exclusion of part-time, casual, and temporary employees from the bargaining unit. From the employers' point of view, excluding such employees from the coverage of the collective agreement is often advantageous because it is thereby possible to pay them at rates less than unionized full-time workers, to avoid providing them with employee benefits, and more generally to treat them as a flexible reserve labour force with few job rights (Commission of Inquiry into Part-Time Work 1983). In the past, unions often tacitly or overtly approved of this strategy, not least because it provided full-time, male workers with greater employment security and higher wages, leaving the predominantly female and young peripheral labour force as an inexpensive cushion against risk.

The dramatic growth in recent years of part-time and other "atypical" forms of employment, as well as the expansion of the services sector in which such jobs are concentrated, has led unions to pay more attention to improving collective agreement provisions for such workers. Some success has been registered recently, as can be seen by a comparison of the number of collective agreements in 1986 and 1994 which contain provisions regarding part-time workers (Figure 13.1). Of the various part-time issues that might be dealt with in a collective agreement, seniority appears to be a central preoccupation; other important issues include various types of leave provisions. Unions have clearly made little progress, however, in having a maximum limit put on the number of part-time workers relative to full-time workers or in negotiating pension coverage and severance pay provisions for part-time workers.

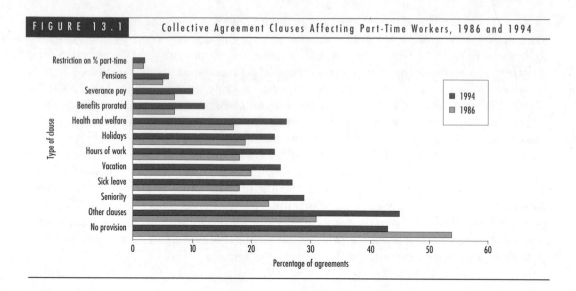

FIGURE 13.1   Collective Agreement Clauses Affecting Part-Time Workers, 1986 and 1994

In any event, the struggle for real recognition and stability does not end with the recognition clause. First, a union is by nature external to the employing organization. Although the members are employees of the organization, the union itself has a separate existence and is only the legal representative of the unionized employees. Hence, a union enjoys no automatic status as a part of the organization. Second, many Canadian employers are hostile to unionism, which means that union members and officials must work continuously to ensure that management respects the role of the union. Third, like any other organization, unions need a degree of institutional stability. Fourth, under existing Canadian labour laws, the collective agreement covers all members of the bargaining unit, not just union members.

For these reasons, unionized workers normally attempt to negotiate a variety of provisions that will allow the union to make its presence felt in the workplace and give it a degree of security. For example, a collective agreement may provide unions with certain types of facilities, such as access to bulletin boards or office space. A minority of collective agreements provide union officials with "super seniority," which places them ahead of their actual position on the seniority list, thus offering protection from possible company harassment and providing continuity in the case of layoffs (seniority is discussed more fully in a later section). The right of the union to appoint shop stewards (whose duties include helping workers prepare and present grievances) also stems from the collective agreement. Sometimes the agreement specifies how many stewards are to be appointed, and it usually spells out the circumstances under which they and other union officials may leave their work stations to attend to union business. An example of such a provision is:

The privileges of stewards to leave their work with no loss of pay to attend to union business is granted on the following conditions:

1. Such business must be between union and management.
2. The time will be devoted to the prompt handling of necessary union business.

3. The steward shall obtain the permission of the foreman before leaving his work.
4. Time away from work will be reported.
5. The company reserves the right to limit such time if it deems the time taken to be excessive. (Sanderson 1979, 89)

The most controversial aspect of union attempts to establish a degree of stability centres on the interrelated issues of union security and the payment of union dues. A variety of types of union security clauses are found in collective agreements. The "closed shop" is a system under which an employer agrees to hire and retain only those workers who are members of the union. The closed shop is usually associated with the existence of "hiring halls," which are arrangements under which unions supply the number of workers needed by an employer. The closed shop is most common in industries such as construction where workers possess needed skills but the work is often temporary or seasonal in nature (Hébert 1992). A "union shop" clause requires that all employees join the union within a specified period of time after having been hired. A "modified union shop" means that at the time the collective agreement is signed (or, in some cases, the initial certification), the current employees are not obliged to join the union, but all employees hired subsequently must join. "Maintenance of membership" clauses require that employees who have joined the union (and those who join in the future) must remain in the union. "Rand formula" clauses do not impose any requirements regarding union membership, but they do require all members of the bargaining unit, whether or not they are members of the union, to pay union dues. Some Rand formula clauses exempt certain workers from this requirement (for example, if they have religious objections to paying union dues) or permit nonunion members to stipulate that their dues be donated to a charity instead of going to the union. If unions are unable to convince their employer to agree to any form of union security, this is known as the "open shop."

The vast majority of major collective agreements in Canada provide for some degree of union security (Figure 13.2). About half of these agreements, because they contain only a Rand formula or no union security provision at all, do not impose any union membership requirements on employees. This proportion has remained virtually

---

FIGURE 13.2   Union Security Provisions in Collective Agreements, 1994 (% of agreements)

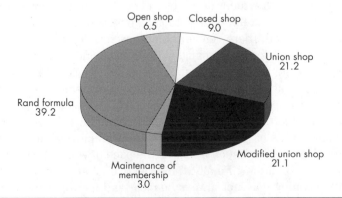

unchanged since 1986. Of the half which do impose some form of requirement, the union shop and the modified union shop continue to predominate. Agreements stipulating a closed shop have grown slightly since the mid-1980s but still represent fewer than 10 per cent of all agreements. Maintenance of membership clauses are found in a very small—and shrinking—number of agreements.

Related to the question of union security is the collection of union dues. "Checkoff" refers to the practice whereby employers agree to deduct union dues from the employees' pay cheques on behalf of the union. The checkoff of union dues is partly a form of security and partly a bookkeeping device to provide the union with a regular cash flow and to protect it against loss of dues (and members) through inadvertence or recalcitrance. The vast majority of collective agreements require some form of checkoff, but here too there are several different types of clauses. Occasionally checkoff is voluntary, but usually it is mandatory either for all union members or, where there is a Rand formula, for all employees in the bargaining unit. A typical Rand formula clause is:

> In the case of an employee covered by this agreement who is not a member of the union and who is not required to become a member of the union, the employer agrees to deduct and forward to the union, monthly, the regular weekly union dues in accordance with the Rand Formula.

The predominance of the Rand formula is related to the wider controversies that swirl around the issues of union security and dues checkoff. On one side, many employers claim that union security clauses infringe upon the rights and freedom of individual workers who may not wish to join a union. On the other side, unions argue that the absence of such clauses can easily undermine their effectiveness by allowing nonunion workers to remain on the job while union workers are out on strike. They also contend that such clauses are needed to discourage "free riders"—those workers who, as members of the bargaining unit, are legally entitled to the benefits and protections negotiated by the union, but who might be tempted to avoid their share of the costs and sacrifices by not joining the union. The Rand formula was devised as a compromise between these two positions; it prevents nonunion workers from taking a free ride but does not entail compulsory unionism.

Workplace Conflict and the Contract

The signing of a collective agreement does not end conflict between workers and management. Although collective agreements establish negotiated terms and conditions of employment for a set period, there remain numerous sources of tension that may spark disputes at any time. Unanticipated changes in market conditions may lead to calls for adjustments, such as wage increases if inflation suddenly surges, or wage reductions or other concessions if profitability drops. Similarly, issues not covered by the agreement may suddenly emerge; an example is technological change in the workplace that threatens jobs or disturbs established patterns of pay. More generally, the day-to-day management of work is a permanent source of potential conflict, since employees and their managers do not necessarily see eye-to-eye on such issues as the pace of work, the style of supervision, and adequate working conditions. Finally, the collective agreement itself may give rise to disputes, since its meaning may not always be clear and its application in particular circumstances may be disputed. For all these reasons, collective agreements usually contain provisions for dealing with conflict.

No-Strike Clause.   One of the chief mechanisms for regulating conflict is the no-strike clause. A typical example is:

> The union agrees that, during the life of the agreement there will be no strike, picketing, slowdown or stoppage of work, either complete or partial and the company agrees that there will be no lockout.

That a majority of collective agreements in Canada contain such a clause is hardly surprising in view of the fact that, with some exceptions, Canadian labour law prohibits the use of strikes or lockouts while the contract is in effect (England 1980). Thus, in theory, collective agreements prevent workers and unions from resorting to the use of industrial conflict to resolve disputes which occur during the life of the agreement (unless they have deliberately provided reopener clauses which permit bargaining on selected issues to occur under specified circumstances).

Theory aside, the legal and contractual prohibitions on the use of work stoppages are not always effective, and illegal strikes during the term of the agreement are not uncommon in Canada (see Chapter 14). However, because arbitrators tend to look askance at such strikes, and have proved willing to assess damages against unions that encourage or condone them, these clauses play an important role in forcing union leaders to restrain their own members, to bring an end to midcontract strikes, or, at least, to remain uninvolved, thus depriving the strikers of legitimacy and organizational support. In addition, employers can use the threat of applying these clauses as leverage to end the strike on terms that are unfavourable to the strikers (Wells 1986). Thus, even if no-strike clauses do not actually prevent conflict from breaking out into the open during the life of an agreement, they play an important role in reducing its incidence and effectiveness.

Grievance Arbitration.   A second conflict-regulation mechanism, found in virtually every collective agreement in Canada, is the grievance arbitration procedure. Grievance arbitration procedures provide a means through which any differences between the parties arising from the application, interpretation, administration, or alleged violation of the collective agreement may be settled. Collective agreements usually require that a grievance be taken first to the immediate supervisor. If the grievance is not resolved there, it may be appealed to one or more higher levels of management. If a settlement still does not occur, collective agreements almost always provide for binding settlement by an outside arbitrator or arbitration board. For our purposes, it is important to stress that such procedures became required in law at the same time that industrial conflict during the collective agreement was banned; indeed, the requirement that grievance arbitration procedures be included in collective agreements was an attempt to provide workers and unions with a method of dealing with problems even while they were legally prevented from exerting pressure through a strike. Grievance arbitration is not a full substitute, however, since the range of disputes that are technically arbitrable include only those covered by the collective agreement; moreover, the rule that workers must usually "obey now, grieve later" means that management's decisions must be followed when they are issued, while the aggrieved employee can only complain through the sometimes cumbersome and lengthy grievance procedure.

So far we have seen that disputes over issues not dealt with explicitly in the collective agreement are considered to fall within the prerogative of management. As well, if the issue is not dealt with in the collective agreement it cannot be the subject of a grievance taken to arbitration, nor can workers legally resort to strikes over these or any other issues during the term of the agreement. In practice, of course, workers and unions can bring their concerns to the attention of management by using a whole range of informal tactics ranging from noncooperation to sabotage (Edwards 1986). It is also common for stewards and supervisors to reach informal agreements in response to grievances that are not technically arbitrable.

Labour-Management Committees.   Collective agreements do sometimes include a special method of raising and discussing noncontractual issues related to labour-management relations—the labour-management committee. Plant-level or firm-level labour-management committees, comprised of representatives from both labour and management, can serve as a forum to discuss matters of mutual interest. These can include health and safety, alcohol and drug abuse, working conditions, work schedules, training and retraining, technological changes, quality and efficiency, reduction of waste, and any other issue, depending on the particular situation. The growth of labour-management committees in recent years has been significant: in 1986, 38 per cent of major collective agreements (covering about 40 per cent of workers) provided for such a committee; by 1994 the number had risen to 53 per cent of agreements (covering more than 60 per cent of employees). The effectiveness of labour-management committees varies considerably, often reflecting the nature of the relationship between the parties. Decisions or recommendations normally require mutual agreement. Participation on such committees does allow workers and their unions an opportunity to influence management decisions, but in the absence of mutual agreement, management's decisions prevail.

Joint Governance Agreements.   Recent years have seen some experimentation with another mechanism designed to regulate the relationship between labour and management—the "joint governance agreement" (Verma and Cutcher-Gershenfeld 1993). These agreements tend to last for four to six years compared to the usual two or three years of a normal collective agreement. They often contain provisions for mid-term or periodic revisions of wage rates subject to binding arbitration if an agreement is not reached by the parties. Such contracts frequently involve a trade-off whereby employers secure concessions designed to reduce labour costs and increase productivity, in return for which unions gain greater job security and more involvement in organizational decision makings. In some of these agreements, mechanisms are established (like joint committees) that allow what is in effect "continuous bargaining" on issues related to the organization of work (Rondeau 1994). In Quebec (where they are known as "social contract agreements"), some thirty of these agreements, covering approximately 30,000 employees, have been negotiated in recent years. While less common, such contracts can also be found in other provinces (Verma and Cutcher-Gershenfeld 1993).

To a certain extent these agreements can be seen as an attempt to put the union-management relationship on a new, more stable and co-operative footing; however, the fact that they have often been negotiated against the background of threatened layoffs or plant closures raises the question of their long term durability. Indeed, although the trade union movement in Quebec has supported the negotiation of such agreements in specific cases, it bitterly opposed the recent amendment to the Quebec Labour Code that dropped the long-standing limit of three years on the maximum length of collective agreements. Although at first glance the stance taken by the union movement seems contradictory, it was rooted in the logic of bargaining power. When a legal limit on the length of collective agreements exists, unions can insist on receiving significant concessions from the employer in return for agreeing to waive the normal limit. However, in the absence of a legal limit on contract duration, unions cannot extract special concessions in return for agreeing to waive that limit (*Le Devoir*, April 20, 1994).

To summarize, collective agreements can affect the union-management relationship and control conflict in a variety of ways—through the delineation of management rights, through provisions for union rights and security, and through the establishment of mechanisms of conflict resolution and communication. It must be emphasized, however, that collective agreements do not themselves establish the contours of the labour-management relationship; rather, every agreement crystallizes in writing the nature of the collective relationship forged between workers and their employer at a particular point in time.

THE WAGE-EFFORT BARGAIN

The essence of the employment relationship is the exchange of work time for remuneration. Employers agree to pay wages and other benefits, and in return they become entitled to control the work activities of employees during the time for which they have paid. Quite naturally, employers and workers often have different opinions as to what constitutes a "fair wage" or a "fair day's work." Thus, from the exchange of remuneration for work time and effort springs a whole range of potentially conflictual issues that are commonly negotiated and set out in collective agreements. Taken together, the provisions in collective agreements that regulate hours of work, compensation, and incentives constitute what is called the wage-effort bargain.

Hours of Work and Scheduling

Most collective agreements specify the number of daily and weekly hours that workers are normally expected to work, the starting and ending times of shifts, the length of meal breaks, rest breaks, wash-up time, and so on. However, for a variety of reasons, the "normal" workday or week is not always possible: 30 per cent of Canadians do not work a regular, daytime schedule (Statistics Canada 1993). As a result, many collective agreements contain special rules regarding work time. In cases of shift work, for example, there may be a negotiated system of rotating shifts among employees, or shift scheduling may be handled by seniority. In addition, there are often a variety of wage premiums negotiated to cover particular circumstances, such as "call-out" or "reporting" pay (for workers called into work for a short period), "standby pay" (for workers who must remain available during nonworking hours), or for shifts including work on weekends.

Collective agreements regulate not only daily and weekly hours, but also the amount of working time over the year. Most agreements, for example, include clauses specifying the length of annual vacations. Usually, the length of vacations is tied to length of service, so that the longer employees remain with an employer, the longer their vacation periods become. The paid holidays that are provided for in collective agreements (usually between ten and thirteen per year) are less often tied to length of service; however, most agreements deny employees the right to paid holidays if they do not work the day before and/or the day after the holiday. In addition to vacations and paid holidays, collective agreements may also specify paid or unpaid leaves of absence of various kinds. Among the most common, of course, is sick leave. In recent years, unions have attempted to expand educational leave provisions, primarily to enable their members to attend job-related or union-sponsored educational programs.

As well, many unions have recently put special emphasis on improving parental leave. Employment standards legislation usually guarantees some minimal maternity leave, and most jurisdictions now provide for leave for fathers and for parents who adopt children. The growing number of women in the labour movement has encouraged unions to seek improvements on these legal minima through collective agreement provisions for expanded monetary benefits, longer leave periods, and the right to accumulate seniority while on maternity leave. Currently, more than half of employees covered by major collective agreements are entitled to some paid maternity leave greater than that provided through unemployment insurance (compared to fewer than 40 per cent in 1986), and nearly 60 per cent have full or partial protection of seniority during maternity leave (compared to fewer than half in 1986). However, coverage has been less than complete, and many workers still have no access to extended parental leave or enhanced income support.

The growing presence of women in the paid labour force has increased the urgency of providing family-related provisions in collective agreements. From 1976 to 1991, the rate of participation in the paid labour force of women with children under the age of six rose from 41 to 68 per cent (Statistics Canada 1992; 1990). As a result, nearly 60 per cent of Canadian families in 1991 were either single-parent families, or had both spouses/partners in the labour force (Statistics Canada 1993). This important dynamic in the labour market has had implications for approaches to work time and work scheduling, as families struggle to balance the demands of work and home. A number of collective agreements now contain flexible work time provisions that offer employees some leeway in choosing their start and finish times, or compressed work weeks (longer hours over fewer days per week). In addition, provisions which permit leaves for the care of a family member, for bereavement, or for responsibilities such as parent-teacher interviews or professional appointments, are intended to build a more "family-responsive" workplace. Here too, however, extension of coverage has not kept pace with social changes; in 1994, three-quarters of collective agreements did not provide for flextime, while nearly two-thirds contained no provision for leave to deal with an illness in the family.

A more traditional contentious issue involves overtime. Employers generally prefer to retain flexibility in determining the hours of work, but employees and their unions prefer that overtime hours be worked on a voluntary basis and that such hours be distributed equally. Most agreements do not, however, give workers the right to refuse overtime, and fewer than half provide for equal sharing of overtime hours. Those agreements that do provide for equal sharing use a wide number of systems, since overtime can be shared on a plant-wide basis, a department-wide basis, within an occupational bracket, by seniority, or some combination of these.

Recently, the issue of working time has gained prominence in the sphere of public policy as well as at the level of collective bargaining. Concern has been expressed that the distribution of working time in Canada has become skewed, so that while the level of unemployment is relatively high, those who are employed are working longer or overtime hours. Although the "standard" weekly hours of work as defined in collective agreements have declined in recent years (Table 13.1), the actual number of hours that some employees work has in fact risen. As a result, hours of work and income levels are becoming increasingly polarized; in 1993, 21.6 per cent of workers usually worked more than 40 hours per week, compared to 18.8 per cent in 1981 (Statistics Canada, unpublished data). It is argued that a redistribution of the available hours of work could act as a mechanism for reducing or curtailing unemployment. Along these lines, the Canadian Labour Congress at its 1994 convention called for a government ban on mandatory overtime and urged unions to seek a reduced work week. As well, in 1994 the federal government set up an Advisory Group on Working Time and the Distribution of Work, in part to examine the feasibility of reductions in working time as one way to help job creation.

Within the collective agreement, a reduction or redistribution of working time could be achieved in several ways: shortening the "standard" work week; restricting the use of overtime; increasing overtime premiums; increasing the availability of leave provisions; or permitting early or phased-in retirement. Several recent collective agreements have introduced provisions aimed at redistributing working time in order to create or preserve jobs. In 1993, Chrysler Canada and the Canadian Auto Workers reduced the standard daily hours of work at the Windsor minivan plant from 8 to 7.5, with no loss of pay. Their collective agreement also implemented a third shift, increased and restructured paid time off, and introduced a phased-in retirement program. The combined effect of these provisions was expected to create an additional 800 new jobs at the plant. Also in 1993, Bell Canada and the Communications, Energy and Paperworkers Union agreed to a two-hour per week reduction in working hours, with a corresponding reduction in pay, in order to avert a threatened layoff. Provisions designed to share work on a voluntary basis have started to become more common; in 1994, 10 per cent of major collective agreements contained clauses permitting two or more employees to share an existing job, up from fewer than 4 per cent in 1986.

TABLE 13.1   Standard Weekly Working Hours under Major Collective Agreements, 1986 and 1994 (% of agreements)

Hours	1986	1994
Less than 35	1.6	2.4
35 to 39	33.2	34.0
40	46.5	43.3
More than 40	4.1	3.0
No provision	14.6	17.3
Totals	100.1%[a]	100.0%
Number of agreements	939	1,053

[a] Does not add to 100 per cent because of rounding.

Compensation

Wages are at the heart of the collective agreement. For most employees the pay cheque is the chief determinant of their living standard and one of the main reasons they are in paid employment. For the employer, wage costs have a significant impact on financial performance. Thus, an important aspect of the collective agreement is the wage level or scale; but just as important is the way the agreement affects the wage structure, the wage system, and wage premiums.

Wage Structures. Sometimes all of the employees covered by a collective agreement receive the same wage or salary, but it is more usual for the agreement to set out a number of wage rates. The pattern of differentials between these rates is known as the wage structure. Two types of such hierarchies are common. First, different jobs may be paid differently. For example, in a pattern common to collective agreements in the steel industry, jobs in the plant are grouped among twenty-eight classes with a differential of 19.7 cents per hour between each. Thus, a general labourer (Job Class 2) is entitled to a $0.197 per hour premium over the base rate; a millwright in Class 16 receives an hourly premium of $2.955; an industrial mechanic (Class 21) benefits from a premium of $3.940; and so on.

The second common way of defining wage structures is through the criterion of length of service. Such systems are common where there are few opportunities to progress upwards through various job classifications. For instance, one agreement covering a medium-sized office sets out five pay steps within each job category, with employees moving up one step every twelve months. In some cases, progression through these increment levels is also tied to satisfactory job performance.

The setting of rates for particular jobs can give rise to much controversy, since subjective judgments about the relative worth of particular tasks and skills cannot be avoided. Jobs predominantly done by women workers have frequently been placed low down on the wage hierarchy because the classification process has been dominated by male assumptions about the nature of skill and ability (see, for example, Lamson 1986). In order to redress this, some collective agreements specify that equal pay be accorded to men and women for performing similar work, or work deemed to be of comparable worth; more than 15 per cent of major agreements now contain such a provision, compared to fewer than 6 per cent in 1986. In addition, several Canadian jurisdictions have introduced legislation to enforce pay equity, requiring equal pay for work of equal value, where value is determined by a gender-neutral job evaluation procedure. As a result of these legislated or negotiated provisions, in 1993 nearly 70,000 workers covered by major collective agreements received pay equity increases averaging 2.2 per cent. On a more general level, some agreements include elaborate provisions for job evaluation systems, which attempt to measure and compare such attributes as skill, responsibility, effort, and stress; but although these systems lend a measure of objectivity to the process, there remains an inherently subjective element. Despite the growing drive for pay equity and the spread of formal job evaluation procedures, the majority of collective agreements still do not contain explicit provisions for either. Thus, the re-examination of traditional wage structures is likely to remain an important and potentially contentious issue in collective bargaining.

Wage Systems. The wage system is the manner in which pay is calculated, and this also is included in the collective agreement. The most common wage systems in Canadian collective agreements are hourly pay, weekly pay, and incentive pay systems; in practice these different systems can be combined. Generally speaking, production employees are paid on an hourly basis, whereas office and professional workers are paid on a weekly or monthly basis. Besides specifying the basic rates, agreements often include special payments for certain circumstances, such as travel allowances for remote work sites, clothing and tool allowances, and so forth.

Incentive pay systems are more complex than hourly or weekly pay systems. For example, a piecework pay system (in which pay is determined, at least in part, by the employee's rate of output) must take into account circumstances like machine breakdown and other necessary interruptions in work. In addition, because each task must have a piecework rate set for it, the administrative costs can be high and the setting of rates may give rise to considerable conflict. For these reasons, only about 4 per cent of contracts (mostly in the clothing and forestry industries) incorporate a piecework system.

Another form of employee-specific pay has been characterized as "pay-for-knowledge," whereby wages are determined by the skills and knowledge that employees possess rather than the particular job that they perform. This is seen by management as a method of encouraging multiskilling of employees and increasing its flexibility and discretion in the deployment of workers and the utilization of labour. However, systems of individualized remuneration rates have generally been resisted by Canadian unions and are contained in only a small number of collective agreements (Holmes and Kumar 1991). Similarly, other forms of pay systems that are based on incentives offered either to individuals or to groups of workers (for example, based on bonuses for productivity) are rarely contained in Canadian collective agreements.

Wage Premiums and Levels. Wage premiums are additions to basic pay that arise from certain circumstances, such as shift work, overtime, or work on holidays. The most usual rate for overtime hours is time-and-one-half, though a small number of agreements simply prescribe straight time for excess hours, and some agreements require more than time-and-one-half. Some collective agreements also have special overtime rates for days worked in excess of the normal work week.

The wage level is the amount of pay for each classification of employee. Since the sharp recession of the early 1980s, Canadian employers have attempted to improve their competitiveness by reducing labour costs. In particular, employers have sought to force many unions to accept small increases, freezes, or even reductions in wages. In 1993, a record number of major agreements contained wage freezes or cuts: 44.8 per cent of agreements negotiated that year, covering nearly two-thirds of unionized workers, provided for no increase or a reduction in wages. This marked a substantial rise from the 4.4 per cent of such agreements a decade earlier. While most of these wage freezes occurred in the public sector—largely as a result of government legislation—the private sector also experienced an unprecedented incidence of wage freezes or cuts; 43.5 per cent of private sector workers covered by major collective agreements settled in 1993 received no increase, or a loss, in wages. To a certain degree the wage freezes and cuts in recent years have reflected the lower rate of inflation. However, over the past decade, real wages (that is, wages adjusted to account for inflation) have actually declined in Canada.

Other Modifications. Wage levels have not been the only focus of recent employer efforts to modify the wage-effort bargain in their favour (Kumar 1987). Citing a need for greater flexibility, employers have attempted to break away from established patterns in order to negotiate settlements tailored to the specific requirements of their operations.

Under "two-tiered" wage structures new employees are paid lower rates than incumbent employees; in some cases these differences disappear as the new employee progresses, but in others the differential is permanent. Unions have fiercely resisted this strategy because it creates two classes of employees, thus threatening the trade union principle of equality of treatment. The prevalence of two-tiered agreements peaked in the latter half of the 1980s and has subsequently declined; in 1993, only four major collective bargaining settlements contained this type of wage structure. Another method of lowering labour costs has been to use lump-sum payments in place of all or part of an increase in actual wage rates. Such payments reduce increases in wage-related benefits and premiums and, because they are not included in wage rates, allow subsequent contract renegotiations to begin from a lower base. Lump-sum payments have received only limited acceptance in Canada, and their use has been diminishing consistently since 1987.

Some employers have attempted to replace wage increases with various forms of employee profit-sharing or share ownership. Some governments in Canada have introduced legislation offering at least minimal support for these initiatives, for example by providing income tax incentives. Most unions have resisted this move, arguing that such systems tie wages to the outcomes of decisions over which workers are given little say. Several major unions have been supportive of employee-ownership plans however. For example, in 1991 members of the United Steelworkers union at Algoma Steel took a wage cut to finance an investment in the firm that gave them part ownership and membership on the board of directors. Although some research indicates that the incidence of broad-based profit-sharing or share ownership increased substantially in Canada in the 1980s (Long 1992), few of these plans have been incorporated into collective agreements.

Recent recessionary times combined with the fall of inflation have seen one other significant trend in collectively agreed compensation—the decline of cost of living allowance (COLA) clauses. COLAs are a special form of premium that began to grow in popularity in the 1950s and became especially common during the inflationary 1970s. The basic idea is that wages should be adjusted to the rate of inflation so that workers' purchasing power is maintained during the life of the agreement, thereby allowing the parties to reach multiyear contracts without risking the erosion of negotiated wages by unanticipated inflation. Actually, very few contracts provide full protection: some COLAs are triggered only above a certain level of inflation; some are capped (limited to a certain amount of increase); some do not cover the whole contract period; and some do not provide for a full adjustment to the rate of inflation (Wilton 1980). The decline in the rate of inflation after 1982 meant that many of the remaining COLAs were not triggered, thus aiding the efforts of employers to remove such protection from collective agreements: whereas nearly 30 per cent of major agreements settled in 1981 contained COLA clauses, only 13.5 per cent of those reached in 1993 contained such clauses (Bureau of Labour Information, *Major Wage Settlements*).

Employee Benefits.   Compensation includes much more than the actual pay received by employees. In fact, more than 30 per cent of total compensation costs in Canada are represented by employee benefits. The most common types of benefits found in collective agreements are pensions, long-term and short-term disability plans, sick leave plans, extended health care, life insurance and dental insurance. The collective agreement usually spells out the details of the various plans, the eligibility rules (often linked to seniority), and the respective contributions of employer and employees towards the costs of the plans. In fact, so widespread are such plans that they can no longer accurately be referred to as "fringe" benefits; they are now central features of the overall compensation package.

Of the various types of benefits that are found in collective agreements, pension plans have probably given rise to the most controversy. It is impossible to delve into the debate over pensions here, but it should be stressed that at the root of the controversy lie philosophical differences between employers and unions. Generally speaking, unions regard pension contributions, whether paid by the employer or the employee, as deferred wages. On this basis, they argue that the administration of pension funds should be the joint responsibility of unions and employers. Moreover, unions have raised concerns about the way some pension plans discriminate against women, about the lack of inflation protection in many pension plans, about vesting rules that do not entitle the employee to take out the employer's contribution if they change jobs, and other matters. Employers have taken a different view. Since most pension plans in the unionized sector are defined-benefit plans that set out the specific pension benefits, employers argue that so long as they ensure that these benefits are paid they should retain control over the funds accumulated.

Currently, fewer than one-quarter of pension plans in major collective agreements provide for union participation in the administration of the fund. An even smaller number give unions unilateral control; many of these are agreements negotiated by the United Food and Commerical Workers' Union and a few are to be found in the construction industry. The question of control over pension funds has been brought to the fore in recent years because some employers have attempted to remove from pension funds the "surplus assets" (i.e., the money in excess of the amount needed to meet the funds' commitments). In recent years, collective bargaining over pensions has focused not only on issues of control and improvement of benefit levels, but also on provisions for earlier or phased-in retirement.

The recent economic and political climate has not been conducive to the introduction of new benefits. Indeed, as with wages, many employers have attempted to reduce benefits or to shift a higher proportion of the costs of benefit packages to workers. Nonetheless, recent years have seen the emergence of one new type of benefit that is likely to grow in popularity in the future—prepaid legal services. The Canadian Autoworkers' Union and the large automakers have negotiated collective agreements providing for a legal services plan, financed by an employer contribution of 3 cents per hour per employee. Under the plan, union members receive a range of free legal services. Recent CAW agreements have also contained such new benefits as employer-sponsored child-care programs and the availability in the workplace of advocates to provide assistance to women facing harassment on the job or abuse at home.

In conclusion, the wage-effort bargain, encompassing provisions on working time, wages, and employee benefits, is a prominent feature of the collective agreement. Indeed, unionization is often seen solely as an attempt by employees to offset the power of the employer to determine the wage-effort tradeoff. However, the employment relationship is much more than a simple exchange of time for money: even after wages and working hours have been agreed on, the organization and control of the workforce and the workplace naturally give rise to a host of issues, many of which centre on disputes between employers and employees over the control of jobs.

THE CONTROL OF JOBS

In the absence of unions, management normally controls decisions that affect the internal labour market and the production process: how many workers to employ, whom to hire, the types of jobs to be established, the assignment of individual employees to particular tasks, how tasks are to be performed, the rate of production, whom to promote, how lay-offs are to be handled, and so on. For management, the criteria for decisions about such matters are rooted in its concern to minimize labour costs and to maximize productivity. In practice, this means that managers want the rules regulating the internal labour market and production process to be as flexible as possible.

These issues look very different from the workers' standpoint. In particular, workers and their unions are concerned that too much managerial flexibility can result in a sense of permanent insecurity for employees, in a lack of autonomy for workers and work groups, and in the abuse of discretion by managers. Thus, unions have traditionally sought to obtain some input into the management of the internal labour market, especially on matters that affect job security. Workers' belief that they are entitled to some basic job rights inevitably conflicts with management's concern with flexibility and control, so collective agreements often contain negotiated provisions arising from the struggle for the control of jobs.

Hiring and Job Assignment

The struggle for control over jobs begins with the processes of hiring and job assignment, which collective agreements regulate in a variety of ways. It is quite common, for example, for agreements to prohibit discrimination on the basis of sex, race, religion, union activity, and other objectionable grounds, not only in hiring decisions but in a range of other areas such as promotion.

Collective agreement provisions also address hiring and job-assignment decisions by: stipulating the minimum qualifications or training for new or reassigned employees; establishing union-management apprenticeship programs; requiring vacancies be filled from within the organization when possible; and restricting supervisors and other nonbargaining unit personnel from performing tasks normally done by union members. Additionally, newly hired employees are usually put on probationary status. About 70 per cent of major agreements specify probationary periods for new employees, usually of less than five months, but occasionally for six months or more. The significance of probationary status is that such employees are often not entitled to a number of the protective features of the collective agreement, particularly protection against dismissal if their performance is not judged acceptable. Thus, the use of a probationary period permits management to retain a considerable amount of control over hiring.

Another method by which collective agreements can affect the hiring process is through closed shop arrangements or hiring halls. As discussed earlier, closed shop agreements are a form of union security—the only one that regulates the hiring decisions of the employer. The longshoring industry offers a good example of the way union hiring halls function. On the Vancouver waterfront the composition of work gangs and the allocation of gangs and individual workers to particular tasks are controlled by the workers themselves through a union hiring hall and a joint union-management dispatch system. In this way, longshore workers have been able to exercise a considerable amount of control over hiring, job assignment, and production, though management has made some inroads in recent years (Foster 1986).

Workforce Reductions and Contracting-Out

Although the hiring process can give rise to conflict, an even more serious issue is that of reducing the workforce. Employers naturally want to be free to reduce the labour force as they see fit, whereas workers and their unions just as naturally want to avoid job losses. Especially during periods of high unemployment, the goal of improving job security becomes paramount for unions.

Collective agreements may regulate workforce reductions in several ways. One basic type of protection is the requirement that employers notify employees and the union of impending layoffs in order to give them time to make adjustment plans. Although one might think that such provisions would be common, only a little more than half of major agreements make any mention of layoff notification, and of these, the vast majority provide for less than forty-five days' notice. It is possible that the existence of legislation requiring advanced notice of layoffs in most Canadian provinces, and at the federal level, makes the achievement of parallel collective agreement provisions less pressing.

Some collective agreements have severance pay plans, and a small number (particularly in the primary metal and transportation equipment sectors) establish supplementary unemployment benefits. Other types of workforce reduction protection in agreements include: provisions regarding the distribution of work among employees during slack periods; rights to new job openings in other establishments run by the employer; early retirement provisions; and the continuation of benefits in the case of layoffs. But layoff notices, severance pay, supplementary unemployment benefits, and the like only cushion the impact of job loss. Although such provisions may help prevent hasty or unnecessarily drastic reductions, employers still retain the power to reduce the workforce at their discretion. Indeed, despite the emphasis that unions have put on improving job security during the 1980s and 1990s, and despite substantial gains in a few cases—including agreements between the federal government and the Public Service Alliance of Canada and between Canada Post and the Canadian Union of Postal Workers—there has been no widespread improvement in any of these types of security.

One particularly contentious area related to workforce reductions is the practice of contracting-out, where an employer hires another firm to do work for it, rather than using existing employees or hiring new employees. For example, many large institutions, such as universities, subcontract their cleaning operations to independent firms. Because contracting-out threatens the jobs of existing employees or prevents growth of the unionized workforce, it is bitterly opposed by workers and their unions. Management, on the other hand, typically wants to be able to contract out, primarily to reduce labour costs (since smaller specialized firms are not likely to be unionized and often pay lower wages), but also to exercise leverage over its existing employees by raising the possibility of contracting-out at the negotiating table.

Unions have had some success in introducing collective agreement provisions restricting the use of contracting-out: between 1986 and 1994, the incidence of such provisions in major collective agreements grew from 36.4 per cent to 43.7 per cent. In most of the cases where there is a restriction, contracting-out is prohibited only if it leads to lay-offs or if the contract is with a nonunionized firm. Only a small minority of agreements provide a complete ban on contracting-out.

Job Rights and Seniority

Workers and managers are concerned not only with the size of the workforce, but also with the criteria used to make decisions about changes within the internal labour market, particularly decisions about promotions, transfers, reassignments, and layoffs. Workers generally favour the principle of seniority—that is, the idea that long-serving employees, because they have invested a considerable portion of their working lives in the organization, are entitled to preferential treatment in job opportunities and security against layoffs. In addition, seniority rights "provide an element of due process by limiting nepotism and unfairness in personnel decisions" and serve "to buttress the bargaining power of unions by curbing competitive and aggressive behaviour that pits one worker against another" (Gersuny 1982, 519). Although some managers favour a limited use of seniority as a means of reducing tensions over promotion and other decisions, most prefer to retain control over such decisions because they believe that they are in the best position to judge which employees are the most (or least) deserving.

In roughly 60 per cent of collective agreements (covering about 50 per cent of employees), promotion decisions must take some account of seniority (Figure 13.3). A small number of these specify that seniority is the only factor to be taken into account; but the great majority provide that seniority will be one criterion (along with skill and qualifications), or that it will be the deciding factor only if all others are equal. Even where qualified by other factors, seniority may still be the most important criterion because skill and

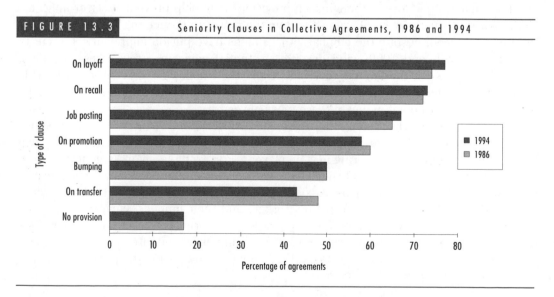

FIGURE 13.3 Seniority Clauses in Collective Agreements, 1986 and 1994

ability can be difficult to assess, and because management sometimes finds it simpler to use seniority in cases in which there is not a great difference in ability (Chaykowski and Slotsve 1986).

The use of seniority is more common with respect to layoffs, where it must be taken into account in about three-quarters of agreements. And seniority is often used to determine the order in which employees are recalled from layoffs. Indeed, as Figure 13.3 indicates, layoff and recall decisions are the issue most frequently governed by seniority.

Collective agreements may also contain bumping rights. "Bumping" is the practice of allowing senior employees who have been laid off to take the jobs of more junior employees, who may, in turn, take the jobs of even more junior employees. Thus, in theory at least, the displacement of a very senior employee can set off a series of bumps down through the seniority list, much like the fall of a row of dominoes. Around half of collective agreements contain bumping provisions, though the great majority restrict a worker's ability to bump, either by limiting it to certain locations, or requiring a certain level of ability.

The notion of job rights linked to seniority is also applied in other areas. For example, seniority may be used to determine the choice of shifts and vacation times, the level of benefits (such as length of vacations), and entitlement to overtime.

Because seniority is used as a criterion in so many decisions, agreements frequently go into considerable detail about how seniority is calculated, and it is not unusual for them to require the posting of seniority lists at regular intervals. In fact, although the basic idea of seniority is easy to grasp, its measurement and application is often extraordinarily complex (Slichter, Healy, and Livernash 1960). For example, seniority can be calculated organization-wide, at the level of the establishment or department, or within an occupational group. A single agreement may use each of these methods for a different purpose.

Figure 13.3 indicates that there has been little change in the pattern of seniority clauses since the mid-1980s. Heightened employee concerns about job security appear to have been offset by employer concerns over flexibility in the management of its workforce. Nonethless, it is possible that the coming years will see the seniority principle called into question for other reasons. Because it favours employees with longer years of continuous service, seniority may be challenged on the grounds that it serves as a mechanism of systemic discrimination against women and other comparatively recent entrants to the labour force (Forrest 1993). Furthermore, it may conflict with the duty of employers to accommodate the needs of disabled workers. In fact, some scholars have suggested that legal challenges to seniority clauses, at least in those collective agreements to which the government is a party, might be launched under the Canadian Charter of Rights and Freedoms (Carter 1987).

Work Rules

The management of the internal labour market involves not only decisions about the allocation and reallocation of job opportunities and losses but also about the way in which the actual work is performed. Management has traditionally regarded decisions about the speed and quantity of production, the way tasks are defined, the number of employees assigned to particular operations, and so on to be within its domain. On the other hand, workers and their unions have sometimes sought to win influence over these matters. The speed of an assembly line or the number of employees allocated to a particular task, for example, is an issue of efficiency from management's point of view. From the point of view of employees, however, it is an issue of quality of working life and the level of employment. The result of this divergence of interests is a struggle over the "frontier of control" (Gilson 1985). Although such struggles often involve informal tactics and result in unwritten arrangements, they are sometimes formalized through the collective agreement.

One type of work rule that is occasionally negotiated is workload. For example, school teachers in several provinces have negotiated average and maximum class sizes. Another type of work rule arises in cases where a job classification system is in place. In such circumstances, it is not unusual for collective agreements to restrict the assignment of individual workers to jobs within their classification or to prohibit supervisors and other employees not in the bargaining unit from performing tasks for which there is a classification. The construction trades in particular attempt to maintain strict control over which workers are permitted to do certain tasks.

Systems of collectively negotiated job classifications have been criticized in recent years by employers on the grounds that they prevent the most efficient allocation of labour. As a result, two types of modifications to existing structures of job classifications have become more common. First, recent research indicates that job classification systems are being simplified through the reduction of the number and types of job classes (Beaucage and Lafleur 1994). Second, some employers and unions have introduced measures in collective agreements to promote multiskilling. Recent collective agreements in the pulp and paper industry, for instance, include clauses requiring tradespeople to carry out any task of which they are capable, rather than only those tasks which are part of their trade. In some cases, multiskilling is encouraged through bonuses, as in the case of an agreement between Cami Automotive and the CAW that provides maintenance workers with a $500 per year multiskilling bonus, or at Dow Chemical in Ontario and Fraser Inc. in New Brunswick where hourly flexibility bonuses have been negotiated. In still other cases, like the MIL Davie shipyard in Lévis, Quebec, multiskilling has been achieved in return for job security provisions.

Technological Change

Although this chapter has discussed separately the issues of work rules, workforce reductions, and job rights, it should be kept in mind that they are closely interconnected, as can be seen in the issue of technological change. Differences between workers and employers over the handling of technological change have been occurring since the industrial revolution, but in times of economic crisis and restructuring, such as the last decade or so in Canada, these disputes become particularly sharp. Management seeks ways to cut labour costs and increase productivity through technology, while workers' concerns with job security and the integrity of their skills are heightened.

Despite employer reluctance to involve employees and their unions in the technological change process through the collective bargaining process, the 1980s and 1990s have seen a slow but steady increase in collective provisions dealing with technological change. Nonetheless, fewer than 50 per cent of major agreements require the employer to

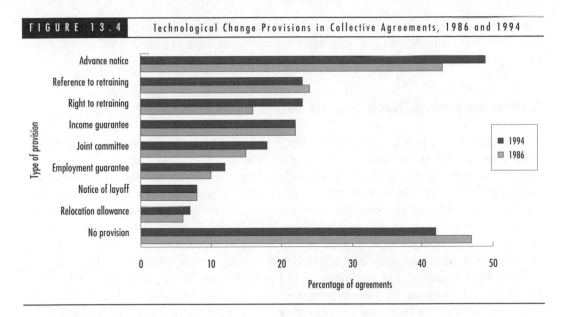

FIGURE 13.4   Technological Change Provisions in Collective Agreements, 1986 and 1994

notify and/or consult with the union in advance of technological changes; fewer than 20 per cent provide for labour-management technological change committees; and fewer than 10 per cent require that special layoff notices be provided to employees affected by technological change (Figure 13.4). Some form of training or retraining of employees affected by technological change is mandated in about a quarter of agreements, and only about one-fifth of workers have any form of income or employment security in the case of technological change. Finally, more than 40 per cent of agreements (covering around one-third of workers) contain no reference at all to technological change. In a few jurisdictions, legislation exists that allows for the reopening of collective agreements, under defined circumstances, on the issue of midterm technological changes. Although the existence of such legislation appears to be an incentive to employers and unions to negotiate procedures to handle technological change (Craig 1986), it has many weaknesses. In general, employers in Canada have been steadfast in their determination to preserve their control over the process of technological change.

THE CONTROL OF WORK BEHAVIOUR AND THE WORK ENVIRONMENT

To this point, we have looked at how collective agreements affect the union-management relationship, the contours of the wage-effort bargain, and the regulation of the internal labour market and production system. To complete the discussion, we must examine a fourth set of issues—those arising from the social and physical environment in which work is performed.

The organization of work necessarily involves social relations between individuals and groups. As well, the physical properties of the workplace have an impact on the people who work there. Collective agreements cannot possibly regulate even a small proportion of the issues, tensions, and relationships that spring from the social and physical setting. However, negotiated rules frequently do come into play in two general areas: workplace behaviour and occupational health and safety.

Behaviour and Discipline at Work

The modern workplace is pervaded by rules established by management to regulate the behaviour of employees. The purposes of such rules include safety concerns (e.g., procedures in nuclear plants), hygiene considerations (e.g., cleanliness in a food-processing factory), attempts to maximize work time (e.g., limitations on break periods), customer relations (e.g., the attempt by one airline to ban the wearing of earrings by its male flight attendants), general standards of decorum (e.g., "no fighting"), and efforts to reinforce the structure of authority (e.g., respecting the decisions of supervisors). In some circumstances, rules may extend to off-the-job behaviour, where the employee's conduct away from work is considered to be damaging to the employer; for instance, some employers have begun demanding that their employees submit to tests for drug use or tests for AIDS. These examples may be rooted in very different circumstances, but they have an important feature in common: they are rules established by management, the enforcement of which entails an array of disciplinary sanctions.

Collective agreements usually grant management the power to institute rules of behaviour and to mete out punishment, subject to the employees' right to grieve. Unions usually prefer not to incorporate specific rules in the collective agreement, since this preserves their right to dispute disciplinary action. For instance, most collective agreements allow management to suspend or discharge employees provided that there is "just cause"—a criterion that is almost always arguable. Some contracts, however, include specific rules and/or penalties. For example:

> Should investigation of a case of absenteeism fail to disclose a bona fide reason, management shall discipline the absentee as follows:
>
> (a) 1st Case—Instruction and verbal warning.
> (b) 2nd Case—Instruction and written warning.
> (c) 3rd Case—Instruction and up to three days off.
> (d) 4th Case—Instruction and layoff subject to discharge.

The imposition of discipline is subject to a number of procedural limitations in some collective agreements, such as the right of an employee to be represented by a union at disciplinary meetings with management, or the requirement that an employee's disciplinary record be "cleared" after a specified period of time (usually one to three years). In addition, disciplinary sanctions are subject to challenge by the employee through the grievance and arbitration procedure contained in collective agreements. In fact, disputes over discipline comprise about one-third of all Canadian arbitration awards annually, and about half of these involve dismissals (Adell 1993). As a result, arbitrators' rulings on these issues over the years are quite important, and have contributed to the development of special rules and procedures in law and practice to handle such cases. For example, a growing number of collective agreements contain provisions for expedited hearings related to discharge cases. In addition, despite the provision in most collective agreements that arbitrators do not have the power to alter any of the terms of the agreement or to substitute any new provisions for any existing provisions, in discharge and disciplinary cases an arbitrator has a wide discretion to vary the particular disciplinary penalties imposed by the employer. As well, in discipline and dismissal cases, unlike most other grievances, the burden of proof lies with the employer (i.e., it is up to the management to justify the discipline that it imposed).

Working Conditions and Health and Safety

Work kills, maims, and sickens at a horrifying rate: in 1992, more than 700 industrial fatalities occurred in Canada; more than 860,000 workers were injured on the job; and more than nineteen *million* worker-days were lost to disabling injuries and illnesses.

Occupational health and safety issues are not solely technical questions. As Sass (1982, 52) points out: "In all technical questions pertaining to workplace health and safety there is the social element. That is, for example, the power relations in production: who tells whom to do what and how fast. After all, the machine does not go faster by itself; someone designed the machinery, organized the work, designed the job." At times the core issue is money. From the point of view of some employers, improved occupational health and safety may involve short-term losses in efficiency, as well as the extra costs of administration and protective equipment. There are allegations that such attitudes were responsible for the 1992 Westray Mine explosion in Nova Scotia that killed many workers. Occasionally, workers themselves resist efforts to increase safety. They may take shortcuts because pay and performance are judged on speed of production (as in some coal mines). Sometimes workers take risks out of bravado or a supposedly macho approach to the job. Nonetheless, at many job sites, health and safety is a matter not of dollars and cents but of life and death.

Some of the clauses in collective agreements already discussed (such as rules affecting the pace of work) have an indirect effect on health and safety. More directly, around half of collective agreements oblige employers to cover the costs of safety equipment in whole or in part. An even greater number of agreements (about 70 per cent) institute safety programs, safety committees, or both. In most Canadian jurisdictions, occupational health and safety committees are required by law, even in nonunionized workplaces. Such legislation usually gives workers the right to refuse to perform tasks that they believe are hazardous or potentially injurious. Recent legislation also requires that information be provided on hazardous materials used in the workplace. Such requirements are typically referred to as Workplace Hazardous Materials Information System (or WHMIS for short). In addition to these legislative requirements, however, the inclusion of provisions in collective agreements—such as those which allow employees to obtain information about and/or refuse unsafe work—enables unions to deal with specific problems through grievance and arbitration procedures rather than having to rely solely on the enforcement of health and safety laws or the policies agreed on by joint committees.

CONCLUSION

Given the largely unfettered power of management to rule over a nonunionized workforce, collective agreements represent a step towards industrial democracy. Yet judged against the democratic standards that govern political life in our society, collective agreements represent only a partial step in the direction of full economic democracy. Collective agreements *do* make a difference, but employers have been quite successful in preventing a real sharing of authority and have been able to maintain many of their traditional prerogatives. Indeed, the manner in which collective agreements are administered, particularly with respect to management residual rights, actually serves to legitimize and bolster managerial powers.

The collective agreement reflects these basic authority relationships and also the ebb and flow of economic and political power in society. For example, the 1980s and 1990s have been marked by recession, high rates of unemployment, and a resurgent conservatism. The bargaining power of unions has deteriorated, and Canadian employers have taken advantage of this situation to launch an offensive against many of the provisions in collective agreements. Unions and workers have been confronted with employer demands to reduce or freeze wages and benefits, to tie compensation more closely to productivity, and to make work rules and job classifications more flexible. Even management proposals for greater employee participation in decision making, jointly managed training and retraining programs, union participation in employee assistance programs, quality circles, and autonomous work groups, have at times been coloured by antiunion motivation, since these techniques often weaken union solidarity.

Nevertheless, the collective agreement remains at the centre of the Canadian industrial relations system. It provides both a detailed set of rules to govern the workplace and a benchmark of union ability (or inability) to win for its members a voice in the management of the workplace. For the union, the negotiation and administration of the collective agreement is the cornerstone of its activity, and to union members it represents the tangible results of union membership. Whatever changes take place in Canadian industrial relations will undoubtedly be reflected in the content and substance of the collective agreement.

QUESTIONS

1. Obtain a collective agreement and categorize its contents according to the four general types of clauses outlined in this chapter.

2. Describe the distinctive characteristics of Canadian collective agreements. Discuss the reasons for these characteristics.

3. Most North American industrial relations scholars see collective agreements bringing "constitutional government" to the place of work. Discuss this contention.

4. Outline the arguments for and against the residual rights theory of managerial prerogatives. In your view, does this doctrine promote or retard organizational effectiveness?

5. Discuss the different types of union security clauses found in collective agreements. In your opinion, does the Rand Formula establish a balance between individual and collective rights?

6. Describe the ways in which collective agreements might be used to remove the barriers to equality faced by women workers and by workers with disabilities.

7. What are the various wage incentive systems? Why are they not commonly found in collective agreements?

8. Discuss how the conflict between management's concern with efficiency and workers' concerns with job security and working conditions is manifested in collective agreements.

9. What aspects of collective agreements give credence to the view that trade union leaders have become "managers of discontent?" What aspects of agreements do not lend support to this view?

10. Discuss the recent moves by Canadian employers to alter many of the traditional features of collective agreements in their favour. What are the likely long-run effects?

11. Why do collective agreements sometimes include provisions that are already required by legislation, such as employment standards legislation, human rights codes, or occupational health and safety legislation? Give examples.

12. What do you think the typical Canadian collective agreement will look like ten years from now and why?

REFERENCES

ADAMS, R.J. 1977. "A Case for an Employer's Organization in Canada." *Labour Gazette* 77 (April): 153-56.

ADELL, B. 1993. "Workplace disciplinary rules and procedures in Canada." *International Labour Review* 132: 583-603.

BEAUCAGE, A., and C. LAFLEUR. 1994. "La négociation concessive dans l'industrie manufacturière canadienne pendant les années 1980." In E. Déom and A. Smith, eds, *Proceedings of the XXXth Annual Conference of the Canadian Industrial Relations Association*. Québec: CIRA.

BUREAU OF LABOUR INFORMATION. HUMAN RESOURCES DEVELOPMENT CANADA. Various issues. *Major Wage Settlements*. Ottawa: Bureau of Labour Information.

CARTER, D.D. 1987. *Canadian Industrial Relations and the Charter—The Emerging Issues*. Queen's Papers in Industrial Relations 1987-2. Kingston, Ont: Industrial Relations Centre, Queen's University.

CHAYKOWSKI, R.P., and A. VERMA. 1992. *Industrial Relations in Canadian Industry*. Toronto: Dryden.

CHAYKOWSKI, R.P., and G.A. SLOTSVE. 1986. "Union Seniority Rules as a Determinant of Intra-Firm Job Changes." *Relations industrielles/Industrial Relations* 41: 720-37.

COMMISSION OF INQUIRY INTO PART-TIME WORK. 1983. *Part-time Work in Canada*. Report. J. Wallace, chair. Ottawa: Labour Canada.

CRAIG, A.W.J. 1986. "Technological Change, Labour Relations Policy, Administrative Tribunals and the Incidence of Technological Change Provisions in Major Collective Agreements." In M. Thompson, ed, *Is There a New Canadian Industrial Relations?* Proceedings of the 23rd Annual Meeting of the Canadian Industrial Relations Association. Québec: CIRA.

CURTIS, C.H. 1966. *The Development and Enforcement of the Collective Agreement*. Kingston, Ont: Industrial Relations Centre, Queen's University.

DRACHE, D., and H. GLASBEEK. 1992. *The Changing Workplace: Reshaping Canada's Industrial Relations System*. Toronto: James Lorimer.

EDWARDS, P.K. 1986. *Conflict at Work*. Oxford: Basil Blackwell.

ENGLAND, G. 1980. "Some Thoughts on the Peace Obligation." *Ottawa Law Review* 12: 521-609.

FISHER, E.G., and L.M. SHERWOOD. 1984. "Fairness and Managerial Rights in Canadian Arbitral Jurisprudence." *Relations industrielles/Industrial Relations* 39: 720-37.

FORREST, A. 1993. "Women and Industrial Relations: No Room in the Discourse." *Relations industrielles/Industrial Relations* 48: 409-40.

FOSTER, J.B. 1986. "On the Waterfront: Longshoring in Canada." In C. Heron and R. Storey, eds, *On the Job: Confronting the Labour Process in Canada*. Toronto: University of Toronto Press.

GERSUNY, C. 1982. "Origins of Seniority Provisions in Collective Bargaining." *Labor Law Journal* 33 (August): 518-24.

GILSON, C.H.H. 1985. "Changes in the Nature of Grievance Issues Over the Last Ten Years: Labour-Management Relations and the 'Frontier of Control'." *Relations industrielles/Industrial Relations* 40: 856-64.

GOLDBERG, A.J. 1985. "Management's Reserved Rights: A Labor View." In A.M. Glassman and T.G. Cummings, eds, *Industrial Relations: A Multidimensional View*. Glenview, Ill.: Scott, Foresman.

HÉBERT, G. 1992. *Traité de négociation collective*. Boucherville: Gaëtan Morin.

HOLMES, J., and P. KUMAR. 1991. "Divergent Paths: Restructuring in the North American Automobile Industry." *Queen's Papers in Industrial Relations, 1991-4*. Kingston: Industrial Relations Centre, Queen's University.

KILLINGSWORTH, C.C. 1969. "Management Rights Revisited." In G.G. Somers, ed, *Arbitration and Social Change*. Washington, DC: Bureau of National Affairs.

KUMAR, P. 1987. *Recent Wage Deceleration: Short-run Response or Structural Change?* Queen's Papers in Industrial Relations 1987-1. Kingston, Ont: Industrial Relations Centre, Queen's University.

LAMSON, C. 1986. "On the Line: Women and Fish Plant Jobs in Atlantic Canada." *Relations industrielles/Industrial Relations* 41: 145-56.

LONG, R.J. 1992. "The Incidence and Nature of Employee Profit Sharing and Share Ownership in Canada." *Relations industrielles/Industrial Relations* 47: 463-88.

MacDOWELL, L.S. 1978. "The Formation of the Canadian Industrial Relations System During World War Two." *Labour/Le Travailleur* 3: 175-96.

RONDEAU, C. 1994. "La négociation continue. Étude théorique et pratiques québécoises." In E. Déom and A. Smith, eds, *Proceedings of the XXXth Annual Conference of the Canadian Industrial Relations Association*. Québec: CIRA.

SANDERSON, J.P. 1979. *The Art of Collective Bargaining*. Toronto: Richard De Boo.

SASS, R. 1982. "Safety and Self-Respect." *Policy Options*, July-August: 50-53.

SLICHTER, S.H., J.J. HEALY, and E.R. LIVERNASH. 1960. *The Impact of Collective Bargaining on Management*. Washington, DC: The Brookings Institution.

STATISTICS CANADA. 1993. *Families, Social and Economic Characteristics*. Ottawa.

———. 1992. *Labour Force Annual Averages 1991*. Cat. no. 71-220. Ottawa.

———. 1990. *Women in Canada: A Statistical Report*. Target Group Data Bases. 2nd ed. Cat no. 890503E. Ottawa.

VERMA, A., and J. CUTCHER-GERSHENFELD. 1993. "Joint Governance in the Workplace: Beyond Union-Management Cooperation and Worker Participation." In B. Kaufman and M. Kleiner, eds, *Employee Representation*. Madison WI: Industrial Relations Research Association.

WELLS, D. 1986. "Autoworkers on the Firing Line." In C. Heron and R. Storey, eds, *On the Job: Confronting the Labour Process in Canada*. Kingston, Ont: McGill-Queen's University Press.

WILTON, D.A. 1980. "An Analysis of Canadian Wage Contracts with Cost-of-Living Allowance Clauses." Discussion Paper 165. Ottawa: Economic Council of Canada.

YOUNG, F. 1975. "Issues in Contracting Out." In H.C. Jain, ed, *Canadian Labour and Industrial Relations*. Toronto: McGraw-Hill.

CHAPTER 14

STRIKES AND DISPUTE RESOLUTION

MORLEY GUNDERSON,
DOUGLAS HYATT, AND
ALLEN PONAK*

THIS CHAPTER PROVIDES AN OVERVIEW OF THE CAUSES AND CONSEQUENCES of strike activity in Canada. First, a description of the frequency, size, and duration of strikes and their distribution by industry and province is presented. The functions and causes of strikes are then discussed, focusing on both economic and noneconomic causes. In addition, the role of dispute-resolution procedures in reducing strike activity is outlined. Finally, the chapter concludes with a brief discussion of the potential consequences of strikes.

* The authors acknowledge material in this chapter that appeared in the previous edition of the textbook by Anderson, Gunderson, and Ponak (1989).

Strikes are one of the most visible outcomes of union-management relations in Canada, and they are often used as a barometer to gauge the health of the industrial relations system. (Hereafter, strikes refer to both strikes and lockouts unless otherwise noted.) Strikes play a variety of functions both in the union-management relationship and in society: they support bargaining demands; reveal information on the parties' true settlement points; establish reputations; place pressure on both sides to make negotiating concessions; solve intraorganizational bargaining problems; provide a release of pent-up frustrations; support or protest government policy; and show solidarity with workers' causes elsewhere in the world. Just as strikes have different purposes, it is also clear there is a complex and wide-ranging set of conditions that are likely to combine to cause a strike. In any given union-management relationship, the prevailing economic conditions, community characteristics, internal dynamics of the union and management organizations, the nature of the relationship, and the history of collective bargaining may contribute to producing a settlement or a strike. Strikes also have costs. For workers a strike almost always means substantial loss of income while the strike lasts. Strike pay may be provided by the union, but the amount is usually only sufficient for basic subsistence needs. If the strike shuts down operations, the employer may be faced with loss of profit, loss of customers, and a permanent decline in market share. The public may also be affected if, for example, the major employer in a small town is shut down or a service on which people rely, such as mass transit, is no longer available.

Because of these costs, Canadian public policy has long been directed towards preventing strikes. Research has shown that effective dispute resolution procedures established through public policy may reduce the probability and duration of a strike. Thus, by understanding the causes and consequences of strikes, policymakers may be able to influence strike activity in Canada.

MEASURING STRIKE ACTIVITY

As with most seemingly simple statistics, the measures of strike activities are replete with problems—problems that are accentuated when comparisons are made over long periods of time or across diverse countries (for a discussion of measurement problems see Cameron 1983; Fisher 1973; Garen and Krislov 1988; Lacroix 1986b; Shalev 1978; Shorter and Tilly 1974; Silver 1973; Skeels 1971; and Stern 1978). These problems include what to count as a strike (in Canada strikes involving a total loss of less than ten working days are excluded), how to treat political strikes or protests, how to classify people who may not officially be on strike but are not working because of the strike, and how to determine when some protracted strikes have ended. Quantitative studies of strike activity are also difficult to compare because of differences in the measures used (Stern 1978). As well, the format for publishing strike statistics can change. For example, prior to 1982 the United States classified work stoppages involving six or more workers as a strike. After 1982, only stoppages involving 1,000 or more workers are included in the series. This has lead some researchers, including Skeels, McGrath, and Arshanapalli (1988), to question the appropriateness of generalizations based on large strikes (although Garen and Krislov [1988] find that small and large strikes both have the same underlying determinants).

Most developed nations, Canada included, publish strike statistics (actually work stoppages that include strikes plus lockouts) in three series: (1) frequency or number of strikes per year; (2) total number of workers involved in strikes; and (3) volume or total days lost through strikes, often expressed as a percentage of estimated working time. These raw measures do not, however, directly indicate the average size of each strike (that is, the average number of workers involved) or the average duration (that is, the average length of time each worker remains on strike). Hence, the raw measures by themselves do not indicate if a high volume of strike activity, as measured by days lost, resulted from a large number of strikes (frequency), a large number of workers involved in each strike (size), a series of long strikes (duration), or some combination of these three components.

As illustrated in Table 14.1, however, some basic manipulations of the raw numbers enable the calculation of the three components of the total volume of strike activity—frequency, size, and duration. These three components, when multiplied together, give the overall volume of strike activity, or total days lost (Forchheimer 1948). Expressed as a percentage of time worked, this is a measure of the relative degree of overall strike activity in the economy.

CANADIAN STRIKE ACTIVITY

Strike activity in Canada has been historically quite volatile. The percentage of working time lost due to strikes has ranged from a low of 0.01 in the Depression of 1930, to a high of 0.60 in 1919 after the First World War and 0.59 in 1976. Even in these years of peak strike activity, less than one per cent of total working time was lost due to strikes. Table 14.1 reveals that there have been distinct phases: moderate levels of strike activity in the prosperous years of the early 1920s; low levels in the depression years of the late 1920s and early 1930s; low levels in the war years 1939-45; a spurt in 1946 followed by moderate levels until the mid-1960s; extremely high levels from 1960 to 1981; moderate and declining levels throughout the 1980s; and a sharp drop in the 1990s.

Strike activity generally drops in periods of recession and stagnant economic activity. Since the recession of the early 1980s, and especially during the 1990s, strike activity has declined markedly, perhaps heralding an end to the wave of strike activity which began in the mid-1960s. Yet on an international basis during the 1970s and even into the 1980s and 1990s Canada ranked second only to Italy in terms of days lost per worker due to strikes (see Chapter 17 of this volume; Lacroix 1986b). This high volume of strike activity occurs in part because strikes in Canada tend to be of long duration.

Components of Strike Activity

The first three columns of Table 14.1 indicate the contribution of each of the components of strike activity—frequency, size, and duration—to the overall volume of strike activity. With the exceptions of both World Wars, Canada has almost always had strikes of fairly long duration compared to most other countries. Over the full period 1901 to 1993, the average strike lasted 18.3 days, though since 1981 strike duration has declined slightly to

TABLE 14.1   Various Measures of Strike Activity, Canada, 1901-1993

	Frequency[a]	Size[b]	Duration[c]	Volume Person-Days Lost[d]	Volume As Percentage of Working Time[e]
1901	99	243	30.6	737,808	____
1902	125	102	16.0	203,301	____
1903	175	219	22.4	858,959	____
1904	103	111	16.9	192,890	____
1905	96	130	19.7	246,138	____
1906	150	156	16.2	378,276	____
1907	188	181	15.3	520,142	____
1908	76	343	27.0	703,571	____
1909	90	201	48.6	880,663	____
1910	101	220	32.9	731,324	____
1911	100	292	62.4	1,821,084	____
1912	181	237	26.5	1,135,787	____
1913	152	267	25.6	1,036,254	____
1914	63	154	50.5	490,850	____
1915	63	181	8.3	95,042	____
1916	120	221	8.9	236,814	____
1917	160	314	22.4	1,123,515	____
1918	230	347	8.1	647,942	____
1919	336	443	22.8	3,400,942	0.60
1920	322	187	13.3	799,524	0.14
1921	168	168	37.1	1,048,914	0.22
1922	104	421	34.9	1,528,661	0.32
1923	86	398	19.6	671,750	0.13
1924	70	490	37.7	1,295,054	0.26
1925	87	333	41.2	1,193,281	0.23
1926	77	310	11.2	266,601	0.05
1927	74	301	6.8	152,570	0.03
1928	98	179	12.8	224,212	0.04
1929	90	144	11.7	152,080	0.02
1930	67	205	6.7	91,797	0.01
1931	88	122	19.0	204,238	0.04
1932	116	202	10.9	255,000	0.05
1933	125	212	12.0	317,547	0.07
1934	191	240	12.5	574,519	0.11
1935	120	277	8.7	288,703	0.05
1936	156	223	8.0	276,997	0.05
1937	278	259	12.3	886,393	0.15
1938	147	139	7.3	148,678	0.02
1939	122	336	5.5	224,588	0.04
1940	168	361	4.4	266,318	0.04
1941	231	377	5.0	433,914	0.06
1942	354	322	4.0	450,202	0.05
1943	402	543	4.8	1,041,198	0.12
1944	199	378	6.5	490,139	0.06
1945	197	488	15.2	1,457,420	0.19
1946	226	614	32.4	4,494,833	0.54
1947	234	442	22.9	2,366,339	0.27
1948	154	278	20.7	885,793	0.10
1949	135	347	22.1	1,036,818	0.11
1950	161	1,200	7.2	1,388,110	0.15
1951	258	392	8.9	901,625	0.09
1952	219	513	24.6	2,765,506	0.29
1953	173	315	24.1	1,312,715	0.15
1954	173	327	25.3	1,430,300	0.15
1955	159	378	31.2	1,875,400	0.19
1956	229	387	14.1	1,245,824	0.11

TABLE 14.1 (cont.)   Various Measures of Strike Activity, Canada, 1901-1993

	Frequency[a]	Size[b]	Duration[c]	Volume	
				Person-Days Lost[d]	As Percentage of Working Time[e]
1957	245	329	18.3	1,477,105	0.13
1958	258	425	24.4	2,673,481	0.24
1959	216	440	23.4	2,226,891	0.19
1960	274	180	15.0	738,701	0.06
1961	287	341	13.6	1,335,081	0.11
1962	311	239	19.1	1,417,361	0.11
1963	332	251	11.0	916,991	0.07
1964	343	293	15.7	1,580,421	0.11
1965	502	342	13.4	2,301,088	0.17
1966	617	667	12.6	5,179,993	0.34
1967	522	483	15.8	3,975,792	0.25
1968	581	385	22.7	5,077,609	0.32
1969	597	514	25.2	7,733,287	0.46
1970	544	481	25.0	6,539,500	0.39
1971	569	421	11.9	2,854,480	0.16
1972	598	1,180	10.9	7,716,287	0.43
1973	724	484	16.4	5,761,150	0.30
1974	1,217	487	15.6	9,222,256	0.46
1975	1,170	431	21.6	10,877,291	0.56
1976	1,040	1,525	7.3	11,544,166	0.59
1977	806	270	15.3	3,320,051	0.17
1978	1,057	379	18.4	7,357,185	0.36
1979	1,049	441	16.9	7,819,351	0.37
1980	1,028	427	20.8	9,129,956	0.42
1981	1,050	326	25.9	8,850,555	0.39
1982	680	683	12.3	5,712,537	0.27
1983	645	511	13.5	4,440,902	0.21
1984	716	261	20.8	3,883,398	0.18
1985	829	196	19.2	3,125,562	0.14
1986	748	647	14.8	7,151,471	0.31
1987	668	871	6.5	3,810,913	0.16
1988	548	377	23.7	4,901,263	0.20
1989	627	709	8.3	3,701,363	0.15
1990	579	467	18.8	5,079,191	0.20
1991	463	547	9.9	2,516,021	0.10
1992	404	370	14.1	2,109,749	0.09
1993	382	266	15.8	1,605,019	0.07

[a] Number of strikes in existence during the year, whether they began in that year or earlier.

[b] Average number of workers involved per strike, calculated as the number of workers involved divided by the number of strikes.

[c] Average days lost per worker on strike, calculated as total person-days lost divided by the number of strikers involved. This is a measure of the average length of time that each worker who is on strike remains on strike. An alternative measure of duration is the average length of each strike, which can be calculated as the days lost divided by the number of strikes.

[d] Product of frequency (strikes) times size (strikers/strikes) and duration (days lost/striker). Numbers are approximate because of rounding.

[e] Beginning in 1975, potential working time is based on employed workers. Prior to 1975, working time is based on paid, nonagricultural workers.

SOURCES: 1901-1945 — Labour Canada, *Strikes and Lockouts in Canada*, various issues.

1946-1993 — Calculations by the authors based on the Bureau of Labour Information, *Work Stoppage File*.

15 days. This recent drop in duration, which has been accompanied by a decline in strike frequency, has resulted in a substantial reduction in the percentage of working time lost due to strikes. The 1970s were a particularly volatile period in Canadian industrial relations and this is reflected in strike activity. Two very large strikes occurred in 1972 and 1976 — the Common Front general strike of public employees in Quebec, and a Day of Protest throughout Canada in opposition to wage controls introduced by the federal government the previous year. The average size of strikes in these two years increased dramatically as a result. The frequency of strikes also increased because the average length of contracts shortened during the inflationary cycle of the 1970s. This meant that more contracts were being negotiated each year and hence the potential for strikes rose.

Contract Status at Time of Strike

It is useful to distinguish strikes by the status of the contract at the time of the strike because different kinds of strikes may well have different underlying causes. First-contract or recognition strikes occur over the establishment of the first collective agreement following the certification of the union; contract-renewal strikes occur over the renegotiation of an existing collective agreement; midcontract strikes occur during the term of an existing collective agreement. (Midcontract and other illegal strikes in Canada have been described and analyzed in Fisher 1982; Fisher and Percy 1983; Jones and Walsh 1984; and Ng 1987. Such strikes in the United States have been examined by Brett and Goldberg 1979, Byrne and King 1982, and Flaherty 1983.)

Table 14.2 provides information on the status of the contract at the time of the strike. From 1986 to 1993, the vast majority of strike activity according to all measures was accounted for by regular end-of-contract disputes that occur during the renegotiation of an existing collective agreement. This result is not unexpected, since the overwhelming majority of contract negotiations occur in this category and since strikes during the term of the collective agreement are illegal. Recognition or first-agreement strikes accounted for 15.5 per cent of strikes and lockouts, but because they tended to occur mainly in small establishments, they involved only 1.3 per cent of workers on strike. In spite of their illegality in all jurisdictions except Saskatchewan, strikes during the term of an existing collective agreement accounted for 7.8 per cent of all work stoppages and 23.9 per cent of workers involved in strikes. Because they were illegal, these strikes tended to be of short duration however, explaining why they only accounted for 3.7 per cent of person-days lost because of strikes.

TABLE 14.2   Strikes and Lockouts by Contract Status for Various Measures of Strike Activity, Canada, 1986-1993

Contract Status	Strikes and Lockouts	Workers Involved	Person-Days Lost
First agreement	15.5%	1.3%	3.5
Renegotiation of agreement	73.3	73.7	91.9
During term of agreement	7.8	23.9	3.7
Other[a]	3.4	1.1	0.9
Total	100.0%	100.0%	100.0%

[a] Includes instances where there was no collective agreement before the work stoppage and where the conclusion of a final agreement was not a basic issue.

SOURCE: Calculations by the authors based on data from the Human Resources Development Canada, *Work Stoppage File.*

Although not shown in the table, midcontract strikes as a proportion of all strikes have declined substantially since the 1970s—from 25.2 per cent in the 1970-79 period to 11.8 per cent in the 1980-85 period, to 7.8 per cent between 1986 and 1993. Research would be needed to establish the reasons for this decline. Two possible explanations include the emergence of new grievance-arbitration procedures (for example, expedited arbitration and grievance mediation), and employment standards innovations (for example, health and safety committees and advance layoff notice) to deal with problems that arise during the term of the collective agreement.

Clearly, the underlying causes of these different types of strikes may differ. Recognition strikes may reflect the inexperience of the parties, an especially important factor because the inexperience is likely to lead to misperceptions and a lack of knowledge about the other's position. They may also arise as a continuation of bitter and difficult union organizing campaigns. Midcontract strikes, on the other hand, usually occur in response to a particular work situation or working condition and may reflect pent-up frustration and lack of confidence in the grievance procedure. Such strikes may also be a way for union members to show discontent over the contract negotiated by their leadership. All too often, the discussion and analysis of strikes assumes that they are a relatively homogeneous phenomenon, and therefore all strikes are analyzed as regular end-of-contract disputes. Most certainly, the determinants of strikes may differ depending on the type of strike.

Industry and Regional Variation

As indicated in Table 14.3, there is considerable industrial and regional variation in strikes in Canada and also considerable variation within an industry or province over brief periods of time. Between 1980 and 1993, the average strike time lost per worker fell almost in half, from 0.60 days to 0.35 days. In the most recent time period, the most strike-prone parts of the economy were the primary industries (e.g., fishing, forestry, and mining), followed by construction, transportation/utilities, and manufacturing. The industries that were *not* strike-prone were agriculture, trade, finance, and services. Public administration was at the average. This ranking of industries by strike activity was the same in the 1980-85 period.

The provincial figures do not exhibit the same degree of variation. Of the larger provinces, British Columbia and Quebec have the highest volume of strike activity. To a large degree, this reflects the concentration of strike-prone industries in those provinces. This is borne out in econometric studies that indicate strike probabilities in the private sector in Canada to be fairly similar across regions when other factors, including industrial distribution, are held constant (Dussault and Lacroix 1980; Gunderson, Kervin, and Reid 1986; Swidinsky and Vanderkamp 1982). The province of Quebec is an exception to this pattern, however. Strike probabilities are significantly higher in Quebec even after controlling for the effect of other variables, including the industrial distribution of the workforce (Gunderson, Kervin, and Reid 1986).

TABLE 14.3   Person-Days Lost per Employed Worker by Industry and Province, Canada, 1980-1993

	1980-85	1986-93
Industry		
Agriculture	0.02	0.01
Other primary industries	1.64	2.02
Manufacturing	1.22	0.63
Construction	1.26	0.97
Transport/utilities	0.80	0.65
Trade	0.14	0.10
Financial	0.15	0.03
Services	0.32	0.14
Public administration	0.46	0.35
Province		
Newfoundland	1.54	0.59
Prince Edward Island	0.15	0.00
Nova Scotia	0.56	0.10
New Brunswick	0.39	0.37
Quebec	0.78	0.39
Ontario	0.43	0.25
Manitoba	0.16	0.12
Saskatchewan	0.33	0.17
Alberta	0.22	0.14
British Columbia	0.94	0.63
Average	0.60	0.35

NOTE: Calculated as person-days lost due to strikes and lockouts divided by the number of employed workers in each industry and province.

SOURCE: Person-days lost: Calculations by the authors based on Bureau of Labour Information, *Work Stoppage File.* Numbers of paid workers: Statistics Canada, cats. 71-529 and 71-100, various issues.

Strike Rates and Settlement Stages

Another measure of strike activity is the strike rate or proportion of collective agreements that are signed after a strike has occurred. This information is provided in Table 14.4, which shows the stage at which each collective agreement was settled (hence the term "settlement stage"). The last column of Table 14.4 indicates that from 1980 to 1993, 13.4 per cent of private sector agreements were signed after a strike. The strike rate was lower (11.4 per cent) in the more recent 1986-93 period than in the earlier 1980-85 period (15.6 per cent). Although not shown separately in the table, the strike rate in the private sector dropped markedly in the 1990s (5.3 per cent in 1991; 11.8 per cent in 1992; and only 2.7 per cent in 1993).

TABLE 14.4   Settlement Stages, Major Collective Agreements Public and Private Sectors, 1980-93

| Settlement Stage | Proportion of Agreements Signed at Each Stage[a] | | | | | |
| | Early Period 1980-1985 | | Later Period 1986-1993 | | Full Period 1980-1993 | |
	Public	Private	Public	Private	Public	Private
Direct Bargaining	40.5	42.7	54.7	53.1	48.6	48.1
Conciliation	9.6	20.6	10.3	14.7	10.0	17.6
Post-Conciliation	3.5	6.9	2.4	5.8	2.9	6.4
Mediation	8.9	12.0	10.9	12.3	10.0	12.2
Post-Mediation	1.6	1.0	2.4	0.4	2.1	0.7
Arbitration	9.1	0.6	6.0	1.2	7.4	0.9
Strike	4.7	15.6	2.7	11.4	3.6	13.4
Legislated[b]	21.1	0.3	10.3	1.0	15.0	0.2
Other, Unknown	1.0	0.3	0.3	0.1	0.4	0.7
Total	100.0	100.0	100.0	100.0	100.0	100.0

[a] In order for the data to be defined consistently across time periods, contracts covering 200 or more workers in the federal jurisdiction were excluded after the 1986 settlement year and construction contracts after the 1983 settlement year. Thus, the table includes nonconstruction contracts covering 500 or more employees.

[b] Includes contracts re-opened under wage controls and the Ontario Social Contract of 1993. These amounted to 4.4 per cent of the 10.3 per cent in the period 1986-93 and 2.5 per cent of the 15 per cent over the full period 1980-1993.

SOURCE: Calculations by the authors based on data from the Bureau of Labour Information's Major Wage Settlements data base, for major collective agreements of 500 or more employees.

In the period of 1986-93, almost half of the private sector agreements were settled at the stage of direct bargaining, with an additional 37 per cent settled with the assistance of conciliation or mediation. The use of third-party arbitration is extremely rare in the private sector (less than 1 per cent)—the parties being loathe to hand this decision over to a third-party arbitrator.

In the public sector, strike rates initially appear considerably lower, at 2.7 per cent in the 1986-93 period. This apparently low rate, however, is misleading. The public sector has a substantial proportion of contracts settled through direct legislative intervention. Unfortunately, "legislated settlements" in Table 14.4 includes ad hoc back-to-work legislation and legislated settlements that were the result of wage controls including the Ontario Social Contract. Thus it is not possible to add the back-to-work legislation (after a strike) to the conventional strike component, to get a measure of total strike activity in the public sector. However, adding the strike category, the legislated category, and the arbitrated category highlights that between 1980 and 1993, public sector collective agreements were achieved by the parties themselves (or through the assistance of a mediator or conciliator) less than 75 per cent of the time. By comparison, private sector negotiations successfully produced collective agreements 85 per cent of the time. (The special problems of the public sector are discussed in Chapter 15.)

Summary of Basic Picture

Historically, there have been wide fluctuations in the various components of strike activity in Canada. From the mid-1960s to the early 1980s, strike activity was particularly high, but it has dropped markedly during the 1980s and especially 1990s. Whether this is simply a short-run phase or the beginning of a long-run trend reflecting greater competitive pressures is an important but unanswered question.

Although most strikes occur during the renegotiation of a collective agreement, a substantial number of illegal strikes occur during the term of the collective agreement. Recognition or first-agreement strikes occur quite often; however, they do not involve many workers and hence do not contribute much to the total person-days lost because of strikes.

There is substantial industry and regional variation. Quebec and British Columbia have the highest volume of strike activity of the larger provinces, in part because they have a concentration of strike-prone industries, including fishing, mining, construction, lumber, and pulp and paper. These strike-prone sectors tend to be particularly sensitive to business cycle conditions or involve a relatively high degree of isolation.

FUNCTIONS AND CAUSES OF STRIKES
Functions of Strikes

Since strikes can serve a variety of purposes and can occur for a variety of reasons, it is not really feasible to talk about a unique cause of strike activity. Strikes may occur to win recognition for a particular union or to win concessions from management. They may serve an important information-generating function through shedding light on the true settlement points of both parties, and on the internal tradeoffs being made within both the union and the firm. They may simply be mistakes or accidents made by the parties, given the complexities and uncertainties of the bargaining process. Strikes may reflect pent-up, unresolved grievances over working conditions or be spontaneous acts in response to a particular working condition. (The latter often results in a strike during the term of an existing collective agreement.) Strikes may be a cathartic event providing a safety valve for pent-up frustration, or they may be a political act of worker solidarity or even a way of getting a vacation. They may also be used by union leaders to solidify the rank and file, to find out what they really want and are prepared to give up, or to lower their expectations as the strike runs its course. The parties may also use strikes to establish or enhance reputations for subsequent rounds of bargaining; this factor can complicate the analysis of strike activity, since the ultimate purpose of the strike may appear unrelated to the events at hand.

Causes or Determinants of Strikes

Theories of the causes of strikes endeavour to relate measures of strike activity to various observable characteristics that are believed to affect strike activity. Such characteristics, or strike determinants, can involve variables related to the social, economic, political, and legal environment in which the parties operate, the characteristics of their respective organizations as well as of the negotiators and the bargaining process itself.

Any theory that tries to indicate how these observable characteristics affect strike activity must confront a basic dilemma; such variables do not have a direct impact on the level of strike activity so long as the variable's effect on each party's bargaining power is understood by both. For example, it is often stated that strike incidence is high at the peak of a business cycle because labour has more bargaining power at that time (since workers have job opportunities elsewhere and employers are reluctant to lose business). To the extent that this is also known by employers, however, management has an incentive to increase its offer to avoid the strike. The factor giving labour more bargaining power, therefore, has implications for the magnitude of the settlement but not necessarily for strikes. Differential bargaining power is a theory of wages, not of strikes. In a world of perfect information, strikes would serve no useful function; each party would realize each other's position and settle accordingly, dividing up the savings from having avoided a costly strike. Hence, the often-cited statement by Hicks (1966, 146-47): "The majority of actual strikes are doubtless the result of faulty negotiation.... Any means which enables either side to appreciate better the position of the other will always make a settlement easier; adequate knowledge will always make a settlement possible."

At the theoretical level, there have been a number of attempts to identify a causal connection between strikes and a variety of observable variables that appear to be determinants of strikes. One procedure is to assume that the parties base their offers and demands on different factors. Rees (1952), for example, argued that unions base their demands on current or lagging indicators such as employment and the cost of living, while management bases its offers on leading indicators such as business failures, security prices, and new contracts. Mauro (1982) theorizes that firms make their offers on the basis of product prices, while employees base their demands on the consumer price index. Kaufman (1982) argues that both parties base their positions on expected inflation, but they have divergent expectations about its expected level. In all these circumstances, the parties' offers and demands may not offset each other's, and strikes may ensue. Although these theories do provide an explanation for strikes, they do not explain why such divergences in expectations or in the determinants of offers and demands should persist.

An alternative perspective (for example, Abowd and Tracy 1989; Hayes 1984; Kennan and Wilson 1989; Tracy 1987) views strikes as serving the purpose of eliciting information from employers, who tend to have more information on the true state of their product market and financial position. Given this situation of asymmetric or private information on the part of employers, unions try to prevent them from bluffing about the true state of their financial position. They do this by compelling the firm to endure a strike if it argues that wage concessions are necessary because of its bad financial position. In such circumstances the firm can endure the strike only if its particular situation is so adverse that the loss of output from the strike is not as costly as a high wage settlement. In essence, the firm is compelled to accept a package involving lower employment (via a strike that is costly) if it insists that its particular situation is adverse; this, in turn, deters bluffing about its true position. We must emphasize that it is the firm's particular situation relative to the general state of the economy that is at issue, not the general state of the economy itself. The former is private information; the latter (that is, the business cycle) is public information.

This asymmetric-information perspective is appealing since it provides a theoretical rationale for the existence of strikes. It is not clear, however, that such private information, held only by the firm, is so important in today's world of sophisticated information processing. In addition, it is not clear why the parties would not agree to contractual arrangements whereby compensation depends upon the true state of the firm, as that information is revealed over time.

A third perspective emphasizes that strikes will depend on the joint or total cost to both parties of using the strike as opposed to other mechanisms for sorting out differences between the parties (Kennan 1980; Reder and Neuman 1980; Siebert and Addison 1981; Cousineau and Lacroix 1986; Gunderson, Kervin, and Reid 1986; Gunderson and Melino 1989; 1990; Maki 1986). That is, as discussed previously, strikes can serve a variety of functions—eliciting information, establishing reputations, solving intraorganizational problems, venting frustrations, protesting government policy, supporting workers' causes elsewhere—or they may just be mistakes or accidents. In other words, strikes help the parties sort out their differences over the division of the wealth of the enterprise and over everyday employment practices. These purposes can also be served by other mechanisms, including continuous bargaining, joint committees, grievance arbitration, voluntary interest arbitration, and even absenteeism and turnover. All of these mechanisms are costly in terms of uncertainty and their use of real resources.

Simply put, the argument for the joint-cost perspective is that whatever the function or benefits of strikes—and there are many—they are used less often and less intensely when they are costly relative to the other mechanisms that can serve the same purposes. Similarly, if strikes are mistakes or accidents, they will be made less often when the costs of such mistakes are high. It is the joint cost to *both* parties that is important. If a certain factor or variable increases the cost of a strike to only one of the parties, that party will have to "bribe" the other with more favourable settlement terms to reduce the likelihood or duration of a costly strike. The fact that a variable has a differential effect on the parties means that it has implications for settlement terms as well as strike incidence.

However, incidence and duration are reduced even though the cost of strikes is higher for one party, since the cost to that party is a component to the total cost to both parties. For example, if unemployment insurance became available to workers on strike, the joint-cost theory predicts that the use of strikes would increase because, in effect, the state would be subsidizing the cost of this method of dispute resolution. It also predicts that settlement terms would be more favourable to the union because, in effect, the bargaining power of the union would be enhanced.

It is interesting that both of the most recent theoretical developments in the strike literature—the asymmetric-information models and the joint-cost perspective—predict that strike activity will be reduced when strikes are costly. The asymmetric-information models predict this on the basis that the firm will opt for the strike to get wage concessions when the cost of the strike to the firm is low. The joint-cost model predicts that strikes will be used more often when the costs are low because strikes are thereby more appealing than the other procedures for solving basic differences at the workplace.

The recent theoretical developments in the strike literature emphasize the importance of strikes as an information-generating mechanism, compelling the parties to articulate their preferences and tradeoffs (including those within the organization) and to reveal what otherwise might be private information. They also emphasize focusing on the costs and benefits of strikes relative to other mechanisms for solving basic differences at the workplace. Although often formidable in their mathematical procedures, these models essentially formalize ideas that have long been recognized in institutional industrial relations. More important, they provide a convenient way of incorporating a wide array of institutional industrial relations variables, including policy variables, as strike determinants. In essence, they suggest the *causal* mechanism whereby the institutional industrial relations variables affect strike activity. That is, strike activity is likely to be higher if the variable increases the need for the strike to elicit information from the parties (if, for example, the variable increases uncertainty, misinformation, divergent expectations, or intraorganizational differences) or if the variable reduces the cost of using the strike as opposed to other mechanisms for solving basic differences at the workplace.

Categorizing Strike Determinants

There are almost as many ways of categorizing the causes of strikes as there are ways of classifying strikes themselves. To a certain degree, the categorization reflects the perspectives of the different disciplines that have contributed to our understanding of strike activity. Economists have focused on the economic environment (notably the business cycle, market characteristics, and inflationary expectations); sociologists have focused at the macro-level on class conflict and dramatic changes in the social system and in the relations of production, and at the micro-level on the process of bargaining and on interpersonal relations; political scientists and historians have emphasized the political environment and the importance of the strike in achieving political ends; and industrial relations analysts have emphasized dispute resolution procedures and characteristics of the bargaining structure and relationship.

For our purposes here, we have categorized the determinants of strikes as either economic or noneconomic factors, the latter including legal and procedural factors, political and historical factors, characteristics of the various actors and of the bargaining structure, and personal and interpersonal relationships. Many of these categories are obviously interdependent and overlapping; they are used simply as a convenient way to summarize the current theoretical and empirical literature and to illustrate its interrelatedness—and at times the isolation of particular disciplinary perspectives.

ECONOMIC DETERMINANTS OF STRIKES

The economic determinants of strikes can be categorized according to the ways in which strikes have been analyzed empirically: the early studies of strikes and the business cycle; the more recent studies of the time pattern of aggregate strike activity; recent cross-section studies that seek to explain variation in strikes across industries, unions, regions, cities, or collective agreements; and recent studies that use hazard-function procedures to analyze determinants of strike duration.

Business Cycles and Strike Cycles

The earliest economic studies of the time pattern of aggregate strike activity focused on the relationship of strikes to the business cycle. The expectation was for a positive relationship with strikes being highest at the peak of a business cycle. The reasoning for this theory (usually derived in an ad hoc fashion) was that at the peak of a business cycle—when unemployment is low and profits are high—workers are willing to incur the cost of a strike, largely because they are then more likely to be able to find jobs elsewhere and because they feel employers can pay more since profits are high and inventories low. This line of reasoning, however, begs the question of why the parties should not settle for large wage increases in such circumstances. More bargaining power in the hands of labour should lead to larger wage settlements, not necessarily more strikes. In spite of their inadequate theoretical explanation, the earliest studies of aggregate strike activity tended, with some notable exceptions, to find a positive relationship between strikes and the business cycle. (Many of these early studies are discussed in Kennan 1986.)

Recent Studies of Time Pattern of Aggregate Strike Activity

The more recent studies of the time pattern of aggregate strike activity differ from the earlier studies both because they endeavour to establish a more rigorous theoretical relationship between strikes and various measures of business cycle activity, and also because they use more sophisticated statistical techniques to try to disentangle the complex relationship between strikes and various measures of economic activity.

Many of the recent studies take as their departure the model developed by Ashenfelter and Johnson (1969). Theirs was the first attempt to develop a formal model whereby strikes resulted from optimizing behaviour. The essence of their model is that a firm decides on the "optimal" profit-maximizing duration of the strike by trading off strike costs with expected future wage costs in its profit-maximizing decision. Subsequent theoretical work has analyzed the analogous decision with respect to unions (Eaton 1972) and for both parties in the same model (Kaufman 1981). In addition, some recent studies have formalized models emphasizing how strikes may result when union leaders and management have objectives that differ not only from each other's, but also from their constituents' (Nelson, Stone, and Swint 1981; Swint and Nelson 1978).

Although the recent studies differ considerably in the precise specification of the variables, most relate various measures of aggregate strike activity to a variety of explanatory variables reflecting measures of aggregate business conditions. Most of the studies use annual or quarterly observations, and some pool both time-series and cross-section data by using the individual contract as the unit of observation. Explanatory variables used to reflect aggregate business conditions include the unemployment rate (or proxies such as job vacancies or the deviation of output from its trend), profits, and real wages (in some cases money wages and inflation are entered as separate explanatory variables). Even though particular studies always have some exceptions, the empirical results generally find economic factors to be important determinants of the time pattern of aggregate strike activity.

Unemployment.   A negative relationship between strikes and unemployment (or its proxies) has been documented in Canada (Abbott 1984; Card 1990; Dussault and Lacroix 1980; Gunderson, Kervin, and Reid 1986; 1989; Harrison and Stewart 1989; Smith 1972; 1976; Swidinsky and Vanderkamp 1982; and Vanderkamp 1970), in the United States (Ashenfelter and Johnson 1969; Dilts 1986; Kaufman 1981; 1982; Nelson, Stone, and Swint 1981; Shalev 1980; Snyder 1977; and Vrooman 1989), and in the United Kingdom (Davies 1979; Pencavel 1970; Sapsford 1975; and Shorey 1977, but the opposite in Ingram, Metcalf, and Wadsworth 1993; and Milner and Metcalf 1993). In general, it appears that the relationship found in the earlier business cycle studies—that strikes are less likely in depressed periods of high unemployment and more likely in periods of prosperity—is also found in the more recent econometric studies, although this relationship does not appear to be as strong or as pronounced in Canada (Snyder 1977; Vanderkamp 1970).

This finding of a positive relationship between strikes and the business cycle at first glance appears to be at odds with the joint-cost perspective, since the cost of strikes would appear to be highest at the peak of a business cycle. Although the costs may be highest at the peak, so may the benefits, to the extent that information problems (for example, uncertainty, asymmetric information, divergent expectations, intraorganizational problems) increase with the business cycle. Further, as emphasized by Reder and Neumann (1980), the parties may have developed a long-run protocol whereby they mutually agree not to be opportunistic by taking advantage of the differing strike costs over the short-run business cycle. In addition, although strike incidence is procyclical, there is some evidence that strike duration is countercyclical (Harrison and Stewart 1989; Kennan 1980) so that the duration pattern is consistent with the joint-cost perspective.

Money Wages.   Increases in money wages tend to be associated with reduced strike activity in the United States (Ashenfelter and Johnson 1969; Kaufman 1981) and in the United Kingdom (Pencavel 1970; Shorey 1977). In contrast, the relationship in Canada has been found to be statistically insignificant (Vanderkamp 1970), of the opposite sign (Cousineau and Lacroix 1976; Frank, Kelly, and MacNaughton 1982), and negative for the number of strikes but statistically insignificant for the size, duration, or volume of strike activity (Walsh 1975). Paldam and Pederson (1982) report an almost uniformly positive relationship between strike activity and aggregate money wage increases across seventeen countries in the Organization for Economic Cooperation and Development (OECD).

Inflation.   Inflation, especially if unanticipated (Blejar 1981; Kaufman 1981) has generally been associated with increased strike activity in Canada (Cousineau and Lacroix 1976; 1986; Fisher and Percy 1983; Smith 1976; Vanderkamp 1970; Walsh 1975), the United States (Ashenfelter and Johnson 1969; Gramm, Hendricks, and Kahn 1988; Kaufman 1981; 1982; 1983a; Nelson, Stone, and Swint 1981; Shalev 1980; Vrooman 1989), and in the United Kingdom (Davies 1979; Pencavel 1970; Sapsford 1975; Shorey 1977). Kaufman (1981), for example, attributes the resurgence of strikes in the United States in the 1970s to the fact that unanticipated inflation created marked divergences in the expectations of the parties.

Real Wages.   Real wages are affected by both money wages and inflation. If money wages increase faster than prices so that real wages rise, strike activity tends to dissipate in the United States (Dilts 1986; Edwards 1978; Kaufman 1981; 1983a; Shalev 1980; Snyder 1977; Swint and Nelson 1978; Vrooman 1989). This has also been true in the United Kingdom in the past (Davies 1979; Pencavel 1970), but not more recently (Ingram, Metcalf, and Wadsworth 1993), nor has it been true in Canada (Abbott 1984; Gunderson, Kervin, and Reid 1986; 1989; Snyder 1977). In addition, Paldam and Pederson (1982) find that increases in real wages had a negative effect on strike incidence in only two of seventeen countries. McLean (1977; 1979) provides some evidence to suggest that a large increase in real wages can raise workers' expectations relative to employers' ability to pay, and this can lead to subsequent increases in strike activity.

Profits.   There does not appear to be a consensus in the empirical literature on the impact of profits on strike activity. In Canada, negative relationships have been noted (Smith 1972; Walsh 1975), but positive and statistically insignificant relationships were found for the size and total-time-lost measures of strike activity (Walsh 1975). In the United States, both negative (Shalev 1980) and positive but statistically insignificant relationships (Ashenfelter and Johnson 1969; Gramm, Hendricks, and Kahn 1988; Kaufman 1981; Skeels 1971) have been found, and in the United Kingdom both positive (Pencavel 1970; Shorey 1977) and statistically insignificant negative relationships (Davies 1979) have been recorded. There is also some evidence that prolonged "strike waves" occur when profits have been steadily eroded by an extended period of rising labour costs (Screpanti 1987; Shalev 1980).

Time Trend.   A positive time trend, indicating an increasing level of strike activity over time when other factors are held constant, has been documented in numerous countries, at least until recently. This is the case in Canada for the period after the Second World War (Smith 1976; Vanderkamp 1970; Walsh 1975) and in the United Kingdom (Pencavel 1970; Sapsford 1975; Shorey 1977). A negative trend has been found in the United States (Ashenfelter and Johnson 1969; Dilts 1986; Kaufman 1981; 1982; Skeels 1971). Kaufman (1983a) found a negative trend in the United States from 1950 until the early 1960s and then a positive trend until the late 1970s. Since the 1980s, however, strike activity has dropped markedly in many countries.

Conclusion. The more recent econometric analysis of aggregate strike activity over time tends to confirm the importance of economic determinants of strikes. In particular, strike activity diminishes in periods of high unemployment and increases in periods of inflation or when real wages are eroded. In Canada, economic factors have been more successful in explaining the frequency of strikes than their size or duration (Fisher 1982; Fisher and Percy 1983; Walsh 1975), and they have been less successful in explaining strikes before the Second World War when union-organizing strikes were prominent (Skeels 1982; Snyder 1977). The ability of economic factors to explain strikes is highest for contract-renewal strikes, second highest for first-agreement strikes, and lowest for strikes during the term of the contract (Walsh 1975). The relationship between economic factors and strike activity is weaker in Canada than either in the United Kingdom or, especially, in the United States.

Canada-United States. This weaker relationship between strikes and economic factors in Canada may occur for a variety of reasons. At this stage only speculation is possible.

1. Because Canada has a smaller population than either the United Kingdom or the United States, its strike activity may be more dominated by "unusual" events. In essence, a few particular strikes may dominate the picture, especially for strike measures that involve size, duration, or person-days lost.

2. To the extent that long-duration strikes are more prominent in Canada and strike duration is not as explicable by economic factors as is strike incidence, Canadian strike activity (at least for measures involving duration) will appear to be less dependent on economic activity.

3. Strikes during the life of the contract are more often illegal in Canada than in the United States, where the right to strike during the contract is often negotiable. Since there is more pressure in Canada to wait until the contract expires before striking, it is less likely that strike activity will reflect economic conditions at the time of the strike. In essence, in Canada there is less flexibility to strike in response to current economic conditions, although illegal midcontract strikes occur frequently, and they appear to be responsive to economic factors (Fisher 1982).

4. As suggested by Vanderkamp (1970), there may simply be differences in the political and sociological environments of Canada and the United States that make Canadian strike activity less dependent on economic activity.

Cross-Section Studies and Economic Variables

The importance of economic factors in explaining strike activity has also been tested in cross-section studies (sometimes pooling time-series data also), which try to explain differences in strike activity across unions (Roomkin 1976), cities (Stern 1978), regions (Burton and Krider 1975; Horn, McGuire, and Tomkiewicz 1982), industries (Creigh and Makeham 1980; Maki and Strand 1984; McLean 1979; Mitchell 1981; Pencavel 1970; Rees 1952; Shorey 1976), or collective agreements. Empirical studies at the micro-level using the collective agreement as the unit of observation are particularly informative since their analysis is at the level of the bargaining unit, where bargaining actually occurs, and they often incorporate numerous explanatory variables describing the negotiation environment (Abowd and Tracy 1989; Card 1990; Cousineau and Lacroix 1986; Dussault and Lacroix 1980; Gramm 1986; 1987; Schell and Gramm 1987; Gunderson, Kervin, and Reid 1986; 1989; Gunderson and Melino 1989; McConnell 1989; 1990; Swidinsky and Vanderkamp 1982; Tracy 1986; 1987).

Unfortunately the cross-section studies of strike activity are exceedingly difficult to compare because of the different units of observations (for example, industry, union, region, collective agreement) and the different variables used to explain strike variation or to control for the other relevant factors. In general, however, it appears that characteristics of the economic environment are not as consistently or quantitatively important in explaining strike activity in the cross-section studies as they are in the aggregate time-series studies. Presumably the effect is dominated by noneconomic factors that do not change much over time (and hence that do not "explain" much of the variation in the time pattern of aggregate strike activity).

HAZARD ESTIMATES OF STRIKE DURATION

A number of recent econometric studies (Card 1990; Gunderson and Melino 1990; Harrison and Stewart 1989; McConnell 1990; Ondrich and Schnell 1993; Tracy 1986; 1987; Vrooman 1989; and earlier references cited in Kennan 1986) have focused on analyzing strike duration by examining the strike settlement probabilities as the strike progresses (termed the "hazard rate"). Generally, as the strike progresses, the probability of settling the next day (the conditional strike probability) declines, implying that the remaining life expectancy of the strike actually increases as the strike progresses. Much of this simply reflects the fact that the composition of the remaining strikes increasingly consists of strikes that are hard to settle, the easy ones having been settled earlier and dropped out of the sample. When these factors are controlled for, the conditional settlement probabilities increase substantially as the strike progresses although there is no consensus on the exact configuration of those settlement rates. The evidence appears to indicate, however, that the expected duration of strikes is countercyclical (that is, decreases at the peak of the business cycle) while strike incidence is procyclical.

NONECONOMIC DETERMINANTS OF STRIKES

It is somewhat of a misnomer to categorize some determinants of strikes as noneconomic since many of these factors (such as a legislative change) may alter the costs and benefits of strikes to the parties. Conversely, many of the economic or market variables may operate through intervening variables categorized as noneconomic.

Numerous studies have emphasized the noneconomic determinants of strikes, focusing on behavioural, organizational, and political aspects. Excellent recent reviews and discussions of many of these studies are given in Edwards (1992) and Kaufman (1993). Many of the studies attempt to relate strike activity to one or more of the following aspects:

characteristics of the community, union and management organizations, the negotiation process, the bargaining parties, the legal and historical context in which bargaining occurs, personality factors, and the broader sociopolitical environment.

Worker and Community Characteristics in Mobilizing Workers

Sociological investigations of the determinants of strike activity have viewed strikes as an example of collective behaviour. The mobilization of workers, while sometimes economic, is also organizational and political in nature. As Stern (1975a, 57) notes:

> There is a need for rapid mobilization of a relatively large number of participants, a well-developed system of communication, a favourable political climate, and the ability to sustain activity over some length of time. These elements may be analyzed as products of organizational characteristics as well as economic conditions.

As a result, sociologists have attempted to identify characteristics of the community and the union that may increase the mobilization and threat potential of the bargaining unit.

Resource-mobilization theories emphasize that strikes are more likely when unions have the strength and resources to mobilize individual workers into collective action (Cohn and Eaton 1989; Korpi and Shalev 1980; Edwards 1981; Franzosi 1989; Snyder 1977). This ability to mobilize resources can be associated with a wide range of factors. For example, Stern (1975b) finds strike activity to be higher in cities that are manufacturing oriented, heavily unionized, and dominated by males in the labour force. Kaufman (1983a) and Leigh (1984) also find that strikes are more prevalent in male-dominated industries. The militancy of union members has been associated with numerous personal characteristics as well as with characteristics of the community (Church, Outram, and Smith 1990; Martin 1986; McClendon and Klass 1993; Ng 1991; 1993; Schutt 1982; Tomkiewicz, Tomkiewicz, and Brenner 1985). Anderson (1981a) finds that a variable measuring the level of strike activity in the community's private sector during the previous three years is consistently important in explaining the incidence of public-sector strikes. Further, the positive relationship between plant size and strike activity is taken as evidence of the importance of alienation and militancy in mobilizing strikes (Britt and Galle 1974; Edwards 1981; Enderwick and Buckley 1982; Shorter and Tilley 1974).

Frustrated Expectations and Collective Action

Wheeler (1985) emphasises that strikes are not so much the result of rational calculations on the part of parties; rather, they tend to occur when individuals are frustrated over the gap between their expectations and their economic and social circumstances. This individual frustration gets translated into collective action when certain preconditions are present, including group solidarity. Many of the worker and community characteristics associated with the translation of individual frustration into collective action were discussed in the previous section. Wheeler indicates how this perspective is able to explain considerable strike behaviour.

Goddard (1992) also emphasizes the importance of strikes as a behavioural manifestation of worker discontent through a "collective voice." Based on Canadian data, his research provides evidence that strikes are more likely in workplaces where there is a lack of autonomy or progressive managerial practices, where union leaders are under pressure to appear militant, and where large operations create a sense of alienation.

Political Environment

A general political environment that is favourable to labour may facilitate the mobilization of workers into forms of collective action like strikes. It may also, however, facilitate labour unions making gains at the political level over social policies that can benefit labour, and this may move the forum for collective action from strikes at the workplace to action at the political level. Overall, therefore, it is not clear whether a general political environment that is favourable to labour will increase or decrease strikes at the workplace. It is also difficult to separate the independent effect of the general political environment from other factors that are at work simultaneously.

Within Canada, Quebec has tended to have a political and legislative environment that "favours" labour, and yet it has a high level of strike activity (see Chapter 16). In the United States, strikes increased in the 1930s under the pro-labour environment of the New Deal, and they decreased in the anti-labour environment of the Reagan era (Goldfield 1991). Kaufman (1993, 112), for example, calculates that strike rates in collective agreements fell to 8 per cent by 1987-89, compared to 16.5 per cent in 1954-75. Cohen (1990) shows that labour is certainly more likely to "lose" strikes in an anti-labour political environment like the 1980s in the United States, and to "win" them in a pro-labour environment like the New Deal era in the United States. Similarly, in Britain, strikes decreased substantially in the 1980s in a political and legal environment that was not supportive of labour (Ingram, Metcalf, and Wadsworth 1993). These examples illustrate that strike activity is likely to increase under a pro-labour political environment and to decrease under an anti-labour political environment. There is, however, also considerable international evidence indicating that strikes appear to be less likely in corporatist, social-democratic political environments where labour has considerable influence over the negotiation of social programs that can benefit labour. Such evidence is discussed in Chapter 17 in this volume, Hibbs (1978), Ross and Hartman (1960), Shorter and Tilly (1974), and Snyder (1975), with a critical assessment given in Edwards (1992 and references cited therein). Clearly, more research in this area would be welcome to sort out the underlying relationship between the general political environment and strike activity.

A number of studies have emphasized strikes as the manifestation of a political struggle between labour and management for power and control at the shop-floor workplace level. (Many of these studies are discussed in Edwards 1986, and Lichtenstein 1985). From this perspective, strike activity can be altered by various institutional and organizational factors; nevertheless, it is an inevitable byproduct of the struggle between labour and capital for control at the workplace.

Union and Management Organization Characteristics

Intraorganizational Conflict. A major component of the bargaining process is the negotiations that occur within the union and management sides (Ghilarducci 1988; Walton and McKersie 1965; Ross and Hartman 1960; Northrup 1984). Often there is a great diversity of interests that results in potentially conflicting goals and priorities for the collective bargaining process. Factions and different degrees of militancy often exist within the union on the basis of age, sex, occupation, seniority, or political affiliation, as well as between union leaders and the rank and file (Ashenfelter and Johnson 1969). Unless mechanisms exist within the union to resolve these conflicts, the potential for a strike may increase because of the inability of union members to agree on management's offers. Stern and Anderson (1978) reveal how, during the 1975 strike of the Canadian Union of Postal Workers, internal differences within the union over the importance of technological change had a great impact on the duration of the strike as well as on its initial occurrence. Recent studies by Gramm and Schnell (1994) and LeRoy (1994) indicate how the decision to cross the picket line and return to work (a decision that signals internal conflict within the union and that can effectively end the strike) is related to the individual characteristics of strikers, characteristics such as seniority, income, and racial identification with union leadership.

Management officials also may have major disagreements over priorities and the stand to be adopted on various issues at the bargaining table. Although this type of conflict is most pronounced in the public sector, where differences between management and elected officials are common, it is not unusual for line and staff managers in the private sector to have disputes during collective bargaining. Research on municipal employees in both Canada (Anderson 1981a) and the United States (Kochan and Baderschneider 1978) indicates that internal conflict tends to increase the probability of negotiations breaking down and a strike being called.

Inadequate Decision-Making Authority. Inadequate decision-making authority, particularly on the management side, increases the probability of a strike; for example, in the 1960s and early 1970s, the final decision on management's position often resided in the US headquarters of Canadian subsidiaries, leading union negotiators to believe that the management negotiators were little more than messengers who ran back and forth between the table and top management. For such situations, the likelihood of a strike can increase for two reasons. First, union leaders may feel that the only way to bring the real decision makers to the bargaining table is to apply pressure through a strike. Second, not having the real decision makers involved in the day-to-day negotiating process increases the likelihood that they have either unrealistic expectations about the point of settlement or inaccurate perceptions of the expectations of the union.

Research suggests that inadequate authority is more likely to be an important cause of breakdowns in negotiations when arbitration rather than the right to strike is the final action to be taken by the parties (Anderson 1981a; Kochan and Baderschneider 1978). However, Chermesh (1982) finds that in Israel strikes have been more prominent in establishments where the managerial bargainers have limited authority. On the union side, Roomkin (1976) examines the role of union policies requiring national approval of subordinate contracts and national approval of all strikes in determining strike frequency. Weak support is found for the hypothesis that more decentralized unions have a greater propensity to strike. The relationship is significant only for those unions functioning in local product markets. Overall, however, the impact of union and management decision-making authority in determining strikes is basically an unexplored area.

Foreign Ownership and Multinationals.   Related to the notion of inadequate decision-making authority that may be involved with foreign-owned firms, a number of studies have examined the extent to which such firms may be more strike-prone than domestically owned firms. The issue is complicated, however, by the fact that foreign-owned firms tend to be large multinationals that have considerable bargaining power because they can diversify their production to other plants (Rose 1991). The issue is especially important in the Canadian context, given the significant role of foreign ownership and multinationals.

Canadian studies that have used statistical techniques to control for the influence of other determinants of strikes, have produced mixed results. Cousineau, Lacroix, and Vachon (1991) find strike activity to be less in foreign-owned firms. Ng and Maki (1988) find it to be the same, but that members of national unions are more likely to strike than are members of international unions. Budd (1994) finds no difference in strike activity between foreign-owned firms and Canadian-owned firms, nor between members of national or international unions. He argues that the differences disappear when adequate control variables are included to control for the effect of other determinants of strike activity, especially industry and firm size.

Canadian research, therefore, has produced no consensus, however, on the effect of foreign ownership on strike activity. Budd (1994) also reviewed the results from a number of similar studies in the United Kingdom and Ireland, and found that there is no consensus regarding the effect of foreign ownership. Foreign-owned multinationals were more strike-prone according to three studies, less strike-prone in one, and the same as domestically owned firms in two studies. Most of these studies, however, suffered from the methodological problem that they did not use statistical techniques to control for the effect of other variables such as industry and firm size.

Size and Number of the Bargaining Units.   Knowing the impact of the size of the bargaining unit on strike activity is important because labour relations boards can influence bargaining unit size in their certification decisions. There is also the perception that some of Canada's poor strike record is attributable to the proliferation of small bargaining units, which characterize its decentralized bargaining structure. The limited empirical evidence that is available on this topic does not support this conclusion, however. On the contrary, other things being equal, strikes are less likely in single-plant bargaining units (Cousineau and Lacroix 1986; Ingram, Metcalf, and Wadsworth 1993; Kaufman 1983b; Schwartz and Koziara 1992; Vanderkamp 1982) and in smaller bargaining units (Goddard 1992; Gramm 1986; Stern 1976; Stern and Anderson 1978; Gunderson, Kervin, and Reid 1986; 1989; Swidinsky and Vanderkamp 1982).

Negotiator and Bargaining-Process Characteristics

Union and Management Trust or Hostility.   Walton and McKersie (1965) indicate that collective bargaining involves the attempts of both parties to structure their opponents' attitudes. Interpersonal sources of conflict may make it extremely difficult for union and management representatives to accept the position of the other side, to back down from an extreme position taken early in bargaining, or to compromise. As a result, hostility and a lack of trust may increase the probability of a strike. For example, Anderson (1981a) and Kochan and Baderschneider (1978) find a measure of attitudinal hostility to be strongly related to the probability of an initial impasse in the public sector. Horn, McGuire, and Tomkiewicz (1982) find mistrust and lack of communication between union and management to be important predictors of teacher strikes.

Negotiator Skills and Experience. As previously noted, Hicks (1966) stated that most strikes are the result of faulty negotiations. Inexperienced negotiators are more likely to provide incorrect cues to their opponents, generating unrealistic expectations about the terms of settlement. Moreover, inexperience may lead a negotiator to become overcommitted to a position that may be unacceptable. Movement from that position may then be impossible without a loss of face, both for the other side and for the negotiator's own constituency. Thus, a lack of skill and experience on the part of either or both negotiators is likely to increase the probability of a strike. Although Anderson (1981a) finds that most measures assessing the skill and experience of union and management negotiators were not significant in predicting the occurrence of Canadian municipal strikes, such strikes were significantly less likely to occur where the management negotiator had received formal training in labour relations (that being one measure of negotiators' possible skills). For teachers, Montgomery and Benedict (1989) found that experience in bargaining was associated with fewer and shorter strikes.

Bargaining History

Whether or not a strike is going to occur in a given round of negotiations may be affected as much by the historical context of the relationship as by current economic and noneconomic conditions. Past struggles and hostilities may well exacerbate subsequent conflict; the parties may develop a habit or pattern of conflict—a "narcotic" effect. Alternatively, strikes may serve as a safety valve and learning experience, thereby decreasing subsequent conflict. The negative experience of a strike may also discourage subsequent conflict through what is known as a "teetotaller" effect.

Using British data, Ingram, Metcalf, and Wadsworth (1993) find no evidence of either a narcotic or teetotaller effect. In contrast, Kochan (1980) presents data from both the private and public sectors in the United States supporting the narcotic effect by showing that the probability of an impasse almost doubles if negotiations have broken down and an impasse had been declared in the previous round of negotiations. Swidinsky and Vanderkamp (1982) also find that strikes in Canada are more likely when the previous bargaining round also involved higher levels of conflict, such as a strike (although Gunderson, Kervin, and Reid (1986; 1989) and Goddard (1992) do not find such an effect). Whether these results reflect the legacy of past strikes in affecting conflict in subsequent rounds of bargaining, or simply the fact that some situations are persistently more strike-prone than others is not answered by such comparisons.

In an attempt to answer this question, Schnell and Gramm (1987) compare strike behaviour over four consecutive negotiations by 147 bargaining units in US manufacturing, after controlling for all observable and unobservable differences that may affect the propensity to strike. This approach enables them to determine whether previous strikes had an independent effect in reducing or exacerbating subsequent conflict. They find strong evidence of a teetotaller effect—that is, that the experience of a previous strike has the sobering effect of reducing the propensity to indulge in a subsequent strike—after controlling for the effect of any innate propensity to strike. Mauro (1982) finds similar evidence of a teetotaller effect in bargaining rounds, after controlling for the effect of unobservable factors that otherwise may lead some bargaining situations to experience persistent strikes. Card (1988) also finds evidence of a teetotaller effect, but only if the previous strike was of long duration (two weeks or more). If the previous strike was short, the unresolved issues apparently carry over into the subsequent round of bargaining, enhancing the probability of a subsequent strike. This suggests that teetotalling only follows a severe hangover; a small taste simply whets the appetite! Ondrich and Schnell (1993) also provide evidence that unresolved issues from previous bargaining rounds tend to lead to longer strikes in subsequent rounds.

DISPUTE RESOLUTION PROCEDURES

All Canadian jurisdictions have established a number of procedures, usually involving the intervention of a neutral third party, to help the parties resolve their disputes (Ponak and Falkenberg 1988). Some purposes of third party intervention are to: provide information and help the parties articulate their preferences and tradeoffs; provide a period for emotions to ebb and hostilities to cool off; solve interpersonal and political problems through enabling the parties to save face by yielding to the suggestions of a third party; bring public awareness to and perhaps pressures on the parties; and in the most extreme form of intervention—compulsory interest arbitration—to provide for a substitute for the strike. These objectives are facilitated to varying degrees by a variety of forms of third-party intervention including conciliation, mediation, factfinding, and arbitration. (The terms "conciliation," "mediation," and "factfinding" are sometimes used interchangeably and are often used differently in different jurisdictions as well as in different labour relations laws. Hence, the terminology used here should be regarded as a common, but not exclusive, way of defining these concepts.)

Types of Dispute Resolution Procedures

Compulsory Conciliation. Canada was one of the few countries to adopt a system of compulsory conciliation during the early 1900s. In the current context, most jurisdictions require conciliation as a precondition to a work stoppage. Typically, at the request of either party, a government conciliator is appointed by the provincial ministry of labour. The conciliator meets with the parties and reports the possibilities of a settlement to the minister of labour. After the report has been filed and a specified period of time has elapsed (usually seven or fourteen days), the union obtains the right to strike and management the right to lock out. In some jurisdictions, if conciliation is unsuccessful, the dispute is forwarded to a conciliation board (usually tripartite), also charged with investigating the dispute and reporting to the minister.

Mediation. Although the terms "mediation" and "conciliation" are sometimes used interchangeably, mediation is often reserved for the voluntary use of a neutral third party, often a nongovernment professional, who gets involved after the conciliation process is exhausted, and possibly when the strike is in progress. Mediation usually is more interventionist than conciliation, with the mediator not just providing information at the early stages, but also suggesting compromises at subsequent stages and ultimately even suggesting proposals and possibly settlement terms. The mediator's views can be used or ignored by the parties (hence the importance of trust and confidence in the mediator); they need not involve a recommendation, and they are usually not made public, except possibly in public sector disputes.

Factfinding. Factfinding, a task often performed by conciliation boards, is a more formal process than mediation. The factfinder (or factfinding board) is charged with the responsibility of investigating the issues in dispute and making formal recommendations to the labour relations board and possibly to the public. As in mediation, however, the recommendations of the factfinder do not have to be adopted by the parties.

Typically, the factfinding process includes formal briefs from both union and management as well as a formal hearing where both parties are allowed to present their views. In some situations, however, the term "factfinding" is used (as the word implies) to refer to a stage in which a third party simply helps the parties compile the relevant facts before any intervention by a conciliator or mediator.

Arbitration. Arbitration is the strongest form of third party intervention, since it involves the establishment of terms and conditions of the collective agreement by a third-party arbitrator. Such arbitration is termed "interest arbitration" to distinguish it from "rights or grievance arbitration," the latter involving a neutral third party to interpret the existing collective agreement. Interest arbitration usually serves as a substitute for the strike in situations in which strikes are banned, as is often the case for various elements of the public sector such as police, firefighters, hospital workers, teachers, and the civil service. Canadian jurisdictions vary considerably in requirements for interest arbitration for the different elements of the public sector (see Chapter 15). Although the arbitration decision itself is binding on both union and management, the decision to engage in arbitration may be voluntary. Such voluntary arbitration is rare, however, compared to compulsory arbitration, which is required by law if the parties cannot come to an agreement.

Arbitration may be either conventional or final-offer. Under conventional arbitration, arbitrators may make any award they believe to be appropriate, selecting some positions of either party or modifying them as necessary. In contrast, under final-offer arbitration, the arbitrator must select the exact position of either the union or management on a total-package basis or an issue-by-issue basis.

Arbitration, especially in its compulsory form, has been criticized as an unacceptable strike substitute since it does not provide the same inducements to the parties to settle as would a strike. Specifically, arbitration has often been found to chill genuine collective bargaining. This "chilling effect" is said to occur because the parties may hold back concessions during bargaining, believing that the arbitrator is likely to split the difference between their final positions. Arbitration has also been criticized because it may create a "narcotic effect," making the parties dependent on the arbitrator to determine their terms and conditions of employment. Evidence of both chilling and narcotic effects has been found in the arbitration system in the Canadian federal public service (Anderson and

Kochan 1977); however, the existing empirical evidence in general (reviewed in Anderson 1981b; Ponak and Falkenberg 1988) does not yield conclusive results.

Other Forms of Dispute Resolution.   In the Canadian public sector, the government has often taken an alternative approach to resolving disputes, especially strikes by public employees. More and more frequently, both the federal and provincial governments have been willing to pass special back-to-work legislation requiring the termination of a strike and forcing the parties back to the bargaining table (see Chapter 15). Thus, strikes may be reduced through mediation and factfinding, prohibited and replaced by arbitration, or ended through special legislation.

Effect of Dispute Resolution and Other Policy Variables

There is very little empirical evidence on the effect of various dispute-resolution procedures or other labour relations policy variables on the level of strike activity. This is particularly unfortunate since, by definition, such variables could be manipulated to reduce the level of strike activity, if this outcome was considered desirable. In contrast, other possible strike determinants, such as the economic variables and the season, region, and industry, are subject to little or no policy manipulation.

Specific Laws.   The few empirical studies that have included policy variables have generally simply added a variable to reflect the impact of a particular law such as the Landrum-Griffin Act (Ashenfelter and Johnson 1969; Nelson, Stone, and Swint 1981), right-to-work laws (Gramm 1986), state penalties for public sector workers who go on strike (Olson 1986), rights for school districts to reschedule teacher strike days to qualify for state aid (Olson 1984; 1986; Montgomery and Benedict 1989), the availability of unemployment insurance for workers on strike (Hutchens, Lipsky, and Stern 1992; Ondrich and Schnell 1993) or an index of labour law changes that affect collective bargaining and union power (Ingram, Metcalf, and Wadsworth 1993). These studies generally find that laws and policies designed to discourage strikes or make them more costly or difficult do tend to reduce strike activity.

Prohibitions on Right-to-Strike in Public Sector.   A number of empirical studies have also examined the extent to which legislative prohibitions on union activity and the right to strike in the public sector have deterred strikes (Currie and McConnell 1991; Ichniowski 1982; 1988; Northrup 1984; Olson 1986; 1988; Peterson 1981; Partridge 1988; Zimmer and Jacobs 1981). Most find public sector strike activity is deterred, but by no means eliminated, by prohibitions and penalties on the right to strike.

Currie and McConnell (1991), for example, analyze the effect of alternative dispute resolution procedures on public sector strikes in Canada over the period 1964-1987. They find that granting public sector workers the right to strike does lead to significantly higher strike frequencies, compared to when the right is prohibited and arbitration is required. Furthermore, the cost per dispute is much higher when the dispute takes the form of a strike rather than an arbitration. For these reasons, dispute costs (strikes plus arbitrations) are higher when the right to strike is granted, compared to when arbitration is required. They argue that this must be traded off against higher wage costs which tend to occur under arbitration.

Hebdon (1991), however, finds that prohibiting the right to strike among public sector workers in Canada leads to more grievances. In essence, restricting the right to strike simply redirects conflict into other costly forms such as grievances. This suggests that while dispute costs (strikes plus arbitrations) may be lower when strikes are prohibited, this may not be true when other forms of dispute, such as grievances, are also considered.

Labour Relations Policy Variables.   A comprehensive analysis of the impact that a wide range of Canadian labour relations policy variables have on strike activity is summarized in Table 14.5, based on the econometric studies cited in the source.

TABLE 12.5   Effect of Labour Relations Policy Variables on Strike Activity

Labour Relations Policy Variable	Effect on Incidence	Effect on Duration
	%	days
Average Incidence and Duration	15.9%	35.0 days
Conciliation officer	-7.9	1.2
Conciliation officer and board	-12.8*	-1.1
Cooling-off period (days)	0.2	0.5
Mandatory strike vote	-11.1*	-7.4*
Employer-initiated vote option	18.9*	-1.5
Dues checkoff	-9.1*	6.4*
Prohibition on replacement workers	24.4*	6.9*
Negotiated reopeners	-5.4	1.5
Automatic reopeners	6.6	-3.4*

* Statistically significant at p < .05 level.
SOURCE: Strike incidence effects are from Gunderson, Kervin, and Reid (1989) based on Labour Canada's Major Collective Agreements (500 or more employees) data base for the years 1971-1985.   Strike duration effects are from Gunderson and Melino (1990) based on Labour Canada's Work Stoppage File for strikes of any size for the years 1967-1985.

A nontechnical summary of these studies, and the qualifications that are appropriate given the nature of the data, are given in Gunderson, Melino, and Reid (1990). The first column gives the effect of each policy variable on strike incidence—that is, the probability that the contract will be settled following the occurrence of a strike. These changes should be interpreted relative to the average strike incidence of 15.9 per cent; that is, over the period 1967-1985 almost 16 per cent of contracts involved a strike. The second column gives the effect of each policy variable on strike duration—that is, the length of strikes that occurred (which averaged 35 days over that period). The discussion here will focus on those variables that had a statistically significant (as denoted by an asterisk [*]) and quantitatively large impact on strike activity, since they are of most policy relevance and are the ones where most confidence can be placed on the relationship.

The existence of a conciliation officer and board is associated with a substantial 12.8 per cent reduction in the likelihood that a strike will occur. A mandatory strike vote (a majority of bargaining unit members must vote in favour of the strike before it can occur) is associated with an 11.1 per cent reduction in strike incidence as well as a reduction of seven days in the duration of strikes. Dues checkoff is associated with a substantial 9.1 per cent reduction in the likelihood of a strike but a 6.9-day increase in the duration of strikes. The existence of automatic reopener provisions (whereby the collective agreement can be reopened in the event of technological change that was unanticipated at the time the contract was signed) is associated with a 3.4-day reduction in the length of strikes.

The most controversial, and perhaps unexpected, result is that legislation prohibiting the use of replacement workers (so called "anti-scab" legislation) is associated with a 24.4 per cent increase in strike incidence and a 6.9-day increase in the length of strikes. While these magnitudes are large they should be regarded with caution since they are based exclusively on the anti-strike breaking provisions that were introduced in Quebec in 1977; other pro-labour legislative changes were also introduced in Quebec at the same time (see Chapter 16). But consistent with these results, Lacroix and Lesperance (1988) also found for the period 1961-81 that bans on replacement workers and laws permitting secondary picketing have led to increased strike incidence in Quebec, Ontario, and British Columbia.

A number of theoretical explanations have been offered for why the restrictions on the use of replacement workers can lead to increased strike activity. In their review of the game-theory analysis of strikes, Kennan and Wilson (1989) indicate that banning replacement workers actually increases the union's uncertainty about the firm's willingness to pay to end the strike since that willingness is no longer constrained by the firm's option of using replacement workers. When the firm could use replacement workers, the union knew that this would place an upper limit on the firm's willingness to pay to end the strike—that upper limit is removed if replacement workers are not an option. As well, a ban on replacement workers makes the strike a more attractive weapon to the union compared to other mechanisms such as continuing to work without a contract (Cramton and Tracy 1992). Whatever the reason, the limited evidence from Canada suggests that legislative bans on replacement workers are associated with an increase in both the incidence and duration of strikes. It will be interesting to examine this relationship in the future once the recent anti-strike replacement legislation adopted in Ontario and British Columbia have had sufficient time to have an impact. It is also useful to recall that banning the use of strike replacements has other policy objectives. It was first introduced in Quebec, for example, to reduce picket line violence, an outcome that has largely been achieved.

CONSEQUENCES OF STRIKE ACTIVITY

Strikes are of policy interest in large part because of their perceived effects on the parties themselves, on third parties, and on the economy as a whole. Canada's poor strike record by international standards has been cited as a possible contributor to its poor productivity performance and as a possible concern to foreign investors and importers. Although conjectures abound, there is very little rigorous statistical analysis of the effects of strikes, certainly much less than the analysis of strike determinants. Nevertheless, a few empirical studies estimate the diverse consequences of strikes.

With respect to the effect of strikes on wages, Canadian studies show mixed results. Lacroix (1980a) cites a substantial number of empirical studies that find that strikes lead to higher subsequent wage settlements; however, his own empirical results suggest that this result is very sensitive to the specifications of the estimation equation. Card (1990) finds no relationship between strikes and subsequent wage settlements, except for very long strikes which lead to lower wage settlements. Reid and Oman (1991) find that the wage gains from shorter strikes are such that they tend to outweigh the costs to workers (see also Eaton 1972 and Gennard 1982). For longer strikes the opposite is the case. This tends to confirm the industrial relations stereotype that unions "win" short strikes, but "lose" long ones. Evidence of monetary losses from a long strike of university faculty in Saskatchewan is also given in Ng (1993). Based on US data, McConnell (1989) finds that strikes lead to lower wage settlements.

There is also evidence that strikes reduce the stock market value of struck firms where they occur (Becker and Olson 1986; Davidson, Worrell, and Garrison 1988; DeFusco and Fuess 1991; Greer, Martinez, and Reusser 1980; Neumann 1980), although they increase the value of nonstruck firms that get additional business because of the strike (DeFusco and Fuess 1991). There is some evidence that strikes have negative psychological consequences on the workers involved in the strike (McBride, Lancee, and Freeman 1981; Stoner and Arora 1987), albeit there is also evidence that strikes can galvanize community support for strikers (Gibson, Spencer, and Granville 1989; MacDowell 1993) as well as have a cathartic and constructive effect on labour-management relations (Beatty and Ganz 1989). However, most empirical studies find that the effects of strikes usually are not dramatic (for example, Gunderson and Melino 1987; Hameed and Lomas 1975; Knight 1989; Maki 1983; Neumann and Reder 1984; Paarsch 1990).

Certainly, the consequences are not as substantial as often portrayed in the media at the time of a strike. Gunderson and Melino (1987), for example, indicate that in the North American auto industry the typical pattern has been for inventories to be built up prior to a strike, through increased production and increased prices, with the latter having deterred consumption. After a strike, inventories were again restored in the same fashion. The authors indicate that "both consumers and producers rationally respond to the expected and the actual event of the strike through a variety of inter-temporal adjustments; and, while the initial effects are in some instances quite pronounced, the long-run effects are usually minimal" (p. 1). But, as the survey evidence of Tang and Ponak (1986) indicates, the perceived costs of strikes differ dramatically across different organizations.

The impact of strikes on productivity has been found to be negative (Flaherty 1987) as well as positive (Knight 1989). McHugh (1991) provides evidence indicating that negative productivity effects were more pronounced in linked industries that supplied or depended upon the struck industries than they were in the struck industries themselves.

Further, it must be emphasized that the empirical literature on strike effects tends to focus on private sector strikes, where customers usually have options in terms of other suppliers or of postponing purchases. In the public sector, the situation is quite different because of the essential nature of many of the services and the lack of alternatives. Here, the third-party effects on the general public can be quite substantial; this is, of course, the rationale for binding interest arbitration as an alternative to a strike. In the quasi-public sector and for regulated utilities (for example, telephone, transportation), the situation is likely to fall in between those of the private and public sectors; third parties (that is, customers) usually have some alternatives, although they are not as readily available as for consumers in the private sector. This threat of a loss of customers puts some pressure on the parties to settle—more so than in the public sector, but less so than in the purely private sector.

CONCLUDING COMMENTS

Although there is a voluminous literature on strike determinants, most of it simply relates measures of strike activity to a variety of variables for which data are available. Little effort is made to understand the causal mechanisms through which these observable factors affect strike activity. Recent theoretical work has somewhat improved on this lack of analysis by emphasizing that strikes have benefits, especially in terms of the information they generate, and that whatever the function of strikes, they will be used less when the joint costs to both parties are great relative to the costs of other mechanisms for achieving the same end.

On the empirical side, the most important recent advances involve the use of large-scale data sets that have the individual contract (that is, the collective agreement) as the unit of observation. This is important, not only because this is the level at which bargaining actually occurs, but also because it can enable the incorporation into the study of a number of characteristics of the bargaining unit. It can also enable the construction of longitudinal data sets involving bargaining rounds for the same bargaining pair. Such longitudinal data, in turn, are important because they facilitate controlling for the effect of otherwise unobserved factors that may give rise to persistent strike-proneness. In addition, a beginning has been made in analyzing the effect of labour relations policy variables, an important consideration since these are the levers that can be manipulated to alter strike activity. The recent theoretical and empirical advances may help explain a variety of phenomena associated with Canadian strike activity: the high level by international standards; the increase, especially from the mid-1960s to the mid-1970s; and the decline since the mid-1970s.

Since the mid-1960s, the Canadian economy has been subject to considerable growth involving new entrants into the market and new unionization. New bargaining relationships carry with them little mutual information about each party's "resistance points" and involve a desire on the part of each to establish a reputation. In addition, in the 1970s the economy was subject to numerous shocks, including oil price changes, unanticipated inflation, and trade shocks, and these increased uncertainty, especially concerning the firm's ability to pay. They put a premium on the strike as a mechanism to elicit information and re-establish the appropriate division of the firm's rents. The greater uncertainly also led to shorter contracts, increasing the number of times the parties are exposed to the risk of an end-of-contract dispute. This, in turn, may have led to an increased use of renegotiation strikes as opposed to midcontract dispute resolution procedures such as grievances, joint committees, and continuous bargaining (although the extent to which these serve as substitute dispute resolution procedures remains empirically unknown and an interesting subject for research).

Canada's high strike record reflects not only these information problems, but also a concentration of strike-prone, resource-based industries which tend to be strike-prone in other countries as well. Information problems are exacerbated by the open nature of the Canadian economy and the extent of foreign trade and possibly even foreign control. In addition, Canadian unions negotiate a wide range of items. In contrast, in many European countries, many of these issues (for example, hours of work) are addressed at the political level, where the unions are involved as partners in establishing a broad social contract.

With respect to the decline in strike activity that has occurred since the mid-1970s, the joint-cost and asymmetric-information perspectives also provide some insights. That period has been characterized by intense international competition and dramatic restructuring and downsizing. It is no longer the case that information is asymmetric with firms knowing more about the true state of demand and ability to pay than do workers; rather, both parties know that economic difficulties prevail, and this has been revealed through the trend towards downsizing and restructuring. There is less uncertainty about the "economic rents" or excess profits to bargain over, since such rents have been dissipated by international competition. In essence, there is less need to fight over the "spoils" when there are no spoils to divide! The joint cost to both parties of engaging in strikes is also higher since competitors from abroad may permanently replace the lost output and the jobs associated with that output. Furthermore, multinationals may locate their new plants and investment in countries where there is less risk of strikes. This is especially the case since just-in-time delivery systems put a premium on being able to deliver products and services with a high degree of certainty and reliability.

In essence, in recent years the cost of using the strike mechanism has increased and the benefits have declined—the latter especially in terms of eliciting information from the parties. This may explain some of the decline in strike activity that has occurred in Canada, at least since the 1970s. Since these economic pressures are stronger in the private sector than in the public sector, this may also explain why strike activity has declined more precipitously in the private sector than in the public sector. The increase in the cost and the decline in the benefits of using the strike mechanism may also explain some of the increased use of alternative dispute resolution procedures and co-operative as opposed to adversarial bargaining that has occurred. These may be necessary for the joint survival of both business and jobs in times of intense international competition and when business investment and plant-location decisions are increasingly made on an international basis. Just as "necessity is the mother of invention," it may also be the mother of innovation in alternative dispute-resolution procedures.

Although these explanations of our changing pattern of strike activity are plausible, it must be admitted that neither the state of theory or evidence in the strike literature gives us a very complete—some would say even adequate—explanation of the various dimensions of strike activity over time or across various industries, regions, countries, and bargaining units. For every generalization and empirical regularity there is an exception; often no generalizations are possible. Strikes remain somewhat of a mystery, an area where we should be modest about our ability to predict behaviour and consequences. This uncertainty reflects the variety of institutional, economic, and process factors that impinge on the parties, as well as the fact that if strikes and their outcomes were completely predictable, they would serve little purpose.

QUESTIONS

1. What measures of strike activity are typical? What information does each provide about strikes?

2. Describe the main function that strikes play.

3. How are the business cycle and strikes related?

4. Describe four main dispute resolution mechanisms.

5. How does mediation work to reduce the likelihood of a strike?

6. In your opinion, what impact do strikes have on the Canadian economy? Why might this impact differ among sectors (private, regulated, public)?

7. "Unequal bargaining power on the part of one of the parties in the negotiation process has implications for wage determination, not for strikes." Discuss.

8. Why may one expect the relationship of strike cycles to business cycles to differ in Canada and the United States?

9. Discuss how strikes may arise because of an asymmetry of information between employers and employees. What does this imply about the effect of changing economic conditions?

10. Discuss the joint-cost perspective as a theory of strike determination. Given this perspective, how would you expect strike activity to be affected by each of the following factors: compulsory conciliation; the availability of unemployment insurance for workers on strike; and an increase in the unemployment rate?

11. What impact would you expect free trade between Canada and the United States to have on strike activity in Canada?

12. Use the joint-cost perspective and the asymmetric-information theories of strike activity to explain the following empirical "facts" about strike activity in Canada: its high level relative to other countries; its increase between the mid-1960s and mid-1970s; and the greater decline in the private sector compared to the public sector.

REFERENCES

ABBOTT, M.G. 1984. "Specification Tests of Quarterly Econometric Models of Aggregate Strike Frequency in Canada." In R. Ehrenberg, ed, *Research in Labor Economics*. London: JAI Press Inc.

ABOWD, J., and J. TRACY. 1989. "Market Structure, Strike Activity, and Union Wage Settlements," *Industrial Relations* 28: 227-50.

ANDERSON, J.C. 1981a. "Determinants of Collective Bargaining Impasses: Effects of Dispute Resolution Procedures." In R. Petersen and G. Bamber, eds, *Industrial Relations and Conflict Management*. New York: Martinus Nijhoff.

————. 1981b. "The Impact of Arbitration: A Methodological Assessment." *Industrial Relations* 20: 129-48.

ANDERSON, J.C., and T.A. KOCHAN. 1977. "Impasse Procedures in the Canadian Federal Service: Effects of the Bargaining Process." *Industrial and Labor Relations Review* 30: 282-301.

ANDERSON, J.C., M. GUNDERSON, and A. PONAK. 1989. "Strikes and Dispute Resolution." In J. Anderson, M. Gunderson, A. Ponak,.eds, *Union-Management Relations in Canada,* 2nd edition. Don Mills ON: Addison-Wesley.

ASHENFELTER, O., and G. JOHNSON. 1969. "Bargaining Theory, Trade Unions, and Industrial Activity." *American Economic Review* 59: 35-49.

BEATTY, C., and J. GANZ. 1989. "After the Strike: Changing the Teacher Board Relationship." *Relations Industrielles/ Industrial Relations* 44: 569-589.

BECKER, B.E., and C.A. OLSON. 1986. "The Impact of Strikes on Shareholder Equity." *Industrial and Labor Relations Review* 39: 425-38.

BLEJER, M. 1981. "Strike Activity and Wage Determination Under Rapid Inflation: The Chilean Case." *Industrial and Labour Relations Review* 34: 356-64.

BRETT, J., and S. GOLDBERG. 1979. "Wildcat Strikes in Bituminous Coal Mining." *Industrial and Labor Relations Review* 32: 465-83.

BRITT, D., and O. GALLE. 1974. "Structural Antecedents of the Shape of Strikes: A Comparative Analysis." *American Sociological Review* 35: 642-51.

BUDD, J. 1994. "The Effect of Multinational Institutions on Strike Activity in Canada." *Industrial And Labor Relations Review* 47: 401-16.

BURTON, J.F., and C.E. KRIDER. 1975. "The Incidence of Strikes in Public Employment." In D.S. Hamermesh, ed, *Labour in the Public and Non-profit Sectors*. Princeton, NJ: Princeton University Press.

BYRNE, D.M., and R.H. KING. 1986. "Wildcat Strikes in U.S. Manufacturing, 1960-1977." *Journal of Labor Research* 7: 387-402.

CAMERON, S. 1983. "An International Comparison of the Volatility of Strike Behaviour." *Relations industrielles/Industrial Relations* 38: 767-84.

CARD, D. 1988. "Longitudinal Analysis of Strike Activity." *Journal of Labor Economics* 6: 147-76.

————. 1990. "Strikes and Wages: A Test of an Asymmetric Information Model." *Quarterly Journal of Economics* 105: 625-659.

CHERMESH, R. 1982. "Strike Proneness and Characteristics of Industrial Relations Systems at the Organization Level: A Discriminant Analysis." *Journal of Management Studies* 19: 413-35.

CHURCH, R., Q. OUTRAM, and D. SMITH. 1990. "British Coal Mining Strikes 1893-1940: Dimensions, Distribution and Persistence." *British Journal of Industrial Relations* 28: 329-50.

COHEN, I. 1990. "Political Climate and Two Airline Strikes: Century Aviation in 1932 and Continental Airlines in 1983-85." *Industrial and Labor Relations Review* 43: 308-23.

COHN, S., and A. EATON. 1989. "Historical Limits on Neoclassical Strike Theories: Evidence from French Coal Mining, 1890-1935." *Industrial and Labor Relations Review* 42: 649–62.

COUSINEAU, J., and R. LACROIX., 1976. "Activite Economique, Inflation et Activite de Greve." *Relations industrielles/Industrial Relations* 31: 341-58.

———. 1986. "Imperfect Information and Strikes: An Analysis of Canadian Experience, 1967-82." *Industrial and Labor Relations Review* 39: 377-87.

COUSINEAU, J., R. LACROIX, and D. VACHON. 1991. "Foreign Ownership and Strike Activity in Canada." *Relations industrielles/ Industrial Relations* 46: 616-29.

CRAMTON, P., and J. TRACY. 1992. "Strikes and Holdouts in Wage Bargaining: Theory and Data." *American Economic Review* 82: 100-21.

CREIGH, S., and P. MAKEHAM. 1980. "Variations in Strike Activity within UK Manufacturing Industry." *Industrial Relations Journal* 11: 32-7.

CURRIE, J., and S. McCONNELL. 1991. "Collective Bargaining in the Public Sector: The Effect of Legal Structure on Dispute Costs and Wages." *American Economic Review* 81: 693-718.

DAVIDSON, W., D. WORRELL, and S. GARRISON. 1988. "Effect of Strike Activity on Firm Value." *Academy of Management Journal* 31: 387-94.

DAVIES, R.J. 1979. "Economic Activity, Incomes Policy and Strikes—A Quantitative Analysis." *British Journal of Industrial Relations* 17: 205-23.

DEFUSCO, R., and S. FUESS. 1991. "The Effects of Airline Strikes on Struck and Nonstruck Carriers." *Industrial and Labor Relations Review* 44: 324-33.

DILTS, D. 1986. "Strike Activity in the United States: An Analysis of the Stocks and Flows." *Journal of Labor Research* 7: 187-99.

DUSSAULT, F. and R. LACROIX. 1980. "Activité de grève: un test des hypothèses explicatives traditionnelles." *Canadian Journal of Economics* 13: 632-44.

EATON, B.C. 1973. "The Worker and the Profitability of the Strike." *Industrial and Labor Relations Review* 26: 670-79.

EDWARDS, P.K. 1978. "Time Series Regression Models of Strike Activity: A Reconsideration with American Data." *British Journal of Industrial Relations* 16: 320-34.

———. 1981. "The Strike-proneness of British Manufacturing Establishments." *British Journal of Industrial Relations* 29: 135-48.

———. 1986. *Conflict at Work: A Materialist Analysis of Workplace Relations.* Oxford: Basil Blackwell.

———. 1992. "Industrial Conflict: Themes and Issues in the Recent Research." *British Journal of Industrial Relations* 30: 361-404.

ENDERWICK, P., and P.J. BUCKLEY. 1982. "Strike Activity and Foreign Ownership: An Analysis of British Manufacturing 1971-73." *British Journal of Industrial Relations* 20: 308-21.

FISHER, E.G. 1982. "Strike Activity and Wildcat Strikes in British Columbia: 1945-1975." *Relations industrielles/Industrial Relations* 37: 284-301.

FISHER, E.G., and M.B. PERCY. 1983. "The Impact of Unanticipated Output of Consumer Prices on Wildcat Strikes." *Relations industrielles/Industrial Relations* 38: 254-74.

FISHER, M.R. 1973. *Measurement of Labour Disputes and their Economic Effects.* Paris: Organization for Economic Co-operation and Development.

FLAHERTY, S. 1983. "Contract Status and the Economic Determinants of Strike Activity." *Industrial Relations* 22: 20-33.

———. 1987. "Strike Activity, Worker Militancy, and Productivity Change in Manufacturing, 1961-1981." *Industrial and Labor Relations Review* 4: 585-600.

FORCHHEIMER, K. 1948. "Some International Aspects of the Strike Movement." *Bulletin of the Oxford University Institute of Statistics* 10: 9-24.

FRANK, J.A., M.J. KELLY, and B.D. MacNAUGHTON. 1982. "Legislative Change and Strike Activity in Canada, 1926-1974." *Relations industrielles/Industrial Relations* 37: 267-83.

FRANZOSI, R. 1989. "One Hundred Years of Strike Statistics: Methodological and Theoretical Issues in Quantitative Strike Research." *Industrial and Labor Relations Review* 42: 348-62.

GAREN, J., and J. KRISLOV. 1988. "An Examination of the New American Strike Statistics in Analyzing Aggregate Strike Incidence." *British Journal of Industrial Relations* 26: 75-84.

GENNARD, J. 1982. "The Financial Costs and Returns of Strikes." *British Journal of Industrial Relations* 20: 247-56.

GHILARDUCCI, T. 1988. "The Impact of Internal Politics on the 1981 UMWA Strike." *Industrial Relations* 27: 371-84.

GILSON, C., I. SPENCER, and S. GRANVILLE. 1989. "The Impact of a Strike on the Attitudes and Behaviour of a Rural Community." *Relations industrielles/Industrial Relations* 44: 785-802.

GODARD, J. 1992. "Strikes as Collective Voice: A Behavioral Analysis of Strike Activity." *Industrial and Labor Relations Review* 46: 161-175.

GOLDFIELD, M. 1991. "The Economy, Strikes, Union Growth and Public Policy During the 1930s." *Proceedings of the 1991 Spring Meeting of the Industrial Relations Research Association.*

GRAMM, C. 1986. "The Determinants of Strike Incidence and Severity: A Micro Level Study." *Industrial and Labor Relations Review* 39:361-75.

———. 1987. "New Measures of the Propensity to Strike During Contract Negotiations, 1971-1980." *Industrial and Labor Relations Review* 40: 406-17.

GRAMM, C., W. HENDRICKS, and L. KAHN. 1988. "Inflation Uncertainty and Strike Activity." *Industrial Relations* 27: 114-29.

GRAMM, C., and J. SCHNELL. 1994. "Difficult Choices: Crossing the Picket Line During the 1987 National Football League Strike." *Journal of Labor Economics* 12: 41-73.

GREER, C., S. MARTIN, and T. REUSSER. 1980. "The Effect of Strikes on Shareholder Returns." *Journal of Labor Research* 1: 217-30.

GUNDERSON, M., J. KERVIN, and F. REID. 1986. "Logit Estimates of Strike Incidence from Canadian Contract Data." *Journal of Labor Economics* 4: 257-76.

———. 1989. "The Effect of Labour Relations Legislation on Strike Incidence." *Canadian Journal of Economics* 22: 779-794.

GUNDERSON, M., and A. MELINO. 1987. "Estimating Strike Effects in a General Model of Prices and Quantities." *Journal of Labor Economics* 5: 1-19.

———. 1990. "The Effects of Public Policy on Strike Duration." *Journal of Labor Economics* 8: 295-316.

GUNDERSON, M., A. MELINO, and F. REID. 1990. "The Effects of Canadian Labour Relations Legislation on Strike Incidence and Duration." *Labor Law Journal* 41: 512-18.

HAMEED, S.M., and T. LOMAS. 1975 "Measurement of Production Losses Dues to Strikes in Canada: An Input-Output Analysis." *British Journal of Industrial Relations* 13: 86-93.

HARRISON, A., and M. STEWART. 1987. "Cyclical Fluctuations in Strike Durations." *American Economic Review* 79: 827-41.

HAYES, B. 1984. "Unions and Strikes with Asymmetric Information." *Journal of Labor Economics* 2: 57-83.

HEBDON, R. 1991. "Ontario's No-Strike Laws: A Test of the Safety Valve Hypothesis." Proceedings of the 28th Conference of the Canadian Industrial Relations Research Association.

HIBBS, D. 1978. "On the Political Economy of Long-Run Trends in Strike Activity." *British Journal of Political Science* 8: 153-75.

HICKS, J. R. 1963. *The Theory of Wages,* 3rd ed. New York: St. Martin's Press.

HORN, R.N., W.J. MCGUIRE, and J. TOMKIEWICZ. 1982. "Work Stoppages by Teachers: An Empirical Analysis." *Journal of Labor Research* 3: 487-96.

HUTCHENS, R., D. LIPSKY, and R. STERN. 1992. "Unemployment Insurance and Strikes." *Journal of Labor Research* 13: 337-54.

ICHNIOWSKI, C. 1982. "Arbitration and Police Bargaining: Prescriptions for the Blue Flu." *Industrial Relations* 21: 149-66.

———. 1988. "Police Recognition Strikes: Illegal and Ill Fated." *Journal of Labor Research* 9: 183-97.

INGRAM, R., D. METCALF, and J. WADSWORTH. 1993. "Strike Incidence in British Manufacturing in the 1980s." *Industrial and Labor Relations Review* 46: 704-17.

JONES, J.C.H., and W.D. WALSH. 1984. "Inter-industry Strike Frequencies: Some pooled Cross-sectional Evidence from Canadian Secondary Manufacturing." *Journal of Labor Research* 5: 419-25.

KAUFMAN, B. 1981. "Bargaining Theory, Inflation, and Cyclical Strike Activity in Manufacturing." *Industrial and Labor Relations Review* 34: 333-55.

———. 1982. "The Determinants of Strikes in the United States, 1900-1977." *Industrial and Labor Relations Review* 35: 473-90.

———. 1983. "Interindustry Trends in Strike Activity." *Industrial Relations* 22: 45-57.

———. 1983. "The Determinants of Strikes Over Time and Across Industries." *Journal of Labor Research* 4: 159-75.

———. 1982. "The Determinants of Strikes in the United States: 1900-1977." *Industrial and Labor Relations Review* 35: 473-90.

———. 1993. "Research on Strike Models and Outcomes in the 1980s: Accomplishments and Shortcomings." In D. Lewin, O. Mitchell, and P. Sherer, eds, *Research Frontiers in Industrial Relations and Human Resources.* Madison, Wisc: Industrial Relations Research Association.

KENNAN, J. 1980. "Pareto Optimality and the Economics of Strike Duration." *Journal of Labor Research* 1: 77-94.

———. 1986. "The Economics of Strikes." In O. Ashenfelter and R. Layard, eds, *The Handbook of Labor Economics.* Amsterdam: North Holland.

KENNAN, J., and R. WILSON. 1989. "Strategic Bargaining Models and Interpretation of Strike Data." *Journal of Applied Econometrics* 4: 87-130.

KNIGHT, K. 1989. "Labour Productivity and Strike Activity in British Manufacturing Industries: Some Quantitative Evidence." *British Journal of Industrial Relations* 27: 365-74.

KOCHAN, T. 1980. *Industrial Relations and Collective Bargaining.* Homewood, Ill: Irwin.

KOCHAN, T., and J. BADERSCHNEIDER. 1978. "Dependence on Impasse Procedures: Police and Fire Fighters in New York State." *Industrial and Labor Relations Review* 31: 431-449.

KORPI, W., and M. SHALEV. 1980. "Strikes, Power and Politics in the Western Nations.: 1900-1976." in M. Zeitlin, ed, *Political Power and Social Theory.* Greenwich, Conn.: JAI Press.

LACROIX, R. 1986a. "A Microeconometric Analysis of the Effects of Strikes on Wages." *Relations industrielles/Industrial Relations* 41: 111-26.

———. 1986b. "Strike Activity in Canada." In W.C. Riddell, ed, *Canadian Labor Relations.* Toronto: University of Toronto Press.

LACROIX, R., and A. LESPERANCE. 1988. "New Labor Laws and Strike Activity." *Relations industrielles/Industrial Relations* 43: 812-27.

LEIGH, J.P. 1983. "Risk Preference and the Interindustry Propensity to Strike." *Industrial and Labor Relations Review* 36: 271-85.

———. 1984. "A Bargaining Model and Empirical Analysis of Strike Activity across Industries." *Journal of Labor Research* 5: 127-37.

LEROY, M. 1992. "Multivariate Analysis of Unionized Employees' Propensity to Cross Their Own Union's Picket Line." *Journal of Labor Research* 13: 285-92.

LICHTENSTEIN, N. 1985. "UAW Bargaining Strategy and Shop-Floor Conflict: 1946-1970." *Industrial Relations* 24: 360-81.

MARTIN, J. 1986. "Predictors of Individual Propensity to Strike." *Industrial and Labor Relations Review* 39: 214-27.

MacDOWELL, L. 1993. "After the Strike: Labour Relations in Oshawa, 1937-1939." *Relations industrielles/Industrial Relations* 48: 691-710.

McBRIDE, A., W. LANCEE, and S. FREEMAN. 1981. "The Psychological Impact of a Labor Dispute." *Journal of Occupational Psychology* 54: 125-33.

McCLENDON, J., and B. KLAAS. 1993. "Determinants of Strike-Related Militancy: An Analysis of a University Faculty Strike." *Industrial and Labor Relations Review* 46: 560-73.

McCONNELL, S. 1989. "Strikes, Wages, and Private Information." *American Economic Review* 79: 810-15.

———. 1990. "Cyclical Fluctuations in Strike Activity." *Industrial and Labor Relations Review* 44: 130-43.

McHUGH, R. 1991. "Productivity Effects of Strikes in Struck and Nonstruck Industries." *Industrial and Labor Relations Review* 44: 722-32.

McLEAN, R. 1977. "Coalition Bargaining and Strike Activity in the Electrical Equipment Industry, 1950-1974." *Industrial and Labor Relations Review* 30: 356-63.

———. 1979. "Interindustry Differences in Strike Activity." *Industrial Relations* 18: 103-109.

MAKI, D. 1983. "A Note on the Output Effects of Canadian Postal Strikes." *Canadian Journal of Economics* 16: 149-54.

———. 1986. "The Effect of the Cost of Strikes on the Volume of Strike Activity." *Industrial and Labor Relations Review* 39: 552-63.

MAKI, D., and K. STRAND. 1984. "The Determinants of Strike Activity: An Interindustry Analysis." *Relations industrielles/Industrial Relations* 39: 77-91.

MARTIN, J.E. 1986. "Prediction of Individual Propensity to Strike." *Industrial and Labor Relations Review* 39: 214-27.

MAURO, M.J. 1982. "Strikes as a Result of Imperfect Information." *Industrial and Labor Relations Review* 35: 522-38.

MILNER, S., and D. METCALF. 1993. "A Century of Strike Activity." In D. Metcalf and S. Milner, eds, *New Perspectives on Industrial Disputes.* London: Rutledge.

MITCHELL, D.J.B. 1981. "A Note of Strike Propensities and Wage Developments." *Industrial Relations* 20: 123-27.

MONTGOMERY, E., and M. BENEDICT. 1989. "The Impact of Bargainer Experience on Teacher Strikes." *Industrial and Labor Relations Review* 42: 380-92.

NELSON, W., G.W. STONE Jr., and J.M. SWINT. 1981. "An Economic Analysis of Public Sector Collective Bargaining and Strike Activity." *Journal of Labour Research* 2: 77-98.

NEUMANN, G.R. 1980. "The Predictability of Strikes: Evidence from the Stock Market." *Industrial and Labor Relations Review* 33: 525-35.

NEUMAN, G.R., and M.W. REDER. 1984. "Output and Strike Activity in U.S. Manufacturing: How Large are the Losses?" *Industrial and Labor Relations Review* 37: 197-211.

NG, I. 1987. "Determinants of Wildcat Strikes in Canadian Manufacturing Industries." *Relations industrielles/Industrial Relations* 42: 386-96.

———. 1991. "Predictors of Strike Voting Behaviour." *Journal of Labor Research* 12: 123-34.

———. 1993. "Strike Activity and Post-Strike Perceptions Among University Faculty." *Relations industrielles/Industrial Relations* 48: 231-47.

NG, I., and D. MAKI. 1988. "Strike Activity of U.S. Institutions in Canada." *British Journal of Industrial Relations* 26: 63-73.

NORTHRUP, H. 1984. "The Rise and Demise of PATCO." *Industrial and Labor Relations Review* 37: 167-84.

OLSON, C.A. 1984. "The Role of Rescheduled School Days in Teacher Strikes." *Industrial and Labor Relations Review* 37: 515-28.

———. 1986. "Strikes, Strike Penalties, and Arbitration in Six States." *Industrial and Labor Relations Review* 39: 539-51.

———. 1988. "Dispute Resolution in the Public Sector." In B. Aaron et al., eds, *Public Sector Bargaining,* 2nd ed. Washington: Bureau of National Affairs.

ONDRICH, J., and J. SCHNELL. 1993. "Strike Duration and the Degree of Disagreement." *Industrial Relations* 32: 412-31.

PAARSCH, H. 1990. "Work Stoppages and the Theory of the Offset Factor: Evidence from the British Columbia Logging Industry." *Journal of Labor Economics* 8: 387-418.

PALDAM, M., and P.J. PEDERSEN. 1982. "The Macroeconomic Strike Model: A Study of Seventeen Countries, 1948-1975." *Industrial and Labor Relations Review* 35: 504-21.

PARTRIDGE, D. 1988. "A Reexamination of the Effectiveness of No-Strike Laws for Public School Teachers." *Journal of Collective Negotiations in the Public Sector* 17: 257-66.

PENCAVEL, J. 1970. "An Investigation into Industrial Strike Activity in Britain." *Economica* 37: 239-56.

PETERSON, A. 1981. "Deterring Strikes by Public Employees: New York's Two for One Salary Penalty and the 1979 Prison Guard Strike." *Industrial and Labor Relations Review* 34: 545-62.

PONAK, A., and L. FALKENBERG. 1989. "Resolution of Interest Disputes." In A. Sethi, ed, *Collective Bargaining in Canada.* Toronto: Nelson.

REDER, M., and G. NEUMANN. 1980. "Conflict and Contract: The Case of Strikes." *Journal of Political Economy* 60: 371-82.

REES, A. 1952. "Industrial Conflict and Business Fluctuations." *Journal of Political Economy* 60: 371-82.

REID, F., and A. OMAN. 1991. "Do Unions Win Short Strikes and Lose Long Strikes?" *Proceedings of the 28th Conference of the Canadian Industrial Relations Association.*

ROOMKIN, M. 1976. "Union Structure, Internal Control and Strike Activity." *Industrial and Labor Relations Review* 29: 198-217.

ROSE, D. 1991. "Are Strikes Less Effective in Conglomerate Firms?" *Industrial and Labor Relations Review* 45: 131-44.

ROSS, A., and P. HARTMAN. 1960. *Changing Patterns of Industrial Conflict.* New York: John Wiley and Sons.

SAPSFORD, D. 1975. "A Time Series Analysis of U.K. Industrial Disputes." *Industrial Relations* 14: 242-49.

SCHNELL, J.F., and C.L. GRAMM. 1987. "Learning by Striking: Estimates of the Teetotaller Effect." *Journal of Labor Economics* 5: 221-41.

SCHUTT, R. 1982. "Models of Militancy: Support for Strikes and Work Actions Among Public Employees." *Industrial and Labor Relations Review* 35: 406-22.

SCHWARZ, J., and K. KOZIARA. 1992. "The Effect of Hospital Bargaining Unit Structure on Industrial Relations Outcomes." *Industrial and Labor Relations Review* 45: 573-90.

SCREPANTI, E. 1987. "Long Cycles in Strike Activity: An Empirical Investigation." *British Journal of Industrial Relations* 25: 99-124.

SHALEV, M. 1978. "Problems of Strike Measurement." In C. Crouch and A. Pizzorno, eds, *The Resurgence of Class Conflict in Western Europe Since 1968.* London: MacMillan.

———. 1980. "Trade Unionism and Economic Analysis—The Case of Industrial Conflict." *Journal of Labor Research* 1: 133-74.

SHOREY, J. 1977. "Times Series Analysis of Strike Frequency." *British Journal of Industrial Relations* 15: 63-75.

SHORTER, E., and C. TILLY. 1974. *Strikes in France, 1830-1968.* London: Cambridge University Press.

SIEBET, W., and J. ADDISON. 1981. "Are Strikes Accidental?" *Economic Journal* 91: 389-404.

SKEELS, J. 1971. "Measures of US Strike Activity." *Industrial and Labor Relations Review* 27: 515-25.

———. 1982. "The Economic and Organizational Basis of Early United States Strikes, 1900-1948." *Industrial and Labor Relations Review* 35: 491-503.

SKEELS, J., P. McGRATH, and G. ARSHANAPALLI. 1988. "The Importance of Strike Size in Strike Research." *Industrial and Labor Relations Review* 41: 582-91.

SMITH, D.A. 1972. "The Determinants of Strike Activity in Canada." *Relations industrielles/Industrial Relations* 27: 663-78.

———. 1976. "The Impact of Inflation on Strike Activity in Canada." *Relations industrielles/Industrial Relations* 31: 139-45.

SNYDER, D. 1975. "Institutional Setting and Industrial Conflict: Comparative Analysis of France, Italy, and the United States." *American Sociological Review* 40: 259-78.

———. 1977. "Early North American Strikes: A Reinterpretation." *Industrial and Labor Relations Review* 30: 325-41.

STERN, R.N. 1975. "Economic and Sociological Explanations of Strikes: Toward an Empirical Merger." In J. Stern and B. Dennis, eds, *Proceedings of the 28th Annual Winter Meeting of the Industrial Relations Research Association.* Madison, Wisc: IRRA.

———. 1976. "Intermetropolitan Pattern of Strike Frequency." *Industrial and Labor Relations Review* 25: 218-35.

———. 1978. "Methodological Issues in Quantitative Strike Analysis." *Industrial Relations* 12: 32-42.

STERN, R.N., and J.C. ANDERSON. 1978. "Canadian Strike Activity: Union Centralization and National Diversity." In J. Stern, ed, *Proceedings of the 30th Annual Winter Meeting of the Industrial Relations Research Association.* Madison, Wisc: IRRA. 132-40.

STONER, C., and R. ARORA. 1987. "An Investigation of the Relationship Between Selected Variables and the Psychological Health of Strike Participants." *Journal of Occupational Psychology* 60: 61-71.

SWIDINSKY, R., and J. VANDERKAMP. 1982. "A Micro-Economic Analysis of Strike Activity in Canada." *Journal of Labor Research* 3: 456-71.

SWINT, J.M., and W.B. NELSON. 1978. "The Influence of Negotiators' Self Interest on the Duration of Strikes." *Industrial and Labor Relations Review* 32: 56-66.

TANG, R.Y.W., and A. PONAK. 1986. "Employer Assessment of Strike Costs." *Relations industrielles/Industrial Relations* 41: 552-70.

THOMPSON, M., and A. PONAK. 1991. "Canadian Public Sector Industrial Relations." *Advances in Industrial Relations* 5: 59-93.

TOMKIEWICZ, J., C. TOMKIEWICZ, and O. BRENNER. 1985. "Why Don't Teachers Strike?" *Journal of Collective Negotiations in the Public Sector* 14: 183-90.

TRACY, J.S. 1987. "An Empirical Test of an Asymmetric Information Model of Strikes." *Journal of Labor Economics* 5: 149-73.

VANDERKAMP, J. 1970. "Economic Activity and Strikes in Canada." *Industrial Relations* 9: 215-320.

VROOMAN, S. 1989. "A Longitudinal Attitude of Strike Activity in U.S. Manufacturing." *American Economic Review* 79: 816-26.

WALSH, W. 1975. "Economic Conditions and Strike Activity in Canada." *Industrial Relations* 14: 45-54.

WALTON, R., and R. McKERSIE. 1965. *A Behavioral Theory of Labor Negotiations.* New York: McGraw Hill.

WHEELER, H. 1985. *Industrial Conflict: An Integrative Theory.* Columbia, S.C.: University of South Carolina Press.

ZIMMER, L., and J. JACOBS. 1981. "Challenging the Taylor Law: Prison Guards on Strike." *Industrial and Labor Relations Review* 34: 531-44.

PART V
INDUSTRIAL RELATIONS IN SPECIAL ENVIRONMENTS

The last major section of this book deals with three aspects of the Canadian industrial relations system that warrant special consideration: the public sector, the province of Quebec, and comparisons with foreign systems. Though each one of these subjects has been referred to from time to time in other chapters, separate treatment here emphasizes their importance and highlights alternative models of union-management relations.

Chapter 15 examines the public sector. Public employees now account for close to half of all union members in Canada, quite a remarkable situation since public sector unionization did not occur on a widespread basis until the 1970s. The rapid growth of collective bargaining in this sector has been controversial because it has produced work stoppages in sensitive areas (in hospitals, for instance) and resulted in rapid wage increases for a number of groups. The chapter reviews these and other issues, focusing in particular on differences between private sector and public sector industrial relations practices.

Industrial relations in the province of Quebec are the subject of Chapter 16. Quebec's cultural, linguistic, and social traditions have given rise to a number of unique institutions and practices in its labour relations arena. For example, the Confédération des syndicats nationaux, a labour federation originally founded with the support of the Catholic church, has no counterpart anywhere in North America. In the legal realm, the province's "anti-scab" law, first introduced in 1977, was a forerunner of similar legislation in Ontario and British Columbia some fifteen years later. In the public sector of Quebec, bargaining has been characterized by an unusual degree of centralization, and it has become far more politicized than in other provinces. These examples notwithstanding, Quebec industrial relations share numerous features with those in other Canadian jurisdictions. Both the similarities and differences are discussed in detail.

The final chapter in this section, Chapter 17, compares industrial relations patterns in Canada to those found in other democratic, industrialized nations. The comparison includes analyses of the development and orientation of labour organizations, union penetration of the workforce, employer organization, legal approaches, industrial conflict, government-union-employer co-operation (tripartitism), bargaining structures, and industrial democracy. Particular attention is paid to successful foreign practices that might be applicable to Canada.

The three chapters in this section should place the country's practices in a broader perspective and highlight the diversity to be found in industrial relations systems within and outside Canada.

CHAPTER 15

PUBLIC SECTOR COLLECTIVE BARGAINING

ALLEN PONAK AND
MARK THOMPSON

THIS CHAPTER REVIEWS THE EVOLUTION, DISTINGUISHING FEATURES, and special problems of collective bargaining in the Canadian public sector. Almost one-third of all Canadian workers and more than half the country's union members are public employees. Widespread collective bargaining in the public sector did not emerge until the late 1960s, but after that bargaining coverage quickly became almost universal.

Experience has demonstrated that collective bargaining functions differently in the public sector than in the private sector, in particular because of some pronounced differences in the decision-making context in which public and private sector employers operate. These differences, as well as other factors, have given rise to persistent and as yet unresolved problems in the areas of dispute resolution and wage determination. More recently, the very role of government itself has been undergoing change. Focusing on concepts and trends, the discussion places the public sector labour-management experience in perspective and raises questions with respect to future developments.

The public sector has been a highly visible part of the industrial relations system for the past twenty-five years. During the 1970s it became the most heavily unionized segment of the Canadian economy as employees in health care, education, and government at all levels embraced collective bargaining in numbers not seen since the industrial unionism drives of the 1930s and 1940s. This massive influx of new union members not only changed the face of the labour movement, it helped make labour relations front page news. The coverage was not always favourable. The collective bargaining process in which these new union members engaged affected the way public services were provided, disrupted those services from time to time, contributed to higher levels of taxation, and created a whole new set of pressures on public managers and government budgets.

The response of governments to these developments has been intertwined with attitudes about the role of government itself. In many respects, Canada was built by public agencies and branches of government carrying out economic policy; this was a legacy of colonialism and the early absence of a strong private sector. Public institutions were created to promote public ends in transportation, communications, cultural spheres, and social endeavours, that is, in the complete infrastructure of a modern society (Thompson and Ponak 1992). As well, Canadian governments generally accepted Keynesian economics, which called for government intervention to reduce major fluctuations in the business cycle and maintain high levels of aggregate demand to achieve full employment (Haiven et al. 1991).

In the 1980s the traditional approach of government underwent critical scrutiny. The questioning of the role of government in an advanced industrial society was not unique to Canada; the debate was mirrored by similar discussions in other developed countries. Both in Canada and elsewhere, governments of all political stripes, from conservative to socialist, embarked on a path leading to the reduction of the role and size of government (Beaumont 1995). In many countries, Canada included, massive public debt levels lent urgency to the debate.

These new policies, sometimes labelled "Thatcherism" or "Reaganism" after their two most prominent political proponents, placed much heavier faith in the unfettered operation of the free market. Rejected, wholly or in part, were the Keynesian strategies that had dominated economic policy since the end of the Second World War. In particular, the intervention of government in the marketplace was seen as the problem rather than the solution—thus by reducing the role of government, it was thought, the economy could flourish (Haiven et al. 1991).

The shift in the role of government in this country has led to the privatization of major government-owned enterprises from airlines and telephone companies to liquor stores. It has also resulted in the contracting out of work formerly performed by public employees, including snow removal, highway maintenance, and safety inspections. Hospitals and recreation centres have been closed, class sizes increased, and new user fees imposed on a variety of services. The move away from Keynesian economics has meant the replacement of full employment policies by those emphasizing debt reduction policies, and this has been the case even with NDP governments. The shift in economic policy approach, with its emphasis on a diminished role for government in favour of greater reliance on the private sector and on the diminished importance of full employment in favour of debt reduction, cannot help but have significant consequences for the employees, unions, and managers in the public sector.

This chapter places the public sector experience into an analytical perspective. Examined in turn are the size and scope of the public sector, the emergence of bargaining, the distinguishing features of public sector labour-management relations, the special problems of public sector dispute resolution and wage determination, and the consequences of the new role for government that emerged in the 1980s.

SIZE AND SCOPE OF THE PUBLIC SECTOR

For purposes of this discussion, the public sector is defined to include federal and provincial civil services, municipalities, health care, education, and government enterprises (for example, the Canadian Broadcasting Corporation, Hydro-Québec). Table 15.1 provides data on public sector employment at the beginning of 1994. Unfortunately, reliable employment information was not available for government enterprises, and they were not included in the table.

Total public employment was estimated at 2.7 million in 1994, comprising more than 28 per cent of all employees in Canada. Including government enterprises like Canada Post and various provincially owned utility companies would undoubtedly raise the public sector proportion of employment to close to one-third of the overall economy. Health care and education are by far the largest components of the public sector, accounting for over two-thirds of all employees. By contrast, the federal government employs relatively few people, contrary to popular perceptions. On an international comparative basis, Canada ranks slightly above the OECD average in terms of the ratio of public to overall employment (Beaumont 1995).

TABLE 15.1   Public Sector Employment (000s), 1986 and 1994

	1986	1994	Average Annual Percentage Change 1986-1994	Average Annual Percentage Change 1991-1994
Education	784.7	928.0	2.28	1.45
Health & welfare	865.9	1107.3	3.48	2.51
Local government	179.9	207.0	1.67	0.69
Provincial government	210.8	227.2	0.97	0.03
Federal government	256.6	261.2	0.27	-0.08
Total public sector	2,297.9	2,730.7		
Total economy	8,882.1	9,690.0		
Public sector proportion	25.9%	28.2%		

SOURCE: Statistics Canada, *Employment, Earnings, and Hours*, cat 72-002, Table 1.1. Figures are for January of reporting year.

Data in Table 15.1 confirm that public sector employment has grown both in absolute terms and proportionately since 1986. After 1990, however, the growth rate of public employment slowed markedly. Since then, provincial civil service growth has been virtually nil and the federal civil service actually shrank in size. The rate of employment growth in health care, education, and local government has declined sharply. To put this recent decline into even sharper perspective, it should be noted that public employment increased at an annual rate of 7 per cent between 1946 and 1975 (Foot and Thadaney 1978).

Given current government policies, the trend of much slower growth, and in some cases absolute decline, is not likely to be reversed soon. Spurred by the necessity to reduce government debt levels (Swimmer and Thompson 1994) and by an emerging orthodoxy on the benefits of less government, a number of government strategies will inevitably lead to a smaller public sector. These include the sale of government assets and enterprises (privatization), the turning over of work previously performed by public employees to private contractors (contracting out), and the reduction of the level of public services (Thompson 1995).

Privatization can take several forms, but most often has involved the sale of Crown corporations to private sector firms engaged in the same or related industry. For example, the federal government sold two aircraft manufacturing firms to Boeing and Bombardier, and the British Columbia government sold its gas distribution system to private sector distribution companies already active in the province (Thompson 1995). Thompson (1995) estimated that there had been over seventy-five privatization transactions by the end of 1992, with the federal government and the provinces of Quebec, Saskatchewan, and British Columbia most actively pursuing this strategy.

The contracting out of services previously performed by public employees to the private sector has also been extensive, particularly at the municipal level, in hospitals, and in educational institutions. The most common candidates for contracting out are solid waste disposal (i.e., garbage collection), building maintenance and security, laundries, food services, snow removal, and road and highway maintenance (Thompson 1995). Canada Post has contracted out janitorial services for some of its facilities, and private firms run many university food services.

A third strategy to reduce government is simply to decrease or eliminate specific public services, reducing employment at the same time. This approach has been especially noticeable in health care with the closure of acute care hospitals, the elimination of certain departments (e.g., surgical wards) or the reduction in the number of beds (Haiven 1995). In Saskatchewan, for example, a number of rural hospitals have been closed, and in Calgary two large acute care hospitals are scheduled to be shut down.[1] Beyond health care, other examples of reduced service include cutting back outdoor ice rinks in Montreal parks, closing university departments, and reducing library operating hours. Taken together, privatization, contracting out, and service reductions will lead to fewer public employees in the years to come.

DEVELOPMENT OF PUBLIC SECTOR COLLECTIVE BARGAINING

Public sector collective bargaining did not become widespread in Canada until the mid-1960s. Previously, few public employees engaged in formal collective bargaining, with the exception of blue-collar municipal workers. Today the situation is totally reversed. It is difficult to find a public employee group not covered by a collective agreement. Three of Canada's five largest unions operate almost exclusively in the public sector, and the level of collective bargaining in the public sector far exceeds that found in the private sector. It is estimated that well over 50 per cent of all union members in Canada work in the public sector (Rose 1995).

Table 15.2 reports the latest available information on union density for various components of the public sector. The level of unionism ranges from more than 90 per cent unionized in provincial government to 50 per cent in health and social services (with the bulk of nonunion employment in health care found in offices of physicians and dentists, which arguably should not be included as public sector at all).[2] The union density rates in the public sector are obviously much higher than the rate of only 35 per cent for the economy as a whole, and the 20 per cent rate for the private sector.

The current levels of public sector union density are reflected in the size and continued growth of public sector unions, shown in Table 15.3. The Canadian Union of Public Employees, with substantial membership among hospital and school board employees and municipal workers, is Canada's largest union with over 400,000 members. Since 1980 it has grown at more than 4 per cent per year. Canada's second largest union is the National Union of Provincial and General Employees, which represents mainly provincial civil servants but has recently started organizing in the private sector (Rose 1995; Fryer 1995). It also has experienced sustained and substantial membership growth. The Public Service Alliance of Canada, the country's third largest union, is an exception among public sector unions in terms of growth rate. Its membership is almost exclusively composed of federal civil servants; when the federal government stopped growing, so too did the PSAC.

TABLE 15.2   Union Members as a Percentage of Paid Workers

	1991
Local government	67.9
Provincial government	94.9
Federal government	72.5
Educational services	75.3
Health and social services	50.9
Overall economy	35.1

SOURCES: Statistics Canada, cat 71-202, *CALURA Labour Unions, 1991*, Appendix I.5 and Unpublished information provided by the Labour Unions Section, Statistics Canada.

TABLE 15.3   Membership and Growth Rates of Public Sector Unions

Unions	1980 (000s)	1994 (000s)	Annual Per Cent Increase
Public Service Alliance of Canada	155.7	167.8	0.6
National Union of Provincial and General Employees	195.8	307.6	4.1
Canadian Union of Public Employees	257.2	409.8	4.2
Teachers' unions	276.8	404.6	3.3
Nurses' unions	78.1	166.5	8.1
Police unions	34.5[a]	43.5	3.3
Firefighers' unions	19.4[a]	27.2	5.0

[a] Membership is for 1986.

SOURCE: Labour Canada, *Directory of Labour Organizations*, 1980 and 1994; and Rose (1995) Table 1.

While local, provincial, and federal employees are represented by their own national unions, teachers and professional health care employees thus far have remained in provincially based independent labour organizations. If nurses or teachers chose to establish national labour organizations, such unions would rank among the largest in the country.

Association-Consultation

The size of public sector unions belies their very recent origins as true labour organizations. Associations of public employees existed before 1900, and then, as now, these workers shared at least some of the many concerns of their private sector counterparts in terms of salaries and employment conditions (Logan 1948).

Early in the twentieth century, Canadian public employees, instead of placing their faith in unionism and collective bargaining, formed associations of public employees. These organizations avoided union tactics, especially strikes. Management personnel, up to the most senior positions, often were active in these associations and even occupied positions of leadership. A major function of these organizations was consultation with the employer, which was regarded as the best means for influencing the salaries and working conditions of their members.

This approach to employer-employee relations is referred to here as "association-consultation." It was the prevalent form of public sector labour relations until the mid-1960s, when it yielded to the more familiar unionism and collective bargaining approach. The transition from association-consultation to union-collective bargaining began in the 1950s, accelerated in the mid-1960s, and was virtually complete by the mid-1970s.

It should be emphasized that not all early organizational activity among public employees followed the association-consultation model. A number of groups, including teachers in several provinces and outside municipal workers in most cities, have a long history of unionism and bargaining with their public employer, some dating back to the First World War period (Frankel and Pratt 1954; Muir 1968). Until the 1960s, however, such groups were in the minority.

Early employee organizations were attracted to association-consultation for several reasons. First, this approach is popular with employees who want to participate in setting their employment conditions but are uncomfortable with trade union methods and tactics. White-collar workers and professionals, a major component of the public sector, have traditionally viewed unionism sceptically (Thompson 1982). Their education and involvement with management produced reservations about collective action and the adversarial tone of Canadian labour relations. As long as consultation was either promised or granted, they avoided collective bargaining (Frankel 1962; Hodgetts and Dwivedi 1974; Muir 1968).

Second, association-consultation was found in situations in which collective bargaining was impossible in practical terms. Until legislative changes were made in the 1960s and 1970s, most public employers strongly opposed collective bargaining for their employees. The foremost basis for opposition lay in the concept of government sovereignty. The point can be simply stated: sovereignty implies that government bodies are vested with certain powers and responsibilities that cannot be shared or taken away; collective bargaining, it was argued, would diminish these powers by forcing, for example, revisions in government budgets.

Relying on the sovereignty concept, governments contended that even if they wished to do so, they could not permit public employees to engage in bargaining. Perhaps the clearest articulation of this position was the 1964 statement of Quebec Premier Jean Lesage: "The Queen does not negotiate with her subjects" (Goldenberg 1973, 11). In a similar vein, Prime Minister Louis Saint-Laurent declared in 1951:

> There can be no bargaining agent for the nation comparable with the employer in industry. The funds from which salaries are paid in the public service have to be voted by Parliament and Parliament alone can discharge that responsibility. (quoted in Frankel 1962, 11)

Public employer opposition also reflected concern over the effect of work stoppages. It was assumed that bargaining would inevitably lead to strikes and that strikes would result in an interruption of services that the government had an obligation to provide, that were often irreplaceable, and that might be essential to the safety of the population. The sovereignty and work-stoppage arguments provided a strong intellectual and moral basis for opposition to public employee bargaining.

Consistent with this position, governments excluded most public employees from labour legislation enacted in the 1940s and 1950s. The lack of legal protection made it much easier for public employers opposed to unionism to discourage bargaining activity. Public employees had few of the protections accorded their private sector counterparts. Given a legal environment unsupportive of collective bargaining, association-consultation was adopted as the most feasible alternative.

Unions and Collective Bargaining

If employee sentiments, employer opposition, and the legislative environment all seemed to favour association-consultation, why did it decline, starting in the 1960s? The answer lies in problems with the "consultation" component of association-consultation, which was based on the belief that consultation was an adequate means for employees to address their employment concerns. In the long run, consultation proved a disappointment. It contained a number of weaknesses not foreseen at the outset that ultimately created great dissatisfaction. Even employees with a long-standing distaste for unions and collective bargaining reluctantly re-evaluated their opposition as difficulties with association-consultation mounted (Bairstow et al. 1973).

In practice, consultation delivered much less than envisioned. The scope of issues open to consultation proved narrower than the employees wanted. Wages were typically the subject of salary briefs only. No mechanisms existed to resolve differences between the parties on contentious issues. The powers of the consulted party were only advisory; if the employer rejected a proposal, the status quo prevailed (Frankel 1960).

Once disenchantment with consultation set in, staff associations switched to advocating collective bargaining. At the same time, they began to model themselves along traditional union lines, excluding management personnel from their membership, hiring full-time staff experts, eliminating no-strike clauses from their constitutions, merging with competing or complementary organizations, and in some cases affiliating with the Canadian Labour Congress.

This transformation did not occur overnight, of course, or without some soul searching, particularly within professional groups (Bairstow et al. 1973; Thompson 1975). Major changes in leadership were often necessary (McLean 1979). Two factors, however, considerably facilitated the transition. Once some momentum towards the union-collective bargaining model had been achieved, a demonstration effect emerged that accelerated developing trends. For example, a huge arbitration award won by Ottawa nurses in 1968 greatly heightened interest in collective bargaining for that occupation throughout Ontario. Also helping the transition was the general climate of social change characteristic of the 1960s. It was the era of the Civil Rights movement, anti-Vietnam War protests, the Quiet Revolution in Quebec, and campus militancy. The public sector was in a period of rapid growth, and newly hired employees brought campus attitudes to their employment. Thus, the social environment was conducive to challenges of authority and of the status quo in general, making the time particularly propitious for public employees to undertake major changes in norms.

The major catalyst in the movement to full collective bargaining was the removal of legal obstacles. Saskatchewan had set a precedent in 1944 by including civil servants under the coverage of the provincial Trade Union Act, undermining the proposition that government sovereignty prevented public sector bargaining. Other governments slowly accepted that certain limitations in their own discretion might be necessary if rights to which public employees now felt strongly entitled were to be ensured. In many jurisdictions, the substitution of arbitration for the right to strike overcame misgivings about work stoppages. Gradually, the legislative environment began to change from one hostile to the collective bargaining model to one that was supportive.

The most important breakthrough for employees wanting collective bargaining occurred in 1963. Astute political lobbying by employee organizations persuaded the newly elected federal government of Prime Minister Lester Pearson to promise collective bargaining rights for the federal civil service (Edwards 1968). The Public Service Staff Relations Act (PSSRA) resulted several years later and more than 100,000 federal employees were soon covered by collective agreements. In 1965, the Quebec Labour Code extended bargaining rights to all public employees in that province, and 40,000 workers started their first round of bargaining. Political pressure mounted for other governments to emulate these examples. One by one, other jurisdictions enacted collective bargaining legislation for various groups of public employees.

By 1975, the rights of virtually all public employees to engage in collective bargaining were established and protected by law. Access to certification procedures, conciliation machinery, and labour boards, together with public employers' acceptance of the unionism and collective bargaining, launched one of the most sustained periods of union growth in Canadian history. Once committed to collective bargaining, public sector organizations wasted little time before exercising their newly acquired rights. Existing associations converted themselves into unions, eliminating the need for extensive membership campaigns, and unionization spread rapidly. By the late 1970s, most eligible public employees in the country were covered by collective agreements.

Implications of Unionization

The pattern of public sector collective bargaining development and the fact that the public sector is now so highly unionized have several implications. First, the rapid replacement of consultation with collective bargaining made growing pains inevitable. The first decade of bargaining was marked by a number of difficult and highly visible strikes, especially those involving postal workers and Quebec public employees, and by large wage demands as employees attempted to "catch up" after years of perceived neglect and the impact of inflation.

Second, the rapid manner in which collective bargaining expanded created a momentum of its own that governments, even if they had second thoughts at the time, could do little to resist. Once the initial organizing and bargaining phase was by and large complete, however, misgivings harboured by some public employers were translated into legislative change and intervention that started to undo the framework initially established. This was especially true with respect to compensation issues and the right to strike.

Third, the rise of public sector unions changed the shape of the Canadian labour movement. Before the 1960s, organized labour in the country was predominantly blue-collar, male, private sector, and linked to unions in the United States. These characteristics are far less prevalent today. The emergence of large public sector unions produced tensions and contributed to divisions in the labour movement (Thwaites 1984; Rose 1995).

Fourth, the experience in the public sector suggests that the high degree of union penetration ultimately achieved would have been unlikely had public employees not gone through the association-consultation phase first. Although adherence to that model delayed collective bargaining for a considerable period, it also set the stage for the very rapid expansion of bargaining coverage.

DISTINGUISHING FEATURES OF PUBLIC SECTOR COLLECTIVE BARGAINING

As public employee unionism spread rapidly, it became obvious that bargaining did not work quite the same way in the public sector as in the private sector. Certain important differences between public and private sector employers, employees, and legislation combined to produce distinctive bargaining dynamics.

Employer Differences

Many of the distinctive features of public sector labour relations stem from differences between public employers and private employers. Decision-making structure and authority differ between the two sectors, typically being much more diffuse in the public sector. For most public employers (a small number of government enterprises excepted) the profit motive is absent, replaced by political considerations. Federal and provincial government employers also enjoy the ability to legislate—an advantage unmatched by their private sector counterparts. Each of these features can have substantial implications for bargaining dynamics in the public sector.

Management Structure.   Management responsibility for collective bargaining is usually well-defined and established in private sector organizations. The public sector is characterized, on the other hand, by "bewildering fragmentation of authority among numerous management officials" (Burton 1979, 103). Typically, responsibility for labour relations decisions are shared between professional managers and elected officials. The political agenda of elected officials and their frequent lack of labour relations experience holds the potential for conflict with line management (Swimmer and Thompson 1995).

The diffusion of management authority in the public sector is to some extent deliberate, reflecting assumptions about the value of checks and balances, political versus nonpolitical decision making, and local versus central control. For example, responsibility for education decisions is typically apportioned between locally elected school boards and a provincial ministry of education; in the civil service, recruitment, transfer, and promotion are vested in an ostensibly apolitical civil service commission, while resource allocation remains a cabinet function; many provinces divide responsibility for managing municipal police forces among a police chief, municipal officials, and a police board.

Public sector funding arrangements also contribute to shared authority. Many public employers are funded from a multiplicity of sources, each of which may seek to influence the way in which the money is spent (Goldenberg 1988). Urban transit commissions offer a good illustration of this point. Urban transit is financed through a combination of user charges, municipal subsidies, and provincial grants. Accordingly, provincial governments, a variety of municipal administrations (where various suburbs are part of a metropolitan system), and citizen groups, as well as transit management itself, all may claim some role in the collective bargaining process and some control over bargaining outcomes. With so many claimants, decision making becomes much more complex.

Furthermore, as higher levels of government have devoted more and more of their budgets to the funding of services, a separation of administrative responsibility and budgetary authority has developed, thereby diluting the decision-making authority of local management. For example,

> while local hospitals and school boards by and large have retained their positions as legal employers, provincial governments are increasingly becoming the effective employer where financial matters are concerned (Goldenberg 1988, 275).

In Quebec and New Brunswick, provincial government officials have become the actual management party at the bargaining table in health care and social services negotiations, while a government observer is part of the employer bargaining team in Saskatchewan hospital negotiations (Haiven 1995).

Third, structural disunity is exacerbated by political competition. Elected management officials may belong to different political parties or speak on behalf of different levels of government. Competition on the basis of party, government level, and so on is an accepted part of the political system, but it further undermines employer cohesion.

Public management's structural complexity has important implications for collective bargaining. Overlapping and unclear authority lines may contribute to unnecessary delay as a variety of internal bargains have to be struck before union proposals can be addressed. There is also strong evidence that the grievance arbitration process takes substantially longer to complete in the public sector than in the private sector (Ponak and Olson 1992).

Canadian public sector employers are still groping for the right organizational form for labour relations (Goldenberg 1988). The Quebec provincial government developed a highly centralized bargaining structure, but a series of major disputes under this format resulted in legislation forcing a degree of decentralization (Boivin 1972; Lemelin 1984; Hébert 1995). The City of Vancouver and a dozen surrounding suburban communities have given full bargaining authority to an employers' association as have several municipalities in the British Columbia interior. As well, many smaller cities that had previously used elected council members at the bargaining table have moved to professional negotiators (Graham 1994). In education, four provinces have local bargaining, three provinces have province-wide bargaining with the Ministry of Education or Treasury Branch in the role of management, and three provinces have master collective agreements with local issues negotiated at the individual school-board level (Thomason 1995).

Political Considerations.   For the private sector employer, the outcomes of collective bargaining are reckoned mainly in economic terms. A new collective agreement must be evaluated in terms of how changes in production efficiency and overall labour costs will affect the firm's costs of production, its ability to remain competitive, and ultimately its profitability. The major employer costs of not reaching a collective agreement stem from consequences generated by any loss of production if employees withdraw their services. These consequences may include short-run revenue loss and decline in long-term market share. Bargaining behaviour must be evaluated in terms of these consequences and their ultimate profit impact.

Public employers must also be aware of the economic consequences of new collective agreements, especially in times of dwindling operating budgets, but the consequences have different implications. Profit-loss considerations do not apply, market share and competitive pressures are rarely relevant, and revenue seldom is linked directly to the quantity of product or service provided.

Instead, the outcomes of collective bargaining have a strong political dimension, with a primary focus on public opinion and the prospects of re-election (Swimmer and Thompson 1995a). This will have an impact on time horizons, which are likely to be short and attuned to the next election, the willingness to take a strike, and preferences for compensation increases (Gunderson 1995).

These kinds of political calculations can be illustrated with respect to work stoppages. On the one hand, whereas strikes normally impose financial hardships on private-sector employers, public employers may actually reap financial benefit from a strike if, as in many cases, revenues are unaffected. For example, a municipality does not stop collecting property taxes when its road crews withdraw their services temporarily. On the other hand, public sector strikes frequently disrupt services that are not easily substituted for (e.g., elementary schools, air traffic control) and that affect large numbers of people. Ultimately, the decision about a work stoppage will involve a political assessment of the consequences on the part of the public employer. In 1987, for instance, a postal strike not only interrupted an important public service, but Canada Post also suffered a negative public response to its relatively inept use of strikebreakers. Where the service is less visible, citizen response may be nonexistent or at least muted, thereby producing few political risks. In any event, this type of political evaluation is something that a private sector employer rarely has to make.

The political element in public sector bargaining translates into substantial efforts by the parties in making their case to the public, particularly with respect to work stoppages. Thus, negotiations may take place not only at the bargaining table but in the media as each side attempts to convince the public that its cause is just. Teachers and hospital workers, for example, usually frame their bargaining demands not in terms of better wages and working conditions but for improvement in the quality of education or health care.[3] Public employers, for their part, take great pains to justify such actions as back-to-work legislation in the name of the public interest, not on the grounds that such tactics enable them to achieve a particular bargaining objective. The 1991 strike of federal government employees was waged as much in the media as in the negotiating arena (Swimmer 1995).

Successfully making a case to the public can pay dividends at the bargaining table. In 1980, nurses in British Columbia achieved a settlement involving an unusually large wage increase. A major factor in their success was a convincing media campaign showing that nurses were greatly underpaid. Canada Post has used paid newspaper advertisements to attack the wage demands of its unions, successfully portraying its employees as overpaid.

Legislative Powers.   The federal and provincial governments play a dual role in labour relations. They are both large employers and holders of sovereign authority over all the people within their territories, with the power to legislate the rules under which they and their employees must function. The power to legislate tempts governments to adjust labour relations rules in their own self-interest as employers.

Several examples are illustrative. In 1978 the federal government introduced amendments to the PSSRA to extend managerial exclusions significantly, to tie arbitration and conciliation criteria for compensation to private sector norms, to restrict the right to strike, and to give the employer the right to lock out. The Public Service Alliance of Canada attacked these proposals, charging that their purpose was to strengthen the employer's negotiating power and protect its political interests in the event of a strike. The government staunchly defended the proposals on the grounds that they protected the public interest. Ultimately, popular opposition to the proposals was so strong that the government withdrew them. In 1982, the government of Alberta amended public sector legislation to make arbitration awards subject to its own fiscal policies, and the following year the Québec government unilaterally amended its own collective agreements to roll back negotiated wage increases. Between 1991 and 1993, the governments of Newfoundland, Nova Scotia, New Brunswick, Québec, Manitoba, and Ontario passed legislation that froze or rolled back wages for all or some public employees (Fryer 1995).

In these cases, governments did not act solely to advance their own interests as employers. They also responded to what were perceived as genuine public concerns about the impact of collective bargaining on government costs in times of fiscal restraint. The important point is that the ability of governments to exercise legislative authority to further their own ends as employers is a potent source of industrial relations power that, if not exercised with restraint, has the potential to fatally undermine collective bargaining. Indeed, some analysts believe this has already occurred. They argue that governments are increasingly willing to rely on back-to-work and wage restraint legislation instead of negotiations to achieve their objectives and that this tactic has permanently ended real collective bargaining in the public sector (Panitch and Swartz 1993). Other observers, although concerned by the trend to substitute legislation for negotiation, believe collective bargaining is resilient enough to survive as long as the restraints do not become permanent (Thompson and Swimmer 1995).

Employee and Union Differences

The degree of public-private sector differences that exists on the employer side is not matched on the employee and union side. There is little evidence to suggest that the pressures on public sector union leaders to achieve collective bargaining objectives are very different than the pressures on their private sector counterparts. While in some cases the subject matter of negotiations might vary between the two sectors, bargaining is still focused around the traditional issues of "wages, hours, and conditions of employment" in both sectors. For a time, it was thought that public employees had little to fear from an exceptionally rich settlement since the demand for their services was considered price-inelastic, but recent experience shows that there is a wage/employment trade-off, sometimes an explicit one (Fryer 1995; Wilton 1986).[4]

The major consequence of strike action—immediate loss of income—also is the same for public and private sector employees. There is little reason to expect that such costs have inherently different consequences for employees in the two sectors, except that public sector workers have little reason to fear their employer will close permanently.

There are, however, several differences between public and private sector employees, and by extension their unions, that are worth noting. Perhaps most significantly, the public sector employs a higher proportion of women than does the private sector. While women make up about 45 per cent of the total labour force, they comprise 80 per cent of persons employed in health and social services, 62 per cent of the labour force in education and 43 per cent of the employees in public administration (Statistics Canada, 1993). Given the higher union density, this means that 60 per cent of public sector union members are female, compared to only 22 per cent in the private sector. The proportion of women union members is highest in education (60 per cent) and health and social services (81 per cent) (Swimmer and Thompson 1995a).

Furthermore, the public sector contains a higher proportion of white-collar workers and professionals than does the private sector. White-collar workers fill more than half of all jobs in the economy as a whole (that is, in the private and public sectors combined). Although specific comparative data are not available, information from a variety of sources (Anderson 1977; Foot and Thadaney 1978; Gunderson 1979) suggests that white-collar employment in municipalities and government enterprises approximates the economy-wide level and substantially exceeds that norm in health care, the provincial and federal civil services, and education. As many as two-thirds of all Canadian professionals may be employed in the public sector (Gunderson 1979).

These differences in employment composition mean that whereas private sector unions are essentially blue-collar and male dominated, public sector unionism is heavily white-collar and female. Similarly, virtually all professionals who engage in collective bargaining are employed in the public sector.

One important implication of these differences is the heightened significance it gives to employment and pay equity issues and anti-discrimination regulations. Public sector unions with a large female membership have been among the strongest advocates of workplace equity. Almost all efforts to implement pay equity (aimed at reducing male/female pay differences) have taken place in the public sector. As well, public employers have taken a more active role in employment equity initiatives (aimed at reducing the segregation of women into "female" jobs) than have private employers (Weiner 1995).[5]

Other collective bargaining objectives also may be affected by the differences in composition between public and private sector unions. While systematic evidence is sketchy, public sector unions might be expected to give higher priority to such issues as day care, maternity benefits, and time off to attend to child rearing responsibilities. Unions composed of professional employees might also be expected to attempt to negotiate over issues relating to professional concerns, possibly creating clashes over managerial prerogatives and policy (Ponak 1981). Teacher unions, for example, have bargained over student/teacher ratios, curriculum development, and limits on the inclusion of handicapped children in the classroom (Thomason 1995). On the other hand, a study comparing the attitudes of activists of an industrial union and a union of provincial civil servants showed remarkably few differences in the bargaining issues considered most important or in the degree of support indicated for joint labour-management programs (Ponak and Fraser 1979).

Early research also suggested that the composition of public sector unions would result in less strike and grievance activity and less militancy in general. Studies conducted up to 1984 of federal civil servants, white-collar public employees, nurses, and university faculty members showed ambivalence about strike activity (Ponak and Haridas 1979;

Swimmer 1984), a preference for arbitration (Ponak and Wheeler 1980), and a lower inci-dence of grievance activity (Begin 1978; Gandz 1979). The experience since the early 1980s, however, indicates that public sector unions account for an increasing proportion of strike volume (Gunderson and Reid 1995) and have high rates of grievance arbitration (Ponak and Olson 1992). Thus, the presence of more women, white-collar employees, and professionals in the public sector has not resulted in a notably less militant form of union-ism.

Policy and Legislative Distinctions

The right of public employees to unionize and engage in collective bargaining is enshrined in law, much as it is in the private sector. Public employers are obliged to recognize and bargain in good faith with labour organizations that enjoy majority support. Public sector collective bargaining legislation is extremely diverse, however, compared to the private sector. Whereas private sector legislation in each of the provinces and at the federal level generally follows principles derived from PC 1003 (enacted in 1944) as well as earlier con-ciliation legislation (see Chapter 3), there is no similarly accepted framework in the pub-lic sector. Hence there are considerable differences in legislation between the public and private sectors and in terms of how different groups of public employees are regulated.

Table 15.4 sets out public sector labour legislation at the federal level, in each province, and in the two territories. It can be readily seen that most jurisdictions have one or more statutes exclusively for public employees. With the notable exception of munici-pal employees, the majority of public employees do not fall under general private sector labour codes. For example, in seven provinces collective bargaining for teachers is gov-erned either by a special statute established for that purpose (e.g., the Teachers Collective Bargaining Act in Nova Scotia) or the basic legislation governing education (e.g., the Public Schools Act in Manitoba).

Even where superficially it may appear that labour relations are governed by the general private sector statute, as in the case of hospital workers in six provinces, there may be special provisions within the general labour code or in other legislation that create dis-tinctive regulatory procedures. In Alberta, for example, a provision of the Labour Relations Code prohibits strikes by hospital workers and sets out an arbitration system. In Québec, other statutes replace the Labour Code for bargaining structure and the maintenance of essential services (Hébert 1995; Haiven 1995).

In addition to the general pattern of excluding much of the public sector from pri-vate sector labour statutes, Table 15.4 also shows that a number of provinces have sepa-rate legislation for different public sector groups. Ontario is perhaps the extreme case. Police, firefighters, hospital workers, teachers, and civil servants each have their own sep-arate statute. Other provinces have not gone quite as far in this direction as Ontario has, but except for British Columbia, all other provinces have at least two separate statutes for public employees. In the private sector, in comparison, there tends to be a unified regula-tory approach within each jurisdiction.

TABLE 15.4 Public Sector Labour Legislation by Jurisdiction

Jurisdiction	General Private Sector	General Municipal	Police	Firefighters	Hospitals	Teachers	Civil Service	Government Enterprise
Federal	Canada Labour Code	Canada Labour Code	Canada Labour Code	Public Service Staff Relations Act	Public Service Staff Relations Act	Public Service Staff Relations Act	Public Service Staff Relations Act	Canada Labour Code
British Columbia	Labour Relations Code	Labour Relations Code	Labour Relations Code	Labour Relations Code	Labour Relations Code	Labour Relations Code	Public Service Labour Relations Act/Labour Relations Code	Labour Relations Code
Alberta	Labour Relations Code	Labour Relations Code	Police Officers Collective Bargaining Act/Police Act	Labour Relations Code	Labour Relations Code	Labour Relations Code	Public Service Employee Relations Act	Labour Relations Code
Saskatchewan	Trade Union Act	Trade Union Act	Police Act	Fire Department Platoon Act	Trade Union Act	Education Act	Trade Union Act	Trade Union Act
Manitoba	Labour Relations Act	Labour Relations Act	Labour Relations Act/Police Act; City of Winnipeg Act	Labour Relations Act/Fire Departments Arbitration Act	Labour Relations Act	Public Schools Act	Civil Service Act	Labour Relations Act
Ontario	Labour Relations Act	Labour Relations Act	Police Services Act/ Public Service Act (Ontario Provincial Police)	Fire Department's Act	Labour Relations Act/Hospital Labour Disputes Arbitration Act	School Boards and Teachers Collective Negotiations Act/Colleges Collective Bargaining Act	Crown Employees Collective Bargaining Act	Crown Employees Collective Bargaining Act
Quebec	Labour Code	Labour Code	Labour Code/Police Act	Labour Code	Labour Code/Public Service Act	Labour Code	Labour Code/Public Service Act	Labour Code/Public Service Act
New Brunswick	Industrial Relations Act	Industrial Relations Act	Industrial Relations Act/Police Act	Industrial Relations Act	Public Service Labour Relations Act	Public Service Labour Relations Act	Public Service Labour Relations Act/Civil Service Act	Public Service Labour Relations Act
Nova Scotia	Trade Union Act	Trade Union Act	Trade Union Act	Trade Union Act	Trade Union Act	Teacher's Collective Bargaining Act	Civil Service Collective Bargaining Act	Trade Union Act
Prince Edward Island	Labour Act	Labour Act	Labour Act/Police Act	Labour Act	Labour Act	School Act	Civil Service Act	Civil Service Act
Newfoundland	Labour Relations Act	Labour Relations Act	Labour Relations Act/Royal Newfoundland Constabulary Act	Labour Relations Act/City of St. John's Fire Department Act	Public Service Collective Bargaining Act	Teacher's Collective Bargaining Act	Public Service Collective Bargaining Act	Public Service Collective Bargaining Act
Yukon	Canada Labour Code	Canada Labour Code			Canada Labour Code	Education Act	Public Service Staff Relations Act	
Northwest Territories	Canada Labour Code	Canada Labour Code					Public Service Act	

SOURCES: Applicable statutes as of September 1994.

This multiplicity of statutes and diversity of approaches governing the public sector reflect both the absence of a generally accepted labour law model for public employees and the dual role of government as employer. As various groups of public employees sought enabling legislation for collective bargaining, legislators experimented freely (Goldenberg 1988), while taking heed to protect their own and the public interest. As well, the early experience with bargaining differed widely across the country, again giving rise to distinct regulatory approaches. For example, Ontario's decision to enact a specific statute to regulate labour relations for teachers, complete with its own tribunal and extensive fact-finding provisions, reflected a particularly volatile initial bargaining experience in that province (Downie 1992).

While it is difficult to generalize, public sector statutes differ most from the private sector model in three areas. First, there tends to be less discretion given to labour relations boards with respect to *certification and recognition.* A number of statutes—for example, the federal Public Service Staff Relations Act (Finkleman and Goldenberg 1983)—established occupational bargaining units, an approach very different from the discretion given labour boards in the private sector. British Columbia established three bargaining units under its provincial civil service law (PSLRA). Also in contrast to private sector practice, a number of organizations were granted statutory representation rights, particularly in the case of teachers' unions, faculty associations, and to a lesser degree, civil service unions. Finally, police are prohibited from affiliating with other labour organizations in four provinces (Jackson 1995). Although the private sector model might not have produced dramatically different bargaining structures, legislating these decisions created a degree of inflexibility in some bargaining regimes that prevented a more natural evolution of the system.

A second area of difference has been the tendency to restrict the *scope of bargaining* in many parts of the public sector. Private sector negotiators are almost universally free to bargain over whatever issues they choose. General private sector labour code requirements that bargaining proceed over "wages, hours, and working conditions" have been interpreted very liberally.

Less negotiating latitude is permitted under a variety of public sector statutes. The PSSRA removes classifications, criteria for promotion, transfers, and layoffs, technological change, and pensions from the scope of bargaining. Similar constraints on bargaining scope are found in a majority of provincial civil service statutes. Local government employees, teachers, and hospital employees are frequently covered by non-negotiable pension plans. The negotiating scope for police and firefighters may be limited, particularly with respect to disciplinary arrangements and superior-subordinate relations, owing to the paramilitary nature of these services. Since early 1980 many governments have legislated temporary wage controls, effectively removing wages from the negotiations during some rounds of bargaining.

These types of restrictions enhance management rights and bargaining power, enabling the employer to achieve through legislation what might be difficult to achieve through negotiations (Swimmer 1995). The restrictions may also be dysfunctional to the bargaining process, creating a degree of frustration on the part of unions that undermines the trust essential for productive negotiations. Moreover, the parties may end up spending a great deal of time discussing what can and cannot legally be bargained, diverting attention from the actual workplace issues that need to be addressed. Similarly, where the restrictions carry over into interest arbitration, as is frequently the case, much of the arbitration may be devoted to legal arguments over the ability of the arbitrator to address various issues.[6]

Dispute resolution procedures provide a third, and the most controversial, major area of legislative difference between the public and the private sectors. Almost all private sector employees enjoy a right to strike over the renegotiation of a collective agreement once certain preconditions have been satisfied. Typically, these preconditions include contract expiration, a strike vote, strike notice, and a conciliation step. Public sector employees, by comparison, are much more fettered. Frequently their right to strike is removed and replaced by arbitration, even in situations, as for New Brunswick firefighters and Alberta nurses, in which a general labour code provides basic statutory coverage. If strikes are permitted, the preconditions are normally more severe than in the private sector. Quebec public employees cannot withdraw their services until agreement is reached on maintaining certain functions deemed essential; federal civil servants must participate in a two-stage conciliation process before their right to strike becomes operative; and fact-finding is a precondition to work stoppages for Ontario teachers. These restrictions notwithstanding, the public sector has accounted for an increasing proportion of Canadian strike activity in recent years.

The proclamation of the Canadian Charter of Rights and Freedoms in 1982 was initially viewed by unions as a vehicle for challenging some of the restrictions in public sector legislation. A series of Supreme Court decisions, however, have indicated that the courts are not likely to intervene, preferring to leave the design of collective bargaining systems to provincial legislatures and the federal Parliament (Swinton 1995). In three decisions that together are referred to as the Labour Trilogy,[7] the Supreme Court ruled that freedom of association does not include the right to strike, the right to bargain collectively, or the right to choose a bargaining agent. These decisions enable governments to continue to restrict the right to strike for certain employees; uphold the legality of imposing various bargaining restrictions, particularly wage controls; and leave unchanged the statutory naming of bargaining representatives. Swinton (1995) concludes that "while the decisions did not give new constitutional protection to the right to strike or bargain collectively, neither did they undermine the strength of unions and recast the courts into the role of labour policy makers." Indeed in a later decision, the highly publicized *Lavigne* case,[8] the Supreme Court upheld the right of public sector unions to compel all bargaining unit members to pay union dues, thus protecting the Rand formula. The decision had the effect of also protecting union political activity (Swinton 1995).

STRIKES AND DISPUTE PROCEDURES

Of all the issues that remain contentious in the public sector, the question of strikes has proved to be the most difficult. Opponents of strike rights for public employees make their case mainly on the grounds that public sector work stoppages impose an unacceptable degree of inconvenience on the public at large. Private sector disputes often do not affect third parties seriously, since there are usually substitutes available for products cut off by strikes. This is in sharp contrast with the public sector. The effects of strikes by teachers, postal workers, air traffic controllers, and transit workers, among others, inevitably go beyond the employees and employers directly involved at the bargaining table, disrupting heavily used and irreplaceable services. In stoppages involving employees such as hospital workers, police, and lighthouse keepers, service interruptions may pose immediate danger to the health and safety of those who by necessity rely on the struck services. For these reasons alone, it is argued, public employees should be prohibited from striking. Additionally, strike opponents have variously contended that the right to strike gives too much power to public sector unions ("holding the public to ransom"); that public sector strikes provoke political confrontations; and that the right to strike was designed for the private sector and does not fit the distinctive characteristics of the public sector (Cohen 1979; Kochan 1979).

These arguments have not gone unchallenged. Analysis of public employee strikes suggests that damage to the public is much less than commonly claimed (Gunderson 1994). Many public sector employees, it is pointed out, perform services that most people, in the short run at least, can do without. It is merely that the few truly disruptive disputes that do take place receive enormous publicity, creating an impression that all public employees perform similarly vital services. In addition, techniques have been developed to protect the public during stoppages, such as requirements that certain essential employees remain at work.

The notion that the right to strike places too much power in the hands of the public sector unions is also contested. It is argued that the financial constraints under which most public employers operate, the decreasing likelihood of public panic in the face of service disruptions, the substantial financial savings a public employer may realize during a strike, and the degree of taxpayer concern over high wage increases place substantial constraints on public employee bargaining power (Cohen 1979; Feuille 1979). Thus, the possibility of a strike plays exactly the role in bargaining that it should: namely, it imposes joint costs on both parties, inducing compromises necessary for a settlement (Gunderson and Reid 1995).

But the strongest argument for favouring the right to strike in the public sector lies in the lack of acceptable substitutes for strikes. Removing the right to strike from the collective bargaining process necessarily implies replacing it with some other mechanism capable of resolving disputes. Many of those who defend the right to strike contend that they are not so much enamoured of the strike weapon as they are disillusioned with the alternatives, such as arbitration and final-offer selection (Weiler 1980). Strike substitutes are criticized on the grounds that they weaken the collective bargaining process, lead to excessive third-party intervention, and generally produce inferior collective agreements (Ponak and Falkenberg 1989).

Given this debate, it is not surprising that policymakers are divided in their opinion, as demonstrated by the diversity of dispute resolution procedures in use.

Public Sector Strike Record

To help assess the debate about the right to strike it is important to begin with an examination of the strike record. Table 15.5 presents annual public sector strike volume (person-days not worked) from 1975 to 1993, inclusive, and also shows public sector strike volume as a proportion of the economy-wide strike volume (public and private sectors combined). Several patterns are apparent. First, there are wide fluctuations from year to year both in terms of absolute public sector strike volume and of the public sector proportion of overall person-days lost. Second, in any given year one or two major strikes often account for 40 per cent or more of total time lost. This is consistent with the general Canadian pattern of large lengthy strikes (Ponak and Falkenberg 1989). Third, there has been a marked decline in annual public sector strike volume since 1984. From 1975 to 1984, the average annual public sector strike volume was relatively constant at approximately 1,800,000 days lost per year. Afterwards, annual public sector strike volume declined by one-third between 1985 and 1989 and by a further 40 per cent in the next four years.

TABLE 15.5   Public Sector Work Stoppages by Year

Year	Person-Days not Worked (000s)	As Percentage of Total Strike Activity	Comments
1975	2,025	18.6	
1976	2,219	19.2	
1977	801	24.1	
1978	1,189	16.1	Nation-wide postal strike
1979	2,385	30.5	Québec public sector, Saskatchewan civil service
1975-79 (mean)	1,724	21.1	
1980	3,194	35.0	Québec teachers' strike 40 per cent of total
1981	2,211	25.0	Nova Scotia health care, BC municipalities, postal dispute account for two-thirds of total
1982	895	15.7	Alberta nurses, BC civil service, 40 per cent of total
1983	2,129	47.9	Québec teachers, BC general strike, two-thirds of total
1984	572	14.7	Recession and public-sector wage controls reduced total
1980-84 (mean)	1,800	28.1	
1985	628	20.1	Ontario Hydro and Air Canada flight attendants half the total
1986	796	11.1	
1987	885	23.2	BC General Strike 38 per cent of total
1988	2,167	44.2	
1989	1,658	44.8	Québec public sector 46 per cent of total
1985-89 (mean)	1,267	27.0	
1990	786	15.5	
1991	1,429	56.5	Federal civil servants account for half of total
1992	496	23.4	
1993	362	22.6	
1990-93 (mean)	768	27.1	

SOURCE: Calculations based on special data request from Bureau of Labour Information, Labour Canada, which included strike and lockout totals for the economy as a whole and for the public sector by year, jurisdiction, and industry.

At the same time as public sector strike volume has been declining, the public sector's share of the economy-wide strike volume has increased. Public employees now account for approximately 27 per cent of all person-days lost in Canada, up from approximately 21 per cent prior to 1980. The increased public sector share of strike volume reflects the substantial decline of private sector strike activity since the mid-1970s, a decline that has been much greater than the decline in strike volume in the public sector. Gunderson and Reid (1995) estimate that since 1988 the public sector has been losing more days to strikes as a percentage of days worked than the private sector.

Across the country, it can be seen from Table 15.6 that average annual public sector strike volume has either declined or remained relatively constant in each of the ten provinces and the federal sector. Nova Scotia, New Brunswick, Quebec, and the federal civil service (PSSRA) recorded particularly large reductions in days lost due to public sector strikes after 1985. Only that part of the public sector governed by the federal Canada Labour Code (for example, Canada Post, government-owned telephone companies, railways, and airlines) showed an increase in strike volume after 1985. Table 15.6 also allows a comparison of the strike record in various provinces adjusted for differences in provincial size.[9] These data also show that relative to the size of the labour force, days lost due to public sector strikes are much higher in Newfoundland, Quebec, and British Columbia than in other provinces. Prince Edward Island, Ontario, and Manitoba have the fewest days lost per capita.

TABLE 15.6   Public Sector Work Stoppages, by Jurisdiction

Jurisdiction	Average Annual Person-Days Lost		Average Annual Person-Days Lost per Thousand Labour Force
	1975-84	1985-93	1975-93
Newfoundland	39,720	36,856	166.1
Prince Edward Island	72	77	1.2
Nova Scotia	37,402	10,618	60.6
New Brunswick	23,828	6,680	49.4
Quebec	706,826	224,034	144.4
Ontario	181,357	179,236	35.2
Manitoba	19,795	17,401	34.9
Saskatchewan	53,283	28,150	84.8
Alberta	86,042	82,672	65.5
British Columbia	209,599	152,061	120.4
Federal-Labour Code	195,904	229,788	n/a
Federal -PSSRA	208,251	90,362	n/a

SOURCE: (1) Person-Days Lost based on unpublished data provided by Bureau of Labour Information, Labour Canada by year and jurisdiction; (2) Labour Force Data based on 1988 total labour force per province as provided in Table 15, pp. 56 - 62, *The Current Industrial Relations Scene in Canada, 1989* (Queen's University Industrial Relations Centre).

TABLE 15.7   Public Sector Work Stoppages by Element of Public Sector

Sector	Average Annual Person-Days Lost 1990-1993	Average Annual Person-Days Lost per Thousand Employees 1990-1993
Education	210,000	216.3
Health & Welfare	148,728	134.6
Federal Government	179,413	685.0
Provincial Government	35,278	153.5
Local Government	43,335	209.7
Other	151,588	n/a

SOURCES: (1) Person-Days Lost based on unpublished data provided by Bureau of Labour Information, Labour Canada by year and industry;
(2) Employment data based on January 1988, Table 7, *Employment, Earnings and Hours*, Statistics Canada, cat 72-002.

From Table 15.7 it can also be seen that some parts of the public sector have experienced more strike activity than others, although the information in this table should be viewed with some caution because of the relatively short time period covered. Because of the nationwide strike of the Public Service Alliance of Canada in 1991, the federal sector has had the most time lost due to strikes since 1990, relative to labour force size. This may well be an anomaly, since previous analyses, using different data sets, have generally shown that federal government employees account for the lowest strike volume after adjusting for size (Thompson and Ponak 1992).

In addition to measuring strike volume, another way of examining the strike record is to look at the stage at which contract negotiations were settled, using each set of negotiations as the level of analysis. This type of analysis is especially useful in showing the proportion of contract negotiations which resulted in a strike. Table 15.8 reports the contract settlement stage in two time periods for both the private and public sectors, for negotiations involving at least 500 employees.[10]

TABLE 15.8   Settlement Stages, Major Collective Agreements, Public and Private Sectors, 1978-93 (Proportion of agreements signed at each stage[a])

Settlement Stage	1980-85		1986-93	
	Public	Private	Public	Private
Direct bargaining	40.5	42.7	54.7	53.1
Conciliation and mediation[b]	23.6	40.5	26.0	33.2
Arbitration	9.1	0.6	6.0	1.2
Strike	4.7	15.6	2.7	11.4
Legislated[c]	21.1	0.3	10.3	1.0
Other, unknown	1.0	0.3	0.3	0.1
Total	100.0	100.0	100.0	100.0

[a] In order for the data to be defined consistently across time periods, contracts covering 200 or more workers in the federal jurisdiction were excluded after the 1986 settlemnt year and construction contracts after the 1983 settlement year. Thus the table includes nonconstruction contracts covering 500 or more employees.

[b] This category includes settlements achieved post-mediation and post-conciliation.

[c] Includes contracts re-opened under wage controls and the Ontario Social Contract of 1993. These amounted to 4.4 per cent of the 10. per cent in the period 1986-93 and 2.5 per cent of the 15 per cent over the full period 1980-1993.

SOURCE: Calculations based on special data request from Labour Canada's Major Wage Settlements data base, for major collective agreements, usually of 500 or more employees.

From the table, several patterns are observable. First, it can be seen that the likelihood that public sector negotiations would be settled by the parties either on their own or with the help of a mediator or conciliator has improved over time. In the most recent period, more than 80 per cent of public sector negotiations were settled at the bargaining table or in mediation/conciliation, a rate that is approaching that of the private sector. Second, as might be expected, arbitration is much more common in the public compared with the private sector because large numbers of public employees do not have the right to strike. The degree of arbitration reliance has been declining over time, a reflection of the increasing ability of public sector unions and management to reach collective agreements through negotiation.

Third, the proportion of negotiations that result in a strike ("strike rate") has also been declining in the public sector and is lower than in the private sector. The degree of difference in strike rates between the two sectors is deceptive, however, because in some cases settlements produced by legislation occurred *after* a strike was already under way. Thus, a truer indicator of the proportion of negotiations that resulted in a strike would combine the "Strike" category with some portion of the "Legislated" category. Unfortunately, because the "Legislated" category includes settlements obtained as a result of wage controls as well as back-to-work legislation, it is not possible to derive a precise strike rate; suffice to say it is greater than the rate shown just in the "Strike" category.

Finally, Table 15.8 highlights the extent to which governments have intervened in the public sector. Since 1986, more than 10 per cent of all collective agreements involving large bargaining units have been settled through either back-to-work legislation or statutory wage controls. This degree of intervention is less than in the past, but it still calls into question whether large public sector bargaining units really enjoy full collective bargaining rights.

Compulsory Arbitration

The use of compulsory arbitration is aimed at eliminating strikes before they can occur. Because public sector strikes can impose hardship and inconvenience on the public and may pose political risks to elected officials, they are frequently prohibited by law and replaced by arbitration. While arbitration can take several forms, the most commonly used format in Canada is *conventional interest arbitration*. Under this system, if the negotiating parties cannot reach a settlement, they submit their differences to an arbitrator (or arbitration panel) who listens to arguments about the merits of the respective positions and then issues a binding award. This award becomes, in effect, the new collective agreement. Under conventional arbitration procedures, arbitrators are free either to accept the position that one of the parties has submitted or to fashion their own solution on any particular issue (they can, for example, split the difference). Some statutes also stipulate criteria that the arbitrator must consider in rendering a decision, though these criteria rarely differ from factors, such as industry patterns, that arbitrators would routinely consider in the absence of such legislative guidance.

There is little question that where compulsory arbitration systems are in place they have been very successful at eliminating work stoppages, since few public sector unions will call illegal strikes (the United Nurses of Alberta are a notable exception). Misgivings about arbitration are not based on its effectiveness at preventing strikes, but rather on the effect it has on the likelihood of the parties reaching agreement during negotiations (Downie 1979; Thompson and Cairnie 1973). Our industrial relations system places a high premium on the ability of labour and management to resolve differences themselves through the give and take of the bargaining process. Almost all available evidence indicates that conventional arbitration systems lead to a lower rate of negotiated settlements than do systems in which strikes are permitted. After a review of major empirical studies up to 1988, Ponak and Falkenberg (1989) estimated that right-to-strike systems achieved settlement rates of 90 per cent but that under conventional arbitration systems settlement rates fell to between 65 and 70 per cent.

The reduced ability of parties to settle their differences under conventional arbitration is attributable to two major factors. First, the possibility of an arbitration award being imposed is often not a sufficient threat to the negotiators to induce the tough compromises necessary to reach a settlement. The possibility of a strike, by comparison, usually is a sufficient threat. Second, conventional arbitration systems may introduce an actual disincentive to compromise because concessions made during negotiations may undermine positions that might be taken in the event of arbitration. Anything that discourages compromise during negotiations reduces the likelihood of settlements. It is important to note, however, that despite these disincentives to settle, the parties do reach agreement in at least 65 per cent of their negotiations, demonstrating that the parties still maintain a fundamental preference for negotiated settlement.

In an effort to eliminate the disincentives to reach agreement under conventional interest arbitration, *final-offer selection* (FOS) has been suggested (Stevens 1966). Under FOS, the arbitrator must choose, without alteration, either the position submitted by management or that submitted by the union. Arbitrators cannot, as they can under conventional arbitration, split the difference between the positions submitted by the two parties; rather, they are obliged to accept one party's position or the other's. Depending on the form of FOS used, the selection of the two positions may be made either issue by issue or as a package. The idea behind FOS is that the two parties would rather make the concessions needed to achieve settlement during negotiations than face the risk of an arbitration award in which the other side's position, in its entirety, could be incorporated into the new collective agreement.

Final-offer selection is required in several statutes in the United States, especially for police and firefighters, but is rarely used in Canada. The US experience generally shows that FOS is capable of producing a higher rate of negotiated settlements than conventional arbitration, typically in the range of 80 to 85 per cent (Ponak and Falkenberg 1989). Despite the ability of FOS to produce higher settlement rates, there is little prospect of it becoming more widespread in Canada. It is rejected by all parties, arbitrators included, on the grounds that it can lead to poor collective agreements (if neither side submits reasonable proposals) and that it produces a damaging win-lose mentality in the labour-management relationship. Under conventional arbitration, in contrast, the arbitrator is able to fashion a decision that is likely to reflect some compromise between the final positions submitted by the two sides.

Choice of Procedures

The drawbacks associated with compulsory arbitration combined with misgivings about an unfettered right to strike have given rise to an intriguing approach known as choice of procedures (COP). Pioneered in 1967 under the PSSRA, where it is still in place, it has also been tried for limited periods in several states and provinces (Ponak and Wheeler 1980). Under PSSRA procedures, the union is given the option of choosing either arbitration or a work stoppage in the event negotiations fail to produce a settlement; the employer must abide by the union's choice.

The experience under COP has been mixed. While there was some early evidence that it is capable of reducing both strikes and arbitration (Ponak and Wheeler 1980), federal employees have increasingly rejected the arbitration option because choosing the strike option has proven more effective in the achievement of union bargaining objectives (Swimmer 1994). After twenty-five years of use, it has not spread beyond the federal sector and in several states and provinces it was abandoned after being tried.

Limited Strike

A second intriguing addition to the public sector dispute resolution framework is the concept of a limited (or controlled) strike. Also first introduced under the PSSRA, it has since been adopted in a majority of provinces for at least some employee groups (Swimmer and Thompson 1995; Haiven 1995; Hébert 1995). The limited strike approach permits work stoppages but requires that certain employees be "designated" to remain on the job to provide essential services. The number and role of such employees is generally subject to negotiation between the parties and, in the absence of agreement, a labour relations tribunal makes the final determination. Under the PSSRA, the proportion of employees designated within a given bargaining unit has varied from 2 per cent or less among librarians and social science support services to 100 per cent of air traffic controllers, firefighters, and veterinary scientists (Swimmer 1995).[11] In Montreal, transit workers may strike but must provide service during rush hour.

In theory, a limited strike system should satisfy the divergent needs of policymakers, unions, and employers. The union is able to exercise its right to strike. It is under pressure to settle because the majority of its members are foregoing their pay cheques and the employer is in partial operation. The employer is under pressure because it is unable to provide the level of service normally counted on and may be forced to mount a herculean effort to maintain even its limited operations. The public interest is protected because the designated employees ensure that essential services are maintained.

In practice, it becomes obvious that designating the "correct" proportion of bargaining unit personnel is crucial to the success of the controlled strike approach. If too many employees are designated, the pressure on the employer may be inconsequential; if too few employees are at work, even minimum service requirements may not be met and the union may enjoy a bargaining advantage. Thus, negotiations between the union and employer to determine the proportion of employees who will not strike are often difficult and protracted. For example, in the face of an impending strike of 2,000 nonprofessional employees at the Vancouver General Hospital, management took the position that all 2,000 employees were essential, while the union claimed that none of its members should have to "scab on their own union's strike" (Weiler 1980). Eventually the labour board designated 100 employees as essential.

An excellent review of essential service procedures during nurses strikes in five provinces between 1988 and 1991 is provided by Haiven (1995). He found that it is extremely difficult for the parties to negotiate essential employee levels in advance of a strike and that such negotiations, as well as any hearings held in the absence of agreement, are often dysfunctionally formal and bureaucratic. He also concluded that labour tribunals tend to set designation levels that are too high, preferring to err on the side of caution. In one Québec hospital 110 per cent of the usual nurse complement was required during a tight labour market for nurses. As well, nurses themselves frequently chose to provide higher levels of coverage than had either been imposed or negotiated. Even with high levels of coverage, Haiven found that many hospitals failed to prepare adequately for strikes, resulting in chaotic conditions. Despite these problems, Haiven concluded that a learning process was under way for all parties and that the limited strike model still represented a desirable approach to public sector dispute resolution.

Back-to-Work Legislation

Legislation to end particular strikes has long been a feature of the public sector. As can be seen from Table 15.9, 62 public employee strikes, the great majority of which were legal under the prevailing labour legislation, were terminated through special legislation between 1965 and 1993. In almost all cases, arbitration was also invoked to resolve the issues in dispute once the strike was terminated.

TABLE 15.9   Back-to-Work Legislation in the Public Sector

Year	Federal Government	Québec	Ontario	British Columbia	Saskatchewan	Other Provinces	Total
1950-64	0	0	0	0	0	0	0
1965-69	0	4	1	0	1	1	7
1970-74	0	2	2	1	0	0	5
1975-79	2	5	6	4	1	0	18
1980-84	0	8	3	1	2	3	17
1985-89	2	3	2	1	3	0	11
1990-93	2	1	0	1	0	0	4
Total	6	23	14	8	7	4	62

SOURCE: Updated from Thompson and Ponak (1992, Table 8.12) and Panitch and Swartz (1993, Appendix I).

The use of special legislation has not been evenly distributed across the country. More than a third of back-to-work laws were enacted in Quebec, a province marked by particularly tumultuous public sector disputes (Hébert 1995) as well as a tradition of legislative intervention in industrial relations (Morin and Leclerc 1986). Given the relatively small size of its workforce, Saskatchewan has also seen a high utilization of legislation to end strikes. Conversely, the federal government has resorted to legislation infrequently.

The incidence of back-to-work legislation peaked in the 1975 to 1984 period and has been declining since. The reasons for the decline as well as the overall impact of government reliance on back-to-work legislation have sparked considerable debate. Some observers believe that the use of special legislation to end otherwise legal strikes is part of a fundamental retreat by governments from any kind of free collective bargaining system for public employees (Haiven et al. 1991; Panitch and Swartz 1993). They argue that a combination of frequent use of back-to-work laws together with wage restraint legislation, the essential service designation policies of the federal government, and the deliberate downsizing of the public sector have resulted in the end of the strike as a viable union option. According to this position, the use of legislation to end strikes has declined because strikes themselves have declined in the face of concerted employer attacks on public employees and collective bargaining.

Other observers are less ready to accept that the decline in back-to-work legislation is associated with the end of free collective bargaining in the public sector (Thompson and Swimmer 1995). They note that strike activity in the private sector has dropped substantially, a function of general economic circumstances, labour market conditions, and mature bargaining relationships. Some of these factors have also contributed to a decline in public sector strike activity. As well, public sector disputes, and the need for governments to intervene, have been reduced by the introduction of sophisticated labour tribunals like the Essential Services Commission in Quebec and the Education Relations Commission in Ontario. Both of these tribunals have had a positive influence on the general atmosphere of bargaining in the sectors over which they have authority. Thus, while these observers are critical of the overuse of back-to-work laws, they also argue that the incidence of such legislation is declining for sound industrial relations reasons.

Which one of these perspectives will ultimately prevail can only be assessed with the passage of time.

Implications

The design of a dispute resolution system requires balancing the multiple objectives of avoiding strikes, minimizing third-party dependence, and maximizing good faith bargaining, protecting the public interest and accountability of elected officials, and in the long run, building the commitment of the parties and the public to a bargaining system that forces the parties to confront their problems effectively (Kochan 1979, 187).

It is not yet clear whether these objectives can be accommodated within a single dispute resolution system. As one reviews the array of alternatives currently available, it is apparent that some techniques come closer to meeting the ideal than others but that there are no easy answers. Continued experimentation and research, combined with a maturation of public sector labour-management relations, may eventually produce a consensus. The first step towards such a consensus, however, must surely be the realization that all procedures are at best imperfect and that the explicit trade-offs between desirable but incompatible objectives (for example, strike avoidance and no third-party dependence) are necessary.

COMPENSATION ISSUES

Questions surrounding public employee compensation, though less visible than those involving dispute resolution, have proven almost as troublesome. During the 1970s, a public perception arose that government employees were overpaid and too successful at winning high and unwarranted wage increases. Private employers complained that government wage settlements established patterns that the private sector, limited by profit-loss considerations, could not match. Union officials countered by claiming that such allegations were untrue and that seemingly high wage increases reflected the need of some groups of low-paid public employees to catch up to the private sector. Furthermore, union officials argued, even if a few government employees were paid more than their private sector counterparts, there was nothing inherently wrong about government being a wage leader. On the contrary, public employers should be model employers, setting a standard to be followed by the rest of the community.

Public-Private Wage Differentials

Philosophies and perceptions aside, the following factors suggest that compensation in the public sector will usually be higher than in the private sector: (1) political pressures are less stringent than the profit constraint; (2) there is pressure on government to be a model employer; (3) the public sector is more highly unionized; (4) demand for labour has generally been greater in the public sector than the private sector, especially in the 1970s and early 1980s; (5) wage surveys on which public sector wage increases are based tend to focus on large, higher-paying private employers; and (6) public employers have the ability to defer costs to future taxpayers (Gunderson 1995).

There are also some offsetting theoretical reasons why public sector compensation should lag behind that for the private sector. First, the public sector has traditionally provided more job security than the private sector, which should lead to a private sector wage premium. Second, the public sector is much more likely to be singled out for special wage restraints, depressing wages. Third, government is much more likely to intervene in public sector strikes, depriving more powerful public sector unions of the opportunity to win large wage increases (Gunderson 1995). For a number of occupations, the public sector is effectively the only employer (monopsony power), giving the employer a bargaining power few private sector employers enjoy.

Empirical studies confirm that the upward bias outweighs the downward pressures, although the difference is not large. These studies show that public employees enjoy a wage premium between 5 and 10 per cent over their private sector counterparts, and that public sector fringe benefits are slightly more generous than in the private sector. The public sector advantage is greatest at the provincial and local level, is larger for women than for men, is greater at the lower ranges of the pay scales, is negative at senior levels, and has been diminishing for a number of years. The research also shows that there is no significant spillover effect from the public to the private sector; i.e., public sector wage levels do not drive up wages in the private sector (Gunderson 1995). It is important to note further that the studies upon which these conclusions are based predate the effects both of the wage controls introduced in the early 1990s and of the recent slowdown in public sector employment growth.

Further insight into public and private sector wage differentials can be gained by examining time series data on wage changes in the two sectors. Table 15.10 reports annual wage increases between 1979 and 1992, based on collective agreements involving 500 or more employees. It shows the wage changes for the private and public sectors as a whole and also disaggregates the public sector data by major group. From the table it can be observed that there has been very little overall difference in wage changes between the two sectors from 1979 to 1992. In that period, private sector wages increased by 129 per cent while public sector wages increased by a slightly lower 125 per cent. In seven of fourteen years private sector wage increases were greater than the wage increases in the public sector, in six years the public sector led, and in 1989 wage increases were the same in both sectors. Looking at the various components of the public sector, we can see in Table 15.10 that local and provincial employees received the largest overall wage increases and that federal government employees received the lowest increases. The table also shows that private sector wage increases have been greater or equal to those in the public sector since 1988.

TABLE 15.10   Average Annual Percentage Wage Changes, Major Collective Agreements

Year	Overall Private	Overall Public	Federal	Provincial	Local	Education/ Health/ Welfare	Crown	Utilities
1979	10.8	9.2	8.4	9.1	9.4	8.2	12.4	9.1
1980	11.6	10.9	11.3	11.3	10.8	10.8	11.1	10.2
1981	12.7	13.2	12.7	13.5	12.7	13.5	12.7	13.3
1982	9.7	10.6	8.3	11.8	12.1	11.4	10.6	12.3
1983	5.4	4.6	5.5	5.0	5.7	3.6	5.6	6.6
1984	3.2	3.9	5.0	5.2	3.3	3.1	4.6	2.6
1985	3.4	3.8	3.2	4.4	4.7	3.4	4.0	3.4
1986	3.0	3.8	3.6	3.9	4.9	3.6	3.7	2.8
1987	3.8	4.2	3.4	4.5	4.2	4.2	2.6	2.0
1988	4.9	3.9	3.5	4.3	4.6	3.8	3.1	3.0
1989	5.3	5.3	4.2	5.7	6.1	5.9	4.0	5.0
1990	5.9	5.6	5.3	5.8	4.9	5.4	4.5	5.3
1991	4.3	3.5	1.7	3.9	5.1	3.8	4.4	2.3
1992	2.3	1.5	1.7	1.0	4.6	1.4	3.0	3.1
Cumulative (%)	129	125	112	136	145	120	129	114

SOURCE: This table is based on Appendix A and Appendix B in Gunderson (1995), both of which were compiled from Labour Canada, Bureau of Labour Information, *Major Wage Settlements*.

Taken together, the empirical studies on wage differentials and the time series data lead to several observations. First, they confirm that, consistent with public perceptions, government employees have been better paid than private sector employees. But the differential has been slight—probably a good deal less than popularly believed—and may in fact have disappeared given wage trends since 1988. Second, the evidence suggests that the public employer is a more egalitarian employer. Women earn comparatively more in the public sector than in the private sector. Public sector wage scales as well may be more compressed, providing employees at the low end with a comparative earning advantage. Thus, intentionally or otherwise, government is in certain respects a model employer if one assumes that equal pay and a higher floor for the lowest-paid workers are laudable objectives. Third, there is no support for the contention that public sector wage settlements have outstripped private sector wage settlements; indeed, the reverse appears to be the case.

Public Sector Wage Controls

One of the most significant elements in public sector industrial relations has been the widespread adoption of wage restraint programs in the 1980s and 1990s. The federal Anti-Inflation Program of 1975 covered both the public and private sectors, but it showed governments that restricting the compensation of public sector workers was attractive politically. Since many people believed that public sector wage settlements were driving up private sector compensation, restraining public sector compensation offered the prospect of restraining general wage levels (Auld and Wilton 1985).

The first round of wage restraint programs aimed exclusively at the public sector was initiated in the early 1980s when the Canadian economy fell into a severe recession, causing government revenues to fall sharply. With the encouragement of Prime Minister Pierre-Elliott Trudeau, every province in the country restricted public sector compensation in 1982 and 1983. Five provinces and the federal government enacted legislation establishing a formal system of wage controls. For example, the federal government enacted its "6 and 5" program, placing a ceiling of six per cent and five per cent wage increases in each of the program's two years (Swimmer 1995). In Quebec, the government legislated a 20 per cent wage rollback in 1982 (Hébert 1995). The remaining five provinces limited spending so that restrictions on compensation would be necessary. In a review of the impact of the restraint programs in British Columbia, Manitoba, Ontario, and New Brunswick, it was concluded that: (1) there was no direct relationship between provincial economic growth and the degree of restraint; (2) wage increases varied considerably among different groups within the public sector of each province; and (3) the number of provincial civil servants rose during the restraint period (Thompson 1988).

The wage restraint programs of the 1980s generally lasted no more than three years (with the exception of British Columbia where controls remained until 1987). However, shortly after collective bargaining over wages resumed in the early 1990s, a new round of wage controls began, again covering only the public sector. The main impetus for the new restraint programs was pressure on government to reduce spending to tackle public debt. The wage control programs also fit well with sentiment in favour of a smaller role for government, and thus wage restraints were part of broader campaigns that included privatization, contracting-out, layoffs, and reduction in services to the public.

Beginning in 1991, seven provinces plus the federal government passed legislation either reducing or freezing wages. In some cases, the controls were introduced in stages, with subsequent stages harsher than the initial stage. In Newfoundland, Nova Scotia, and Manitoba, wage freezes introduced in 1991 were followed by wage rollbacks in 1994 (Fryer 1995). To reduce some of the pain, the rollbacks were often achieved at least partially through unpaid days off work.

Three provinces, Prince Edward Island, Saskatchewan, and Alberta, did not impose wage controls through legislation but negotiated wage restraints with unions after significant public sector funding reductions. The Alberta provincial government, for example, embarked on a program to reduce funding to health care, education, and its own administration by more than 20 per cent over three years. At the same time, public employees were asked to take a 5 per cent pay cut. In the collective bargaining that followed, most groups agreed reluctantly to wage reductions, usually in the form of a combination of unpaid days off and outright salary decreases. In Saskatchewan, on the other hand, negotiations with civil servants produced a five-year collective agreement that provided very modest wage increases toward the end of the contract, which expires in 1996 (Fryer 1995).

British Columbia, with the country's most dynamic economy, attempted to achieve cost reduction in a different way. An effort was made to expand the bargaining agenda to reduce the focus on wages by paying greater attention to public sector restructuring issues, job security, and training and career development. Negotiations are to take place on a sectoral basis in seven sectors: the civil service; health care; social services; Crown corporations, boards, and agencies; elementary and secondary education; colleges and institutes; and universities. The first set of sectoral negotiations took place in health care and resulted in a collective agreement that provided a modest wage increase, a reduced work week, strong job security, and a plan to cut 5,000 jobs at acute-care hospitals. According to Fryer (1995) the BC approach "guarantees job security in return for flexibility and cost savings." Planned increases in nonhospital health care have progressed slowly.

The British Columbia experience stands in sharp contrast to the situation in Ontario which saw the legislation of a so-called "social contract" amid the most controversy since the Québec general strikes in the 1970s and 1980s. As in BC, the Ontario NDP government also attempted to negotiate a combination of cost savings and public sector restructuring with public sector unions. The similarities end there, however. First, rather than negotiate on a sectoral basis, the Ontario government attempted to bargain with close to one million public employees and numerous different unions at the same time. Second, the government also asked that existing collective agreements be reopened and scheduled wage increases rescinded. Third, whereas the British Columbia government had paved the way for its program with a commission of inquiry that invited public input, preparatory discussions were very limited in Ontario. As a result, public sector unions bitterly opposed the Ontario government's approach. While negotiated agreements were ultimately achieved with unions representing two-thirds of public employees, bargaining took place under a government deadline after which the Social Contract Act was to go into effect. The legislation contained the government's contract objectives. Needless to say, labour organizations that had helped elect the NDP government felt betrayed (Fryer 1995).

C O N C L U S I O N

Public sector collective bargaining has gone through three distinct phases since its widespread emergence in the 1960s. The first phase, which lasted until the early 1980s, was marked by rapid unionization, the liberalization of labour laws, strong public sector employment growth, and high wage settlements as unions sought to "catch up" to the private sector. This phase, then, can be thought of as an expansionary one both in terms of public sector collective bargaining and of the role of government in general.

The second phase, which lasted through most of the 1980s, was one of restraint. It was characterized by wage controls aimed exclusively at public employees and by low wage settlements even in the absence of formal controls. Employment growth began to slow, unions reached a saturation point in terms of public sector organizing opportunities, and strike volume began to decline, although at a slower rate than in the private sector. Public sector labour laws remained largely intact, but it was obvious that governments could and would suspend such laws to impose wage controls, issue back-to-work orders, or deem entire groups of employees as essential and hence unable to strike. Federal and provincial governments, though proclaiming the virtues of the emerging philosophies favouring less government, had not as yet abandoned Canada's traditional commitment to an active public sector.

The third phase in public sector collective bargaining, a period of retrenchment, began in the 1990s. This phase has been characterized by a commitment on the part of governments to reduce the size of the public sector through privatization and contracting out and through outright decreases in government services. Layoffs have become a common feature of public employment, reversing a long tradition of job security as an important ingredient of government employment. The 1990s have also seen the widespread renewal of public sector wage restraints, with significant wage decreases for many employees. Time lost due to public sector strikes has continued to decline.

The events in this latest phase of public sector collective bargaining have been driven by two developments. One has been an increasing change in the way in which governments view their own role, resulting in reductions in the role of governments in many spheres of economic, social, and cultural activities. In addition, the rethinking of the philosophical limits of government has coincided with a period of recession and high public debt, which has placed practical limits on the scope of government undertakings. The result of these two forces has been to place severe pressures on the public sector collective bargaining system as unions, employees, and public sector managers all attempt to cope with a very different environment than the one which shaped the original contours of the system.

The future of collective bargaining for public employees will depend on several factors. First, it is difficult to envision a genuine collective bargaining system if wages and benefits are excluded from negotiations because of legislated wage controls (or the threat of legislation, which has much the same effect). Since the early 1980s, public employees in the federal jurisdiction and in most provinces have seen their wages controlled through legislation for long periods. The first period of controls lasted approximately three years, after which there was a return to wage bargaining, and then a second round of controls was introduced. By the end of 1994, this second round had also lasted for three years and it was unclear when controls would be lifted. The 1990s wage controls were introduced ostensibly to address accelerating government debt which had been exacerbated by a severe recession. If this indeed constituted the main motivation, it can be expected that controls will be lifted as the economy improves and public debt begins to stabilize. Meaningful collective bargaining might then be restored.

Alternatively, wage controls may become a fixture in the public sector, both as a way of continuing to attack the debt and, more importantly, because controls on public employee compensation may be seen as consistent with the goal of reducing government. Moreover, politicians have correctly concluded that controlling the wages of public employees is politically popular and that union attempts to fight controls have thus far been largely ineffectual. As a result, wage control programs hold few political risks, making them relatively easy to establish. While it is true that some provinces have attempted to negotiate with their unions to bring about desired changes (successfully in British Columbia, unsuccessfully in Ontario) these attempts have been in the minority and restricted to NDP governments. A meaningful system of collective bargaining is unlikely under permanent wage controls.

The place of the right-to-strike is a second factor that will affect the future development of industrial relations in the public sector. Strike volume in the public sector has declined sharply since the mid-1980s, a trend consistent with the drop in private sector strike activity. However, the decline in public sector strikes may be attributable to the effect of wage controls (which removes an often contentious issue from negotiations) and the propensity of governments to use back-to-work legislation. If wage controls are lifted, one result might be a dramatic increase in public sector strike activity, especially if employees attempt to recoup perceived losses during the control period. This in turn could produce more legislation to end strikes. A collective bargaining system in which one of the more important rules (i.e., the right to strike) constantly changes is one that is likely to be marked by a great deal of frustration, mistrust, and turbulence.

A third factor that will help determine the future direction of public sector collective bargaining is the response of unions. Unions representing public employees are the largest in the country and make up more than half the labour movement. Despite this apparent strength, they have been unsuccessful at reversing policies that are clearly contrary to the interests of their members. Contracting-out frequently results in the transfer of jobs to nonunion and lower-paid workers, the sale of government assets typically results in job losses, and reductions in government services usually mean layoffs. Even where services have been diminished, union leaders have seldom been able to rally a general public that is more likely to see public sector unions as a narrowly based interest group.

Given this environment, a number of union strategies have been suggested. One set of strategies involves relying on the traditional union tool of negotiations to attempt to obtain contract language that will protect union members. Reliance on negotiations often is buttressed by extensive use of litigation before arbitration tribunals, labour boards, and courts (Thompson 1995). The Canadian Union of Postal Workers has employed this strategy to achieve, among other things, limits on contracting-out and a high degree of job protection in the event of work rationalization. At least one observer has suggested that the viability of this approach is dependent on the internal efficiency of the union itself and that a number of public sector unions need to significantly improve the delivery of union services to their membership if they hope to advance their collective bargaining agenda (Rose 1995).

A second set of strategies involves enhancing overall union power through the building of coalitions and alliances with other unions and with community-based groups (Panitch and Swartz 1993; Rose 1995). It has been noted that unions have not even been able to co-ordinate their activities within a particular sector. For instance, the four or five health care unions found in each province (e.g., nurses, support staff, technicians) have rarely established strong working relationships. Where inter-union alliances have been formed, they have strengthened union power considerably. Examples include Quebec Common Front actions involving most of the province's public sector unions, the coalition of private and public sector unions formed in British Columbia in 1983 to oppose anti-union legislation, and the co-operation between the National Union of Provincial and General Employees and the Public Service Alliance of Canada during the latter's nation-wide strike in 1991. In each one these cases, the co-ordination contributed to whatever degree of union success was achieved.

Community-based coalitions also may assist public sector unions to achieve their objectives. Labour organizations have become involved in wider efforts to save social programs and preserve standards in education and medicare. The results of these efforts are difficult to assess, but unions, with their large organizations and considerable resources, certainly are in a position to enhance the lobbying and other activities of such groups. For example, in British Columbia public sector unions generated support from more than a hundred municipalities to oppose (unsuccessfully) the privatization of highway maintenance (Thompson 1995).

A third strategy lies in partisan political action. A 1991 Supreme Court of Canada decision[12] ruled that public employees cannot be restricted in speaking out on employment questions and other issues of the day, thus providing a much greater scope for political activity by all public employees, and civil servants in particular (Swinton 1994). In 1993, the Public Service Alliance of Canada actively campaigned for the defeat of the federal Conservative government. More campaigns of this kind might be undertaken, although organized labour's experience, even with NDP governments which it helped elect, has not always been positive.

Finally, a former public sector union leader suggests that unions must be much more willing to jettison their traditional adversarial mentality if they are to have any hope of achieving tangible gains for their members (Fryer 1995). It is argued that the economic realities of the 1990s give governments very little choice but to reduce the level and scope of the public sector. While recognizing that problem solving is a two-way street, Fryer argues that public sector unions can be most effective by attempting to work together with governments to bring about necessary changes while protecting the interests of their members. The approach taken in British Columbia through sectoral negotiations is seen as a model for this kind of strategy.

Even if union leaders prove capable of devising new strategies, it is likely that the expansion phase of public sector collective bargaining is gone forever. The kinds of economic, political, and social changes under way in Canada also are under way, to varying degrees, in other advanced industrial societies. As a result, the role of governments is likely to continue to contract for some period of time.

There is no inherent reason why collective bargaining cannot flourish, even in the face of public sector decline. It has proven resilient in private sector industries, like textiles and clothing, which have been in a state of decline and restructuring for decades.

Indeed, meaningful collective bargaining can assist the process of change to the benefit of all participants. Such a scenario is possible in the public sector if both parties are prepared to abandon old habits. For employers this means refraining from legislative intervention that eliminates wage negotiations, ends legal strikes, and otherwise manipulates the rules in a way guaranteed to sow mistrust and anger. For unions it means accepting that the expansion years of the 1960s and 1970s are over and cannot be re-created and therefore that adjusting to the economic realities of the 1990s is a necessity. Perhaps then the next phase of public sector collective bargaining will be one of renewal.

QUESTIONS

1. Explain the role consultation played in the development of public sector collective bargaining.

2. Describe the key differences between private and public sector employers and discuss the implications of these differences for collective bargaining in the public sector.

3. Some public employees (for example, most municipal employees) fall under general private sector labour legislation, while others (for example, federal civil servants) are governed by special public sector statutes. Discuss the merits of the respective approaches.

4. Why is the question of dispute resolution procedures such an important issue in the public sector?

5. "Public employees should have the right to strike." Discuss.

6. Describe the approach taken by the Supreme Court of Canada in the Labour Trilogy cases and assess the implications of these decisions for collective bargaining in the public sector.

7. "Public sector wage controls are justified by the necessity of keeping public sector wage increases behind private sector wage increases." Discuss.

8. Describe the changes in the role of government during the past ten years and indicate the implications of these changes for public sector collective bargaining.

9. If you were a public sector union leader, how would you respond to the changing role of government in order to best advance the interests of union members?

REFERENCES

ANDERSON, J.C. 1977. *Union Effectiveness: An Industrial Relations Systems Approach.* PhD dissertation. Cornell University, Ithaca, NY.

AULD, D., and D.A. WILTON. 1985. "Wage Settlements in the Ontario Public Sector and the Ontario Controls Program." In D. Conklin, T. Courchene, and W. Jones, eds, *Public Sector Compensation.* Toronto: Ontario Economic Council.

BAIRSTOW, F., H. LEBEL, B.M. DOWNIE, and A. KLEINGARTNER. 1973. The Professional Employee in the Public Service of Canada." *Journal of the Professional Institute* 52: 4-55.

BEGIN, J.P. 1978. "Grievance Mechanisms and Faculty Collegiality: The Rutgers Case." *Industrial and Labor Relations Review* 31: 295-309.

BEAUMONT, P. 1995. "Canadian Public Sector Industrial Relations in a Wider Setting." In G. Swimmer and M. Thompson, eds, *Public Sector Collective Bargaining: The End of the Beginning or the the Beginning of the End.* Kingston: Queen's University, IRC Press.

BOIVIN, J. 1972. "Collective Bargaining in the Province of Quebec Public Sector." *Relations industrielles/Industrial Relations* 27: 708-17.

BURTON, J. F. 1979. "The Extent of Collective Bargaining in the Public Sector." In B. Aaron, J. Grodin and J. Stern, eds, *Public Sector Bargaining.* Madison, Wisc: Industrial Relations Research Association.

COHEN, S. 1979. "Does Public Employee Unionism Diminish Democracy?" *Industrial and Labor Relations Review* 32: 189-95.

DOWNIE, B.M. 1979. *The Behavioural, Economic and Institutional Effects of Compulsory Interest Arbitration.* Discussion Paper 147. Ottawa: Economic Council of Canada. 1984.

———. 1992. "Industrial Relations in Elementary and Secondary Education: A System Transformed." In R. Chaykowski and A. Verma, eds, *Industrial Relations in Canadian Industry.* Toronto: Dryden.

EDWARDS, C. 1968. "The Public Service Alliance of Canada." *Relations industrielles* 23: 634-41.

FEUILLE, P. 1979. "Selected Benefits and Costs of Compulsory Arbitration." *Industrial and Labor Relations Review* 33: 64-76.

FINKELMAN, J., and S. GOLDENBERG. 1983. *Collective Bargaining in the Public Service: The Federal Experience in Canada.* 2 vols. Montreal: Institute for Research on Public Policy.

FOOT, D. K., and P. THADANEY 1978. "The Growth of Public Employment in Canada." In D.K. Foot, ed, *Public Employment and Compensation in Canada: Myths and Realities.* Scarborough, Ont: Butterworths.

FRANKEL, S. 1960. "Staff Relations in the Canadian Federal Public Service: Experience with Joint Consultation." In J.E. Hodgetts and D.C. Corbett, eds, *Canadian Public Administration.* Toronto: Macmillan.

———. 1962. *Staff Relations in the Civil Service.* Montreal: McGill University Press.

FRYER, J. 1995. "Provincial Public Sector Labour Relations." In G. Swimmer and M. Thompson, eds, *Public Sector Collective Bargaining.* Kingston: Queen's University, IRC Press.

GANDZ, J. 1979. "Grievance Initiation and Resolution: A Test of the Behavioural Theory." *Relations industrielles/Industrial Relations* 34: 778-92.

GOLDENBERG, S. 1973. "Collective Bargaining in the Provincial Public Services." In J.F. O'Sullivan, ed, *Collective Bargaining in the Public Service.* Toronto: Institute of Public Administration of Canada.

———. 1988. "Public Sector Labour Relations in Canada." In B. Aaron, J. Grodin, and J. Stern, eds, *Public Sector Bargaining.* 2nd ed. Madison, Wisc: Industrial Relations Research Association.

GRAHAM, K. 1995. "Collective Bargaining in the Municipal Sector." In G. Swimmer and M. Thompson, eds, *Public Sector Collective Bargaining*. Kingston: Queen's University, IRC Press.

GUNDERSON, M. 1979. "Professionalization of the Canadian Public Sector." In M. Bucovetsky, ed, *Studies in Public Employment and Compensation in Canada*. Scarborough, Ont: Butterworths.

———. 1980. "Public Sector Compensation in Canada and the US." *Industrial Relations* 19: 257-71.

———. 1995. "Public Sector Compensation" In G. Swimmer and M. Thompson, eds, *Public Sector Collective Bargaining*. Kingston: Queen's University, IRC Press.

GUNDERSON, M., and F. REID. 1995. "Public Sector Strikes in Canada" In G. Swimmer and M. Thompson, eds, *Public Sector Collective Bargaining*. Kingston: Queen's University, IRC Press.

HAIVEN, L. 1994. "Industrial Relations in Health Care: Regulation, Conflict and Transition to the 'Wellness Model'" In G. Swimmer and M. Thompson, eds, *Public Sector Collective Bargaining*. Kingston: Queen's University, IRC Press.

HAIVEN, L., S. McBRIDE, and J. SHIELDS. 1991. "The State, Neo-Conservatism, and Industrial Relations" In L. Haiven, S. McBride, and J. Shields, *Regulating Labour*. Toronto: Garamond Press.

HARDY, J., and A. PONAK 1983. "Staff Relations in the Royal Canadian Mounted Police. *Journal of Collective Negotiations* 12: 87-97.

HÉBERT, G. 1995. "Public Sector Bargaining in Quebec: The Rise and Fall of Centralization" In G. Swimmer and M. Thompson, eds, *Public Sector Collective Bargaining in Canada*. Kingston: Queen's University, IRC Press.

HODGETTS, J.E., and O.P. DWIVEDI. 1974. *Provincial Governments as Employers*. Montreal: McGill Queen's University Press.

JACKSON, R. 1995. "Police and Firefighter Labour Relations in Canada" In G. Swimmer and M. Thompson, eds, *Public Sector Collective Bargaining*. Kingston: Queen's University, IRC Press.

KOCHAN, T.A. 1974. "A Theory of Multilateral Collective Bargaining in City Governments". *Industrial and Labor Relations Review* 27: 525-42.

———.1979. "Dynamics of Dispute Resolution in the Public Sector." In B. Aaron, J. Godin, and J. Stern, eds, *Public Sector Bargaining*. Madison, Wisc: Industrial Relations Research Association.

LEMELIN, M. 1984. *Les Négociations collectives dans les secteurs public et parapublic*. Montréal: Éditions Agence d'Arc.

LEWIN, D., and J. DELANEY. 1987. "Public Sector Unionism, Bargaining and Dispute Resolution in the United States." Paper presented to Pacific Rim Labour Policy Conference, Vancouver.

LOGAN, H.A. 1948. *Trade Unions in Canada*. Toronto: Macmillan.

McLEAN, B. 1979. *A Union amongst Government Employees. A History of the BC Government Employees' Union*. Vancouver: BC Government Employees' Union.

MORIN, F., and C. LECLERC. 1986. "The Use of Legislation to Control Labour Relations: The Quebec Experience." In I. Bernier and A. Lajoie, eds, *Labour Law and Urban Law in Canada*. Toronto: University of Toronto Press.

MUIR, J.D. 1968. *Collective Bargaining by Canadian Public School Teachers*. Ottawa: Task Force on Labour Relations.

PANITCH, L., and D. SWARTZ. 1993. *The Assault on Trade Union Freedoms*. Toronto: Garamond Press.

PONAK, A. 1981. "Unionized Professionals and the Scope of Bargaining." *Industrial and Labor Relations Review* 34: 396-407.

PONAK, A., and L. FALKENBERG. 1989. "Resolution of Interest Disputes." In A. Sethi, ed, *Collective Bargaining in Canada*. Toronto: Nelson.

PONAK, A., and C.R.P. FRASER. 1979. "Union Activists Support for Joint Programs." *Industrial Relations* 18: 197-209.

PONAK, A., and T.P. HARIDAS. 1979. "Collective Bargaining Attitudes of Registered Nurses in the United States and Canada." *Relations industrielles/Industrial Ralations* 34: 576-90.

PONAK, A., and C. OLSON. 1992. "Time Delay in Grievance Arbitration." *Relations industrielles/Industrial Relations*, 47: 690-708.

PONAK, A., and M. THOMPSON. 1979. "Faculty Attitudes and the Scope of Bargaining." *Industrial Relations* 18: 97-102.

PONAK, A., and H. WHEELER. 1980. "Choice of Procedures in Canada and United States." *Industrial Relations* 19: 292-308.

ROSE, J.B. 1995. "The Evolution of Public Sector Unionism." In G. Swimmer and M. Thompson, eds, *Public Sector Collective Bargaining*. Kingston: Queen's University, IRC Press.

SCARROW, H. 1960. "Employer-Employee Relationships in the Civil Services of the Canadian Provinces." In J.E. Hodgetts and D.C. Corbett, eds, *Canadian Public Administration*. Toronto: Macmillan.

STEVENS, C. 1966. "Is Compulsory Arbitration Compatible with Bargaining?" *Industrial Relations* 5: 38-52.

SWIMMER, G. 1984. "Resolution in the Ontario Public Sector: What's So Wrong about the Right to Strike?" In D. Conklin, T. Courchene, and W. Jones, eds, *Public Sector Compensation*. Toronto: Ontario Economic Council.

———. 1995. "Collective Bargaining in the Federal Public Service of Canada - The Last Twenty Years." In G. Swimmer and M. Thompson, eds, *Public Sector Collective Bargaining*. Kingston: Queen's University, IRC Press.

SWIMMER, G., and M. THOMPSON. 1995a. "Collective Bargaining in the Public Sector — An Introduction." In G. Swimmer, and M. Thompson, eds, *Public Sector Collective Bargaining*. Kingston: Queen's University, IRC Press.

———. 1995b. *Public Sector Collective Bargaining: The Beginning of the End or the End of the Beginning.* Kingston: Queen's University, IRC Press.

SWINTON, K. 1994. "The Charter of Rights and Public Sector Labour Relations." In G. Swimmer and M. Thompson,eds, *Public Sector Collective Bargaining*. Kingston: Queen's University, IRC Press.

THOMASON, T. 1995. "Labour Relations in Primary and Secondary Education." In G. Swimmer and M. Thompson, eds, *Public Sector Collective Bargaining*. Kingston: Queen's University, IRC Press.

THOMPSON, M. 1975. "The Development of Collective Bargaining in Canadian Universities." *Proceedings of the Twenty-Eighth Annual Meeting of the Industrial Relations Research Association.* Madison, Wisc: IRRA.

———. 1988. "Public Sector Industrial Relations in Canada: The Impact of Restraint." In B. Dennis, ed, *Proceedings of the Annual Spring Meeting, 1988, of the Industrial Relations Research Association*. Madison, WI: IRRA.

———. 1995. "The Industrial Relations Effects of Privatization: Evidence from Canada." In G. Swimmer and M. Thompson, eds, *Public Sector Collective Bargaining*. Kingston: Queen's University, IRC Press.

THOMPSON, M., and J. CAIRNIE. 1973. "Compulsory Arbitration: The Case of British Columbia Teachers." *Industrial and Labor Relations Review* 27: 3-17.

THOMPSON, M., and A. PONAK 1984. "Industrial Relations in Canadian Public Enterprises." *International Labor Review* 123: 647-63.

———. 1991. "Canadian Public-Sector Industrial Relations: Theory and Practice." *Advances in Industrial Relations* 5: 59-93.

———. 1992. "Restraint, Privatization,and Industrial Relations in the Public Sector in the 1980s." In R. Chaykowski and A. Verma, eds, *Industrial Relations in Canadian Industry*. Toronto: Dryden.

THOMPSON, M., and G. SWIMMER. 1995. "The Future of Public Sector Industrial Relations." In G. Swimmer and M. Thompson, eds, *Public Sector Collective Bargaining*. Kingston: Queen's University, IRC Press.

THWAITES, J. 1984."Tensions Within the Labour Movement in Quebec: Relations Between the Public and Private Sector in Three Case Studies from 1972 to 1982." In M. Thompson and G. Swimmer,eds, *Conflict or Compromise: The Future of Public Sector Industrial Relations*. Montreal: Institute for Research on Public Policy.

WEILER, P.C. 1980. *Reconcilable Differences: New Directions in Canadian Labour Law Reform*. Agincourt, Ont: Carswell.

WEINER, N. 1995. "Workplace Equity." In G. Swimmer and M. Thompson, eds, *Public Sector Collective Bargaining*.

WETZEL, K., and D. GALLAGHER. 1979. "The Saskatchewan Government's Internal Arrangements To Accommodate Collective Bargaining." *Relations industrielles/Industrial Relations* 34:452-70.

WILTON, D., 1986. "Public Sector Wage Compensation." In W. Riddell, ed, *Canadian Labour Relations*. Toronto: University of Toronto Press.

END NOTES

1   The closure of hospitals has been justified on the grounds that the primary purpose is to improve health care by rationalizing the system and offering alternative forms of care. Sceptics are concerned that the sole motivation is cost cutting (Haiven 1995).

2   Given the way in which union density statistics are reported by Labour Canada it was not possible to exclude private medical offices from other parts of health and social services in calculating density rates.

3   For a good illustration of how parties attempt to publicly frame bargaining issues for strategic advantage see the discussion of the 1987 Toronto teachers' strike in Thomason (1995).

4   According to Fryer (1995), in 1991 the federal finance minister, Michael Wilson, offered federal civil servants a choice: agree to a wage freeze or face substantial layoffs.

5   Pay and employment equity programs do not focus exclusively on women, but normally include visible minorities, persons with disabilities, and aboriginal people. For purposes of labour relations, however, the focus on women is most significant.

6   In a police arbitration presided over by one of the authors, 75% of the three-day hearing was devoted to legal arguments over what issues the arbitrator could include in his award. Ultimately the arbitrator ruled that most of the union's proposals could not be the subject of an arbitration award since these issues were legislatively defined as being within management's sole authority.

7   These cases are as follows: 1) Reference re *Public Service Employee Relations Act*, *Labour Relations Act*, and *Police Officers Collective Bargaining Act* (1987) 38 D.L.R. (4th) 161 (S.C.C); 2) *Public Service Alliance of Canada* v *The Queen in Right of Canada* (1987) 38 D.L.R. (4th) 249 (S.C.C.); and 3) *Government of Saskatchewan* v *Retail, Wholesale, and Department Store Union* (1987) 38 D.L.R. (4th) 277 (S.C.C.).

8   *Lavigne* v *Ontario Public Service Employees Union* (1991) 81 D.L.R. (4th) 545 (S.C.C.).

9   The usual way to adjust strike volume for differences in size is through a measure of days worked. Because this kind of data was not available, labour force size was chosen as a way to permit comparisons among the provinces in Table 15.6 and among the different components of the public sector in Table 15.7. We were not able to obtain the necessary data for the federal sector in Table 15.6.

10   We are indebted to Doug Hyatt and Morley Gunderson for providing this table based on their analysis of Labour Canada data.

11   A 1982 court decision significantly altered the designation process under the PSSRA. The federal government can now declare that full service must be maintained, virtually guaranteeing that almost all employees providing the service will be deemed essential. For example, prior to the ruling, approximately 10 per cent of air traffic controllers were deemed essential because most commercial aviation would be suspended during a strike. Following the ruling, 100 per cent of air traffic controllers must remain on the job because the government has decreed that commercial aviation must continue normally (Swimmer 1995). This has removed in practice the ability of a number of groups to engage in even a limited strike.

12   *Osborne* v *Canada (Treasury Board)* (1991) 82 D.L.R. (4th) 321 (S.C.C.).

CHAPTER 16

LABOUR-MANAGEMENT RELATIONS IN QUEBEC

JEAN BOIVIN AND
ESTHER DÉOM

THIS CHAPTER IDENTIFIES FEATURES OF THE QUEBEC INDUSTRIAL relations system, emphasizing characteristics of labour-management relations that most depart from those found in the rest of Canada.

These characteristics include particular sociopolitical and industrial relations contexts, a unique situation of union pluralism, and specific provisions of the labour legislation in which Quebec played a leading role such as the right to strike for public employees or the restrictions on the use of temporary replacement workers during labour conflicts. Other legislative provisions found only in Quebec that are considered in this chapter include the decree system, the labour relations framework of the construction industry, and an essential services commission to deal with conflicts threatening the health and safety of the public.

The chapter also addresses aspects of employment policies such as labour standards, pay and employment equity, and occupational health and safety.

Should the Quebec industrial relations system be thought of as essentially different from the industrial relations system found elsewhere in Canada? Or do the similarities outweigh the differences? The perspective advanced in this chapter is that many fundamental characteristics of the Canadian industrial relations system prevail in Quebec, but that there are nonetheless specific conditions and practices unique to the Quebec situation. We will mostly focus on these unique aspects with only limited attention to those characteristics which are found elsewhere in Canada and which are abundantly described elsewhere in this book.

This chapter covers four general areas: the environment in which labour-management relations evolve, the structure of employer and employee organizations, the legislative framework for collective bargaining, and, public policy on work.

THE ENVIRONMENT

The Economic Context

Table 16.1 describes the Quebec economy relative to the rest of Canada in general, and Ontario in particular. In 1993, Quebec's gross domestic product (GDP) was 22.6 per cent of the Canadian total, compared to the largest share of 40.3 per cent in Ontario. Quebec's standard of living, as represented by personal income per person has risen from 81.5 per cent of the Canadian average in 1946, to 94.5 per cent by 1993. In contrast, it has declined slightly in Ontario, although personal income in Ontario is still higher than the national average.

Although Quebec's income per capita has risen relative to the rest of Canada, that relative improvement stopped during the 1970s. Over the decade of the 1980s, slow pro-

TABLE 16.1   Economic Indicators — Quebec, Ontario, Canada

	Years	Quebec	Ontario	Canada	Quebec/ Canada (%)	Quebec/ Ontario (%)	Ontario/ Canada (%)
Population (in thousands)	1946	3,629	4,093	12,622	28.8	88.7	32.4
	1976	6,234	8,265	22,993	27.1	75.4	35.9
	1992	7,151	10,611	28,436	25.1	67.4	37.3
Labour Force (in thousands)	1946	1,337	1,702	4,829	27.7	78.6	35.3
	1976	2,689	3,882	10,203	26.4	69.3	38.0
	1993	3,404	5,362	13,946	24.4	63.5	38.4
Participation Rate (%)	1946	53.6	55.8	55.0	97.4	96.1	101.5
	1976	58.3	63.8	61.1	95.4	91.3	104.4
	1993	62.2	66.9	65.2	95.4	93.0	102.6
Employment (in thousands)	1946	1,283	1,654	4,666	27.5	77.6	35.5
	1976	2,456	3,643	9,477	25.9	67.4	38.4
	1993	2,960	4,793	12,383	23.9	61.8	38.7
Unemployment (in thousands)	1946	54	48	163	33.1	112.5	29.5
	1976	233	239	726	32.1	97.5	32.9
	1993	444	569	1,562	28.4	78.0	36.4
Unemployment Rate (%) (June 1994)	1946	4.0	2.8	3.4	117.6	142.9	82.4
	1976	8.7	6.2	7.1	122.5	140.3	87.3
	1994	11.8	9.5	10.3	114.6	124.2	92.2
Value of manfacturing shipments (in million $)	1946	2,498	3,755	8,036	31.1	66.5	46.7
	1976	25,803	49,851	98,281	26.3	51.8	50.7
	1993	74,786	163,059	309,852	24.1	45.9	52.6
Gross Domestic Product (in million $)	1961	10,608	16,674	40,586	26.1	63.6	41.1
	1976	47,697	78,188	197,916	24.1	61.0	39.5
	1993	160,170	285,367	707,651	22.6	56.1	40.3
Personal Income per Person (in $ of the current year)	1946	655	930	804	81.5	70.4	115.7
	1976	6,481	7,570	6,877	94.2	85.6	110.1
	1992	20,648	23,593	21,858	94.5	87.5	107.9

SOURCES: For 1946, 1961 and 1976: P. Fréchette et J.P. Vézina. *L'économie du Québec*, Montréal: Éditions études vivantes, 1990. For 1992, 1993, 1994: Statistics Canada, Catalogue 11010, *Canadian Economic Observer*, May 1994; Catalogue 71201, *Historical Labour Force Statistics* (1993); and Catalogue 31001, *Value of Manufacturing Shipments* (1993).

ductivity growth, combined with rising taxes (in part to pay for the increasing public debt), has left residents of Quebec and citizens elsewhere in Canada far worse off economically than they were at the beginning of the 1980s.

Labour force participation rates have increased substantially since 1946, although by 1993, at 62.2 per cent, they were still below the national average of 65.2 per cent and the Ontario rate of 66.9 per cent. Similarly, the unemployment rate has steadily increased and remains above the national average. In Ontario, the increase in the unemployment rate has been even more pronounced, going from 82.4 per cent of the national average in 1946, to 92.2 per cent of the national average by June 1994.

Structure of the Quebec Economy

As in the rest of Canada, Quebec's economy has now become a "service" economy with three out of four employees working in the tertiary sector. This is 12 percentage points more than twenty years ago. As a consequence, the manufacturing sector has seen its share of total employment drop from 31.7 per cent to 22.4 per cent between 1971 and 1992, similar to the change throughout Canada (Fréchette and Vézina 1990, 121).

Although Quebec accounts for 27.8 per cent of manufacturing employment in Canada, its share of the total value in manufacturing is only 22.7 per cent. This is because Ontario is characterized by capital-intensive industries, whereas Quebec depends for the most part on labour-intensive industries such as textiles and clothing that involve lower value added per employee.

Quebec's economy is also largely dependent on the development of its natural resources, namely, hydroelectric power, forestry, and mining. This explains why Quebec is a major producer of aluminum, paper, asbestos, and copper. The Quebec economy is also characterized by more locally owned small and medium-size firms. This is in contrast to Ontario which depends more on branches of foreign owned multinational corporations.

Such major structural differences between the Quebec and Ontario economies partly explain the diametrically opposed stances taken by the two provinces during the heated debates on the Free Trade Agreement (FTA) with the United States. While most economic groups and the Ontario government campaigned strongly against the deal, the situation was exactly the opposite in Quebec, where only the labour movement openly opposed it.

This may appear surprising in view of the fact that an important part of Quebec's economy relies on labour-intensive industries, which are more likely to be affected by low wage competition. However, many business leaders in industries such as garment manufacturing have opted to develop specialized product niches, which could benefit from expanded market opportunities, rather than compete on the basis of costs. They have transformed their production lines and invested in the training of their employees to meet these new challenges. Obviously, some firms were adversely affected by free trade with the US, especially those that did not already enjoy a competitive advantage and were not able to adjust to the new situation. However, the new economic environment has overall yielded more positive than negative results for Quebec firms.

Quebec also favored the FTA because of what Matthew Fraser (1987) called Quebec Inc.—a new spirit of business entrepreneurship, exemplified by success stories such as Bombardier, Cascades, Canam-Manac, and Quebecor. A growing number of locally owned firms strongly believe that they can successfully compete in foreign markets.

Moreover, many of these new entrepreneurs feel that they can succeed whether Quebec remains part of Canada or not.

Sociopolitical Context

The most obvious difference between Quebec and the rest of Canada is that the former has a population that is more than 80 per cent French speaking and accordingly has a specific cultural background and traditions. This situation accounts for the perennial political turmoil over the type of relationship that should exist between Quebec, the other provinces, and the federal government. This turmoil has particularly dominated the political scene since the failure of the Meech Lake Accord in June 1990.

The 1993 federal election witnessed a breakdown of traditional politics in Canada with the almost total disappearance of the Conservative Party and the rise to official opposition status of the Bloc Québécois, a party that is devoted to achieving the separation of Quebec from Canada. Moreover, outside Quebec, another new political group, the Reform Party, was able to attract a large portion of the traditional Conservative vote as well as lure many supporters away from the NDP. In this context, even though the federal Liberal government—and many Canadians outside Quebec—wish to forget about the constitutional debate and deal with more urgent economic issues, the mere presence of the Bloc Québécois in the House of Commons is a constant reminder to all Canadians of the constitutional problem.

The strength of the nationalist mood in Quebec was vividly expressed at the September 1994 provincial election which was won by the separatist Parti Québécois. The PQ has promised to hold a referendum on Quebec's independence within one year of its election. At the time of writing, the outcome of such a referendum is rather unpredictable because opinion polls taken just prior to the provincial election showed that only 40-45 per cent of respondents would have voted in favour of Quebec's independence.

Officially, the Quebec Federation of Labour (QFL) (Fédération des travailleurs et travailleuses du Québec) is the only central labour organization to endorse the Parti Québécois. In the months immediately preceding and following the national referendum of 1992, however, many labour organizations in the province adopted platforms favouring Quebec's independence, and most union activists strongly supported the Bloc Québécois in the 1993 federal election.

The overwhelming prominence enjoyed by the constitutional issue in Quebec's sociopolitical environment probably explains why no left-wing party has ever had electoral success in Quebec. The New Democratic Party has never been able to win a seat in any general provincial or federal election in Quebec. Its best performance was a mere 12 per cent of the popular vote in the 1965 federal election. The NDP's only electoral success came in 1990 when it won a by-election in a riding near Montreal, a victory due more to the popularity of the candidate than to the appeal of the party itself.

Some observers maintain that a left-wing party would be superfluous in Quebec because the socio-democratic program of the Parti Québécois has the strong support of union members. For two reasons, this is only partly true. First, only one central labour organization officially endorses the PQ, and even the type of support given by the QFL is more symbolic and tactical than practical. The relationship between the QFL and the PQ is very different in nature from the one that exists between the unions affiliated with the CLC and the NDP. There is no formal affiliation of local unions with the PQ. Support is given through a formal resolution adopted at a special general convention which the QFL always calls before each election. However, this support was withheld in the 1985 election because of the position taken by the PQ government against public sector unions in the previous round of negotiations.

Second, the socioeconomic program of the Parti Québécois is not much further to the left than that of the Liberal Party. Obviously, in opposition it was easy for the PQ to criticize some Liberal government decisions on privatization. However, when asked what his government would have done in similar circumstances, the leader of the PQ (Jacques Parizeau) did not reject outright the principle of privatization.

Thus, in Quebec, the debate about sovereignty-association or independence is at the top of the political agenda and it permeates the industrial relations system. However, it is not possible to predict with any certainty the kind of impact that a rupture of the federal link would have on the industrial relations context. We will now describe that context in some detail.

The Industrial Relations Context

The industrial relations context in Quebec has undergone a complete turnabout over the last ten years. This transformation can be seen both in the reduction of work stoppages and in the new cooperative attitude which prevails in an increasing number of work places.

In regard to strike activity, the number of collective bargaining situations involving work stoppages, which ranged from 15 to 20 per cent in the 1970s, dropped to 5-6 per cent at the end of the 1980s and early 1990s (Lacroix 1987; Les relations du travail au Québec 1989; 1993). Radical union leaders who occupied a predominant place in the industrial relations scene of the 1970s, have been replaced by new leaders who are more inclined to accept labour-management cooperation in order to enhance productivity and protect jobs.

The Quebec Federation of Labour's Solidarity Fund

The major cause of this transformation has been the economic situation. The 1981-82 recession, the worst economic crisis in Quebec since the Great Depression of the 1930s, raised the unemployment rate to approximately 15 per cent. In the spring of 1982, the Quebec government organized a socioeconomic summit meeting to make employer and union representatives sensitive to the urgent need for creating jobs. From that meeting consensus emerged to stimulate residential construction through an investment fund called "Corvée-Habitation." The idea was to allow buyers of new houses to have access to mortgages at lower than market rates. The fund was financed by a special tax levied on financial institutions and by contributions from all employers and employees operating in the construction industry. Three years after its inception, the program was responsible for 57,000 new construction jobs and twice as many in related industries (Fournier 1991, 27).

However, the Quebec Federation of Labour, which had supported the idea of Corvée Habitation, maintained that this program was insufficient by itself to cope with the severe employment problems in Quebec. The QFL wanted to develop a large investment fund to help maintain and create permanent jobs in Quebec. Since the Quebec government was supportive of the idea, it passed legislation on June 23, 1983 creating the QFL Solidarity Fund, which began to operate in February 1984. The Fund accepts savings not only from QFL members but also from the public. Contributors enjoy the tax deferral advantages of both a Registered Retired Savings Plan and Quebec's Equity Savings Plan, which means a tax deduction of up to 80 per cent of the original investment.

According to a legislative amendment adopted in 1986, the Fund must maintain the equivalent of 60 per cent of its assets as equity participation in small and medium-sized firms, the rest being invested in financial institutions. The Fund plays a key role in promoting training for workers in firms in which it has invested and in promoting labour-business cooperation through increased participation by workers in managing their own firms. To this effect, the Fund requires first that workers be allowed access to the books of their firms and that they be able to interpret them. To achieve this goal, the Fund has set up an education and economic development foundation, largely funded by employers' contributions. Subsequent stages include the development of diverse forms of participative management in which the union becomes in effect a partner with the financial owners (Fournier 1993, 89).

The QFL Solidarity Fund was at first greeted with a certain degree of skepticism by other labour organizations. Most union leaders in Quebec, however, now agree that setting up the Fund not only allowed thousands of jobs to be created and maintained, but also helped develop greater economic democracy in the workplace. (This view is not shared, though, by one of the key labour organizations, the Centrale des syndicats démocratiques.)

As of October 31, 1993, the Fund had a little less than 200,000 subscribers, of whom slightly less than half were QFL members. The net worth of the Fund was $797.1 million, and its equity participation in some 100 small and medium-sized enterprises was $395 million, representing approximately 50 per cent of all risk capital invested in Quebec (Rapport annuel 1993). The Fund has also created two other investment tools: specialized sectorial funds in biotechnology, environment, and aerospace; and regional funds, which are operating with the participation of other financial institutions such as the Caisse de dépôt et de placements, the Société d'investissements Desjardins, banks, and local investors.

It is probably an exaggeration to say that the creation of the Solidarity Fund was the major cause of the growth of labour-management cooperation in Quebec in the 1980s. We believe, however, that the existence of the Fund has certainly been an important contributing factor to the change in the industrial relations climate in Quebec and an important factor in explaining why the level of strike activity did not increase during the recovery years of 1984-89, as is usually the case after a recession.

Social Contracts

The most recent economic recession (1990-92), which severely hit North American and European countries, further reinforced labour-management cooperation in Quebec. In April 1991, the SAMMI-Atlas company, a branch of SAMMI Steel Company Ltd. of South Korea, signed a collective agreement with the union representing its production workers that was described by the Quebec Minister of Industry and Commerce as a "social contract." Many characteristics of the SAMMI-Atlas agreement were soon to be adopted by other firms, and the term "social contract" rapidly became the new symbol for cooperative union-management relationships in Quebec. This is in contrast to Ontario, where the same term refers to the constraints imposed on public sector employees' working conditions by the NDP government in 1993 in an attempt to avoid layoffs.

The provincial Department of Industry and Commerce was instrumental in influencing the SAMMI-Atlas deal. It made the government's financial participation in modernization of the company conditional upon several key features that included a commitment to six years of industrial peace, a minimum level of employment, a training program, work flexibility, and total quality management.

Although government financial participation in a company is not a necessary condition for firms to develop a social contract, it has become common practice for institutions such as the QFL Solidarity Fund and the Industrial Development Society (a Quebec government agency designed to increase capitalization of Quebec companies) to require that most of the elements of the social contract are included before the investment is made. The Department of Industry and Commerce has even published guidelines identifying the seven basic elements that a social contract should contain: 1) labour relations stability that is ensured by long-term peace agreements; 2) employment stability; 3) human resources development and training; 4) flexibility and mobility in work organization; 5) total quality management; 6) economic transparency, i.e., information provided to employees on the financial situation of the firm; 7) joint administration of the agreement (MIC 1992).

It should be noted that many elements of social contracts are not integral parts of collective agreements. They are usually included in a memorandum of agreement that complements the collective agreement. In fact, some of these elements, such as the long-term commitment to industrial peace, would even be illegal if they were part of the agreement because the Labour Code stipulates a maximum contract duration of three years. The Quebec government has recently amended the Labour Code to allow the signing of collective agreements for a period of up to six years (Bill 116, adopted May 17, 1994).To compensate for the fact that the union cannot use its right to strike until the end of the period covered by the social contract, most memorandums of agreement provide for arbitration of monetary clauses after three years, usually in the form of final offer selection.

Social contracts are found predominantly in two industrial sectors, pulp and paper and metalworks. They are more likely to involve CSN (Confederation of National Trade Unions) affiliates than national or international unions belonging to the QFL/CLC, although the Steelworkers' Union, the Communication, Energy, and Paper Workers' Union, and the Amalgamated Clothing and Textile Union have also been involved. The number of social contracts is still relatively low—less than twenty were in existence at the beginning of 1994—but their number is steadily increasing. More important, but almost impossible to appraise quantitatively, is the greater number of other types of labour-management arrangements that have not officially been labelled "social contracts" but are nevertheless based on the same principles of cooperative rather than adversarial relationships.

The new institutional arrangements between labour and management in Quebec must be assessed within the wider North American context. First, they possess some of the characteristics of the so-called "concession bargaining agreements" that were signed in the US in the early and mid-1980s, namely the trade-off between greater managerial flexibility and long-term industrial peace in exchange for employment security. But, in contrast to these arrangements which labour unions reluctantly had to accept, the seven elements contained in social contracts go much further in terms of making the union a partner in the implementation of the agreement.

Another distinguishing feature of Quebec experiments in labour management cooperation is the substantial amount of political and institutional support given by two key actors: the Quebec government and prominent union leaders. In addition to the role played by public agencies such as the Société de développement industriel, the Department of Industry and Commerce, and the Department of Labour in promoting and implementing social contracts, the Quebec government also uses its fiscal policy to promote greater employer-employee partnership in small and medium-size firms. The "Régime d'intéressement des travailleurs dans un contexte de qualité totale" provides tax deductions for both employees and employers who are involved in a profit sharing plan in a context of total quality management. The employee tax deduction can reach $3,000 a year with a maximum of $6,000 in five years, and the employer non-refundable tax credit represents 15 per cent of the sums paid to the employees.

Leaders of the major labour organizations have often been involved in discussions about the establishment of "social contracts," such as in the case of SAMMI-Atlas where the president of the CNTU played a decisive role. They have also used their annual conventions to encourage widespread debates within their membership around issues such as new human resource management techniques, work organization, and work sharing. More than anything else, they have displayed a great awareness of the major employment problems affecting the Quebec economy. As the former president of the QFL once said: "What good is it to have the best union in the world, the best collective agreement if you don't have a job, if your firm closes down?" (Fournier 1993, 89).

This new economic pragmatism by Quebec union leaders is in singular contrast to the official position adopted by other Canadian labour organizations such as the Canadian Labour Congress or the Canadian Automobile Workers. According to Kumar (1993), these organizations have developed "a culture of resistance to change within an adversarial framework."

One of the outstanding features of the transformation of the industrial relations context in Quebec is that it has been accomplished in an environment characterized by the highest level of unionization and the most liberal collective bargaining legislation in North America.

EMPLOYER AND EMPLOYEE ORGANIZATIONS

The next section of this chapter is devoted to describing the major labour organizations in Quebec (the FTQ, the CSN, the CSD, the CEQ) as well as the major employer organization (the Conseil du Patronat du Québec).

Trade Union Structure and Membership

The Quebec Federation of Labour (QFL)/(Fédération des travailleurs et travailleuses du Québec)

The Quebec Federation of Labour (QFL) is by far the largest central organization in Quebec (Table 16.2). In 1993 the QFL represented more than 35 per cent of all employees covered by collective agreements under the jurisdiction of the provincial labour code (that is, all employees except construction workers and workers under the federal jurisdiction).

TABLE 16.2   Distribution of Workers According to Union Affiliation and Sectors to Which They Belong,[a] 1993

Unions	Public Provincial Civil Service	Parapublic Health and Education	Quasi-Public Utilities & Government Enterprises	Private	Municipal Administration	All sectors
			% of workers[b]			
CEQ	–	26.6	1.5	0.5	–	9.6
CSD	–	1.1	0.3	6.5	2.7	3.6
CSN	–	39.4	18.7	18.6	11.0	24.3
FTQ	–	12.2	54.0	54.8	51.0	35.9
Independent[c]	100	20.7	25.3	17.1	35.3	25.3
Others[d]	–	–	0.1	2.9	–	1.4
All Unions	100	100	100	100	100	100
(% in Each Sector)	(6.5)	(34.9)	(6.7)	(46.7)	(5.1)	(100.0)
			Number of workers			
CEQ	–	88,843	995	2,270	–	92,108
CSD	–	3,823	207	29,187	1,345	34,562
CSN	–	131,833	12,068	83,448	5,423	232,772
FTQ	–	41,778	34,930	243,931	25,044	344,683
Independent	62,789	69,363	16,356	76,721	17,318	242,547
Others	–	–	85	13,085	5	13,175
All Unions	62,789	334,640	64,641	448,642	49,135	959,847

[a] These data exclude the federal sector and workers subject to the Construction Decree.
[b] Ratio of number of workers per union to total number of workers per sector.
[c] The term "Independent" means non-affiliation with the following organizations: CEQ, CSD, CSN, FTQ.
[d] The category "Others" includes: the American Federation of Labor-Congress of Industrial Organizations (AFL-CIO), the Canadian Labour Congress (CLC), the Confederation of Canadian Unions (CCU), the Canadian Federation of Labor (CFL) and the Union des producteurs agricoles (UPA).

SOURCE: Statistics compiled by the authors from *Les relations du travail 1993*, Ministère du travail, Québec, 1994, 28.

The bulk of its membership comes from the private sector, where it represents more than 54 per cent of all unionized employees, but it also has considerable strength in the municipal sector and significant representation in the parapublic sectors. As well, its affiliates in the construction industry have always obtained the largest share in the representation elections held periodically under the Loi sur les relations du travail dans l'industrie de la construction (the Construction Industry Labour Relations Act). Almost all unionized employees who come under the jurisdiction of either the Canadian Labour Code or the Public Service Staff Labour Relations Act are affiliated with the QFL.

The affiliation of local unions with provincial federations such as the QFL is not mandatory under the CLC constitution. Once a local union has joined a national or international union that belongs to the CLC, the local itself decides whether or not to affiliate with the provincial body. Thus, it is important to note that the QFL has been able to increase substantially its percentage of CLC union affiliates. It gradually raised its share from a mere 37 per cent one year after the historic 1956 merger of the TLC and the CCL, to between 65 and 70 per cent in the 1970s. Today the QFL represents virtually all CLC affiliates in Quebec.

Special Status within the CLC.   The Quebec situation of trade union pluralism and cultural specificity has led the QFL to behave like an independent labour body. Unlike other provincial federations, which quickly achieved a monopoly status in their respective jurisdiction after the 1956 merger, the QFL must compete with three other major labour organizations to obtain union members' allegiance. This unique situation has gradually led QFL leaders to ask for additional powers and more autonomy from their parent body, the CLC.

As early as 1967, the QFL leadership developed the argument that CLC success in Quebec depended on a strong provincial federation. In practice, this meant that the CLC should recognize that QFL representatives were in a better position than CLC officials to understand the specific needs and problems of Quebec workers. To be successful in attracting workers to CLC unions, the argument ran, the organization should grant the QFL more powers, more autonomy, and hence more money. The process of gaining more autonomy has recently led to an agreement that was labelled by the QFL as a "sovereignty-association" agreement. However, the process of gaining this new status has been a long one and took place in two stages: the first at the 1974 CLC convention in Vancouver, and the second at the 1994 convention in Toronto.

In 1974, delegates to the CLC national convention in Vancouver accepted the Quebec delegation's three major requests: 1) that the QFL would henceforth have full jurisdiction over labour education services in Quebec, a prerogative exercised by the CLC itself in all other provinces; 2) that the CLC would bargain with the QFL over a formula that would permit the latter to recoup funds for services that Quebec union members pay for but do not benefit from because of linguistic, cultural, or political differences (for example, a unilingual newspaper); 3) that the CLC would yield full jurisdiction over local labour councils to the QFL—an agreement implying jurisdiction over staff providing the appropriate services and hence over the sums of money that those staff members disburse.

Although it took some years for these resolutions to be realized in practice, the QFL has been able to increase its presence in most regions where it was formerly weak (or nonexistent) through hiring additional union staff appointed to local councils. The QFL has also extensively expanded its education services.

From "Special Status" to "Sovereignty-Association."   From 1974 to 1994, many unique situations were created by the particular status of the QFL. Those situations led to informal agreements between the QFL and the CLC. But in one case, it also led the QFL to take actions forbidden under the CLC constitution but that had been more or less tolerated. In the mid-1970s, contrary to the CLC constitution, the QFL maintained among its affiliates organizations that had either severed their affiliation with, or refused to join, an international trade union. Asked to justify this irregularity, QFL leaders always publicly affirmed that the situation was temporary. Their rationale was based on the unique situation of the QFL, namely the trade-union pluralism in Quebec. For this reason, the QFL kept those organizations within its ranks, pending their final decision to return to their former organizations or to affiliate with some other CLC organization (QFL, Constitution 1977, c. art. 5f). Many building trade unions affiliated with the AFL-CIO threatened to leave the CLC if the latter did not order the QFL to end the situation of dual unions within its ranks. The CLC leadership, under the presidency of Dennis McDermott of the United Automobile Workers, decided to stand behind the QFL and refused to expel the dual unions. As a result, in March 1981, the CLC Executive Council suspended fourteen international building trade unions, with more than 229,700 members, for non-payment of affiliation dues. One year later, ten of these international building trade unions participated in the establishment of a new labour federation: the Canadian Federation of Labour (CFL).

The 1994 agreement constitutes a logical result of the 1974 agreements. It also became a necessity because of the deterioration in relations between the QFL and CLC after the electoral failure of the QFL candidate at the CLC national convention in June 1992. This "sovereignty-association" agreement was adopted unanimously by the CLC delegates at the national CLC convention held in Toronto in May 1994. Under its provisions, in addition to occupying a seat on the CLC Executive Council, the QFL president automatically becomes a full voting member of the CLC executive committee. This agreement also gives the QFL the right to observe its own protocols on such important issues as internal jurisdictional disputes and union education, and it gives it control over the corresponding sums of money. It systematically includes the QFL in the CLC international representation by inviting the QFL to designate officers or representatives to participate in activities or organizations such as the International Labour Office Annual Conference, meetings of the International Confederation of Trade Unions Executive Board, as well as other international conferences, particularly whose associated with Francophone countries. With this agreement between equal partners, the QFL evolved from having a "special status" to "sovereignty-association."

The Confédération des syndicats nationaux

The Confédération des syndicats nationaux (CSN) was originally a confederation of Catholic trade unions created in 1921. At the time, it represented approximately 26,000 workers and was known as the Confédération des travailleurs catholiques du Canada (CTCC). By 1993, it included more than 232,000 workers, representing more than 24 per cent of all Quebec workers covered by collective agreements under the provincial labour code (excluding the construction sector). In contrast to the QFL, the majority of whose members come largely from the private sector, more than half of the membership of the CSN is in the parapublic sector, particularly in health care.

Since its creation in 1921, the CSN has undergone profound changes in the composition of its membership, its structure, and its ideology. Rapid industrial expansion drew large numbers of French Canadians to major urban centres, where they came in contact with other workers. This led the CTCC to remove the Catholics-only clause from its constitution in 1943. Vigorous organizing campaigns by the TLC and the CCL in Quebec also forced Catholic organizations such as the CTCC to be more militant than they were at the outset, when they were so strongly influenced by Catholic priests and bishops. This new militancy brought the CTCC into conflict with the Union Nationale regime of Maurice Duplessis on more than one occasion. Many historians consider the violent strike at Asbestos in 1949 as the turning point in the evolution of the Catholic confederation.

At the time of the great union mergers that brought an end to the rivalry between the American Federation of Labour (AFL) and the Congress of Industrial Organizations (CIO) in the United States as well as their counterparts—the TLC and CCL—in Canada, the CTCC was urged to join the unification movement. However, the CTCC wanted to join as a unit in order to preserve its distinct character and identity, and the CLC was structurally designed to accommodate only individual unions organized on the basis of particular trades or industries. Thus, instead of achieving structural unity, the Quebec labour movement remained divided and continued to be prone to rivalry and conflict between the two main union bodies, the CTCC and the CLC's new Fédération du travail du Québec (QFL).

At its 1960 convention, the CTCC dropped the last vestiges of its identification with the Catholic Church and renamed itself the Confédération des syndicats nationaux (CSN). It subsequently reorganized and centralized its structure (for example, it established a single strike fund financed by all of its affiliates) in order to be in a better position to compete with QFL's affiliates.

The CSN grew rapidly in size and in influence during the Quiet Revolution of the 1960s. It benefited most from the organization of professional and other salaried employees in the public service, but it also won certification campaigns over the CLC-QFL on many occasions. After the 1965 departure of CSN president Jean Marchand for Ottawa, where he became an influential minister in Pierre Trudeau's Liberal cabinet, the leaders who came to power showed a much greater propensity for radical, even revolutionary viewpoints. The early 1970s were propitious to union radicalism within both the CSN and the QFL. One important consequence of this growing radicalism was serious splits within the CSN: the first led to the creation of the Centrale des syndicats démocratiques (CSD) in May 1972. Then in September 1972, 30,000 civil servants also pulled out of the CSN; they decided to remain an independent labour organization rather than join either the QFL or the CSD. One year later, some 5,000 workers in the aluminum industry also left the CSN and formed another independent organization, the Fédération des syndicats du secteur aluminium.

The loss in membership suffered by the CSN during the 1970s, compounded by the severe economic crisis of the early 1980s, has contributed to a reduction in the influence of the radical elements within the CSN. Once strongly opposed to cooperation with management, the CSN, as well as other labour organizations such as the QFL, is now actively involved in labour-management cooperation experiments. For instance, as noted above, the president of the CSN played a decisive role in the establishment of the social contract at SAMMI-Atlas. This move from a quasi-Marxist orientation in the mid-1970s to a more pragmatic one in the mid-1980s was reflected in the themes debated by the delegates at the 1994 convention, Work Sharing and Work Organization.

The organizational structure of the CSN resembles any other labour federation. Local trade unions are affiliated with professional "federations," which are the equivalents of national or international unions, and with local labour councils. The professional federations do not possess their own strike funds; rather, the money is centralized at the CSN. However, a great deal of autonomy is left to local unions over how they conduct their negotiations, and the strike fund is available to any of these locals, almost without restriction. Between biannual conventions, the CSN's administration is handled by two intermediate bodies: the Bureau Confédéral (Confederal Bureau), which is made up of the top senior officials (the Executive Committee), twenty-two representatives from the professional federations, and twenty-two from the local labour councils; and the Conseil Confédéral (Confederal Council), which includes all members of the Bureau Confédéral plus sixty-five representatives appointed by local labour councils and fifty-three representatives from the professional federations. The Council meets four times a year, and the Bureau meets every month.

Even though the 1976 convention increased the representation of professional federations (to the number described above), the structure of the CSN remains highly political because of the weight given to local labour councils. It is well known that the latter are functionally oriented toward broader political issues while the professional federations tend to focus on bread-and-butter issues.

Unlike the typical North American model of a craft union federation, the CSN does not affiliate construction workers on a trade-by-trade basis. All its members in this sector are grouped within a single industrial-like professional federation. Although apparently unusual, this type of union structure does conform with Quebec's special legislation regulating labour relations in the construction industry.

The Centrale des syndicats démocratiques

Created in 1972, the CSD is structured on the same model as the CSN except that affiliation to professional federations and labour councils is not mandatory for local unions. Since its creation in 1972, the CSD has not succeeded in significantly increasing its membership. With approximately 30,000 members in 1972, the membership increased to 40,000 by 1985, only to decrease to approximately 34,000 members by 1993. The CSD represents 3.6 per cent of employees covered by collective agreements under the provincial labour code. The majority of its members (84 per cent) work in the private sector, mainly in three major industrial sectors: metal-works, chemical products, and clothing.

As a matter of philosophy, the CSD wants to remain absolutely neutral vis-à-vis political parties. It does not profess any particular social doctrine, and it even has an article in its constitution whereby the adoption of a particular ideological orientation by the organization would require a referendum of the whole membership.

The Centrale de l'enseignement du Québec

The unionization of teachers in Quebec dates from 1936; the first provincial federation was formed ten years later. Like most other union organizations, the Corporation des instituteurs et institutrices catholiques du Canada had a very rough time during the Duplessis regime. It dropped its confessional name in 1967 and became the Corporation des enseignants du Québec (CEQ). That year also saw the first confrontation between teachers and the provincial government, which led for the first time to special legislation to end the wave of teachers' strikes throughout the province.

Like the CSN at the beginning of the 1970s, the CEQ went through a substantial ideological reorientation. One aspect of this reorientation was the transformation of the organization from a "corporation"—in which membership was mandatory according to a government charter and restricted to elementary and secondary school teachers—to a genuine labour organization, the Centrale de l'enseignement du Québec (still CEQ). This meant that after the CEQ asked the government to revoke its charter, it had to seek certification from all its existing local units according to the rules of the Quebec Labour Code. By doing so, the CEQ opened its ranks to all categories of workers in the field of education, from caretakers to classroom teachers, and at the elementary, secondary, and postsecondary levels. As a consequence, the CEQ competed with CSN, CSD, and QFL affiliates in representation elections for certain categories of employees. Nonetheless, more than 90 per cent of the CEQ's membership is still made of elementary and secondary school teachers.

Independent Labour Unions

Despite the presence of four major labour federations in Quebec, one-quarter of the province's union members are not affiliated with any of these organizations. The most important independent unions are the Syndicat de la fonction publique du Québec (the

Civil Service Union) and the nurses' associations. This situation has been a major concern for the four main labour organizations because it was a growing phenomenon: independent labour organizations represented approximately 15.5 per cent of unionized workers in 1975 (Delorme and Veilleux 1980, 17). Even though this figure rose to 27.0 per cent in 1987, it now seems to have reached a saturation point: from 1987 to 1993, the independent labour organizations represented approximately 25 per cent of unionized workers.

Employer Organizations

There are many types of employer organizations in Quebec including sectoral groups directed towards economic and social interests, economic promotion groups, business groups, professional associations, and even employer associations responsible for negotiating with trade unions. There are approximately ninety employer associations in Quebec representing approximately 25,000 employers. The latter act mainly in the construction sector and in sectors governed by the Collective Agreement Decrees Act (Delorme, Fortin, and Gosselin 1994, 169).

More importantly, Quebec is characterized by the existence of a prominent confederation of employer associations, the Conseil du patronat du Québec (CPQ). This organization was created in 1969 to address three specific goals: 1) to have a single spokesperson for employers to deal with the Quebec government, which wanted to deal with a single organization during consultation with employers; 2) to integrate those Anglophone businesses that, since the Quiet Revolution, had felt isolated from the Francophone majority; and 3) to highlight the employers' perspective on labour legislation (Boivin 1989).

The CPQ is mainly a group of associations, not individual companies. Furthermore, contributions from individual firms or corporate members represented 46 per cent of the CPQ's total revenue in 1993. However, corporate members are not part of the CPQ decision-making structure. These members form the Bureau des Gouverneurs which acts only as a consultative body. It is estimated that employers directly or indirectly represented by the CPQ employ 70 per cent of the Quebec labour force (Leclerc and Quimper 1994, 211).

Over the years, the CPQ has managed to become the spokesperson for the employers' community in Quebec. It represents management in the majority of existing tripartite structures including the Advisory Council on Labour and Manpower and the Superior Education Council. The CPQ presents briefs on all questions that are likely to be of interest to its members, takes part in conventions and press conferences, publishes studies, states opinions, and organizes colloquia and conferences on these questions as well. In fact, the CPQ performs all the activities that are usually expected from a representative organization in labour relations, with the exception of collective bargaining. There are also Quebec branches of the Canadian Manufacturers Association and the Chamber of Commerce, just as in any other province.

LABOUR LEGISLATION AND COLLECTIVE BARGAINING

Collective bargaining in Quebec takes place in the context of one of the highest unionization rates in North America and one of the most liberal labour legislation regimes. Although Quebec's collective bargaining framework is rooted in the basic principles of the Wagner Act in the United States, it possesses many features which guarantee that employees will have a significant influence on their working conditions. Some of these features are shared by other Canadian jurisdictions, which have sometimes borrowed from Quebec, while others are unique to Quebec.

To illustrate our argument about the "liberalism" of Quebec labour legislation, particular features of the Labour Code as well as other legislation such as the Act Respecting the Process of Collective Negotiation and the Collective Agreements in the Public and Parapublic Sectors, the Collective Agreement Decrees Act and the Construction Labour Relations Act are presented below.

The Labour Code

The Labour Code provides the basic legal framework for collective bargaining in both the private sector (with the exception of the construction industry) and the public sector, although in the latter case, it is complemented by another piece of legislation that organizes bargaining structures.

Public Employees' Right to Strike

When the Labour Code was enacted in 1964, its major objective was to update a legislative framework that had been adopted twenty years earlier and that was modelled on the US Wagner Act. It included several modifications, the most daring of which was granting the right to strike to all public employees except police and firefighters. Quebec was the first government in North America to produce a positive law in this regard, most other jurisdictions having restrictive laws or court interpretations applying to public sector employees. In the next few years, Quebec's lead would be followed by the Canadian federal government, most provincial governments, and two American states.

Antistrikebreaking Provisions

In 1977, the same year that a reform bill that would have brought positive modifications to the National Labor Relations Act in the US failed to be adopted in Congress, Quebec introduced a series of amendments to its Labour Code that went far beyond what the failed US bill would have achieved. Once again, Quebec took a major (and controversial) step forward in the protection and promotion of employees' right to bargain collectively by becoming the first jurisdiction in the world to ban the use of replacement workers during a work stoppage. A few American states and three Canadian provinces already had statutes prohibiting the use of "professional strikebreakers." As well, there are general restrictions in Canada on permanently replacing striking employees. However, the legislative ban on the use of replacement workers is more extensive in Quebec than in any other jurisdiction.

The bill was passed amidst strong opposition from employers and in a sociopolitical context that was quite similar to that in Ontario when the NDP passed similar legislation in 1992. The Parti Québécois, which had been elected the year before, never tried to conceal its "pro-labour" orientation. This legislation, which also included other measures enhancing the status of labour unions and collective bargaining, provided the occasion to fulfill a promise made when the party had been in opposition.

According to article 109.1 of the Labour Code, employers cannot use the services of other persons to do the work usually done by their own employees if the latter are in a situation of legal strike or lockout. Amendments made in 1983 further reinforced the restrictions after a court decision had upheld the practice developed by employers of subcontracting work done by workers on strike. Consequently, the only persons who are now allowed to work during a legal strike in Quebec are the employer's supervisory personnel, and even then only those individuals who were hired prior to the start of collective bargaining.

Despite the early fears expressed by employers, the antistrikebreaking provisions have not had any negative impact on the process of collective bargaining, nor have they forced employers to surrender to unrealistic bargaining demands by the unions. There is some evidence to show that the antistrikebreaking provisions in Quebec might be associated with an increase in strike activity, both in terms of incidence (Gunderson, Kervin, and Reid 1989) and duration (Gunderson and Melino 1990). The authors of these studies point out, however, that although their analyses do control for the impact of other determinants of strikes, it is exceedingly difficult to assess the independent impact of a single provision, such as a ban on replacement workers. Our judgement is that the antistrikebreaking provisions have had a positive effect on the climate of labour relations in Quebec since there has been a substantial decrease in the amount of violence during work stoppages. This was indeed the major reason advanced by the government to justify the implementation of this very controversial measure, and in this regard, the objective has clearly been achieved.

A study by Fleury (*Marché du travail* 1991) examined the frequency with which the provisions banning the use of replacement workers were invoked during the period 1978–1989. In roughly one-third of the work stoppages, the union requested an investigation to determine whether replacement workers were being utilized. Twenty-five per cent of these cases did not proceed because a settlement was reached by the parties either before or during the investigation. The investigators found the employers to be in violation of Article 109.1 in slightly more than 50 per cent of the remaining cases. This meant that the overall percentage of labour conflicts where strikebreakers were officially used was approximately 13 per cent. However, people involved in the investigation procedures reported that in many instances, employers were not even aware that they were in violation of the statute. Most employers would immediately rectify the situation after being warned by the investigator. Unfortunately, the exact number of these cases is not recorded; no doubt it would decrease considerably the 13 per cent violation rate.

In fact, there have been very few cases where sanctions have been levied against employers (a maximum fine of $1000 per day, for each day of infraction) after a union has filed an official complaint with the Labour Tribunal. Moreover there have been very few civil injunctions issued by the courts. Both of these procedures have been available to unions to stop employers from using strikebreakers.

The perceived success of these antistrikebreaking provisions explains why two other provinces, Ontario and British Columbia, adopted similar measures, in 1992 and 1993 respectively. Such legislation is also being considered in the United States.

Other Pro-Labour Amendments Introduced in 1977

The 1977 amendments to the Labour Code also included other measures that were beneficial to labour organizations. These included first-collective-agreement arbitration and automatic deduction of union dues from all employees included in the bargaining unit whether or not they were members of the union. The same legislation also compelled labour organizations to hold a secret ballot as a precondition to a strike and prior to accepting or rejecting an employer's settlement proposals in bargaining.

Essential Services in Labour Disputes

In 1982, the government passed new amendments to the Labour Code, this time to protect the public's health and safety during labour disputes. The 1970s were characterized by a high level of strike activity, and the effects were particularly felt in the public sector. For example, the Montreal Urban Community's Transport Commission was affected by twenty-one complete or partial work stoppages (nineteen of which were illegal) between 1975 and 1982. Quebec City's public transit system was completely shut down for a period of nine months in 1979, and Montreal blue-collar workers stayed on strike for forty-two days in 1980. Very often, these conflicts were settled through injunctions or special back-to-work legislation, and each time they provoked great sociopolitical upheaval.

The government wanted to protect the health and safety of citizens while at the same time preserving the right to strike of public employees. To achieve this objective, it set up the Essential Services Council, which is an administrative tribunal whose main function is to manage and maintain essential services during work stoppages affecting public services. The Quebec Labour Code makes a distinction between "public services" such as the ones enumerated below and over which the Council has jurisdiction, and "the public and parapublic sectors" which refer to those services where the provincial government is either the direct employer (civil service) or indirect employer (education and social affairs). Health and social services are thus included in both categories. The Council is composed of eight members appointed by the government. The president and vice-president are appointed for a five-year term and the six other members are appointed for three years. Two of these members are appointed after consultations with employee associations and another two after consultations with employer associations deemed the most representative in public, health, and social services. The remaining two members are named after consultations with entities such as the Civil Rights Commission, the Youth Rights Commission, the Office of Handicapped Persons, and the Quebec Ombudsperson.

At the beginning, the Council's jurisdiction was restricted to few situations: municipal corporations; a telephone service falling within the provincial constitutional jurisdiction; a home-garbage removal and refuse incineration service; transport services carried out by boat; an ambulance service enterprise; services operating a waterworks sewer, or water treatment system; undertakings engaged in the production, transmission, distribution, or sale of gas or electricity; the Canadian Red Cross; private reception centres; regional health and social service centres; or agencies that have been mandated by the government. In June 1985, the Council's jurisdiction was extended to encompass establishments in the area of health and social services. However, the Labour Code also sets out, for different categories of establishments, a fixed percentage of employees (from 55 per cent to 90 per cent) who must ensure essential services in the event of a work stoppage. The Council's role in this particular instance is thus reduced to an evaluation of whether the services set out in an agreement or a list correspond to the percentage prescribed by the law.

The primary task of the Council consists of evaluating whether the essential services set out in a list or an agreement are sufficient to ensure public health or safety during a strike and to verify that these essential services are being provided during a strike. It is the local parties' responsibility to try to come up with an agreement on the definition of essential services prior to the start of any strike. If no agreement is reached, the local union's list of proposed services is sent to the Council for approval, just as the contents of any agreement reached by the parties must also be approved.

The Council also has the power to act upon its own initiative as soon as it is informed of a labour dispute. In all of its interventions, mediation is the preferred means of action even if the Council possesses strong remedial powers. A team of mediators and investigators are available to help the parties and to brief the Council on each situation.

Between 1982 and 1993, 380 agreements and 206 lists of essential services were submitted to the Council. The municipal sector was by far the most frequent participant, representing 40 per cent of all essential services lists and agreements received in 1983, rising to 73 per cent by 1992. Moreover, 76 per cent of the lists or agreements have been declared satisfactory upon submission, and an additional 20 per cent became satisfactory after the additions or changes recommended by the Council. This left only 2 per cent of the lists or agreements (10 cases) that were deemed unsatisfactory (Conseil des services essentiels 1993, 28).

Given the obligation to maintain essential services, bargaining strategies in public services have changed considerably. Unions have widely abandoned strategies calling for general strikes of unlimited duration and have opted instead for shorter strikes that might be repeated if necessary. For example, more than 70 per cent of strikes held in 1991/92 have lasted 72 hours or less (Conseil 1993, 39). The reduction of the duration of strike periods also diminishes the impact of the strike on the services provided to the public during the dispute. Thus, a profound change of attitude has occurred in regard to essential services; labour organizations now consider it normal to maintain such services so as not to compromise public health or security during work stoppages. They can also refer to the jurisprudence developed by the Council to help reach an agreement or to draw up a list of essential services. Strikes that completely eliminate essential services have, for all intents and purposes, disappeared in Quebec.

The Council has a wide range of remedial powers at its disposal. These include ordering a union to refrain from or stop an action, requiring the parties to resume dialogue, accelerating an arbitration procedure, and requiring the union to inform its members of the consequences of their action. The most widely used remedial powers have been those ordering workers back to work or to refrain from using pressure tactics. The Council also has the power to set up a fund for the benefit of users of public services when it believes that a given conflict has interfered with a service to which the public is entitled, or when the essential services stipulated in an agreement or a list have not been provided. Since 1985, remedial orders demanding compensation have been rendered only in four instances in public services and in fifteen instances in health and social services. Twelve of these orders were issued following massive work stoppages during the bargaining rounds of 1986 and 1989 (Conseil 1993, 54).

The credibility of the Council is now firmly established, at least in a number of areas. First, it has educated the parties involved about their responsibility for the continuity of services that are considered essential by the general population. Second, the unions involved have discovered that maintaining essential services has not prevented them from meeting their bargaining objectives, although they must spend more time in negotiations than in the past (Grant and Racine 1993). Third, the courts have established the legitimacy of the Council after it was systematically challenged in the early years. Ten years of maintaining essential services has had the effect of changing attitudes within the labour relations milieu in Quebec. When work stoppages do occur, the public knows that essential services will be maintained.

Unfortunately, these findings are not true in the health and social services sector, where the enforcement of the law relating to essential services has proved to be difficult. For instance, requiring that a minimum percentage of employees be maintained per establishment in the event of a strike, certainly has the advantage of imposing an objective criterion that can reassure the population. However, the uniform application of these minimum percentages in all establishments throughout the province, without consideration given to geographic and social specificities or to the difference in the services provided, has made it more difficult to determine the level of services that are essential in each establishment.

Because the explicit aim of the legislation is not to prohibit the workers from exercizing their right to strike but rather to ensure that the health or safety of the public not be put at risk during work stoppages, it has been suggested that percentages not be used at all in health and social services. Instead, the Council could be allowed to assume a more active role and set essential services on a case-by-case basis as it does in the municipal sector. Such a possible modification, even if quite hypothetical in the current context, is based on the assumption that there will still be a collective bargaining system in the public sector. This question will now be addressed.

The Public Sector

The collective bargaining system in the Quebec public sector has a hybrid legal framework. Although officially under the general jurisdiction of the Labour Code, the negotiation process is largely determined by the Act Respecting the Process of Negotiation and the Collective Agreements in the Public and Parapublic Sectors (referred to as the Negotiation Act). In addition, civil servants are also covered by the Civil Service Act. For their part, the provincial police have their own special collective bargaining legislation.

The Negotiation Act establishes a two-tier bargaining structure—provincial and local—within the three sectors of education, social affairs, and government agencies. According to this legislation, the most important matters, such as salaries, fringe benefits, and job security, are to be negotiated at the provincial level between the various certified agents and the management negotiating committees. In education, for example, separate collective bargaining groups must be established for teachers, nonteaching professionals, and support staff in each of the following sub-sectors: Catholic school boards, Protestant school boards, and colleges. Management negotiating committees include representatives from both the employers' association (such as the Federation of Catholic School Boards) and the provincial departments concerned (such as the Department of Education). In matters of government interest, all negotiation mandates must be approved by the Treasury Board.

Local negotiations in education and social affairs can only take place after provincial negotiations have been completed. Excluded from bargaining are any matters that have been settled at the provincial level. Local bargaining deals with questions such as disciplinary measures, union dues, and health and safety. In case of disagreement during local negotiations, the parties must resort to a mediation-arbitration system; they cannot use the strike or lockout.

Chapter V-1 of the Labour Code sets up a detailed calendar for the orderly conduct of negotiations within the framework of the Negotiation Act. Clauses relating to salary and salary scales are to be bargained every three years but are in effect only for the first year of the contract. In each of the two subsequent years, determination is to be made through government regulations after a consultation process with the unions. In practice, this procedure has never been followed, and salaries have always been determined for each year of the three-year period covered by collective agreements.

A right to strike or to lockout during provincial negotiations can be applied in each sector (education, social affairs, civil service) twenty days after a mediation report has been issued, provided the party has given a seven-day prior notice indicating the time it intends to resort to a strike or lockout. However, in social affairs, there are additional restrictions. Depending on the type of institution involved, a minimum percentage of employees (ranging from 55 per cent to 90 per cent) must be maintained at work, and no strike can be declared unless the Essential Services Council has approved the list of employees designated as essential. Also, the lockout is prohibited.

These severe restrictions on the use of the right to strike, which were adopted by the PQ in 1985, were the consequence of the public's exasperation with the repeated work stoppages that had occurred since 1964. Nonetheless, this did not deter the major union involved in health and social services (its general employees affiliated with the CNTU) from scheduling a general strike in the first bargaining round that followed the enactment of these amendments. The newly elected Liberal government retaliated with special legislation outlawing the possible strike and providing for very harsh penalties in case of non-compliance. Among these penalties, an employee would incur a loss of one year of seniority and a loss of one extra day of pay for each day of a strike. The union would lose twelve weeks of dues deductions for each day of a strike. Heavy fines for workers, union officials, and the union itself were also included in Bill 160.

Every local union complied with this special legislation, and the government did not have to apply the penalties. However, such was not the case in the next round when the nurses' union, a group of some 40,000 workers, struck without respecting the essential services percentages mentioned in the Labour Code. They were soon followed by general employees affiliated with the CNTU. Even though essential services were provided by the unions according to their codes of ethics, and despite the fact that the Essential Services Council found very few cases where the level of services was deemed deficient (Conseil des services essentiels 1992, 23), the strike was still illegal according to the Labour Code. As a result, the harsh penalties included in Bill 160 applied automatically, to the great dismay of union members.

TABLE 16.3   Conflicts Involving the Six Major Bargaining Agents in the Quebec Public Sector, 1966–1989

	1966	1968	1972	1976	1979	1982	1985	1989	Total (1966-89)
Hospital Employees									
Strikes	1		1	1	1		1	1	6
Legislative Intervention	1		1		1	1	1		5
Illegal			1	1	1			1	4
Nurses									
Strikes			1	1	1		1	1	5
Legislative Intervention			1	1		1	1		4
Illegal								1	1
Teachers									
Strikes	1		1	1	1	1			5
Legislative Intervention	1		1	1	1	2			6
Illegal						1			1
Civil Servants									
Strikes			1						1
Legislative Intervention			1		1	1			3
Illegal									0
Professionals									
Strikes	1		1			1			3
Legislative Intervention			1		1	1			3
Illegal						1			1
Hydro									
Strikes			1		1			1	3
Legislative Intervention			1		1			1	3
Illegal									0
All Agents									
Strikes	3	0	6	3	4	2	2	3	23
Legislative Intervention	2	0	6	2	5	6	2	1	24
Illegal	0	0	1	1	1	2	0	2	7

SOURCE: Jean Boivin, "Bilan de la négociation collective dans les secteurs public et parapublic québécois," in La négociation collective du travail, C. Bernier, R. Laflamme, F. Morin, G. Murray, et C. Rondeau, eds, 48e congrès du Département des relations industrielles de l'Université Laval, Ste-Foy: Presses de l'Université Laval, 1993, 177.

The history of collective bargaining in the Quebec public sector is fraught with legal and illegal strikes, conflict, and special back-to-work legislation, not only in the health and social services sector but also in education and government agencies. Table 16.3 shows the level of conflict of the six most important bargaining agents over the eight rounds of provincial negotiations in which they have been involved since the adoption of the Labour Code in 1964. The six bargaining agents and the eight rounds of bargaining mean that there were 48 bargaining situations over the period. In addition to the settlement without conflict, there could be more than one form of conflict (i.e., legal strikes, legislative interventions, or illegal strikes) associated with each bargaining situation.

Nearly half of the bargaining situations have resulted in legal strikes (23/48), with an equivalent number of special legislative interventions (24/48). Illegal strikes have occurred less frequently (7/48), but this proportion is substantially higher than what is found in the private sector, where these situations are so unusual that the Department of Labour does not even keep track of such statistics. Such militancy among public sector unions in Quebec has continued throughout the 1980s, a phenomenon which is in sharp contrast with the general decline observed across the rest of the economy.

There has not been any collective bargaining in the public and parapublic sectors since 1989. The provincial government, faced with severe economic constraints, twice asked and twice obtained from the various unions an extension of the collective agreements that had expired in December 1991. However, in June 1993, instead of resuming the process of negotiation, the government adopted legislation which froze salaries for two years (until June 30, 1995), and ordered all public employers to reduce their wage bill by one per cent in each of these two years. This reduction was to be achieved through instituting 2.6 unpaid holidays, unless an agreement could be reached with the respective unions on other means to realize the savings. Bill 102 also allowed municipalities to be covered by the legislation if they so choose. Approximately half of the municipalities with a population of 5,000 or more agreed to be covered by the legislation.

A few days before adopting Bill 102, the government adopted another piece of legislation that also infuriated public sector unions. Bill 198 required all government departments and public agencies to reduce their supervisory personnel by 20 per cent between 1993 and 1996 and the rest of their workforce by 12 per cent between 1993 and 1998.

Public sector unions felt betrayed by these measures because they had already agreed to extend their collective agreements for 18 months. They tried to mobilize their members and the population against the government's adoption of Bills 102 and 198, but to no avail. While unions recognized that Quebec had serious financial problems, they claimed that employees' involvement in a major work reorganization scheme would yield greater long-term benefits than the short-term approach of saving money by penalizing workers. More than anything else, though, the unions were concerned—and rightly so—about the future of their right to bargain collectively in the public sector.

The Decree System

There exists in Quebec a system of extending collective agreements to non-unionized sectors of an industry. This is unique in North America. The Act Respecting Collective Agreement Decrees gives the minister of labour the power to take the results of collective negotiations between a group of employers and a union or a group of unions and apply certain provisions of this agreement to all employers and all employees in a given industry and in a given region. This system of juridical decree or extension has been in force since 1934, and it has not been amended in any substantial manner since it was adopted.

When it was first established, the decree system had two main goals. First, it was supposed to encourage collective bargaining and allow non-unionized workers to benefit from the better working conditions found in collective agreements. (It should be remembered that the legislation mandating collective bargaining was to be adopted only in 1944.) Second, it was aimed at eliminating competition over wages and working conditions among firms operating in the same industry.

The system basically works as follows. First, the unionized firms, usually the largest ones in a particular sector, negotiate their collective agreement as they would normally under the Labour Code. Second, the employers and the unions interested in having their agreement extended determine the contents of the agreement that would eventually be binding on all employers and employees. The parties involved must also determine the scope of the decree by defining the type of activity that will be covered as well as the geographical area, whether the whole province or just a region. Third, the text of the agreement is sent to the minister of labour, who publishes it in the *Gazette officielle du Québec* and in one French and one English newspaper. Third parties have thirty days to file any objections. Finally, "the Minister, if he deems the provisions of the agreement have acquired a preponderant significance and importance for establishing conditions of labour, without serious inconvenience resulting from the competition of outside countries or the other provinces, may recommend the approval of the petition . . . with such changes as are deemed expedient, and the passing of a decree for such purpose" (Section 6 of the legislation). It should be noted that the minister has the discretionary power to change some provisions of the agreement before he or she recommends extension.

Not all the provisions of the agreement can be included in the decree. In fact, their number is rather limited since they comprise only the following items: wages, hours of work, working days, vacations with pay, social security benefits, classification of operations, and classes of employees and employers.

Another interesting characteristic of the system is that it makes the parties responsible for ensuring that the decree is adhered to by all employers included in its scope of application. For this purpose, a joint committee is formed that includes an equal number of representatives from employers and unions who have signed the agreement. The minister may also add an equal number of members recommended by employers and employees who are not parties to the agreement. The committee appoints a general manager, a secretary, and a certain number of inspectors. It also acts on behalf of the employees in the enforcement of the decree before the courts. The operating costs of the committee are mainly covered by employers' and employees' dues, which amount to one-half of one per cent of the employers' payrolls and the same percentage of the employees' salaries. The joint committee becomes the natural forum where negotiations for the renewal of the decree take place. For this reason, the extension system is a type of multi-employer and, sometimes, multi-union collective bargaining.

The decrees are mainly found in low-wage sectors characterized by a large number of small- and medium-sized firms that operate in highly competitive markets. Despite the fact that many of the companies involved have disappeared over the years, the number of employers and employees covered by decrees has remained stable over the past twenty years. This is so because, as the more traditional trades in the manufacturing sector were covered less and less by decrees, new ones were enacted in sectors such as security guards, building services, solid waste, and the installation of petroleum equipment. At the end of 1993, 15,300 employers and 125,000 salaried workers (five per cent of total employment) were covered by 29 decrees in the following sectors: garages; services such as bread distributors, building services, road haulage, security guards, and solid waste; clothing, which includes handbags, leather gloves, men's clothing, millinery, shirts, and women's clothing; hairdressers; and other industries such as building materials, caskets, flat glass, furniture, paper boxes, woodworking, petroleum equipment, non-structural metals, and corrugated paper boxes. (Construction is discussed later.)

During its sixty years of existence, the decree system has often been the subject of strong criticisms. At one time, labour organizations complained that the system prevented them from increasing their representation in the sectors involved. They said that unorganized workers had no incentive to join a union since they were already benefiting from some of the working conditions negotiated by unions without having to pay union dues. However, this argument is not supported by facts because union density has been higher in sectors covered by decrees than it has in the Quebec economy as a whole, at least until recently (St-Laurent 1983, for the period 1974-1981; and Bernier 1993, for the period 1982-1989).

More recently, criticisms have come mostly from employers who complain that higher labour costs imposed by the decrees put them at a competitive disadvantage vis-à-vis firms located outside Quebec. Consequently, many employers' associations are presently requesting either a complete abolition of the decree system or, at least, that decrees not apply to sectors exposed to foreign competition. The Quebec Branch of the Canadian Manufacturers' Association is part of the first group while the Province of Quebec Chamber of Commerce is in the second one. The Conseil du patronat du Québec, who has always considered the decree system as a lesser evil when faced with the alternative of multi-employer certification sought by labour organizations, has taken a neutral position since its association members are to be found on each side of the issue. For their part, all labour organizations are in favour of keeping the current system.

At the time of writing, the government was consulting with all interested parties on the possibility of modifying the current legislation. It is, however, not possible to predict which course of action will be followed.

The Construction Industry

The labour relations system of the Quebec construction industry is unique in North America. Its legal framework dates to 1934, since construction was one of the sectors to which the Collective Agreement Decrees Act applied. In those days, collective bargaining was practiced on a multitrade basis at the regional level, and the minister of labour would extend by decree the terms of a collective agreement to all employers and employees in a given geographical area. There were fifteen regional decrees throughout the province and a few provincial decrees. Some trade unions were occasionally able to bargain individually in some regions and obtain advantages not provided in the decree, but these situations were exceptional.

This system was in force until 1968, when the government imposed a new legal framework through the Construction Industry Labour Relations Act. The legislation retained multitrade bargaining and the juridical extension principles of the old decree system, but it established a single industry-wide structure of bargaining. One reason for this new act was the necessity to reduce the fierce rivalry between locals of international unions affiliated with the QFL and the regional associations affiliated with the CNTU. Therefore, traditional trade union certification under the Labour Code was eliminated and replaced by a new system of representative associations.

Although the original purpose of the act was achieved—the elimination of labour conflicts resulting from inter-union rivalry—many additional pieces of legislation were needed to facilitate the determination of working conditions. The latest amendments to the legislative framework were adopted in December 1993, and many provisions were not yet in effect at the time of writing. That is why the description that follows presents the most important characteristics of the system as they relate to the experience of the last twenty-five years, while at the same time attempting to assess the impact of the new amendments.

Trade Union and Employer Associations

Contrary to the general situation which comes under the jurisdiction of the Labour Code, certification does not exist in the Quebec construction industry. Instead, union pluralism exists based on a system of "closed shop by law" whereby all workers must belong to one of the five associations recognized as the sole representatives of construction workers' interests. These are (with membership share in parentheses): the QFL-Construction (41.9 per cent); the Quebec Council of Construction Trades (31.7 per cent); the CSN-Construction (14.9 per cent); the CSD-Construction (10.2 per cent) and the North Shore Association (1.0 per cent) (Marché du travail 1993). All associations continue to exist during the course of the collective agreement.

Local unions affiliated with the QFL-Construction were formerly part of the Quebec Council of Construction Trades. But they were recognized as a separate entity through an amendment to the Construction Act following the internal conflict that erupted within the CLC and the QFL over the issue of dual unions in the early 1980s.

Workers can change their affiliation from one association to another prior to the negotiations leading to the renewal of the decree. However, there is a disincentive to disaffiliate because the only workers who have to vote in a ballot supervised by the Quebec Construction Commission are those who want to change their affiliation; those who do not vote keep their previous affiliation. To be eligible to vote, workers must possess a competency card issued by the Quebec Construction Commission and they must have worked at least 300 hours in the construction industry the year before.

As regards management, the legislation recognizes five distinct contractors' associations; three of which represent the main sectors of the industry (residential, industrial and commercial, and road building and engineering) and two are trade associations (the electricians and the pipe mechanics trade corporations). The legislation also requires these five associations to set up an employers' association for the purpose of collective bargaining: the Association des entrepreneurs en construction du Québec (AECQ), or the Quebec Association of Building Contractors.

Collective Bargaining: Structures and Process

The AECQ is the sole bargaining agent for all contractors, but for the unions, the legislation tries to reconcile the principle of majority rule with the reality of pluralism that has always prevailed in the industry. Hence, an association representing at least 15 per cent of the workers has a right to be part of the union negotiating side and to present proposals in relation to the contents of the collective agreement. However, negotiations cannot start unless one or more association can claim to represent at least fifty per cent of workers. The same majority principle applies to the final acceptance of a collective agreement.

Once the parties have concluded their negotiations, the minister of labour then proceeds to the juridical extension of the collective agreement, which becomes a decree covering the whole industry. This decree has the force of law.

Prior to the 1993 amendments, there was only one decree which applied to all trades. Under the new scheme envisaged by the legislation, four collective agreements are to be negotiated leading to as many decrees in each of the following sectors: residential, industrial, institutional and commercial, and engineering and road building. It is expected that some clauses will be common to the four sectors while others will be specific to each sector.

The AECQ will remain the bargaining agent for the four collective agreements, but each sectoral employers' association will be empowered to accept or reject the clauses applying to its sector. On the union side, the representativeness of each association will have to be established in each sector, and bargaining agents will be determined according to the same formula that existed under the former bargaining system (see above).

The most controversial provision of the 1993 amendments was the deregulation of labour relations in the residential sector applying to housing projects of eight or less units. This sector is now being excluded from coverage under the Construction Act, meaning that workers no longer need to belong to a union to work on a small residential construction site. Needless to say, this major modification infuriated labour organizations which organized a series of wildcat strikes in December 1993. The government retaliated with special legislation unilaterally extending the decree until December 31, 1994 and ordering all strikers back to work under the threat of stiff penalties similar to the ones already adopted in the public sector some years previously.

It is difficult to predict whether the new institutional arrangements will yield better bargaining results than the previous one. There is no doubt that before the 1993 amendments were brought in by the Liberal government, all interested parties were requesting changes, albeit for quite different reasons. Employers were complaining that a province-wide, multitrades bargaining structure was imposing labour costs that were too onerous for most contractors in the residential sector. Some unions wanted sectoral employers' associations to be more actively involved in the determination of their sector's working conditions, but none went so far as proposing that the single province-wide bargaining structure be replaced by sectoral negotiations leading to separate collective agreements.

In the end, both the unions and the employers' associations were lamenting that it had become almost impossible for the parties involved in collective negotiations to come to an agreement without the government having to intervene in the bargaining process. In practice, this meant that the government very often imposed the terms and conditions of the decree upon the parties.

Hiring Practices

The placement of workers on construction sites is done under the supervision of the Quebec Construction Commission, a tripartite administrative machine managed by the parties and government appointed-representatives. In order to get a job in the construction industry, a worker must have a competency card issued by the QCC. There are three categories of competency cards: journeyman, apprentice-journeyman, and general occupation. Twenty-five different trades have been officially recognized and the ratio of apprentice to journeymen varies from 1:1 to 1:5. There are also fifty general occupations. Seventy-five per cent of all construction workers carry on a trade and two thirds of these are journeymen.

One of the objectives put forward by those who devised the labour relations system of this industry some twenty years ago was to ensure that construction jobs would be awarded to "genuine" construction workers. In order to achieve this goal, while taking into consideration the chronic economic instability and insecurity that is typical of this industry, the government decided to erect a web of regulations that applied to both the hiring of workers and the licensing of contractors.

Originally, the hiring of workers was done on the basis of both a regional priority mechanism and a requirement that a minimum number of hours had been worked in the industry in Quebec within a given period. This last condition was dropped in 1987 and replaced by the system of competency cards. However, the prerequisite for regional priority was still very much in force. Until 1987, regional priority had been based on residency in Quebec, thus restricting construction jobs to Quebec residents and preventing nonresidents of Quebec from having access to these jobs. That year, the rule of residency was changed to allow nonresidents of Quebec to work in Quebec under certain conditions. Out-of-province workers could choose a region in which they wanted to be employed, but they also had to take a sixty-hour safety course and join one of the five representative associations. These conditions were waived in the case of very qualified and specialized trades like pipeline welders.

Even more severe restrictions applied to contractors because, until the 1993 amendments, all contractors had to have a place of business in Quebec in order to work in the province's construction industry. Although the number of nonresident workers and contractors who were effectively prevented from working in Quebec was relatively low, the principle involved (greater restrictions for nonresidents of Quebec to work in Quebec than for Quebec residents to work in other provinces) became a hot political issue, particularly in the neighbouring provinces of Ontario and New Brunswick. After these two governments adopted measures preventing Quebec workers and contractors from having access to their respective construction industries, the Quebec government had no other choice but to remove its last restrictions.

Conclusion

Despite the rigorous measures adopted by the Quebec government to guarantee its construction workers a type of job security similar to that found in the manufacturing sector, the number of hours worked by "genuine" construction workers has systematically declined over the years. For example, the percentage of workers who had not worked a single hour in the industry after having worked the previous year jumped from 14.3 per cent in 1989 to 21.2 per cent in 1992. Also, that same year, 69 per cent of workers had worked less than 1,000 hours (Secrétariat du Sommet 1993, 11).

Although the 1990-92 recession provides a partial explanation of these numbers, it was not the only factor explaining the precarious situation of the industry. According to the AECQ, 25 million hours had been worked illegally in 1992, a figure representing 26 per cent of the total hours officially registered. The QCC estimated that such illegal activities had deprived various government agencies of some $420 million in revenues in 1991 (Secrétariat du Sommet 1993, 12).

To a certain degree, the excessive regulation of the industry might have led the unions to price their members out of the market. The latest legal changes reflect the government's awareness of the necessity to restore a greater degree of competitiveness in the industry. These changes, which have allowed for sectoral bargaining, deregulated the residential sector and removed the last restrictions preventing nonresident contractors and workers from gaining access to construction sites, were introduced at the risk of triggering a wave of labour unrest on construction sites. Only time will tell if the risk was worth taking.

PUBLIC POLICY ON WORK

Labour Standards

The regulation of minimum working conditions constitutes one of the oldest forms of government intervention in the area of paid work (Trudeau 1990, 1087). In Quebec, the first government interventions date back to the end of the nineteenth century and were aimed especially at fighting against the exploitation of women and child labour. In 1937, the Quebec legislature set a minimum wage rate that was to be applied universally. In 1940, the Fair Wage Act was amended and became the Minimum Wage Act. From 1940 to 1979, there were numerous rulings to complete the intent of the legislation and modify the working conditions it aimed at originally.

Minimum working conditions are presently governed by the Labour Standards Act, which was adopted in 1979. This act replaced the Minimum Wage Act and mainly constituted a codification of the numerous rulings previously adopted. This act did not make any particular provisions that would distinguish it from other legislation at provincial and federal levels. As elsewhere in Canada, the application of the law was left to the Commission des normes du travail (Labour Standards Commission), which essentially operates through a complaint procedure.

However, it was by providing recourse to a complaint procedure accessible to workers covered by the act that Quebec once again distinguished itself when it adopted the Labour Standards Act. The 1979 act introduced an innovative complaint procedure (Trudeau 1990). This provision granted protection against unjust dismissal of workers who have been in continuous service of an employer for five years or more. This in fact represents the equivalent of the arbitration proceeding for unjust dismissal that workers covered by collective agreements enjoy.

Arbitration proceedings took place before an arbitrator appointed by the Labour Standards Commission but paid for by the employer and worker. The arbitrator's decision was final and was not subject to appeal. Even though this provision was innovative, it was criticized because of the costs of the arbitration proceedings, which were divided between the parties, and which would obstruct the use and effectiveness of the complaint procedure (Trudeau 1990, 1114).

In 1990, the Labour Standards Act was changed substantially. First, in terms of content, provisions were introduced that aimed at making working conditions for people with family responsibilities more flexible. These new provisions allowed for parental leave, pregnancy leave, and leave for family duties. Improvements were also made to maternity leave and leave for childbirth or an adoption.

In terms of recourse to complaint procedures, the government decided to change substantially the arbitration procedure related to unfair dismissal, which had been adopted in 1979, to reduce costs incurred by both parties. As of June 1, 1991, complaints about this subject have been referred to labour commissioners, whose main mandate relates to the certification procedure provided for in the Labour Code. While making the state bear the costs of the arbitration proceedings, and thus addressing criticisms of these costs, this change has also raised concern because the new labour commissioners who were appointed to settle complaints had not had the time to develop expertise as grievance arbitrators.

Even though it is still too early to analyze the impact of changes made to this procedure, the labour commissioners have indicated that they will maintain the jurisprudence developed by the earlier grievance arbitrators on this subject. This will certainly help facilitate the transition from one system to another. The 1990 changes also reduced the years of required continuous service, from five to three, in order to allow more employees access to the complaint procedure described above.

In brief, the labour standards and complaint procedures that are provided for in the Quebec law generally conform to what is provided for in other legislation at provincial and federal levels.

Pay and Employment Equity

In all spheres of social and economic activity, the 1970s and 1980s were characterized by an organized and systematic fight against discrimination towards certain groups, especially women. This movement had substantial impacts in the workplace. This section will first present the tools adopted by the province of Quebec to counter discrimination at work and ensure employment equity. Secondly, it will depict the current situation as regards employment equity in the public and private sectors. Even though current laws are meant to tackle discrimination against several so-called target groups, it is women who are at the forefront of the anti-discrimination movement. Thus reference will most often be made to their situation.

Discrimination at Work and Policy Responses

The presence of women in the labour market is no longer surprising. Although women have made some breakthroughs in the areas of training and employment previously occupied almost exclusively by men, the majority of women workers are still concentrated in certain sectors of activity and employment categories, and they are largely, even totally absent from certain other fields. Indeed, even though women represented almost half (44 per cent) of the labour force in 1991, they remained confined to certain jobs: 42.1 per cent of women in the workforce were found in the ten principal occupations for women (Gouvernement du Québec 1993). This phenomenon of occupational segregation is not the only negative effect of discrimination against working women.

In 1991, women workers in Quebec who were employed full-time for the entire year earned only 70.1 per cent of the income of men in a similar situation. In 1992, the ratio increased to 73.9 per cent suggesting an improvement in women's salary situation

(Statistics Canada 1993). In the present economic circumstances, however, it is possible that the narrowing of the wage gap is more due to a deterioration of men's economic situation (particularly due to the loss of jobs in the manufacturing sector where salaries are relatively high) rather than to an improvement in women's position.

Thus, in spite of some narrowing of the wage gap between men and women since the end of the 1960s, the gap between men and women's average income was barely reduced at all during the last ten years. It is remarkable that the gap remained so wide despite the adoption of laws dealing specifically with this problem.

The two major problems related to labour market discrimination against women are the existence of wage differentials between men and women within the salary structures of firms, and the prevalence of occupational segregation. The latter involves the *concentration* of women in a limited number of jobs in the labour market and the *feminization* of these jobs (the fact that women occupy the majority of these jobs). Thus, women not only face the problem of access to certain jobs considered to be men's jobs, but they also suffer a wage deficit which has not really been reduced. These two aspects are part of the issue of discrimination against women in the labour market, however they are different in nature and therefore require the development of different methods to counter them.

1. *Equal access* aims first to eliminate discrimination in all human resources management practices in order to guarantee equal opportunity to each individual: this is the dimension of equality of opportunity. A further objective of equal access is equal representation of members of groups that have been discriminated against in all jobs offered by a firm: this is the dimension of equality of outcome.
2. *Pay equity* is specifically aimed at obtaining equal pay for work of equal value, which would help narrow the wage gap between men and women.

These two aspects of anti-discrimination policy are dealt with in the Quebec Charter of Human Rights and Freedoms.

Charter of Human Rights and Freedoms

In Quebec, legislators chose to address employment discrimination and employment equity in a Charter which also guarantees fundamental freedoms. The Charter of Human Rights and Freedoms, ratified in 1975, is intended to be the preferred tool in the fight against discrimination at work.

Quebec is alone among Canadian legislatures in having adopted a definition of discrimination. Thus, to say that discrimination exists, the following three elements must be found:

- a distinction, an exclusion or a preference
- based on prohibited grounds (there are thirteen of them, pregnancy being a distinct prohibited ground for discrimination)
- which has the effect of destroying or compromising the right to full and equal recognition and exercise of human rights and freedoms.

Formulated in this way, this definition identifies two types of discrimination: direct discrimination which is "the fact of a distinction, exclusion or preference directly and explicitly based on a prohibited ground for discrimination" (Côté and Lemonde 1988, 17) and systemic discrimination, that is, discrimination resulting from customs and practices rooted in systems such as the employment programs of some organizations.

Thus the Charter's objective in the area of employment is to "neutralize" work environments by eliminating all manifestations of discrimination. To achieve this goal, two distinct and complementary series of measures have been included in the Charter. They are the provisions prohibiting discrimination and the provisions that are aimed at promoting the rights of groups that have been discriminated against in the past.

Quebec's human rights commission is the organization responsible for overseeing, in the first instance, the application of the Charter. Created in 1975, the commission was for fifteen years the only organization overseeing the Charter. Essentially, the commission functions on the basis of complaints filed by people, groups or organizations. It may also carry out investigations on its own initiative. Given its limited resources and the fact that it must oversee the application of all Charter provisions, the commission has only been able to react to complaints, thus limiting the Charter's impact, which is in theory universal. Until 1990, the commission restricted its role to conciliation and was empowered to make recommendations only. The commission had to go to court if it wished to have its recommendations enforced.

The establishment of a human rights tribunal in 1990 did not alter this fundamental operating characteristic of the commission. The tribunal hears appeals against the commission's recommendations, however the commission is still the starting point for all Charter-related complaints.

When compared to the proactive laws adopted by Ontario and some other provinces to guarantee pay equity, this method of functioning can be described as passive because it relies on complaints being filed. Even if organizations are required to respect the Charter, in reality the law of "nothing seen, nothing done" applies. This method of functioning is based on the idea that discrimination in the labour market is an exception rather than the rule.

Equal Access

When it was adopted in 1975, the Charter recognized only the principle of *equality of opportunity* in employment between men and women; it addressed problems of access only by prohibiting discrimination in human resources management practices. At the time, it was believed that it was sufficient to give everyone equal opportunity so that the employment systems of organizations would reflect better the diversity of the labour force. In the light of experiences with these measures and the relative failure of programs that only addressed equal opportunity, the objective of equal access was reinforced in 1982 by the introduction of the concept of equality of outcome. The Charter was then amended to include a section related to equal access programs. However, it was not until 1985 that this section came into effect.

Regulations providing for equal access programs hold that they must include equality of opportunity measures whose goal is to eliminate discriminatory practices permanently, as well as corrective measures aimed at correcting the under-representation of groups discriminated against. Nevertheless, for private sector firms, equal access programs are still voluntary, and participation in such programs remains largely dependent on a favourable economic context and an awareness of the situation by the management of particular firms.

Equal access has a dual objective:

1. on the one hand, to detect all sexist and discriminatory aspects of employment policies and practices and eliminate them, and on the other hand,
2. to increase the representation of women (and members of other target groups) in jobs where they are actually under-represented and thus eliminate occupational segregation.

Pay Equity

Since it came into effect in 1976, the Charter has recognized the principle of "equal pay for work of equal value" by stipulating that "Every employer *must*, without discrimination, grant equal salary or wages to the members of his personnel who perform work of equal value at the same place" (emphasis added).

The term "work of equal value" refers to a reality which is quite different from that referred to by the term "equal work." The early antidiscrimination laws included the notion of equal pay for equal work in order to end *obvious* sources of wage discrimination. The application of this principle entailed, for example, the disappearance of different wage scales for men and women doing the same jobs (e.g., male cashier and female cashier). Given persistent occupational segregation, the application of this one principle could have an effect on only a small part of the wage gap between men and women, since men and women do not always have the same jobs.

According to the principle of pay equity, an employer must pay a secretary the same wage as that of a playground maintenance worker if the two jobs are of *equal value*. The notion of equal work was similar to comparing apples with apples. With the concept of pay equity, different jobs are compared, and thus apples can be compared with oranges. Just as apples and oranges can be compared for their calories, vitamins, weight, appearance, and how easy they are to eat, so jobs can be broken down into various factors and compared using the common denominators.

Even though the Charter does not indicate a specific method for measuring equivalence, the commission has nevertheless clarified in numerous documents and reports that job evaluation is a particularly useful method in this regard. The criteria for measuring equivalence have not been included in the Charter, and to date there are no regulations concerning this subject. However, the commission has specified that equivalence may be determined according to four factors that are essentially the same as those found in the majority of laws dealing with pay equity: 1. abilities (intellectual, technical, and professional capacities); 2. responsibilities for people, equipment, material, products, etc.; 3. effort (physical and mental demands); and 4. working conditions.

In the absence of a methodology and precise tools, it is therefore possible for union and management organizations who get involved in this area to do almost anything. The lack of direction and models may result in organizations using inadequate and imperfect tools and setting up processes that cannot ensure that the principle of pay equity will be achieved.

Review of the Current Situation

Pay Equity. The Quebec Charter may have been unusually generous in its early recognition of the principle of pay equity in 1976, but since its introduction the situation in Canada has changed considerably. For example, in Ontario all public sector employers and all private firms with 10 or more employees must achieve pay equity according to implementation deadlines established in 1988. The example of Ontario is not unique. Numerous other provinces have also adopted a so-called proactive approach to pay equity that is quite different from the passive complaints-based approach maintained in Quebec.

The passive approach on which the Quebec Charter is structured, the cumbersome complaint process that puts the burden of proof on the complainant, and the reproaches often made about the commission for its weak and ineffective process for dealing with complaints (Côté and Lemonde 1988) help explain why few real gains have been made with regard to pay equity, and why most successes have been achieved in unionized sectors.

Thus in Quebec, experiences with pay equity have mostly been through negotiation, occasionally through the filing of complaints, and sometimes through both channels. Negotiations are mostly undertaken in the Quebec public and parapublic sectors under pressure from union organizations. Even an agreement between the collective bargaining parties may be called into question by complaints filed with the human rights commission, as was the case with the Government of Quebec's professionals.

The Quebec Treasury Board has always refused, until very recently, to talk about pay equity, wanting instead to negotiate salary relativities that include, among other things, pay equity. According to the Treasury Board, the "salary relativity" exercise for the public and parapublic sectors has for all practical purposes been completed. A document submitted by the minister responsible for the status of women at the end of 1993 stated that ". . . in the civil service, in the health, social service and education networks and in colleges, the salary scale for the majority of this female-dominated labour force has been adjusted. In 1990 and 1991 an amount of 330 million dollars was invested to this end" (Politique 1993, 19). While recognizing the importance of the jobs that were subjected to a wage adjustment, Quebec's council on the status of women notes "that by not attending exclusively to inequalities shown between traditionally female and male occupations, firms may minimize the scope of potential adjustments" (CSF 1993).

Only the CSN has refused to negotiate with the treasury board, preferring instead to use the complaint procedure. Faced with a slow process for settling the first complaints, which were filed in 1987, in December 1992 the CSN filed a request for a mandamus order (a written order from the superior court to force a public organization to carry out its responsibility as required by law) against Quebec's human rights commission to force it to complete its investigation of their outstanding complaints. At the moment, having been required by the court to fulfill the functions for which it was created, the commission is continuing its investigation and doing the best it can with its current budget.

Thus, only a superficial analysis would lead us to believe that the issue of pay equity has been settled in the public and parapublic sectors. Complaints filed by the CSN, by professionals within the government, and by other organizations in the health care sector have not always resulted in a settlement. The province's network of universities has also undertaken negotiations on pay equity. These negotiations have been carried out using the public sector model and have not yet been completed.

This first round of negotiation on pay equity has therefore been limited mainly to the public and parapublic sectors as well as to the university network. The private sector, "which nevertheless includes a large proportion of the female work force, clearly lags behind" (CSF 1993, 18). At the beginning of 1995, it is impossible to talk about an imminent settlement of the pay equity issue in the workplace, in particular in non-union environments in the private sector where the wage gap attributable to discrimination is likely to be the most pronounced.

Equal Access.   As previously mentioned, the Quebec Charter is the main source of reference for the development of equal access programs. However, pursuant to the Charter these programs are voluntary (with the exception of the civil service), which explains why they have not been adopted more widely.

Since 1986, equal access programs have been introduced in government departments and organizations. In addition, pilot projects allowing for the establishment of such programs have been set up in 76 organizations in the parapublic, private, and municipal sectors. This has had an effect on nearly 900 establishments and 150,000 people (Politique 1993, 19). Following an initial evaluation of equal access programs carried out by the province's women's directorate in 1991, Quebec's council on the status of women estimated that "the quantitative effect of equal access programs on the distribution of women in employment will be limited due to the short duration of programs and the weakness of measures adopted. At the qualitative level, it appears that, instead of being genuine equal access programs with established numerical goals and corrective measures, projects put into place more often resemble equal opportunity programs" (CSF 1993, 21).

In 1989, the government established a contractual obligation program modelled on the Federal Contractors Program. The latter continues to apply to firms with a federal government contract. The Quebec program requires all firms with more than 100 employees, and with a Quebec government grant or contract for goods or services in the amount of $100,000 or more, to introduce an equal access program. According to a report submitted by the minister responsible for the status of women, these initiatives have not produced the expected results: "only 5.6 per cent of firms with more than 100 employees are establishing an equal access program under contractual obligation" (Gouvernement du Québec, 1993 p. 20).

Conclusion

Interest in the issues of employment equity and discrimination in general has existed for several decades, however it has resulted in the development of a false perception of reality. The attention given to examples of women who have succeeded in breaking through traditionally male professions or trades has had a consequence not anticipated by women's groups: it has been forgotten that these examples are most often exceptions which now and in the past have had little to do with the reality of the occupational segregation that persists in the labour market.

Even though Quebec was a pioneer in its adoption in 1976 of the Charter of Human Rights and Freedoms, which includes the principle of pay equity, it is now falling behind in both dimensions of equal access and pay equity.

Quebec's slowness in taking action on pay equity was one of the reasons behind the creation in 1990 of the Quebec Coalition for pay equity. Since its creation, the Coalition's increased efforts to have Quebec adopt a proactive law similar to that of Ontario have been relatively successful. This slow development is recognized by all organizations concerned with equity:

- in March 1991, Quebec's human rights commission organized public consultations on a proactive pay equity law;
- the commission's report, submitted to the Quebec minister of justice in February 1992, recommended that a proactive law be adopted by the Government of Quebec;
- in May 1993, the province's council on the status of women, in a notice sent to the minister responsible for the status of women, recommended the adoption of a law that would include two components: a pay equity component, applicable to all private, public, and parapublic sectors; and an equal access component, applicable to the public, and parapublic sectors only. According to these recommendations, private sector firms would only be affected by the contractual obligation program;
- a few months later, at the beginning of 1994, the policy on the status of women was made public by the minister responsible for the status of women. Concerning employment equity, this policy is essentially based on the model proposed by the council on the status of women.

On March 8, 1994, at the opening of the legislative session the premier of Quebec, Daniel Johnson, announced a bill on employment equity to be presented in autumn 1994. However, between now and then, elections will have taken place; for this reason, the ultimate outcome remains uncertain.

Occupational Health and Safety

There are two laws in Quebec that provide the framework for the two main aspects usually considered in an occupational health and safety system: prevention and compensation. The Occupational Health and Safety Act, which was passed in 1979, encompasses the entire area of prevention, while the Workers' Compensation Act, which was passed in 1985, regulates compensation. The occupational health and safety commission was created to oversee the application of these two laws. Although Quebec was one of the last provinces to adopt health and safety laws, in so doing it has been able to benefit from experiences elsewhere and include some innovative provisions in the law, especially in the field of prevention.

As regards compensation, the situation in Quebec is very similar to that which exists in other provinces and at the federal level; similar provisions include the no-fault principle, the collective responsibility of employers, and mandatory insurance guaranteed by a state fund. However, from one province to another, differences can be found in such factors as employers' obligations under the law, payments of claims, the internal operations of commissions, and the extent to which compensation is based on wage loss or simply on the nature of the injury.

However, the situation is much less homogeneous in the area of prevention. Quebec, along with certain other provinces including Ontario, Manitoba, and Alberta, is at the forefront of prevention programs. Both earlier and now, certain provisions such as the precautionary cessation of work by pregnant workers and the recognition of the right of an injured worker or victim of an occupational disease to return to work, have been seen as innovative since they have not been included in the laws of other provinces. However, the originality of Quebec is found especially in the way in which the law is applied. When the province's Occupational Health and Safety Act was passed in 1977, the government set up three mechanisms to ensure parity for and the participation of both parties:

1. The board of directors of the occupational health and safety commission, which has jurisdiction over all aspects of occupational health and safety (prevention, inspection, compensation and funding) is a joint body.

2. Occupational health and safety committees in firms are also joint committees. Most provinces also provide for the establishment of such committees.

3. Joint consultation at the sectoral level was also established through sectoral occupational health and safety associations. This joint consultation between the parties at the sectoral level is a unique feature of the Quebec occupational health and safety system. These associations are *voluntary* groupings of union and management associations that exist within the same sector of activities.

Appeals can be made through an appeals tribunal which is external to the occupational health and safety commission and is under the authority of the minister of justice. This body, which is called the Workers' Compensation Appeals Tribunal, can intervene in all appeals against rulings by the occupational health and safety commission. This is another original feature of the administration of Quebec's system of occupational health and safety. Another particularity of this mechanism can be found in the fact that the appeals tribunal can play a conciliatory role between the parties. Over the years this has led to the unblocking of the system through out-of-court settlements of outstanding compensation claims.

Currently, the main inter-related preoccupations of the occupational health and safety system are the costs of administering the system, reducing the length of time taken to settle cases, and reducing the emphasis on legal aspects in the processing of files by the occupational health and safety commission. In regard to costs, it should be noted that despite a decrease in the number of accidents at work in the past few years, the costs of administering the system have continued to increase. This is due mainly to a general increase in the average period of compensation and more particularly to an increase in the duration of relapses. However, for the first time since its creation, in 1995 there will be a decrease in the average rate of employer contributions.

As regards the waiting periods for the settlement of cases and the weighty legal proceedings related to the process, the most likely scenario will be that changes will be put forward to restructure the appeal mechanisms by eliminating an internal level of appeal within the occupational health and safety commission.

CONCLUSION

The growth of nationalism in Quebec may soon lead this province to separate from the rest of Canada and try to proceed on its own as a distinct country. Although this is far from a certainty given the recent opinion polls on the issue, it is tempting to speculate on the impact that the new political environment could have on the state of labour-management relations. Such prediction, however, is almost impossible to make because so much depends on the economic consequences of independence for Quebec.

Labour-management relations are presently adjusting to the new economic environment created by greater national and international competition, and these adjustments are taking forms (for example, greater union-management cooperation) that very few observers would have predicted ten years ago.

The same uncertainty exists with regard to the evolution of labour-management relations in an independent Quebec. If the economic consequences of separation are negative, would the new situation reinforce union-management cooperation in the same way that the two previous recessions did; or, on the contrary, would it lead to a weakening of the labour movement and a major decline in unionization? On the other hand, if independence happens to be the cure to the many economic ills and wastes that the PQ and BQ have identified with the present federal system, would the new prosperity be conducive to greater militancy by the unions and a return to the type of labour-management relations that existed in the 1970s; or would the recent experiences with labour-management cooperation continue and be even more institutionalized?

Whatever the political outcome, competitive pressures will continue to be felt by private enterprises, and the government's debt burden will still seriously impair its capacity to intervene in the economy, let alone maintain intact the actual social programs. This is why some unique features of Quebec industrial relations, such as the decree system and the highly centralized labour relations regimes of the public sector and the construction industry, have recently experienced some profound transformations or are presently under reconsideration.

QUESTIONS

1. Explain why the Quebec government and business leaders were endorsing the passage of the Free Trade Agreement with the United States while most interest groups in Ontario were opposing this deal.
2. What is the official platform adopted by most central labour organizations in Quebec with regard to this province's future political status?
3. Describe the functioning of the Quebec Federation of Labour's Solidarity Fund.
4. What is meant by "social contracts" in Quebec?

5. Explain the particular relationship that exists between the CLC and QFL.

6. Explain the ideological transformation that occurred within the CSN in the late 1980s.

7. What role does the Conseil du Patronat du Québec play in Quebec's labour relations systems?

8. Assess the impact that the antistrikebreaking provisions of the Labour Code have had on the process of collective bargaining in Quebec.

9. Compare the effectiveness of the role played by the Essential Services Council in public services and in the public and quasi-public sectors respectively.

10. What remedial powers can the Essential Services Council utilize in its interventions in labour disputes? And what approach is most often used by the Council in these disputes?

11. Under what conditions can the legal right to strike be exercised in Quebec social affairs (hospital) sector?

12. What lessons can be drawn from the experience of collective bargaining in Quebec public and quasi-public sectors between 1964 and 1994?

13. Describe how the decree system works in Quebec.

14. What are the particular features of the labour relations system in Quebec Construction industry?

15. Explain the two aspects of anti-discrimination policy in Quebec.

16. What is the main difference between Quebec and Ontario as regards their general approach toward pay equity?

17. Overall, would you say that Quebec public policy on work is substantially different from the rest of Canada?

REFERENCES

BERNIAR, J. 1993. "Juridical Extension in Quebec: A New Challenge Unique in North America." *Relations industrielles/Industrial Relations*, 48: 745-761.

BOIVIN, J. 1993. "Bilan de la négociation collective dans les secteur public et parapublic québécois," *La négociation collective du travail*, C. Bernier, R. Laflamme, F. Morin, G. Murray et C. Rondeau, eds, 48e congrès des relations industrielles de l'Université Laval. Ste-Foy: Presses de l'Université Laval.

———. 1989. *Les relations patronales-syndicales au Québec. 2nd ed.* Chicoutimi, Que: Gaétan Morin.

COMMISSION DE LA CONSTRUCTION DU QUÉBEC. 1992. *Résultats du scrutin.*

CONSEIL DES SERVICES ESSENTIELS. 1993. *1982-1992: Dix Ans à maintenir avec vous l'essentiel.* Québec: Direction des communications.

CONSEIL DU STATUT DE LA FEMME. 1993. *Même poids, même mesure. Avis sur l'équité en emploi.* Québec: Direction des Communications.

CÔTÉ, A., and LEMONDE, L. 1988. *Discrimination et Commission des droits de la personne.* Montréal, Qué: Saint-Martin.

DELORME, F., FORTIN, R., and L. GOSSELIN. 1994. "L'organisation du monde patronal au Québec: un portrait diversifié." In *Les relations industrielles au Québec. 50 ans d'évolution*. Québec: Presses de l'Université Laval, 167-201.

DELORME, E., and D. VEILLEUX. 1980. *Les syndicats indépendants au Québec: un aperçu de leur situation*. Québec: Ministère du Travail et de la main-d'oeuvre

FLEURY, G. 1991. "Les dispositions anti-briseurs de grève: 1978-1989." *Le marché du travail* 12: 6-8, 71-86.

FONDS DE SOLIDARITÉ DES TRAVAILLEURS DU QUÉBEC. 1993. *Rapport annuel*.

FOURNIER, L. 1991. *Solidarité Inc.* Montréal: Québec-Amérique.

———. 1993 "The Quebec Solidarity Fund: A Profound Revolution in the Labour Movement." *Inroads: A Journal of Opinion*. Ottawa: Inroads Inc.

FRASER, M. 1987. *Quebec Inc.* Montréal: Éditions de l'Homme.

FRÉCHETTE, P., and J.P. VÉZINA. 1990. *L'économie du Québec*. Montréal: Éditions études vivantes.

GOUVERNEMENT DU QUÉBEC. 1993. *La politique en matière de condition féminine. Femmes des années 1990 - Portrait statistique*. Québec.

GRANT, M., and F. RACINE. 1992. "Les services essentiels et la stratégie de négociation dans les services publics." *Le marché du travail*, 13: 6-8, 73-78.

GUNDERSON, M. J. KERVIN, and F. REID. 1989. "Effects of Labour Relations Legislations on Strike Incidence." *Canadian Journal of Economics* 22: 779-794.

GUNDERSON, M., and A. MELINO. 1990. "The Effects of Public Policy on Strike Duration." *Journal of Labor Economics* 8: 295-316

KUMAR, P. 1993. *Canadian Labour's Response to Work Reorganization*. QPIR 1993-96. Working Paper Series, School of Industrial Relations-Industrial Relations Centre, Queen's University: Kingston.

LECLERC, M., and M. QUIMPER. 1994. *Les relations du travail au Québec: une analyse de la situation dans le secteur public*. Sainte-Foy, Qué: Presses de l'Université du Québec.

MINISTÈRE DE L'INDUSTRIE, DU COMMERCE, DE LA SCIENCE ET DE LA TECHNOLOGIE. 1993. *Un modèle d'entente de partenariat: le contrat social en entreprise*. Québec: Direction générale des politiques.

MINISTÈRE DES FINANCES. CONSEIL DU TRÉSOR. 1993. *Les finances publiques: Vivre selon nos moyens*. Québec: Gouvernement du Québec.

ST-LAURENT, R. 1983. "La syndicalisation dans les secteurs à décrets de convention collective." *Le marché du travail* 4: 57-60.

SECRÉTARIAT DU SOMMET SUR L'INDUSTRIE DE LA CONSTRUCTION. 1993. *Document de consultation*. Québec: Ministère du travail du Québec.

STATISTICS CANADA. 1993. Earnings of Men and Women, 1992. Catalogue 13-217.

TRUDEAU, G. 1990. "Les normes minimales du travail: bilan et éléments de prospective." *Vingt-cinq ans de pratique en relations industrielles au Québec*. Cowansville. Qué: Yvon Blais Inc.

CHAPTER 17

CANADIAN INDUSTRIAL RELATIONS IN COMPARATIVE PERSPECTIVE

ROY J. ADAMS

THIS CHAPTER CONSIDERS MAJOR ASPECTS OF INDUSTRIAL RELATIONS systems in several countries and examines Canadian practice in light of foreign experience. Particular topics include the development of labour movements and the reasons for the different strategies chosen by trade unions; employer and government reactions to the emergence of organized labour; current structures and practices of job regulation; and the results of the systems in terms of industrial conflict and terms and conditions of employment.

The Industrial Revolution, which "took off" in western Europe in the eighteenth century, produced enormous changes in society of which modern industrial relations systems are one result (Kerr et al. 1964). In this chapter, the focus is limited to advanced industrialized countries that adhere to liberal democratic principles. All of these countries have a labour movement which is largely free from government and employer control. They all rely on a combination of market forces and institutions for the regulation of employment relations. Free collective bargaining is a major element of the institutional configuration.

THE DEVELOPMENT OF LABOUR MOVEMENTS IN EUROPE AND NORTH AMERICA

Modern-day labour movements trace their roots to local organizations that began to appear in the eighteenth century. Typically, these organizations were founded by craftsmen such as printers, shoemakers, shipwrights, seamen, tailors, cigar makers, and bakers. Many began as friendly societies whose original purpose was mutual insurance against death, unemployment, sickness, and retirement (Slomp 1990). When employment problems were experienced as a result of inflation, recession, or the introduction of new technology, these societies chose spokesmen to present petitions to the employer regarding the situation. Work stoppages tended to be spontaneous protests directed towards the employer and sometimes towards government authorities. Trade unions were fragile, blossoming in good times and wilting during depressions. In the early years, they were faced with substantial opposition from employers and from governments.

As industrialization proceeded, the economic concepts of free trade, free enterprise, and competition began to win favour. In several countries, unions were outlawed on the theory that they were conspiracies in restraint of trade (Hepple 1986; Slomp 1990; Adams 1994). Employers frequently refused to deal with unions, arguing that they were an infringement of the legitimate rights of the owner. Labour was regarded as a commodity to be purchased and sold on the free market. The Protestant ethic, derived from Calvinism, suggested that one's economic destiny depended solely on one's ability to work and save. Poverty, once considered an inevitable phenomenon, was now regarded as the reward for sloth (Dunlop 1972). The unemployed were often arrested as indigents and made to labour in workhouses.

Despite these negative forces, union membership and influence grew, if slowly. Periodic outbreaks of labour protest resulted in the overturning of the various laws against union activity during the latter part of the nineteenth century. Workers eventually won the right of association and the right to strike. In 1868, the first national trade union federation that would endure, the Trades Union Congress, was established in Great Britain. During the next thirty years, union federations emerged in most of the countries of Europe and North America.

The Rise of Marxism

To counter the political and legal obstacles to their existence, these emerging labour movements required a philosophy or ideology to justify their existence, provide direction to their efforts, and inspire their members. At this critical juncture, Karl Marx put forth his grand sociopolitical theory of economic evolution (Hyman 1975; Larson and Nissen 1987).[1] He argued that capitalist society essentially comprises two classes: workers (who depend on wages for their living) and capitalists (who own the means of production). The income of the capitalists results from their expropriation of a part of the value added to raw products by labour—value that should, according to Marx, rightfully go to the worker. Over time, he said, the capitalist class would be reduced in size as a result of competition and economic cycles, and workers would become conscious of the exploitative nature of capitalist society. Eventually, workers would overthrow the remaining capitalists and set up a socialist government that would, in time, fade away into classless communism. A labour strategy designed only to win better terms and conditions of employment could not succeed because of the competitive dynamics of the economic system; a political strategy was required. Moreover, because capitalist philosophy and class power pervaded every aspect of society including education, religion, government, and the press, capitalism could be replaced only by a complete and violent overthrow of the system.

Fundamental Marxism was challenged, embellished, or limited by other socialist intellectuals. Democratic socialists, such as the British Fabians, accepted the Marxist dictum that a political strategy was appropriate for labour but believed that the political change could be brought about by democratic means. They urged workers to seek change within the context of democracy (Webb and Webb 1920). Syndicalists, on the other hand, were opposed to party politics. They accepted the Marxist proposition that capitalism could be defeated only by drastic means but felt that the general strike should be used as the principal tool (Landauer 1959; van der Linden 1990).

Between 1870 and 1920, the mainstream of the labour movements in Europe adopted some combination of these ideas. In some countries, labour or socialist parties acted as the central bodies for the unions for several years. In others, unions were instrumental in founding political parties.

The growing acceptance of socialist ideas gave rise to counter movements. The Catholic Church was particularly concerned with the antireligious and violent nature of the Marxist philosophy. In 1891, Pope Leo XIII issued the encyclical *Rerum Novarum*, which stimulated the establishment of trade unions based on Christian principles. The result was the development of a Christian trade union movement that acquired importance in several European countries including France, Italy, the Low Countries, and Germany (Fogarty 1957), as well as in Quebec (see Chapter 16).

American "Exceptionalism"

Marxist thought also inspired several North American union movements, including the Industrial Workers of the World, the One Big Union, the Workers' Unity League and many independent unions. However, in the United States the American Federation of Labour

(AFL) in 1886 established nonMarxist principles that would eventually be adopted by the majority of American unionists. Rejecting all variants of socialism, the AFL set its strategy as organizing skilled craftsmen into strong unions, one for each trade, capable of winning job and income security from employers by the application of bargaining power. The AFL did not seek major social change. Rather, it accepted the capitalist system, rejected the idea of any alliance with a political party, and distrusted any government action (Hattam 1993). On the political front, its policy was to "reward friends and punish enemies."

Socialists condemned this "exceptional" approach for being misguided, elitist, and hard-hearted. In the 1920s, American "exceptionalism" found a champion in Selig Perlman, a reformed socialist and professor at the University of Wisconsin. Perlman (1928) argued that socialist intellectuals were not really concerned with the well-being of "flesh-and-blood" workers; instead, they saw the world in terms of abstract forces and abstract masses of labour. European unionists, according to Perlman, were beguiled by the elegant and grandiose schemes of the socialists and had failed to recognize the real needs of workers.

Instead of being backward and myopic, American unions, Perlman argued, were in the vanguard. It was the Europeans, not the Americans, who were immature. In time, as workers grew more confident of themselves, "pure and simple" unionism, rather than socialist unionism, would emerge triumphant. American unions had matured sooner because of conditions special to the United States that made socialism unattractive as a guiding philosophy. For example, to embrace socialism, one must accept the dictum that society is divided into antagonistic classes. That proposition, however, ran counter to the deeply ingrained American ethic of egalitarianism. In the United States, the fast rate of economic growth, the early emergence of free education, mass male suffrage, and a two-party political system, as well as the strong pull of immigrants' ethnic identities, all militated against the development of a cohesive and militant working class. In addition, early legislative successes were often followed by judicial emasculation of the legislative intent, thus helping to turn American unions away from politics (Forbath 1991, Hattam 1993).

Over time the pillars of US labour ideology weakened and a few fell. Thus, when the unskilled began to organize en masse during the 1930s, the AFL decided to give up its elitist craft union approach and to organize unskilled and semiskilled workers. The alternative was to become overshadowed by the rapidly expanding Congress of Industrial Organizations (CIO). This competition weakened substantially the tenet of "one union for one jurisdiction." In several industries, both an AFL and a CIO union were taken into the new AFL-CIO in 1955.

From its formation in the 1930s, the CIO provided considerable support to the Democratic Party, and since the 1955 merger, the alliance between that party and organized labour has continued for the most part. The AFL-CIO has been much more active politically than was the old AFL. However, the idea that the primary aim of unions is to win better terms and conditions of employment for their own members still pervades the thought of the American labour movement (Galenson and Smith 1978; Brody 1991).

The Canadian Labour Movement

In Canada, the labour movement had developed no firm philosophy by 1900. There were political-reform unions affiliated with the US-based Knights of Labor, "pure and simple" unions—some affiliated with the AFL and some Canadian only—and unions (and union-ists) who adhered to various shades of socialism.

In 1902 the AFL pressured the Canadian Trades and Labour Congress (TLC) to expel its "dual" unions and adopt a craft union strategy. The TLC reluctantly did so but did not fully accept the antipolitical attitude of the AFL. Over the next sixty years there would be many debates about (and some moves toward) developing a party link. In the late 1950s trade union leaders and political activists worked together to create the New Democratic Party, which since then has received the support of the Canadian Labour Congress (CLC), Canada's dominant trade union federation. The NDP has a philosophy similar to those of the British Labour Party and the Social Democratic parties of Scandinavia and Germany (Horowitz 1968, Whitehorn 1992). The link between the CLC and the NDP has continued to be controversial, however. In the early 1980s, the outspoken CLC president's support for the party was one of the reasons behind the breakaway from the Congress of several inter-national craft unions that continued to adhere to the AFL tradition. They set up a new organization, the Canadian Federation of Labour, which is politically neutral (Rose 1983). More recently, because of disagreements with the policies of the NDP government, the Ontario Federation of Labour withdrew its support of the party in that province, and those active in the party and the trade union movement across the country began reconsidering the mission of the party and the union-party link.

Explaining European-North American Differences

The "exceptional" strategy chosen by the US labour movement has long been a focus of thought in America. In the 1960s Adolf Sturmthal (1966; 1973) proposed a theory that attempted to reconcile the contrary views of Marx and Perlman. He suggested three fac-tors as critical determinants of labour strategy: the nature of the problems faced by work-ers, the membership base of the labour movement, and the state of the labour market. American workers, he said, considered their major problem to be job and income security. European workers had similar security problems, but they also had political problems, which American workers did not have. During the nineteenth century the great majority of workers in most European countries did not have the right to vote, did not have ready access to education, and were treated by those in power as an inferior class of human beings. Differences of dress, speech, social behaviour, and other vestiges of feudal society emphasized adherence to a class system. In contrast, the American egalitarian ethic "stressed the ideas of classlessness, individual initiative, and opportunity" (Bok 1971, 1403). Even though real upward mobility was probably no greater in America than it was in Europe, egalitarian ideology persisted. Male suffrage and access to education became widespread earlier in the United States than they did in many European countries.

The AFL considered its problem to be primarily economic rather than political. Therefore, it decided to limit membership primarily to workers who had a critical position in the production process. Since the American economy was developing rapidly, these workers were often in short supply and thus had significant economic bargaining power. On the other hand, because the AFL represented only a small fraction of society, its polit-ical power was at best modest. In Europe, where the dominant problems were considered to be political, the labour movements organized broadly. By doing so they weakened their potential economic bargaining power (unskilled workers could be easily replaced in the event of a strike) but became more influential politically.

Over time, the labour movements on both sides of the Atlantic have changed their strategies somewhat. Instead of a general movement towards socialism as predicted by Marx or towards pure and simple unionism as Perlman predicted, there has been a convergence. American unions have become much more politically active than their predecessors were in the old AFL, although they certainly have not become radically socialist. European trade unions are now heavily engaged in economic bargaining with employers, although they continue to pursue political objectives. These changes are congruent with Sturmthal's theory. Since the 1930s, the US government has intervened more deeply in the economy than ever before. Thus, more issues important to workers are being determined politically. Moreover, in the 1930s the membership base of the American labour movement expanded significantly, and it became representative of a wider constituency. In Europe, as basic political freedoms were won and as the economies grew, political objectives became less critical and collective bargaining expanded (Slomp 1990).

Although Sturmthal's theory provides considerable insight, it is not entirely satisfactory. There are some cases that do not seem to fit well. For example, Danish unions adopted socialism early in their existence even though they were organized on a craft basis at the time and have continued to use that organization form widely up to the present (Scheuer 1992). The French have an egalitarian tradition almost as strong as that of the United States, and they achieved general male suffrage early; but the mainstream of the French labour movement adopted a radical philosophy. It continues today to be among the most radical movements in the Western world despite political and economic developments apparently similar to those in other European countries (Lorwin 1954; Sellier 1973; Goetschy and Rosenblatt 1992).

These deviations from the pattern that one would expect on applying Sturmthal's theory probably need to be explained by reference to conditions specific to those countries. For example, Sellier (1973) demonstrates that the persistent leftism of the mainstream of the French labour movement owes more to the habitual intervention of the state into union-management relations, fostering a dependence by labour on government action, than it does to objective economic conditions.

Finally, it does not seem to be accurate to think of the AFL strategy as the result of a decision taken by American workers in general when so few of them benefited by it. Instead, it was the choice of a small group of unionists, which, as a result to its success, probably hindered the development of a broader-based movement. Left-wing movements were very severely repressed in America and the courts regularly undermined whatever legislative gains labour made (Moody 1988; Forbath 1991; Hattam 1993).

Canadian developments have been similar to those in the United States. Movement has been away from "pure and simple" towards political unionism, but an additional factor noted by Sturmthal—the migration of ideas—has been important in Canada. Since its emergence, the labour movement has been pulled between the moderate, democratic socialism of Great Britain and the nonpolitical approach of US labour. Perhaps because of the British link, moderate socialism is more acceptable in Canada than in the United States. Nevertheless, many Canadian unionists subscribe fully to the US approach.

In Quebec, the Canadian Catholic Confederation of Labour was part of a wider movement set in motion by *Rerum Novarum*. Over time, the confederation evolved from being Church-dominated, to "pure-and-simple," to quite radical during the 1970s, and back to a more moderate but still socially conscious character during the 1980s and early 1990s (see Chapter 16). Interestingly, the Catholic union movement underwent a similar evolution in France (Kassalow 1971).

OTHER DEVELOPMENT PATTERNS

In advanced, industrialized countries outside North America and Europe, one finds patterns similar to those already noted, with interesting individual variations. For example, in Australia the unions have been closely allied with the Labour party in a manner similar to that of Britain and Sweden since early in their existence (Bamber and Snape 1993; Gardner and Palmer 1992). After several major strikes in the 1890s, pressure for recognition exerted by unions and the party against determined employer resistance led to the establishment of a national system of arbitration. Unions may submit claims regarding conditions of work to tribunals, whose decisions are binding. Australian unions today continue to have close party links while making extensive use of the arbitration system to advance the employment interests of their members.

In Japan, where industrialization began later than in the west, unions were suppressed for the first two decades of the twentieth century and, after a short period of legitimacy, were again subdued under the military rulers who held power during the Second World War (Gordon 1985; Shirai 1983; Vogel 1979; Weiler 1986; Koike 1988; Kuwahara 1993). Unions grew rapidly after the war under the occupying administration, which encouraged collective bargaining on the American model. However, when the two major union federations adopted socialist philosophies (one more radical than the other), government policy towards unions cooled considerably. The right to strike was outlawed in the public sector in 1948 following a number of major, disruptive strikes (Matsuda 1993).

Despite the adherence of Japan's national federations to leftist ideology, enterprise unions adopted a much more conservative position, and it is at the firm level that the weight of union activity and decision-making authority rests (Shirai 1983). Enterprise unions, composed typically of all company employees below the middle-management rank, have attracted world-wide attention because of the concern that they typically demonstrate for the success of the company.

EMPLOYERS IN INDUSTRIAL RELATIONS

In continental Europe, worker political action was successful and labour-socialist parties grew rapidly in the early decades of the twentieth century (Slomp 1990). The very different strategic decisions taken by labour movements in North America and Europe produced divergent employer reactions.

Socialist ideology threatened the fundamental existence of the capitalist system. European employers, realizing that they could not destroy the labour movement, established associations with the objective of stabilizing relations with the unions (Windmuller and Gladstone 1984; Adams 1994). These associations eventually drew together under national federations that represented the industrial relations interests of employers to government, to the public, and to union federations. In many countries, employers' associations decided (often under government pressure) to recognize unions as legitimate bargaining agents for workers on a broad scale. "Basic agreements" providing such recognition, were recorded in Denmark during the 1890s, in Sweden in 1906, in Germany in the era after the First World War, and in Switzerland and France during the 1930s (Lorwin 1954; Windmuller and Gladstone 1984; Slomp 1990). In return for recognition, unions were expected by employers' associations to negotiate agreements on an industry-wide basis and to recognize management's right to manage.

A major objective of this strategy was to reduce or check the potential influence of unions in the workplace. European employers were prepared to negotiate industry-wide agreements with unions, but they were not prepared to allow unions to become involved in the day-to-day management of the firm.

Employer reactions to unions were entirely different in the United States. Because the mainstream unions organized narrowly along craft lines and accepted the maxims of capitalism, they did not acquire political power and thus did not pose a threat to fundamental employer interests. Left-wing unions were severely and successfully suppressed by the state. As a result, employers generally concluded that they might indeed be able to contain or destroy unions. Where associations were formed, their main priority often was to stay union-free, negotiating with the unions only if compelled to do so. Under such circumstances, unions were generally forced to seek recognition on a plant-by-plant basis, and the process of recognition took on the characteristic of a battle for the hearts and minds of the workers involved. Where the union won, it was typically powerful enough to require management to sign a collective agreement that, over time, became increasingly elaborate. This development gave nonunion companies more reason to oppose unions because, unlike the situation in Europe, union recognition did come to imply significant union incursion into day-to-day management authority (Adams 1994). In Canada, employer reaction and the resultant plant-by-plant struggles for recognition were very similar to those in the United States.

The US Wagner Act of the 1930s sought to change the situation by imposing a duty on employers to negotiate with unions freely chosen by their employees. The act made illegal many unfair labour practices designed by employers to penalize employees for union sympathies. It also forbade employers to establish "company unions," that is, employer-dominated representation schemes. This stipulation had the unintended effect of removing from unorganized employers the duty to negotiate with any employee organization that was unable to survive the rigours of a hotly contested certification campaign. The Taft-Hartley Act of 1947 gave approval to employer attempts to convince employees to reject collective bargaining and thus any form of independent, government-certified representation in the formulation of their conditions of work. Subsequently, few employers recognized unions voluntarily, and union-organizing campaigns continued to be an open struggle for the loyalty of the workers involved. Unionization came to be thought of as a punishment for management failure (Adams 1993). Consequently, the possibility of the US system's evolving in the direction of European models grew more and more remote. Since nonunionized employers had good prospects of remaining union-free, they had no incentive to associate with unionized employers for the purpose of dealing with unions. Indeed, many nonunionized companies formed groups openly hostile to the fundamental existence of trade unions, a development that would not have been tolerated in most other democratic countries (Adams 1974; 1994; Wheeler 1993).

Thus, in the United States today, the extent of employer organization for industrial relations purposes is much less than elsewhere. Although associations do exist in some industries, particularly those characterized by small unionized firms whose bargaining power relative to unions is low, most US employers conduct labour relations policy individually. There are an estimated 200,000 collective agreements in effect in the United States, or one for approximately every 85 union members (Mills 1994). There is no US employer federation that has the prominence and authority regarding social matters comparable to the federations that exist in most other advanced countries (Windmuller and Gladstone 1984).

The situation in Canada is similar to that in the United States (Davies 1986; Craig and Solomon 1993). There are many associations representing the interests of business, but none with the dominant authority of employer organizations found in most liberal democratic countries (Fournier 1986). Probably the most important business organization in Canada is the Business Council on National Issues (BCNI) which was formed in the 1970s in response to the wage and price control programme of the federal Liberal government. During its short life it has actively consulted with both government and labour. However, the BCNI has neither the will nor the desire to represent the interests of Canadian business as a whole. In the view of some business leaders, the formation of a broad-based national employers' organization, competent to express the views of business on employee-relations matters, would have the effect of recognizing that there are fundamental class divisions in society.

JOB REGULATION[2]

Canada and the United States

In Canada and the United States, the dominant job-regulation process is collective bargaining between a single union and a single employer. Other typical attributes include written, formal, and comprehensive collective agreements; union organizations that are strong at the workplace and have important duties at that level; and well-developed grievance procedures ending in binding arbitration. These arrangements are unusual in comparative international perspective. The following example from Germany illustrates common themes found in much of European bargaining (Streeck 1984; Thelen 1991; Turner 1991).

Germany: An Illustration of European Patterns

The principal union federation in Germany is the German Federation of Trade Unions (DGB). Unlike most of its European counterparts, it is formally apolitical. However, its pre-Nazi predecessor had close links with the Social Democratic Party, and many German union leaders continue to be actively involved in SDP activities.

When the DGB was reconstituted after the Second World War, it decided not to officially endorse a political party. The objective of discouraging factionalism was only partially achieved. Germany also has the small Christian Federation (CGD), the Association of German Civil Service Officials (DDB), and the German Salaried Employees Union (DAG). However, about 80 per cent of all union members belong to DGB-affiliated unions. The DGB is composed entirely of industrial unions, with the largest affiliate being IG Metall, the metalworkers' union.

On the other side of the labour market, the industrial relations interests of employers are pursued by the German Employers' Confederation (BDA). It is composed largely of associations of employers organized by industry. Approximately 90 per cent of all German private enterprises (employing about 95 per cent of the workforce) belong to an employers' association, and most are affiliated with the BDA.

Union-management collective bargaining is typically conducted between an industrial union and an employers' association. The resulting collective agreements are binding on employers in given provinces or regions of the country. In the metalworking industry, wage bargaining typically takes place annually between the employers' association and IG Metall. For steel companies, jobs are broken down into several categories, and, for each category, minimum wages, average increases, overtime rates, and other generally applicable wage issues are negotiated. In addition to the wage contract, IG Metall has several contracts with the association on specific issues. There are, for example, agreements regarding the procedures that an employer must follow with respect to layoffs, vacations, technological change, apprenticeships, union shop stewards, and the "humanization" of work. These agreements do not expire at the same time, and some last for several years. In the mid-1980s, collective agreements providing greater flexibility began to appear. For example, the 1984 metal-trades agreement on hours of work called for a 38.5 hour week, but the specific implementation formula was left to be worked out at the enterprise level (Turner 1991; Thelen 1991).

Legally, collective agreements apply only to union members. As a matter of practice, however, the terms are applied to all relevant employees regardless of union status. As in Canada, unions are not permitted to strike for higher wages while a wage agreement is in effect.

The employers' association in the metal industry also negotiates with a DAG white-collar union. However, most white-collar workers are, in fact, in IG Metall, and the negotiations with the white-collar union tend to follow the dominant pattern.

Within the metalworking industry, white-collar workers have a choice of joining IG Metall, which is affiliated to the DGB, or the white-collar union affiliated to the DAG. They may also become members of the Christian trade union. Thus, in the same office, different clerks may belong to different unions; others may belong to no union. There are no mandatory union membership provisions in German collective agreements. German unions do not believe in compelling people to join, and such agreements would probably infringe the right of free association and thus be illegal.

Most relevant employers in the metalworking industry belong to the employers' association. The terms of the agreement may be extended through legislative decree to non-member companies based on joint approval by the union and the employers' association. This is one reason why so many employers have decided to join the relevant association.

Within each individual enterprise, there is the need to deal with numerous additional employment issues, including actual hours of work, wage payment procedures, holiday scheduling, piece rate systems, recruitment and selection standards, job classification, transfers, and individual dismissals. In Germany, such issues are not negotiated by a local union. Instead, they are established unilaterally by the employer or negotiated by a works council elected by all relevant employees, whether union members or not. German law requires the establishment of such councils. However, since enforcement procedures are lax, there are many companies, especially small firms, in which there is no functioning council. These bodies have no formal connection with the union, but IG Metall is entitled to nominate candidates to the council, and in practice most councillors are active trade unionists. The councils are not permitted to call strikes, but impasses concerning many issues may be taken to binding arbitration. In addition to negotiating substantive terms and conditions of employment, the councils also monitor the collective agreements and the application of employment law on matters such as human rights and labour standards. They are also entitled to receive data concerning the economic performance of the firm.

German workers with a grievance may turn to their supervisor, works councillor, or shop steward, or they may go directly to the local union office. In the 1970s, IG Metall made strenuous efforts to establish a network of union shop stewards in plants, but even where they do exist their functions and stature are restricted. Workers may also take their grievance to the Labour Court if they receive no satisfaction from their initial efforts. A worker who does so most likely will ask the union to represent the case. The courts are staffed by professional judges, familiar with labour law and practice, appointed only after consultation with employers and unions. The Labour Court will entertain grievances not only over the application of the collective agreement but also on alleged infringement of law or agreements between works councils and employers. Before handing down judgements, the Court attempts to conciliate disputes (Gladstone 1993).

Sweden: An Illustration of Centralized Bargaining

In Germany the major union federation (DGB) does not negotiate collective agreements with the Employers' Federation (BDA), but in several European countries bargaining does take place at this centralized national level. In Sweden, for example, the Social Democratic Labour Federation (LO) negotiated an annual "frame" or national centralized agreement with the Swedish Employers Confederation (SAF) from the 1950s to the mid-1980s (Martin 1986). This agreement typically called for an average increase in the wage bill of employers and often contained more detailed provisions for certain categories of workers, such as women, youths, and supervisors. Within that frame, more detailed agreements were negotiated at the industry level, and within the confines of the industry still more detailed agreements were reached between local union "clubs" and enterprise or plant managements. In addition to periodic wage bargaining, the LO and the SAF concluded several long-term agreements on such issues as industrial conflict, safety, training, layoffs, and work study. This model, which evolved slowly, came under great pressure after the deep world-wide recession of 1981 and 1982. Seeking more flexibility in order to respond to an increasingly competitive global economic system, Swedish employers demanded more decentralized bargaining and in recent years most bargaining has commenced at the industry rather than the national level (Hammarström 1993). Thus, Swedish bargaining is becoming more like that in Germany.

Tripartism

Over and above their direct negotiations, trade unions and management organizations are able to exert a considerable amount of influence on social policy. Formal, tripartite consultation regarding government policy takes place in several countries. In the Netherlands, for example, the Social-Economic Council, consisting of union, management, and crown-appointed public members, advises the government on policy initiatives. The government is required by law to consult the council on all important social and economic issues, and consensus recommendations generally become government policy (Windmuller 1969; Visser 1992). In Sweden, important employment issues are investigated by ad hoc commissions on which union and management organizations always have representation. As in the Netherlands, government rarely rejects consensus recommendations. Through such agencies, labour and management in many European countries engage in what amounts to the negotiation of socioeconomic policy (Juris, Thompson, and Daniels 1985; Crouch 1993). Although this practice waned in the 1980s and 1990s after peaking in the 1970s, it is still of considerable importance in many European countries as well as in Japan and, more recently, in Australia (Treu 1992).

Works Councils and Workers' Participation in Enterprise Decisions

Works councils are found in most European countries. In some cases, they have their basis in law, in other cases in collective agreements (Rogers and Streeck 1994). In several countries, works councils came about because of the vacuum created by the generally successful employer strategy of agreeing to multi-employer bargaining in return for union recognition of the employers' right to autonomy in hiring and firing and organizing work. In West Germany, the Netherlands, and France, unions were not able to establish a viable shop floor presence. When councils were first proposed, the unions were suspicious because they feared that such bodies would usurp their collective bargaining functions and therefore reduce union influence. Employers feared that councils would make inroads on managerial prerogatives. On the other hand, the council idea was consistent with the socialist philosophy of class representation. And from the employers' perspective, it was better to deal with a council of representatives elected by all employees than with outsiders.

For many decades the arrangement worked in favour of the employers who, by and large, were able to dominate the councils and conduct business as usual. However, political pressure for reform built up during the 1950s and 1960s, and during the 1970s the councils were strengthened significantly in several countries. Moreover, European labour movements began to demand significant worker input into more general management policies dealing with production lines and schedules, plant closures, financial administration, investments, mergers, and organizational changes.

To socialist labour movements, workers' participation in management (if not workers' control of industry) had long been an objective. During this period, unions began to mobilize their energies to advance towards this goal. The result was legislation strengthening works councils and requiring the appointment of workers' representatives to the boards of large corporations, much to the chagrin of management (International Labour Office 1985; 1987). The process has gone furthest in West Germany, where workers have parity with shareholders in choosing directors in the coal and steel industry and near parity in large companies in other industries. Despite the fears of business, labour-management parity on German boards has not resulted in economic disadvantage to the firms. The workers' representatives have acted responsibly. In fact, explosive situations have been avoided because the employment implications of issues such as the introduction of new technology and plant closures have been seriously considered at an early stage (Thelen 1991).

Other Features of European Industrial Relations

Multiple unionism, another common feature of European industrial relations systems, resulted from the controversial choice of socialism as the doctrine of much of the labour movement. This, in turn, led to a proliferation of countersocialist and apolitical union organizations as well as the fragmentation of the left. Because of this political factionalism, union security clauses and exclusive representation of the North American variety are largely unworkable in Europe.

Another notable characteristic of European practice is the existence of collective bargaining extension legislation whereby collective agreements are extended by legislative decree throughout the industry. Such procedures free employers from low-wage competition and allow the benefits of unionism to extend beyond union members. Moreover, the existence of these clauses helps to explain why employers' associations in Europe have generally been successful in attracting most large corporations into membership. In order to influence decisions that affect their work forces, companies must be association members. They also stand to be whipsawed if they remain outside of the association.

Labour courts are also found in most European countries. They perform functions similar to those of private arbitrators or arbitration boards, but their jurisdiction is much broader. In most countries, the labour courts hear cases regarding disputes over the application of work rules, whether such rules were established by custom and practice, statute, collective agreement, or an agreement between the works council and the employer. European labour courts have developed standards of just treatment very similar to those that have been developed by arbitrators under collective bargaining in North America. In the typical European country, however, all employees enjoy the benefit of these "just cause for discipline" standards whereas in North America, such standards do not apply to employees outside of the collective bargaining system who may be dismissed for any or no reason (Adell and Adams 1993). Since union recognition is not a significant issue throughout most of Europe, agencies similar to North American labour relations boards do not exist.

Recent Developments

The "Great Recession" of the early 1980s produced lower inflation, higher unemployment, and a significant decline in strike frequency. In the new milieu governments felt less of a need to negotiate restraint with unions. As a result, tripartite negotiation of incomes policy, which had been very widespread in the 1970s, was practiced less often. In the United Kingdom, the Conservative government forsook any attempt to reach agreement with unions and instead vigorously pursued free-market policies that had the effect of weakening labour organizations (Ferner and Hyman 1992). Somewhat similar but much less harsh deregulatory, market-liberating policies were adopted in, for example, the Netherlands, Belgium, and Germany.

At the level of the firm, there has been a noticeable slowing of movement towards more "industrial democracy." The policy focus shifted from ways to achieve more democracy to ways to achieve more economic efficiency and competitiveness. Faced with intensifying international competition, employers throughout Europe, like those in Sweden and Germany, demanded more flexibility in the establishment of wages, hours, and conditions of work; and towards that end they exerted pressure for more decentralized bargaining. *Lean production*, a form of work organization generally modelled on Japanese practice (see below), began to make headway among European firms (International Institute for Labour Studies 1993).

Increasing competition from both Asia and North America also provided impetus for a drive from the mid-1980s towards a single European market. Major efforts have been made to remove various regulatory barriers to trade including barriers to the movement of labour (Ulman et al. 1993; Nielsen and Szyszczak 1991). Labour's price for supporting this move was the establishment of a social charter that would put in place general social standards (such as the right of freedom of association and collective bargaining; the right to vocational training; sexual equality; and the right of workers to information, consultation, and participation in employment decision making) applicable across the European Community (now known as the European Union). That charter was adopted by all member states except the UK in 1989, but movement towards common standards has not been dramatic. Most progress has been made in the relatively uncontroversial areas of occupational health and safety and the standardization of qualifications. The expansion of the market has sparked speculation that collective bargaining may soon follow suit and be done on a Europe-wide basis. However, movement to date in that direction has been very modest (Addison and Siebert 1992). A few companies have agreed to meet and confer about employment issues with Europe-wide works councils, and a few transnational meetings between UNICE (the European Organization of Employer Associations) and ETUC (the European Organization of Trade Unions) have occurred. But no fundamental changes in bargaining patterns have yet taken place.

North American Parallels

In North America there are no tripartite consultative mechanisms with the stature and influence of those in Europe. Some consultative bodies do exist; however, no tradition has been established obligating government to seek consensus and to follow through on the decisions arrived at as a result of such consensus.

North American developments in the 1970s moved to some extent in a European direction (Adams 1985). The Canadian Labour Congress argued forcefully for a greater say in policymaking, and the federal government consulted with the unions to a much greater extent. These initiatives led to some agreements on minor issues, but no national deal could be struck on major issues such as wages, prices, and tax reform. Together with the BCNI, the CLC pressured the federal government to establish the National Labour Market and Productivity Centre, which came into existence in 1984 (Adams 1985). That agency has pursued a cooperative agenda throughout the 1980s and early 1990s. It has generally focused on issues such as training and labour market information, issues on which labour and management might most readily find common ground. In the early 1990s, the CLMPC convinced the federal government to set up a Canadian Labour Force Development Board with particular responsibility for developing a labour force training and development strategy. Also during the 1980s joint labour-managment organizations came into existence at the industry level. The exemplary organization was the Canadian Steel Trade and Employment Congress. This organization had great success in retraining and redeploying workers made redundant as the result of massive restructuring in the steel industry.

There was even some movement in the United States during the 1970s toward European norms. For example, in the latter part of the decade the AFL-CIO and the administration of President Jimmy Carter arrived at a national understanding on wage restraint in return for government action to create jobs (Flanagan 1980). However, when Ronald Reagan was elected president in 1980, the accord became moot.

During the Reagan and Bush administrations of the 1980s, the US government adopted a policy antagonistic to unions and collective bargaining. Employer activities designed to avoid or escape collective bargaining were benignly tolerated—some would say encouraged—even though in many cases the tactics adopted were blatantly illegal. Like the British government, the US government followed a union-exclusion policy. No attempt was made to achieve a tripartite national consensus (Wheeler 1993). That exclusionist policy seemed to change with the election in 1992 of Democrat Bill Clinton, who in 1993 set up a commission to recommended changes to labour law likely to produce more labour-management cooperation in pursuit of competitiveness.

European-style vehicles of industrial democracy, such as works councils and worker representation on boards of directors, historically had not been considered necessary or attractive by North American unions. The belief was that strong local unions and hard bargaining provided workers with a substantial say in establishing those work rules in which they were most interested. Nevertheless, developments in the 1970s and 1980s tended toward European models. Almost all Canadian jurisdictions have passed laws requiring the establishment of health and safety committees in workplaces, whether a union is involved or not. Proposals by assorted commissions and task forces have called for the use of statutory joint committees (essentially equivalent to works councils) to handle issues such as training, technological change, pension management, profit-sharing, and redundancy; but few of these proposals were implemented (Adams 1986). As the extent of collective bargaining, especially in the private sector, continued to decline in the United States, mandatory representation through works councils became the subject of increasing discussion in the public arena. By the early 1990s several prominent labour experts were calling for the establishment of works councils, and it was one of the options being actively entertained by Clinton's Commission on the Future of Worker-Management Relations (see, for example, Weiler 1990; Adams 1993; Freeman and Rogers 1993).

In the United States, trade unions acquired seats on the boards of directors of several companies (for example, Chrysler, United Airlines, Eastern Airlines and a number of steel companies) in exchange for wage and benefit concessions that management claimed were essential for the survival of the enterprise. In Canada, neither concessions nor the acquisition of board seats had become as prevalent as in the United States (Kumar, Coates, and Arrowsmith 1987).

JAPANESE INDUSTRIAL RELATIONS

In recent years Japanese industrial relations practices have attracted detailed attention from the West, primarily because of the enormous success of the Japanese economy and because of the imputed link between that success and the country's employment relations practices. At the enterprise level especially, unions and management have developed practices that seem to be consistent with achieving high and increasing levels of productivity and competitiveness as well as meeting, to a large degree, employee goals of security and equity.

Although antecedents to the present system can be traced far back in Japanese history, the specifics of current practice took shape only in the 1950s and 1960s (Gordon 1985). After several very difficult strikes, labour and management came to an informal but generally respected accord that has been maintained largely intact since then. Unlike the basic agreements negotiated in many European countries, this accord was worked out on a company-by-company basis between enterprise unions (comprising essentially all corporate employees except upper management) and corporate managers. As a result, there are differences from firm to firm, but the same broad outlines are found in most large corporations.

Basically, unions have negotiated for job security, objective (seniority-based) wages and promotions, and egalitarian treatment in exchange for their willingness to embrace enthusiastically management-initiated policies designed to achieve high productivity and competitiveness (Gordon 1985; Shirai 1983; Vogel 1979; Kuwahara 1993). Job security has been achieved by granting employees instant tenure. Employers agree not to dismiss anyone, individually or collectively, except in the most drastic circumstances. Should they encounter difficulties, large Japanese firms cut back on dividends, bonuses, and hours and then provide incentives for people to leave voluntarily before dismissing anyone.

Another part of the accord is an understanding that all regular members of the production community have roughly similar rights. All employees, managers and workers alike, are entitled to share in profits via bonus wages; all employees use the same cafeterias and washrooms. All employees (at least all those working in the production facilities) wear similar uniforms. High-level managers often have their desks in the same large room as first-level supervisors. The wage differential between top officers and the lowest paid employee is a fraction of the differential in the West.

In return for these concessions, management demands and has generally received a commitment from employees that they devote their full energies—intellectual and emotional as well as physical—to the success of the enterprise. Employees are asked to cooperate on the shop floor in order to bring about continual improvements in production and quality, and generally they have done so. Employees are expected to learn not only one job but many jobs in a general production cluster. Employees are expected to socialize after work with their co-workers and immediate supervisor, and continually consider ways to improve the welfare of the entire enterprise. They are expected to arrive early to work to do calisthenics and sing company songs with their co-workers and to take only half or less of the vacation time to which they are entitled. They are evaluated not only on their work performance but also on their attitude. Those who do not perform at the high level expected of all employees are first counselled, then pressured, and then harassed until they leave the firm "willingly." (Being forced out of a firm has serious consequences because large, high-paying Japanese companies generally do not hire midcareer employees from other organizations).

Flexibility and responsiveness to the environment are achieved in this system through widespread use of casual and part-time employees (a large percentage of whom are women) who are not admitted to the union and do not enjoy tenure. Management may also make changes in the hard and soft technology of production without concern for labour protest. Since core employees do not fear for their jobs, they have not opposed the introduction of new technology or the rearranging of jobs. Because of the bonus system, the wage bill can expand and contract with the fortunes of the company.

Japanese firms that have established branches in Europe and North America have transplanted several of these practices, apparently successfully since Japanese business has been almost as successful in the West as it has been on its native soil (Shimada and MacDuffie 1986; Womack et al. 1990). Thus, quality circles, multiple-skills training (with resulting broad job classifications), careful selection, and relatively permanent employment have travelled well from East to West. The Japanese have not attempted to export their wage and promotion schemes, which do not fit well into Western industrial relations systems. Many Japanese branches have attempted to operate without a union in fear that Western union traditions would not be easily reconcilable with Japanese management practices. In Britain they have promoted single-union relationships contrary to the multiple-union character of the typical British workplace.

Japanese techniques, especially quality circles, multiple-skills training combined with broad job classifications, and guarantees of greater job security, have been emulated in the West by an increasing number of companies during the 1980s. Wage flexibility has also been discussed a good deal, but pay schemes that cause worker income to vary with profits have not been widely introduced.

NAFTA AND MEXICO

In 1992 Canada, the United States, and Mexico signed the North American Free Trade Agreement (NAFTA). It significantly liberalized trade among the three countries but not to the same extent as in the European Union. Nevertheless, labour movements in both Canada and the United States were opposed to the pact as they were to the Canada-US free trade pact that was passed in 1989 (Bognanno and Ready 1993). Even though most economic forecasters predicted that economic growth would be stimulated in all three countries as a result of the agreement, unions feared that many jobs would be lost as a result of companies shifting production to Mexico. Despite labour's objection, the supposedly labour-friendly Clinton Administration in the United States strongly supported the passage of NAFTA. In an attempt

TABLE 17.1   Volume, Frequency, and Duration of Industrial Conflict, Annual Averages, 1970-92

	Days Lost per 1000 Paid Workers (*volume*)	Number of Strikes per 100,000 Workers (*frequency*)	Days Lost per Worker on Strike (*duration*)	Workers Involved per Strike (*size*)
Italy	678	13	2	2891
Canada	571	7	14	541
Australia	367	31	2	527
New Zealand	280	24	3	348
United Kingdom	263	5	8	707
United States	205	3	14	475
Sweden	104	2	6	673
France	98	13	2	371
Japan	39	3	3	558
West Germany	32	—	5	—
Netherlands	23	0.5	5	952
Austria	5	0.2	1	2348

NOTES: Italy reported hours lost which were converted to days by dividing by seven. From 1983 to 1992 the United States reported only days lost from strikes of 1000 or more workers; those numbers were inflated by 1.6, the average difference between all strikes and strikes of 1000 or more workers between 1976-1981 for which both series are available. An equivalent procedure was used to estimate the number of workers on strike. France reports average number of strikers per month which were converted to years by multiplying by 12.

SOURCES: International Labour Office, *Yearbook of Labour Statistics,* various issues.

to assuage union objections, the Clinton government was able to negotiate labour and environmental side accords (Lemco and Robson 1993). The labour side accord has many clauses that echo those in the European Social Charter such as the right to bargain collectively, the freedom of association, the elimination of employment discrimination, and the need for policies designed to prevent occupational injuries and diseases. However, each country is allowed to implement these principles in its own manner, and mechanisms for enforcement are weak. As a result, they did not satisfy either the AFL-CIO or the Canadian Labour Congress.

The major voice of labour in Mexico, the Confederation of Mexican Workers (CTM), is closely tied to the Institutional Revolutionary Party (PRI) that has held power throughout most of the twentieth century (Middlebrook 1991). Although originally populist and revolutionary, the party has ruled in a basically conservative fashion for several decades. In the 1980s it initiated a major deregulation of the Mexican economy. Because of its control over the leadership of the CTM, it did not encounter much labour opposition to this effort even though the move resulted in the deterioration of material conditions for many workers. Although reliable information on labour union activity in Mexico is not readily available, many incidents of the government undermining independent trade unions have been reported. Oddly, many legislated employment standards are more favourable to employees in Mexico than in the US or Canada. For example, the hiring of strikebreakers is prohibited, profit sharing is required, and overtime is supposed to be remunerated at twice the regular pay rate. However, enforcement procedures are apparently very lax. Because of the passage of NAFTA, interest in Mexico by Canadians and Americans is bound to increase significantly.

TABLE 17.2   Mean Strike Volume Before and After the Second World War

	1918-1938	1944-1972	% Change
Norway	2079	100	-1979
Sweden	1713	40	-1673
United Kingdom	1210	210	-1000
Netherlands	700	50	-650
Denmark	810	170	-640
Belgium	500	370	-130
Italy	690	710	+20
France	500	630	+130
Canada	400	550	+150
United States	500	700	+200
Finland	510	730	+220
Japan	50	300	+250

NOTE: Volume is average number of days lost per year because of strikes. Countries are ranked from high to low in terms of the change in strike volume.
SOURCE: Derived from Hibbs 1978.

INDUSTRIAL CONFLICT

As Table 17.1 indicates, the number of days lost because of industrial conflict in Canada exceeds that of most industrialized countries. This widely publicized observation has given rise to much popular discussion. On the basis of such figures it is often said that "Canada's industrial relations record is the worst among industrialized nations except Italy" (Malles 1977, 1). However, when one disaggregates the available strike data, a clearer picture of Canada's situation emerges. Strikes do not occur with inordinate frequency in Canada. The incidence of strikes is much higher in Australia, New Zealand, Italy, and France and close to the Canadian rate in the United Kingdom. However, Canadian strikes, like those in the United States, last much longer than strikes in other industrialized countries. Strike volume (that is, worker-days lost because of strikes) is high because of the combination of moderate strike frequency and long duration (Malles 1977; Lacroix 1986).

Canada's position near the top of the strike-volume chart is of relatively recent origin. Before the Second World War, many countries, including Sweden, Norway, Great Britain, Denmark, and the Netherlands, experienced higher overall levels of industrial conflict. By the late 1950s, it appeared that strikes were "withering away" (Ross and Hartman 1960). However, in a study carried out in the late 1970s, Hibbs demonstrated that since the Second World War strike volume decreased to very low levels in some countries and increased in others (see Table 17.2). He also showed that the level of industrial conflict was closely related to changes in socialist-labour and Communist party cabinet representation and to the size of the public budget. In countries with a high "social wage" (as represented, for example, by the level of social services), Hibbs argued,

> political competition and conflict between left-wing and right-wing parties in the electoral arena (and political market place) has, to a great extent, replaced industrial bargaining and conflict between labour and capital in the private sector (the economic market place) as the process shaping the final distribution of national income.

On the other hand, in

> countries governed more or less continuously by bourgeois parties of the centre and right, the state budget or public economy remains comparatively small,

and

> the economic market place is therefore the primary locus of distributional conflict in these nations. (Hibbs 1978, 165)

From an industrial relations perspective, Hibbs's findings may be interpreted somewhat differently. In European countries with a low level of industrial conflict, a large part of the total labour package is legislatively determined. In part, this is the result of the competition of political parties. However, much social legislation is the result of consensual agreements on the part of labour, management, and government, given effect through law. For several reasons, strikes are an unlikely result of high-level wage negotiations. National bargaining requires a high degree of professionalism. The parties are constrained to take into account the consequences of their decisions on the economy. If they did not, they would lose credibility and, therefore, political and social support. Moreover, an irresponsible use of power could result in higher rates of inflation or the precipitation of recession, outcomes that would have negative consequences for their constituents. Failure to agree at the national level might result in the shutdown of the economy. This dynamic is also in place in countries with decentralized bargaining, such as Japan, where wage bargaining takes place at regular intervals and is coordinated by high-level employer and union organizations (Soskice 1990).

The available data suggest that few breakdowns occur at centralized levels of bargaining in Europe. If they did so, one would expect many thousands of workers to be involved in each strike, but the data indicate that the average strike in most countries has fewer than 1,000 participants (see Table 17.1). One may conclude that when strikes do take place in those countries, they generally occur at lower levels in the bargaining structure. Since many issues have been removed from consideration by the time they reach lower levels, the range of issues in dispute is likely to be narrow.

In Canada and the United States, where bargaining is concentrated at the establishment level, the scope of the issues to be negotiated is wider. Thus, the stakes are higher and the bargaining process is probably more complicated, resulting in larger and more detailed agreements. Considering such circumstances, North American bargaining works remarkably well. When strikes do occur, they tend to be long and drawn out in contrast to strikes that occur at lower levels of multilevel bargaining systems, which are relatively short. In the most successful multilevel systems, both the duration and the incidence of strikes are lower than in predominantly single-level systems.

Industrial relations experts in North America have long presumed that conflict is primarily a problem of the bargaining process. They have, therefore, spent an enormous amount of time and effort seeking to develop techniques such as conciliation, arbitration, "med-arb," factfinding, and final-offer selection. From an international perspective, however, conflict appears to be more strongly related to structure than to process. As long as uncoordinated decentralized bargaining continues in North America, it is unlikely that the overall level of conflict will be reduced to the levels common in Northern Europe.

On both sides of the Atlantic, industrial conflict can be expected to vary in response to the general economic climate. Research has established that strike incidence tends to be high in periods of brisk economic growth, especially when prices are rising rapidly (thus provoking a widespread sense of grievance) and unemployment is low (thereby enhancing union bargaining power). In the period from the mid-1960s until the early 1980s, those characteristics were to be found in most industrialized market countries (Juris, Thompson, and Daniels 1985). However, by the mid-1980s price inflation had receded and unemployment in many countries reached levels not seen since the 1930s. One result was a general decrease in the level of overt industrial conflict that continued into the 1990s.

TERMS AND CONDITIONS OF WORK

Workers in the United States and Canada who belong to strong trade unions receive total compensation equivalent to or better than that of workers in most other nations. Average wages in the United States and Canada have historically exceeded those in other nations. During the past twenty years, however, the North American wage advantage over Europe and Japan has eroded substantially. Today workers in many advanced nations enjoy a standard of living close to if not better than that of their counterparts in Canada and the United States.

In addition to achieving high overall compensation, North American unions have also been successful in negotiating extensive employee benefits, such as vacations, holidays, sickness insurance, pensions, supplementary unemployment insurance, and severance benefits. Through collective bargaining and grievance procedures, unionized North American workers have been able to participate in the establishment and administration of procedures for job classification, discipline, transfers, layoffs, promotions, subcontracting, staffing schedules, plant location, and the effects on employees of technological change (Lewin 1978; Wheeler 1993). The industrial jurisprudence that has been developed within the context of collective bargaining provides working people with a set of known standards on which they may rely in contrast to the authoritarian character of employment relations when there is no collective representation. Decentralized bargaining provides individual workers with opportunities to participate closely in decision making regarding these issues (Brooks 1960). Thus, the strategy of North American unions to focus most efforts on winning concessions from individual employers has provided significant benefits to the workers involved.

TABLE 17.3   Estimates of Union Density and Bargaining Coverage, Early 1990s

	Union Density %	Bargaining Coverage %
Austria	55-60	90+
Belgium	60-70	90+
Sweden	85-90	90+
Germany	40-45	90
Netherlands	25-30	80
Norway	55-60	75
United Kingdom	40	47-55
Switzerland	25-30	65
France	7-10	80
Canada	35-40	40-45
United States	10-15	15-20
Japan	24-28	25-30

SOURCES: Estimates based largely on Ferner and Hyman 1992 and Bamber and Lansbury 1993.

These benefits have been most substantial in those cases where union bargaining power is strongest. North American legislation (unlike works council law in Germany, for example) does not require management to reach agreement with worker representatives on issues in dispute. Where management power exceeds that of the union involved, many of the issues just listed remain within the discretion of the employer. In contrast to Europe, where works council legislation and board representation provide most employees with a legal right to participate in employment decision making via elected officials, and where labour courts have developed standards similar to those developed under arbitration in Canada and the United States, a large percentage of North American workers have no collective representation rights whatsoever (Wheeler and Rojot 1993; Adams 1994). They may opt for unionization if they so choose, but to do so is often thought to be disloyal, insulting, and openly critical of the employer and thus a step to be taken only as a last resort (Adams 1993).

Extent of Unionization and Collective Bargaining

As just noted, the majority of employees in North America do not belong to trade unions, largely because of employer opposition and the structure of the law. As a result, most workers depend on individual bargaining and the action of legislators as their methods for participating in employment decisions. Table 17.3 presents estimates of comparative union density and bargaining coverage in several countries. The table illustrates that not only are European workers more likely than their North American counterparts to be members of trade unions, but also they are much more likely to be covered by collective agreements. Even in countries such as Germany, the Netherlands, and Switzerland, where the level of unionization is moderate, most workers are covered by collective agreements. This is the result of the basic agreements mentioned above and the consequent broad extent of union recognition for bargaining purposes. In countries such as Canada, the United States, and Japan, where recognition must be acquired on an employer-by-employer basis, both union density and bargaining coverage are restricted. Since the "Great Recession" of the early 1980s, there has been a great deal of restructuring in many countries, and unemployment has increased to levels unknown since the 1930s. One result is that union membership has declined in several countries. In a few, however, (Sweden, Denmark, Belgium) it has increased. In these countries the unions administer the unemployment insurance scheme, and because of high unemployment many previously uninsured employees, especially those in the white-collar ranks, have signed up both for insurance benefits and for union membership. Because collective bargaining is not as closely linked to union membership as it is in North America, bargaining coverage in most European countries has remained stable despite the decline in union density. Indeed, in France bargaining coverage during the 1980s increased substantially as a result of a government policy that required employers to initiate annual negotiations. In Britain, however, bargaining coverage did fall significantly due to bargaining decentralization and the withdrawal of many companies from employer associations (Edwards et al. 1992).

Managerial Discretion

Until recently, North Americans who participated in the collective bargaining system had a clear advantage over their European counterparts in terms of their ability to hold management accountable for decisions related to the terms and conditions of employment and to participate in making those decisions. Although the bargaining coverage of the European work force was greater, the participatory procedures were weaker. However, with the introduction of new legislation granting works councils more rights and providing for workers' representatives on boards of directors, and with union efforts to strengthen their workplace organizations, the situation has significantly changed. Clearly, the opportunity for European workers to participate in management decisions has improved considerably, while there have been fewer such gains in North America. Indeed, in the United States, industrial democracy has receded substantially because of the difficulties of unorganized workers to establish collective bargaining in the face of intensive employer opposition.

Social Benefits

The early, intensive, and continuous political efforts of European labour have produced more and better social benefits than have the relatively recent and more modest efforts of the US and Canadian labour movements. As indicated in Table 17.4, the United States, relative to other industrialized countries, has one of the lowest social wages (as represented by expenditure on social security benefits as a percentage of gross domestic product). In Canada, where a unified labour movement has pursued a consistent policy of lobbying and party support for the past twenty years, the social wage is somewhat higher. Unlike the United States, Canada has, for example, universal medical coverage and legally mandated holidays and vacations with pay.

TABLE 17.4   Expenditures on Social Security Benefits as a Percentage of Gross Domestic Product, 1986 and 1991

	1986	1991
Sweden	31.3	35.2
Netherlands	28.6	28.4
Denmark	26.3	28.3
France	28.6	n/a
Germany	26.4	n/a
Belgium	25.4	24.0
Austria	23.4	23.6
Canada	16.2	18.6
United Kingdom	20.4	18.3
United States	12.5	12.0
Japan	12.2	n/a

NOTE: "Social security" is here defined to include medical care, sickness benefits, unemployment benefits, old-age benefits, employment-injury benefits, family benefits, maternity benefits, invalidity benefits, and survivor's benefits.
SOURCE: 1986: International Labour Office 1989. 1991: International Labour Office 1994.

In European countries, the political strategy of labour was put into effect earlier and more thoroughly than in North America. It has also been more successful. Labour and social democratic parties have contested the primacy of moderate and conservative parties at the national level for several decades. As a result, the social wage in most European countries is considerably higher than in either Canada or the United States. Indeed, it had become so large by the 1980s that it was beginning to be considered detrimental to economic performance. As a result, steps were taken to reduce or contain it in several countries. Among the major industrialized nations, the social wage is the lowest in Japan, where the strategy from the end of the Second World War until fairly recently was to concentrate resources on productive investment instead of on social consumption (Shirai 1983).

Job Security

North American workers also have had less job security than their European counterparts. Unemployment rates in Canada and the United States exceeded those in Europe for most of the post-Second World War years. In the early 1980s, however, unemployment rates soared in several countries. Although rates are still very low in Japan and Switzerland, they have either reached or gone beyond the US level in the Netherlands, Belgium, France, West Germany, and the United Kingdom. Subsequent to a major recession in the early 1990s and the policies of a conservative government, unemployment in Sweden topped 8 per cent in 1993, by far the highest rate experienced since the 1930s. At the same time as unemployment rates have increased, employer demands for more flexibility have led to a loosening of restrictions against dismissal and mass layoffs (Evans, Nedzynski, and Karlsson 1985). Job creation has been slower in Europe than it has been in North America. However, this is probably due more to demographics and the lower unemployment insurance benefits in Canada and the US (due perhaps to the political weakness of the labour movements) rather than to the superiority of labour policy in these countries (Wilensky 1992; Rowthorn 1992).[3]

TABLE 17.5   Overall Economic Performance, 1970-1990

	Growth[1]	Inflation[2]	Unemployment[3]	Socio-economic Performance Index[4]
US	1.8	6.3	6.6	8.9
Canada	2.8	6.8	8.0	8.0
Sweden	1.9	8.4	2.2	11.3
Germany	2.5	3.9	4.6	14.0
Japan	3.9	5.7	2.1	16.1

[1] Real GDP Per Capita, average year-to-year percent change (*SOURCE:* OECD Economic Outlook, Historical Statistics).

[2] Consumer Price Indices, average annual percentage changes (*SOURCE:* OECD Economic Outlook, Historical Statistics).

[3] Average rate of unemployment as a percentage of total labour force (*SOURCE:* OECD Labour Force Statistics).

[4] The sum of the figure for inflation subtracted from 10, the figure for unemployment subtracted from 10, and the figure for growth. I developed this index in the course of writing Industrial Relations Under Liberal Democracy, (1994) where it is calculated for a broader range of countries.

LABOUR RELATIONS AND OVERALL ECONOMIC PERFORMANCE

It has been well established in the past decade that the institutions of industrial relations can have a major impact on overall economic performance. Numerous studies have concluded that labour-management-government relations based on the acceptance of labour as a major actor in the economic arena produce better economic results than conflictive relations based on adversarial assumptions and labour exclusion. Although many North American analysts have called for more labour-management cooperation, Canada and the United States continue to be marked by a high degree of conflict, in contrast to countries such as Germany, Japan and, until recently, Sweden. The negative impact of this conflictive culture is suggested by Table 17.5. During the past two decades Germany, Japan, and Sweden, countries in which labour is assimilated into a consensus decision-making culture, have outperformed Canada and the United States by a considerable margin. Data assembled on a broader range of countries confirm the generality of this effect (Adams 1994).

FUTURE OUTLOOK

At the end of the 1970s, it appeared that the general trend in the industrialized market countries was towards an industrial relations model with the following characteristics: national tripartite bargaining over incomes and social policy; multi-employer negotiations at the industry level over an expanding range of conditions of employment; and workers' participation in decisions at the enterprise level via a combination of works councils, board representation, and local unions. By the mid-1980s, however, broad-based bargaining was under pressure in many countries, and the trend towards an expansion of workers' participation in enterprise decisions had largely ceased. Whereas labour organizations had been in the ascendant during the 1960s and 1970s, they were now in retreat, fighting defensive battles against the erosion of jobs and income. Employers in several countries had seized the strategic initiative to introduce substantial changes. That pattern continued, to a large extent, into the 1990s.

Since there is currently such diversity and turbulence, it is impossible to predict with any confidence the likely contours of industrial relations for the remainder of the 1990s. At one pole there is the continuing attraction of an articulated industrial relations system in which labour and management (with the participation of government where relevant) co-decide issues of importance at the national, industry, and enterprise levels. At the other pole, the ultimate conclusion of the exclusionist policies pursued in the United States during the Reagan-Bush era and in Great Britain since 1979, when Margaret Thatcher took power, would seem to be an industrial relations system in which employees would have no representative mechanism through which to influence employment decisions critical to their welfare. No doubt a wide variety of patterns between these poles will continue to exist, but labour exclusionism seems to have been generally rejected outside of Britain and North America. Indeed, tripartism seems to be the primary method emerging in the countries of east and central Europe as they attempt to reshape industrial relations after decades of totalitarianism.

In Canada, several cooperative ventures between labour, management, and the state at the national, provincial, and industrial levels hold out the promise for significant movement toward more positive labour relations in the coming years. On the other hand, intense business opposition to mild labour law reform initiatives in Ontario and British Columbia suggests that high levels of labour-management animosity are not a thing of the past.

Canada, of course, will not be able to avoid the winds of change. If the past is a competent guide to the future, however, Canada is not likely to adopt extreme practices. By the year 2000, the Canadian industrial relations system is unlikely to have become a model of articulated co-operation, but it is equally unlikely to be union-free. Change will occur, but most likely both the rate and the form will be moderate.

QUESTIONS

1. North American labour movements have emphasized an "economic" strategy for seeking their goals; the approach of continental European labour movements has been more political. What have been the practical consequences of these different strategies for the conditions of the average worker?

2. A typical North American collective agreement might contain a management's rights clause, a union security clause, actual wages to be paid per job class, seniority provisions regarding promotions and layoffs, and a grievance procedure ending in binding arbitration. How would these same issues be handled in a typical European situation? Use examples from at least two countries.

3. Sturmthal's thesis on "Economic Development and the Labour Movement" can be thought of as an attempt to resolve the differences between Marxist philosophy and Perlman's theory of the labour movement. How does Sturmthal go about doing this? Is his thesis convincing?

4. In Europe today, the great majority of employers accept trade unions as necessary and legitimate institutions. Conversely, large numbers of North American employers continue to resist unionism and do not recognize the necessity of trade unions. What factors account for these differences?

5. Works councils are common agencies of job regulation in Europe, but they do not exist in North America. Why have they appeared in Europe and not North America? What functions do they serve? What advantages and disadvantages do they have over the North American approach to these same functions?

6. Collective bargaining has been described as the American approach to industrial democracy. What advantages and disadvantages does American-style collective bargaining have over the other forms of industrial democracy found in Europe?

7. Describe the present-day pattern of industrial conflict in Canada and at least two countries outside North America (these countries should exhibit patterns different from each other). Provide an explanation for these three patterns.

8. In some developed countries, industrial conflict has increased in the long run; in others it has decreased. How can these different patterns be explained?

9. Most North American industrial relations experts explicitly or implicitly assume that industrial conflict is primarily a problem of the bargaining process. How well does this assumption hold up against the international experience?

10. What are the differences in the social wage between the typical European country and North America? To what extent are these differences the result of variations in the industrial relations systems? What is the relationship between the social wage and the volume of industrial conflict?

11. Japanese industrial relations are widely believed to be helpful in allowing industry to achieve high levels of productivity, security, and equity simultaneously. Describe the theory underlying that belief, and review the reservations held by critics of Japanese practice.

12. What is the relationship between the character of labour-management-government relations (adversarial vs. cooperative) and socioeconomic performance? What does the comparative experience suggest that Canada might do to move from an adversarial to a more consensus-based system of employment relations?

REFERENCES

ADAMS, R.J. 1974. "Solidarity, Self-Interest and the Unionization Differential between Europe and North America." *Relations industrielles/Industrial Relations* 29: 497-511.

————. 1985. "Industrial Relations and the Economic Crisis: Canada Moves towards Europe." In H. Juris, M. Thompson, and W. Daniels, eds, *Industrial Relations in a Decade of Economic Change.* Madison, WI: Industrial Relations Research Association.

————. 1986. "Two Policy Approaches to Labour-Management Decision Making at the Level of the Enterprise." In W.C. Riddell, ed, *Labour-Management Cooperation in Canada.* Toronto: University of Toronto Press.

————. 1993. "The North American Model of Employee Representational Participation: "A Hollow Mockery." *Comparative Labor Law Journal* 15: 4-14.

————.1994. *Industrial Relations under Liberal Democracy: North America in Comparative Perspective,* Columbia: University of South Carolina Press.

ADAMS, R.J., and C.H. RUMMEL. 1977. "Workers' Participation in West Germany: Impact on the Worker, the Enterprise and the Trade Union." *Industrial Relations Journal* 8: 4-22.

ADELL, B., and R.J. ADAMS. 1993. "Discipline and Discharge for Theft in Ten Countries," *Industrial Relations Research Association,* proceedings of the annual meeting held at Anaheim, California, January 5-7, Madison, WI: IRRA.

ADDISON, J., and W.S. SIEBERT. 1992. "The Social Charter: Whatever Next?" *British Journal of Industrial Relations* 30: 495-514.

BAMBER, G., and R.D. LANSBURY, eds. 1993. *International and Comparative Industrial Relations,* 2nd ed. London: Allen & Unwin.

BAMBER, G., and E. SNAPE. 1993. "Industrial Relations in Britain." In G. Bamber and R.D. Lansbury, eds, *International and Comparative Industrial Relations,* 2nd ed. London: Routledege.

BOGNANNO, M., and K. READY, eds. 1993. *The North American Free Trade Agreement, Labor, Industry and Government Perspectives.* Westport, CT: Praeger.

BOK, D.C. 1971. "Reflections on the Distinctive Character of American Labor Laws." *Harvard Law Review* 84: 1394-463.

BRODY, D. 1991. "Labor's Crisis in Historical Perspective," in G. Strauss, D. Gallagher and J. Fiorito, eds, *The State of the Unions.* Madison, WI: Industrial Relations Research Association.

BROOKS, G.W. 1960. "Unions and the Structure of Collective Bargaining." In A. Weber, ed, *The Structure of Collective Bargaining.* Glencoe, Ill: Free Press.

CRAIG, A., and N. SOLOMON. 1993. *The System of Industrial Relations in Canada,* 4th ed. Scarborough, Ont.: Prentice Hall.

CROUCH, C. 1993. *Industrial Relations and European State Traditions.* Oxford: Clarendon.

DAVIES, R.J. 1986. "The Structure of Collective Bargaining in Canada." In W.C. Riddell, ed, *Canadian Labour Relations.* Toronto: University of Toronto Press.

DERBER, M. 1984. "Employers Associations in the United States." In J. Windmuller and A. Gladstone, eds, *Employer Associations and Industrial Relations.* Oxford: Clarendon.

DUNLOP, J.T. 1972. "The Development of Labor Organization: A Theoretical Framework." In R. Marshall and R. Perlman, eds, *An Anthology of Labor Economics.* Toronto: John Wiley.

EDWARDS, P., M. HALL, R. HYMAN, P. MARGINSON, K. SISSON, J. WADDINGTON, and D. WINCHESTER. 1992. "Great Britain: Still Muddling Through." In A. Ferner and R. Hyman, eds, *Industrial Relations in the New Europe.* Oxford: Blackwell.

EVANS, J., R. NEDZYNSKI, and G. KARLSSON. 1985. *Flexibility and Jobs: Myths and Realities.* Brussels: European Trade Union Institute.

FERNER, A., and R. HYMAN, eds. 1992. *Industrial Relations in the New Europe.* Oxford: Blackwell.

FLANAGAN, R.J. 1980. "The National Accord as a Social Contract." *Industrial and Labor Relations Review* 34(1): 35-50.

FOGARTY, M. 1957. *Christian Democracy in Western Europe, 1820-1953.* London: Routledge and Kegan Paul.

FORBATH, W. 1991. *Law and the Shaping of the American Labor Movement,* Cambridge: Harvard University Press.

FOURNIER, P. 1986. "Consensus Building in Canada: Case Studies and Prospects." In K. Banting, ed., *The State and Economic Interests,* Toronto: University of Toronto Press.

FREEMAN, R., and J. ROGERS. 1993. "Who Speaks for Us? Employee Representation in a Nonunion Labor Market." In B. Kaufman and M. Kleiner, eds, *Employee Representation: Alternatives and Future Directions.* Madison, WI: Industrial Relations Research Association.

GALENSON, W., and R.S. SMITH. 1978. "The United States." In J.R. Dunlop and W. Galenson, eds, *Labor in the Twentieth Century.* New York: Academic Press.

GARDNER, M., and G. PALMER. 1992. *Employment Relations: Industrial Relations and Human Resources Management in Australia.* South Melbourne: Macmillan.

GLADSTONE, A. 1993. "Settlement of Disputes over Rights." In R. Blanpain and C. Engels, eds, *Comparative Labour Law and Industrial Relations in Industrialized Market Economies,* 5th ed. Deventer: Kluwer.

GOETSCHY, J., and P. ROSENBLATT. 1992. "France: The Industrial Relations System at a Turning Point?" In A. Ferner and R. Human, eds, *Industrial Relations in the New Europe.* Cambridge: Blackwell.

GORDON, A. 1985. *The Evolution of Labor Relations in Japan: Heavy Industry 1853-1955.* Cambridge, Mass: Harvard University Press.

HAMMARSTRÖM, O. 1993. "Industrial Relations in Sweden." In G. Bamber and R.D. Lansbury, eds, *International and Comparative Industrial Relations,* 2nd ed. London: Routledge.

HATTAM, V. 1993. *Labor Visions and State Power: the Origins of Business Unionism in the United States.* Princeton: Princeton University Press.

HEPPLE, B. 1986. *The Making of Labour Law in Europe: A Comparative Study of Nine Countries Up to 1945.* London: Mansell.

HIBBS, D.A., Jr. 1978. "On the Political Economy of Long-Run Trends in Strike Activity." *British Journal of Political Science* 8: 153-75.

HOROWITZ, G. 1968. *Canadian Labour in Politics.* Toronto: University of Toronto Press.

HYMAN, R. 1975. *Industrial Relations: A Marxist Introduction.* London: Macmillan.

INTERNATIONAL INSTITUTE FOR LABOUR STUDIES. 1993. *Lean Production and Beyond, Labour Aspects of a New Production Concept.* International Labour Office: Geveva.

INTERNATIONAL LABOUR OFFICE. 1987. *Collective Bargaining in Industrialized Market Economies.* Geneva: ILO.

———. 1989. *The Cost of Social Security: Thirteenth International Inquiry, 1984-86.* Geneva: ILO.

———. 1985. *World Labour Report 2.* Geneva: ILO.

———. 1994. *World Labour Report 7.* Geneva: ILO.

———. Various issues. *Yearbook of Labour Statistics.* Geneva: ILO.

INTERNATIONAL ORGANIZATION OF EMPLOYERS. 1970. *Structure, Scope and Activities of National Central Employer Organizations.* London: IOE.

JURIS, H., M. THOMPSON, and W. DANIELS, eds. 1985. *Industrial Relations in a Decade of Economic Change.* Madison, WI: Industrial Relations Research Association.

KASSALOW, E. 1971. "The Transformation of Christian Trade Unionism: The Recent Evolution of the French CFDT." *Proceedings of the Twenty-Fourth Annual Meeting of the Industrial Relations Research Association.* Madison, WI: IRRA.

KERR, C., J.T. DUNLOP, F. HARBISON, and C.A. MYERS. 1964. *Industrialism and Industrial Man.* New York: Oxford University Press.

KOIKE, K. 1988. *Understanding Industrial Relations in Modern Japan.* Basingstoke: Macmillan.

KUMAR, P., with M.L. COATES and D. ARROWSMITH, eds. 1987. *The Current Industrial Relations Scene in Canada.* Kingston, Ont.: Industrial Relations Centre, Queen's University.

KUWAHARA, Y. 1993. "Industrial Relations in Japan." In G. Bamber and R.D. Lansbury, eds, *International and Comparative Industrial Relations,* 2nd ed. London: Routledge.

LACROIX, R. 1986. "Strike Activity in Canada." In W.C. Riddell, ed, *Canadian Labour Relations.* Toronto: University of Toronto Press.

LANDAUER, C.A. 1959. *European Socialism.* 2 vols. Berkeley: University of California Press.

LARSON, S., and B. NISSEN, eds. 1987. *Theories of the Labor Movement.* Detroit: Wayne State University Press.

LEMCO, J., and W. ROBSON, eds. 1993. *Ties Beyond Trade, Labor and Environmental Issues Under the NAFTA,* Toronto: C.D. Howe Institute in conjunction with the National Planning Association (USA).

LEWIN, D. 1978. "The Impact of Unionism on American Business: Evidence for an Assessment." *Columbia Journal of World Business* 13: 89-103.

LORWIN, V. 1954. *The French Labor Movement.* Cambridge, Mass: Harvard University Press.

MALLES, P. 1977. *Canadian Industrial Conflict in International Perspective.* Ottawa: Information Ltd.

MARTIN, A. 1986. "The End of the 'Swedish Model': Recent Developments in Swedish Industrial Relations." Cambridge, Mass: Center for European Studies, Harvard University.

MATSUDA, Y. 1993. "Japan." In S. Deery and R. Mitchell, eds, *Labour Law and Industrial Relations in Asia.* Melbourne: Longman Cheshire.

MIDDLEBROOK, K. 1991. *Unions, Workers and the State in Mexico.* San Diego: Center for U.S.-Mexican Studies.

MOODY, K. 1988. *An Injury to All: The Decline of American Unionism.* New York: Verso.

MILLS, D. 1994. *Labor-Management Relations,* 5th ed. New York: McGraw-Hill.

NIELSEN, R., and E. SZYSZCZAK. 1993. *The Social Dimension of the European Community,* 2nd ed. Copenhagen: Munksgaard.

PERLMAN, S.A. 1928. *A Theory of the Labor Movement.* New York: Macmillan.

ROGERS, J., and W. STREECK, eds. 1994. *Employee Participation and Works Councils.* Chicago: University of Chicago Press.

ROSE, J.B. 1983. "Some Notes on the Building Trades-Canadian Labour Congress Dispute." *Industrial Relations* 22: 87-93.

ROSS, A.M., and P.T. HARTMAN. 1960. *Changing Patterns of Industrial Conflict.* New York: John Wiley.

ROWTHORN, B. 1992. "Corporatism and Labour Market Performance." In J. Pekkarinen, M. Pohjola, and B. Rowthorn, eds, *Social Corporatism: A Superior Economic System?* Oxford: Clarendon.

SCHEUER, S. 1992. "Denmark: Return to Decentralization." In A. Ferner and R. Hyman, eds, *Industrial Relations in the New Europe.* Oxford: Blackwell.

SCHMITTER, P.C., and W. STREECK. 1986. *The Organization of Business Interests.* Berlin: de Gruyter.

SELLIER, F. 1973. "The French Workers' Movement and Political Unionism." In A. Sturmthal and J.G. Scoville, eds, *The International Labor Movement in Transition.* Urbana, Ill: University of Illinois Press.

SHIMADA, H., and J.P. MacDUFFIE. 1986. "Industrial Relations and 'Humanware.'" Working Paper 1855-88, Sloan School of Management, Massachusetts Institute of Technology.

SHIRAI, T., ed. 1983. *Contemporary Industrial Relations in Japan.* Madison, WI: University of Wisconsin Press.

SLOMP, H. 1990. *Labor Relations in Europe: A history of issues and developments.* New York: Greenwood.

SOSKICE, D. 1990. "Wage Determination: The Changing Role of Institutions in Advanced Industrialized Countries." *Oxford Review of Economic Policy* 6, 36-61.

STREECK, W. 1984. *Industrial Relations in West Germany: A Case Study of the Car Industry.* London: Heineman.

STREECK, W., and D.C. SCHMITTER, eds. 1985. *Private Interest Government: Beyond Market and State.* London: Sage.

STURMTHAL, A. 1966. "Economic Development and the Labour Movement." In A.M. Ross, Jr., ed, *Industrial Relations and Economic Development.* London: Macmillan.

———. 1973. "Industrial Relations Strategies." In A. Sturmthal and J.G. Scoville, eds, *The International Labor Movement in Transition.* Urbana: University of Illinois Press.

THELEN, K. 1991. *Union of Parts: Labor Politics in Postwar Germany.* Ithaca: Cornell University Press.

TREU, T., ed. 1992. *Participation in Public Policy-Making: The Role of Trade Unions and Employers' Associations.* Berlin: deGruyter.

TURNER, L. 1991. *Democracy at Work: Changing World Markets and the Future of Labor Unions.* Ithaca: Cornell University Press.

ULMAN, L., B. EICHENGREEN, and W.T. DICKENS, eds. 1993. *Labor and an Integrated Europe.* Washington: Brookings Institution.

VAN DER LINDEN, M. 1990. *Revolutionary Syndicalism: An International Perspective.* Brookfield, Vt.: Gower.

VISSER, J. 1992. "The Netherlands: The End of an Era and the End of a System." In A. Ferner and R. Hyman, eds, *Industrial Relations in the New Europe.* Cambridge: Blackwell.

VOGEL, E. 1979. *Japan as Number One.* Tokyo: Charles Tuttle.

WEBB, S., and B. WEBB. 1920. *Industrial Democracy.* London: Longman.

WEILER, J.M. 1986. "The Japanese Labour Relations System: Lessons for Canada." In W.C. Riddell, ed, *Labour-Management Cooperation in Canada.* Toronto: University of Toronto Press.

WEILER, P. 1990. *Governing the Workplace: The Future of Labor and Employment Law.* Cambridge: Harvard University Press.

WHEELER, H. 1993. "Industrial Relations in the United States of America." In G. Bamber and R.D. Lansbury, eds, *International and Comparative Industrial Relations*, 2nd ed. London: Routledge.

WHEELER, H., and J. ROJOT, eds. 1992. *Workplace Justice: Employment Obligations in International Perspective.* Columbia: University of South Carolina Press.

WHITEHORN, A. 1992. *Canadian Socialism: Essays on the CCF-NDP.* Toronto: Oxford University Press.

WILENSKY, H. 1992. "The Great American Job Machine in Comparative Perspective." *Industrial Relations* 31: 473-488.

WINDMULLER, J. 1969. *Labor Relations in the Netherlands.* Ithaca, NY: Cornell University Press.

WINDMULLER, J., and A. GLADSTONE, eds. 1984. *Employer Associations and Industrial Relations.* Oxford: Clarendon.

WOMACK, J., D. JONES, and D. ROOS. 1990. *The Machine that Changed the World.* New York: Maxwell Macmillan International.

END NOTES

1. Volume I of *Das Capital*, Marx's most comprehensive theoretical work, was published in 1867. However, the ideas of Marx and his collaborator Engels appeared in the form of articles, pamphlets and books on particular topics, such as *The Condition of the Working Class in England*, beginning in the 1840s.

2. This term is usually attributed to Alan Flanders, a British professor of industrial relations who was prominent in the 1960s and 1970s. It is used to refer to any process such as collective bargaining, government establishment of minimum standards, or unilateral employer action to establish terms and conditions of work very broadly conceived.

3. Wilensky (1992), for example, could find no relationship between job creation and public policy instruments for eighteen countries over several decades. He did, however, find significant relationships between "job creation" and demographic variables such as immigration (more immigrants, more jobs), divorce (more divorce, more single mothers in the labour force, and more jobs), and age (more young people, more jobs).

CHAPTER 18

FUTURE DIRECTIONS FOR CANADIAN INDUSTRIAL RELATIONS

ALLEN PONAK AND MORLEY GUNDERSON

THIS CHAPTER REVIEWS THE MAJOR FEATURES OF UNION-MANAGEMENT relations in Canada, following the modified industrial relations systems model presented in Chapter 1. Examined in turn are the environment, the actors, the conversion processes, and the outcomes of the industrial relations system. The purpose of the discussion is to highlight significant changes that are under way and to assess the implications of these changes for the practice of industrial relations in the future. A major conclusion of the analysis is that the initiative in union-management relations has swung to the employer and that the Canadian labour movement faces serious challenges in the years ahead.

CANADIAN INDUSTRIAL RELATIONS IN TRANSITION

Projecting the future on the basis of past events is always risky. A number of recent developments, however, have profoundly affected union-management relations in this country and in all likelihood will continue to leave their imprint into the next century. The huge Canadian debt and its impact on public sector industrial relations is one example in this regard. Furthermore, certain patterns that had been evident in the past became much more prominent as the 1990s unfolded (for example, management emphasis on employee involvement programs).

The Environment

Canadian industrial relations do not take place in a vacuum. Unions and management themselves, as well as the nature of their interactions, are shaped by the economic, social, political, and historical forces at work in the country. Sometimes the relationship is direct and obvious, as when political decisions are made to end economically disruptive work stoppages. This has occurred frequently in the Canadian grain export industry where legislation to end strikes (or the threat of legislation) has become commonplace. At other times, the relationship is less obvious. For example, the demographic profile of the labour force has been changing slowly for a considerable period of time, but now the cumulative impact of these changes is posing a significant challenge to the future strength of the Canadian labour movement. Failure on the part of Canada's unions to adjust to the new labour market reality of more white-collar, female, part-time, and casual employees could result in a decline in union membership.

Economic Environment

Labour and management cohabit in an economic world. Commodity price fluctuations, the level of unemployment, the rate of inflation, growing international competition, and the growth of the overall economy all affect union-management interactions. Numerous studies attest to these relationships (see Chapter 2).

Several developments during the past decade were particularly important, and all had the effect of reducing union strength. First, high unemployment rates became a persistent feature of the Canadian labour market, even when the economy grew. A host of reasons has been offered for the "jobless recovery" of the late 1980s and early 1990s. Innovative technologies have allowed fewer workers to control more and more production, corporate restructuring has resulted in the elimination of large numbers of administrative jobs, and lower tariffs have made overseas production more cost effective. The continuing high level of government debt has meant the end of high levels of public sector job creation.

The large number of unemployed workers has been an important factor in enabling employers to seize the initiative in collective bargaining. People with jobs have become much more interested in job security than in pursuing new demands. Militancy, as expressed by the willingness to go on strike, has declined significantly. One result is that unions are hard-pressed to retain gains made in the past, and many workers have experienced a reduction in real wages. Where it was once common for unions to enter negotiations with a lengthy list of contract changes, now it is often employer negotiators who arrive with the long list of proposals.

A second important labour market development is the changing nature of the workforce. While the increasing proportion of white-collar workers, the higher participation rate of women, the increased use of part-time and casual employees, and the aging of the labour force are trends that had been under way for years, these changes came to the forefront during the 1980s and 1990s. With them came a new set of bargaining issues and other challenges. Employment opportunity, pay equity, maternity leave, and child care became priorities for many employees, and these issues increasingly found their way into negotiations and litigation. A workforce gradually growing older started paying closer attention to retirement issues, leisure time, and pensions. The use of part-time and casual employees, a crucial element in the flexibility of many employers, and the rights and remuneration of such employees were often highly contentious issues in collective bargaining.

The changes in the nature of the workforce brought with them potentially profound consequences for the prospects of union growth. Outside the public sector, unions have traditionally held only limited appeal to white-collar and service workers. Part-time and casual employees, a disproportionate number of whom are women, have also provided difficult organizing terrain for many unions. The failure of the bank-organizing campaign in the early 1980s and the major department store drives later in the decade highlighted the weakness of the labour movement. If labour leaders prove unable to devise strategies that can convince such employees to sign union cards, then the long-run prospects of the labour movement will be dim (see Chapters 7 and 8).

At the macro level, a third important economic development has been the commitment of virtually all governments in Canada, regardless of political affiliation, to what can loosely be called a "free market" orientation. The poverty of the Soviet bloc and the conversion of China to capitalism ended most debate about the virtues of socialism and heavily regulated economies. Huge government debt heightened the practical appeal of less government. The most visible aspects of such free market commitment in Canada have been privatization in the public sector, the deregulation of some industries (e.g., trucking), and the negotiation of free trade agreements with the United States and Mexico .

Organized labour has opposed these developments, partly on philosophical grounds but mainly for reasons of job security and economics. Privatization and contracting-out reduce union membership. For example, postal stations located in convenience stores are much less likely to be unionized than outlets run directly by Canada Post; the same is true of university cafeterias run by franchise rather than the university directly. Deregulation, to the extent it permits nonunion firms to enter the marketplace, often places substantial pressure on wage and benefit levels and on working conditions. This certainly has been the experience in the United States (Kochan, Katz, and McKersie 1986). Free trade places even more pressure on unions. The level of unionization in the United States is now so low that Canadian firms will invariably be competing much more frequently against nonunion operations. They will also now be competing with Mexico's vastly lower wage rates, though current productivity differences will shield the impact in the near term.

In short, the economic environment of the 1990s poses unprecedented challenges for the Canadian labour movement. It must adjust to an often insecure workforce that is very different than its traditional membership base and cope with a much more open economy subject to great competitive pressures. At the same time the economic changes have enhanced employer bargaining power, placing management in a strong position to achieve its bargaining agenda and to introduce workplace innovations that unions may view with little enthusiasm. Labour market changes also create more opportunities for employers to pursue union avoidance strategies, if they are so inclined.

Legal Environment

Industrial relations, whether it involves unionized or nonunionized employees, takes place within a legal framework. For unionized employees and their employers, collective bargaining legislation provides basic rights, protections, rules, and enforcement procedures (see Chapter 3). The statutory framework for the private sector in all Canadian jurisdictions, with the partial exception of Quebec (see Chapter 16), derives from the US Wagner Act and has been in place since the end of the Second World War. This framework protects the right of employees to form unions free from employer interference, provides certification mechanisms, obliges unions and employers to bargain in good faith, permits either side to use economic sanctions once certain prerequisites have been met, and establishes labour relations boards to administer and enforce the legislative regime.

The past decade has seen an important modification to this basic model with the extension of strike replacement prohibitions to British Columbia and Ontario. First introduced in Quebec in 1977 to discourage strike-related violence, these laws ban the use of replacement workers during a legal work stoppage, making it much more difficult for an employer to operate during a strike. The Quebec approach was not emulated elsewhere in Canada until NDP governments in Ontario and British Columbia passed similar legislation in the early 1990s. As a result, approximately three-quarters of employees covered by collective agreements in Canada no longer face the possibility of being replaced while on strike, decreasing the bargaining power of those employers who might otherwise attempt to hire replacement workers. This change marks a significant departure from the Wagner Act framework, which accepted the right to hire strike replacements as a legitimate part of management's arsenal in its exercise of economic sanctions.

The public sector also has seen an important change in the legal environment. Public sector legislation has been in place for less than twenty years in most jurisdictions. It lacks a widely accepted unifying model, and, as a result, has been marked by diversity and volatility (see Chapter 15). Although virtually all public employees enjoy the right to unionize, their rights in the collective bargaining arena have been circumscribed with respect to bargaining structure, negotiable issues, and permissible work stoppages.

Significant new restraints in the form of wage control programs have now been added. Between 1982 and 1985 and then beginning again in 1991, the federal government and most provinces introduced legislation that effectively removed wages from the negotiating table. Although the specifics varied among jurisdictions, control programs included wage freezes and rollbacks, upward wage limits, discretionary ability-to-pay guidelines, funding cutbacks, and explicit wage/job trade-offs. Whether these wage controls prove to be temporary or permanent is still open to debate. If permanent, they will weaken public sector unions and greatly alter the collective bargaining process and outcomes in that sector.

General employment legislation continued to exercise a significant influence in industrial relations (see Chapter 4). Unlike collective bargaining law, laws pertaining to employment standards, health and safety, and human rights regulate all employees, whether or not they are covered by collective agreements. Such employment legislation is usually designed to provide a safety net of basic, minimal standards for the workplace. In unionized settings, these legislative requirements generally constitute the floor upon which the collective agreement builds. As the legislative floor is raised, through amendment or automatic adjustment, so too are union targets raised. For the unorganized sector, employment law is intended to provide protection that might otherwise not be forthcoming in areas as diverse as holiday entitlement, equal opportunity, health and safety, and layoff. In some instances, the standards are set higher than society's minimum and may serve to introduce new elements to the employment environment (mandatory health and safety committees for example).

During the past decade, the basic framework of employment legislation expanded in two notable ways. First, the Ontario government (under the Liberal Party) introduced comprehensive pay equity legislation in 1988. Based on the concept of equal pay for work of equal value, the law was designed to ensure that persons in female-dominated jobs would receive the same pay as persons in male-dominated jobs of the same value, where value was to be determined by a gender-neutral job evaluation procedure. The distinguishing feature of this legislation was its application to the private sector and not just the public sector, and its proactive provision that required employers to demonstrate that their workplaces complied with the pay equity guidelines. In contrast, statutes in other provinces generally applied only to the public sector and usually required employees to file complaints alleging noncompliance, a process far less likely to result in widespread adoption of pay equity. The Ontario approach represents a much more activist orientation to employment standards than has been true in the past.

A second expansion in employment law took place through the judiciary. One set of court decisions has significantly increased the responsibilities of employers and unions to accommodate employees with disabilities or with special religious needs, up to the point where the employer experiences "undue hardship."[1] The concept of the "duty to accommodate" is now widely applicable in the employment setting and has been the subject of numerous arbitration and human rights tribunal decisions. Another court decision greatly enhanced the rights of pregnant employees by prohibiting sick leave insurance programs that excluded pregnancy-related illness and incapacity from coverage.[2] As a result, significant changes to collective agreements and sick leave and maternity policies were introduced.

These court decisions are notable in and of themselves but they also signify an important trend in employment standards. The 1990s has seen a slowdown in legislative initiatives with respect to general employment law. For example, proposals to prorate employee benefits for part-time employees were shelved by NDP governments in British Columbia and Saskatchewan. In contrast, major expansions in employment law principles have occurred through a judiciary receptive to the rights of individual employees and through arbitration and human rights tribunals. Thus, the focus of attention in employment standards has moved from legislation to litigation.

Social, Cultural, and Political Environment

The Canadian public and polity have held conflicting attitudes towards industrial relations over the years. On the one hand, support for collective bargaining has been entrenched in the private sector for more than forty years, public sector employee rights are fairly well developed (especially compared with those in the United States), and the New Democratic Party, whether in opposition or in power provincially, has often succeeded in advancing labour's agenda. On the other hand, significant segments of the general public are very critical of the labour movement, hold its leaders in low esteem, and believe strikes are excessive and ought to be replaced by arbitration (Riddell 1986a; Kumar 1986). Furthermore, public policy, having irrevocably accepted labour's right to exist, has been uncomfortable with the consequences. The result has been a passion for strike prevention (see Chapters 3, 14, and 15) and periodic episodes of wage control. More recently, the openness and legitimacy of employer antiunion strategies appear to have increased, largely as a result of events in the United States (see Chapter 5).

This environment has created a certain defensiveness on the part of the union movement and its leaders, a natural reaction to an environment perceived as hostile. This attitude, in turn, leads to suspicion and a hesitation to co-operate with management or government. As the president of the Energy and Chemical Workers Union, a union known for its willingness to participate in employee involvement programs, stated:

> I am involved in a number of quality of work life programs. But wherever I have one that works, I have a dozen more that are simply designed to get rid of a union if it is there, or keep it out if it is not there. (Basken 1988, 121)

In an increasingly competitive world, the attitudes and conditions that foster this type of continued mistrust cannot fail to be dysfunctional, not only for the direct participants but for the country as a whole.

The Actors

The three major actors in the Canadian industrial relations system are unions, employers, and government. A fourth set of actors, independent third-party neutrals, are also briefly discussed.

Unions

Canada's more than four million union members belong to close to five hundred national and local independent unions and sixty US-linked international labour organizations. Most of these unions are affiliated with one of five competing labour federations. Yet, because collective bargaining tends to occur at the local level—and there are more than 16,000 local unions—Canada's labour movement can be properly characterized as decentralized and fragmented (see Chapter 7). This remains true in the 1990s despite a number of union mergers and amalgamations. Also unchanged is the adherence of the mainstream of the labour movement to the relatively conservative philosophy of business unionism. "Business unionism" connotes an approach to labour relations in which emphasis is given to attaining workplace improvements in wages and conditions for union members through direct negotiation with their employers. Broader social and political goals, although articulated and pursued, have been given lower priority in practice, particularly at the local level.

Changes within the Canadian labour movement are difficult to pinpoint. The early 1990s have been mainly characterized by the continuation of patterns already under way. Earlier, the typical union member was a blue-collar male working in manufacturing or construction and affiliated with an international union. By the 1990s, largely as a result of public sector organizing successes, the typical unionist was likely to work in an office for government or one of its agencies, probably belonged to a union with its headquarters in Ottawa rather than Washington, and stood a 40 per cent chance of being a woman. The number of union members in Canada increased by more than 400,000 in the ten-year period ending in 1993. While this rate of growth was slower than in the past, it was noteworthy compared to patterns in United States, where total union membership actually declined during the same period (see Chapter 7).

The fact that Canada's unions continued to add members tended to obscure other trends, which painted a different picture. First, throughout the 1980s most new members were added in the public sector, which, by general consensus, is the easiest place for unions to organize. Second, absolute membership growth slowed markedly in the 1990s and in fact fell between 1992 and 1993. Third, union density declined between 1984 and 1990. It began to increase again in 1991, but union density still remained lower in 1993 than in 1984. In other words, the addition of new members in the past decade did not keep pace with the growth in the labour force. Moreover, public sector cutbacks, which are bound to have a negative impact on union membership, have not yet been reflected in membership data.[3] Thus, although there is little question that Canadian unions have proved more adept at responding to social and economic change than their American counterparts, there are indications that the labour movement will come under increasing pressure to maintain its status.

Employers

The study of how managers plan and deal with union-management relations has been largely ignored in the industrial relations literature. For example, the comprehensive examination of Canadian labour relations undertaken on behalf of the Macdonald Commission (Riddell 1986a; 1986b) has no chapters devoted exclusively to management practice. Similarly, until recently, few industrial relations textbooks included specific chapters on the employer. This omission may partly be explained by a tendency to view management in unidimensional terms: the employer's goal is to maximize output at minimum cost with minimum union interference, especially with respect to work practices. Although this objective may well be true of most employers, a great deal more needs to be said about how employers pursue this objective, the various options that may be available, and the circumstances that affect the options managers select.

To this end, strategic-choice theory has been recently applied to the study of management's actions in industrial relations (see Chapters 1 and 5). Employers' strategic options range from union acceptance to union avoidance. Management's actual selection of these options is conditioned by the rate and pattern of unionism, the competitiveness of the product market, the firm's overall business strategy, and a host of other factors. Moreover, the same firm may well apply different strategies to different parts of its operations, perhaps taking a union-acceptance approach to production workers and a union-avoidance strategy with respect to its office staff.

The available Canadian evidence, much of it presented for the first time in Chapter 5 of this book, indicates that union acceptance remains the predominant approach of unionized companies in Canada and that there does not appear to be a strong link between overall business strategy and industrial relations decisions. These conclusions are important. Strategic-choice theory was developed in the United States to help explain the precipitous decline of unionism in that country, a decline attributed to the adoption of union-removal and union-avoidance strategies by American firms (Kochan, Katz, and McKersie 1986). There has yet to be a study of the strategic choices of the nonunion sector in Canada, but in the unionized sector it is increasingly evident that US practices are not being imported—even by US firms. Thus, while management may be taking the initiative in industrial relations in Canada, this initiative is being exercised within the context of union acceptance. Employers attempt to achieve their objectives within the collective bargaining arena rather than outside it through a nonunion strategy. The evidence from Canada suggests that the strategic-choice approach may have to be modified for its application to the circumstances of this country (see also, Chaykowski and Verma 1992).

Government

Government plays a dual role in the industrial relations system. First, it regulates, through collective bargaining and employment legislation, the interaction among unions, employers, and employees (see Chapters 3 and 4), a role it has played for most of this century (see Chapter 6). In filling this role, the federal and provincial governments also collect statistics on union membership, strikes and lockouts, contract expirations, workplace accidents, and other data relevant to industrial relations. As well, governments have established mediation or conciliation services to help resolve potential or actual labour disputes. Occasionally, they step beyond such passive regulation to intervene actively in a dispute that is deemed too harmful to the economy or to the safety or well-being of the general public.

The second and more controversial role played by government is that of a major employer. More than one-quarter of the workers in Canada are employed by the various levels of government and their agencies, and the vast majority of these employees belong to unions (Chapter 15). In fact, half of all union members in Canada work in the public sector. As a result, the decisions of Canadian governments as employers reverberate throughout the country's industrial relations system. For example, the Ontario Social Contract not only directly affected a million public employees, but severely damaged the relationship between the Ontario NDP party and many private sector unions. The introduction of public sector wage freezes and rollbacks by most governments in Canada is likely to dampen wage increases in the private sector as well. In many Canadian jurisdictions, the introduction of pay equity, though generally limited to public employers, cannot but affect the private sector. This is also true of the implementation of employment equity (affirmative action) in the federal jurisdiction and for federal contractors. In addition to providing a demonstration effect (intended or otherwise), governments as employers attract attention whenever their employees strike. Given the nature of government services, work stoppages often inconvenience the public in some way, thus ensuring substantial media coverage.

Being both regulators and major employers, governments are ensured that their actions will continue to be a major determinant of future outcomes in industrial relations.

Third-Party Neutrals

A fourth set of actors in the industrial relations system are individuals who serve as independent arbitrators and mediators. Generally drawn from the legal community or academia, such people normally serve ad hoc under the mutual agreement of the employer and the union. For the vast majority of them, arbitration and other third-party activities (mediation, fact finding, and so on) are a sideline to their main employment. For example, many of the contributors to this textbook are full-time professors but also serve as arbitrators. The presence of a corps of experienced neutrals acts as a lubricant in the industrial relations system, permitting the parties to draw on the expertise of individuals who are not affiliated with labour, management, or government.

Conversion Processes

Shaped by their environments, the various actors in the industrial relations system bring an array of expectations and objectives to their mutual interactions. Through a variety of processes, these often conflicting objectives are converted into a set of agreements, rules, and policies that govern the workplace. In nonunion settings, most workplace rules are determined unilaterally by the employer. The main conversion processes in unionized settings are collective bargaining and grievance procedures. In the public sector, interest arbitration is often used in conjunction with bargaining. In both union and nonunion enterprises, employee involvement programs are becoming increasingly important as conversion processes at the workplace level.

Collective Bargaining

Collective bargaining lies at the heart of Canada's industrial relations system. Every year more than 10,000 collective agreements are negotiated between representatives of unions and representatives of management. The vast majority of these negotiations are peacefully resolved without a work stoppage, sometimes with the assistance of a mediator. Reflecting the adversarial nature of the process, a strike or lockout occurs approximately 10 per cent of the time. Eventually the costs of the dispute to the parties produce the compromises necessary for settlement (see Chapters 9 and 14).

A particular feature of the Canadian collective bargaining system is its decentralized nature. Unlike bargaining in countries such as Sweden or West Germany, where major union federations confront associations of employers in "mega-negotiations" involving entire industries (see Chapter 17), bargaining in Canada most often takes place at a single location and is restricted to employees at that location and their employer. Moreover, it is not uncommon for an employer to have to deal separately with more than one union at a single location. For example, the production and the maintenance employees in many industrial plants have different unions, and a typical hospital may have as many as five unions representing various groups of employees (for example, nurses, custodial workers, maintenance workers, residents and interns, and technicians). Because the decentralized bargaining system may contribute to the high strike frequency in Canada and to other inefficiencies in the country's industrial relations system, there have been repeated calls for more centralized structures. During the 1970s, such calls appeared to have had an effect, and centralized negotiations increased in the early 1980s. Since then, however, the trend has been in the opposite direction, with the dismantling of some national structures (meatpacking) and some provincial bargaining structures (BC forestry, Quebec public sector). The deregulation of some industries, to the extent it increased internal competitive pressures, has accentuated this trend. As well, pattern linkages between some major Canadian and American industries (for example, the auto industry) have greatly weakened. Thus, decentralized bargaining remains firmly entrenched in Canada.

The most important contemporary change in the collective bargaining arena has been a decisive shift in bargaining power and initiative from unions to employers. Pressed by a particularly harsh economic landscape, many employers attempted to control the agenda during negotiations in a sharp reversal of the roles that have prevailed for many years. Traditionally, it was the union that entered negotiations with a long list of proposals. Management demands, if any, were often put forward for trading off in an effort to retain the status quo. This situation changed in the private sector as recessionary conditions, increased foreign competition, deregulation, and increasingly aggressive management attitudes combined to produce concession bargaining. No longer content simply to maintain the status quo, many employers entered negotiations with their own long lists of proposals, many of these aimed at changing long-standing contract provisions. Favoured changes included lower entry wages (two-tier wage structures), fewer job classifications, and increased flexibility with respect to part-time and casual employees and contracting-out. In the public sector, huge government debt and a philosophy favouring less government saw management negotiators roll back wages and reduce employment levels.

Not surprisingly, unions have fought vigourously and often successfully against attempts to "undo" the contract, especially in the private sector. Where concessions have been granted, increased job security often was gained in return (Thompson and Verma 1989). In the public sector, the ability of the employer to legislate desired changes and to outlaw strikes made it much more difficult for unions to mount an effective opposition. The developments in both sectors are a strong reminder that collective bargaining is a two-way street and that unions can no longer assume that the existing agreement is a floor on which further improvements can be expected.

Interest Arbitration

As a conversion process, interest arbitration is really a specialized case of collective bargaining in that it is used only after negotiations (and usually mediation) have failed to produce agreement. On an institutional basis, it is restricted almost exclusively to the public sector and even there to bargaining that involves only certain groups (for example, police in most provinces). Where available, however, it may be used to resolve as many as one-third of all contract negotiations (see Chapter 15). Its importance lies in the fact that, when used, it replaces the face-to-face resolution of problems between the parties with the ruling of an outsider, albeit an experienced outsider who is acceptable to both parties. Thus, a major benefit of collective bargaining—the joint solving of problems—is lost. Despite these shortcomings, interest arbitration is likely to continue to play a prominent role in public sector dispute resolution.

Grievance Procedures

Collective agreements are in force for fixed periods of time with negotiations occurring at one- to three-year intervals. It is inevitable that during the term of the agreement questions will arise with respect to the interpretation and application of the contract. For example, it may fail to deal with a situation that was not foreseen. The wording may be unclear or ambiguous. Is "spouse" intended to apply to same-sex relationships? Were correct criteria used in making a promotion decision? Is the employer entitled to subcontract work, even if it means layoffs? Was there in fact "just cause" for suspending an employee for three days? The grievance process is designed to handle these and a myriad of similar situations through joint discussion at progressively higher levels of the union and management hierarchies. Failure to reach a mutually satisfactory solution leads to grievance arbitration with the rendering of a binding interpretation by an independent arbitrator (see Chapter 10).

The development and institutionalization of the grievance process has been a significant achievement of the Canadian industrial relations system. Issues arising during the term of the agreement can be handled without resort to a work stoppage (in contrast to the situation in countries such as Australia), and individual employees and the union have the opportunity to challenge management decisions. Its benefits notwithstanding, however, the grievance procedure, particularly arbitration, has been subject to increasing criticism during the last twenty years on the grounds that it is too slow, too costly, and too legalistic. The past decade has witnessed a number of changes to alleviate some of these problems. Grievance procedures have been streamlined and provisions have been made for the acceleration of certain types of grievances (such as dismissal cases). Expedited arbitration and grievance mediation have been adopted in a number of contracts and made available by statute in several jurisdictions. Arbitrators themselves have also devised ways for reducing time and expense (for example, through preset hearing days). Thus, after many years of accumulated complaints, some positive steps are being taken to ensure the continued acceptability of the grievance process.

Employee Involvement

The growth of employee involvement programs, designed to enable the actors to achieve their goals through the direct participation of employees in decision making, may well prove to be one of the most important recent developments. Unionized workers have long enjoyed participation in decision making through their union representatives, but current initiatives are different in both kind and scope. Quality circles, self-managed work teams, and quality-of-work-life programs are all examples of direct forms of employee participation that take place in the workplace (see Chapter 11). Collective bargaining in contrast is an indirect kind of participation that occurs outside the workplace (though it has an impact in the workplace).

While employee involvement programs are still not widespread in Canada, international competitive forces should accelerate their adoption. The rise of newly industrialized countries in Southeast Asia and elsewhere means that countries like Canada are finding it difficult, if not impossible, to compete on either labour costs or standardized technologies. Rather, the advantage of advanced industrial nations lies in flexible work processes that emphasize quality. Such work processes demand adaptable, highly educated workers whose input into decision making is essential to success. The assumptions of scientific management—that management knows the best way of achieving production goals and the job of workers is to obediently carry out instructions—are ill-suited to such work processes. Indeed, direct forms of employee involvement rest on the contrary belief that management cannot possibly know everything and that workers have substantial information that can enhance efficiency. Successful employee involvement programs are ones that create a structure and process for the two-way sharing of information and for motivating workers to want to share information with management.

As noted throughout Chapter 11, this is easier in theory than in practice. Comprehensive employee involvement programs cannot operate in isolation within a traditional organizational structure. Thus, substantial changes may be necessary in compensation practices, supervisory procedures, communications systems, performance evaluation, resource allocation, and authority relationships. These types of changes are far from trivial and many programs fail because of low commitment, or outright resistance, on the part of front-line supervisors and middle management. Unions too are often threatened by employee involvement programs, partly because such programs have been used in the past by nonunion companies as a part of a union avoidance strategy. In addition, to the extent that employee involvement programs blur the lines between employees and managers, commitment to the union may decline. From this perspective, joint governance, which combines indirect participation through collective bargaining with more direct forms of employee involvement, may constitute a very useful model for the spread of new programs.

The importance of creative approaches and commitment to new relationships in the workplace was summed up by one prominent observer of Canadian industrial relations:

> There will always be an adversarial element to our industrial relations system because we are bound to fight over who gets what share of the pie. The only question is whether the pie is going to be growing. If we do not start to go beyond the adversarial system to enter into more consultative and cooperative relations, we are not going to have a bigger pie to fight over; it is going to get smaller. (Crispo 1988, 128-129)

Industrial Relations Outcomes

The major outcomes of the industrial relations system are highly visible. The media regularly report important contract settlements, especially wage increases. Prominent attention is given to work stoppages, even though they occur in a small fraction of negotiations. Furthermore, strikes and lockouts are transitory in the sense that the vast majority are eventually resolved; the firm resumes its business and the employees return to work. The collective agreement is more permanent. It forms the basis for the rules of the workplace and has been likened to a constitution. Although the key provisions are not imbedded in stone, significant alterations are not easily achieved. On a day-to-day basis, the impact of unions on the terms of the agreement are the most important product of the various industrial relations conversion processes.

The Collective Agreement

The collective agreement governs a large part of the daily relationship between the employer and its employees and their union. It stipulates everything from how much an employee will be paid to how job openings should be allocated (see Chapter 13). The contract contains procedures for resolving questions of what its provisions mean and how they should be applied (see Chapter 10). In some instances, collective agreements are several hundred pages in length, though most are considerably shorter.

The contract is the major outcome of the union-management negotiation process and is subject to periodic revision. In practice, however, the majority of provisions remain unaltered from negotiation to negotiation, either because both parties are satisfied with the way the provision is operating or because one side is opposed to suggested changes and has sufficient bargaining power to ensure that the status quo is maintained. A major exception lies in compensation provisions, particularly wages, which are almost always changed each time the contract is renegotiated. Traditionally, such changes have always been upwards, related to changes in the consumer price index, the level of employment, and relative bargaining power (see Chapter 12). The 1980s and 1990s saw an important reversal in traditional wage trends: employers often succeeded in negotiating wage reductions (especially in the public sector) or no wage increase at all. Relatively low levels of inflation, high levels of unemployment, increased international competition, wage concessions in the United States, and public sector wage controls shifted bargaining power, leading to this outcome. Despite the slower movement of negotiated wage increases, a significant wage advantage still prevailed in favour of unionized over nonunionized employees (see Chapter 12).

Equally important were efforts by many employers to change long-standing contract provisions, especially those affecting management flexibility. Employers targeted clauses that restricted the use of part-time and casual employees, constrained contracting-out or the introduction of new technology, made it difficult for employees to perform more than one job, made changes in staffing levels difficult, or otherwise interfered, in management's view, with optimum efficiency. Such proposals had a much better chance of acceptance in situations in which the employer was willing to trade off something in return. For example, Canada Safeway in Alberta was able to obtain concessions on classifications and Sunday premiums from the United Food and Commercial Workers Union by offering greater job security for full-time staff. Clothing manufacturers in Quebec were able to remove restrictions on technological change by agreeing to an engineered incentive system with union involvement (Grant 1993).

Overall, the last decade has been marked by more careful attention by management to those parts of the collective agreement that were perceived to affect work productivity and by unions to those that affect job security provisions.

Work Stoppages

No aspect of the Canadian industrial relations system attracts more attention than labour disputes. Many Canadians are as familiar with the country's ranking in terms of time lost because of strikes (second behind Italy) as they are with the results of the last Canada Cup. Compared to other countries, Canada certainly has a high incidence of time lost to work stoppages. Its average of approximately half a day lost per worker per year between 1970 and early 1992 was more than twice the rate of the United States and Britain, and twenty times that of Holland (see Chapter 17). Like many countries, however, strike activity in Canada declined dramatically in the late 1980s and early 1990s, particularly in the private sector (See Chapter 14).

The literature on strike determinants is extensive, with particular attention paid to economic factors capable of explaining year-to-year fluctuations in strike activity for the country as a whole (see Chapter 14). Because collective bargaining in Canada is so decentralized, aggregate-level strike analyses, though interesting, provide only limited insight into what is occurring at the local level, where the negotiations actually take place. Thus, new work is being conducted using individual sets of negotiations as the unit of analysis.

These studies, reviewed in Chapter 14, have shown, among other things, that strikes are more likely in situations where the firm is growing and that a statutory requirement for conciliation reduces the chances of a work stoppage. This type of analysis has also shown that among large bargaining units in the private sector a strike or lockout occurs in 15 per cent of the negotiations, a higher proportion than generally thought.

Strike statistics, however, fail to reveal much in terms of economic or social impact. Is the employer shut down or are operations maintained (as they are in most telephone strikes, for example)? Does the work stoppage spill over into other sectors, causing layoffs and other dislocations? Was the stoppage unexpected, or have employees, customers, and management had sufficient advance warning to cushion the worst effects? Does Canada's reputation for high strike incidence deter investment? Unfortunately, there are few answers to such questions because most research to date has focused on the causes of strikes rather than their consequences. Given the relatively high strike propensity of the Canadian economy, additional research directed toward the impact of strikes would be both a fruitful and important area for further study.

INDUSTRIAL RELATIONS INTO THE NEXT CENTURY

It should be clear from the preceding discussion that Canadian industrial relations are in the midst of some important changes. Because an industrial relations system is a complex melding of forces, with each element being affected by and in turn affecting the other elements, change in one part of the system will almost invariably produce change elsewhere in the system. Appreciating the interrelationships is crucial to understanding where union-management relations are headed in the decade ahead.

The point of departure for the discussion is an analysis of union prospects. This is a logical place to begin since the formation and activities of the labour movement, themselves shaped by broader social and economic forces, historically have provided the impetus for most of the interactions and processes within the industrial relations system. This remains true today even with the ascendency of management as the more powerful actor within the system.

If recent developments have proved difficult for Canada's unions, the future may be even more difficult. Continuing labour force changes, a more open and competitive economic environment, high rates of unemployment, and a more proactive employer approach will present severe challenges to the Canadian labour movement. Union growth since the 1970s was largely fuelled by unionization in the public sector, but that sector is now so heavily organized that growth potential there is limited. The organizing opportunities of the future lie in office towers, bank and insurance branches, department stores, and shopping malls. As yet, Canada's unions have failed to devise a strategy capable of convincing sufficient numbers of such employees to sign union cards. Furthermore, in highly publicized campaigns, Canadian banks and major retailers demonstrated the will and the expertise to combat nascent union efforts through the adoption of union-avoidance and union-removal strategies.

If union density declines, employers may be tempted to reassess their union acceptance strategies. In the United States, the decline of the labour movement was hastened by the development of a strong nonunion sector (Kochan, Katz, and McKersie 1986). As long as the union sector commanded approximately one-third of the workforce, it tended to lead the way for the rest of the economy with respect to employment conditions, including wages. Once union density fell far enough, the unionized sector lost its influence as a pattern-setter. This loss considerably reduced the benefits of unionism, making it difficult for the American labour movement to hold onto existing members, let alone attract new ones. It also made it much easier and more socially acceptable for US employers to declare openly their union avoidance predispositions.

This type of experience could well be repeated in Canada if the union sector clearly begins to lose ground relative to the nonunion sector, especially in the private sector. Though unionized employers in Canada have followed a union acceptance approach to date, the analysis in Chapter 5 showed that this approach was chosen because of an absence of feasible alternatives, not because of any enthusiasm for collective bargaining. The expansion of a nonunion sector could provide the alternatives.

These kinds of outcomes are by no means inevitable, but a reversal of current patterns will require imaginative responses from Canadian labour leaders (see Chapters 7 and 8). White-collar workers in the private sector are often not attracted to the traditional approaches of the labour movement. Office and sales employees do not necessarily feel kinship with the struggles of workers elsewhere. Indeed, many may not see themselves as "workers" in the usual sense of the word, identifying as much with management as with co-workers. Sacred union bargaining objectives, such as obligatory membership, seniority-based job opportunities, and internal wage equality (or compression) often hold little appeal. Least appealing is the idea of going on strike. Union advocacy of voluntary arbitration or a choice-of-procedures system similar to that found in the federal public sector would enhance the acceptability of union representation for many white-collar workers. So too would union campaigns that stress the importance of rewarding and protecting individual achievement and co-operation with management.

Even a rethinking of union strategy may not be enough. One of the remarkable aspects of the past decade was the manner in which the Canadian industrial relations system detached itself from the American one. The most obvious manifestation was union density: after years of parallel development in the two countries, unionization rates in Canada became more than double those of United States by the 1990s. Differences between the two systems were also evident in Canadian unions' greater propensity to strike, their greater ability to resist contract concessions, and their relative reluctance to engage in co-operative programs. The waning influence of international unions within the Canadian labour movement also contributed to the divergence between the two systems. A crucial difference also lay in the role assumed by American management. With an aggressiveness only rarely seen in Canada, American employers embraced union-resistance, union-removal, and union-avoidance strategies. Even in union-acceptance situations, US management was much more likely to pursue major contract concessions and become more involved in labour-management co-operative ventures aimed at increased productivity. American observers (for example, *Business Week,* May 11, 1981) labelled the strategic approaches adopted by employers as the "new industrial relations" and concluded that employers were responsible for most of the fundamental changes in US union-management relations.

The close business, educational, and communications linkages between Canada and the United States, plus the free trade agreements, are powerful forces that work against the long term divergence of the two industrial relations systems. Even with a weakened labour movement and favourable labour market conditions, however, it is unlikely that Canadian employers would be able to fully emulate their American counterparts, assuming they wanted to do so. Public sector unions are much stronger in Canada than in the United States and will provide an irreducible minimum base of support for unionism, recent setbacks notwithstanding. The New Democratic Party, for which there is no US equivalent, will continue to offer alternative models of industrial relations where it is in power. Where it is not in power, it will continue to constitute a source of succour and support for the labour movement. Private sector labour law in Canada, relative to US labour law, will continue to make it more difficult for employers to counter union-organizing campaigns or to promote decertifications. Indeed, the spread of legislation prohibiting the use of strikebreakers makes union-removal strategies exceedingly difficult. Further, Canada has no equivalent of the US sunbelt with its deeply conservative, antiunion traditions.

For these reasons, organized labour still remains a powerful enough force to block, or make prohibitively expensive, the pursuit of a nonunion option for most unionized employers. Nevertheless, union bargaining power is comparatively weaker than it has been at any time since the Second World War (see Chapter 8). Accordingly, the most likely scenario for the remainder of the 1990s is the continued predominance of union acceptance strategies, but with management enjoying more freedom of action. The key question concerns the objectives employers will choose to pursue with this freedom. Clearly there will be some variation across industries and companies. Common trends will be the continuation of contract "tightening" through the elimination of unproductive work practices, and cost containment through modest wage changes and employment reduction. But such changes are at best incremental and may not be sufficient to address the competitive challenges that lie ahead.

One approach that might address the conflicting as well as mutual interests of the actors is a more widespread adoption of direct forms of employee involvement within prevailing collective bargaining structures. Such an approach, labelled "joint governance" (Verma and Cutcher-Gershenfeld 1993) and described in Chapter 11, can offer tangible benefits to all parties. For employers, successful direct employee involvement programs (like self-managed work teams) can greatly enhance efficiency, flexibility, and product quality. While joint governance implies a substantial increase in power-sharing with the union, direct employee involvement programs require a devolution of authority in any event. Most importantly, convincing the union to be a partner in the program, not an adversary, greatly enhances the overall likelihood of program success.

For unions, joint governance permits some degree of control over programs that may occur with or without their participation. Undoubtedly, unions face risks in choosing to become management's partner. Employee involvement programs have been used to undermine unions in the past and there is always the possibility that union leaders will be accused by opponents of selling out their members. On the other hand, the real partnership that joint governance entails places union leadership in a better position to protect their members than would otherwise be the case. Moreover, worker satisfaction increases with increased participation in decision making; as a partner in the process unions can share some of the credit for positive outcomes.

Indeed, joint governance contains the seeds of a new organizing strategy for the labour movement. This would involve a dual track approach that combines the advocacy of traditional collective bargaining to enhance wage and job protection with the endorsement of the new direct forms of employee involvement. Such an approach might well appeal to nonunion employees who desire more co-operative and participative relationships in the workplace but are still concerned about job security and their standard of living. Unions that championed employee involvement under the umbrella of collective bargaining could find the receptive audience among the unorganized that they have long been seeking.

BACK TO THE FUTURE

The net effect of these converging forces is an industrial relations system in obvious transition. As in the United States, the new industrial relations are taking root in Canada, but because Canadian unions are stronger than US unions, the outcomes have not been as dramatic. It is possible that the strong endorsement by both parties of workplace participation within a union-acceptance framework could move the industrial relations system in exciting new directions. A look to the south should provide a constant reminder to Canadian unions of what the implications will be of a failure to grapple with ongoing changes.

In looking to the future of the industrial relations system, however, it is important not to ignore the lessons of the past. History tells us that the fortunes of the major actors in the system are constantly changing. Management ascendance and union travail will in all likelihood prove a transitory condition, part of yet another era in the long evolution of Canadian industrial relations. Each era leaves its stamp on contemporary practices. The challenge for the future is to ensure that the positive lessons of the past twenty years are retained when the next stage comes, as surely it must.

QUESTIONS

1. What major environmental changes will have the most impact on union–management practices in the future? Explain the impact.

2. If you were a Canadian labour leader, what steps would you take to avoid the kind of decline in membership and power that has been experienced by US unions?

3. As the head of a unionized firm, how would you respond to a union request for a joint governance type of system through which a direct form of employee involvement could be achieved? What factors would you consider in developing a response?

4. Would a general weakening of the labour movement and an accompanying growth of the nonunion sector be a positive or a negative development for Canada? What role, if any, should governments play in such developments?

5. If you could change any aspect of the current Canadian industrial relations system, what would you want to change? Why?

REFERENCES

BASKEN, R.C. 1988. "Foreign Lessons and Applications—Discussant." In A. Ponak, ed, *The Future of Alberta Labour Relations.* Calgary: University of Calgary.

CHAYKOWSKI, R., and A. VERMA, eds. 1992 *Industrial Relations in Canadian Industry.* Toronto: Dryden.

CRISPO, J. 1988. "Conclusions." In A. Ponak, ed, *The Future of Alberta Labour Relations.* Calgary: University of Calgary.

GRANT, M. 1993. "Industrial Relations in the Clothing Industry: Struggle for Survival." In R. Chaykowski and A. Verma, eds, *Industrial Relations in Canadian Industry.* Toronto: Dryden.

KOCHAN, T.A., H.C. KATZ, and R.B. McKERSIE. 1986. *The Transformation of American Industrial Relations.* New York: Basic Books.

KUMAR, P. 1986. "Union Growth in Canada: Retrospect and Prospect." In W.C. Riddell, ed, *Canadian Labour Relations.* Toronto: University of Toronto Press.

RIDDELL, W.C., ed. 1986a. *Canadian Labour Relations.* Toronto: University of Toronto Press.

————. 1986b. *Labour-Management Cooperation in Canada.* Toronto: University of Toronto Press.

THOMPSON, M., and A. VERMA. 1989. Managerial Strategies in Industrial Relations in the 1980s: Comparing the US and Canadian Experience." *Proceedings of the Forty-First Annual Meeting*, Industrial Relations Research Association, 1989.

VERMA, A. and J. CUTCHER-GERSHENFELD. 1993. "Joint Governance in the Workplace: Beyond Union-Management Cooperation and Worker Participation." In B. Kaufman and M. Kleiner, eds, *Employee Representation.* Madison WI: Industrial Relations Research Association.

END NOTES

1   See, for example, *Central Alberta Dairy Pool* v *Alberta (Human Rights Commission)*, [1990] 2 S.C.R. 489 and *Renaud* v *Board of School Trustees, School District No. 23 (Central Okanagon) and CUPE et al.* (1992) S.J.C. No. 75.

2   *Brooks* v *Canada Safeway* (1992) 26 C.C.E.L. 1 (S.C.C.).

3   There is likely to be a lag between public sector layoffs and union membership declines because laid off union members are often carried "on the books" as union members for a period of time.

INDEX